Uncertainty, Information Management, and Disclosure Decisions

This volume integrates scholarly work on disclosure and uncertainty with the most up-to-date, cutting edge research, theories, and applications. Uncertainty is an ever-present part of human relationships, and the ways in which people reduce and/or manage uncertainty involves regulating their communication with others through revealing and concealing information. This collection is devoted to collating knowledge in these areas, advancing theory, and presenting work that is socially meaningful.

This work includes contributions from renowned scholars in interpersonal uncertainty and information regulation, focusing on processes that bridge boundaries within and across disciplines, while maintaining emphasis on interpersonal contexts. Disciplines represented here include interpersonal, family, and health communication, as well as relational and social psychology. Key features of the volume include:

- A comprehensive volume integrating the latest research on disclosure, information seeking, and uncertainty.
- Highly theoretical content, socially meaningful in nature (e.g., applied to real-world contexts).
- An interdisciplinary approach that crosses sub-fields within communication.

This volume is a unique and timely resource for advanced courses in interpersonal, health, or family communication. With its emphasis on theory, the book is an excellent resource for graduate courses addressing theory and/or theory construction, and it will also appeal to scholars interested in applied research.

About the Editors

Tamara D. Afifi (Ph.D., University of Nebraska-Lincoln) is an Associate Professor in the Department of Communication at the University of California, Santa Barbara. She has published over 50 articles and chapters in numerous national and international outlets, and she was the recipient of the Young Scholar Award from the International Communication Association in 2006.

Walid A. Afifi (Ph.D., University of Arizona) is an Associate Professor in the Department of Communication at the University of California, Santa Barbara. He is author of more than 50 articles and chapters, has served as Associate Editor for both the *Journal of Social and Personal Relationships* and *Personal Relationships*, and has been active as a member of several editorial boards.

Uncertainty, Information Management, and Disclosure Decisions

Theories and Applications

Edited by
Tamara D. Afifi
and
Walid A. Afifi

Routledge
Taylor & Francis Group

NEW YORK AND LONDON

First published 2009
by Routledge
270 Madison Avenue, New York, NY 10016

Simultaneously published in the UK
by Routledge
2 Park Square, Milton Park,
Abingdon, Oxon OX14 4RN

*Routledge is an imprint of the Taylor & Francis Group,
an informa business*

© 2009 Taylor & Francis

Typeset in Sabon by
Book Now Ltd, London
Printed and bound in the United Kingdom on acid-free paper by
CPI Antony Rowe, Chippenham, Wiltshire

All rights reserved. No part of this book may be reprinted or
reproduced or utilised in any form or by any electronic, mechanical,
or other means, now known or hereafter invented, including
photocopying and recording, or in any information storage or
retrieval system, without permission in writing from the publishers.

Trademark Notice: Product or corporate names may be trademarks
or registered trademarks, and are used only for identification and
explanation without intent to infringe.

Library of Congress Cataloging in Publication Data
Uncertainty, information management, and disclosure decisions:
theories and applications / Tamara D. Afifi, Walid A. Afifi, editors.
    p. cm.
Uncertainty. 2. Risk assessment. 3. Disclosure of information.
4. Management. I. Afifi, Tamara D. II. Afifi, Walid A.
HB615.U554 2009
303.48'33—dc22   2009010319

ISBN10: 0–415–96515–2 (hbk)
ISBN10: 0–415–96516–0 (pbk)
ISBN10: 0–203–93304–4 (ebk)

ISBN13: 978–0–415–96515–6 (hbk)
ISBN13: 978–0–415–96516–3 (pbk)
ISBN13: 978–0–203–93304–6 (ebk)

This book is dedicated to the two girls that guide us through our experiences with uncertainty, information, and disclosure: Leila Zeinab and Rania Cyrine.

Contents

List of Illustrations

Figures

Tables

List of Contributors

Tamara D. Afifi
Department of Communication
University of California–Santa Barbara

Walid A. Afifi
Department of Communication
University of California–Santa Barbara

Austin S. Babrow
Department of Communication
Ohio University

Leslie A. Baxter
Communication Studies Department
University of Iowa

Dawn O. Braithwaite
Communication Studies Department
University of Nebraska–Lincoln

Dale E. Brashers
Department of Speech Communication
University of Illinois

John P. Caughlin
Department of Speech Communication
University of Illinois

Mark Dechesne
Center for Terrorism and Counterterrorism (CTC)
University of Leiden—Campus The Hague
The Netherlands

Rutger C. M. E. Engels
Institute of Family and Child Care Studies
Radboud University Nijmegen

Catrin Finkenauer
Department of Social Psychology
VU University Amsterdam

Daena J. Goldsmith
Department of Communication
Lewis and Clark College

Kathryn Greene
Department of Communication
Rutgers University

Timothy P. Hogan
Center for Management of Complex Chronic Care
Edward Hines, Jr. VA Hospital
U.S. Department of Veterans Affairs

J. David Johnson
College of Communications and Information Studies
University of Kentucky

Andrea Joseph
Department of Communication
University of California–Santa Barbara

Anita Kelly
Department of Psychology
University of Notre Dame

Peter Kerkhof
Department of Communication
V University Amsterdam

Leanne K. Knobloch
Department of Speech Communication
University of Illinois

Michael W. Kramer
Department of Communication
University of Missouri

Arie W. Kruglanski
Department of Psychology
University of Maryland

Kaska E. Kubacka
Department of Social Psychology
VU University Amsterdam

Serena C. Lo
Department of Psychology
George Washington University

Diane Macready
Department of Psychology
University of Notre Dame

Tara McManus
Department of Communication Studies
University of Nevada, Las Vegas

Marianne S. Matthias
Department of Communication
Butler University

Chris R. Morse
Department of Communication
Bryant University

Sandra Petronio
Department of Communication Studies Core Faculty, IU Center for
    Bioethics, Indiana School of Medicine, Adjunct Faculty, IU School of
    Nursing, School of Informatics
Indiana University Purdue University Indianapolis (IUPUI)

Paul J. Poppen
Department of Psychology
George Washington University

Artemio Ramirez, Jr.
Hugh Downs School of Communication
Arizona State University

Jennifer Reierson
Department of Communication
North Dakota State University

Rajiv N. Rimal
Department of Health, Behavior and Society
Johns Hopkins University

Michael E. Roloff
Department of Communication Studies
Northwestern University

Kristen L. Satterlee
Department of Speech Communication
University of Illinois

Paul Schrodt
Department of Communication Studies
Texas Christian University

Monique Mitchell Turner
Department of Communication, Center for Risk
   Communication Research
University of Maryland

Anita L. Vangelisti
Department of Communication
University of Texas–Austin

Joseph B. Walther
Department of Communication
Michigan State University

Courtney N. Wright
School of Communication Studies
University of Tennessee

María Cecilia Zea
Department of Psychology
George Washington University

Introduction

Tamara D. Afifi and Walid A. Afifi

The notion of *uncertainty*, as studied in interpersonal contexts, is variously defined but generally reflects one of two conceptualizations: one focused on a perceived inability to predict behaviors, attitudes, or outcomes, and the other focused on a perceived inability to understand the meaning behind particular attitudes, behaviors, or outcomes. The nature of uncertainty's association with *information* has also been the subject of considerable attention and the target of controversy. On the one end, we find conceptualizations of uncertainty as a direct and linear function of an objective quantity of information—such that each bit of information that is acquired decreases uncertainty by that precise amount—and on the other end we find conceptualizations of uncertainty that have no relation, or perhaps more appropriately, a seemingly random association, to acquired information. In the middle, we find scholars struggling with the nature of the association.

On another, but related, front, we find scholars interested in information management decisions (e.g., information seeking, information providing, information avoidance, self-disclosure). Again, we find controversies here. For example, the nature of disclosure's association with closeness has been the subject of voluminous work. On one end, we find suggestions that self-*disclosure* is a direct and linear function of relational closeness. On the other end, we find suggestions that *avoidance* is a direct and linear function of relational closeness. And again, in the middle, we find scholars struggling with the nature of the association.

What we do not find much of, though, is an effort to bring together scholars in areas that share considerable theoretical and applied overlap. This book represents an effort to bring together the best scholarship in the domains of uncertainty, information management, and disclosure. In so doing, we encourage scholars and readers alike to consider places where separation is central to understanding and other places where possibilities for overlap can flourish.

Individuals face numerous macrolevel stressors (e.g., losing a job, having a child, getting married, illness, war) and microlevel stressors (e.g., balancing work and family, relational conflict, identity threats) that affect uncertainty

levels across a variety of relationship types (e.g., friendships, romantic relationships, workplace relationships, families) and manifest themselves in different ways. A central premise of early work on uncertainty is that people
long to reduce their uncertainty in order to explain and predict the world
around them. However, as other scholars have since pointed out (e.g., see
Babrow and Matthias's chapter on problematic integration theory, Baxter
and Braithwaite's chapter on reconceptualizing uncertainty, Hogan and
Brashers's chapter on uncertainty management theory, Afifi and Morse's
chapter on the theory of motivated information management, Dechesne and
Kruglanski's chapter on need for closure), there are times when people do not
want to reduce their uncertainty, but instead choose to manage it or even
wish to increase it.

One method by which people reduce, manage, or increase their uncertainty
involves regulating their communication with others through revealing and
concealing information. This is accomplished by avoiding communication,
secrecy, managing one's privacy or the privacy of others, and disclosure.
People often have to make difficult decisions about their disclosures, including if and when to disclose or keep the information private, the conditions
under which they would disclose, and potential consequences of the disclosure (or secrecy) for themselves, others, and their relationships.

Regulating uncertainty also involves managing, seeking, or filtering the
information that is likely to affect the degree of uncertainty that is felt. For
instance, in an effort to reduce their uncertainty, people may seek information about the issue in question. Of course, that may backfire and increase
their uncertainty instead. They may seek a wide array of information to
manage their uncertainty or they may seek information that only supports
their point of view. Individuals sometimes also avoid seeking information
because they are afraid of the outcome. In this instance, individuals may
prefer not to know the information for fear of what might happen as a
result or because not knowing offers them a sense of hope.

Consequently, as we noted at the start of this introduction, the concepts of
"uncertainty," "information management," and "disclosure decisions" often
go hand in hand. Researchers who study one of these domains (e.g., uncertainty) also tend to cross over into one of the other domains (e.g., disclosure
decisions) in an effort to understand how people make sense of the world
around them. For instance, researchers who study uncertainty often examine
whether or not people seek information or avoid information in order to
manage their uncertainty. Recently, researchers have also investigated what
happens to another person's uncertainty as a result of one's disclosures of
relational transgressions, health-related information (see Goldsmith's chapter
on communal coping, uncertainty, and disclosure), and divorce (see Afifi,
Schrodt, and McManus's chapter on divorce disclosures).

These research areas have garnered significant attention from top journals and books in recent years. For instance, special issues of the *Journal of
Communication* (2001) and *Human Communication Research* (2002) were

devoted to the study of uncertainty and information seeking. Moreover, within the past 5 years alone, work in these areas has appeared in the *Journal of Personality and Social Psychology*, the *Journal of Applied Psychology*, *Personal Relationships*, the *Journal of Social and Personal Relationships*, *Social Science and Medicine*, the *Journal of Computer-Mediated Communication*, *International Journal of Intercultural Relations*, *Health Communication*, *Health Psychology*, and the *Journal of Organizational Behavior*, among many others. There have also been a good number of books that have made important contributions to the area of uncertainty and disclosure decisions. Among these are Berger and Bradac's (1982) book on uncertainty in interpersonal encounters (*Language and Social Knowledge*), Pennebaker's (1995) book linking emotion, disclosure, and health, Petronio's (2002) book outlining her theory of communication privacy management (*Boundaries of Privacy: Dialectics of Disclosure*), Case's (2002) book on information behavior, Greene et al.'s (2003) book on disclosure of HIV, Goldsmith's (2004) book on *Communicating Social Support* (where she addresses social support from an uncertainty and disclosure perspective), Kruglanski's (2004) book on closemindedness and the need for closure, and Kramer's (2004) book on uncertainty in organizations, among many others. Many of these have been recognized through awards and all have gained considerable attention from scholars across disciplines. Of course, there are also tens of edited books that contain a chapter here or there on uncertainty, information seeking, and disclosure decisions that have made significant contributions.

What was *lacking*, until now, was an edited book that focuses on uncertainty, information management, disclosure decisions, and their overlap. The number of articles in top journals and the surge of books in these research areas in recent years illustrate a genuine interest in these processes and the need to pull together these bodies of work into one edited book. In fact, an edited volume on these issues is far overdue, lagging well behind the dramatic growth in original theory and research in these areas during the past 15 years. This book is entirely devoted to collating knowledge in these three areas, knowledge that not only advances theory, but that is socially meaningful.

A second goal of this book is to focus on processes that bridge boundaries within and across disciplines, but that still focus on interpersonal contexts. Because uncertainty and disclosure decisions are processes that cross different types of contexts, we asked scholars studying interpersonal relationships, organizations, technology, family, and health to write chapters. While the book is broad in its contexts, it simultaneously focuses on a specific type of audience: scholars interested in understanding uncertainty, information seeking, and disclosure processes from an interpersonal perspective. We perceive interpersonal communication to be a broad rubric that encompasses initial interactions, informal and formal contexts where people establish relationships, and families. To ensure that the volume was comprehensive in its breadth, we recruited scholars from across a wide array of disciplines.

A third goal entering this project was to provide a book that emphasizes both theory and socially meaningful research. All of the authors who contributed to this book have work that is very strongly grounded in theory, and their chapters are a reflection of this orientation. In fact, most of the authors have developed their own theory of uncertainty, information seeking, and/or disclosure decisions or have developed a distinct approach to viewing these processes. In fact, several of the chapters in this book (e.g., Greene's chapter; T. Afifi's chapters) represent new theories or models. If they do not present new theories or models, they enhance existing theories (e.g., Babrow and Matthias's chapter on problematic integration theory; Hogan and Brashers's chapter on uncertainty management theory; W. Afifi and Morse's chapter on the theory of motivated information management; Rimal and Turner's chapter on risk perception attitude; Kramer's chapter on the theory of managing uncertainty) or completely reframe the way that people think about uncertainty or disclosure (e.g., Baxter and Braithwaite's chapter on reclaiming uncertainty; Caughlin and Vangelisti's application of multiple goals theory to explain secrets). Other authors challenge the existing paradigmatic thinking of these processes (e.g., Kelly and Macready's chapter on secrets). All of the authors advance the theory and research in their areas and generate future avenues of research that have heuristic value for the readers of this book. Many of the chapters also bridge uncertainty, information seeking, and disclosure decisions and show how these areas are interrelated and inform one another.

In addition to the theoretical rigor of their work, the scholars represented in this book also engage in research that is socially meaningful or that has significant social implications. We asked all the authors to address both the theoretical and applied/socially meaningful nature of their work in some way. All of the chapters demonstrate how theoretically rich research can be applied in interpersonal relationships in ways that have an impact on people's lives. The research that is described in this book has been applied in community-based contexts and offers insights that can enhance the everyday lives of others. All of the theories that are discussed in this book have been tested in important applied social settings and/or with critical issues, including cancer, HIV, sexual health, organ donation, terrorism, physician–patient communication, parent–child encounters, and divorce, among others.

This book is divided into two major sections: (1) uncertainty and (2) disclosure decisions. The first major section on uncertainty is further broken down into three subsections. The first subsection encourages readers to reconsider central issues that have come to define work in uncertainty or information management. The scholars in this section advance new ways of thinking about their theories or challenge existing ways of thinking about uncertainty and information. The second subsection for uncertainty highlights the intersection between uncertainty and information seeking. The final subsection examines information seeking in specific contexts.

The second major section focuses on disclosure decisions. This section is further broken down into three subsections. The first subsection examines the intersection between uncertainty and disclosure. These authors provide excellent examples of how these two bodies of literature can inform one another. The second subsection explores the potential consequences, both positive and negative, of avoidance and secrecy. Like work on uncertainty, the area of information regulation or disclosure decisions, as we are referring to it here, has seen an explosion of interest in recent years, stemming in large part from the contribution of Baxter's Relational Dialectics Theory (see Baxter and Braithwaite's chapter where they apply the theory to uncertainty) and Petronio's Communication Privacy Management Theory (see Petronio and Reierson's chapter on confidentiality and CPM theory). Since their emergence, these theories have shaped much of the inquiry in this domain and spawned other approaches to understanding these processes.

An overarching goal with these two major sections is to examine both the experience of uncertainty and the strategies used to manage it. Each chapter in this book focuses on a theory, model, or set of propositions that help us account for individuals' decisions to reduce, manage, or increase their uncertainty and how they might seek or choose not to seek information in the face of uncertainty. They also examine how people disclose or conceal information to particular audiences, their motivations for doing so, and the consequences of these decisions. All of the chapters are written by scholars who are the originators of their concepts or theories and are leaders in their area of scholarship.

Our book revolves around processes that are not only strongly related and have a long history of research but have also witnessed an explosion of scholarly attention. The processes are also central to multiple disciplines and subdisciplines but still focus on interpersonal contexts. We hope that this book will advance knowledge in these areas and contribute to continued growth in our understanding of them.

Part I

Uncertainty

Conceptualizations of Uncertainty and Information Management

1 Generally Unseen Challenges in Uncertainty Management

An Application of Problematic Integration Theory

Austin S. Babrow and Marianne S. Matthias

A colleague of ours was talking with a dear friend, a very bright guy who prided himself as something of a polymath, when the latter declared, with evident pride in the chestnut he was about to impart, that Aristotle was the last living person to know all there was to know. Not long after, our friend was reading a work by Czech author Milan Kundera, where she encountered the claim that the French encyclopedist, Denis Diderot, was the last person alive who knew everything. Intrigued, she submitted the evidently controversial issue to a search on Google. Although she surveyed only the first 20 or so of the more than 8.5 million hits, she quickly found that there were several other contenders for the crown (e.g., Milton, Jefferson).

We commence this chapter with the foregoing anecdote because it illustrates several phenomena relevant to the enterprise of this book. Most obvious are the chimera of omniscience and its apparent antitheses, uncertainty and ignorance. A bit less obviously, the story illustrates the value we place on knowledge, various forms of uncertainty (insufficient, overwhelming, and conflicting information, and perhaps an intimation of the unknowable), and the interplay of interpersonal relations and mass media that shapes these experiences.

The present volume displays an impressive range of inquiries into these phenomena that have been developing in the last couple of decades. Kruglanski's (2004) elegant theory offers penetrating insights into the shifting motivational bases of information search and the plasticity of lay epistemology (or, as we'd say, into the uncertain, and apparently irresolvable, nature of knowing; see Babrow, 2001, note 2). Thanks largely to the efforts of Brashers (2007), the field of communication is ever more broadly in possession of the insight that we are often motivated to avoid information. And in works like those of Afifi and Weiner (2004), Johnson (1997), Petronio (2002), and Greene (2000), we have growing awareness of the complex array of incentives and disincentives, facilitators and barriers involved in uncertainty and information regulation.

In this chapter we take up what we believe is the most essential, yet largely neglected, issue in research on communication and uncertainty: the importance of more discriminating analysis of uncertainty itself. While this topic is not new (see Babrow, 2001, 2007a; Babrow, Kasch, & Ford, 1998; Friedman, Dunwoody, & Rogers, 1999; Mishel, 1988, 1990), in our view it has not received the careful attention it merits. As a consequence, enormously important issues have been given too little attention. At the very least, significant avenues for theory, research, and practice have been overlooked. In some areas, neglect of these issues may exacerbate the very problems we hope to remedy. In the following, we use problematic integration theory to illuminate the nature of uncertainty and to begin to identify neglected problems and opportunities for developing theory and application. We commence with an overview of the conceptual framework.

Problematic Integration Theory

Problematic integration (PI) theory is a general perspective on communication and human being rooted in a conception of the nature of mind and meaning. It can be summarized in several basic claims (Babrow, 2007a). The theory's most basic propositions are that humans are continually constructing and reconstructing the meanings of their experience, and indeed of life itself, in the form of "probabilistic" and "evaluative orientations." Probabilistic orientations are associations (Babrow, 2001), such as definitions, beliefs and expectations, and perceived similarities (e.g., perceived isomorphism, metaphor), by which we come to understand the nature and meaning of our world. Applied to the interpersonal world, for example, these meanings answer questions such as, "When did our marriage begin to come apart?" "What does it mean to be a 'good enough parent'?" Moreover, as the theoretical label emphasizes, these associations are said to be probabilistic orientations because they are held with varying levels of assurance, certainty, or probability. The label *probabilistic orientation* also emphasizes that, no matter how deeply we hold any such association, it can be called into question and thereby transformed into uncertainty.

PI theory also holds that we orient to, make sense of, or come to understand the meaning of life in evaluative terms. Indeed, the theory asserts that evaluative orientations, from the most extreme positive through neutral to the most extreme negative interpretations of concrete experiences and abstractions, are as basic to human meaning as are the associations by which we understand the structure of life. For instance, predicting how another person will react to a prospective line of action is not a sufficient basis for determining how to behave; reasoned action requires evaluation of the other's reaction as well (Fishbein & Ajzen, 1975).

PI theory offers a third proposition in the assertion that probabilistic and evaluative orientations are integrated in human experience. To explain this assertion, it is important first to note the theory's insistence that knowledge and value judgment are distinguishable. In countless ways, we realize the truth that what we believe to be so is not necessarily the same as what we wish would be so. PI theory also recognizes that there is much to be gained in efforts to separate probabilistic and evaluative orientations; the accomplishments of science attest to the revolutionary positive change that results from efforts to separate belief from value. But PI theory's third proposition recognizes that human sense making very forcefully inclines us toward the integration of these forms of meaning.[1]

Integration entails several processes. For one, probabilistic and evaluative orientations are interdependent: Our probabilistic judgments influence value judgments, and vice versa. Even a cursory inspection of experience and relevant research literature attests to the wide variety of ways that we make wishful and defensive adjustments of probability and value estimates (Weinstein & Klein, 1996). We also routinely act in ways that change expectations about valued outcomes, such as adopting healthier lifestyles or becoming politically active.

Probability and evaluation also are integrated through reciprocal processes that link these orientations to a given focus of thought with such orientations to other objects of thought. For example, accepting a proposal of marriage not only establishes the strength of a relational bond and *eo ipso* ratifies the value of the relationship, but its meaning also simultaneously shapes beliefs and evaluations having to do with identity, surrounding social relationships, career, leisure, and a host of other aspects of the partners' lives.

In short, probabilities and values are not isolated. Rather, as PI theory and many other perspectives recognize, they are integrated with one another and with broader complexes of knowledge, feelings, intentions, and ongoing behavior. PI theory begins to diverge from other frameworks by focusing on a fourth proposition: The integration of probabilistic and evaluative orientations is often problematic.

In its most rudimentary form, such problematic integration occurs because of the interdependence of probabilistic and evaluative orientations. In other words, because of their reciprocal influences, probability and value orientations can destabilize one another. For example, both perceived probability and value may influence one another, shifting to and fro repeatedly over the course of time, as partners consider the prospects of divorce, parents consider their child's future in a highly demanding but prestigious college, or loved ones and friends witness a young man's life with AIDS.

The nature of PI is further explicated in a fifth claim: The experience of PI entails processes by which a particular integrative dilemma is transformed in various ways. In other words, PI involves "chaining out" of meanings in a variety of different directions. For one, problematic meanings chain from one focal issue to other related issues ("chaining across foci"). For example, James Bradac's (2001) personal recollections on his experiences of living for the past 12 years with amyotrophic lateral sclerosis ("Lou Gehrig's disease") traversed questions of diagnosis, cause, prognosis, the meaning of numeric odds, interaction patterns and interpersonal relationships, and identity. In other words, the experience of substantial PI sets in motion cascading waves of change that extend the length, breadth, and depth of psychological and relational systems.

Another way that meanings chain out in the experience of integrative dilemmas involves the transformation of one *form* of PI into another. Indeed, PI theory identifies several major forms of problematic integration: divergence (e.g., incompatible expectations and desires), uncertainty (of some desire or dread), ambivalence (e.g., equally appealing but mutually exclusive alternatives, objects of thought with mutually exclusive and opposite evaluative meanings), and unpleasant impossibility/certainty. For example, perceived impossibility (e.g., of a couple staying together) is often refashioned into diverging expectation and desire (e.g., a ray of hope), which is in turn reconstructed as uncertainty (e.g., one comes to doubt the trustworthiness of information about the likelihood of obtaining what one wants, or the likelihood comes to be seen as indeterminate), and so on (Babrow, 2007a).

In addition to chaining across problematic topics and issues (foci) and forms of integrative dilemmas, problematic meanings also chain across levels of experience. This idea is more fully explicated in one final proposition: Communication is the primary medium, source, and resource in PI experiences (Babrow, 1992, 2007a). In other words, PI is not only an individual psychological process, but it is also inherently a communicative phenomenon. We learn much and perhaps most of what we know about the composition of the world and its evaluative meanings, and particularly problematic meanings, through communication. Communication is also a coping resource in that it can be used to encourage reappraisal of a specific probability or evaluation, or to facilitate a more holistic transformation or reframing of PI (Babrow, 1992). As examples of the latter, unknown chances of realizing a heart's desire can be recast as a test of faith or character (Babrow, 2001, 2007a). Although these very transformations may bring relief from the original PI, the resulting new orientations themselves can be problematic, thus prompting an ongoing search for meaning. In short, communication is not only a major source of probabilistic and evaluative orientations, it is also integral to struggles over elusive and/or troubling meanings.

While PI theory has been applied to a variety of phenomena (e.g., Gill & Babrow, 2007; Matthias, 2009; Matthias & Babrow, 2007; Shi & Babrow, 2007; see Babrow, 2007a, for a review), it has very often been used as a lens for examining the relationship between communication and uncertainty (Babrow, 2001). Further, the experience of uncertainty is nowhere more powerfully embodied than when uncertainty arises in relation to the body itself. As a result, PI theory has been applied extensively to issues in health communication, although its implications extend to any domain in which we want to study the relationship between communication and frustrations of our strong inclination to make sense of the world. In this regard, the framework has much to suggest for theory, research, and practice related to what the current volume terms *uncertainty* and *information regulation*. The following section traces some of these implications, with particular attention to those often overlooked or neglected.

Frequently Neglected Issues in the Study of Uncertainty and Information Regulation

Recognizing the Different Meanings of Uncertainty: Beyond the Linguistic Catch-All

PI theory joins countless perspectives across the humanities and social sciences that posit the idea that humans are ordering, constructive, sense-making, meaning-making beings (Babrow, 2007a). The broadly recognized human propensity toward sense making is often accompanied by several corollaries (see Babrow, 2001, for more thorough explication): We are discomfited by disorder or uncertainty, our dominant response to uncertainty is information seeking, and the main aim and most significant outcome of any encounter with uncertainty is its reduction (or frustration of this aim). This sort of thinking is a prime motivation for the basic impulse toward what is very often termed *informational support* in the interpersonal realm and for the explosion of information now available on the Internet. But if we pause and reflect, we realize that there are subtle and not so subtle differences in the nature of uncertainty. If we pause and reflect, we realize that these differences must be recognized and each one addressed on its own terms. Indeed, we strongly believe that the most basic, important, and commonly overlooked issue in studies of communication and uncertainty is the necessity of more careful analysis of this concept.

Several past essays on PI theory have attempted to press the idea, voiced over a decade ago by linguist Paul Atkinson (1995), that the term uncertainty has been a sort of linguistic "catch-all." While more recently we have seen increasing recognition of various meanings, these often take the form of definitions that string together disparate senses of the term in a seemingly unfocused manner. The result is that discussions of this vitally important concept very often range indiscriminately across quite diverse meanings.

In contrast, PI theory offers a systematic analysis that provides several useful insights into the nature of uncertainty. These insights stem from the ideas that (a) meaning is associational, (b) associations are fundamentally probabilistic (although, surely, much meaning is experienced without doubt; see Babrow, 2001, 2007a), and (c) such probabilistic associations are themselves shaped by and in turn shape surrounding evaluative and other meanings. In what follows, we emphasize point (a) and weave instances of point (c) through the discussion, but before turning to these issues we wish to comment briefly on point (b).

The idea that associations are probabilistic, which is reflected in enormous literatures in statistics, economics, finance, insurance, engineering, medicine, and information science, inclines many in these areas to conceptualize uncertainty in quantitative terms. In other words, although we may not be certain of some association (e.g., that we will observe or experience some event; that a message has some specific, definite meaning), we might try to quantify the likelihood of association, as in a frequency statistic or Bayesian probability.

Such quantification may or may not be prescriptively meaningful or useful (see Babrow et al., 1998, for a discussion in reference to formal decision analysis), but we believe there is little evidence that it has much relevance to the ways people ordinarily construct their understandings of the world or experience uncertainty (thus the appeal of research on decisional heuristics and the birth of "behavioral economics"). Rather, as indicated by the enormous range of available words, we believe that probabilistic orientations most often take the form of relatively imprecise conceptions of probability, likelihood, or chance ("ordinal" at times, dichotomous at others).[2]

If meaning is associational, and if such associations are in some form probabilistic, then PI theory suggests that any hindrance to these associations can be said to be a form or meaning of uncertainty. Moreover, the associations that provide meaning, understanding, belief, or "truth" can be troubled in many ways. In short, there appear to be numerous forms of uncertainty. Our aim here is not to catalogue these forms (cf. Babrow, 2007a; Babrow et al., 1998). Rather, it is to establish the significance of better recognition, understanding, and appreciation of the variety of ways that uncertainty can be experienced. To illustrate the importance of such variance, we offer a discussion of a small subset of the myriad meanings of uncertainty.

Consider an obvious distinction alluded to in this chapter's introductory narrative: the difference between uncertainty rooted in having too little information versus uncertainty born of information overload. Obviously these experiences require different responses. When we lack information—when we are ignorant—information seeking and provision are clearly sensible responses. By contrast, excessive information requires not more information but strategies for dealing with overload. Coping with ignorance is clearly quite different than managing overwhelming information.

Perhaps less clearly, the more we assume people need additional information, the more we create the circumstances that give rise to information overload, that is, indiscriminate, undigested, uncoordinated avalanches of information. And, because health and other well-intentioned communicators *do* assume that uncertainty is rooted in insufficient information far more often than they recognize the problem of information overload, we rarely see efforts to help people cope with the latter. The topic is largely off the radar for most communication scholars and practitioners. We believe it is off the radar more generally in society—except insofar as we hear people complaining about overload. But how often do you hear constructive suggestions about how to cope other than the mirages offered by various search engines and automated "news" tracking services? In short, insufficient and overabundant information give rise to different experiences of uncertainty, each with its own requirements. Unfortunately, in areas like health communication, scholarship and practice are overwhelmingly devoted to educating, to disseminating information. We thereby neglect the growing need to develop coping strategies even while we heighten the problem by our actions.

Consider another meaning of uncertainty suggested by the story that opened this chapter: the experience of inconsistent information. As we said about having too little or too much information, this third form of uncertainty has its own distinctive implications and requires its own distinctive responses. But again, the hugely predominant assumption in areas like health communication is that uncertainty is rooted in ignorance. As a result, we teach ever-larger numbers of undergraduate and graduate students in communication programs and many allied disciplines how to disseminate information. We thereby create not only overload but also the inescapable challenges of inconsistent information.

In fact, if you think about the very nature of this domain, you realize that it is bursting with opportunities to create inconsistent messages. For instance, health (e.g., pregnancy, menopause) and illness (or marital infidelity, divorce, and many other stressors) are complex, far more complex than most communicators care to imagine. As a direct result, unprincipled and often inconsistent simplifications abound. As another example, health research (among so many other areas) is booming. It is constantly turning up new, often contradictory, information. Unfortunately, the result is that knowledge of health and illness becomes ever more complex, creating the context for ever more breathtaking oversimplification. In addition, communicators of every sort can afford ever less time to digest any one piece of new information before they feed it into burgeoning communication media ravenous for content. Moreover, consider the democratization of information through the World Wide Web and its effect on "authority." In the age of community knowledge projects such as Wikipedia, anyone can assert expertise; everyone is a potential editor. In this age, the only constant is knowing that knowledge can be revised.

And lest interpersonal scholars dismiss this as a problem for media researchers and practitioners, we should note that it is vital to the ever-growing number of us who are seamlessly wired. More and more of us willingly—even greedily—carry the tools of constant Internet access into every corner of our lives. As a result, the unmet need to help people deal with information overload is joined by the unmet need to help us deal with information inconsistency. Paradoxically, some significant forms of uncertainty have never been greater than in the maturing information age.

Another distinct but generally overlooked form of uncertainty can be seen by reconsidering the notion that we are often uncertain in the sense that we lack information. This is commonly called ignorance. But if we take time to reflect, we soon recognize that ignorance can have several differently consequential forms or meanings.

For example, there is a historically important set of distinctions in the medical education literature, introduced by Renee Fox (1957, 1976) in her work on training for uncertainty, which is relevant far beyond this very narrow context. We refer here to the idea that one can be personally ignorant of information that others possess, or one can be ignorant of something that nobody knows any better than we do (call the latter *universal igno-rance*). Fox noted that still another uncertainty is knowing which of the preceding two possibilities fits a given situation. In the past this was a rela-tively distinctive challenge for medical students, who must master enormous—and also enormously incomplete—bodies of knowledge. They have also had to learn how to determine whether in any given situation they are person-ally ignorant or ignorance is universal. Hence, Fox characterized medical education as "training for uncertainty."

However, with the contemporary explosion of information and access to it, the problem described by Fox has come to affect people across all knowl-edge domains. Many of us wonder: Is our personal ignorance or the igno-rance of *experts* surmountable by a broader search for knowledge, or is our ignorance universal? While there has been attention to this distinction and how to deal with it in medical school,[3] there is little consideration of how to deal with it outside of medical education. With the happy exception of Afifi and Weiner's (2004) recognition of the importance of perceived "effi-cacy" in the information-seeking process, it is not on the radar for most people who study uncertainty, information seeking, and information provi-sion. However, there is more here than Fox recognizes in the idea of train-ing for uncertainty or contemporary information-seeking models capture with the notion of efficacy. In other words, we ought to differentiate among forms of universal ignorance.

To develop this point, we offer a story. In graduate school one of us formed a fast friendship with a man who had had kidney failure in his early twenties. When we met him, he was in his late twenties and managing the rigors of a demanding doctoral program while undergoing dialysis several nights each week. What was remarkable about his story was that he had a twin brother who had all along been willing to donate a kidney. The match was as good as could be had. Yet despite the ready availability of an opti-mal match, our friend chose to put off the transplant. For how long? He chose to endure the awesome rigors of dialysis, the neuropathy and joint pains and damage to his circulatory system, and so on, for 15 years.

Our friend took this course of action because of what he was able to learn—but, more importantly, what was unknown when his kidneys first failed. He learned then that transplant success was not very high, that his best chance for success was the one kidney his brother offered, that if that gift failed him his chances of success plummeted, and that, even if the trans-plant was successful, the immunosuppressive therapy he would face for the rest of his life had its own nightmarish side effects. In view of all this, he chose to postpone the transplant for as long as he could bear it, giving as much time as he could for the relevant medical research to advance and improve practice. He finally received his brother's kidney in his mid-thirties. Almost certainly as a direct result, he is still alive today, 20 years later.

The reason we tell this story is because it teaches an important lesson about the unknown, or universal ignorance. There is a very big difference in how we experience and live ignorance when we believe that desired information is unknown but conceivably knowable within some time frame, most especially in time to save our life or that of a loved one, versus the information being unknown but conceivably knowable at some unspecified time in the future. Moreover, these circumstances can be further differentiated from the desire to know what is fundamentally unknowable. As our friend's story illustrates, these distinctions are important. Unfortunately, they are not on the agenda in most research on communication and uncertainty (in illness or otherwise).

Another commonly overlooked distinction that has been profitably developed in work based on problematic integration is that between epistemological and ontological meanings of uncertainty (Babrow, 2001, 2007a; Gill & Babrow, 2007; Matthias, 2009; Matthias & Babrow, 2007). In brief, ontological uncertainties arise in conceptions of the nature of the world, such as the enormous diversity of life (e.g., debates about a variety of different scientific classification systems), the complexity of causal structures, or the play of random or chance influences on events (Anderson, 1996; Babrow, 2001). As an example, the trajectory of any given interpersonal relationship may be seen as fundamentally uncertain because so many factors, both physical and social, can impinge on its movements. Moreover, many of these factors can be understood as fundamentally unpredictable, an idea suggested most forcefully, we think, in the notion that human behavior is underdetermined insofar as it involves choice or agency (Anderson, 1996). So we conceive uncertainty in an ontological sense when we understand it to be inherent in the nature of the world.

By contrast, uncertainty takes on an epistemological cast when it arises in relation to the nature of our knowledge of the world (e.g., inconsistent information, knowledge of questionable relevance to one's interests). While ontological and epistemological uncertainties are interrelated in various ways, they are distinguishable. Even in areas thought to be relatively free of ontological uncertainty (i.e., relatively mechanistic systems), we might have too little or too much information; the information might be from an untrustworthy source; we might trust the source's motives but think, nonetheless, that the data are unreliable, invalid, of questionable relevance, and so on.

In summary, then, at times we are uncertain in the sense that we conceptualize what we are trying to understand as itself inherently uncertain. By contrast, we might be uncertain in the sense that we recognize the limits of our knowledge. PI theory terms the former as *ontological* and the latter as *epistemological* meanings or forms of uncertainty. The theory also emphasizes the consequentiality of this distinction (e.g., Babrow & Dutta-Bergman, 2003). For instance, when a person expresses uncertainty in relation to some aspect of an interpersonal relationship or relevant feature of the world (e.g., what others think about us, what prevailing economic conditions will do to us), she may conceptualize the uncertainty as a matter rooted in the inadequacy of available knowledge. Alternatively, she may understand the uncertainty as fundamentally ontological or a characteristic of the nature of reality. Conceptualized in epistemological terms, information seeking or provision may be helpful. (Of course, as noted above, whether information seeking or provision will be helpful depends in turn on the specific form of epistemological uncertainty involved!) But if the uncertainty is understood ontologically, as a basic feature of interpersonal reality, information seeking or provision, or other behaviors better suited to other epistemological forms of uncertainty, will be seen as irrelevant, a denial of reality, or interacting in bad faith (e.g., a diversion or dissembling).

Consider an example in the domain of romantic relationships. Based on belief that romantic relationships are inherently unpredictable, Dana might express uncertainty about the prospect of living with Gerry. Hearing Dana's uncertainty as epistemological, Gerry might offer reassurances of affection and note corroborating evidence of commitment. Given Dana's ontological uncertainty, Gerry's words might seem naïve or perhaps desperate. Unfortunately, the distinction between epistemological and ontological meanings is rarely noticed in research on uncertainty and information regulation.

To this point in the chapter, we have considered several frequently overlooked distinctions in the meaning of uncertainty and briefly discussed the implications of these oversights. Although we could easily identify more distinctions, it is perhaps more important to dilate on the need for greater attention to these various meanings. Most obviously, insofar as meanings of uncertainty vary, the variance is socially significant, and scholars and practitioners neglect this variance, inquiry and understanding must suffer. For example, prediction and control are left to the chance confluence of underspecified or imprecise conceptual and empirical concoctions. Interpretive research, in which the central question is meaning, in all its dense, nuanced complexity, is also threatened by vague and unreflective understandings of the meaning of uncertainty. From the standpoint of PI theory, unpacking the meanings or forms of uncertainty, their relationships with evaluation, and the chaining across forms or meanings is the essential interpretive task (e.g., see Gill & Babrow, 2007; Shi & Babrow, 2007). Hence, there is much to be gained by more careful understanding of this central concept.

It is also quite likely that neglect of variations in the meanings of uncertainty fosters actions that at times compound the problems of living with uncertainty (e.g., overwhelming information, contradiction, oversimplification and unnecessary complexification, and excessive or inadequate information seeking). These considerations approach but do not quite reach yet another largely overlooked issue in this area of scholarship. We turn now to a brief discussion of this concern.

The More We Learn, The Less We Know

Another enormous but grossly under analyzed challenge in an age besotted with information is that uncertainty reduction begets new uncertainties. In other words, answering any one question about health or substantial inter-personal relations very commonly gives rise to new questions. For example, diagnosis of nontrivial illness (just as information acquisition about any substantial issue) begets a cascading series of questions (see Babrow & Dutta-Bergman, 2003). As other examples, experiences such as parenting, chronic health conditions, and even an effective higher education give rise to lifelong learning. Indeed, basic discoveries themselves surface whole new classes of questions, as we have seen, for example, in the mapping of the human genome. In view of the fact that learning invariably begets new questions, and resolution of a given uncertainty ushers in the uncertainties of a newly discovered world, perhaps we would be wise to think of com-munication about uncertainty in wholly different ways.

For instance, to cope with the cascading sequence of uncertainties that is often the very nature of substantial problems, perhaps the main goal of communication should be relational rather than informational or educa-tional. What we mean by this is that people caught up in complex problems (e.g., marital infidelity, divorce, infertility, birth defects) might find far more value in interactions that secure relations with surrounding networks of loved ones, care providers, friends, and employers. But when our research is focused on uncertainty about illness or a specific relational problem, as it is so often, broader relational issues are secondary considerations, if they are not completely out of mind.

Insofar as we wish to keep uncertainty in mind—the initially problematic uncertainty or the cascade of uncertain sequelae—we encounter the challenges of living with sustained uncertainty and the opportunity to come to a new understanding of these experiences. We refer here to the idea that our under-standing of uncertainty itself can change through time. Fortunately, some theory and research has recognized this important change (e.g., Brashers, 2001; Cohen, 1993; Mishel, 1990). We believe the significance of this insight has been undercut by foundational orientations that are overlearned because they are continually and massively reinforced by contemporary Western culture.

Students of communication can readily and fruitfully recognize and meditate on several relevant ideas that receive little attention in our litera-ture. Western culture enforces the presumption that uncertainty is bad, that certain knowledge is our highest intellectual calling, and that uncertainty reduction should, therefore, be our aim in all but narrowly circumscribed contexts (see Babrow & Kline, 2000). The most frequently noted counter-claim is the idea that uncertainty is a requirement for hope in threatening situations (e.g., Babrow, 2007a; Brashers, 2007; Mishel, 1988, 1990). A somewhat less common realization is that people who confront sustained uncertainty, such as those who live with substantial chronic health problems over a period of time, eventually come to see and accept uncertainty as a basic feature of existence (most notably, see Mishel, 1990). Even less com-mon is the recognition that we do not have to experience ill health or other adverse events to accept—and even embrace—the uncertainty in life. For instance, having children entails a host of intrinsically unknowable future realities, yet fills us with excitement and joy as we anticipate their birth (see Matthias, 2009; Matthias & Babrow, 2007). In the words of PI theory, experiences such as these reflect an ontological (and in this case positively valued) conception of uncertainty.

What is even less frequently recognized, to the point of vanishingly small attention, is the fact that Westerners who approach the ontological insight that uncertainty is the most fundamental characteristic of existence must do so in a culture that is not merely opposed but actively hostile to such acceptance.[4] We would like to see attention devoted to how people who embrace the idea that existence is fundamentally uncertain negotiate with people opposed to this idea. What are these conversations like? When, why, and how do they operate as opposing views, as argument or debate, as persuasion or pleading, as recrimination or cajoling? By contrast, when, why, and how are people able to achieve dialogic openness to uncertainty when profound values are at stake? We believe that these may be among the most pressing questions in an age that seems destined to perfect the modernist paradox: The more we learn, the less we know.

We refer to "dialogic openness" in the preceding because we believe that it is a requirement of truly open and searching discussion when people with vastly different worldviews attempt to talk about profoundly difficult issues. Only by being fully available to one another, without artifice, without the intent to influence, can we approach one another's truth in conversations as fraught with risk as these (see Buber, 1957). These questions have implications of the greatest importance when they arise in relation to highly valued issues such as those having to do with our health or the health of loved ones. Indeed, in our research we have seen the impact of differing views of uncertainty on key health care interactions, such as coping with the uncertainties and decision making in pregnancy (e.g., Matthias & Babrow, 2007).

In addition to dialogic openness, there are several other perspectives for approaching and perhaps surmounting the aforementioned conundrum. For instance, social constructionism quite handily accommodates the issue by recognizing that all knowledge claims are born out of the application and, at times, the development of available constructions or "typifications" (Berger & Luckmann, 1966). As the stock of typifications increases, the materials for and hence the production of new understandings, new constructions, and new questions increase. The recognition of new ways of seeing, new understandings that frequently contradict the old, necessarily heightens our sensitivity to the truth that the more we know (especially, the more ways of understanding we recognize), the more we see the extensiveness of the unknown.

Another way of understanding the conundrum of knowledge begetting ignorance is to cultivate the sort of worldview espoused by traditions such as Buddhism and Daoism (see Babrow, 2007b; Bradac, 2001). Here the challenge for Westerners is that acceptance of fundamental uncertainty can have different meanings. It is likely that much of the time, for Westerners, acceptance means grudging resignation to an inescapable unpleasantness. By contrast, it can also mean positive embrace, such as the realization that life is alive with possibility; this is a key feature of social constructionism for at least one major proponent (see Gergen, 2000). And as still another contrast, acceptance can be a neutral *being with* uncertainty as opposed to *operating on* uncertainty; the latter is essentially the nature of grudging resignation and positive embrace. If this notion of being with uncertainty is unclear, this may reflect the possibility that it transcends linguistic formulation. Words by their nature impose order (Gergen, 2000), so they are likely to be inadequate vehicles for comprehending the experience of being with, being in, or existing noninstrumentally with uncertainty.

Insofar as words structure our perceptions, thoughts, actions, and relationships, we wish to call attention to a formulation that we find troubling. Here we refer to the idea that uncertainty can or should be *managed* or *regulated*. This notion, which has been advanced most elegantly and consistently in Brashers' (2001, 2007) uncertainty management theory, crystallized an important idea and fostered a significant advance in thinking about uncertainty and communication. However, we have come to believe that the terms *uncertainty management* and *information regulation*, if not theories in these names, are limiting; they imply that uncertainty is inherently an experience that can and should be controlled. To explain what we mean here, we want to tell one more story.

One of us (AB) enthusiastically embraced the phrase *uncertainty management* in earlier writing (e.g., Brashers & Babrow, 1996; Ford, Babrow, & Stohl, 1996), but began to change views when treated to a lesson in cultural presumption. A reviewer for the international journal, *Social Science & Medicine*, taught the lesson in response to the first draft of a paper critical of the "ideology of uncertainty reduction" that permeated discourse on breast self-examination (eventually published by Babrow & Kline, 2000). In the first draft of that paper we argued that the ideology was damaging; it ought to be replaced by more forthright recognition of the inescapable uncertainties and the necessity of their management rather than reduction in the realm of breast health. The reviewer gently rebuked us for the "American presumption" of control, arguing persuasively that the idea of "managing uncertainty" partakes of the very control orientation that supports uncertainty reduction. Following this lesson, we have tried to use the phrase *coping with* rather than *managing uncertainty*. However, this too seems to connote something other than acceptance in the sense of simply "being with uncertainty" in a thoroughly noninstrumental, nonwillful way. By contrast, it is useful to think of the idea of "flowing" with the Dao or the Buddhist acceptance of karma.

In any case, and as suggested above, it is difficult to find words for alternatives to managing uncertainty. One unfortunate consequence, we believe, is that the deeply embedded presumption of control is likely to intrude into otherwise insightful cultural critiques of the ideology of uncertainty reduction when guided by the idea of "uncertainty management" (e.g., see Goldsmith, 2001). Hence, the clear implication of control in this wording makes us hope for alternatives. In any case, there is much to be gained by searching analyses of the frequently neglected and suppressed idea that, the more we learn, the less we know.[5]

Conclusion

At this point, the reader might be wondering, how should we orient to uncertainty? We hope you do not think this chapter is meant to suggest that we throw in the towel, that we embrace ignorance or faithlessness. Nothing could be further from our aim. What we do hope is that our readers understand these ideas as an invitation to embrace the ultimate challenge of communication about profound interpersonal uncertainties: to think with greater complexity, subtlety, and humanity about significant uncertainty and the role of communication in these experiences. To do otherwise, to oversimplify, to ignore significant nuances, is to embrace delusion. In the end, if we are to have any hope of communicating well about life's challenges, we must overcome the commonly accompanying delusions. We must meet the real challenges, many of which involve uncertainty about the meanings we hold most dear.

Notes

1 While it is easy to point to the breathtakingly grand accomplishments of science, made possible by heroic efforts to separate knowledge and values, it is just as easy to see that these very accomplishments have brought about equally incomprehensibly dire threats to our existence. It is also foolishness to deny the constructive power of wish and desire on actuality; much of what we now know and experience was motivated originally by desires out of step with what was then current "reality." Humans may be better served in the long run, and in general, by more thoughtfully recognizing and grappling with—rather than trying to deny—the interdependence of probabilistic and evaluative meanings.
2 But note the following qualification:

> Depending upon historical and cultural context, probabilistic orientations will be more or less differentiated and elaborated. In some cultures, there appears to be habitual certainty, or what we might stretch to term *dichotomous probabilistic orientations* (e.g., either "It was/is/will be" or "It was not/is not/never will be"). This would seem to be natural in cultures where people cleave strongly to a clear and compelling cosmology, and where challenges to the cosmology are rare.
>
> (Babrow, 2001, p. 566)

By contrast, contemporary culture as reflected in American English offers words for many gradations of probability, just as contemporary risk communicators have developed probability-scale "magnifiers" that visually enhance sensitivity to very fine probability gradations (e.g., among very low probability events).

3 Atkinson (1984) issued a trenchant challenge to Fox's thesis. In brief, he argued that, not only is medical education *not* training for conscious and explicit grappling with uncertainty, but it is rather more a matter of developing frames of mind that *ignore* or transform uncertainty into confident authority. His provocative thesis may apply as well to extramedical struggles with the paradoxical increase in uncertainty ushered in by the seemingly unlimited access to information through the Internet.

4 Some readers might be tempted to counter this claim with the observation that society actively encourages childbearing and parenting, experiences which this chapter previously used to illustrate sustained, inherent uncertainty. However, we believe that individuals engage in these activities *in spite of* the intrinsic uncertainty of these processes, rather than as a manifestation of the acceptance of uncertainty. This belief is supported by the powerful commitment in contemporary American society to mitigate these uncertainties. Such attempts at uncertainty reduction are nowhere more apparent than in obstetric care in which technology and intervention are heavily employed in order to exert control over reproductive processes (Lupton, 2003). Similarly, note the ever-expanding library of hugely popular books on "what to expect when you're expecting" (Murkoff, Eisenberg, & Hathaway, 2002).

5 None of the preceding should be taken to mean that PI theory denies the power of human interest in knowing, understanding, prediction, and control. On the contrary, the theory recognizes this power in proposing that probabilistic orientation is a central characteristic of human being. The current chapter merely recognizes that worldviews such as Daoism and Buddhism suggest good reasons to lessen the grip of this orientation and offer means to this end. One reading of the strife of world history is that it may manifest the difficulty of achieving this shift (see Babrow, 2007b). Of course, a thorough discussion of these issues is well beyond the scope of this chapter.

References

Afifi, W. A., & Weiner, J. L. (2004). Toward a theory of motivated information management. *Communication Theory, 14*, 167–190.

Anderson, J. A. (1996). *Communication theory: Epistemological foundations*. New York: Guilford.

Atkinson, P. (1984). Training for certainty. *Social Science and Medicine, 19*, 949–956.

Atkinson, P. (1995). *Medical talk and medical work*. London: Sage.

Babrow, A. S. (1992). Communication and problematic integration. *Communication Theory, 2*, 95–130.

Babrow, A. S. (2001). Uncertainty, value, communication and problematic integration. *Journal of Communication, 51*, 553–573.

Babrow, A. S. (2007a). Problematic integration theory. In B. B. Whaley & W. Samter (Eds.), *Explaining communication: Contemporary theories and exemplars* (pp. 181–200). Hillsdale, NJ: Lawrence Erlbaum.

Babrow, A. S. (2007b, November). *Using problematic integration theory, a perspective on communication and human suffering, to promote dialogue across spiritual and other world views*. Paper presented at the annual meeting of the National Communication Association, Chicago, IL.

Babrow, A. S., & Dutta-Bergman, M. J. (2003). Constructing the uncertainties of bioterror: A study of U.S. news reporting on the anthrax attack of Fall, 2001. In C. B. Grant (Ed.), *Rethinking communicative interaction: New interdisciplinary horizons* (pp. 297–317). Amsterdam: John Benjamins.

Babrow, A. S., Kasch, C. R., & Ford, L. A. (1998). The many meanings of "uncertainty" in illness: Toward a systematic accounting. *Health Communication, 10,* 1–24.

Babrow, A. S., & Kline, K. N. (2000). From "reducing" to "coping with" uncertainty: Reconceptualizing the central challenge in breast self-exams. *Social Science and Medicine, 51,* 1805–1816.

Berger, P. L., & Luckmann, T. (1966). *The social construction of reality: A treatise in the sociology of knowledge.* Garden City, NY: Anchor.

Bradac, J. J. (2001). Theory comparison: Uncertainty reduction, problematic integration, uncertainty management, and other curious constructs. *Journal of Communication, 51,* 456–476.

Brashers, D. E. (2001). Communication and uncertainty management. *Journal of Communication, 51,* 477–497.

Brashers, D. E. (2007). A theory of communication and uncertainty management. In B. B. Whaley & W. Samter (Eds.), *Explaining communication: Contemporary theories and exemplars* (pp. 201–218). Hillsdale, NJ: Lawrence Erlbaum.

Brashers, D. E., & Babrow, A. S. (1996). Theorizing health communication. *Communication Studies, 47,* 243–251.

Buber, M. (1957). Elements of the interhuman. *Psychiatry, 20,* 105–113.

Cohen, M. H. (1993). The unknown and the unknowable—Managing sustained uncertainty. *Western Journal of Nursing Research, 15,* 77–96.

Fishbein, M., & Ajzen, I. (1975). *Belief, attitude, intention, and behavior: An introduction to theory and research.* Reading, MA: Addison-Wesley.

Ford, L. A., Babrow, A. S., & Stohl, C. (1996). Social support messages and the management of uncertainty in the experience of breast cancer: An application of problematic integration theory. *Communication Monographs, 63,* 189–207.

Fox, R. C. (1957). Training for uncertainty. In R. K. Merton, G. G. Reader, & P. L. Kendall (Eds.), *The student-physician* (pp. 207–241). Cambridge, MA: Harvard University Press.

Fox, R. C. (1976). Medical evolution. In J. J. Loubser, R. C. Baum, A. Effrat, & V. M. Lidzz (Eds.), *Explorations in general theory in social science* (pp. 773–787). New York: Free Press.

Friedman, S. M., Dunwoody, S., & Rogers, C. L. (1999). *Communicating uncertainty: Media coverage of new and controversial science.* Mahwah, NJ: Lawrence Erlbaum.

Gergen, K. J. (2000). *An invitation to social construction.* London: Sage.

Gill, E. A., & Babrow, A. S. (2007). To hope or to know: Coping with uncertainty and ambivalence in women's magazine breast cancer articles. *Journal of Applied Communication Research, 35,* 133–155.

Goldsmith, D. E. (2001). A normative approach to the study of uncertainty and communication. *Journal of Communication, 51,* 514–533.

Greene, K. (2000). Disclosure of chronic illness varies by topic and target: The role of stigma and boundaries in willingness to disclose. In S. Petronio (Ed.), *Balancing the secrets of private disclosures* (pp. 123–135). Mahwah, NJ: Lawrence Erlbaum.

Johnson, J. D. (1997). *Cancer-related information-seeking*. Cresskill, NJ: Hampton Press.

Kruglanski, A. W. (2004). *The psychology of closed mindedness: Essays in social psychology*. New York: Psychology Press.

Lupton, D. (2003). *Medicine as culture*. London: Sage.

Matthias, M. S. (2009). Problematic integration in pregnancy and childbirth: Contrasting approaches to uncertainty and desire in obstetric and midwifery care. *Health Communication, 24,* 60–70.

Matthias, M. S., & Babrow, A. S. (2007). Problematic integration of uncertainty and desire in pregnancy. *Qualitative Health Research, 17,* 786–798.

Mishel, M. H. (1988). Uncertainty in illness. *Image: Journal of Nursing Research, 20,* 225–232.

Mishel, M. H. (1990). Reconceptualization of the uncertainty in illness theory. *Image: Journal of Nursing Research, 22,* 256–262.

Murkoff, H., Eisenberg, A., & Hathaway, S. (2002). *What to expect when you're expecting* (3rd ed.). New York: Workman.

Petronio, S. (2002). *Boundaries of privacy: Dialectics of disclosure*. Albany, NY: SUNY Press.

Shi, X., & Babrow, A. S. (2007). Challenges of adolescent and young adult Chinese American identity construction: An application of problematic integration theory. *Western Journal of Communication, 71,* 316–335.

Weinstein, N. D., & Klein, W. M. (1996). Unrealistic optimism: Present and future. *Journal of Clinical Psychology, 15,* 1–8.

2 Reclaiming Uncertainty
The Formation of New Meanings

Leslie A. Baxter and Dawn O. Braithwaite

The purpose of this chapter is to reclaim uncertainty along different conceptual lines from the traditional approach evidenced by many of the chapters in this volume. In particular, we reconceptualize (un)certainty away from an individual's ability to predict and explain outcomes, viewing it instead as a characteristic of discourse; more specifically, uncertainty is framed as the interplay of different, often competing, discourses. This reconceptualization is grounded in relational dialectics theory (RDT), which extends the dialogism work of the Russian cultural and literary theorist Mikhail Bakhtin to communication in familial, personal, and social relationships. In contrast to the traditional conceptualization in which communication is positioned as a strategy by which to reduce or manage uncertainty, a dialogic reconceptualization argues that uncertainty is an inherent feature of communication and the key process through which meaning is created. Thus, uncertainty is framed positively, not negatively, in an RDT reconceptualization. Totalizing certainty is to be guarded against, for it holds potential for calcification of meaning and thus potentially can extinguish creativeness by relationship parties. The chapter opens with a discussion of the traditional conceptualization of (un)certainty and then articulates in the second section a dialogically grounded reconceptualization. The third section of the chapter examines implications of this reconceptualization for researchers of communication and relationships.

The Traditional Conceptualization

Contemporary theoretical approaches to (un)certainty owe an intellectual debt to the classic work by Shannon and Weaver (1949) in which uncertainty was conceptualized as the number of alternative outcomes possible in a given situation and the relative likelihoods of their occurrence—uncertainty increased as the number of alternatives increased and as the probabilities of the alternatives became equal. Shannon and Weaver applied this conceptualization to information bits. Thus, for example, if given the letter "T" in English, there are several possible alternatives for the subsequent letters "h," "V," "a," "e," and so forth, each with a given likelihood of occurrence. A popular televised game show capitalizes on this understanding of uncertainty, as contestants guess letters from the emergent clues of surrounding letters and words.

Uncertainty reduction theory (URT; Berger & Calabrese, 1975) extended this classic conceptualization to (un)certainty surrounding another person's (or one's own) behaviors during initial interaction situations. They argued that people were motivated to reduce uncertainty, desiring certainty instead. Berger and Calabrese distinguished proactive certainty (the ability to predict the most likely alternative action the other person might take) from retroactive certainty (the ability to explain another's actions after the fact from several possible alternative explanations). Later applications of URT extended its scope beyond initial interactions to include certainty about an individual at any point in a relationship's history (for a useful review, see Knobloch, 2008).

Subsequent research has extended the certainty concept to a variety of outcome domains. Berger and Bradac (1982) further distinguished cognitive certainty (certainty about one's own or another's attitudes and beliefs) from behavioral certainty (the extent to which another's [or one's own] behavior is predictable in a given situation). Berger and Bradac also differentiated certainty about an individual from certainty about a relationship, arguing that the two kinds of certainty were of different logical types. Other scholars have elaborated on relationship-level (un)certainty (e.g., Knobloch & Solomon, 1999, 2002). Baxter and Montgomery (1996) reported (un)certainty with respect to several different phenomena, including individual cognitions, attitudes, personality, and behaviors; continuity in scheduling the next meeting between parties; the level of excitement and stimulation afforded by interaction episodes; the emotional excitement of "romance"; and the state of the relationship. Health communication scholars have extended the uncertainty concept to include an individual's prediction and explanation of health outcomes (e.g., Babrow, 2001; Brashers, 2001). Thus, people can have varying degrees of predictive/explanatory confidence about a variety of possible phenomena beyond those identified in the 1975 articulation of URT.

In contrast to Berger and Calabrese's (1975) early conceptualization of certainty as positive and uncertainty as negative, subsequent research has indicated a more complex view (see Baxter & Montgomery, 1996, pp. 112–118, for a review of this research). In fact, Berger and Gudykunst (1991) noted that certainty does not appear to be universally positive and can even be negative for relationship parties under certain conditions.

Later work on (un)certainty has embraced this more complex view in which uncertainty can be positive to individuals under certain circumstances. In particular, three uncertainty management theories have arisen in recognition of the fact that people sometimes seek to reduce uncertainty and sometimes do not: problematic integration theory (PIT; Babrow, 1992, 2001); uncertainty management theory (UMT; Brashers, 2001; Brashers et al.,

1999); and the theory of motivated information management (TMIM; Afifi & Weiner, 2004; for a useful review of these theories, see Afifi & Matsunaga, 2008).

Recognition that uncertainty is not universally negative led Baxter and Montgomery (1996) to argue for a dialectical approach to certainty and uncertainty, an approach that recognized the value of both certainty and uncertainty to relationship parties. However, this early argument for a dialectical approach was still positioned largely within the conceptualization of (un)certainty in the Shannon and Weaver (1949) tradition—an individual's confidence in his or her ability to predict an outcome among several alternatives. In this chapter, we mount a different RDT argument, one which shifts the conceptual grounds for the (un)certainty construct. Baxter and Montgomery referred to this alternative conceptualization as the tension between the given and the new, but they failed to develop it fully. In particular, this reconceptualization challenges four central assumptions to existing work on (un)certainty: (a) the assumption that both individuals and relationships are finalizable, which makes certainty about them conceptually possible; (b) the still-present presumption in favor of certainty; (c) the either-or logic that undergirds (un)certainty research and theory; and (d) the location of (un)certainty outside of communication rather than positioning it as an integral part of communication. We briefly address each of these assumptions as a segue to the dialogic reconceptualization detailed in the next section of the chapter.

Assumptions of Existing Research on (Un)certainty

The uncertainty reduction/management theory and research is predicated on a taken-for-granted assumption that the objects of our effort—largely individuals and relationships—are finalizable. That is, the view of the human being and of his or her relationships is that one can achieve certainty and should strive to do so. Individuals and relationships are presumed to have self-contained essences, knowable with the appropriate information acquisition strategies. These essences are preformed and do not provide conceptual room to "unfold an emerging, shifting and open horizon of human possibilities, which . . . emerge as a property of the ongoing dialogue itself" (Sampson, 1993, p. 24). In short, the objects of uncertainty reduction/management are positioned as closed systems, theoretically knowable should one be so motivated and skilled. By contrast, a dialogic reconceptualization of (un)certainty argues that individuals and relationships are potentially ongoingly open.

Although later work on (un)certainty has recognized that uncertainty is not always negative, the shift to uncertainty management, as opposed to uncertainty reduction, still privileges certainty. Language use is not without tendency; thus, it is significant to note that PIT, UMT, and TMIM are theories of uncertainty management, not theories of certainty management. Thus, the presumption is that it is uncertainty that requires management—sometimes managed toward reduction and sometimes not. The prospect that certainty requires management—including the possibility of reducing it—goes unconsidered. In this sense, extant theory and research still privileges certainty, while recognizing exceptions under which parties are not motivated to reduce it. As we will pursue in the next section, an RDT perspective on certainty upends this valencing, finding certainty suspect as a general theoretical position.

Consistent with the Shannon and Weaver (1949) conceptualization of certainty, extant research and theory views the various alternative outcomes as discrete, either-or alternatives. Certainty is one's confidence to predict and explain which single alternative outcome will be enacted, and this, in turn, is based on a probabilistic judgment about the likelihoods of the various options. When one alternative outcome is predicted, the other possible outcomes fade away in an either-or choice-making enterprise. As we develop in the next section, a more dialogic conceptualization of the certainty–uncertainty complex is one in which alternatives hold the potential to interpenetrate with one another in the emergent meaning-making process. This is a both-and logic instead of an either-or logic that characterizes the traditional conception.

The fourth assumption of extant research and theory is that communication, for the most part, rests outside of (un)certainty. (Un)certainty is located in the individual's mind—it is one's confidence to predict or explain some external outcome. Communication is positioned largely as a strategy of management, a mechanism by which uncertainty is reduced, managed, or contained. Thus, for example, the uncertainty reduction and uncertainty management literature focuses extensively on how communication can be deployed as an information-gathering mechanism to gain knowledge that will reduce, or manage, one's uncertainty level (for a useful review, see Knobloch, 2008). To be sure, communication can itself be a source of uncertainty, functioning to subvert our predictive and explanatory confidence (e.g., Brashers, 2001). But the dominant view is that communication is a mechanism of reduction/management, consistent with the Shannon and Weaver (1949) presumption that information = certainty. However, no work in the uncertainty reduction/management tradition argues that communication is inherently an engine of uncertainty and that this quality is essential to meaning making, which is the argument to be developed in the next section.

In reviewing the traditional approach to uncertainty reduction/management, we have identified four important assumptions that scaffold its research and theory. Next, we develop an alternative conceptionalization, one which seeks to reclaim uncertainty along different lines.

A Dialogic Alternative: The Indeterminacy of Intertextuality

Dialogism, the label Holquist (2002) has given to the corpus of work by Russian cultural/literary theorist Mikhail Bakhtin (1981, 1984a, 1984b, 1986, 1990), is a theory of language use and meaning making. Baxter and Montgomery (1996) extended dialogism to communication in relationships in articulating RDT. From the perspective of dialogism, meaning making is a profoundly unfinalizable process. As Bakhtin scholars Morson and Emerson (1990) have written,

> Bakhtin advances the term unfinalizability (nezavershennost) as an all-purpose carrier of his conviction that the world is not only a messy place, but is also an open place. The term appears frequently in his works and in many different contexts. It designates a complex of values central to his thinking: innovation, "surprisingness," the genuinely new, openness, potentiality, freedom, and creativity—terms that he also uses frequently. (pp. 36–37)

Throughout his 50-year scholarly career, Bakhtin was suspicious of closure, certainty, finalizability—semantic unity in any form—referenced by the term *monologue*. By contrast, *dialogue* referenced all forms of unfinalizability or uncertainty. Bakhtin's theory of dialogism is a theory about the ongoing struggle between dialogue and monologue, unfinalizability and closure, uncertainty and certainty. A political victim of the Stalinist regime, Bakhtin resisted all monologic inclinations. In an oft-quoted statement that cuts to the heart of the dialogic project, Bakhtin observed that "any utterance . . . is a contradiction-ridden, tension-filled unity of two embattled tendencies in the life of language" which "serves as a point where centrifugal as well as centripetal forces are brought to bear" (Bakhtin, 1981, p. 272). This struggle is not "between individual wills or logical contradictions" (Bakhtin, 1981, p. 273) but rather reflects Bakhtin's conception of language use as "ideologically saturated," riddled with "worldviews" that represent more dominant, centralized, "official," or finalized systems of meaning (i.e., centripetal tendencies) in play with less dominant, marginalized, "unofficial," or open systems of meaning (i.e., centrifugal tendencies). Meaning emerges in the moment out of the interplay of these different, often competing, systems of meaning or discourses. As Bakhtin (1981) has vividly stated,

> Any concrete utterance . . . enters a dialogically agitated and tension-filled environment of alien words, value judgments and accents, weaves in and out of complex interrelationships. . . . The living utterance, having taken meaning and shape at a particular historical moment in a socially specific environment, cannot fail to brush up against thousands of living dialogic threads woven by socio-ideological consciousness around the given object of an utterance; it cannot fail to become an active participant in social dialogue. After all, the utterance arises out of this dialogue as a continuation of it and as a rejoinder to it—it does not approach the object from the sidelines. (pp. 276–277)

This "dialogically agitated" dynamic is referred to by Allen (2000) as *intertextuality*. As Barthes (1977, p. 159) has noted, the original meaning of the word *text* is "a tissue, a woven fabric." The term *intertextuality* thus builds on the image of a woven fabric of meaning that is created from the play of different threads of meaning.

But where do these competing discourses come from? Building upon Bakhtin's (1986) conception of communication as a "chain of speech communion" (p. 93), four different sites of discourse hold potential for communication of relationship parties (Baxter, in press; Baxter & Montgomery, 1996). First, some of the links in the speech-communion chain can be quite distant in space and time; these distal links represent the cultural already-spoken utterances of the past. Whenever we speak, argued Bakhtin, we potentially use words that are already populated with others' prior utterances. Utterances in the here-and-now "speak culture" and can be riddled throughout with any number of already circulating social/cultural ideologies. Second, other utterances in the chain of speech communion may be more proximal: prior utterances in the parties' relational history or prior utterances in the immediate conversation at hand. These discursive links represent dialogic overtones with the already-spokens of the current interaction event, inflecting the present utterance with relational themes from the relationship's past (Wood, 1982). The third and fourth sites of discourse shift attention from the past to the anticipated future. Utterances not only can reverberate with dialogic perspectives of already-spokens but they can also be laced with the dialogic overtones of utterances that are anticipated to follow. Similar to the proximal and distant perspectives of the already-spokens, proximal and distant voices can be identified with the not-yet-spokens in the chain of speech communion. An utterance can take into account the immediate addressee's possible responses, the third kind of discourse. But an addressee can be distant, as well—others who are not a fellow participant in the immediate conversation but who may respond to the utterance at some future point. The anticipated addressee could be a specific person or the generalized "other" of Bakhtin's (1986) superaddressee. The superaddressee is akin to people in general or society, and invokes communicators' conception of what is regarded as normative or ideal.

A given utterance exchanged between relationship parties can create a variety of possible meaning outcomes, depending on how the struggle of competing discourses unfolds; that is, whether or not the meanings that emerge in the moment of interaction function reproductively to instantiate dominant discourses or to formulate new meanings, meaning outcomes will still unfold. Such meanings of the moment are a kind of certainty, but a contingent certainty, a certainty that is unfinalized and that holds the potential to be abandoned in the next interaction moment. This contingent certainty is the only kind of certainty that is valued from a dialogic perspective, but it becomes monologic if it becomes calcified over time.

The threat of monologue is ever-present. As the terms *centripetal* and *centrifugal* suggest, not all threads in Bakhtin's cloth of meaning making are positioned equally. Centripetal discourses have the advantage; they are more likely to function presumptively as taken-for-granted meaning. By contrast, centrifugal discourses are more marginalized; they carry a heavier semantic burden to challenge, dislodge, or disrupt commonly accepted meanings. Thus, from a dialogic perspective, the problem is not how to achieve certainty. The dialogic project is one of vigilance to keep the struggle for meaning open—to embrace uncertainty and the creative bricolage that it allows.

Centripetal discourse can be reproduced in a variety of ways. The most harmful from Bakhtin's perspective is complete monologue in an authoritative discourse so dominant that other, competing discourses are virtually absent. Authoritative discourse "demands our unconditional allegiance" (Bakhtin, 1981, p. 343). He describes authoritative discourse as "the word of the fathers" (Bakhtin, 1981, p. 342), fused with tradition and authority that give it taken-for-granted status. It is "not surrounded by an agitated and cacophonous dialogic life" (Bakhtin, 1981, p. 344), but rather functions with hard-edged finality as "Truth." Bakhtin viewed authoritative discourse as a state of totalizing certainty. Instead of Shannon and Weaver's (1949) view that certainty is information rich, Bakhtin viewed the monologue of authoritative discourse as the death of creativity; it represents "inertia," "semantic finiteness," and "calcification" (Bakhtin, 1981, p. 344). Monologic authoritative discourses are central to the process of reproduction in which dominant meanings become instantiated. They become accepted as stable "reality" (Berger & Luckmann, 1966).

Even when centrifugal discourses are in play with centripetal discourses, the latter can still win the semantic dance of meaning making. Fairclough (2003) has usefully summarized three ways in which centripetal discourses can reproduce the marginalized positioning of centrifugal discourses in the prosaic struggles of everyday interaction. The first is an accentuation of difference in the form of conflict-laden utterances, in which marginalized discourses are explicitly recognized as worthy of response. However, this response is a polemic one that functions to defeat all but the centripetal discourse. The second response is also explicit in its recognition of a centrifugal discourse; however, utterances function to resolve the discrepancy between competing discourses, albeit in a manner that still centers the centripetal discourse. For example, utterances which assert that a centrifugal discourse has already been taken into account in the centripetal discourse function through cooptation to accomplish resolution in favor of the centripetal discourse. The third form of reproduction work involves a bracketing of centrifugal meanings, a communicative effort to give them a token nod that functions to trivialize or to contain them. This third form of engaging centrifugal discourses is the most subtle; Bakhtin (1984a) describes it as the "word with a sideward glance" (p. 208). "Sideward glances" are evident in a variety of communicative practices, according to Bakhtin, including parody, use of diminutives, and the expression of reservations, among others.

Other meaning outcomes are more disruptive, functioning to unseat dominant discourses in some manner. Relationship parties can jointly construct meanings that involve an inversion across time with respect to which discourses are centered and which discourses are marginalized (Baxter & Montgomery, 1996). This diachronic ebb and flow moves back and forth, with centered and marginalized discourses changing places in the meaning-making process. Such ebb-and-flow inversions are common patterns of meaning making by relationship partners (Baxter, 2004), but they elide discursive struggles by constructing them in the form of either-or dilemmas. For example, a couple who negotiate autonomy on some occasions and connection on others illustrates this ebb-and-flow pattern.

Relationship parties can also elide discursive struggles by constructing a segmented system, usually organized along topical lines (Baxter & Montgomery, 1996). On Topic X, one discourse is accepted as authoritative, or taken for granted, for example, a discourse of privacy. On Topic Y, a competing discourse is centered as authoritative, for example, a discourse of openness. Such segmentation practices are also common patterns of meaning making by relationship parties but also work by constructing the interplay of discourses as an either-or dilemma (Baxter, 2004).

Discursive struggles are also skirted when relationship parties construct ambiguous or equivocal conditional meanings. Ambiguity centers neither the dominant nor marginalized discourse, instead functioning as a discursive lubricant that allows meaning to maneuver between discourses. Ambiguity is arguably a creative act of meaning making because it functions to undermine all given systems of meaning, whether dominant or not. However, its creativity works through absence, not presence. That is, it creates a void in meaning rather than crafting a new meaning. Nonetheless, ambiguity can open a space for subsequent meaning making that moves beyond given discourses (Eisenberg, 1984).

Bakhtin's idealized dialogue transpires when centripetal and centrifugal discourses are in play with and against one another. Out of this open, fluid, give-and-take dynamic of different value-laden perspectives, new meanings can emerge. To Bakhtin, such meaning making best realizes the creative potential of language use, and the dialogic project is committed to nurturing this potentiality. Idealized dialogue is a process of bricolage, creating new meanings out of the givens of already-spoken and anticipated not-yet-spoken discourses.

Baxter and Braithwaite (in press) discuss two specific kinds of creative meaning making discussed by Bakhtin. The first form of creativity is what Bakhtin (1981, p. 358) called a *hybrid*—a mixing of discrete discursive meaning systems. Think of hybrids as salad dressing made by mixing oil and vinegar. The discourses (oil, vinegar) are distinct, yet they combine to form a new meaning—salad dressing. Another kind of discursive mixture is what Bakhtin (1990, p. 67) referred to as an *aesthetic moment*; that is, meaning making in which discourses are no longer framed as oppositional but instead merge in a way that profoundly alters each meaning system. These aesthetic meanings of consummation are crafted along new discursive lines. Think of aesthetic moments as akin to what chemists call reactions. For example, two molecules of hydrogen combine with one molecule of oxygen to produce an entirely new entity—water.

In returning to the four assumptions that undergird the traditional conception of certainty discussed in the first section of the chapter, the contrast afforded by our dialogic reconceptualization becomes clear. We underscore that the issue at stake is not which conceptualization is better or worse; rather, our point is that the two conceptualizations hold very different assumptions which in turn hold radically different implications for research on (un)certainty, a matter we turn to in the last section of the chapter.

Rather than presuming that individuals and relationships are closed, finalizable systems of meanings that are knowable, a dialogic perspective privileges instead the opposite presumption: Individuals and relationships, like all objects of meaning making, are open with the potential to change in new, unanticipated ways that emerge out of interaction. Rather than focusing on how persons achieve closure on one another, and on their relationship, the dialogic project would have scholars focus instead on how communication can be used to create space for individuals and relationships to change.

Instead of privileging certainty, and reducing or managing uncertainty, a dialogic perspective instead adopts a suspicious stance toward certainty and embraces uncertainty. Uncertainty in the form of intertextuality is the key requisite to creativity. The meanings that emerge in the moment are conditional certainties, always open to overthrow in the next interactional moment. By contrast, the totalizing certainty of monologue results in stagnant systems of meaning.

Although relationship parties often appear to respond to intertextuality in the either-or activities of cycling inversion and segmentation, the dialogic ideal is a free-flowing interplay of different, often competing, discourses. It is the interplay of discourses that holds the greatest potential for creativity, not choosing one discourse over another as characterizing an either-or logic.

Finally, a dialogic reconceptualization of uncertainty shifts communication to the center of the phenomenon. Communication is inherently an intertextual affair, and the uncertain play of different discourses is what allows meaning making in the moment. Thus, uncertainty is not an impediment to meaning, nor a sign of ineffective or incomplete communication. It is essential to the realization of communication's potential to construct new meanings from given discourses. In this reconceptualization, communication is not viewed as a means of uncertainty reduction or management; rather, it is the play of uncertainty and certainty.

What are the implications for research on (un)certainty from a dialogic perspective? We address some possible directions for research in the final section of the chapter.

Implications for Research

RDT-based work on communication and relationships privileges uncertainty, not certainty, because it is through uncertainty that new meanings are invented for all types of relationships. Creativity has received scant attention by scholars of interpersonal communication. Those few who attend to creativeness tend to view it as an individual accomplishment of message production (e.g., Greene, 2008). The kind of creativity envisioned by an RDT approach is not something an individual achieves; rather, it emerges in the talk between interactants—it is a joint accomplishment. Further, creativity is not envisioned as the production of a message; rather, it is the achievement of an emergent meaning that somehow adds a new discursive voice to the swirl of given discourses that are circulating. Dialogic creativity is thus no small feat to accomplish. In fact, we suspect that much of our interaction experiences are quite devoid of it, instead functioning to reproduce dominant, taken-for-granted meanings. Nonetheless, it is an important process to understand, for dialogic creativity is central to change, how individuals as well as relationships grow and change as a consequence of interaction. A focus on this creative capacity of communication shifts our attention to issues and questions that are different from those engaged by a traditional approach to (un)certainty. We will discuss three implications in this section in terms of individual self/identity as open, relating as intertextual, and dialogic genres of communication.

Individual Self/Identity as Open

Existing research and theory in interpersonal communication tends to presume a preformed self, that is, an individual's identity is formed prior to the interaction and becomes knowable through his or her self-disclosure revelations and through the other's information acquisition strategies, consistent with the traditional approach to (un)certainty. By contrast, the perspective developed in this chapter asks a different question: How are individual selves and identities constructed through communication with others? Baxter and Montgomery (1996) have argued that the key marker of relationship closeness is not how much relationship partners know one another but rather how much they facilitate one another's growth through their joint interaction experiences. From this perspective, self-disclosure is not approached as an informational device but rather as an utterance in a chain of speech communion in which discourses from an individual's already-spoken past are put into play with utterances of the conversation at hand and the anticipated evaluations of the not-yet-spokens. Self-disclosure becomes a conversational move that then is jointly negotiated between parties in producing a meaning of the moment. That meaning may function reproductively, reinforcing the individual's sense of self and identity, which entered the interaction encounter and its dominant discourses, or it may alter that self or identity in some modest or profound manner.

From a dialogic perspective, it is the fact that partners are different from one another that affords the opportunity to create new individual selves and identities. As Holquist (2002, p. 18) noted, central to the dialogic perspective is the presumption that "the very capacity to have consciousness is based on otherness." The "other" has a unique horizon of seeing (Bakhtin, 1990) different from one's own perspective. Through interaction, an individual's horizon of seeing is put into play with the other's horizon of seeing, both are fluid, and the result of such interplay is an emergent self and identity. In short, the other's difference is important in creating individual selves and identities.

The traditional approach to (un)certainty regards difference negatively, instead valuing similarity as an important mechanism of uncertainty reduction. Relational communication scholars have overwhelmingly emphasized the study of partner similarity in personal relationships for over four decades (e.g., Byrne, 1971; Newcomb, 1961), to the relative neglect of partner differences. Partners clearly value their similarities (see Baxter & West, 2003, for a review).

Scholars know considerably less about the role of differences. Byrne and Lamberth (1971) early on suggested that difference need not be damaging to a relationship, and early research on need complementarity or compatibility (e.g., Schutz, 1960; Winch, 1958) found that complementary differences could be positive for relationship parties.

In general, more recent research on partner differences suggests that relationship partners hold an ambivalent attitude toward their differences. Wood, Dendy, Dordek, Germany, and Varallo (1994) interviewed marital partners about the role of difference in their marriage, finding that spouses could identify both positive and negative aspects of difference. Felmlee's (1998) research program in fatal attractions has suggested that partners may initially be attracted to prospective partners because they are different from oneself, yet those very differences can later come back to haunt the parties and prove fatal to the relationship. The theory of self-expansion (e.g., Aron, Aron, & Smollan, 1992) suggests that both similarities and differences can be sources of interpersonal attraction, as they can increase the pool of available perspectives and resources available to each individual. Grounded in RDT, Baxter and West (2003) asked relationship partners jointly to reflect on their positive and negative similarities and differences. Although partners were able to identify a few negatively functioning similarities and both positively and negatively functioning differences, the data were dominated by the identification of various bases of similarity that were perceived to function positively. Although less salient than similarities, differences were clearly a source of ambivalence for these participants. In support of the RDT argument, the foremost perceived advantage of partner difference was its capacity to enable the partners' selves to grow, but differences were also perceived to bring discomfort and conflict.

In an effort to see how this ambivalence plays itself out in partner talk, Baxter, Foley, and Thatcher (2008) recently conducted an RDT-positioned study to analyze how partners talk about their similarities and differences, concluding that partners embraced their similarities but interacted in ways to contain and limit their differences. Relationship partners used four primary practices to symbolically erase their differences: silencing, relationship distancing, negative valencing, and marking discomfort. Silencing included several communicative practices, including topic shifts when differences were introduced, self-censorship that functioned to stop difference talk, denial of difference, interruption when the partner discussed differences, efforts to minimize differences, and reframing differences as similarities. Relationship distancing involved the use of nonimmediacy cues and metatalk that explicitly equated similarity with closeness and difference with distance. Negative valencing involved a variety of practices, including the use of justifications to rationalize differences, pejorative terms to describe differences, and explicit metatalk indicating that differences were negative while similarities were positive. Last, partners marked their discomfort with their differences through several communication features, including nervous laughter, dysfluencies, and explicit metatalk about their level of discomfort in discussing their differences compared to their similarities. These communication practices collectively indicate that partner differences were treated by them as problems for their relationship. By comparison, partners tended to vocalize and positively valence their similarities, indicating that partners framed their similarities as beneficial to relationships. This study suggests that partners negotiate the intertextuality of similarity and difference by reproducing their positive attitudes toward similarity, while muting difference. Nevertheless, if differences are important to the creation of selves and identities, as a dialogic perspective argues, partners may be limiting their opportunities for individual growth.

Ironically, a dialogic approach to the creation of individual selves and identities returns scholars to the humanistic roots of interpersonal communication in the human potential movement of the 1960s. However, in contrast to the "warm and fuzzy" stereotype often attached to that era, the dialogic creation process has a harder edge, based on discursive struggle rather than affirmation.

Relating as Intertextual

The creativeness afforded by the uncertainty of intertextuality is also important in the construction of relationships. By its very definition, change presumes a shift in meanings to something new. The traditional approach to (un)certainty positions communication as an information carrier, allowing parties to determine whether getting closer is sufficiently rewarding to them personally (e.g., Altman & Taylor, 1973). Thus, the engine of relationship change, from a traditional perspective, is psychological—the extent to which the parties find the relationship rewarding or gratifying. By contrast, an RDT perspective locates the engine of change inside of communication itself, specifically in intertextuality. In the parties' interaction encounters, one definition of the relationship jockeys with alternative possible definitions, and which definition emerges in the moment—whether a dominant given discourse, a marginalized discourse, or a newly emergent definitional bricolage—depends on how the talk unfolds.

Existing research does not provide us with many examples of how relationships are created out of discursive struggle. But we can certainly discuss how such research might usefully proceed. Elsewhere (Baxter & Braithwaite, in press), we have discussed the qualitative method by which a dialogic analysis ought to proceed—what Bakhtin (1984a) labeled *contrapuntal analysis* (p. 221). Contrapuntal analysis is a specific kind of discourse analysis that focuses on the "collision" (p. 184) or "counterpoint" (p. 221) of different discourses. In general terms, a contrapuntal analysis proceeds by asking and answering these three analytic questions: (a) What discourses, or systems of meaning, are circulating in the talk of relationship parties; (b) Where are these discourses located with respect to the already-spokens and not-yet-spokens of the chain of speech communion; and (c) How do these discourses interanimate to create meanings in the moment. With respect to the emergent meaning of the relationship, the issue becomes that of identifying competing relationship definitions and where they are located in the speech communion chain, and examining their "collision" in talk.

An obvious place to begin a research program in relationship change is to study relationship processes that, on their face, display competing discourses in bold relief. For example, transition relationships that could be defined by a discourse of "platonic friendship" or a discourse of "romantic relationship" make interesting candidates for study at the fine-grained level of partner talk. In contrast to the traditional approach to (un)certainty, which might examine the extent to which confidence in predicting a partner's attitudes and behaviors is correlated with progression from friendship to romantic involvement, RDT researchers could usefully analyze naturally occurring talk between partners to see how "friendship talk" and "romantic partner talk" interweave, or researchers could analyze interview data to see how these two discourses circulate in partner sense making of their relationship. The discourse of friendship and the discourse of romance are also at play in the negotiation of cross-sex heterosexual pairs. Other relationships where competing discourses are obvious include divorcing parents where a discourse of parental cooperation is in play with a discourse of disaffected ex-ship, adolescent–parent relationships or adult child–elderly parent relationships where a discourse of dependence is in play with a competing discourse of independence, and fictive/voluntary kin relationships where a discourse of family based on biology and law competes with a discourse of family based on mutual affection, to identify just a few.

Our own research program has focused on two other sites of relationship definition where competing discourses are at play: older marriages and the stepfamily. In three studies we have examined discursive struggles faced by long-term marital couples. Two of these studies (Baxter & Braithwaite, 2002; Braithwaite & Baxter, 1995) examined the marital renewal vow ceremony as a site of performance for what "marriage" means. We identified several competing discourses, providing alternative definitions of marriage: marriage as a public institution versus marriage as a private culture of two, marriage as unique versus marriage as conventionalized, marriage as stable versus marriage as ongoingly adaptive, and marriage as a life-long commitment of responsibility versus marriage as a contingent relationship of gratification. Continuing our focus on older married pairs, we have also examined the competing discourses that surround the "married widowhood" (Rollins, Waterman, & Esmay, 1985) of women whose husbands have moved to a nursing home because of the onset of adult dementia from Alzheimer's disease and related disorders (Baxter, Braithwaite, Golish, & Olson, 2002).

In a series of studies, we have examined the competing discourses that animate stepfamily life, especially stepchild relationships with parents from the family of origin (residential and nonresidential) and with stepparents (Baxter, Braithwaite, Bryant, & Wagner, 2004; Baxter et al., 2007; Braithwaite & Baxter, 2006; Braithwaite, Baxter, & Harper, 1998; Braithwaite, Toller, Daas, Durham, & Jones, 2008). Across these studies, we have seen discursive struggles of the "old family" of origin in play with and against the "new family" of the stepfamily household, and a struggle of the discourse of family in which the marital relationship is centered versus a discourse of family in which the parent–child relationship is centered.

However, as Bakhtin would remind us, competing discourses are omnipresent in the prosaics of everyday relational life; we do not need to confine our scholarly gaze to relationship definition processes where discursive struggle beckons us with a blow horn. As illustration of this point, we turn to an interesting dialogically based study by Taylor (1995) in which a dinner conversation was tape-recorded in a family. One competing discourse—favored by the parents—was that the parents were merely having a discussion over a particular topic while eating; a competing discourse—suspected by the children—was that the parents were fighting. The parents talked with the children in ways that functioned to extinguish the "fight" framing in favor of the "discussion" framing. Thus, the meanings at stake in the moment are not necessarily limited to large-scale issues of the relationship's definition; they can deal with more mundane matters as well, such as what kind of interaction encounter is unfolding at the moment.

Dialogic Genres of Communication

In opening up space for communication to be conceptualized as something more than a device of information sharing/acquisition, a dialogic perspective usefully poses the question of which communication genres are more and less likely to function dialogically. For our purposes, a genre simply refers to a speech event with a commonly recognized organizational pattern—greetings, having a fight, and so forth (Bakhtin, 1986; Goldsmith & Baxter, 1996). Although all language use holds potential for dialogue, according to Bakhtin (1981), it is more easily realized in some genres over others.

Arguably among the most dialogic genres is the carnival event, in which life-as-usual is suspended and overturned temporarily (Bakhtin, 1984a, 1984b). Hierarchies are inverted, and mockery challenges all that is serious. Carnivalesque interactions create space for alternative meanings to emerge, in that "the behavior, gesture, and discourse of a person are freed from the authority of all hierarchical positions . . . defining them totally in noncarnival life" (Bakhtin, 1984a, p. 123). Although relationships do not have carnivalesque events on the grand scale of the Mardi Gras, they appear to be characterized by episodes of ritualized playfulness in which everyday life is temporarily suspended (Baxter, 1992). We know little of such events, and most important, we do not know whether they function in a carnivalesque manner to construct new meanings for relationship parties or merely to punctuate the reproduction of old habituated systems of meaning.

In a series of studies, we have examined the ritual as another speech genre that, when executed successfully, functions dialogically. As a number of ritual scholars have observed, successfully performed rituals pay homage to multiple, often competing, discourses (for a review of the vast rituals literature, see Baxter & Braithwaite, 2006). Such homage places discourses on equal footing and may constitute aesthetic moments in which the oppositional quality of discourses is reframed along different lines. For example, the marriage vow renewal ceremony appears to seamlessly construct "marriage" as both public and private, both unique and conventional, both stable yet fluid, both individualistic and communal (Baxter & Braithwaite, 2002; Braithwaite & Baxter, 1995). When stepfamilies are able to craft family rituals that pay homage to both the "old family" of origin and the "new family" of the stepfamily household, they arguably accomplish an aesthetic moment of celebration. Most recently, we have examined the remarriage ceremony between a parent and a stepparent from the stepchild's perspective (Baxter et al., 2007). Although this ceremony sometimes functioned to pay homage to the marriage of the adults, the "old family" of origin, and the "new" stepfamily unit, more typically, our informants told us of empty rituals in which only the marriage was honored while both the "old family" and the "new family" were symbolically ignored. Clearly, more dialogic work on the rituals of relating is warranted.

In inquiring about dialogic and monologic speech events, we shift the question from how communication is used strategically to reduce or manage uncertainty to ask which kinds of communication practices best realize the potential for creative bricolage in meaning making. To answer this question fully also requires a response to the opposite question of which speech genres function monologically, calcifying dominant meanings and muting more marginalized systems of meaning. The specter of monologue is one best met by a critical paradigmatic perspective, complementing the postpositivistic paradigm that currently dominates the study of interpersonal communication (Braithwaite & Baxter, 2008).

Conclusion

We fully appreciate that the perspective represented in this chapter is "odd man out" from that found in other chapters in this volume, and we applaud the intellectual openness of the editors for soliciting its inclusion. The dialogic reconceptualization of (un)certainty that we have articulated suspends four critical assumptions of the traditional conceptualization first articulated by Shannon and Weaver (1949) and extended in URT and the uncertainty management theories. Uncertainty is reconceptualized away from an individual's level of predictive and explanatory knowledge about a person, relationship, or other phenomenon to a view of it as an inherent quality of communication: intertextuality. Intertextuality is uncertain, and it is a requisite to meaning making. Sometimes, meaning making in the moment functions to reproduce given dominant discourses, risking calcification of individual selves and relationships. However, communication also holds the potential for dialogic creativity—the construction of new meanings. The potential for bricolage frames communication as jazz, consisting of "many voices joined in the simultaneous play of 'the already existing' with the 'new and unrepeatable'" (Baxter & Montgomery, 1996, p. 131).

References

Afifi, W. A., & Matsunaga, M. (2008). Uncertainty management theories: Three approaches to a multifarious process. In L. A. Baxter & D. O. Braithwaite (Eds.), *Engaging theories in interpersonal communication* (pp. 117–132). Thousand Oaks, CA: Sage.

Afifi, W. A., & Weiner, J. L. (2004). Toward a theory of motivated information management. *Communication Theory, 14*, 167–190.

Allen, G. (2000). *Intertextuality*. New York: Routledge.

Altman, I., & Taylor, D. (1973). *Social penetration: The development of interpersonal relationships*. New York: Holt, Rinehart, and Winston.

Aron, A., Aron, E., & Smollan, D. (1992). Inclusion of Other in the Self Scale and the structure of interpersonal closeness. *Journal of Personality and Social Psychology, 63*, 596–612.

Babrow, A. S. (1992). Communication and problematic integration: Understanding diverging probability and value, ambiguity, ambivalence, and impossibility. *Communication Theory, 2*, 95–130.

Babrow, A. S. (2001). Uncertainty, value, communication, and problematic integration. *Journal of Communication, 51*, 553–573.

Bakhtin, M. M. (1981). *The dialogic imagination: Four essays by M. M. Bakhtin* (M. Holquist, Ed.; C. Emerson & M. Holquist, Trans.). Austin, TX: University of Texas Press.

Bakhtin, M. M. (1984a). *Problems of Dostoevsky's poetics* (C. Emerson, Ed. & Trans.). Minneapolis, MN: University of Minnesota Press.

Bakhtin, M. M. (1984b). *Rabelais and his world* (H. Iswolsky, Trans.). Bloomington, IN: Indiana University Press.

Bakhtin, M. M. (1986). *Speech genres and other late essays* (C. Emerson & M. Holquist, Eds.; V. McGee, Trans.). Austin, TX: University of Texas Press.

Bakhtin, M. M. (1990). *Art and answerability: Early philosophical essays by M. M. Bakhtin* (M. Holquist & V. Liapunov, Eds.; V. Liapunov & K. Brostrom, Trans.). Austin, TX: University of Texas Press.

Barthes, R. (1977). *Image – Music – Text* (S. Heath, Trans.). London, UK: Fontana.

Baxter, L. A. (1992). Forms and functions of intimate play in personal relationships. *Human Communication Research, 18*, 336–363.

Baxter, L. A. (2004). Distinguished scholar article: Relationships as dialogues. *Personal Relationships, 11*, 1–22.

Baxter, L. A. (in press). The distinctiveness of communication research: A dialogic perspective. In D. Carbaugh & P. Buzzanell (Eds.), *Distinctive qualities of communication research*. New York: Routledge.

Baxter, L. A., & Braithwaite, D. O. (2002). Performing marriage: The marriage renewal ritual as cultural performance. *Southern Communication Journal, 67*, 94–109.

Baxter, L. A., & Braithwaite, D. O. (2006). Family rituals. In L. H. Turner & R. West (Eds.), *The family communication sourcebook* (pp. 259–280). Thousand Oaks, CA: Sage.

Baxter, L. A., & Braithwaite, D. O. (2008). Relational dialectics theory: Crafting meaning from competing discourses. In L. A. Baxter & D. O. Braithwaite (Eds.), *Engaging theories in interpersonal communication* (pp. 349–362). Thousand Oaks, CA: Sage.

Baxter, L. A., & Braithwaite, D. O. (in press). Relational dialectics theory, applied. In S. W. Smith & S. R. Wilson (Eds.), *New directions in interpersonal communication*. Thousand Oaks, CA: Sage.

Baxter, L. A., Braithwaite, D. O., Bryant, L., & Wagner, A. (2004). Stepchildren's perceptions of the contradictions of communication with stepparents. *Journal of Social and Personal Relationships, 21*, 447–467.

Baxter, L. A., Braithwaite, D. O., Golish, T. D., & Olson, L. N. (2002). Contradictions of interaction for wives of elderly husbands with adult dementia. *Journal of Applied Communication Research, 30*, 1–16.

Baxter, L. A., Braithwaite, D. O., Koenig Kellas, J., LeClair-Underberg, C., Lamb-Normand, E., Routsong, T., & Thatcher, M. (2007, November). *Empty ritual: Young-adult stepchildren's perceptions of the remarriage ceremony.* Paper presented at the annual meeting of the National Communication Association Convention, Chicago.

Baxter, L. A., Foley, M., & Thatcher, M. (2008). Marginalizing difference in personal relationships: A dialogic analysis of how partners talk about their differences. *Journal of Communication Studies, 1*, 33–55.

Baxter, L. A., & Montgomery, B. M. (1996). *Relating: Dialogues and dialectics.* New York: The Guilford Press.

Baxter, L. A., & West, L. (2003). Couple perceptions of their similarities and differences: A dialectical perspective. *Journal of Social and Personal Relationships, 20*, 491–514.

Berger, C. R., & Bradac, J. J. (1982). *Language and social knowledge: Uncertainty in interpersonal relationships.* London: Edward Arnold.

Berger, C. R., & Calabrese, R. J. (1975). Some explorations in initial interaction and beyond: Toward a developmental theory of interpersonal communication. *Human Communication Research, 1,* 99–112.

Berger, C. R., & Gudykunst, W. B. (1991). Uncertainty and communication. In B. Dervin & M. J. Voight (Eds.), *Progress in communication sciences* (Vol. 10, pp. 21–66). Norwood, NJ: Ablex.

Berger, P. L., & Luckmann, T. (1966). *The social construction of reality.* New York: Doubleday & Company.

Braithwaite, D. O., & Baxter, L. A. (1995). "I do" again: The relational dialectics of renewing marriage vows. *Journal of Social and Personal Relationships, 12,* 177–198.

Braithwaite, D. O., & Baxter, L. A. (2006). "You're my parent, but you're not": Dialectical tensions in stepchildren's perceptions about communication with the nonresidential parent. *Journal of Applied Communication Research, 34,* 30–48.

Braithwaite, D. O., & Baxter, L. A. (2008). Introduction: The state of theory in interpersonal communication. In L. A. Baxter & D. O. Braithwaite (Eds.), *Engaging theories in interpersonal communication* (pp. 1–18). Thousand Oaks, CA: Sage.

Braithwaite, D. O., Baxter, L. A., & Harper, A. M. (1998). The role of rituals in the management of the dialectical tension of "old" and "new" in blended families. *Communication Studies, 48,* 101–120.

Braithwaite, D. O., Toller, P., Daas, K., Durham, W., & Jones, A. (2008). Centered, but not caught in the middle: Stepchildren's perceptions of contradictions of communication of co-parents. *Journal of Applied Communication Research, 36,* 33–55.

Brashers, D. E. (2001). Communication and uncertainty management. *Journal of Communication, 51,* 477–497.

Brashers, D. E., Neidig, J. L., Cardillo, L. W., Dobbs, L. K., Russell, J. A., & Haas, S. M. (1999). "In an important way, I did die." Uncertainty and revival among persons living with HIV or AIDS. *AIDS Care, 11,* 201–219.

Byrne, D. (1971). *The attraction paradigm.* New York: Academic Press.

Byrne, D., & Lamberth, J. (1971). Cognitive and reinforcement theories as complementary approaches to the study of attraction. In B. I. Murstein (Ed.), *Theories of attraction and love* (pp. 59–84). New York: Springer.

Eisenberg, E. M. (1984). Ambiguity as strategy in organizational communication. *Communication Monographs, 51,* 227–242.

Fairclough, N. (2003). *Analyzing discourse: Textual analysis for social research.* New York: Routledge.

Felmlee, D. (1998). Fatal attraction. In B. H. Spitzberg & W. R. Cupach (Eds.), *The dark side of close relationships* (pp. 3–32). Mahwah, NJ: Lawrence Erlbaum.

Goldsmith, D., & Baxter, L. A. (1996). Constituting relationships in talk: A taxonomy of speech events in social and personal relationships. *Human Communication Research, 23,* 87–114.

Greene, J. O. (2008). Action assembly theory: Forces of creation. In L. A. Baxter & D. O. Braithwaite (Eds.), *Engaging theories in interpersonal communication* (pp. 23–36). Thousand Oaks, CA: Sage.

Holquist, M. (2002). *Dialogism* (2nd ed.). New York: Routledge.

Knobloch, L. K. (2008). Uncertainty reduction theory: Communicating under conditions of ambiguity. In L. A. Baxter & D. O. Braithwaite (Eds.), *Engaging theories in interpersonal communication* (pp. 133–144). Thousand Oaks, CA: Sage.

Knobloch, L. K., & Solomon, D. H. (1999). Measuring the sources and content of relational uncertainty. *Communication Studies, 50,* 261–278.

Knobloch, L. K., & Solomon, D. H. (2002). Intimacy and the magnitude and experience of episodic relational uncertainty within romantic relationships. *Personal Relationships, 9,* 457–478.

Morson, G. S., & Emerson, C. (1990). *Mikhail Bakhtin: Creation of a prosaics.* Stanford, CA: Stanford University Press.

Newcomb, T. M. (1961). *The acquaintance process.* New York: Holt, Rinehart and Winston.

Rollins, D., Waterman, D., & Esmay, D. (1985). Married widowhood. *Activities, Adaptation, and Aging, 7,* 67–71.

Sampson, E. E. (1993). *Celebrating the other: A dialogic account of human nature.* San Francisco: Westview Press.

Schutz, W. C. (1960). *FIRO: A three-dimensional theory of interpersonal behavior.* New York: Holt, Rinehart, and Winston.

Shannon, C. E., & Weaver, W. (1949). *The mathematical theory of communication.* Champaign, IL: University of Illinois Press.

Taylor, C. E. (1995). "You think it was a fight?": Co-constructing (the struggle for) meaning, face, and family in everyday narrative activity. *Research on Language and Social Interaction, 28,* 283–317.

Winch, R. F. (1958). *Mate selection: A study of complementary needs.* New York: Harper and Row.

Wood, J. T. (1982). Communication and relational culture: Bases for the study of human relationships. *Communication Quarterly, 30,* 75–83.

Wood, J. T., Dendy, L. L., Dordek, E., Germany, M., & Varallo, S. M. (1994). Dialectic of difference: A thematic analysis of intimates' meanings for differences. In K. Carter & M. Prisnell (Eds.), *Interpretive approaches to interpersonal communication* (pp. 115–136). New York: SUNY Press.

3 The Theory of Communication and Uncertainty Management

Implications from the Wider Realm of Information Behavior

Timothy P. Hogan and Dale E. Brashers

How people manage uncertainty has become an increasingly popular focus of research in the communication discipline (e.g., Berger, 2005; Goldsmith, 2001; Knobloch & Solomon, 2005), and across the social and behavioral sciences (e.g., Clayton, Mishel, & Belyea, 2006; Dawson, Savitsky, & Dunning, 2006). The research and the theories represented in this volume demonstrate both the broad range of interests in this area, as well as the complexity of processes central to *uncertainty management*. The purpose of this chapter is to describe and to elaborate one theoretical basis for understanding those processes: the theory of communication and uncertainty management, also referred to as uncertainty management theory (UMT).

UMT was developed to understand communication processes in the management of illness-related uncertainty (Brashers, 2001, 2007), following Merle Mishel's (1988, 1990) important research on uncertainty in illness. Brashers and his colleagues originally began development of the theory in a study of people living with HIV or AIDS (Brashers, Hsieh, Neidig, & Reynolds, 2006; Brashers, Neidig, & Goldsmith, 2004; Brashers et al., 2000, 2003). Applying Mishel's theory, they conducted a series of focus groups in which participants described their sources of uncertainty, strategies for managing uncertainty, challenges and dilemmas associated with those strategies, and ways of managing the challenges and dilemmas. Since those beginnings, UMT has been cited in research contexts ranging from communication in long-distance relationships (Maguire, 2007) to organizational communication and corporate risk reporting (Deumes, 2008) to uncertainty management for adoptees (Powell & Afifi, 2005) and for health care administrators in the face of natural disasters (McCaughrin & Mattammal, 2003). It also has been used to further elaborate explanations of why people avoid health information (Barbour, Rintamaki, Ramsey, & Brashers, 2007) and has been applied in reference to cancer (Thompson & O'Hair, 2008), organ transplantation (Stone, Carnett, Scott, & Brashers, 2008), and Alzheimer's disease (Stone & Jones, 2008).

At a fundamental level, UMT offers a means to sort through and make sense of the relationships that exist between the experience of uncertainty and interaction with information. UMT research thus far has focused primarily on the seeking of information and, at times, its avoidance, as uncertainty management vehicles—in addition to cognitive strategies such as accepting chronic uncertainty (see Mishel, 1990) or reframing decision-making tasks (Brashers et al., 2000). In other words, the theory holds that seeking and avoiding information are two ways in which individuals can reduce, maintain, or increase uncertainty. Ample support for this position is apparent in the published literature, including the aforementioned studies; however, conceptual advances across a number of fields suggest that there are other activities associated with information, beyond seeking and avoiding, which have implications for UMT.

In what follows, we adopt a broad view of how people interact with information and explore a wider universe of behaviors that have yet to receive much attention in UMT research. We use the term *information behavior*, which Wilson (2000) defined as the "totality of human behavior in relation to sources and channels of information" (p. 49), as an overarching concept to frame our exploration. We begin with an overview of UMT, including what it posits about the nature of uncertainty, uncertainty appraisals, the meaning of management, and the processes that are central to effective uncertainty management. We conclude this overview by presenting a series of nine principles (Brashers & Hogan, in press) that articulate the organizing framework of UMT. From there we transition to a discussion of information behavior. Drawing on the literature from a number of fields, we present three categories of information behavior: (a) information acquisition, (b) information handling, and (c) information use. Beyond accounting for information seeking and avoiding, these categories suggest a multitude of other information-based behaviors, the understanding of which may significantly contribute to the further development of UMT. We conclude the chapter with a reexamination of the organizing framework of UMT in light of the wider realm of information behavior and take stock of the practical implications inherent in such theoretical advances.

Communication and Uncertainty Management

The theory of communication and uncertainty management holds that uncertainty emerges from many sources and takes many forms. As Brashers (2001) noted, "because it is primarily a self-perception about one's own cognitions or ability to derive meaning, a person who believes himself or herself to be uncertain is uncertain" (p. 478). As evident from existing descriptions, uncertainty can pertain to ambiguity, unpredictability, possibility, complexity, probability, insufficient or conflicting information, lack of clarity, and the unknown or unknowable (see Babrow, Kasch, & Ford, 1998). Brashers et al. (2003), for example, classified the uncertainty of people living with HIV as medical, personal, and social. The medical forms of uncertainty (also see Mishel, 1988) were *insufficient information* about the diagnosis (including *unclear meaning* of diagnostic tests), *ambiguous* symptom patterns (including *unknown* and *unknowable* etiology of symptoms), *complex* systems of treatment and care (including *insufficient information* about experimental medications), and *unpredictable* disease progression (including *possible* illness recurrence). The personal forms of uncertainty were *complex or conflicting* roles and *unclear* financial consequences of the illness. The social forms of uncertainty were *unpredictable* interpersonal reactions or *unclear* relational implications of the illness. Other scholars have characterized uncertainty in contexts with different dimensions and/or sources. As part of their explication of the social norms concept, Lapinski and Rimal (2005) described "ambiguity," or a "situation in which the appropriate course of action is unclear to the actor," as an important influence on the relationship between descriptive norms and behavior (pp. 139–140). Shaha, Cox, Talman, and Kelly (2008) found that research on breast, prostate, and colorectal cancer uncertainty yielded "three main themes: uncertainty because of limited or lack of information, uncertainty concerning the course and treatment choices related to the disease, and uncertainty related to everyday life and coping with the disease" (p. 60). Even unexpected events that are generally thought of as positively valenced (e.g., improvements in physical health—see Brashers et al., 1999; Siegel & Schrimshaw, 2005) have been described as sources of uncertainty, if they challenge meaning or lead to additional ambivalence, ambiguity, or complexity.

What people do when facing uncertainty may depend on what resources they have available or how they appraise what they are experiencing (Brashers, 2001; Brashers & Hogan, in press). Our preference for talking about *uncertainty management* (rather than uncertainty reduction) rests on the growing and compelling evidence that uncertainty is sometimes, but not always, negative (e.g., Afifi & Schrodt, 2003; Dawson et al., 2006; van Dijk & Zeelenberg, 2006); therefore, a variety of options, strategies, or pathways might be implicated in its management. If uncertainty is appraised as a danger (e.g., when not knowing something might lead to harm or the inability to make a decision or solve a problem), people may wish to reduce it through information seeking. They also may need to manage emotions (e.g., anxiety or fear) that the uncertainty-as-danger appraisal generates (Mishel, 1988). When uncertainty is appraised as opportunity (e.g., when *not knowing* is preferable to *knowing*), individuals then might avoid information to maintain their uncertainty or seek information that can create uncertainty. Other times, uncertainty management may involve acceptance of, or adaptation to, chronic uncertainty (Mishel, 1990), reappraisal of uncertainty (Brashers et al., 2004), or redefining decision-making situations (Brashers et al., 2000). Uncertainty due to complexity of information will be managed differently than uncertainty due to ambiguity or due to conflicting information. We might handle the unknown by seeking information, but labeling a thing as unknowable implies that no information is available to seek, and other strategies (e.g., emotion management) may be necessary.

Table 3.1 Principles of Uncertainty Management (Brashers & Hogan, in press)

Principle One:	Uncertainty is a perception about insufficient knowledge, which has both cognitive and affective components.
Principle Two:	There are many sources and forms of uncertainty.
Principle Three:	There are many sources and forms of information.
Principle Four:	The relationship between information and uncertainty is not straightforward.
Principle Five:	Uncertainty is appraised for its meaning.
Principle Six:	Interacting with information can reduce, maintain, or increase uncertainty.
Principle Seven:	Encountering new information fuels the re-appraisal of uncertainty.
Principle Eight:	Gathering information is often a social process, and includes collaborators in an individual's social network.
Principle Nine:	Uncertainty is not inherently good or inherently bad, but something that is managed.

One example of the complexity of uncertainty and its management involved research on social network members of people with a communication-debilitating illness or injury (e.g., dementia, stroke, or head trauma). Donovan-Kicken and Bute (2008) found that these individuals experienced uncertainty both about the injury or illness and about how to communicate with the ill or injured member of their network. Social network members managed their uncertainty by seeking information about the illness or injury, changing how they communicated with their friend or family member, using inferential processes, or accepting or maintaining their uncertainty. This study demonstrates how multiple sources of uncertainty can manifest from an event—in this case, illness or injury—and how different management processes might be called on in response to different forms of uncertainty.

In sum, experiences, appraisal, and management of uncertainty are important aspects of many events and situations. Based on that assumption and previous research, Brashers and Hogan (in press) recently described nine principles for theorizing about communication and uncertainty management (see Table 3.1). These principles provide an overview of the organizing framework of UMT, including the role that information plays in the theory. The remaining sections of this chapter expand those principles by elaborating on what the wider realm of information behavior can add to our understanding of the uncertainty management process. In line with UMT, we recognize that information behavior of any kind applies only to the management of certain types of uncertainty; this is because for some people information would be insufficient (or even counterproductive) as a remedy.

Information Behavior

An appropriate place to begin our exploration of information behavior is with a description of information itself. Brashers, Goldsmith, and Hsieh (2002) defined information as "stimuli from a person's environment that contribute to his or her knowledge or beliefs" (p. 259). These stimuli can include messages from others, observations of behaviors, or other environmental cues. The various needs that people have for information and the ways in which they draw upon it serve a variety of purposes across different contexts. It is what people do with this information, the entirety of possible responses, and potential modes of interaction which constitute the realm of information behavior.[1]

Although they may not label them as such, scholars working across various fields, including communication and library and information science, have described a multitude of information behaviors. To facilitate our discussion in this chapter, we grouped this literature into three broad categories that, when juxtaposed, suggest a process-oriented perspective on information behavior: (a) information acquisition, (b) information handling, and (c) information use. Figure 3.1 depicts these categories and situates them within the context of UMT. As suggested by the overlap among the circles, they are not mutually exclusive. Behaviors in one category may impact or shape behaviors in another, and some behaviors may be understood as instances of one or more categories. As represented by the smaller, dotted circle, existing UMT research has focused largely on behaviors representative of the information acquisition category, namely information seeking (and conversely, avoidance). As we explain in greater detail below, the remainder of the acquisition category remains relatively unaccounted for, as do the information handling and use categories.

Although it is desirable to pull apart theoretical categories of the kind we propose here and treat them separately for analytic purposes, we acknowledge that it is somewhat artificial to do so. Still, we believe that exploration of each supports a more nuanced understanding of information behavior as a whole and can help to extend UMT. We begin our exploration with information acquisition.

Information Acquisition

Information can enter our respective worlds in a variety of ways. We use the expression *information acquisition* to reflect the diverse means by which people come into contact with information in the course of their daily lives. The phrase *information seeking* also has been used at times to refer to this same broad spectrum of experiences and activities; however, doing so blurs meaningful conceptual distinctions between seeking and other means of acquiring information, a point that we address in more detail below. Across disciplines, increasing numbers of scholars are calling attention to the differences between information acquisition that is more intentional, purposive, and goal-directed and that which is fairly unintentional, inadvertent, and

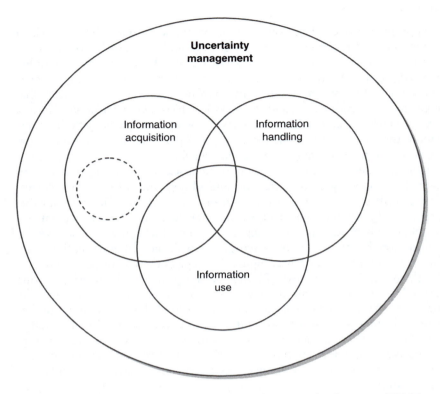

Figure 3.1 Three Categories of Information Behavior in the Context of UMT

happenstance (e.g., Berger, 2002; Niederdeppe et al., 2007; Williamson, 1998). To facilitate this discussion, we might envision plotting instances of information acquisition on a simple continuum on which the most deliberate behaviors are clustered toward one end and unintended information events fall toward the opposite end.

To date, the vast majority of research regarding the ways in which people acquire information has focused on the purposive gathering of information. As Ross (1999) noted, emphasis on the pursuit of information to resolve a problem that an individual has, or to address some problematic situation, is quite common. Others have suggested that the phrase *information seeking* be defined purely in relation to the purposive pursuit of information, "as a consequence of a need to satisfy some goal" (Wilson, 2000, p. 49). From this perspective, information seeking encompasses the gathering of information from all manner of sources through all manner of intentional acts—be it question asking, observing others, or searching formal information systems like libraries or databases. Although often not explicitly acknowledged, existing uncertainty management research also has focused mostly on purposive information seeking, framing it as a behavioral response that follows uncertainty appraisals. From Berger's uncertainty reduction theory (Berger & Bradac, 1982; Berger & Calabrese, 1975), which described interactive, active, and passive information-seeking activities in developing personal relationships and which Berger (2002) later described as "strategic approaches to information acquisition" (p. 289) to studies of health information-seeking behaviors (HISB) in coping with illness (Lambert & Loiselle, 2007), this research is part of a larger body of work that addresses the communicative activities that surround information seeking.

What enables or motivates information seeking has stimulated research relevant to uncertainty management. For example, uncertainty or lack of information may be necessary, but not sufficient, to stimulate information seeking—recent investigations suggest that individual characteristics or attitudes also have predictive value. Niederdeppe, Frosch, and Hornik (2008) found that newspaper coverage of cancer can motivate information seeking for some (e.g., those who typically attend to health news through various media and those with a family history of cancer), yet many do not seek additional information after hearing cancer news stories. Self-efficacy also has emerged as an important influence on information-seeking behavior. According to the theory of motivated information management (TMIM), propensity to seek information is a function of the person's perceived efficacy for the search (Afifi & Weiner, 2004)—those who do not believe that they can find information or use sources appropriately or effectively are less likely to seek information. Internet self-efficacy, for example, can predict the use of Web sites for health information (Rains, 2008). Similarly, in a study of women with breast cancer, self-efficacy moderated the relationship between negative emotions and information seeking— for women with high self-efficacy, negative emotions and information seeking were positively related, and for women with low self-efficacy, negative emotions and information seeking were negatively related (Lee, Hwang, Hawkins, & Pingree, 2008).

Just as individuals make conscious choices to seek information in response to uncertainty, they also may decide to make an intentional effort to thwart the entry of particular information into their lives. As such, avoiding information is another area of research that has developed in response to our desire to understand how people manage uncertainty. Case, Andrews, Johnson, and Allard (2005) described a long history of theory and research on information avoidance in communication and in psychology, including theories of information seeking. The simplest explanation, that people simply do not want bad news, has been a useful starting point for uncertainty management. But recent research supports a more nuanced version of that proposition. People may maintain positive mood by maintaining uncertainty, when they believe that the outcome will be positive (Wilson, Centerbar, Kermer, & Gilbert, 2005), or when avoiding information about a negative outcome allows for maintaining hope (Brashers et al., 2000). Some suggest that too much information can decrease hope, and lead to increased risk behavior (Brashers, 2001). For example, research on HIV prevention suggests that in a perceived "high-risk environment" (e.g., among gay men, or injecting drug users) in which substantial information about risk has been disseminated, individuals may have low levels of hope (e.g., a sense of fatalism) that might hinder efforts toward prevention; conversely, individuals in a perceived "low-risk environment" (e.g., individuals believed to be in monogamous relationships) might maintain hope, which can improve capacity of HIV prevention (Bernays, Rhodes, & Barnett, 2007, p. S8).

As information acquisition is multifaceted, avoiding information also is a complex activity itself. It is not as simple as *not seeking* information: avoiding information, like seeking, implies intended and goal-oriented behavior. Not seeking information implies a passive state; that is, one is simply not actively pursuing information about a topic. But avoiding information implies that situations and channels in which information is delivered are evaded (e.g., doctors appointments are missed or not scheduled, people who likely have information are avoided, news is not watched or read). Nevertheless, perhaps for that reason, avoidance of information may be seen as nonnormative. For example, there may be a "perceived social pressure to be informed" about health risks (i.e., informational subjective norms—Kahlor, Dunwoody, Griffin, & Neuwirth, 2006, p. 163; also see Kahlor, 2007), which might cause people to seek information, even when their instinct is to avoid it. Moreover, individuals may struggle with competing needs in information seeking and avoiding in some contexts, simultaneously wanting and not wanting to know (Wahlin, 2007).

Returning to the image of a continuum, at the opposite end from purposive acquisition (or avoidance) behaviors are activities and experiences that yield information but are not intended to do so. Research from different fields now underscores the point that, beyond deliberate seeking, people often find information of all kinds without necessarily trying, and that failing to account for this wider realm of experience may limit or unintentionally skew our understanding of the ways in which people acquire information. Williamson (1998, p. 35) suggested that the notion of "being informed" as opposed to "seeking information" may more appropriately represent the reality of people's information acquisition patterns and used the concept of "incidental information acquisition" to describe the findings in a study of information behavior among older Australian adults. Participants explained how they incidentally acquired information through their intimate and wider personal networks, including family, friends, clubs, and churches, and from mass media sources like newspapers and television. Erdelez (2004) similarly offered the expression *opportunistic acquisition of information* (OAI) to refer to situations in which individuals find valuable information without (obviously) purposeful action. From Erdelez's perspective, our contemporary information environment is extremely conducive to OAI "because it emphasizes users' mobility and facilitates disappearance of traditional task-oriented silos in acquisition of information" (pp. 1013–1014). Drawing parallels to his earlier research regarding information acquisition strategies in the context of interpersonal communication, Berger (2002) likewise described the important role that "nonstrategic information acquisition" plays in people's lives:

> Even when people do not intentionally seek information about others, they may acquire considerable information through nonstrategic processes . . . the net result is that information that was never sought or was perhaps actively avoided is acquired, and information so acquired could be as consequential, if not more consequential, than information gleaned through strategic means. (p. 289)

The implications of Berger's statement for UMT are substantial. The experience of uncertainty may not always motivate information seeking or avoidance, but information inadvertently gleaned from different sources could impact an individual's uncertainty in unexpected ways. This point foregrounds the nature of the appraisal process in UMT and suggests that, in the face of unintentionally acquired information, reappraisals and the notion of continuing appraisal may be of considerable significance.

The unintentional acquisition of information can transpire across contexts, during the course of different activities or events. In some cases, an individual may be engaged in a routine or everyday task, like driving to work or grocery shopping, when he or she comes across information (e.g., a new billboard is seen or a conversation is overheard) that is in some way meaningful to them. In other cases, unexpected but useful information may be found in the course of another, albeit unrelated information activity (e.g., an individual is listening to a radio news program and hears a story that is relevant to his or her work or is searching the Web to find information about a newly prescribed medication only to stumble across a story regarding an alternative treatment). Various concepts have been put forth to describe situations akin to the latter, including "information encountering" defined as "an instance of accidental discovery of information during an active search for some other information" (Erdelez, 2005, p. 180) and "serendipitous information retrieval triggered by chance encounters, or the point in human interaction with an information system when a human makes an accidental and often sagacious discovery" (Toms, 2000, p. 2). Niederdeppe et al. (2007) differentiated between seeking and scanning behaviors for cancer-related information, based primarily on the purposiveness of the activity. In terms of UMT, these ideas suggest that the deliberate seeking or avoiding of information that sometimes follows the appraisal of uncertainty must be framed as part of a larger information environment of which incidentally acquired information is an important component. Moreover, UMT holds that any experience or event has the potential to engender multiple sources and forms of uncertainty for an individual. The phenomenon of unintentional information acquisition raises questions of multiple or parallel management efforts; that is, in the course of responding to one uncertainty (e.g., actively seeking or avoiding information), information may be encountered that holds implications for a different uncertainty, thus inviting uncertainty reappraisals and potentially altered management goals.

We have dedicated much of this section to a discussion of purposive and unintentional information acquisition behaviors and their respective implications for UMT. In concluding, we want to make a final point that is relevant to the range of behaviors along the acquisition continuum and suggests another direction for future and sustained development of UMT, namely that acquiring information can be a collaborative activity between individuals and their social network members (Brashers et al., 2002). Recent studies have, for example, demonstrated that a family member's health literacy can help determine how a patient manages illness and uncertainty about the illness (Bevan & Pecchioni, 2008), and that cancer survivors who seek additional information are more likely than those who do not seek information to have family members who help in their search (Niederdeppe et al., 2008). In another investigation, researchers explored the collaborative nature of information seeking in oncology interactions and found that patients brought companions 86% of the time, and that those companions asked more questions than did the patients (Eggly et al., 2006). Relationships and collaboration between patients/clients and health care providers also reveals insights to information acquisition and dimensions of the uncertainty management process. Miller (2007) noted that one aspect of compassion that human service workers show to clients is to understand when information is needed (or not needed) and how it should be provided. Deschepper et al. (2008) similarly found that patients in hospice and professional caregivers "agreed that truth-telling should be a 'dosed and gradual' process" (p. 52). Beyond the health domain, other scholars have demonstrated how *browsing*, a concept that has historically been used to connote the casual or impromptu gathering of information, has collaborative elements that can be supported in online information retrieval environments (Twidale, Nichols, & Paice, 1997). Finally, there is also evidence that suggests that social network members can collaborate in (or challenge) information avoidance. T. Afifi and Schrodt (2003) found that family members may avoid communicating to maintain uncertainty about the state of the family, especially in postdivorce, single-parent families, and stepfamilies. Brashers et al. (2004) found that well-meaning friends and family members provided information, even when the person living with HIV wanted to avoid it, thus signaling an incongruity in information acquisition goals that could defy uncertainty management.

Information Handling

Although aspects of information acquisition have been addressed in UMT, much less attention has been paid to how information is handled in the management of uncertainty. When asked what they do with acquired information, individuals might say that they commit it to memory, remember it, or store it in their heads; however, when we examine the various settings where people live and work, we see that information with a kind of physical presence—the visible, tangible, material *stuff* we call information—is also something that people frequently retain (Hogan & Rintamaki, 2006). Information in more ephemeral forms may be translated into concrete manifestations for storage purposes (e.g., a conversation with a colleague might be captured in jotted notes), and thanks to the capacities of current information and communications technologies (ICTs), digital text, audio, video, and other kinds of electronic information now can easily be saved.

Retaining and organizing compilations of information are pervasive human activities. For some, they are ongoing, routine aspects of everyday life; for others, they may be more episodic tasks, emerging in conjunction with particular life events or problems. The apparent range of motivations that underlie these behaviors is expansive and includes identifying information that is immediately valuable, anticipating a future need for particular instances of information, reminding or prompting action, inducing memories, sharing with other people, and helping others handle information that they may not be in a position to handle themselves (Bruce, 2005; Marshall & Bly, 2005; Moen & Flatley Brennan, 2005). This list of motivations suggests that collaboration may at times also be integral to the retention and organization of information, just as it is to the acquisition of information. In 1988, Lansdale used the expression "personal information management" to refer to how individuals "handle, categorise and retrieve information on a day-to-day basis" (p. 55). *Personal* was intended to convey the idea of information that belongs to an individual and is intended for his or her own use. Lansdale characterized information management as a collation of different activities and drew a meaningful distinction between "information handling," which he described as "what people do when they have got information," and the subsequent retrieval of that information (p. 64). Other characterizations of personal information management (PIM) have since followed (e.g., Teevan, Jones, & Bederson, 2006), which retain Lansdale's emphasis on the importance of maintaining and organizing information, regardless of how it was originally acquired (e.g., purposefully or incidentally), to support the activities of daily life.

The idea that we actively manage and handle different kinds of information in the course of our everyday lives is tied closely to repositories of personal information. Bruce, Jones, and Dumais (2004) defined a "personal information collection" (PIC) as "a collection of information sources and channels that we as individuals have acquired, cultivated, and organized over time and in response to a range of stimuli" (p. 1). Bruce and colleagues explained that PICs may include information in different forms (i.e., print or digital), pointers to other information sources, and structures intended to facilitate the organization of material in the collection. As one might imagine, the properties of PICs can be as varied and diverse as the people to whom they belong. In many ways, personal collections are manifestations of that which is important to us as individuals—our joys, accomplishments, problems, worries, and fears. The subject focus and overall nature of the content that comprises them also may represent, in visible, tangible forms, the aspects of our lives around which we experience uncertainty. In as much as they are conveniently located and easily accessible stockpiles of salient information, personal collections can also function as tools of uncertainty management. One can imagine how individuals may maintain a collection of personal investment and budget information, for example, to reduce lingering uncertainty over their own financial security.

In light of the preceding, it should also come as no surprise that there are a wide range of activities related to the handling of personal information. As Kelly (2006) explained, these activities tend to exist at different levels of granularity. Although we can speak of *storing, organizing*, and *maintaining* a personal collection, these activities often are comprised of a multitude of other tasks like labeling, filing, reviewing, weeding, and discarding. Because a given activity may hold different meanings for different people, it also may encompass correspondingly different sets of tasks. For example, the notion of organizing one's collection of brochures and magazines about diabetes self-management may for one individual mean identifying and disposing of older content; for another, however, it may mean retaining all content old and new, but storing it in a chronological manner. Recent studies have identified distinct strategies used by individuals for storing health information (primarily in paper form) within their homes: *just-in-time*, in which information is kept with a person in anticipation of use; *just-at-hand*, in which information is stored in visible or highly familiar, accessible locations; *just-in-case*, in which information is kept away but is readily accessible for future use; and *just-because*, in which information with a temporal relevance is kept, but without much further strategizing (Moen & Flatley Brennan, 2005).

For our purposes in this chapter, it is not necessary to provide a comprehensive review of activities associated with the handling of personal information; however, given its centrality to the development of personal collections and its implications for UMT, one particular activity, "keeping," does warrant explication here. As Bruce et al. (2004) explained, the act of keeping information represents a kind of intervention performed by an individual, the goal of which is to have information on hand, in an accessible form, and in an available location ready for use whenever necessary. Yet keeping is also a kind of balancing act (Marshall & Jones, 2006) wherein the benefits of having ready access to an instance of needed information outweigh the associated temporal and cognitive costs (Bruce, 2005). This raises the question of the "keeping decision," which Jones (2004) described as "fundamental to the management of personal information and fundamentally difficult to do" (p. 21). As Jones went on to explain, the decision, whether to keep or not to keep, is shaped by a multitude of factors and often plagued by mistakes, including instances in which unhelpful information is kept and helpful information is passed over or relinquished.

The multileveled, eclectic domain of activities associated with the handling of personal information has implications for the management of uncertainty. According to UMT, information-based activities, specifically information seeking and avoidance, can follow from uncertainty appraisals. The handling of personal information, however, is not divorced from seeking or avoiding; on the contrary, it sometimes follows on their heels or is intertwined with them. Individuals living with HIV or AIDS have, for example, described how filing information away about their disease before they read it, perhaps in a drawer, box, or other storage location, can serve dual purposes. On one hand, quickly filing disease-related information offered peace of mind. Individuals knew they had the information in their possession and it would be available for future use should a need arise. On the other hand, filing without reading was also a way to get disease-related information out of sight and out of mind. It offered a break, or "holiday," from potentially stressful, uncertainty-inducing information (Brashers et al., 2000). Diligently tending to a personal collection of information may serve to provide a sense of control over a source of stress-inducing, chronic uncertainty, yet existing research also suggests that, in some circumstances, personal collections of information can be a source of stress and anxiety in and of themselves. Home-based studies of individuals living with HIV or AIDS have shown that simply having treatment-related information in one's personal environment introduces the possibility for unpredictable, potentially problematic interactions with others, and can hold unclear, possibly troubling implications for one's own identity. In such circumstances, it is not uncommon for individuals to conceal or hide information in their home or to consult it only in secluded spaces within their home (Hogan, 2007).

Based on this discussion, we might think of the acquisition of information as a kind of stepping-off point to the domain of information handling. In some cases, personal collections of information can represent the experiences or events in our lives about which we feel uncertain, and can serve as tools of uncertainty management. Similar to the continuum of information acquisition behaviors discussed above, there is also reason to believe that the activities of handling personal information have the potential to reduce, increase, and maintain uncertainty.

Information Use

Beyond acquisition and handling, a third major category of information behavior involves the ways in which people process and use information (e.g., Kahlor, 2007). Understanding who uses what, why, how, and to what effect are fundamental questions surrounding information use. Across contexts, information can help individuals develop and/or elaborate cognitive frameworks for organizing activities and managing situations (e.g., understanding events, making decisions, solving problems, interacting with others). It can facilitate creating meaning, labeling and categorizing, providing options, and making choices. It also can help people negotiate the everyday and the extraordinary. Feldman-Stewart, Brennenstuhl, and Brundage (2007), for example, argued that information allows patients "to organize their thoughts, to understand their situation, to decide on treatment, to plan for their future, to provide emotional support to others, and to discuss issues" (p. 311). Thus, information use, as we intend it here, includes the cognitive and expressive processes of incorporating information into cognitions and into activities. Given the encompassing scope of this category, we use this section to characterize it in broad terms.

Wilson (1997) described information processing and learning (i.e., information use) as part of information behavior; activities that help situate the person in context, and that may lead to additional information need. He later added that information-use behavior

> consists of the physical and mental acts involved in incorporating the information found into the person's existing knowledge base. It may involve, therefore, physical acts such as marking sections in a text to note their importance or significance, as well as mental acts that involve, for example, comparison of new information with existing knowledge.
>
> (Wilson, 2000, p. 50)

In his analysis of experienced information users and the "different uses to which information is put" as they attempt to solve problems, Taylor (1991, pp. 229–230) identified eight classes of information use: to contextualize and make sense of a situation (*enlightenment*); to comprehend a problem in more specific terms (*problem understanding*); to determine what and how to do something (*instrumental*); to bring precise data to bear (*factual*); to verify other instances of information (*confirmational*); to develop future-oriented estimates and probabilities (*projective*); to promote one's own involvement (*motivational*); and to manage one's situation, standing, and relationships with others (*personal or political*). Similarly, Todd (1999) described *information utilization* as a synonym to information use, and argued that definitions of information utilization or use are largely dependent on how one defines information but that a pervading sense of "people 'doing something' with information they have sought and gathered themselves or [that was] provided by someone else" unified definitions of the terms (p. 852).

Sometimes, the activity or "doing something" involves a relatively straightforward, direct translation of information into a product. For example, some jobs require translation of scientific information into everyday practice (e.g., knowledge translation in medicine) and may require procedures to support those daily efforts (e.g., "outcomes-focused knowledge translation"—see Doran & Sidani, 2006). At the other end of the spectrum, decisions sometimes must be made in situations in which new information is coming quickly, aspects of the situation are changing rapidly, and everyday procedures may fail. Sweeny (2008) explicated *crisis decision theory* to explain how decisions are made in emergent situations. The decision maker assesses the severity of the event (with information on causes, comparisons to other events, and information about consequences), determines response options (with attributions about controllability of the event and feasibility of response options), and evaluates the response options (with understanding of the resources required and the direct and indirect consequences of each option). The use of information becomes important and obvious at several junctures in Sweeny's theory, and different forms of information clearly are needed. Beyond making decisions, information is also the metaphorical "fuel" that can facilitate problem solving and sustain responsiveness in the midst of complex situations. Gorman et al. (2000), for example, found that expert clinicians rely on bundles, "organized collections of highly selected information," to support their work within intensive care units (p. 280). Based on their fieldwork, Gorman and his colleagues concluded that bundles of information are particularly useful "in settings that are characterized by a high degree of uncertainty, a low level of predictability, and potentially grave outcomes, where time and attention are highly constrained and interruptions are frequent, and where interdisciplinary teamwork is essential" (p. 287).

Intense, demanding circumstances such as those just described encourage us to consider the role of emotions in information use and the ways in which it connects to the goals of uncertainty management theory. Emotions are a major component of uncertainty appraisals, and can yield information about what meaning uncertainty has for an individual. Encouraging and supporting emotional expression in conjunction with information use can be important in uncertainty management. Austenfeld and Stanton (2004) argued that emotion-focused coping strategies are unfairly maligned in research and clinical communities, and that "acknowledging, understanding, and expressing emotion" is an important aspect of "emotional-approach coping" (p. 1335), which may be related to improved health outcomes. In their theory, emotional approach strategies are contrasted with emotional avoidance strategies, such as mental or behavioral disengagement. From this perspective, it may be that informational support is an insufficient basis for uncertainty management interventions. Edwards et al. (2008) reviewed educational programs aimed at helping genetics clinic participants engage in effective decision making about their health. The 16 communication-based interventions showed positive effects on cognitive outcomes (e.g., knowledge) and no harmful effects on mood (e.g., anxiety); "however, often it was the emotional or supportive elements of counselling that provided benefits to users, rather than the informational or educational elements" (p. 4).

Theorizing about uncertainty management requires that we understand the processes involved in information use, perhaps most especially in situations in which information may be imperfect or insufficient for the task at hand. For example, decision making can occur in situations in which uncertainty remains. In the context of genetic testing, results may be equivocal or the long-term outcomes might be probabilistic, and decision making may require an approach that allows for uncertainty (Frost, Venne, Cunningham, & Gerritsen-McKane, 2004). Individuals may avoid decision making or relegate decisions to others in response to "emotionally challenging choices" (Löckenhoff & Carstensen, 2004, p. 1416). They may also find that it is, in some ways, easier to make decisions under conditions of uncertainty than when outcomes are certain; that is, actors may be more constrained in environments in which they feel that outcomes are definite and defined (van Dijk & Zeelenberg, 2006). This raises a final point, that in the context of UMT, we must be sensitive to what some might think of as atypical uses of information. Some research suggests, for example, that people who are ambivalent toward a topic (e.g., smoking) may seek information to move themselves to a more valenced position (Zhao & Cai, 2008). People also may engage in what Sweeny (2008) called motivated reasoning, that is, information search and use that is biased by the desire to confirm existing beliefs. In some instances then, information use may be less about finding an adequate solution to a problem or making an effective decision and more about mounting a response to particular emotional or cognitive demands.

Conclusion

Understanding the role of communication and information in uncertainty management requires a more complete accounting of information behaviors, including information acquisition, information handling, and information use. Research to date on the role of information in uncertainty management has focused primarily on information acquisition behaviors— the addition of information handling and use behaviors should help clarify and expand the role of information in uncertainty management. Information can help individuals manage uncertainty and extend cognitive frameworks for organizing and managing the events of everyday life; however, how information is handled and used certainly will help determine outcomes of these processes. UMT holds that the experience of uncertainty does not always motivate information seeking and that information can have any number of effects on uncertainty. UMT and related research to date would suggest that a similar web of relationships exists between uncertainty and information handling and between uncertainty and information use; however, these are empirical questions that have yet to be addressed. Returning to the contents of Table 3.1 that we presented earlier in this chapter, the more comprehensive explication of information behavior suggests a 10th principle for UMT: "Variations in information acquisition, handling, and use can be important to the effectiveness of uncertainty management."

The additional principle about the categories of information behavior presented here suggests the importance of examining the relationships between categories and activities across categories. For example, how does the seeking of information and the subsequent organizing and storing of information work together as a unified uncertainty management strategy? Is one category (e.g., acquisition, handling, or use) more essential than another when it comes to managing uncertainty? How are judgments made about the effectiveness or appropriateness of information acquisition, handling, and use strategies? Are there situations in which the categories of behavior are at odds with one another and interfere with uncertainty management efforts (e.g., a person wants to avoid information about a particular topic but his or her situation is such that he or she must handle related information—perhaps on behalf of someone else)? How are we to understand situations in which information is sought and stored, but never consulted (e.g., does the collection of information offer a sense of security?)?

Far from offering a comprehensive accounting of information behavior, our goal in this chapter was to encourage readers to reflect on the organizing framework of UMT and to begin to explore how that framework might be meaningfully expanded. The wider realm of information behavior invites us to think about interaction with information in uncertainty management as a process that has important temporal and contextual dimensions. High levels of worry or anxiety might, for example, lead to increased information seeking, but subsequently inhibit information processing (Beckjord, Rutten, Arora, Moser, & Hesse, 2008); therefore, what looks like a calculated effort to reduce uncertainty may not succeed, even with the successful acquisition of information, because of a problem of information use. Moreover, activities like serendipitous information discovery, information encountering, even information handling and use, may bring a person into contact with different kinds of information and could have the subsequent effect of introducing new and different uncertainty. These complexities deserve our sustained attention as we continue to theorize about communication and uncertainty management.

Note

1 Brashers et al. (2002) defined "information management" as "communicative and cognitive activities such as seeking, avoiding, providing, appraising, and interpreting . . . environmental stimuli" (p. 259). The current chapter expands that definition by including other activities, such as information handling and use.

References

Afifi, T. D., & Schrodt, P. (2003). Uncertainty and the avoidance of the state of one's family in stepfamilies, postdivorce single-parent families, and first-marriage families. *Human Communication Research, 29*, 516–532.

Afifi, W. A., & Weiner, J. L. (2004). Toward a theory of motivated information management. *Communication Theory, 14*, 167–190.

Austenfeld, J. L., & Stanton, A. L. (2004). Coping through emotional approach: A new look at emotion, coping, and health-related outcomes. *Journal of Personality, 72*, 1335–1363.

Babrow, A. S., Kasch, C. R., & Ford, L. A. (1998). The many meanings of *uncertainty* in illness: Toward a systematic accounting. *Health Communication, 10,* 1–23.

Barbour, J., Rintamaki, L. S., Ramsey, J., & Brashers, D. E. (2007, November). *Reasons for avoiding health information.* Paper presented at the annual meeting of the National Communication Association, Chicago.

Beckjord, E. B., Rutten, L. J., Arora, N. K., Moser, R. P., & Hesse, B. W. (2008). Information processing and negative affect: Evidence from the 2003 Health Information National Trends Study. *Health Psychology, 27,* 249–257.

Berger, C. R. (2002). Strategic and nonstrategic information acquisition. *Human Communication Research, 28,* 287–297.

Berger, C. R. (2005). Theoretical perspectives: Future prospects. *Journal of Communication, 55,* 415–447.

Berger, C. R., & Bradac, J. (1982). *Language and social knowledge.* London: Edward Arnold.

Berger, C. R., & Calabrese, R. J. (1975). Some explorations in initial encounters and beyond: Toward a developmental theory of interpersonal communication. *Human Communication Research, 1,* 99–112.

Bernays, S., Rhodes, T., & Barnett, T. (2007). Hope: A new way to look at the HIV epidemic. *AIDS, 21*(Suppl. 5), S5–S11.

Bevan, J. L., & Pecchioni, L. L. (2008). Understanding the impact of family caregiver cancer literacy on patient health outcomes. *Patient Education and Counseling, 71,* 356–364.

Brashers, D. E. (2001). Communication and uncertainty management. *Journal of Communication, 51,* 477–497.

Brashers, D. E. (2007). A theory of communication and uncertainty management. In B. Whaley & W. Samter (Eds.), *Explaining communication theory* (pp. 201–218). Mahwah, NJ: Lawrence Erlbaum.

Brashers, D. E., Goldsmith, D. J., & Hsieh, E. (2002). Information seeking and avoiding in health contexts. *Human Communication Research, 28,* 258–271.

Brashers, D. E., & Hogan, T. P. (in press). The appraisal and management of uncertainty: Implications for information-retrieval systems. *Information Processing and Management.*

Brashers, D. E., Hsieh, E., Neidig, J. L., & Reynolds, N. R. (2006). Managing uncertainty about illness: Health care providers as credible authorities. In R. M. Dailey & B. A. Le Poire (Eds.), *Applied interpersonal communication matters* (pp. 219–240). New York: Peter Lang.

Brashers, D. E., Neidig, J. L., Cardillo, L. W., Dobbs, L. K., Russell, J. A., & Haas, S. M. (1999). "In an important way, I did die." Uncertainty and revival among persons living with HIV or AIDS. *AIDS Care, 11,* 201–219.

Brashers, D. E., Neidig, J. L., & Goldsmith, D. J. (2004). Social support and the management of uncertainty for people living with HIV. *Health Communication, 16,* 305–331.

Brashers, D. E., Neidig, J. L., Haas, S. M., Dobbs, L. K., Cardillo, L. W., & Russell, J. A. (2000). Communication in the management of uncertainty: The case of persons living with HIV or AIDS. *Communication Monographs, 67,* 63–84.

Brashers, D. E., Neidig, J. L., Russell, J. A., Cardillo, L. W., Haas, S. M., Dobbs, L. K., Garland, M., McCartney, B., & Nemeth, S. (2003). The medical, personal, and social causes of uncertainty in HIV illness. *Issues in Mental Health Nursing, 24*, 497–522.

Bruce, H. (2005). Personal anticipated information need. *Information Research, 10*, paper 232. Available from http://InformationR.net/ir/10-3/paper232.html

Bruce, H., Jones, W., & Dumais, S. (2004). Information behavior that keeps found things found. *Information Research, 10*, paper 207. Available from http://InformationR.net/ir/10-1/paper207.html

Case, D. O., Andrews, J. E., Johnson, J. D., & Allard, S. L. (2005). Avoiding versus seeking: The relationship of information seeking to avoidance, blunting, coping, dissonance, and related concepts. *Journal of the Medical Library Association, 93*, 353–362.

Clayton, M. F., Mishel, M. H., & Belyea, M. (2006). Testing a model of symptoms, communication, uncertainty, and well-being, in older breast cancer survivors. *Research in Nursing and Health, 29*, 18–39.

Dawson, E., Savitsky, K., & Dunning, D. (2006). "Don't tell me, I don't want to know": Understanding people's reluctance to obtain medical diagnostic information. *Journal of Applied Social Psychology, 36*, 751–768.

Deschepper, R., Bernheim, J. L., Vander Stichele, R., Van den Block, L., Michiels, E., Van Der Kelen, G., et al. (2008). Truth-telling at the end of life: A pilot study on the perspective of patients and professional caregivers. *Patient Education and Counseling, 71*, 52–56.

Deumes, R. (2008). Corporate risk reporting: A content analysis of narrative risk disclosures in prospectuses. *Journal of Business Communication, 45*, 120–157.

Donovan-Kicken, E., & Bute, J. J. (2008). Uncertainty of social network members in the case of communication-debilitating illness or injury. *Qualitative Health Research, 18*, 5–28.

Doran, D. M., & Sidani, S. (2006). Outcomes-focused knowledge translation: A framework for knowledge translation and patient outcomes improvement. *Worldviews on Evidence-Based Nursing, 4*, 3–13.

Edwards, A., Gray, J., Clarke, A., Dundon, J., Elwyn, G., Gaff, C., et al. (2008). Interventions to improve risk communication in clinical genetics: Systematic review. *Patient Education and Counseling, 71*, 4–25.

Eggly, S., Penner, L. A., Greene, M., Harper, F. W. K., Ruckdeschel, J. C., & Albrecht, T. L. (2006). Information seeking during "bad news" oncology interactions: Question asking by patients and their companions. *Social Science and Medicine, 63*, 2974–2985.

Erdelez, S. (2004). Investigation of information encountering in the controlled research environment. *Information Processing and Management, 40*, 1013–1025.

Erdelez, S. (2005). Information encountering. In K. E. Fisher, S. Erdelez, & L. E. F. McKechnie (Eds.), *Theories of information behavior* (pp. 179–184). Medford, NJ: Information Today, Inc.

Feldman-Stewart, D., Brennenstuhl, S., & Brundage, M. D. (2007). A purpose-based evaluation of information for patients: An approach for measuring effectiveness. *Patient Education and Counseling, 65*, 311–319.

Frost, C. J., Venne, V., Cunningham, D., & Gerritsen-McKane, R. (2004). Decision making with uncertain information: Learning from women in a high risk breast cancer clinic. *Journal of Genetic Counseling, 13*, 221–236.

Goldsmith, D. J. (2001). A normative approach to the study of uncertainty and communication. *Journal of Communication, 51*, 514–533.

Gorman, P., Ash, J., Lavelle, M., Lyman, J., Delcambre, L., Maier, D., Weaver, M., & Bowers, S. (2000). Bundles in the wild: Managing information to solve problems and maintain situation awareness. *Library Trends, 49*, 266–289.

Hogan, T. P. (2007). *Information and the management of treatment in chronic illness: A qualitative study of people living with HIV disease.* University of Illinois at Urbana-Champaign: Dissertation Abstracts International (UMI No. 3290247).

Hogan, T. P., & Rintamaki, L. S. (2006, January). *The information work associated with taking medications: A qualitative study of U.S. veterans receiving treatment for HIV disease.* Paper presented at the Association for Library and Information Science Education (ALISE) annual conference, San Antonio, TX.

Jones, W. (2004). Finders, keepers? The present and future perfect in support of personal information management. *First Monday, 9.* Available from http://firstmonday.org/htbin/cgiwrap/bin/ojs/index.php/fm/article/view/1123/1043

Kahlor, L. A. (2007). An augmented risk information seeking model: The case of global warming. *Media Psychology, 10*, 414–435.

Kahlor, L. A., Dunwoody, S., Griffin, R. J., & Neuwirth, K. (2006). Seeking and processing information and impersonal risk. *Science Communication, 28*, 163–194.

Kelly, D. (2006). Evaluating personal information management behaviors and tools. *Communications of the ACM, 49*, 84–86.

Knobloch, L. K., & Solomon, D. H. (2005). Relational uncertainty and relational information processing. *Communication Research, 32*, 349–388.

Lambert, S. D., & Loiselle, C. G. (2007). Health information-seeking behavior. *Qualitative Health Research, 17*, 1006–1019.

Lansdale, M. (1988). The psychology of personal information management. *Applied Ergonomics, 19*, 55–66.

Lapinski, M. K., & Rimal, R. N. (2005). An explication of social norms. *Communication Theory, 15*, 127–147.

Lee, S. Y., Hwang, H., Hawkins, R., & Pingree, S. (2008). Interplay of negative emotion and health self-efficacy on the use of health information and its outcomes. *Communication Research, 35*, 358–381.

Löckenhoff, C. E., & Carstensen, L. L. (2004). Socioemotional selectivity theory, aging, and health: The increasingly delicate balance between regulating emotions and making tough choices. *Journal of Personality, 72*, 1395–1424.

Maguire, K. C. (2007). "Will it ever end?" A (re)examination of uncertainty in college student long-distance dating relationships. *Communication Quarterly, 55*, 415–432.

Marshall, C. C., & Bly, S. (2005). Saving and using encountered information: Implications for electronic periodicals. In *Proceedings of CHI 05: The Conference on Human Factors in Computing Systems* (pp. 111–120). New York: ACM Press.

Marshall, C. C., & Jones, W. (2006). Keeping encountered information. *Communications of the ACM, 49*, 66–67.

McCaughrin, W. C., & Mattammal, M. (2003). Perfect storm: Organizational management of patient care under natural disaster conditions. *Journal of Healthcare Management, 48*, 295–310.

Miller, K. I. (2007). Compassionate communication in the workplace: Exploring processes of noticing, connecting, and responding. *Journal of Applied Communication Research, 35*, 223–245.

Mishel, M. H. (1988). Uncertainty in illness. *Image: Journal of Nursing Scholarship, 20*, 225–232.

Mishel, M. H. (1990). Reconceptualization of the uncertainty in illness theory. *Image: Journal of Nursing Scholarship, 22,* 256–262.

Moen, A., & Flatley Brennan, P. (2005). Health@Home: The work of health information management in the household (HIMH): Implications for consumer health informatics (CHI) innovations. *Journal of the American Medical Informatics Association, 12,* 648–656.

Niederdeppe, J., Frosch, D. L., & Hornik, R. C. (2008). Cancer news coverage and information seeking. *Journal of Health Communication, 13,* 181–199.

Niederdeppe, J., Hornik, R. C., Kelly, B. J., Frosch, D. L., Romantan, A., Steven, R. S., Barg, F. K., Weiner, J. L., & Schwartz, J. S. (2007). Examining the dimensions of cancer-related information seeking and scanning behavior. *Health Communication, 22,* 153–167.

Powell, K. A., & Afifi, T. D. (2005). Uncertainty management and adoptees' ambiguous loss of their birth parents. *Journal of Social and Personal Relationships, 22,* 129–151.

Rains, S. A. (2008). Seeking health information in the information age: The role of internet self-efficacy. *Western Journal of Communication, 72,* 1–18.

Ross, C. S. (1999). Finding without seeking: The information encounter in the context of reading for pleasure. *Information Processing and Management, 35,* 783–799.

Shaha, M., Cox, C. L., Talman, K., & Kelly, D. (2008). Uncertainty in breast, prostate, and colorectal cancer: Implications for supportive care. *Journal of Nursing Scholarship, 40,* 60–67.

Siegel, K., & Schrimshaw, E. (2005). Stress, appraisal, and coping: A comparison of HIV-infected women in the pre-HAART and HAART eras. *Journal of Psychosomatic Research, 58,* 225–233.

Stone, A. M., Carnett, S. N., Scott, A. M., & Brashers, D. E. (2008, April). *Uncertainty and information management for transplant patients.* Paper presented at the Kentucky Conference on Health Communication, Lexington.

Stone, A. M., & Jones, C. (2008, November). *Sources of uncertainty in Alzheimer's disease.* Paper presented at the annual meeting of the National Communication Association, San Diego.

Sweeny, K. (2008). Crisis decision theory: Decisions in the face of negative events. *Psychological Bulletin, 134,* 61–76.

Taylor, R. S. (1991). Information use environments. *Progress in Communication Sciences, 10,* 217–255.

Teevan, J., Jones, W., & Bederson, B. B. (2006). Personal information management. *Communications of the ACM, 49,* 40–43.

Thompson, S., & O'Hair, H. D. (2008). Advice-giving and the management of uncertainty for cancer survivors. *Health Communication, 23,* 340–348.

Todd, R. J. (1999). Back to our beginnings: Information utilization, Bertram Brookes and the fundamental equation of information science. *Information Processing and Management, 35,* 851–870.

Toms, E. G. (2000, December). *Serendipitous information retrieval.* Paper presented in the Proceedings of the First DELOS Network of Excellence Workshop on Information Seeking, Searching and Querying in Digital Libraries, Zurich, Switzerland. Available from http://www.ercim.org/publication/ws-proceedings/DelNoe01/3_Toms.pdf

Twidale, M. B., Nichols, D. M., & Paice, C. D. (1997). Browsing is a collaborative process. *Information Processing and Management, 33,* 761–783.

van Dijk, E., & Zeelenberg, M. (2006). The dampening effect of uncertainty on positive and negative emotions. *Journal of Behavioral Decision Making, 19,* 171–176.

Wahlin, T. R. (2007). To know or not to know: A review of behaviour and suicidal ideation in preclinical Huntington's disease. *Patient Education and Counseling, 65,* 279–287.

Williamson, K. (1998). Discovered by chance: The role of incidental information acquisition in an ecological model of information use. *Library and Information Science Research, 20,* 23–40.

Wilson, T. D. (1997). Information behavior: An interdisciplinary perspective. *Information Processing & Management, 33,* 551–572.

Wilson, T. D. (2000). Human information behavior. *Informing Science, 3,* 49–55.

Wilson, T. D., Centerbar, D. B., Kermer, D. A., & Gilbert, D. T. (2005). The pleasures of uncertainty: Prolonging positive moods in ways people do not anticipate. *Journal of Personality and Social Psychology, 88,* 5–21.

Zhao, X., & Cai, X. (2008). The role of ambivalence in college nonsmokers' information seeking and information processing. *Communication Research, 35,* 298–318.

4 Information Seeking and Interpersonal Outcomes Using the Internet

Artemio Ramirez, Jr. and Joseph B. Walther

The Internet provides a magnificent engine for information seeking for just about everything, from replacement parts and obscure facts to interpersonal information. That the Internet provides modes for initiating and managing relationships is a fact (see Duck, 2008). More and more new applications come into being for the primary purpose of gathering and sharing personal information among friends and acquaintances, to discover and appraise possible social partners, and to maintain relationships. As a result of these new applications, people are able to gather not just more, but different, kinds of information about others than the Internet, or other conversational means, formerly allowed. Not long ago, the interpersonal information people exchanged online was verbal (typed), and under the relatively complete control of the sender: What you said about yourself, explicitly or implicitly, was reflected in your e-mail, your discussion-board postings, or your chat room comments. The early World Wide Web added more modalities—photos and linking—and although control remained with the page author, the effects of additional visual information produced complex effects on impressions and relations. As the Internet has developed, more information about people becomes available through involuntary sources—database archives of past behavioral traces and third-party comments—which further complicate issues of control and the impact of information. The manner in which people use these archives and socially shared commenting systems can be understood conceptually by mapping their actions and online resources to a model of Internet information-seeking strategies. This chapter examines recent models, findings, and promising new research directions related to the way people seek and share interpersonal information via the Internet. It will attempt to illuminate that social information-seeking phenomena (seeking personal, interpersonal, and descriptive information about other people) via the Internet sometimes results in counterintuitive effects on basic impressions and evaluations of others. These ironic effects of more information, particularly the influence of photos, raise challenges for traditional models of computer-mediated communication (CMC), and add interesting new boundaries to the hyperpersonal model of communication in online settings. This chapter further examines a recent model of online information seeking that expands the traditional typology of information-seeking strategies and encompasses new applications like search engines, databases, and social network sites. Finally, it examines new concepts and new directions in research premised on the notion that the Internet now often presents multiple information sources— information by target people and information left by others about target people—and how these developments, too, may affect social information seeking and social information processing on the Internet.

Perspectives on Multimodality via the Internet

While text-only communication continues to be the dominant form of online interaction, multimodal, multichannel, and multisource forms of Internet communication are increasing in popularity. Some of these technologies offer new venues for traditional information seeking and self-presentation, but many also provide novel and unique ways of gathering social information about people.

When we discuss multimodal and multichannel systems, we refer to technologies that convey multiple cue systems, such as text and photos or video. Examples include online match-making sites where users build "profiles" by answering stock questions and describing themselves using text, as well as uploading photographs. Social network sites such as Facebook do the same, but add additional sources of information, as one's Facebook friends post comments to an individual's profile, supplementing (or subverting!) the information one presents about oneself. Thus, in addition to being multimodal, Facebook and other network sites are *multisource* systems in that the profile owner and his or her friends are both sources of information about the profile owner. Other examples of multisource systems are seen in eBay and other commercial sites where users rate sellers or products: In addition to a seller or persuader promoting some item, as one source, comments from another source are a click away, in the form of past customers' feedback about the seller/persuader's prior transactions (see, for example, Flanagin, 2007). We will examine issues related to multisource systems in greater detail later in this chapter.

The emergence of multimodal forms of CMC prompts us to reexamine the scope and boundaries of existing theories, and the extent to which they inform our understanding of technologies for information acquisition and management online. Conventional thinking about CMC sometimes seems to adopt a linear view of the utility of multiple cue systems: A little more cues is a little better, and a lot more cues is a lot better, in terms of communication effectiveness and interpersonal regard. Several early theoretical perspectives, dubbed the "cues-filtered-out perspective" by Culnan and Markus (1987), shared the assumption that nonverbal cues were irreplaceable features for detecting individuality and developing warm relations with other people. In other words, if a medium lacks multimodality, it severely limits a communicator's ability to acquire social information and alter uncertainty levels. As a result, some research claims that CMC users reorient themselves, and do not seek social information about target partners (see for review Walther & Parks, 2002). Conversely, multimodal media, such as those supplying audio and/or visual information, would be expected to reduce uncertainty levels as an automatic result of the amount of cues provided to communicators; their use would be predicted to result in warmer, more positive communication and a heightened sense of connection with partners. Although much early research supported the cues-filtered-out perspective, other empirical studies have established boundary conditions regarding the circumstances under which communicators are disabled and/ or disinterested with regard to social information seeking, and when they gain advantage from the use of multimodal interfaces in fulfilling social functions of communication online (Walther & Parks, 2002). That is, studies have shown that the simple addition of any kinds of visual or audio information does not have uniform linear or additive effects on uncertainty reduction and relationship development.

The social information processing theory of CMC (SIP; Walther, 1992) offered a rebuttal to cues-filtered-out thinking and a different view of multimodal information. SIP argues that multimodal information is not necessary to reduce uncertainty online. Rather, communicators utilize the verbal features of CMC such as content, linguistic, and stylistic devices, as well as the use of chronemic cues (i.e., the interpretation of time usage and signals). The theory holds that, when time is limited, communicators focus on fulfilling task functions, foregoing social functions. The development of impressions and relationships requires a longer period of time to achieve a level comparable to those formed through face-to-face (FtF) interaction. Therefore, when time is ample and exchanges are frequent, communicators develop relationships quite as well as they do offline, only without seeing or hearing one another to do so.

It can be said of each of these models—cues-filtered-out and SIP—that multimodal information is conceived to offer a linear increase in the social information available to online communicators. In the case of the cues-filtered-out perspective, multimodality is necessary and sufficient for uncertainty reduction. In SIP, it can be said that multimodality may be sufficient, but is not necessary. Indeed, the latter perspective has been suggested in a recent reevaluation of SIP, which discussed the addition of photographs and other cues to plain-text CMC. Westerman, Van Der Heide, Klein, and Walther (2008) argued that the addition of multimodal information sources such as photographs provide a greater amount of social information in a shorter time interval than would be possible via text message exchange only. When photographic information is exchanged at the onset of relations, it is likely to provide communicators with a visual "head start" that minimizes the need for verbally discussing characteristics such as obvious physical features. Note the assumption of linearity: More information equals more, not better or worse. That is, in the SIP perspective, adding photos does not cause any big surprises or unexpected changes in the trajectory of uncertainty reduction and interpersonal evaluation that would not have accrued over time using smaller increments of interpersonal information from other modes.

Another model of CMC takes a somewhat different view about the impact of visual information on impressions and relationship development online. The hyperpersonal perspective, a special case of the social information-processing theory, describes how relationships that form online may develop greater levels of affinity and sociability than those achieved through FtF (Walther, 1996). Communicators who engage in message exchange over an extended period of time may develop idealized impressions of their partners and exaggerated relational expectations. Text-based CMC systems allow communicators greater control over key aspects of the communication process, thereby reducing the likelihood of inadvertently sharing undesirable information through nonverbal cues. The increased ability to think through, compose, and revise messages in text formats allows communicators to engage in selective self-presentation and enhance the relational communication dimensions of their exchanges (Walther, 2007). Receivers in turn are prone to overattribute partners' characteristics by elaborating on ambiguous or missing information (i.e., filling in the blanks) in their messages, which serve as the basis for feedback provided to senders. In this sense, information exchanged becomes magnified through a reciprocal process of subtle influence between communicators, resulting in assessments that exceed those found in comparable offline relations.

The hyperpersonal model suggests that realistic, photographic information is liable to render a different kind and quality of impressions and relations than that which can be achieved by text. On one hand, text is malleable and need not be tied to the features of ourselves that we do not wish to emphasize, whereas visual images carry the bad with the good. Again, text-based interactions can be tweaked and selectively interpreted, whereas visual information, voice qualities, and other multimodal information cannot be manipulated as easily. This model suggests a nonlinear relationship between the kind of information presentable through text and that which transmits visually. Ironically, despite the evolution of multimodal systems, much evidence seems to support the hyperpersonal perspective. What has become apparent through research is that attributes of CMC usage—from the kinds of information it depicts to the timing with which multimodal information becomes apparent—trigger various cognitive heuristics and biases that distort, refocus, or amplify the effects of social information on uncertainty.

The addition—or intrusion—of visual information about CMC partners seems to affect relationships differently depending on when, developmentally, it happens. Users, too, seem to be well aware of the liberties of text and the constraints of images. Research about online match-making systems finds that exaggerations that might otherwise appear in one's textual and categorical self-descriptions on online dating sites are less extreme when photos are exchanged in the early stages of relationship formation (Ellison, Heino, & Gibbs, 2006). But well beyond restraining would-be exaggerations, providing visual information may lead to *undesirable* effects when it becomes available to partners whose text-only affiliations have reached more advanced stages of development (Jacobson, 1999; Ramirez & Wang, 2008; Ramirez & Zhang, 2007; Walther, Slovacek, & Tidwell, 2001). As we review below, research has begun to accumulate compelling evidence about these paradoxical effects.

Recent studies suggest that the effect of adding multimodal forms of communication to previously text-only associations may introduce social information that may *increase* rather than decrease uncertainty. In a field experiment involving international collaborative groups, Walther et al. (2001) examined whether teams of varying duration would benefit from being presented with pictures of their previously visually anonymous partners. The researchers manipulated if and when the teams were presented with photographs of their members and then assessed the impact of the photos on judgments of attractiveness (task, social, and physical) and intimacy/affection. The introduction of photographs benefited *newly formed, short-term groups* by fostering greater social attraction and intimacy/affection. However, in the case of *long-term groups*, the availability of photographs dampened intimacy/affection. Moreover, the more that those whose pictures were displayed tried to manage their impressions verbally via CMC, the less attractive their partners perceived them to be, suggesting greater uncertainty or discrepancy between the fixed level of attractiveness reflected in the photos and the variability attempted by participants behaviorally. Walther et al. (2001) concluded that team members who were allowed to interact over time through text alone, without photos, remained unconstrained by multimodal information in order to achieve desired impressions, whereas the addition of visually cued social information circumvented the use of discretionary uncertainty-reducing mechanisms, muddying the waters with respect to the development of hyperpersonal relations.

Whereas participants in the Walther et al. (2001) study continued to interact online even after a second mode of information, photographs, was added to their exchanges, other studies address the effect of shifting interactions from a text-based system to an even more multimodal system with respect to effects on relational processes and outcomes, including postinteraction uncertainty levels. Ramirez and Zhang (2007) examined the effect of FtF meeting following varying lengths of time interacting via text-based CMC ("modality switching") on relational communication assessments. They hypothesized that the intrusion of physical reality in visually anonymous virtual partnerships should dampen relational communication in long-term associations but augment it in short-term ones. They posited that initial FtF meetings occurring in partnerships formed over an extended period hold a greater potential (than such meetings occurring in short-term partnerships) for introducing social information that may contradict already-held partner knowledge. As a result, such meetings are likely to lead partners to reevaluate said knowledge.

In order to test this argument, Ramirez and Zhang (2007) assigned individuals to collaborative partnerships that were required to complete three tasks over a 9-week period. Participants were randomly assigned to complete the tasks via an e-mail-like computer conferencing system only, through FtF interaction only, or some combination of the two modalities, with the combinations varying in terms of how far along in the relationship a medium switch took place. The results indicated that those who remained online and never met in person reported greater intimacy and social attraction than did any of the conditions in which FtF interaction occurred. When the CMC-initiated conditions are considered independently, partnerships that remained online reported greater social orientation and more positive forecasts of the partnership's future than the two conditions that shifted to FtF meeting (immediately following completion of the initial task or the second task). With respect to postinteraction uncertainty, long-term partnerships in which FtF meetings occurred reported a curvilinear trend over time; reduced uncertainty was reported following completion of the two initial tasks followed by an increase following the in-person meeting. Information-seeking behavior, however, was reported as increasing over time for all of CMC-initiated conditions, suggesting the influence of switching modality was minimal.

Drawing upon expectancy violations theory (Burgoon, 1993; see also Afifi & Metts, 1998), Ramirez and Wang (2008) proposed that the dampening of affinity and elevation of uncertainty in long-term virtual partnerships following the introduction of multimodal social information was likely the result of violated expectations. They argued that the social information provided by photographs and in-person meetings were likely inconsistent with the expectations partners formed of each other through text-only interaction (Jacobson, 1999), resulting in less positive evaluations and increased uncertainty in the long-term condition. In the short-term condition, however, because expectations were less well-formed due to limited partner knowledge, the social information aided in their further development, thereby reducing uncertainty. Ramirez and Wang (2008) evaluated the accuracy of this explanation of modality-switching effects in a 2 (short-term vs. long-term association) by 2 (in-person meeting vs. no meeting) design. The results showed that, relative to remaining online, the social information acquired by the in-person meeting was rated as expectancy violating irrespective of the timing of when it was received. Dyads in the short-term condition evaluated the social information as more positive and uncertainty reducing, relative to those remaining online. In contrast, dyads in the long-term condition evaluated the information as more negative and uncertainty provoking relative to their online counterparts.

The overall pattern of findings in this line of research stands in contrast to the early cues-filtered-out perspective reviewed above that assumed the presence of more nonverbal and social cues would inherently lead to more positive interpersonal evaluations. These studies suggest other moderators need to be considered, particularly when examining the uncertainty effects associated with shifts from one modality to another.

Social Information-Seeking Strategies and Internet Tools

The research described above reflects that large amount of activity where individuals can wrestle with the decision of whether to share multimodal information or to withhold it. In other respects, their control over that decision is mitigated. We began this chapter by pointing out that one of the changes in Internet capacities is that the social information that is available about a person is no longer under the exclusive control of the person to whom it refers. There is more and more social information about individuals available online, and more places it resides. The aggregation, storage, and persistence of users' past Internet forays continue to mount in online databases made ever more searchable and retrievable through data mining and search engine queries. Search engines offer potent ways to uncover information that can reveal personal details about targets without their knowledge; take the degree to which the phrase "I Googled him/her" has become common in the lexicon.

Not long before the widespread adoption of these social network sites, dating systems, and other information-sharing utilities, a conceptual model of Internet information seeking was introduced that helps make clear the advantages and uses to which these new, as well as older, Internet information systems are put. This model of communication technology in information seeking, developed by Ramirez, Walther, Burgoon, and Sunnafrank (2002), is timely enough, sufficiently robust, and adequately flexible to illuminate the dynamics of communication technologies that have arrived on the scene even after the model's introduction (such as social network sites like MySpace and other applications). The model focuses on a conventional taxonomy of information-seeking strategies, and applies its principles to new technology attributes and practices.

The model advances a critical observation regarding information-seeking behavior via CMC: It depicts how new technologies offer more than information-seeking opportunities that also occur using traditional forms of communication. Like other forms of interaction, technology helps to connect individuals. Just as one can talk to a prospective relational partner face to face, or call a mutual friend on the phone to share impressions, one can use e-mail and chat via the Internet to reduce uncertainty in similar ways. The Internet, however, also presents communicators new and unique ways to seek information about others. Online information seeking is not only multifaceted but multiply enacted. Communicators can employ several approaches to information acquisition sequentially or simultaneously in order to reduce uncertainty. They can employ multiple forms of technology to acquire different kinds of information during the course of a single episode or interface. The potential for the simultaneous use of e-mail, instant messaging, search engines, and archival message retrieval, any and all of which may be utilized concurrently while engaging in a voice or text-based conversation with a target, provide an almost endless set of tools that communicators have at their disposal. The ways in which information from these different sources and channels complement or supersede one another is just beginning to be explored.

Ramirez et al.'s (2002) model identified several factors that may influence the use of distinct information-seeking strategies in the pursuit of social information online. Central to the model are three information-seeking strategies initially identified by Berger and Kellermann (1983) in the context of FtF interaction: passive, active, and interactive information-seeking strategies. Ramirez et al. (2002) illuminated how each may be enacted via CMC, with the majority of prior research having focused on interactive strategies, which are also those that are best documented offline. Comparative CMC versus FtF research has been able to capitalize on these findings. However, Ramirez et al. offer a fourth information-seeking strategy that is native to Internet information systems: extractive information-seeking strategies. The next section of this chapter reviews and updates the manner in which reference to these strategies can organize recent research on online social information-seeking behavior.

Passive Strategies

Certain virtual environments are amenable to unobtrusive or passive information seeking, which requires no interaction with a target. Passive strategies were conceptualized as information acquisition through unobtrusive target observation. Observational opportunities are most likely to occur in the context of online communication forums structured for large group interaction. Environments such as discussion boards, chat spaces, gaming sites, social network sites, and multimodal settings (e.g., Second Life) provide communicators the ability to review contributions, profiles, or simply lurk in relative obscurity. To a lesser extent, other technological innovations allow for similar information seeking at the interpersonal level. Most personal blogs, for instance, allow interested parties the opportunity to read author postings without the requirement of a response. The prevalence of this form of information acquisition online is also supported by studies reporting that only about 20% of forum members contribute to discussions, whereas the remaining members "lurk," or only read contributions that were made by other people (Barnes, 2001; Nonnecke & Preece, 2000; Seabrook, 1997).

The potential beneficial effects of passive information-seeking behavior are illustrated in Flanagin's (2007) study of consumer-to-consumer auctions on eBay. Employing both uncertainty reduction and predicted outcome value theories, Flanagin (2007) argued that these vendor–consumer relationships were prone to the same theoretically expected influences from information gathering as would occur in traditional, offline interaction, except that the outcome of uncertainty reduction manifests itself in economic behavior such as the number of bids and final bid prices for items up for auction. Flanagin (2007) noted that this type of information "can be viewed as a means by which individuals decrease behavioral uncertainty through passive information-seeking in online environments" (p. 416).

Other recently published research suggests participants, who use interactive information-seeking strategies, and lurkers, who use passive information-seeking strategies, may differ in how they perceive social information acquired in text-based discussions. In a series of three studies, Ramirez and colleagues (2007) examined differences between participants' and lurkers' interpretations of relational tone in CMC interpersonal (Study 1) and group text-based interactions (Studies 2 and 3). Study participants were assigned to either engage in or observe an online discussion and then provide their perceptions of its tone along Burgoon and Hale's (1984) dimensions of relational communication. Across the three studies, participants and observers reported consistent differences in the manner in which they interpreted the relational messages conveyed in the discussions: Although both participant and lurker ratings of relational tone were in the same direction (positive or negative), ratings provided by the prior consistently exceeded those provided by the latter.

The utility of this paradigm for experimentally examining information-seeking behavior in multimodal contexts remains to be investigated. Virtual environments such as Second Life, an avatar-based chat system with advanced graphical capabilities and rich with visual information, may offer additional opportunities for examining differences between passive information seeking and other approaches. Second Life players can choose how to represent themselves physically by means of on-screen avatars, and players chat with others in public spaces. Because of these features, users can observe others without actually interacting with them, and make judgments about those others by assessing their virtual physical appearance, clothing, and accoutrements choices, and by the manner in which they represent themselves. Such completely volitional cues by actors provide observers with overt and covert cues about the real-life personae of the user, without having to engage the target directly.

In addition, Second Life players can unobtrusively watch how players interact with each other in the virtual environment without having to engage in the conversation him or herself. Making inferences about others by watching conversations without being in them and by observing how a target interacts with the environment constitutes "active strategies" for uncertainty reduction, which CMC also provides in several other ways.

Active Strategies

Beyond connecting individuals directly, or allowing them to observe one another unobtrusively, communication technologies also provide communicators with abilities to gather social information from members of targets' social networks. Active strategies are conceptualized as indirect information acquisition without employing direct interaction with the target (Berger & Kellermann, 1983). The prototypical active strategy would be the use of third-party, human information sources, who may provide insight into the target. Sociotechnical advances in multimodal social network sites have provided new venues for assessing the role and effects of active strategies in impression formation. In the aforementioned study by Flanagin (2007) examining online auctions, information about a vendor's reputation, as indexed by comments provided by past customers, offered one form of information that was acquired actively by potential business partners and significantly predicted both the number of bids and the final bid price in online auctions.

In their study assessing how evaluations of Facebook-profile owners are influenced by their friends' physical appearance and behavior, Walther, Van Der Heide, Kim, Westerman, and Tong (2008) illuminate another path by which active strategies influence social judgments. Their experiment manipulated the apparent attractiveness of profile owners' friends by using different photos and comments posted to the "wall" (a space where friends' comments and photos appear) on a mock-up Facebook profile, in order to assess their effects on perceptions of the profile owner. The results indicate that third-party sources have a significant impact upon how others evaluate targets. Specifically, findings showed that when friends' wall postings contained prosocial comments, profile owners were perceived to be more credible as well as more socially attractive and task attractive. Male profile owners were also perceived as more physically attractive when friends posted negatively valenced messages about moral behaviors (e.g., drinking), whereas female owners were perceived as less so. Moreover, profile owners who had photos posted of physically attractive friends were also rated as more physically attractive themselves. Thus, the overall results suggest that comments made available on networking sites in conjunction with multimodal information sources such as photographs hold the potential to influence social judgments in a manner beneficial (or detrimental) to profile owners, dependent on the nature of the photos and comments.

Interactive Strategies

The most obvious manner in which new media and technology aid in information seeking is by providing communicators with a variety of opportunities for engaging in direct interaction. Interactive strategies are conceptualized as involving different tactics enacted during direct interaction between the communicator(s) and target(s). The assumption underlying the use of these strategies is that communicators actively adjust their behavior based on the feedback received from the target. Tactics may take the form of direct questioning, reciprocal disclosure, or eliciting relaxation as means of procuring the information desired.

Studies examining the use of interactive strategies reveal that the pattern of questions employed by CMC communicators parallels that explicated in relationship development theories (e.g., Altman & Taylor, 1973). In their content analysis of e-mails exchanged between senior citizens and school-aged youths over a 6-month period, Pratt, Wiseman, Cody, and Wendt (1999) reported that question asking was higher in initial stages of relationship development than in later ones. Consistent with most theories of relationship formation, demographic and other surface-level questions dominated initial stages with questions about internal states (e.g., attitudes, opinions) appearing more commonly in subsequent stages. Other research reports that CMC communicators rely on question-asking to a greater extent than do their FtF counterparts. Research by Tidwell and Walther (2002) found that communicators employed questioning and self-disclosure at a proportionately greater level when interacting via CMC than FtF. Moreover, question-asking was perceived to be more conversationally effective in CMC than in FtF interaction. In addition, the personal questions and self-disclosures communicated via CMC conveyed greater depth than those exchanged FtF. We now move to the next strategy, one which is original to the Internet, and one which has come to represent an ever-growing list of Internet applications.

Extractive Strategies

Ramirez and colleagues (2002) explicated a special case of active strategies which are unique to communication technology and not available in FtF interaction. Extractive strategies involve the use of electronic searches as means of gathering social information about targets. Search engines such as Google and Yahoo!, database queries of electronic list postings and government records, and other similar tools provide communicators with covert electronic, third-party sources of information, which may offer insight into a target above and beyond that commonly available through other information acquisition approaches.

Utilization of such tools for the purpose of searching for information about others has become pervasive in society, yet scholars have mostly overlooked their use. The exceptions shed light on the phenomenon. For example, studies of online dating report that individuals commonly seek online information about prospective dating partners prior to initial in-person meetings (e.g., Gibbs, Ellison, & Heino, 2006). Moreover, a recent study conducted by the Pew Internet & American Life Project (Madden, Fox, Smith, & Vitak, 2007) sheds light on the online search for information about *ourselves*. The study is noteworthy because it is the only one to date that has explicitly documented the use of search engines in pursuit of social information about individuals and past or current members of their social networks. Their survey of 1,623

Internet users revealed that 42% of the sample searched for information about themselves via search engines—an increase from 22% only 5 years earlier. Those most likely to conduct searches on themselves were under the age of 50 years, more educated, and of higher-income levels than those who were not; males and females were equally likely to conduct such a search. In addition, the same study reported that 53% of the sample had used search engines to find information about at least one personal or professional acquaintance, with the most common searches being for a past relation with whom they had lost contact. The users most likely to conduct online searches on others were between the ages of 39 and 49 years, with males and females being equally likely to have done so.

Employing extractive strategies, however, does not guarantee the quality of the information acquired. Of those in the Pew study reporting that they had conducted a search on themselves, 62% reported that the information acquired matched expectations of what they would find. However, 21% were surprised by the large quantity of personal information available, and 13% were surprised by how little emerged. A different picture emerges with respect to how successful communicators are in locating desired information about others. Only 19% of participants reported "always or almost always" finding what they were searching for, whereas 23% reported succeeding in their search "most of the time," and 21% reported succeeding "hardly ever." With the continued growth in popularity of Web 2.0 tools such as YouTube and social networking sites, which thrive on user-generated content made available to a mass audience, it is likely more and more Internet users will utilize extractive strategies as means of monitoring their online presence as well as that of past or current associates.

Future Research on Uncertainty and Information Management via New Media

This chapter has addressed how new developments in Internet information-seeking supplement or subvert uncertainty reduction processes, compared both to conventional plain-text CMC and to FtF communication. It is already clear that the introduction of multimodal information does not bestow a simple, linear addition to the process of generating social inferences. The timing, modality, and apparent source of different information sources may well interact with the nature of the information itself to disrupt or augment interpersonal impressions developed and cultivated online. As our communication toolkit continues to present multimodal and multi-source interfaces and information resources, new questions arise with regard to the weights and credence that users will place on different sources, and how they will use the vast information resources available to them not only to generate social inferences but to attempt other social goals as well. The remainder of this chapter suggests new research directions, and initial forays in those directions that may help scholars make sense of emerging information and communication technologies online. We highlight recent and current studies that conceptualize new technologies and interfaces as providing multiple simultaneous sources of influence, and how an analysis of the kinds of sources they represent—persuaders or peers—can provide insights into the dynamics of social inferences and social influence online.

Warranting and Multiple Sources

The warranting principle is a relatively new construct that describes the kind of data sources that affect information seekers' impressions most strongly when the veracity of online impressions become critical to an information seeker. If people meet in a chat room, a discussion list, an online game, in Second Life, or some other Internet venue where people have the ability, if not the inclination, to fabricate or distort their self-presentations, a partner may sustain a level of uncertainty for some time. It can be part of the game or the flirtation to fabricate or bend one's self-presentation in online settings where inventing a fictive persona is a given (see, e.g., Roberts & Parks, 1999). Even in settings such as online dating sites, where, if all goes well, prospective partners will meet FtF, there is still a general level of suspiciousness about the accuracy of self-presentations online (Cornwell & Lundgren, 2001). When there is doubt about whether individuals are who they say, partners may want to ascertain what disclosures are bona fide and which, if any, are false. In order to do so, Walther and Parks (2002) suggested, users rely more strongly on information that is difficult to manipulate by the targets. Information that has "warranting" value connects the online persona to an offline person in less malleable ways than self-description does. For example, members of an individual's social network may be sought for information about that person because they are likely to reveal information that will be more trusted than that which the individual may disclose—online or offline. On the Internet, a Web page photo uploaded by the Webmaster for an institutional Web site may connote a more accurate photo than the one that the same target herself posts on an online dating site. A source has self-serving motives to selectively self-present and to gain favor through potential distortion, whereas disinterested third parties should be perceived to be more objective and accurate.

The warranting principle has received preliminary support in empirical research. Walther, Van Der Heide, Hamel, and Shulman (in press) used Facebook mock-ups to see whether contradictions between individuals' self-descriptions on certain traits, and the contents of their friends' "wall postings," tipped evaluations in the directions of the friends' rather than profile owners' claims. Results provided mixed support for the warranting hypothesis with regard to claims of extraversion, which in retrospect may not be as delicate a subject for self-presentation distortions as may other traits. Results from contradictory claims about the target's physical attractiveness, however, more clearly supported the warranting principle: Friends' allusions to the target's good looks or bad looks dominated the impact of the target's self-statements about their appearance. We expect that warranting effects pervade numerous online settings. Extending these principles to other Internet settings, Carr et al. (2008) suggested that users should be more likely to trust a product review on a vendor's commercial site if that review is posted by another user rather than the manufacturer or the vendor.

Carr et al. (2008) further suggested that communication research offers particularly useful conceptualizations with which to understand multisource information interfaces. In many Internet applications, there are several sources of potential social influence, which we may categorize using familiar labels, invoking rather well-known information-processing dynamics in response. On the eBay site, for instance, there is a seller describing the attributes of products trying to persuade others to spend increasingly greater money for his wares. On the very Web page where the seller posts, there are also feedback scores—reputation coefficients—generated by other eBay users who have purchased items from the same seller in the past. We may presume that these other buyers are perceived as peers—invisible and individually anonymous peers. Once we classify them this way, their potential social influence on other Internet buyers should be predictable through the mechanisms of social identification/deindividuation theory. They are perceived as exceptionally similar to ourselves (all eBay users), and they reflect group norms (they all posted feedback), and thus they should have significant influence on our attitudes (our reactions to the seller). It may be these dynamics that underlie Resnick, Zeckhauser, Friedman, and Kuwabara's (2000) empirical findings that reputation coefficients have real economic impact, in terms of the greater bidding prices that a large accumulation of positive ratings garner. We prefer online information that appears to be selected by people just like ourselves (Sundar & Nass, 2001).

The process of information seeking is being transformed by these interfaces. Many Internet applications, like those described above, especially those referred to as "Web 2.0," are designed to capture input from other users and present it alongside the original content. We can conceptualize this arrangement as presenting both a primary persuader or central information source, and a simultaneous second source that provides information about the primary source. How users relate to these secondary sources and what these sources say about the primary information should have a great deal to do with the attention, interpretation, and retention users direct to the primary source. Web 2.0 systems provide uncertainty-reducing information about the central claim or claimant, and reduce the effort of information-seeking to eyeballing the screen or clicking the mouse. Even without the added influence of social clues, we expect that the ease and availability of simultaneous/parallel information is likely to trigger information-processing biases such as anchoring effects and other heuristics (see Tversky & Kahneman, 1974), whether or not the influence of these sources is magnified by social factors. A case in point is the finding that health information seekers tend to forgo extended searching and source evaluations and rely instead on the relative ordering of the information sources that search engine queries display (Eysenbach & Köhler, 2002). When social cues stimulate further levels of credence, and warrant or challenge central claims, the potency of this information convergence may be great.

Our research is beginning to explore these dynamics in some of the popular, potentially potent, Internet environments on the current scene. For instance, we are exploring the manner in which observer-generated comments that appear alongside YouTube videos affect others' perceptions of the messages and sources belonging to those videos, when videos contain deliberate persuasive messages. This work involves benchmarking users' perceived similarity to message posters, and whether features of the comments themselves affect the manner in which they relate. It involves analysis of the strength of the original message content in terms of arguments and appeal, as well as the focus of the posted comments with respect to their counter-arguments, evaluations of aesthetic issues, and attributions about the original message creators. Elsewhere, we are examining whether social identification or interpersonal attraction affect information-seeking and information-processing behaviors during (or when anticipating) chat room discussions. In visually anonymous, text-based interactions such as these, positive or negative social pressures can be quite strong, and may shape selective searching, and selective perception and retention of what might otherwise have been objective information gathering, in order to appease, impress, conform, or contest invisible others (see, e.g., David, Cappella, & Fishbein, 2006).

Thus, an agenda for future research on online uncertainty and information seeking and using includes the following conceptual suggestions that researchers might employ in order to advance understanding of emerging Internet-based social technologies with respect to their effects on uncertainty and information management processes. First, we may conceptualize many Web 2.0 applications as systems presenting parallel information sources, obviating certain offline information-seeking efforts, and promoting impressions and decisions based on that which the interface presents. Second, for any specific application, we attempt to classify the information sources using familiar types (e.g., institutional mass media messages or persuaders, peers, members of the source's social network and/or the observer's, or interpersonal sources). Third, we apply extant knowledge about how users process information that they glean from these various types of sources, in terms of the effects of presumed motivations and trustworthiness, reliability, expertise, and homophily/heterophily with respect to the user. Fourth, we identify other relevant message characteristics that may be expected to moderate social influence (such as language characteristics or expectancy violations). Using these factors, researchers can bring to new interfaces and seemingly novel information appliances the benefits of theoretical knowledge that has been established in traditional domains. There is good reason to believe that the dynamics that have been established in traditional domains will also obtain in new media environments, just as there is a good chance that technology attributes and source dynamics will produce interesting interaction effects that will spark further explorations and thinking about information-processing technology and information-seeking dynamics that are manifested in Internet environments.

References

Afifi, W. A., & Metts, S. (1998). Characteristics and consequences of expectation violations in close relationships. *Journal of Social and Personal Relationships, 15,* 365–392.

Altman, I., & Taylor, D. A. (1973). *Social penetration: The development of interpersonal relationships.* New York: Holt, Rinehart, & Winston.

Barnes, S. B. (2001). *Online connections: Internet interpersonal relationships.* Cresskill, NJ: Hampton Press.

Berger, C. R., & Kellermann, K. (1983). To ask or not to ask: Is that a question? In R. Bostrom (Ed.), *Communication yearbook 7* (pp. 342–368). Beverly Hills, CA: Sage.

Burgoon, J. K. (1993). Interpersonal expectations, expectancy violations, and emotional communication. *Journal of Language and Social Psychology, 12,* 13–21.

Burgoon, J. K., & Hale, J. L. (1984). The fundamental topoi of relational communication. *Communication Monographs, 51,* 193–214.

Carr, C., Choi, S., DeAndrea, D., Kim, J., Tong, S. T., Van Der Heide, B., & Walther, J. B. (2008, May). *Interaction of interpersonal, peer, and media influence sources online: A research agenda for technology convergence.* Paper presented at the annual meeting of the International Communication Association, Montreal.

Cornwell, B., & Lundgren, D. C. (2001). Love on the Internet: Involvement and misrepresentation in romantic relationships in cyberspace vs. realspace. *Computers in Human Behavior, 17,* 197–211.

Culnan, M. J., & Markus, M. L. (1987). Information technologies. In F. M. Jablin, L. L. Putnam, K. H. Roberts, & L. W. Porter (Eds.), *Handbook of organizational communication: An interdisciplinary perspective* (pp. 420–443). Newbury Park, CA: Sage.

David, C., Cappella, J. N., & Fishbein, M. (2006). The social diffusion of influence among adolescents: Group interaction in a chat room environment about anti-drug advertisements. *Communication Theory, 16,* 118–140.

Duck, S. (2008). A past and a future for relationship research. *Journal of Social and Personal Relationships, 25,* 189–200.

Ellison, N., Heino, R., & Gibbs, J. (2006). Managing impressions online: Self-presentation processes in the online dating environment. *Journal of Computer-Mediated Communication, 11.* Retrieved January 10, 2008, from http://jcmc.indiana.edu/vol11/issue2/ellison.html

Eysenbach, G., & Köhler, C. (2002). How do consumers search for and appraise health information on the World Wide Web? Qualitative study using focus groups, usability tests, and in-depth interviews. *British Medical Journal, 324,* 573–577.

Flanagin, A. J. (2007). Commercial markets as communication markets: Uncertainty reduction through mediated information exchange in online auctions. *New Media & Society, 9,* 401–423.

Gibbs, J. L., Ellison, N. B., & Heino, R. D. (2006). Self-presentation in online personals: The role of anticipated future interaction, self-disclosure, and perceived success in Internet dating. *Communication Research, 33,* 1–26.

Jacobson, D. (1999). Impression formation in cyberspace: Online expectations and offline experiences in text-based virtual communities. *Journal of Computer-Mediated Communication, 5.* Retrieved March 22, 2006, from http://jcmc.indiana.edu/vol5/issue1/jacobson.html

Madden, M., Fox, S., Smith, A., & Vitak, J. (2007, December 16). Digital footprints: Online identity management and search in the age of transparency. *Pew Internet & American Life Project.* Retrieved December 20, 2007, from http://www.pewinternet.org

Nonnecke, B., & Preece, J. (2000, April). Lurker demographics: Counting the silent. *Proceedings of CHI 2000 Conference, The Hague, Netherlands* (pp. 73–80). New York: Addison-Wesley/ACM Press.

Pratt, L., Wiseman, R. L., Cody, M. J., & Wendt, P. F. (1999). Interrogative strategies and information exchange in computer-mediated communication. *Communication Quarterly, 47,* 46–66.

Ramirez, Jr., A., Walther, J., Burgoon, J. K., & Sunnafrank, M. (2002). Information seeking strategies, uncertainty, and computer-mediated communication: Towards a conceptual approach. *Human Communication Research, 28,* 213–228.

Ramirez, Jr., A., & Wang, Z. (2008). When on-line meets off-line: An expectancy violation theory perspective on modality switching. *Journal of Communication, 58,* 20–39.

Ramirez, Jr., A., & Zhang, S. (2007). When online meets offline: The effect of modality switching on relational communication. *Communication Monographs, 74,* 287–310.

Ramirez, Jr., A., Zhang, S., McGrew, K., & Lin, S.-F. (2007). Relational communication in computer-mediated interaction: A comparison of participant–observer perspectives. *Communication Monographs, 74,* 492–516.

Resnick, P., Zeckhauser, R., Friedman, E., & Kuwabara, K. (2000). Reputation systems. *Communications of the ACM, 43,* 45–48.

Roberts, L. D., & Parks, M. R. (1999). The social geography of gender-switching in virtual environments on the Internet. *Information, Communication, and Society, 2,* 521–540.

Seabrook, J. (1997). *Deeper: A two-year odyssey in cyberspace.* New York: Simon & Schuster.

Sundar, S. S., & Nass, C. (2001). Conceptualizing sources in online news. *Journal of Communication, 51,* 52–72.

Tidwell, L., & Walther, J. B. (2002). Computer-mediated communication effects on disclosure, impressions, and interpersonal evaluation: Getting to know one another one bit at a time. *Human Communication Research, 26,* 317–348.

Tversky, A., & Kahneman, D. (1974). Judgment under uncertainty: Heuristics and biases. *Science, 185,* 381–391.

Walther, J. B. (1992). Interpersonal effects in computer-mediated interaction: A relational perspective. *Communication Research, 19,* 52–89.

Walther, J. B. (1996). Computer-mediated communication: Impersonal, interpersonal, and hyperpersonal interaction. *Communication Research, 23,* 3–43.

Walther, J. B. (2007). Selective self-presentation in computer-mediated communication: Hyperpersonal dimensions of technology, language, and cognition. *Computers in Human Behavior, 23,* 2538–2557.

Walther, J. B., & Parks, M. R. (2002). Cues filtered out, cues filtered in: Computer-mediated communication and relationships. In M. L. Knapp & J. A. Daly (Eds.), *Handbook of interpersonal communication* (3rd ed., pp. 529–563). Thousand Oaks, CA: Sage.

Walther, J. B., Slovacek, C., & Tidwell, L. C. (2001). Is a picture worth a thousand words? Photographic images in long term and short term virtual teams. *Communication Research, 28*, 105–134.

Walther, J. B., Van Der Heide, B., Hamel, L., & Shulman, H. (in press). Self-generated versus other-generated statements and impressions in computer-mediated communication: A test of warranting theory using Facebook. *Communication Research.*

Walther, J. B., Van Der Heide, B., Kim, S., Westerman, D., & Tong, S. T. (2008). The role of friends' behavior on evaluations of individuals' Facebook profiles: Are we known by the company we keep? *Human Communication Research, 34*, 28–49.

Westerman, D. K., Van Der Heide, B., Klein, K. A., & Walther, J. B. (2008). How do people really seek information about others? Information seeking across Internet and traditional communication channels. *Journal of Computer-Mediated Communication, 13*, 751–767. Retrieved June 4, 2008, from http://www.black well-synergy.com/doi/pdf/10.1111/j.1083-6101.2008.00418.x

Factors Impacting the Association Between Uncertainty and Information Management

5 Expanding the Role of Emotion in the Theory of Motivated Information Management

Walid A. Afifi and Chris R. Morse

The surge of interest in uncertainty and information seeking is evidenced by the fact that at least 10 active programs of research in this area have either started or grown considerably in the past decade (Afifi, 2009). One of the more recent such programs is the development and subsequent testing of the theory of motivated information management (TMIM; Afifi & Weiner, 2004). To date, the theory has been tested for its utility as a perspective from which to understand information-seeking decisions across several contexts, including relationally relevant issues, broadly (Afifi, Dillow, & Morse, 2004), partner's sexual health status (Afifi & Weiner, 2006), family attitudes regarding organ donation (Afifi et al., 2006), and adolescent topic avoidance with parents (Afifi & Afifi, in press). The theory has also been the subject of several review chapters and encyclopedia entries (e.g., Afifi, 2009, in press; Afifi & Lucas, 2008). We have reflected, in several of these manuscripts, on the incompleteness in the coverage of emotion in the framework and have argued that revisions to the theory need to extend its reach in that domain. This chapter is our first effort to do so. The end product is a revision of the first two (of seven original) propositions in TMIM's structure and the addition of two new propositions—in other words, a significant change to the theory's propositional structure.

Theory of Motivated Information Management

The theory of motivated information management (see Figure 5.1) was developed as a result of dissatisfaction with some aspects of existing uncertainty frameworks, most notably their predictive specificity, their tendency to overlook the role of efficacy, and their limited treatment of the interactive nature of the information management process (see Afifi, 2009; Afifi & Weiner, 2004). Afifi and Weiner (2004) began their theoretical statement by articulating scope conditions for the theory. First, they restricted the theory's applicability to important (as opposed to mundane) issues as recognition of the unlikelihood that actors would engage such a process for issues of little relevance to them. Second, the theory was limited to

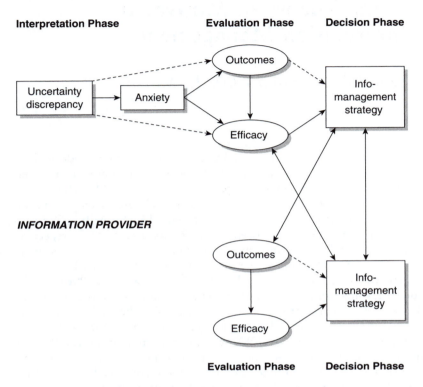

Figure 5.1 Graphical Model of TMIM's Propositional Structure

interpersonal contexts due to the belief that interpersonal exchanges involved unique challenges and opportunities not present to information managers in other contexts.

The theory proposes a three-phase process of information management that actors (i.e., the potential information seeker) go through in deciding a course of action. The process starts with an awareness that the desired level of uncertainty about an important issue is at odds with the actual level of uncertainty on that issue. Our reliance on uncertainty discrepancy (the label given that difference between actual and desired levels of uncertainty) as the starting point for the process, as opposed to actual uncertainty levels alone, reflected a recognition that individuals are sometimes motivated to change low levels of uncertainty or maintain high levels of uncertainty, depending on circumstance (e.g., Babrow, 1992, 2001; Brashers, 2001, 2007). In that sense, uncertainty discrepancy, a notion adopted from Chaiken's (1987) heuristic-systematic model, moved us away from an uncertainty reduction paradigm to an uncertainty management paradigm (see Afifi, 2009, for elaborated discussion). The TMIM framework then adopted a control theory (see Afifi, 2009) account for the emotional consequence of uncertainty discrepancy. Specifically, those theories argue that the difference between desired and actual goal states produce anxiety. According to TMIM, that experience of anxiety theoretically ended the first phase of the process (i.e., the interpretation phase) and directly influenced the cognitive assessments made in the next phase (the evaluation phase).

Afifi and Weiner (2004) adopted a social cognitive theory framework (Bandura, 1997) to account for perceptions that actors make in the evaluation phase. The phase consists of two sets of assessments: outcome expectancies and efficacy. Outcome expectancies, in TMIM, reflect beliefs about the outcomes of a particular information management strategy (Afifi & Weiner, 2004). It includes both process- and outcome-related costs and benefits. The former reflects perceived outcomes associated with the simple *act* of, for example, seeking information from a particular source (e.g., costs and benefits expected to come from the mere act of seeking information about a partner's past relational partners). The latter involves outcomes that are expected to come from, to continue our example, seeking information from that source (e.g., costs and benefits expected to come from the information itself). These outcome expectancies are then predicted to directly influence a set of three efficacy assessments: communication efficacy, coping efficacy, and target efficacy. Communication efficacy involves actors' assessments of their ability to competently engage in the information management action (e.g., seek information) from the target source. Coping efficacy reflects the actors' judgments of whether they have the resources (emotional and otherwise) to "handle" the outcomes of a particular information management strategy. Finally, target efficacy assessments address beliefs about whether the target has access to the sought-after information and is likely to be honest in her or his transmission of the information. Together, these three efficacy assessments directly influence the actors' information management decisions and serve as partial mediator of outcome expectancy's impact on that front.

The final phase—the decision phase—involves a selection among three information management strategies: seek information, avoid information, or engage in cognitive reassessments. All three options potentially affect the actors' uncertainty levels and may either solve the uncertainty discrepancy or reinitiate the information management process.

The outcome of the process depends, in part, on the actions of a potential information target. Afifi and Weiner (2004) also advanced a two-phase process associated with the information provider but did not elaborate fully on that aspect of the theory. Research since then has still failed to do so.

As noted earlier, almost immediately following publication of the theory, Afifi and colleagues addressed the need for a more thorough recognition of the role played by emotion in the information management process (e.g., Afifi, Morse, Dillow, & Weiner, 2005; for review, see Afifi, 2009). What follows is our first attempt at doing so.

Appraisal Theories of Emotion

Appraisal theories of emotion outline a sequential relationship of evaluations directed toward understanding emotions and their function in guiding particular action (Frijda, 1986; Frijda, Kuipers, & ter Schure, 1989). In the remainder of the chapter, we examine the potential role of emotion in the TMIM framework by recasting the response to uncertainty discrepancy from the perspective of appraisal theory and considering the impact of such appraisals on evaluation-phase assessments. In the end, we argue that this approach reveals the limitations of the existing TMIM approach, vis-à-vis the role of emotions, and allows the theory to recognize the breadth of possible emotional responses to uncertainty discrepancy and the unique potential of each to affect information management decisions. We will start with a brief overview of appraisal theories before moving on to their implications for TMIM.

Appraisal theorists argue that individuals respond to events in their environment by making assessments (i.e., appraisals) of their surroundings. These appraisals, in turn, account for the assignment of emotion labels to their physiological experience. The emotion labels then serve as signaling functions that instigate particular responses or actions (Eysenck, 2000; Lazarus, 1991a; Roseman & Smith, 2001). The outcome of the process is highly dependent on individuals' needs and experiences, and is influenced by their relationship with the event, as well as what that event means to their personal goals (Smith & Kirby, 2001a). Although there are several structural appraisal models put forth (Roseman, 1991; Scherer, 2001), we rely mainly on Lazarus's approach to guide us (Lazarus, 1991a, 1991b).

According to Lazarus's model, individuals make two sets of appraisals that ultimately combine to result in the experience of discrete emotions (e.g., happiness/joy, anger, guilt, sadness, hope, relief, shame): primary appraisals and secondary appraisals (Lazarus, 1991b). *Primary appraisals* reflect "whether something of relevance to the person's well-being has occurred" (Lazarus, 1991b, p. 133) and involve three "appraisal components": assessments concerning goal relevance, goal congruence, and ego involvement (Lazarus, 1991a, 1991b). *Goal relevance* captures the degree to which the appraisal-generating event is important for goal attainment. Assessments that the event is of low importance typically result in the abortion of the cognitive evaluation process and only rarely produce an emotional response (Lazarus, 1991b). In contrast, events assessed to have implications for goal attainment are further evaluated along the remaining appraisal components. With *goal congruence*, individuals appraise the extent to which the event coincides with their goals. Situations that are congruent are perceived as desirable and encourage the experience of positive emotions, whereas situations that are incongruent with goal attainment are experienced as undesirable and generally produce negative emotions (Lazarus, 1991b). Finally, *ego involvement* concerns judgments of the event's impact on ego- or identity-relevant goals (Lazarus, 1991b). Threats or benefits to self-esteem, personal identity, health, or judgments of close others, among many other similar concerns, make up the sort of factors that determine the degree to which the event involves ego. This assessment is often the distinction between similar emotions. For example, one way to consider the difference between guilt and shame is the specific aspect of ego that comes under threat by the event. Guilt is activated by a perceived failure to live up to personal standards of moral behavior that make up our personal identity, and shame is experienced as a result of the failure to live up to someone else's perception of who we are (i.e., judgments of close others). Both involve ego, but activate different types of ego involvement and, as such, produce different emotions.

Together, these three assessments reflect a judgment about the investments that one has in the outcome of the event. They are considered *primary* because the approach assumes that emotions *only* occur in response to events with implications for outcomes in which we are invested (Lazarus, 1991a; Smith & Kirby, 2001a). Following cases where these primary appraisals indicate some level of investment in the outcome, individuals proceed to another set of "appraisal components," which together make up *secondary appraisals.*

While primary appraisals determine whether any sort of emotion is experienced and, when relevant, direct the general valence of the emotional experience, secondary appraisals ultimately result in identification of the specific emotion (Lazarus, 1991b). Here, individuals examine their accountability for the event, future expectancies associated with the event, and their ability to cope with the event (Lazarus, 1991a; Smith, Haynes, Lazarus, & Pope, 1993). *Accountability* is conceptualized as the degree to which there is personal responsibility for the event. Specifically, individuals attribute a certain degree of credit or blame to themselves (or others) for the event and assess the degree to which they (or others) were in control of its occurrence (Lazarus, 1991a). *Future expectancies*, consistent with earlier elaboration of outcome expectancies in TMIM, reflect individuals' beliefs about the positive and/or negative consequences that are expected to come from the event. Finally, *coping ability* involves individuals' perceptions of whether they feel able to handle the repercussions of the event (Lazarus, 1991b). Differences along any of these dimensions trigger unique emotional responses. For example, a goal-relevant, goal-incongruent, and ego-involving event that is attributed to another person (high other accountability) is likely to result in anger, and the same event, if attributed to the self (high personal accountability), typically results in shame or guilt (Smith & Kirby, 2001a). In the same vein, a negative emotion with low coping potential and negative-outcome expectancies may result in sadness, whereas a negative emotion with high coping potential and positive-outcome expectancy might produce hope (Smith et al., 1993). Each emotional experience comes with its own unique response set.

The cognitive and/or behavioral responses to the appraisal process are referred to as *action tendencies* (Lazarus, 1991a; Smith & Kirby, 2001b). For example, the emotion of *fear* typically motivates individuals to be cautious of their surroundings and to avoid or flee that which threatens potential harm. *Pride* can encourage individuals to call attention to positive events that meet or exceed positive standards in life. With the experience of *disgust*, individuals often defend themselves by removing or avoiding situations that are deemed offensive. *Anger*, on the other hand, often motivates a desire to attack the responsible agent. The emotion of *guilt* may produce a desire either to make amends or to receive punishment for wrongdoings. Finally, *sadness* generally induces a withdrawal pattern or inspires inaction, in order to achieve comfort or deal with loss (for elaboration on these action tendencies, see Lazarus, 1991b).

In sum, Lazarus's (1991a, 1991b) appraisal theory argues that individuals appraise the goal relevance, goal congruency, and ego involvement associated with an arousing event. Then, when that set of appraisals leads to the identification of a general emotional experience, individuals follow by appraising their accountability for the event, the likely consequences of the event, and their perceived coping ability. These two appraisal sets are then argued to produce a specific emotion which, in turn, affects individuals' cognitive and behavioral responses. Applying this framework to TMIM's approach to the information management process reshapes our thinking about individuals' response to uncertainty discrepancy, specifically, and shifts our predictions about individuals' information management decisions, generally.

Appraisal Theory in TMIM

The original form of TMIM argues that the information management process starts when individuals realize that the amount of actual uncertainty they have about an important issue differs from the amount they desire on the issue (i.e., the experience of uncertainty discrepancy). Relying on well-established principles from activation theory (Ursin, 1988) and control theory (for review, see Carver & Scheier, 1998), Afifi and Weiner (2004; see also Afifi, 2009) argued that such disequilibrium between actual and desired states produces anxiety. The framework for that prediction is solid, and the empirical evidence for the association between uncertainty discrepancy and anxiety associated with that discrepancy is strong. Afifi and colleagues' published program of research on TMIM has consistently found the association between uncertainty discrepancy and related anxiety to be statistically significant and has reported standardized path estimates ranging from .29 (Afifi & Afifi, in press) to .81 (Afifi & Weiner, 2006). Nevertheless, the existing explanatory mechanism is limiting in that it restricts the emotional product of uncertainty discrepancy to anxiety. As such, it fails to account for the breadth of emotional responses to uncertainty discrepancy and the impact of that variance on the rest of the information management process. Adopting an appraisal approach to the experience of uncertainty discrepancy expands the lens from which we can understand the process. A brief review of evidence from the emotion literature sheds light on its implications for both the interpretive and evaluative phases of TMIM.

Impact of Uncertainty Discrepancy on Emotions

Fitting an appraisal theory account into TMIM's calculus for the emotional implications of uncertainty discrepancy is relatively simple once one considers the overlap between TMIM's treatment of the information management process and the specific assessments that make up the primary appraisal process. First, Afifi and Weiner (2004, p. 174) note that "the information-management process begins with individuals becoming aware of an important issue for which they desire more or less uncertainty than they have." This notion of a specific starting point to the process is consistent with appraisal theory's identification of an arousal-producing *event* that initiates the appraisal process. Second, Afifi and Weiner's (2004, pp. 170–171) explicit statement that the theory applies only to issues that "surpass a certain threshold of importance" means that it is also restricted, in the language of appraisal theory, to events that are considered goal relevant (Lazarus, 1991a, 1991b)—the first assessment among the primary appraisals. Third, because uncertainty discrepancy is conceptualized in TMIM as a mismatch between the desired and actual state of uncertainty about an issue, it implies goal incongruence. Put another way, uncertainty discrepancy entails a disconnect (i.e., an incongruency) between the amount of uncertainty one desires (the goal state) and the amount one has (the current state). In fact, Lazarus (1991b, p. 150) explicitly defines *goal congruence* or *incongruence* as "the extent to which a transaction is consistent or inconsistent with what the person wants." Indeed, the description of uncertainty discrepancy in the TMIM framework matches perfectly with an appraisal theory description of events that are assessed as goal relevant and goal incongruent. Such appraisals are the hallmark of negatively valenced emotions (Lazarus, 1991a; Roseman, 2001). The ego involvement assessment then serves as a dial, in some sense, of the intensity with which that uncertainty discrepancy-initiated negative emotion is experienced.

Therefore, how is this account different from that found in the original TMIM framework? At the point of primary appraisals, the differences may be considered relatively small: Activation theory and control theory propose that uncertainty discrepancy leads to anxiety, whereas appraisal theory proposes that it produces a negative emotion. The difference between the accounts is in the breadth of possible emotions, not their valence. The significance of that difference becomes clear once we consider the role of secondary appraisals.

Remember that individuals follow primary appraisals with three assessments that, together, make up secondary appraisals. Those judgments involve their accountability for the event, the future expectancies associated with the event, and their ability to cope with the event. Individuals determine who is responsible, who has control of the event, whether they are able to handle the demands of the event, and whether they believe that matters are likely to improve or get worse (Lazarus, 1991a). These judgments serve to refine the general emotional valence assessments made after primary appraisal into a specific emotional experience (e.g., happiness/joy, hope, relief, compassion, anger, sadness, fear, guilt). When applied to the context of TMIM, we would predict that uncertainty discrepancy, which passes through primary appraisals as a negatively valenced event, could produce a wide range of specific emotions once the situation is assessed through secondary-appraisal lenses. In fact, among the candidate emotions associated with uncertainty discrepancy are anxiety, anger, fear, disgust, jealousy, envy, and hope (conceptualized in appraisal theory as a negative emotion that begets positive appraisal). Anxiety is the one emotion that overlaps in both the original version of TMIM and in one that includes an appraisal theory approach. Whereas activation theory explains the experience of anxiety as a response to disequilibrium between actual and desired states, appraisal theory ultimately argues that anxiety is defined by a particular type of ego involvement that separates it from other emotions. Specifically, Lazarus (1991a) proposed that anxiety occurs in response to existential threat—a unique type of ego involvement. Interestingly, that linkage of anxiety to the assessment of existential threat may also account for the strength of the earlier-reported associations between uncertainty discrepancy and the experience of discrepancy-related anxiety. After all, several scholars have argued that levels of uncertainty affect the salience of existential concerns (for review, see Afifi, 2009).

The benefit of an appraisal approach to the emotional consequence of uncertainty discrepancy is that it also allows for emotions other than anxiety (Lazarus, 1991b). For example, anger, as opposed to anxiety, is likely if the discrepancy between the actual and desired level of uncertainty is appraised as having been under an actor's control. In contrast, jealousy may be the emotional product of uncertainty discrepancy if it is appraised as threatening the longing for another's affection (a type of ego involvement), and there is a clear target on which to assign blame (accountability appraisal). While these reflect examples of appraisals that would produce responses to uncertainty discrepancy other than anxiety, one emotional by-product of uncertainty discrepancy—hope—requires special attention.

Hope occupies a particularly important place as an emotional reaction in this context for two reasons. First, recent literature commonly discusses hope as a possible emotional response to uncertainty. Second, it seems inconsistent, on the face of it, with appraisal theory claiming that uncertainty discrepancy, by definition, produces negative emotions. We will briefly address each issue in turn.

Evidence for individuals' experience of uncertainty as hope has been steadily mounting since Babrow's (for review, see Babrow & Matthias, this volume) and Brashers's (for review, see Hogan & Brashers, this volume) theoretical elaborations on the reasons for positive emotional responses to uncertainty. Babrow and colleagues (e.g., Ford, Babrow, & Stohl, 1996; Gill & Babrow, 2007) have shown that uncertainty can be experienced as positive "if it is seen as a source of possibility and hope" (Babrow & Kline, 2000, p. 1811). Relatedly, Brashers (2001, p. 477) argued that the "fundamental challenge of refining theories of communication and uncertainty is to abandon the assumption that uncertainty will produce anxiety," a conclusion that he reached from consistently finding that individuals who are diagnosed with a terminal illness seek uncertainty because it offers hope.

That experience of hope in response to uncertainty was not something for which the original TMIM framework could account; however, what if we are to adopt an appraisal theory approach to experience of uncertainty discrepancy? At initial glance, it seems similarly problematic, given that appraisal theory assigns negative emotional experiences to goal-incongruent events such as uncertainty discrepancy. A closer examination of Lazarus's position vis-à-vis the emotion of hope, though, reveals the theoretical route to the experience of hope in the face of negatively valenced primary appraisals. Lazarus (1999, p. 653), in a detailed discussion of hope as an emotion, defined hope as the belief that "something positive, which does not presently apply to one's life, could still materialize." He reiterated that conceptualization by noting that "hope arises, in part, from a strong desire to be in a different situation than at present, and from the impression that this is possible" (p. 663). The crux of the appraisal theory position is that the experience of hope rests on two secondary appraisals—coping potential and future expectancies. Specifically, hope arises when appraisal features associated with sadness meet against positive future expectancies and elevated coping potential.

In other words, hope signals a secondary-appraisal shift during the appraisal of events associated with sadness (Lazarus, 1991b). The primary-appraisal judgments linked to sadness and hope are the same. The distinguishing features between sadness and hope are that the former involves assessments that coping potential is low and future expectancies are bleak, while the latter involves judgments of elevated coping potential and bright future expectancies.

The benefits of recognizing the possibility of a wide range of emotional responses to uncertainty discrepancy go beyond bringing TMIM in closer alignment with evidence about the experience of uncertainty as hope (although that is certainly an important consideration). Doing so also allows the framework to account for differential effects that such variance in emotional experience has on information management decisions. Existing data unequivocally demonstrate that emotions affect outcome expectancies and efficacy assessments (the two variables in TMIM's evaluation phase) in unique ways.

Impact of Emotions on Evaluation Phase Assessments

The original TMIM framework argued that anxiety about uncertainty discrepancy influenced both outcome assessments and efficacy ratings. Empirical tests mostly supported that prediction (e.g., Afifi & Afifi, in press; Afifi et al., 2004, 2006). By adopting an appraisal approach, the argument remains that emotional experiences influence these evaluation-phase assessments, but refines the prediction to emotion-specific effects. First, we turn to the argument that emotions affect cognitions. Then, we examine evidence that emotions influence the specific assessments in question (i.e., outcome expectancies and efficacy assessments).

The suggestion that emotion affects cognitive assessments has a long history of empirical evidence behind it (for review, see Frijda, Manstead, & Bem, 2000) and is not a controversial position. In fact, emotion theorists have articulated the case in very direct (and sometimes theatrical) ways. For example, Frijda and Mesquita (2000, p. 45) reflected on "beliefs through emotions" by saying, "Emotions influence beliefs. This is a classical assumption." In a similar vein, Isen (2004, p. 265) concluded that "affect influences the content and process of cognition," and Adolphs and Damasio (2001, p. 28) argued that "emotions color virtually all aspects of our lives. What we pay attention to, what we decide to do, what we remember, and how we interact with other people are all influenced by emotions." Most recently, neuropsychological models of affect have contributed further evidence for cognitive effects of emotional experiences by linking emotions to the activation of neural pathways associated with information processing (Davidson, Scherer, & Goldsmith, 2003). But what evidence do we have for specific effects on outcome expectancies and efficacy? Here, we take a brief detour to discuss a pattern that has developed among those studying affect. It revolves around those scholars who investigate mood and those who attend to emotions, the two domains that, although related in important ways, have progressed in relatively independent paths (Forgas, Wyland, & Laham, 2006). Forgas et al. describe each this way: Moods are "relatively low-intensity, diffuse, subconscious, and enduring affective states that have no salient antecedent" while emotions are "more short-lived, conscious, and intense[, and] usually have a highly accessible and salient cause" (pp. 6–7). While both have been shown to influence cognition, mood researchers have generally focused on the cognitive and behavioral *consequences* and emotion researchers have mostly attended to their *antecedents* (Forgas et al., 2006). In this chapter, we sometimes use emotion and mood interchangeably to discuss broader effects of affect on TMIM. More specifically, though, our reliance an appraisal theory parts us squarely in the emotions (vs. mood) camp.

Influence on Outcome Expectancies

Decades of scholarship has shown that moods play a consistent role in our judgment of expected outcomes. Specifically, individuals in good moods make rose-colored assessments of outcomes, while those in bad moods make pessimistic outcome expectancies (for review, see Forgas, 2001; Loewenstein & Lerner, 2003). That trend occurs in two ways: those in negative moods (a) are likely to expect negative outcomes to be probable, and (b) they weigh the consequences of those outcomes as severe. In contrast, those in positive moods tend to see the likelihood of negative outcomes to be small and weigh those outcomes as relatively harmless. As a result, they view their surroundings to be relatively benign (Gasper & Isbell, 2007). On another front, research into affective forecasting has shown that individuals have a hard time envisioning a future that is radically different, in terms of feeling states, than the present (e.g., Loewenstein, O'Donohue, & Rabin, 2003). Loewenstein and colleagues (for review, see Loewenstein & Lerner, 2003) have also found that we rely on our own affective states to anchor our perceptions of others' states. In other words, we have difficulty believing that others are in radically different emotional states than we are. Finally, research has shown a wide range of mood-related differences in the nature and depth of information processing (for review, see Clore, Gasper, & Garvin, 2001; Forgas, 2006; Trope, Igou, & Burke, 2006). Among the supported patterns are that negative moods often narrow attention focus and trigger more careful processing of information, as compared to positive moods.

Two programs of research are especially relevant to our purposes because they rely heavily on Lazarus's appraisal approach. As a result, they also measure emotion, not mood. The first of these approaches, is Keltner and colleagues' (e.g., Keltner, Ellsworth, & Edwards, 1993; Lerner & Keltner, 2000) *appraisal tendency approach*. Consistent with Lazarus (1991b), their perspective is premised on the notion that the primary and secondary appraisals direct actors to features of the environment most relevant to the appraisal components that produced the emotion. Those features then shape resultant cognitions. For example, Keltner et al. (1993) manipulated participants' emotional state (sad vs. angry) and asked them to predict the likelihood of a negative event and to attribute its potential cause of the event. Findings were consistent with the appraisal-specific features of those particular emotions. The target-specific accountability associated with anger led participants in the anger condition to expect a target-caused negative event, while the ambiguous accountability nature of sadness directed participants in that condition to expect situation-caused negative events. Similarly, Lerner and Keltner (2001) found that individuals in angry emotional states made optimistic assessments of risk, while those in states of fear made choices that were considered less risky, reactions that, again, are consistent with the emotion-specific appraisal components.

The second approach, by Nabi (1999, 2002, 2003), contributes to this knowledge base by also relying on Lazarus's framework, but, in this case, to examine the influence of emotions on information-processing depth. Preliminary data support her *cognitive-functional model*'s ability to replicate some of the processing-related findings from the mood literature. For example, Nabi (2002) reported that emotion manipulations affected the processing of persuasive messages in a manner consistent with the cognitive-functional model. Specifically, anger led to more thorough information processing than fear. Importantly, in both these two approaches, the findings suggest an ability to make fine-tuned differences in predictions based on the specific emotion experienced, as opposed to generalized predictions about positive versus negative states.

Influence on Efficacy Assessments

Bandura (1986) explicitly identifies emotions as having a direct impact on self-efficacy and summarizes some evidence in support of that claim. There is also considerable evidence suggesting that moods affect self-perceptions of personal coping and skill, two of the three components of efficacy in TMIM. Specifically, studies have shown that individuals in sad moods nearly mirror the characteristics of individuals low in efficacy. They have low perceptions of coping ability, are cautious, do not stay persistent in the face of possible failure, and generally consider themselves incompetent (for review, see Gasper & Isbell, 2007). In contrast, those in happy moods expect success, persist in the face of possible failure, see themselves as competent, and move forward with abandon.

Emotions also indirectly affect efficacy assessments through their influence on outcome expectancies. After all, TMIM and other approaches argue that outcome expectancies shape perceptions of efficacy. One interesting and important side note on this front is that those in positive emotional states may not weigh efficacy assessments as much as their low-efficacy counterparts. They may not attend to efficacy information sufficiently to have it influence decisions. Instead, they simply move forward with the expectation that positive outcomes will result. That suggestion is consistent with the possibility advanced by Afifi and Weiner (2004), that efficacy may play a more significant role in some circumstances than others, and the empirical evidence associated with TMIM showed efficacy to play a less important role in positive-expectancy situations (Afifi & Weiner, 2006; see also Afifi, 2009).

One more aside—it is likely that close readers of this chapter have noted the similarity between the assessments made in the secondary-appraisal process and those proposed in TMIM's evaluation phase. Indeed, there is nearly 100% overlap between the two evaluation-phase assessments (i.e., outcome expectancies and the three types of efficacy) and two of the three secondary-appraisal components (i.e., future expectancies and coping efficacy). While the overlap clearly reflects some scholarly agreement (e.g., Bandura, 1997; Lazarus, 1991b) on the important cognitive considerations that individuals go through in responding to goal-relevant situations, the *target* of these assessments is a critical consideration and the factor that separates these processes in TMIM. The appraisal theory assessments reflect beliefs about consequences related to the *event* (i.e., awareness of an uncertainty discrepancy about an important issue). The evaluation-phase assessments involve beliefs about consequences related to a *particular information management strategy* (e.g., information seeking, information avoiding). In other words, TMIM now proposes that individuals make these assessments twice, each time with a different target: once in the emotion appraisal process and once during the TMIM evaluation phase.

In sum, considerable empirical and theoretical evidence points to emotion-specific impacts on TMIM's evaluation-phase assessments. The literature also suggests possible direct influences of emotion on information management decisions. Together, the various emotion-relevant approaches that we reviewed suggest revisions to TMIM's propositional structure.

Revisions to TMIM's Propositional Structure

The first two propositions in TMIM's original structure were as follows (Afifi & Weiner, 2004, p. 175):

> Proposition 1: The size of the mismatch between actual and desired levels of uncertainty (i.e., uncertainty discrepancy) about an important matter leads, in a linear fashion, to uncertainty-related anxiety (hereafter labeled anxiety).

> Proposition 2: Anxiety partially mediates the association between uncertainty discrepancy and the information management process.

Replacing a control theory approach to understanding uncertainty discrepancy with Lazarus's appraisal theory framework results in the following revisions (see Figure 5.2).

INFORMATION SEEKER

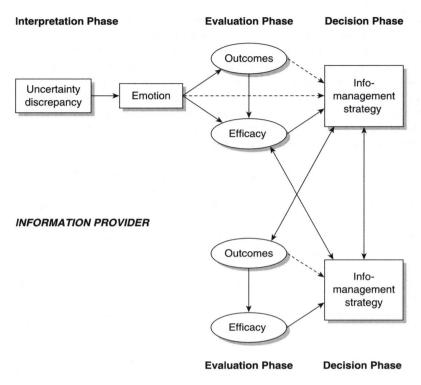

Figure 5.2 Graphical Model of TMIM's Revised Propositional Structure

Proposition 1R: A mismatch between actual and desired levels of uncertainty (i.e., uncertainty discrepancy) about an important matter produces an emotional response, the specific type of which depends on emotion appraisals.

Proposition 2R: The emotional response resulting from uncertainty discrepancy mediates uncertainty discrepancy's effects on the information management process.

The revision to the first proposition reflects our shift from an anxiety-based model of uncertainty discrepancy to one that allows more varied emotional responses. That shift also necessitates a transition from discrepancy size as the knob for intensity of the anxiety experience to the set of appraisal components as the knob for the specification of the type of emotional experience itself. The revision to the second proposition involves two noteworthy changes. The first is the obvious shift from anxiety as the sole emotional response to a more open-ended set of possible emotions. The second, more subtle, change is replacing the suggestion of partial mediation with language that implies full mediation. Our adoption of the emotion-appraisal approach comes with a rather dramatic shift that we had not yet addressed—from understanding uncertainty discrepancy as a cognitive experience that inevitably leads to anxiety but is still distinctly separate from that emotion, to understanding uncertainty discrepancy as wholly defined *by* the set of appraisals that result in a particular emotion. In so doing, TMIM now shares more in common with other appraisal-oriented approaches to the experience or uncertainty (e.g., Babrow, 1992; Brashers, 2001).

In recognizing evidence for both direct and indirect effects of emotion on behavior (for review, see Loewenstein & Lerner, 2003), and consistent with the appraisal tendencies approach (Lerner & Keltner, 2000), it also seems important that we add two propositional statements not previously included in TMIM's structure.

Proposition 2B: The emotional response resulting from uncertainty discrepancy influences the information management decision both directly and indirectly.

Proposition 2C: The emotional response resulting from uncertainty discrepancy influences outcome expectancies and efficacy assessments in a manner consistent with the appraisals from which the emotion developed.

Future Directions

Having finally addressed one of the issues in TMIM that has long troubled us, we find ourselves curiously torn in our emotional response. Like structural engineers who wonder whether this particular attempt at tinkering with an already functional device may do more harm than good, or parents who wonder whether their latest chat with their mostly well-adjusted teenager about responsibility could boomerang, we find ourselves asking whether this change is an improvement to the theory's heuristic utility or adds a burden of predictive complexity that does more damage than repair. Although we feel confident in the advantages of the appraisal approach over the control and equilibrium approaches in this context, the answer likely falls somewhere in the middle. Four issues will ultimately determine the success of these revisions.

First, we need more specificity about each emotion's unique impact on the evaluation-phase assessments. The current revision leaves readers with general guidance on that front but with less predictive specificity than the original theoretical statement. Second, we need a better sense for the frequency with which uncertainty discrepancy produces emotional responses other than anxiety. Indeed, it is quite likely that anxiety *is* the predominant emotional reaction to uncertainty discrepancy. If that is the case, the question becomes whether the gain in breadth of predictive accuracy is sufficiently large to overcome the cost in predictive complexity. Third, we need data on whether two of the subtle but important changes—removing the direct effects of uncertainty discrepancy on evaluation-phase assessments and adding a direct effect from emotional response to behavior—withstand empirical scrutiny in the context of information management decisions. Finally, we need to explore operational strategies that capture the added emotional complexity of the revised framework while continuing to allow precision in testing the theoretical linkages. Space limitations restricted our ability to fully address some of these concerns and it will take time to gather data to test others, but we are optimistic.

Of course, other related issues still exist. We did not address the many other ways how emotions unrelated to uncertainty discrepancy may influence evaluation-phase assessments and, ultimately, the information management decision. Furthermore, as has been the pattern in discussions of TMIM, we failed to address the role of emotions in the information provider's response. These are important concerns that should be taken up in the future. In the end, we have offered a TMIM revision that we hope adds functionality and predictive breadth. We continue to view the process of theory building as a very iterative process and, as such, look forward not only to testing the success of these revisions but also to further research (by ourselves and others)—and to the mixed emotional responses that come with it.

References

Adolphs, R., & Damasio, A. R. (2001). The interaction of affect and cognition: A neurobiological perspective. In J. P. Forgas (Ed.), *Handbook of affect and social cognition* (pp. 27–49). Mahwah, NJ: Lawrence Erlbaum.

Afifi, W. A. (2009). Uncertainty and information management in interpersonal contexts. In S. Wilson & S. Smith (Eds.), *New directions in interpersonal communication* (pp. 94–114). Thousand Oaks, CA: Sage.

Afifi, W. A. (in press). Theory of Motivated Information Management. In S. Littlejohn & K. Foss (Eds.), *Encyclopedia of communication theory*. Sage.

Afifi, W. A., & Afifi, T. D. (in press). Avoidance among adolescents in conversations about their parents' relationship: Applying the Theory of Motivated Information Management. *Journal of Social and Personal Relationships*.

Afifi, W. A., Dillow, M., & Morse, C. (2004). Seeking information in relational contexts: A test of the theory of motivated information management. *Personal Relationships, 11*, 429–450.

Afifi, W. A., & Lucas, A. (2008). Information seeking in relationship initiation and development. In S. Sprecher, J. Harvey, & A. Wenzel (Eds.), *Handbook on relationship beginnings* (pp. 135–152). New York: Psychology Press.

Afifi, W. A., Morgan, S. E., Stephenson, M., Morse, C., Harrison, T., Reichert, T., & Long, S. D. (2006). Examining the decision to talk with family about organ donation: Applying the theory of motivated information management. *Communication Monographs, 73,* 188–215.

Afifi, W. A., Morse, C., Dillow, M., & Weiner, J. (2005, May). *Caring for a newborn in the land of theory: The theory of motivated information management.* Paper presented at the annual conference of the International Communication Association, New York.

Afifi, W. A., & Weiner, J. L. (2004). Toward a theory of motivated information management. *Communication Theory, 14,* 167–190.

Afifi, W. A., & Weiner, J. L. (2006). Seeking information about sexual health: Applying the Theory of Motivated Information Management. *Human Communication Research, 32,* 35–57.

Babrow, A. S. (1992). Communication and problematic integration: Understanding diverging probability and value, ambiguity, ambivalence, and impossibility. *Communication Theory, 2,* 95–130.

Babrow, A. S. (2001). Uncertainty, value, communication, and problematic integration. *Journal of Communication, 51,* 553–573.

Babrow, A. S., & Kline, K. N. (2000). From "reducing" to "coping with" uncertainty: Reconceptualizing the central challenge in breast self-exams. *Social Science & Medicine, 51,* 1805–1816.

Bandura, A. (1986). *Social foundations of thought and action: A social cognitive theory.* Englewood Cliffs, NJ: Prentice Hall.

Bandura, A. (1997). *Self-efficacy: The exercise of control.* New York: Freeman.

Brashers, D. E. (2001). Communication and uncertainty management. *Journal of Communication, 51,* 477–497.

Brashers, D. E. (2007). A theory of communication and uncertainty management. In B. Whaley & W. Samter (Eds.), *Explaining communication theory* (pp. 201–218). Mahwah, NJ: Lawrence Erlbaum.

Carver, C. S., & Scheier, M. F. (1998). *On the self-regulation of behavior.* New York: Cambridge University Press.

Chaiken, S. (1987). The heuristic model of persuasion. In M. P. Zanna, J. M. Olson, & C. P. Herman (Eds.), *Social influence: The Ontario symposium* (Vol. 5, pp. 3–39). Hillsdale, NJ: Erlbaum.

Clore, G. L., Gasper, K., & Garvin, E. (2001). Affect as information. In J. P. Forgas (Ed.), *Affect and social cognition* (pp. 121–144). Mahwah, NJ: Lawrence Erlbaum.

Davidson, R. J., Scherer, K. R., & Goldsmith, H. H. (2003). Introduction: Neuroscience. In R. J. Davidson, K. R. Scherer, & H. H. Goldsmith (Eds.), *Handbook of affective sciences* (pp. 3–7). Oxford: Oxford University Press.

Eysenck, M. W. (2000). Anxiety, cognitive biases, and beliefs. In N. H. Frijda, A. S. R. Manstead, & S. Bem (Eds.), *Emotions and beliefs: How feelings influence thoughts* (pp. 171–184). Cambridge: Cambridge University Press.

Ford, L. A., Babrow, A. S., & Stohl, C. (1996). Social support messages and the management of uncertainty in the experience of breast cancer: An application of problematic integration theory. *Communication Monographs, 63,* 189–207.

Forgas, J. P. (Ed.). (2001). *Affect and social cognition.* Mahwah, NJ: Lawrence Erlbaum.

Forgas, J. P. (2006). Affective influences on interpersonal behavior: Towards understanding the role of affect in everyday interactions. In J. P. Forgas (Ed.), *Affect in social thinking and behavior* (pp. 269–290). New York: Psychology Press.

Forgas, J. P., Wyland, C. L., & Laham, S. M. (2006). Hearts and minds: An introduction to the role of affect in social cognition and behavior. In J. P. Forgas (Ed.), *Affect in social thinking and behavior* (pp. 3–18). New York: Psychology Press.

Frijda, N. H. (1986). *The emotions.* New York: Cambridge University Press.

Frijda, N. H., Kuipers, P., & ter Schure, E. (1989). Relations among emotion, appraisal, and emotional action readiness. *Journal of Personality and Social Psychology, 57,* 212–228.

Frijda, N. H., Manstead, S. R., & Bem, S. (2000). The influence of emotions on beliefs. In N. H. Frijda, S. R. Manstead, & S. Bem (Eds.), *Emotions and beliefs: How feelings influence thoughts* (pp. 1–9). Cambridge: Cambridge University Press.

Frijda, N. H., & Mesquita, B. (2000). Beliefs through emotions. In N. H. Frijda, S. R. Manstead, & S. Bem (Eds.), *Emotions and beliefs: How feelings influence thoughts* (pp. 45–77). Cambridge: Cambridge University Press.

Gasper, K., & Isbell, L. M. (2007). Feeling, searching, and preparing: How affective states alter information seeking. In K. D. Vohs, R. F. Baumeister, & G. Lowenstein (Eds.), *Do emotions help or hurt decision making?* (pp. 93–116). New York: Russell Sage Foundation.

Gill, E. A., & Babrow, A. S. (2007). To hope or to know: Coping with uncertainty and ambivalence in women's magazine breast cancer articles. *Journal of Applied Communication Research, 35,* 133–155.

Isen, A. M. (2004). Some perspectives on positive feelings and emotions: Positive affect facilitates thinking and problem solving. In A. S. R. Manstead, N. Frijda, & A. Fischer (Eds.), *Feelings and emotions: The Amsterdam symposium* (pp. 263–281). Cambridge: Cambridge University Press.

Keltner, D., Ellsworth, P. C., & Edwards, K. (1993). Beyond simple pessimism: Effects of sadness and anger on social perception. *Journal of Personality and Social Psychology, 64,* 740–752.

Lazarus, R. S. (1991a). Progress on a cognitive-motivational-relational theory of emotion. *American Psychologist, 46,* 819–834.

Lazarus, R. S. (1991b). *Emotion and adaptation.* Oxford: Oxford University Press.

Lazarus, R. S. (1999). Hope: An emotion and a vital coping resource against despair. *Social Research, 66,* 653–678.

Lerner, J. S., & Keltner, D. (2000). Beyond valence: Toward a model of emotion-specific influences on judgments and choice. *Cognition and Emotion, 14,* 473–493.

Lerner, J. S., & Keltner, D. (2001). Fear, anger and risk. *Journal of Personality and Social Psychology, 81,* 146–159.

Loewenstein, G., & Lerner, J. S. (2003). The role of affect in decision making. In R. J. Davidson, K. R. Scherer, & H. H. Goldsmith (Eds.), *Handbook of affective sciences* (pp. 619–642). Oxford: Oxford University Press.

Loewenstein, G., O'Donohue, T., & Rabin, M. (2003). Projection bias in predicting future utility. *Quarterly Journal of Economics, 118,* 1209–1248.

Nabi, R. L. (1999). A cognitive-functional model for the effects of discrete negative emotions on information processing, attitude change and recall. *Communication Theory, 9,* 292–320.

Nabi, R. L. (2002). Anger, fear, uncertainty and attitudes: A test of the cognitive-function model. *Communication Monographs, 69,* 204–216.

Nabi, R. L. (2003). Exploring the framing effects of emotion: Do discrete emotions differentially influence information accessibility, information seeking, and policy preference? *Communication Research, 30,* 224–247.

Roseman, I. J. (1991). Appraisal determinants of discrete emotions. *Cognition and Emotion, 5,* 161–200.

Roseman, I. J. (2001). A model of appraisal in the emotion system: Integrating theory, research, and applications. In K. R. Scherer, A. Schorr, & T. Johnstone (Eds.), *Appraisal processes in emotion: Theory, methods, research. Series in affective science* (pp. 68–91). New York: Oxford University Press.

Roseman, I. J., & Smith, C. A. (2001). Appraisal theory: Overview, assumptions, varieties, controversies. In K. R. Scherer, A. Schorr, & T. Johnstone (Eds.), *Appraisal process in emotion: Theory, methods, research* (pp. 3–19). New York: Oxford University Press.

Scherer, K. R. (2001). Appraisal considered as a process of multilevel sequential checking. In K. R. Scherer, A. Schorr, & T. Johnstone (Eds.), *Appraisal process of emotion: Theory, methods, research* (pp. 92–120). New York: Oxford University Press.

Smith, C. A., Haynes, K. N., Lazarus, R. S., & Pope, L. K. (1993). In search of the "hot" cognitions: Attributions, appraisals, and their relation to emotion. *Journal of Personality and Social Psychology, 65,* 916–929.

Smith, C. A., & Kirby, L. D. (2001a). Affect and cognitive appraisal processes. In J. P. Forgas (Ed.), *Handbook of affect and social cognition* (pp. 75–92). Mahwah, NJ: Lawrence Erlbaum.

Smith, C. A., & Kirby, L. D. (2001b). Toward delivering on the promise of appraisal theory. In K. R. Scherer, A. Schorr, & T. Johnstone (Eds.), *Appraisal process in emotion: Theory, methods, research* (pp. 121–138). New York: Oxford University Press.

Trope, Y., Igou, E. R., & Burke, C. T. (2006). Mood as a resource in structuring goal pursuit. In J. P. Forgas (Ed.), *Affect in social thinking and behavior* (pp. 217–234). New York: Psychology Press.

Ursin, H. (1988). Expectancy and activation: An attempt to systematize stress theory. In D. H. Hellhammer, I. Florin, & H. Weiner (Eds.), *Neurobiological approaches to human disease* (pp. 313–334). Toronto, Canada: Huber.

6 Relational Uncertainty
Theory and Application

Leanne K. Knobloch and Kristen L. Satterlee

An array of questions arise for individuals who are negotiating close relationships (Berger & Bradac, 1982; Knobloch, 2008). "Why did he do that?" "What should I say?" "Does this person want to invest in a relationship?" "How should we spend our time together?" "Does she care about me?" "Do I still want to be involved in this relationship?" "What does the future hold for us?" Communication is key to how people navigate the questions they have about participating in close relationships. Individuals possess a variety of communication options for dealing with uncertainty: They can constructively seek information, destructively seek information, constructively avoid information, or destructively avoid information (e.g., Knobloch & Solomon, 2003; Planalp & Honeycutt, 1985). People's choice of how to manage their questions has important consequences for the well-being of their relationships. Indeed, how individuals communicate under conditions of uncertainty may determine whether their relationships develop or dissolve (Planalp, Rutherford, & Honeycutt, 1988).

Relational uncertainty is the degree of confidence individuals have in their perceptions of involvement within interpersonal relationships (Knobloch & Solomon, 1999, 2002a). A growing body of research has examined relational uncertainty as a predictor of how people regulate information (for review, see Knobloch, 2007a). In fact, we suspect that a critical moment now exists: A burgeoning collection of findings has accumulated to date, but those results are somewhat scattered across the literature. We believe a set of overarching propositions would help organize the diverse data. As an added bonus, it would be useful for garnering practical insight into people's everyday experiences of relational uncertainty. It also would be valuable for identifying priorities for future research.

Our goal in this chapter is to theorize about the link between relational uncertainty and information regulation. We begin by explicating the history and the substance of the relational uncertainty construct. Next, we advance a series of propositions about how relational uncertainty corresponds with communication. After discussing the pragmatic applications of our reasoning, we conclude by recommending avenues for future research that meld theory and application.

The Nature of Relational Uncertainty

History

Relational uncertainty is a fundamental human experience (e.g., Berger & Bradac, 1982). Hence, it is not surprising that scholarship on relational uncertainty and related constructs emanate from diverse theoretical perspectives and multiple academic disciplines. Some scholars have investigated personality differences in how people experience ambiguity within social situations, focusing on constructs such as tolerance for uncertainty (Dugas et al., 2005), uncertainty avoidance (Vishwanath, 2003), uncertainty orientation (Shuper, Sorrentino, Otsubo, Hodson, & Walker, 2004; Sorrentino, Holmes, Hanna, & Sharp, 1995), and need for closure (Dechesne & Kruglanski, this volume). Other researchers have considered how individuals cognitively appraise situations when they are experiencing uncertainty about their identity (McGregor & Marigold, 2003). Still others have studied how dyadic well-being is predicted by people's ambivalence about a relationship (Huston, Caughlin, Houts, Smith, & George, 2001), oscillating feelings of satisfaction (Arriaga, 2001), and fluctuating perceptions of a partner's commitment (Arriaga, Reed, Goodfriend, & Agnew, 2006). Although these programs of research conceptualize uncertainty in a variety of ways, they coalesce around the claim that questions about relating are central to dyadic interaction.

Perhaps the most extensive body of work on ambiguity within close relationships, and the one we focus on in this chapter, stems from the discipline of interpersonal communication. The relational uncertainty construct has its roots in several landmark theories of interpersonal communication, most notably uncertainty reduction theory (URT), the pioneering framework on ambiguity within interpersonal interaction (Berger & Calabrese, 1975; Berger & Gudykunst, 1991). URT drew on two other seminal theories to conceptualize how uncertainty operates within acquaintance. Following information theory (Shannon & Weaver, 1949), URT argued that uncertainty occurs when individuals are faced with a number of outcomes that may occur. Following attribution theory (e.g., Heider, 1958; Kelley, 1973), URT proposed that people are motivated to understand social situations. URT built on these two premises to theorize that uncertainty is prominent when strangers meet for the first time. Furthermore, URT advanced seven axioms about uncertainty during initial interaction (Berger & Calabrese, 1975):

Axiom 1: As verbal communication increases, uncertainty decreases.
Axiom 2: As nonverbal affiliative expressiveness increases, uncertainty decreases.
Axiom 3: High uncertainty increases information-seeking behavior.
Axiom 4: High uncertainty decreases the intimacy of communication content.

Axiom 5: High uncertainty produces high reciprocity.
Axiom 6: Similarities between people reduce uncertainty.
Axiom 7: Increases in uncertainty produce decreases in liking.

Although their original explication of URT was limited to the context of acquaintance, Berger and Calabrese (1975) saw the potential for expansion to more developed relationships. They concluded: "For the present time, we have elected to confine our theory to the initial stages of interaction between strangers. Obviously, a full blown theory of interaction development would have to stipulate broader boundary conditions than the present one" (p. 110). Their call for expanded theorizing was overlooked, however, in the first investigations of URT within close relationships. Scholars borrowed URT's acquaintance-focused definition of uncertainty rather than tailoring the construct to the questions people experience within intimate associations. Indeed, early studies privileged ambiguity about a partner's attributes by employing the Clatterbuck Uncertainty Evaluation Scale (CLUES; Clatterbuck, 1979) to measure uncertainty (e.g., Gudykunst, 1985; Planalp & Honeycutt, 1985). The CLUES scale solicits people's knowledge about their partner's personality features, behaviors, and lifestyle preferences (sample items include "How confident are you of your general ability to predict how the person will behave?" and "How well do you think you know the person?").

Of course, questions about a partner's attributes are salient within the context of acquaintance because strangers have limited knowledge about each other. Within the context of close relationships, however, uncertainty about other issues may trump questions about a partner's personality (e.g., Afifi & Burgoon, 1998; Siegert & Stamp, 1994; Turner, 1990). The relational uncertainty construct was formulated to capture the doubts individuals experience within intimate associations (Knobloch & Solomon, 1999). This conceptual shift marked a move from theorizing about partner predictability issues to theorizing about relationship involvement issues (e.g., Afifi & Reichert, 1996; Knobloch & Solomon, 2002a).

Definition

Relational uncertainty refers to the questions people have about participating in an interpersonal relationship (Knobloch & Solomon, 1999, 2002a). It can be conceptualized on both global and episodic levels. On a global level (Knobloch & Carpenter-Theune, 2004; Knobloch & Donovan-Kicken, 2006), relational uncertainty involves people's general sense of ambiguity about participating in a relationship ("How uncertain am I about...?"). On an episodic level (Bevan, 2004; Emmers & Canary, 1996; Knobloch & Solomon, 2003), relational uncertainty encompasses the doubts sparked by a specific event ("This event made me more uncertain about..."). Both levels of relational uncertainty are apparent in relationships between siblings (cf. Bevan, 2004; Bevan, Stetzenbach, Batson, & Bullo, 2006), friends (cf. Afifi & Burgoon, 1998; Planalp & Honeycutt, 1985), dating partners (cf. Knobloch, 2005; Knobloch & Donovan-Kicken, 2006), and spouses (cf. Knobloch, 2008; Turner, 1990).

Relational uncertainty arises from a trio of sources (Knobloch & Solomon, 1999, 2002a). *Self uncertainty* includes the questions people have about their own involvement in a close relationship ("How certain are you about where you want this relationship to go?"). *Partner uncertainty* indexes the ambiguity individuals experience about their partner's involvement in a close relationship ("How certain are you about where your partner wants this relationship to go?"). *Relationship uncertainty* involves the doubts people encounter about the partnership itself ("How certain are you about the norms for this relationship?"). In comparison to self and partner uncertainty, which refer to questions about individuals, relationship uncertainty exists at a higher level of abstraction because it encompasses questions about dyads (Berger & Bradac, 1982; Knobloch & Solomon, 1999, 2002a).

Content

Whereas self, partner, and relationship *sources* of relational uncertainty are applicable to partnerships of all types (Berger & Bradac, 1982; Knobloch, 2007a), the *content* of relational uncertainty varies by dyadic context. For example, the themes of relational uncertainty within courtship cluster around doubts about the compatibility of partners (Knobloch, 2007a; Knobloch & Solomon, 1999). Dating couples grapple with questions about their desire for a relationship, their evaluation of its worth, their goals for its progression, the norms for behavior, the mutuality of feelings between partners, the definition of the relationship, and the future of the relationship (Knobloch & Solomon, 1999). In contrast, the themes of relational uncertainty within marriage often stem from life changes that could modify the relationship. Spouses experience ambiguity about children, career issues, finances, health, extended family, sex, and retirement, among other issues (Knobloch, 2008; Turner, 1990).

The content of relational uncertainty perhaps is best illustrated by people's own words. Here are some comments individuals provided when asked to describe the issues of relational uncertainty they experience within their romantic relationships (Knobloch, 2008; Knobloch & Solomon, 2003).

"Sometimes I wonder if he may have a roaming eye because I have experienced cheating with him before."

"I met someone who I thought I might want to spend time with. It made me question if I wanted to take a step back from my current relationship."

"Does my wife have the values I thought she had? (Does she value money more than me? Does she love family less? Does she have the same spiritual beliefs?)"

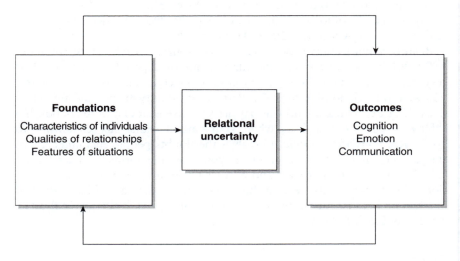

Figure 6.1 Foundations and Outcomes of Relational Uncertainty

Source: Figure adapted from Knobloch (2007a).

"Perhaps one of the biggest struggles is how, despite four years of dating, we married people we thought we knew very well—and were wrong."

"My boyfriend questioned my love for him because I doubted whether our relationship is secure enough for us to be independent and live away from my family."

"When we retire will our marriage change?"

"Does she wish she was married to someone else?"

Not only do these remarks illustrate the variety of questions that can arise within romantic relationships, but they also convey the poignant emotions embedded in people's experiences of relational uncertainty.

A growing body of research has sought to identify the foundations and outcomes of relational uncertainty (see Figure 6.1). To date, scholars have focused on three categories of predictors: (a) qualities of individuals, (b) features of relationships, and (c) attributes of situations. Scholars also have considered three classes of outcomes: (a) cognitions, (b) emotions, and (c) behaviors. Because the foundations and outcomes of relational uncertainty have been described extensively elsewhere (see Knobloch, 2007a, 2010), we do not tackle that task here. Instead, we embrace the theme of this book by theorizing about the link between relational uncertainty and communication.

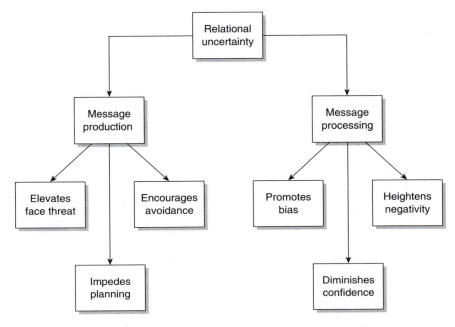

Figure 6.2 Propositions about Relational Uncertainty and Communication

Relational Uncertainty and Message Production

As we noted at the outset of this chapter, we believe the time is right to generate theoretical logic to organize scholarship on relational uncertainty. We tackle that task by delineating six propositions about how relational uncertainty may correspond with features of interpersonal communication (see Figure 6.2). First, we examine the role of relational uncertainty in how people produce messages, and then we consider the role of relational uncertainty in how individuals process messages. Although our propositions are necessarily speculative because the literature is just beginning to take shape, we hope they will provide a useful framework for synthesizing the findings that have emerged to date.

Relational Uncertainty and Face Threat

Our first proposition is that **relational uncertainty escalates the severity of the face threats individuals experience when communicating with a partner.** *Face* is the identity people portray when interacting with others (Goffman, 1967). *Face threats* occur when an individual's preferred image is contested, challenged, or criticized (Brown & Levinson, 1987). Face-threatening messages discredit the image a person wants to project (Brown & Levinson, 1987; Wilson, Aleman, & Leatham, 1998).

Relational uncertainty may heighten the degree of face threat individuals experience when producing messages for two reasons. First, crafting messages may be hazardous under conditions of relational uncertainty because people may inadvertently damage their image, their partner's image, or their relationship (Knobloch, 2006; Knobloch & Carpenter-Theune, 2004). When individuals lack information about potential quagmires, they run a greater risk of jeopardizing face. People could appear unattractive, behave incompetently, embarrass themselves, offend their partner, garner disapproval, disturb the status quo, or discover issues of incompatibility between partners (Afifi & Burgoon, 1998; Baxter & Wilmot, 1985). Indeed, message production may be more face threatening under conditions of relational uncertainty because individuals do not have a clear sense of the boundaries for appropriate and inappropriate behavior.

A second reason that relational uncertainty may elevate the severity of face threats is that individuals must attend to all possible risks. According to politeness theory, people use information about their social environment to assess potential threats to face (Brown & Levinson, 1987). Their knowledge of the surrounding circumstances helps them anticipate plausible risks and rule out implausible risks. But when individuals lack information about the status of their relationship, they do not have the luxury of discounting any potential face threats. They must consider every possible risk. Thus, message production may be more face threatening when people are unsure because they are unable to dismiss any potential risks.

Two studies are compatible with our logic. A first investigation examined the link between relational uncertainty and topic avoidance within the context of courtship (Knobloch & Carpenter-Theune, 2004). In the study, 216 individuals involved in a dating relationship reported their perceptions of relational uncertainty. They also listed topics they avoid talking about with their partner. In a final step, participants evaluated how threatening it would be to talk about each topic with their partner. They completed items measuring their perceptions of self threat (e.g., how embarrassing, how threatening to their image) and relationship threat (e.g., how damaging to the relationship). Bivariate findings indicated that self, partner, and relationship uncertainty were positively associated with both self threat and relationship threat. Structural equation modeling results revealed statistically significant paths from relationship uncertainty to self threat and to relationship threat. Taken together, these findings suggest that talking about sensitive topics may be more face threatening when people are experiencing relational uncertainty.

Complementary results are apparent in the domain of marriage (Knobloch, Miller, Bond, & Mannone, 2007). Participants were 125 married couples who completed self-report measures of relational uncertainty and then engaged in two 10-minute videotaped conversations. After each conversation, individuals rated their interaction with their spouse. Hierarchical linear modeling findings demonstrated that relational uncertainty was positively associated with spouses' reports that the conversations were threatening to themselves and to their marriage. These data imply that relational uncertainty corresponds with a heightened degree of face threat in conversation.

Relational Uncertainty and Planning Messages

Our second proposition predicts that **relational uncertainty increases the difficulty of planning messages**. A *plan* is a cognitive representation of behaviors used to accomplish a goal (Berger, 1997). Theories of message production argue that plans guide how individuals craft messages (Berger, 1997; Dillard, 1990). Relational uncertainty may compromise people's ability to plan messages in two ways. First, individuals draw on knowledge of their surroundings to select a suitable strategy, construct a message, and anticipate their partner's response (Brown & Levinson, 1987; Planalp & Rivers, 1996). If relational uncertainty diminishes people's confidence in their understanding of the situation, then their capacity to plan is likely to be disrupted. Second, individuals have to work harder to plan messages when they are juggling multiple goals and addressing multiple face threats (Berger, 1997). If relational uncertainty escalates the complexity of crafting an utterance, then people's capacity to plan is likely to be impaired. We utilize this logic to propose that relational uncertainty makes planning messages more challenging.

One implication of our prediction is that relational uncertainty corresponds with less fluent messages. *Fluency* is the extent to which messages are polished, articulate, and free of mistakes (Burgoon, Buller, & Floyd, 2001; Greene & Lindsey, 1989). Research implies that when individuals have trouble planning, their messages are less fluent and more error-prone (Berger, 1995). Hence, we follow theories of message production in conceptualizing fluency as an observable marker of people's planning difficulty.

A recent investigation is consistent with theorizing that individuals experiencing relational uncertainty produce less fluent messages (Knobloch, 2006). In the study, 248 participants involved in a dating relationship completed items assessing self, partner, and relationship uncertainty. Then, they simulated leaving a date-request voice-mail message for their partner with the goal of making plans. Independent judges rated the smoothness of each message and counted the dysfluencies in each message. Results demonstrated that the three sources of relational uncertainty shared small negative associations with smoothness, and self and relationship uncertainty shared small positive associations with the number of dysfluencies. These findings provide initial evidence that people construct less fluent messages under conditions of relational uncertainty.

Relational Uncertainty and Avoidance

Our third proposition posits that **relational uncertainty leads individuals to avoid communicating directly about sensitive issues**. *Avoidance* is purposely evading explicit communication with a partner (Afifi, Caughlin, & Afifi, 2007). Avoidance occurs on a topic level when people strategically refrain from broaching an issue with their partner (e.g., Baxter & Wilmot, 1985). It occurs on a conversation level when individuals strategically avoid directly discussing a topic raised in interaction (e.g., through sidestepping the issue, distracting their partner, speaking evasively; Afifi et al., 2007; Caughlin, 2002). We propose that relational uncertainty sparks both topic-level and conversation-level avoidance of sensitive issues that could damage people's image, their partner's image, or the status of the relationship.

Under conditions of relational uncertainty, individuals may avoid communicating directly about vulnerable topics because they do not want to risk negative outcomes. People experiencing relational uncertainty, by definition, are not confident in their perceptions of the status of the partnership (Knobloch & Solomon, 1999, 2002a). Individuals may refrain from discussing sensitive issues because they are not sure how their partner will respond (e.g., Afifi & Burgoon, 1998; Baxter & Wilmot, 1985). In particular, direct communication is hazardous when ambiguity is salient because individuals could tarnish their image, upset their partner, or harm their relationship (e.g., Baxter, 1987; Knobloch, 2006; Knobloch & Solomon, 2002a). Moreover, if relational uncertainty heightens face threat and hampers planning, then people may decide it is easier to avoid talking about sensitive topics than risk unpleasant consequences.

A sizable body of work suggests a link between relational uncertainty and avoidance on both topic and conversation levels. For example, people grappling with questions about their relationship engage in more topic avoidance within cross-sex friendships (Afifi & Burgoon, 1998), dating relationships (Knobloch & Carpenter-Theune, 2004), parent–child relationships (Afifi & Schrodt, 2003), and sibling relationships (Bevan et al., 2006). Individuals experiencing partner-focused and relationship-focused doubts are unwilling to tell their dating partner about behaviors that irritate them (Theiss & Solomon, 2006b). People are less likely to express feelings of jealousy when they are unsure about the state of their courtship (Theiss & Solomon, 2006a). Moreover, individuals who have questions about their relationship prefer to avoid discussing unexpected events with their dating partner (Knobloch & Solomon, 2002b). When people are not sure whether their partnership is a platonic or romantic one, they treat their relationship as a taboo topic (Baxter & Wilmot, 1985). With respect to conversation-level avoidance, individuals who are uncertain about the platonic versus romantic status of their relationship employ indirect methods to seek information (e.g., joking, hinting, escalating touch, waiting for the partner to initiate contact; Baxter & Wilmot, 1984). People experiencing relational uncertainty also craft date-request messages that are less explicit and less relationally focused (Knobloch, 2006). As a set, these studies suggest that relational uncertainty results in avoidance at both topic and conversation levels.

We devoted this section to offering three propositions about the connection between relational uncertainty and message production. We reasoned that relational uncertainty may magnify face threats, hinder people's ability to plan what they are going to say, and motivate them to steer clear of risky topics. We also reviewed empirical evidence consistent with our logic. Next, we shift our attention to how relational uncertainty may shape the ways individuals interpret messages. Our theorizing about the connection between relational uncertainty and message processing is a bit more tentative, partly because scholars have tended to conceptualize ambiguity as a predictor of message production rather than message processing (Knobloch, 2007a). One conclusion is clear from the data, however: Relational uncertainty and message processing share close ties.

Relational Uncertainty and Message Processing

Relational Uncertainty and Information-Processing Biases

Our fourth proposition contends that **relational uncertainty diminishes people's ability to draw accurate conclusions from their partner's messages.** This claim flows from the idea that interpreting messages is a challenging task under conditions of relational uncertainty. A hallmark claim about message processing is that individuals utilize knowledge of their environment to decode incoming information (Dillard, Solomon, & Samp, 1996; Planalp & Rivers, 1996). People grappling with relational uncertainty, by definition, face an information deficit (Berger & Bradac, 1982; Knobloch & Solomon, 1999, 2002a). Accordingly, their capacity to make sense of messages in a top-down fashion may be compromised. If individuals experiencing relational uncertainty do not have adequate background information upon which to rely, then relational uncertainty may escalate the difficulty of interpreting messages.

We further propose that, if relational uncertainty complicates message processing, then people may employ heuristics to simplify the task. An established principle of message processing is that individuals who are under a high cognitive load use shortcuts to make their job more manageable. For example, theories of persuasion contend that people process messages superficially when they are unable or unwilling to devote extensive cognitive effort to the task (e.g., Petty & Cacioppo, 1986). Similarly, relational framing theory argues that individuals simplify message processing by framing cues in terms of either dominance or affiliation (Dillard et al., 1996). We follow this theorizing to argue that people may utilize information-processing heuristics to reduce their cognitive load when they are unsure.

A *tentativeness bias* may emerge in the context of courtship as a shortcut for processing information under conditions of relational uncertainty. Daters who are experiencing relational uncertainty may have difficulty drawing concrete conclusions from conversation. What does this logic imply operationally? When relational uncertainty is high, people's responses to closed-ended items assessing their partner's affiliative behavior should cluster around the scale midpoint. Knobloch and Solomon (2005) evaluated this possibility by recruiting 120 dating couples to complete measures of relational uncertainty, engage in a 10-minute videotaped conversation, and report how much affiliation their partner showed in the conversation. Findings indicated that people endorsed midrange assessments of their partner's affiliation under conditions of relational uncertainty. These results imply that relational uncertainty may spark tentative information processing within courtship.

A *pessimism bias* may arise in the context of marriage as a heuristic for decoding messages when spouses are uncertain. Stated differently, individuals may react negatively to their spouse's behavior when they are unsure about their marriage. Knobloch, Miller, Bond, et al. (2007) tested this idea by asking 125 married couples to report on relational uncertainty, participate in two 10-minute videotaped conversations, and judge how much affiliation, dominance, and involvement their spouse conveyed in each conversation. Knobloch, Miller, Bond, et al. (2007) also trained independent judges to rate how much affiliation husbands and wives displayed. Results revealed that relational uncertainty did not predict judges' ratings of affiliation, but relational uncertainty was negatively associated with people's ratings of their partner's affiliation. In other words, spouses who were experiencing relational uncertainty saw their partner's behavior as less warm even though independent judges did not detect less warmth. Knobloch, Miller, Bond, et al.'s (2007) data suggest that relational uncertainty may promote a pessimism bias within marriage.

We have argued that relational uncertainty may lead to a tentativeness bias in courtship but a pessimism bias in marriage. Why the divergence? We propose that it stems from the dyadic context. Within courtship, people may see relational uncertainty as a normal part of discerning whether they have found a life partner (e.g., Baxter & Wilmot, 1984, 1985). They may be cautious about drawing hard-and-fast conclusions and may refrain from making snap judgments (Knobloch & Solomon, 2005). If doubts about involvement in courtship hamper comprehension, then individuals may have trouble making firm judgments about their partner's behavior. Within marriage, in contrast, spouses may experience relational uncertainty negatively because it is not part of their schema for what marriage should be like. Marriage constitutes a long-term, legal commitment that is difficult to dissolve (e.g., Johnson, Caughlin, & Huston, 1999), so spouses grappling with ambiguity may feel discouraged because relational uncertainty could prefigure divorce. If doubts about involvement in marriage sour people's outlook, then spouses may view their partner's behavior in a negative light. We posit that the unique parameters of the dyadic context account for the tentativeness bias in courtship versus the pessimism bias in marriage.

If the information-processing bias of relational uncertainty is manifest differently in courtship versus marriage, then our reasoning underscores the importance of attending to the dyadic context when theorizing about relational uncertainty. Of course, individuals may grapple with different themes of relational uncertainty within courtship (Knobloch & Solomon, 1999, 2002a), marriage (Knobloch, 2008; Turner, 1990), friendship (Afifi & Burgoon, 1998), and family relationships (Afifi & Schrodt, 2003; Bevan, 2004). We take a step further to propose that the dyadic context may shape not only *what* people are unsure about, but also *how* they process messages. If our logic is correct, then scholars face the thorny task of accumulating universal insights while also tailoring their logic to the context under investigation. This is a complex challenge, without a doubt, but one that is necessary for knowledge to accrue in a systematic fashion.

Relational Uncertainty and Confidence in Communication Ability

According to our fifth proposition, **relational uncertainty shakes people's confidence in their ability to communicate with their partner.** Our previous theorizing provides twin foundations for this claim. If individuals sense that their ability to produce messages is inhibited when they are grappling with questions about involvement, then they may lack confidence in their own effectiveness. Similarly, if people recognize that their message-processing capacity is curtailed under conditions of relational uncertainty, then they may feel insecure about their own interaction skill. We draw on these assertions to reason that relational uncertainty may prompt people to doubt their own communication performance.

Tangential support for our proposition stems from research by Murray, Holmes, and colleagues on people's self-worth. For example, low self-esteem individuals who doubt themselves view their partner's feelings for them as less favorable (Murray, Holmes, MacDonald, & Ellsworth, 1998) and underestimate their partner's regard for them (Murray, Holmes, & Griffin, 2000). Moreover, people plagued by self-doubt are more insecure about their partner's feelings for them and less hopeful about the state of the relationship (Murray, Holmes, Griffin, Bellavia, & Rose, 2001). Whereas individuals with low self-esteem react to relationship threats by reducing closeness, individuals with high self-esteem react to relationship threats by drawing closer to their partner (Murray, Rose, Bellavia, Holmes, & Kusche, 2002). These studies, although focused on insecurity about self-worth rather than relational uncertainty, imply that individuals facing ambiguity may underestimate their own attractiveness.

More concrete evidence emerges from the investigation of date requests that we discussed previously (Knobloch, 2006). Participants in that study were 248 individuals involved in a dating relationship. After reporting on relational uncertainty, they role-played leaving a date-request voice-mail message for their partner. Next, they completed items assessing how effective they perceived their request to be. Independent judges also rated the effectiveness of each message. Findings indicated that relational uncertainty shared negative associations with both insider and outsider ratings of effectiveness. More notably, the negative association between relational uncertainty and

insider perceptions of effectiveness remained after covarying outsider perceptions of effectiveness. Not only did individuals experiencing relational uncertainty perform less effectively, but they *thought* they performed less effectively
even after controlling for the ratings of independent observers. They did not
communicate well and believed they communicated even worse than they
did. Hence, people may have a self-deprecating view of their own communication performance under conditions of relational uncertainty.

An implication of our fifth proposition is that individuals who need to
glean knowledge the most are least confident in their communication skills.
In other words, people experiencing relational uncertainty appear to face
double jeopardy: They lack information about the nature of their relationship and lack assurance in their ability to communicate effectively (Knobloch,
2006). Viewed from a different angle, our logic implies that individuals
who are certain about their relationship may be overly sanguine about the
quality of their communication skills. Perhaps confidence in the status of a
relationship bolsters people's belief that they communicate well, regardless
of how effective their performance appears to independent observers.
Additional research is necessary to tease out whether the link between relational uncertainty and people's confidence in their communication ability
stems from acute pessimism under conditions of relational uncertainty or
acute optimism under conditions of relational certainty.

Relational Uncertainty and Negativity

Our final proposition is that **relational uncertainty prompts individuals to
view their partner and their relationship more negatively.** We deduce this
proposition from the logic that preceded it. If relational uncertainty impedes
people's ability to produce messages (Knobloch, 2006), then their difficulty
may color their perceptions of their partner and their relationship. Moreover,
if relational uncertainty hampers people's ability to process messages via
either tentativeness or pessimism (Knobloch, Miller, Bond, et al., 2007;
Knobloch & Solomon, 2005), then their frustration may shape how they
appraise their partner and their relationship. Consequently, we expect that
individuals who are unsure about involvement should have a more dismal
outlook on their partner and their relationship (Knobloch, 2007a, 2008).

A growing body of research suggests that relational uncertainty predicts
negativity. Within the context of courtship, individuals who are grappling
with relational uncertainty describe their dating relationship as less stable
(Knobloch, 2007b). They also experience more negative emotion, including
anger, sadness, fear, and jealousy (Knobloch, Miller, & Carpenter, 2007;
Knobloch, Solomon, & Cruz, 2001; Theiss & Solomon, 2006a). Dating partners who are unsure appraise their friends and family members as less supportive of their courtship (Knobloch & Donovan-Kicken, 2006). Individuals
judge irritating partner behavior (Solomon & Knobloch, 2004; Theiss &
Solomon, 2006b) and unexpected events (Knobloch & Solomon, 2002b)

as more severe under conditions of relational uncertainty. Similarly, people experiencing relational uncertainty are more reactive to relationship threats, particularly when their commitment to the courtship is low (Arriaga, Slaughterbeck, Capezza, & Hmurovic, 2007). Within the context of marriage, spouses who are experiencing relational uncertainty feel more anger, sadness, and fear in conversation with their spouse (Knobloch, Miller, Bond, et al., 2007) and report less satisfaction with their marriage (Knobloch, 2008). These studies imply that relational uncertainty corresponds with more negative views of partners and relationships.

To this point, we have sought to organize the literature by advancing propositions about how relational uncertainty corresponds with communication. We posited that relational uncertainty may impair message production by escalating face threats, interfering with planning, and encouraging avoidance. We also argued that relational uncertainty may complicate message processing by sparking information-processing biases, diminishing people's confidence in their communication ability, and heightening negativity. Taken together, these claims coalesce around the idea that producing and processing messages may be challenging under conditions of relational uncertainty. A recent study supports our general claim: Individuals reported that conversing with their dating partner was more difficult when they were grappling with questions about their courtship (Knobloch & Solomon, 2005).

Applications

Theoretical ideas possess limited value if they do not have practical applications. In this section, we turn our attention to the applied dimensions of our theorizing. We discuss the practical ramifications of our propositions by identifying paradoxes that confront individuals when relationships are ambiguous. By delineating these paradoxes, we hope to clarify the pragmatic issues people face under conditions of relational uncertainty.

One paradox is that individuals who most need insight into their relationship are least well-equipped to glean it (e.g., Knobloch & Solomon, 2005). If relational uncertainty diminishes people's propensity to communicate directly and interpret messages accurately, then individuals who are grappling with questions about their relationship also are facing the greatest obstacles to obtaining answers. They may be unwilling to ask their partner directly because they do not want to risk embarrassment, anxiety, discomfort, and relationship damage (e.g., Afifi & Burgoon, 1998; Knobloch & Carpenter-Theune, 2004). They may lack faith in their interpretation skills because they are having difficulty deciphering incoming cues (e.g., Knobloch, Miller, Bond, et al., 2007; Knobloch & Solomon, 2005). Hence, one paradox is that people experiencing relational uncertainty are disadvantaged in any quest to gain insight.

A related paradox is that individuals who are unsure may be trapped in an ongoing cycle of ambiguity and avoidance. If both partners eschew direct communication in favor of avoidance, then both will have trouble discerning the status of the relationship (e.g., Baxter & Wilmot, 1984, 1985; Knobloch & Carpenter-Theune, 2004). How long will this sequence of ambiguity, avoiding, more ambiguity, and more avoiding repeat itself? We are not aware of any research that has examined when and why partners break the cycle, but ending the pattern would require individuals to either (a) ignore the face threats and communicate explicitly, or (b) deescalate the relationship because the risks of directness are too high. Both prospects may seem less than ideal to people lodged in the situation.

A third paradox is that relational uncertainty may be simultaneously helpful and harmful to people's well-being. Although ambiguity about involvement may impede message production and processing, it also may shield individuals and relationships from problems. For example, relational uncertainty may insulate people from communicating poorly when their partnership is fragile. If individuals refrain from boldly defining their relationship when doubts are salient, then their cautious approach may protect them from making communicative mistakes (Knobloch, 2007a; Knobloch & Solomon, 2002a). Relational uncertainty also may safeguard people from monotony. Indeed, questions about involvement may provide a much-needed dose of excitement, vigor, and zest to a partnership that has languished (e.g., Aron, Norman, Aron, McKenna, & Heyman, 2000; Baxter & Montgomery, 1996). We have emphasized the detrimental effects of questions about involvement in our theorizing, but a paradox of relational uncertainty is that it furnishes both obstacles *and* opportunities for participants in close relationships (Knobloch, 2007a).

As this trio of paradoxes makes clear, practical guidelines for people grappling with relational uncertainty are neither obvious nor straightforward. Advice to assertively ask a partner where the relationship is headed ignores the inherent risks involved in explicit communication. Advice to embrace the benefits of ambiguity ignores the anxiety people may feel when relationships are unpredictable. Perhaps our best recommendation is for individuals to recognize that relational uncertainty is a common, widespread, and normal part of relating (e.g., Afifi & Schrodt, 2003; Afifi & Burgoon, 1998; Babrow & Matthias, this volume; Solomon & Knobloch, 2001). We suggest that people expect to experience mysterious moments throughout the life cycle of relationships rather than be caught off-guard by the unpredictability of the process (e.g., Baxter & Montgomery, 1996).

Melding Theory and Application in Future Research

We believe that a fruitful strategy for obtaining further theoretical and pragmatic insight into relational uncertainty is to integrate established theories of interpersonal communication. As one example, consider the advances that could stem from juxtaposing relational uncertainty and Fitzpatrick's (1988; Fitzpatrick, Vangelisti, & Firman, 1994) typological approach to marriage.

Her theory argues that people's schemas of marriage vary across three dimensions: (a) desire for interdependence, (b) conventional versus unconventional views of family life, and (c) tolerance for conflict (Fitzpatrick et al., 1994). Approximately 40% of married couples disagree on one or more dimensions of their schemas (Fitzpatrick, 1988). We suspect that couples with divergent marital schemas may be more prone to experiencing relational uncertainty throughout the life span of their marriage. We also speculate that people's marital schemas may predict how they communicate under conditions of ambiguity. More broadly, we think that scholarship on relational uncertainty could benefit from piggybacking on Fitzpatrick's (1988) typological framework.

A better understanding of the connection between relational uncertainty and power could be obtained by capitalizing on the chilling effect framework (Cloven & Roloff, 1993; Solomon & Samp, 1998). According to the chilling effect framework, individuals hesitate to voice grievances when they perceive their partner to possess dependence power or punitive power. Partners accrue dependence power when they appear uncommitted to the relationship (Solomon & Samp, 1998); partners accrue punitive power when they appear capable of engaging in symbolic and/or physical aggression (Cloven & Roloff, 1993). The conceptual distinctions among self, partner, and relationship sources of ambiguity, coupled with the chilling effect framework, raise questions that merit consideration. Do individuals accrue dependence power by advertising the doubts they have about their own involvement in a relationship? Do dependence power and punitive power exert stronger effects on people's willingness to communicate openly when they are grappling with questions about their partner's involvement? Do people's perceptions of their partner's power contribute to the ambiguity they experience about the future of the relationship? We believe these questions warrant investigation.

Other advances could stem from assimilating relational uncertainty with communication privacy management theory (Petronio, 2002; Petronio & Caughlin, 2006). This theory posits that participants in close relationships regulate the flow of private information by negotiating privacy boundaries with each other and with social network members. Individuals decide to reveal or conceal private information based on the rules for privacy they have constructed. When privacy rules are unclear or misunderstood, security breaches are likely to occur (Petronio & Caughlin, 2006). We speculate that the process of developing, articulating, and clarifying privacy rules is rife with relational uncertainty. Not only may people have difficulty managing the flow of private information within the dyad when they are unsure about their relationship, but they also may have trouble coordinating privacy boundaries with their surrounding social networks. Accordingly, pairing relational uncertainty and communication privacy management theory could be useful for illuminating how individuals regulate private information when ambiguity is salient.

A final suggestion is to explore the role of relational uncertainty in how couples communicate about compulsive behavior. Inconsistent nurturing as control theory argues that a close relationship between an individual afflicted with an addiction (e.g., eating disorder, gambling, alcoholism, drug abuse) and his or her functional partner is marked by paradoxes that make it difficult to extinguish the compulsive behavior (Le Poire & Dailey, 2006; Le Poire, Hallett, & Erlandson, 2000). One paradox is that the functional partner must sacrifice his or her needs to assist the afflicted partner during bouts of addiction, but in so doing, the afflicted partner becomes dependent on the help. Another paradox is that the functional partner is caught between wanting to eliminate the addiction and wanting to provide nurturing; the functional partner may worry that the afflicted partner will no longer need the relationship if the compulsion is extinguished. To these paradoxes, we add the dilemma of communicating under conditions of relational uncertainty: If partners discuss their uncertainties about the addiction openly, they put themselves at risk for face threats and relationship damage. Inconsistent nurturing as control theory suggests that intermittent patterns of caregiving and punishment actually reinforce compulsive behavior rather than eliminate it. Does the difficulty of communicating under conditions of relational uncertainty further compromise people's ability to break the cycle of addiction? We await future research on this question.

Conclusion

More than three decades have elapsed since URT first highlighted the salience of uncertainty within acquaintance. The initial scholarly glimpses of ambiguity within close relationships echoed Berger and Calabrese's (1975) prediction that uncertainty is relevant beyond initial interaction (e.g., Berger & Bradac, 1982; Planalp & Honeycutt, 1985; Turner, 1990). Recent years have seen an explosion of work on relational uncertainty in partnerships among parents and children, siblings, friends, dating partners, and spouses (e.g., Afifi & Schrodt, 2003; Afifi & Burgoon, 1998; Bevan et al., 2006; Knobloch, 2006). Now is an exciting time for scholars of relational uncertainty: Advanced theorizing, coupled with an expanding base of empirical findings, implies that the next generation of work is ready to flourish. These conceptual and empirical innovations, in turn, will generate more extensive practical advice for how people should communicate under conditions of relational uncertainty.

References

Afifi, T. D., Caughlin, J. P., & Afifi, W. A. (2007). The dark side (and light side) of avoidance and secrets. In B. H. Spitzberg & W. R. Cupach (Eds.), *The dark side of interpersonal communication* (2nd ed., pp. 61–92). Mahwah, NJ: Lawrence Erlbaum.

Afifi, T. D., & Schrodt, P. (2003). Uncertainty and the avoidance of the state of one's family in stepfamilies, post divorce single-parent families, and first-marriage families. *Human Communication Research, 29,* 516–532.

Afifi, W. A., & Burgoon, J. K. (1998). "We never talk about that": A comparison of cross-sex friendships and dating relationships on uncertainty and topic avoidance. *Personal Relationships, 5,* 255–272.

Afifi, W. A., & Reichert, T. (1996). Understanding the role of uncertainty in jealousy experience and expression. *Communication Reports, 9,* 93–103.

Aron, A., Norman, C. C., Aron, E. N., McKenna, C., & Heyman, R. E. (2000). Couples' shared participation in novel and arousing activities and experienced relationship quality. *Journal of Personality and Social Psychology, 78,* 273–284.

Arriaga, X. B. (2001). The ups and downs of dating: Fluctuations in satisfaction in newly formed romantic relationships. *Journal of Personality and Social Psychology, 80,* 754–765.

Arriaga, X. B., Reed, J. T., Goodfriend, W., & Agnew, C. R. (2006). Relationship perceptions and persistence: Do fluctuations in perceived partner commitment undermine dating relationships? *Journal of Personality and Social Psychology, 91,* 1045–1065.

Arriaga, X. B., Slaughterbeck, E. S., Capezza, N. M., & Hmurovic, J. L. (2007). From bad to worse: Relationship commitment and vulnerability to partner imperfections. *Personal Relationships, 14,* 389–409.

Baxter, L. A. (1987). Cognition and communication in the relationship process. In R. Barnett, P. McGhee, & D. Clarke (Eds.), *Accounting for relationships* (pp. 192–212). London: Methuen.

Baxter, L. A., & Montgomery, B. M. (1996). *Relating: Dialogues and dialectics.* New York: Guilford.

Baxter, L. A., & Wilmot, W. W. (1984). "Secret tests": Strategies for acquiring information about the state of the relationship. *Human Communication Research, 11,* 171–201.

Baxter, L. A., & Wilmot, W. W. (1985). Taboo topics in close relationships. *Journal of Social and Personal Relationships, 2,* 253–269.

Berger, C. R. (1995). Inscrutable goals, uncertain plans, and the production of communicative action. In C. R. Berger & M. Burgoon (Eds.), *Communication and social influence processes* (pp. 1–28). East Lansing, MI: Michigan State University Press.

Berger, C. R. (1997). *Planning strategic interaction: Attaining goals through communicative action.* Mahwah, NJ: Lawrence Erlbaum.

Berger, C. R., & Bradac, J. J. (1982). *Language and social knowledge: Uncertainty in interpersonal relationships.* London: Edward Arnold.

Berger, C. R., & Calabrese, R. J. (1975). Some explorations in initial interaction and beyond: Toward a developmental theory of interpersonal communication. *Human Communication Research, 1,* 99–112.

Berger, C. R., & Gudykunst, W. B. (1991). Uncertainty and communication. In B. Dervin & M. J. Voigt (Eds.), *Progress in communication sciences* (Vol. 10, pp. 21–66). Norwood, NJ: Ablex.

Bevan, J. L. (2004). General partner and relational uncertainty as consequences of another person's jealousy expression. *Western Journal of Communication, 68,* 195–218.

Bevan, J. L., Stetzenbach, K. A., Batson, E., & Bullo, K. (2006). Factors associated with general partner uncertainty and relational uncertainty within early adulthood sibling relationships. *Communication Quarterly, 54,* 367–381.

Brown, P., & Levinson, S. (1987). *Politeness: Some universals in language use.* New York: Cambridge University Press.

Burgoon, J. K., Buller, D. B., & Floyd, K. (2001). Does participation affect deception success? A test of the interactivity principle. *Human Communication Research, 27*, 503–534.

Caughlin, J. P. (2002). The demand/withdraw pattern of communication as a predictor of marital satisfaction over time: Unresolved issues and future directions. *Human Communication Research, 28*, 49–85.

Clatterbuck, G. W. (1979). Attributional confidence and uncertainty in initial interaction. *Human Communication Research, 5*, 147–157.

Cloven, D. H., & Roloff, M. E. (1993). The chilling effect of aggressive potential on the expression of complaints in intimate relationships. *Communication Monographs, 60*, 199–219.

Dillard, J. P. (1990). A goal-driven model of interpersonal influence. In J. P. Dillard (Ed.), *Seeking compliance: The production of interpersonal influence messages* (pp. 41–56). Scottsdale, AZ: Gorsuch Scarisbrick.

Dillard, J. P., Solomon, D. H., & Samp, J. A. (1996). Framing social reality: The relevance of relational judgments. *Communication Research, 23*, 703–723.

Dugas, M. J., Hedayati, M., Karavidas, A., Buhr, K., Francis, K., & Phillips, N. A. (2005). Intolerance of uncertainty and information processing: Evidence of biased recall and interpretations. *Cognitive Therapy and Research, 29*, 57–70.

Emmers, T. M., & Canary, D. J. (1996). The effect of uncertainty reducing strategies on young couples' relational repair and intimacy. *Communication Quarterly, 44*, 166–182.

Fitzpatrick, M. A. (1988). *Between husbands and wives: Communication in marriage.* Newbury Park, CA: Sage.

Fitzpatrick, M. A., Vangelisti, A. L., & Firman, S. M. (1994). Perceptions of marital interaction and change during pregnancy: A typological approach. *Personal Relationships, 1*, 101–122.

Goffman, E. (1967). *Interaction ritual: Essays in face-to-face behavior.* Chicago: Adrine.

Greene, J. O., & Lindsey, A. E. (1989). Encoding processes in the production of multiple-goal messages. *Human Communication Research, 16*, 120–140.

Gudykunst, W. B. (1985). The influence of cultural similarity, type of relationship, and self-monitoring on uncertainty reduction processes. *Communication Monographs, 52*, 203–217.

Heider, F. (1958). *The psychology of interpersonal relations.* New York: Wiley.

Huston, T. L., Caughlin, J. P., Houts, R. M., Smith, S. E., & George, L. J. (2001). The connubial crucible: Newlywed years as predictors of marital delight, distress, and divorce. *Journal of Personality and Social Psychology, 80*, 237–252.

Johnson, M. P., Caughlin, J. P., & Huston, T. L. (1999). The tripartite nature of marital commitment: Personal, moral, and structural reasons to stay married. *Journal of Marriage and the Family, 61*, 160–177.

Kelley, H. H. (1973). The process of causal attribution. *American Psychologist, 28*, 107–128.

Knobloch, L. K. (2005). Evaluating a contextual model of responses to relational uncertainty increasing events: The role of intimacy, appraisals, and emotions. *Human Communication Research, 31*, 60–101.

Knobloch, L. K. (2006). Relational uncertainty and message production within courtship: Features of date request messages. *Human Communication Research, 32*, 244–273.

Knobloch, L. K. (2007a). The dark side of relational uncertainty: Obstacle or opportunity? In B. H. Spitzberg & W. R. Cupach (Eds.), *The dark side of interpersonal communication* (2nd ed., pp. 31–59). Mahwah, NJ: Lawrence Erlbaum.

Knobloch, L. K. (2007b). Perceptions of turmoil within courtship: Associations with intimacy, relational uncertainty, and interference from partners. *Journal of Social and Personal Relationships, 24*, 363–384.

Knobloch, L. K. (2008). The content of relational uncertainty within marriage. *Journal of Social and Personal Relationships, 25*, 467–495.

Knobloch, L. K. (2010). Relational uncertainty and interpersonal communication. In S. W. Smith & S. R. Wilson (Eds.), *New directions in interpersonal communication research*. Thousand Oaks, CA: Sage.

Knobloch, L. K., & Carpenter-Theune, K. E. (2004). Topic avoidance in developing romantic relationships: Associations with intimacy and relational uncertainty. *Communication Research, 31*, 173–205.

Knobloch, L. K., & Donovan-Kicken, E. (2006). Perceived involvement of network members in courtships: A test of the relational turbulence model. *Personal Relationships, 13*, 281–302.

Knobloch, L. K., Miller, L. E., Bond, B. J., & Mannone, S. E. (2007). Relational uncertainty and message processing in marriage. *Communication Monographs, 74*, 154–180.

Knobloch, L. K., Miller, L. E., & Carpenter, K. E. (2007). Using the relational turbulence model to understand negative emotion within courtship. *Personal Relationships, 14*, 91–112.

Knobloch, L. K., & Solomon, D. H. (1999). Measuring the sources and content of relational uncertainty. *Communication Studies, 50*, 261–278.

Knobloch, L. K., & Solomon, D. H. (2002a). Information seeking beyond initial interaction: Negotiating relational uncertainty within close relationships. *Human Communication Research, 28*, 243–257.

Knobloch, L. K., & Solomon, D. H. (2002b). Intimacy and the magnitude and experience of episodic relational uncertainty within romantic relationships. *Personal Relationships, 9*, 457–478.

Knobloch, L. K., & Solomon, D. H. (2003). Responses to changes in relational uncertainty within dating relationships: Emotions and communication strategies. *Communication Studies, 54*, 282–305.

Knobloch, L. K., & Solomon, D. H. (2005). Relational uncertainty and relational information processing: Questions without answers? *Communication Research, 32*, 349–388.

Knobloch, L. K., Solomon, D. H., & Cruz, M. G. (2001). The role of relationship development and attachment in the experience of romantic jealousy. *Personal Relationships, 8*, 205–224.

Le Poire, B. A., & Dailey, R. M. (2006). Inconsistent nurturing as control theory: A new theory in family communication. In D. O. Braithwaite & L. A. Baxter (Eds.), *Engaging theories in family communication: Multiple perspectives* (pp. 82–89). Thousand Oaks, CA: Sage.

Le Poire, B. A., Hallett, J. S., & Erlandson, K. T. (2000). An initial test of inconsistent nurturing as control theory: How partners of drug abusers assist their partners' sobriety. *Human Communication Research, 26*, 432–457.

McGregor, I., & Marigold, D. C. (2003). Defensive zeal and the uncertain self: What makes you so sure? *Journal of Personality and Social Psychology, 85*, 838–852.

Murray, S. L., Holmes, J. G., & Griffin, D. W. (2000). Self-esteem and the quest for felt security: How perceived regard regulates attachment processes. *Journal of Personality and Social Psychology, 78*, 478–498.

Murray, S. L., Holmes, J. G., Griffin, D. W., Bellavia, G., & Rose, P. (2001). The mismeasure of love: How self-doubt contaminates relationship beliefs. *Personality and Social Psychology Bulletin, 27*, 423–436.

Murray, S. L., Holmes, J. G., MacDonald, G., & Ellsworth, P. C. (1998). Through the looking glass darkly? When self-doubts turn into relationship insecurities. *Journal of Personality and Social Psychology, 75*, 1459–1480.

Murray, S. L., Rose, P., Bellavia, G. M., Holmes, J. G., & Kusche, A. G. (2002). When rejection stings: How self-esteem constrains relationship-enhancement processes. *Journal of Personality and Social Psychology, 83*, 556–573.

Petronio, S. (2002). *Boundaries of privacy: Dialectics of disclosure.* Albany, NY: SUNY Press.

Petronio, S., & Caughlin, J. P. (2006). Communication privacy management theory: Understanding families. In D. O. Braithwaite & L. A. Baxter (Eds.), *Engaging theories in family communication: Multiple perspectives* (pp. 35–49). Thousand Oaks, CA: Sage.

Petty, R. E., & Cacioppo, J. (1986). *Communication and persuasion: Central and peripheral routes to attitude change.* New York: Springer-Verlag.

Planalp, S., & Honeycutt, J. M. (1985). Events that increase uncertainty in personal relationships. *Human Communication Research, 11*, 593–604.

Planalp, S., & Rivers, M. (1996). Changes in knowledge of personal relationships. In G. J. O. Fletcher & J. Fitness (Eds.), *Knowledge structures in close relationships: A social psychological approach* (pp. 299–324). Mahwah, NJ: Lawrence Erlbaum.

Planalp, S., Rutherford, D. K., & Honeycutt, J. M. (1988). Events that increase uncertainty in personal relationships II: Replication and extension. *Human Communication Research, 14*, 516–547.

Shannon, C. E., & Weaver, W. (1949). *The mathematical theory of communication.* Champaign, IL: University of Illinois.

Shuper, P. A., Sorrentino, R. M., Otsubo, Y., Hodson, G., & Walker, A. M. (2004). A theory of uncertainty orientation: Implications for the study of individual differences within and across cultures. *Journal of Cross-Cultural Psychology, 35*, 460–480.

Siegert, J. R., & Stamp, G. H. (1994). "Our first big fight" as a milestone in the development of close relationships. *Communication Monographs, 61*, 345–360.

Solomon, D. H., & Knobloch, L. K. (2001). Relationship uncertainty, partner interference, and intimacy within dating relationships. *Journal of Social and Personal Relationships, 18*, 804–820.

Solomon, D. H., & Knobloch, L. K. (2004). A model of relational turbulence: The role of intimacy, relational uncertainty, and interference from partners in appraisals of irritations. *Journal of Social and Personal Relationships, 21*, 795–816.

Solomon, D. H., & Samp, J. A. (1998). Power and problem appraisal: Perceptual foundations of the chilling effect in dating relationships. *Journal of Social and Personal Relationships, 15*, 191–209.

Sorrentino, R. M., Holmes, J. G., Hanna, S. E., & Sharp, A. (1995). Uncertainty orientation and trust in close relationships: Individual differences in cognitive styles. *Journal of Personality and Social Psychology, 68*, 314–327.

Theiss, J. A., & Solomon, D. H. (2006a). Coupling longitudinal data and multilevel modeling to examine the antecedents and consequences of jealousy experiences in romantic relationships: A test of the relational turbulence model. *Human Communication Research, 32,* 469–503.

Theiss, J. A., & Solomon, D. H. (2006b). A relational turbulence model of communication about irritations in romantic relationships. *Communication Research, 33,* 391–418.

Turner, L. H. (1990). The relationship between communication and marital uncertainty: Is "her" marriage different from "his" marriage? *Women's Studies in Communication, 13,* 57–83.

Vishwanath, A. (2003). Comparing online information effects: A cross-cultural comparison of online information and uncertainty avoidance. *Communication Research, 30,* 579–598.

Wilson, S. R., Aleman, C. G., & Leatham, G. B. (1998). Identity implications of influence goals: A revised analysis of face-threatening acts and application to seeking compliance with same-sex friends. *Human Communication Research, 26,* 64–96.

7 Motivated Cognition In Interpersonal Contexts

Need for Closure and its Implications for Information Regulation and Social Interaction

Mark Dechesne and Arie W. Kruglanski

Recent years have witnessed immense growth in communication and information sharing. Internet, as well as mobile and satellite, communications are just a few examples of innovations that have contributed significantly to the alteration of everyday social realities. People are functioning in contexts of communication of greater complexity and diversity than ever before. While this diversity and complexity has the potential to enrich, it may also bring about feelings of uncertainty, and lack of guidance. Depending on personality and situations, these feelings may substantially affect cognition and interpersonal interaction and communication, for better, or for worse.

Over the course of the past decades, research on lay epistemic theory (Kruglanski, 1989) and the need for closure (NFC; e.g., Kruglanski & Webster, 1996) has yielded insights relevant to these concerns. NFC research has documented the role of motivation in the emergence and maintenance of knowledge, and extended its analysis to the realm of social interaction and communication (see e.g., Kruglanski, Pierro, Mannetti, & De Grada, 2006; Kruglanski & Webster, 1996). The types and amounts of (social) information to which we are exposed on a daily basis determine what we consider "knowledge," or "truth." Motivation plays a critical role in this process. We may want to know particular things, and therefore favor particular types of information. Also, we may feel an urge to "know" in order to avoid uncertainty and ambiguity, and thereby we may be disposed to accept the first hypothesis that comes to mind, and to stop considering alternatives once a particular opinion has been formed.

These insights have important implications for understanding the interplay of feelings of uncertainty, information regulation, and social interaction. In what is to come, we derive four propositions from lay epistemic theory and research on the NFC to elucidate the dynamics of uncertainty, information regulation, and social interaction.

We start with the proposition that uncertainty has a profound impact on mental functioning. The extent and way in which uncertainty affects information regulation can only be understood by taking attitudes of intolerance and tolerance toward uncertainty into account. Our second proposition is that such attitudes, referred to as the NFC, vary across situations and individuals.

Third, we propose a particularly negative attitude toward uncertainty; that is, a high NFC entails an information regulation strategy characterized by a tendency to quickly "seize" and rigidly "freeze" on judgments afforded by early information. In contrast, a positive attitude toward uncertainty, that is, a high need to avoid certainty, results in the absence of such tendencies, and the continual search for further and novel information. With a fourth proposition, we consider the impact of uncertainty and information regulation in the social domain. We specifically propose that the seizing and freezing tendencies triggered by uncertainty, and the aversion toward uncertainty, operate quite similarly in the social domain as they operate in the nonsocial domain. In presenting the four propositions and describing converging research findings, we present an evidence-based, comprehensive framework for understanding the triangular relation of uncertainty, information regulation, and social interaction.

Proposition 1: Uncertainty Has a Profound Impact on Psychological Functioning

The concept of knowledge is critical within the lay epistemic tradition (Kruglanski, 1989). Knowledge functions to disambiguate the environment, and thereby affords decisions and action. Conversely, uncertainty, or the lack of knowledge, hampers action, and effects a kind of mental paralysis. Given the centrality of action to human functioning, the management of uncertainty should, therefore, play a critical role in psychological functioning.

Lay epistemic theory is based on these notions. It assumes that human judgment involves a process of quasi-syllogistic inference whereby the appropriate juxtaposition of a major premise (i.e., an if–then inference rule) with some form of evidence (i.e., a minor premise) leads the individual to consider a particular statement as true. For example, once combined with the belief that "If it is 8 a.m. then it is time to go to work" the information "It is 8 a.m." should induce the conviction that it is time to go to work.

More important, the extent to which the information given will lead to a given inference depends on several factors, such as the strength of association between the antecedent and consequent terms of the major premise, the accessibility of that premise (the if–then rule it embodies), the salience of the relevant pieces of information, the degree of effort required to affirming the minor premise and examine its fit to the major premise (i.e., is it the X in the "if X then Y" premise?), and the cognitive capacity required to cope with the difficulty and motivation to expend the required effort.

Lay epistemic theory places particular emphasis on motivational factors that affect the extent to which information yields judgment. It identifies two types of motivation, both considered as bipolar continua. The first continuum ranges from a need for a specific closure to the need to avoid that closure. For instance, a particularly positive work attitude may motivate an individual to be especially attentive to information that it is time to head for the office. Conversely, fatigue and a lack of sleep may enhance the need to avoid such information.

The second continuum ranges from the need to seek the state of certainty and closure to the need to avoid those states. Any answer, as long as it is definite, may help to alleviate the feelings of uncertainty and ambiguity. The need for nonspecific closure encapsulates this motivational propensity. It is the extent to which an individual is motivated to accept a particular notion as true in order to avoid uncertainty and ambiguity. The need to avoid nonspecific closure thus refers to the extent to which one is motivated to abstain from considering alternative conceptions and from forming a definitive opinion. The motivational tendency fostered by the need for non-specific closure affects the extent to which information is considered in the course of judgment formation. We will elaborate on this notion while considering the subsequent propositions.

Proposition 2: Attitudes of Intolerance and Tolerance toward Uncertainty Vary across Situations as Well as Individuals

There are a variety of reasons for why uncertainty may be considered aversive. The need for (nonspecific) closure (hereby referenced as "the need for closure" [NFC]) may arise in situations in which feelings of uncertainty are considered particularly intolerable. For example, if a quick decision is required, and there is little time to consider alternatives, any type of certainty may be preferred over uncertainty. Similarly, limits inherent to our information-processing system may make exposure to diversity and ambiguity particularly unpleasant and may create the need for simplicity and singularity.

In this vein, a wide variety of situational factors are assumed to influence the NFC. The NFC may be heightened in situations where a decision is required immediately, as, for example, under time pressure (see Kruglanski & Freund, 1983; Chiu, Morris, Hong, & Menon, 2000) or in situations where a judgment is needed, as opposed to those in which the individual is at liberty to abstain from a definite decision. In addition, a variety of conditions that render information processing subjectively difficult, laborious, or otherwise unpleasant may increase the NFC because closure renders further processing unnecessary. Such conditions include environmental noise (Kruglanski, Webster, & Klem, 1993), tedium and dullness of the cognitive task (Webster, 1993a), fatigue or low energy, the arduousness of information processing (Webster, Richter, & Kruglanski, 1996), and alcoholic intoxication, which limits the capacity for systematic thought (Webster, 1993b). The NFC is also heightened when closure is known to be valued by significant others because closure may earn their esteem and appreciation (Mayseless & Kruglanski, 1987).

Conversely, the NFC may be diminished in situations that highlight the costs of closure and the benefits of openness. In some circumstances, the costs of closure may be rendered salient by the fear of invalidity (Kruglanski & Freund, 1983), which stems from concerns about committing a costly judgmental error. Validity and closure are not necessarily at odds, but they may pull information processing in opposite directions. For example, when the NFC is elevated, an individual may consider limited information, relying on preconceived notions or stereotypes, but when the NFC is diminished, one may consider ample evidence before making up one's mind. Such epistemic dynamics prompted by the NFC are not assumed to be consciously accessible to the knower, but rather to exert their effects implicitly and outside of awareness.

Individuals may exhibit stable personal differences in the degree to which they value closure. Some people may form definitive, and perhaps extreme, opinions regardless of the situation, whereas others may resist making decisions even in the safest environments. Webster and Kruglanski (1994) have developed the NFC scale (NFCS), which has since been translated into several languages (e.g., Cantonese, Croatian, Dutch, French, German, Hebrew, Italian, Japanese, Korean, Mandarin, and Spanish), affording a cross-cultural investigation of closed and open mindedness. The results of numerous studies indicate that the NFCS has the same basic meaning and structure cross-nationally, and that the ratings can be meaningfully compared across different countries and cultures.

Proposition 3: Uncertainty Avoidance Entails the Seizing and Freezing on Information

To the extent that situations or individual dispositions give rise to enhanced closure seeking, this motivation will trigger a tendency to quickly seize and rigidly freeze on judgments afforded by early information (Kruglanski & Webster, 1996). Indeed, this has been a central notion in the lay epistemic framework.

Uncertainty is reduced by means of knowledge formation. Knowledge formation processes entail the generation and validation of hypotheses. Greater closure motivation leads to a quicker seizing of a generated hypothesis, and a stronger need for this hypothesis to be assessed as valid. In other words, the NFC accelerates the acceptance of particular knowledge, and strengthens the perseverance of beliefs.

The NFC may manifest itself in two general tendencies during the regulation of information: the urgency tendency and the permanence tendency (Kruglanski & Webster, 1996). The urgency tendency refers to the tendency to quickly consider particular possibilities as certainties (i.e., to quickly come to a closure when considering various options). Individuals experiencing uncertainty as aversive are particularly inclined to exhibit this tendency because quickly reaching closure entails considerable uncertainty reduction. The permanence tendency refers to the desire to hang on to a closure. It entails the tendency to freeze on knowledge that is already established, and to refrain from considering alternatives, even in the presence of information that viable alternatives may exist.

As noted earlier, people often generate multiple hypotheses to account for known facts and choose among those hypotheses on the basis of further relevant evidence. By enhancing seizing and freezing tendencies, the NFC may restrict the generation of alternative hypotheses. Accordingly, Mayseless and Kruglanski (1987) conducted an experiment in which participants were shown photos of parts of mundane objects (e.g., a comb, a toothbrush) taken from unusual angles and were asked to generate hypotheses regarding the actual nature of those objects. Generally, individuals dispositionally high in NFC were observed to generate fewer hypotheses than did their low-NFC counterparts. Apparently, they were quicker to seize and freeze on any of the ideas they generated, hence refraining from more extensive processing. Moreover, as a consequence of a (motivationally based) inability to come up with further hypotheses, participants high in NFC were particularly confident about those hypotheses that they generated.

The foregoing tendencies have also been apparent in work on impression formation. Specifically, individuals high in the NFC seem to seek less information about a target person before forming a judgment. In one study, Webster, Richter, and Kruglanski (1996) asked participants to judge the suitability of various job candidates, using various pieces of information. Participants high in NFC were found to request significantly fewer pages of relevant information prior to forming their impression of the job candidate. Low (vs. high) NFC individuals sought more information about the candidate prior to forming their judgments.

The research affords two hypotheses regarding the role of the NFC in information regulation. It could be that individuals high in NFC simply prefer less information when forming a judgment. Another possibility is that individuals with high, relative to low, NFC are more likely to rely on information that comes early, and quickly form impressions (reaching closure), obviating the need for further information search. Research on primacy effects in impression formation supports the latter possibility.

In the context of impression formation, a primacy effect refers to the tendency to base one's social impressions on early information about that person, to the relative neglect of subsequent, equally relevant information. From the present perspective, primacy effects exemplify the seizing and freezing tendencies. As such, they can be expected to be stronger for individuals high in the NFC. In this vein, Webster and Kruglanski (1994) showed that individuals high on the NFC exhibited particularly pronounced primacy effects. In addition, the magnitude of those effects strengthened as the individual's NFC increased.

The "correspondence bias" (Jones, 1979), or the "fundamental attribution error" (Ross, 1977), refers to the attributor's tendency to overascribe an actor's behavior to her or his unique attitudes or personality and underestimate the effect of context. The correspondence bias can be considered an instance of a primacy effect. That is, prior research has shown that, in making an attribution, people first focus on the actor's attributes, before attending to situational factors that may have instigated a behavior (e.g., Gilbert, Pelham, & Krull, 1988). Thus, to the extent that high-NFC individuals are especially likely to exhibit primacy effects, they are also especially likely to exhibit a correspondence bias. Webster (1993a) asked participants to complete a typical attitude–attribution task, in which they estimated a target's attitude after hearing her deliver a speech criticizing student exchange programs with foreign universities. The speech was allegedly prepared under high- or low-choice conditions. The findings showed that in both the high- and low-choice conditions, participants reported that the student's actual attitude was similar to the perspective taken in the essay. This effect held despite the information in the low-choice condition that the target was denied any choice in writing the essay, and it was magnified for individuals with high versus low NFC.

The use of culturally prevalent stereotypes constitutes another instance of a primacy effect. Cultural stereotypes represent highly accessible knowledge structures that come to mind readily, and hence may be particularly likely to serve as bases for judging stereotyped targets when the perceiver is high (vs. low) in NFC. This possibility was supported in several studies and with several different stereotypic contents. High NFC was shown to induce more stereotypical judgments of Ashkenazi and Sephardic Israelis (Kruglanski & Freund, 1983), stronger stereotyping of women in management (Jamieson & Zanna, 1989), and stereotyping of soccer hooligans as well as nurses (Dijksterhuis, Van Knippenberg, Kruglanski, & Schaper, 1996).

The foregoing effects may be attributed to the tendency among high-NFC individuals to seize on available and accessible knowledge (such as stereotypes) rather than paying attention to case-specific, individuating information. Indeed, Ford and Kruglanski (1995) found that, as compared to low-NFC individuals, high-NFC individuals generally relied more on a previously primed concept when judging an ambiguous target. This finding also suggests, however, that individuals with high NFC are not more sensitive to primacy effects per se, but to available and accessible knowledge in general, at least in the absence of a previously formed opinion. High NFC may thus also exhibit stronger recency effects, but again, only when no prior opinion had been formed. Thus, when the impression formation goal exists from the start, high NFC should predict an enhanced primacy effect, a seizing and freezing on the initial information. However, when the impression formation goal is introduced following exposure to the stimulus materials, participants should rely on their memory of the information, and high (vs. low) NFC should predict a stronger recency effect. Data from pertinent experimental studies confirm these predictions (Richter & Kruglanski, 1999).

Taken together, the research on intrapersonal processes demonstrates that individuals who are high (vs. low) in NFC seek less information, generate fewer hypotheses and rely on early, initial information when making judgments. Ironically, despite the reliance on a lesser amount of information, such individuals tend to display greater confidence in their judgments and decisions.

Proposition 4: The Seizing and Freezing Tendencies Extend to the Social Domain

Knowledge formation is to a great extent a social phenomenon. Social communities and interactions constitute the primary contexts in which beliefs about the world are generated and validated. To the extent that social interactions involve the generation and validation of beliefs, NFC is likely to influence seizing and freezing tendencies in the social domain. The seizing tendency is reflected in the tendency of high-NFC individuals to more readily accept novel perspectives in the absence of *a priori* formed conviction. The freezing tendency is reflected in individuals' tendency to seek out like-minded others and to be more reluctant to accept other perspectives, once a particular opinion or belief has been formed. Hence, the processing of social information is, in essence, quite similar to the processing of nonsocial information. In both domains, the generation and validation of hypotheses play a critical role.

Interpersonal phenomena. Take the ability to engage in perspective taking, which is of considerable importance in social interaction. It often requires substantial cognitive effort because one needs to overlook one's own vantage point and divine the perspective of others. To the extent that the NFC closure reduces the individual's readiness to put effort into mental processing and predisposes the individual to seize and freeze on early information, it may reduce perspective taking and empathetic concerns when individuals high in the NFC interact with dissimilar others. To explore these possibilities, Webster-Nelson, Klein, and Irvin (2003) had participants read descriptions of a person who was either similar or dissimilar to themselves. Under heightened NFC, the ability to take a different perspective was reduced when the target was dissimilar from the participant. Similarly, the ability to show empathy was decreased when the target was dissimilar. No differences in perspective taking and empathy emerged when the target and participant were similar to each other.

Perspective taking also plays an important role in public speaking. Speakers often take the audience's perspective into account and make reference to shared realities and common grounds. However, it has been found that, under time pressure, speakers are less likely to refer in their communicative attempts to the common ground they may share with their interlocutors. As time pressure has been one of the major ways in which NFC has been operationalized (Kruglanski & Freund, 1983; Shah, Kruglanski, & Thompson, 1998), it is likely that a high level of this need may reduce the amount of effort communicators invest in their search for common ground. Statements by high-NFC individuals may hence be excessively biased in the direction of the communicator's own perspective, which might reduce their comprehensibility to the listeners. Accordingly, Richter and Kruglanski (1999) demonstrated that higher NFC is associated with a tendency to be brief and sketchy in describing particular objects, with the consequence that outside observers were less able to relate to the perspective of the participant.

Individuals' conversation style is also affected by the NFC. NFC induces the tendency to seek permanent knowledge and reduce ambiguity. It is, therefore, likely to be associated with a preference for abstraction because abstraction implies unification and consistency across specific instances. Ample research testifies to this assertion (e.g., Boudreau, Baron, & Oliver, 1992; Mikulincer, Yinon, & Kabili, 1991). In this vein, Rubini and Kruglanski (1997) showed that high (vs. low) NFC individuals have a tendency to ask abstract rather than concrete questions in the context of a simulated interview. As a result of this tendency, high-NFC individuals also elicited more abstract answers from respondents. The level of abstraction was, in turn, related to liking, with more abstract (and hence more impersonal) questions eliciting less liking from respondents.

High-NFC individuals prefer abstract labels because they can be applied across a variety of situations, implying permanence. In goal-systemic terms (Kruglanski et al., 2002), abstract expressions are more multifinal, that is, they satisfy multiple goals with one means, and thus should be preferred. Consistent with this idea, a set of recent studies by Chun and Kruglanski (as described in Kruglanski et al., 2002) demonstrated that high-NFC individuals preferred proverbs that espoused the multifinality idea (e.g., "killing two birds with one stone") compared to proverbs that argued the opposite (e.g., "if you run with two hares, you will catch neither").

In summary, individual differences in the NFC have important implications for social interaction. High-NFC (vs. low-NFC) individuals have greater difficulty taking another person's perspective and empathizing with them. While communicating with others, high-NFC individuals are focused on their own perspective, making it more difficult for others to comprehend their communications. Also, high (vs. low) NFC individuals prefer to use abstract labels, which can be applied across various situations, as opposed to concrete, situation-specific descriptions.

Group-level phenomena. Within a group, individuals typically strive toward a homogeneity of opinions (Festinger, 1950). From the NFC perspective, such uniformity is essential for epistemic certainty. Individuals high in NFC should thus show a heightened tendency to seek out consensual validation of beliefs through group membership. Thus, to an individual high in the NFC, a group may provide a source of certainty and the validation of beliefs. In situations of uncertainty, and among individuals who have a particularly high NFC, group membership may be considered a particularly valued asset. Hence, any threat to the epistemic benefits of group membership, for example the existence of opinion deviates, or salient outgroups differ in their views from the ingroup, may fan particularly strong reactions in individuals under high NFC.

In line with this reasoning, studies by De Grada, Kruglanski, Mannetti, and Pierro (1999) show that high-NFC group members tend to feel greater pressure toward opinion uniformity than do low-NFC members. Post hoc coding of group members' discussions in this study further showed that high-NFC individuals actually exert more conformity pressures on their fellow members. Such conformity pressures were also manifest in a study by Webster (1993b). She found that, among participants in discussion groups, participants high in NFC showed a tendency to bring up information that was consensually shared. Individuals can also seek consensus by rejecting members who deviate from the majority opinion (Festinger, 1950). Kruglanski and Webster (1991), for example, showed that in a situation where groups were required to reach consensus on an issue, individuals high (vs. low) in the NFC showed greater rejection of an opinion deviate.

Because the ingroup represents a source of shared reality—of particular value to high-NFC individuals—such persons should exhibit an especially pronounced tendency toward ingroup favoritism. This hypothesis was investigated by Shah et al. (1998). In their study, participants were led to believe that they would be competing in groups of two against another pair of individuals. After reading alleged self-descriptions of their partner and competitor, high-NFC individuals reported greater liking for their own teammate and less liking toward the member of the other team compared to low-NFC individuals.

If high-NFC individuals are particularly motivated to have a stable social reality, they should prefer groups that are homogeneous in their composition, hence more likely to reach consensus about various matters, to heterogeneous groups that are less likely to arrive at consensus. However, this should only be true to the extent that the homogeneous group is in agreement with the individual. Thus, high-NFC individuals should prefer homogeneous groups, especially those similar to the self (i.e., groups with whose views one is likely to agree). Relevant to these issues, Kruglanski and colleagues (2002) found that individuals high in NFC exhibited a greater preference for homogeneous (vs. heterogeneous) groups but only when the homogeneous groups were similar (vs. dissimilar) to the self.

The desire for consensus by high-NFC members may be also reflected in their leadership preferences. Specifically, individuals high in NFC are particularly likely to support leaders who make quick and confident decisions. This preference may culminate in the preference for autocratic leaders. The available data are consistent with these possibilities. Autocratic leadership implies greater centrality of the leaders and less openness for diversity. Indeed, a number of studies have found that groups composed of high-NFC individuals encourage the emergence of autocratic leadership to a greater extent than are groups composed of low-NFC individuals (see De Grada et al., 1999; Pierro, Mannetti, De Grada, Livi, & Kruglanski, 2003).

Group membership may not only provide certainty via contemporaneous consensus, but also by providing a sense of continuity of knowledge across time. In this respect, participants high in NFC are likely to be especially averse to changes that occur within the group. In accordance with these ideas, Livi (2003) found that the norms established at initial stages of group existence were more stable across time and across change in membership for groups whose members were high in the NFC than for ones who were low in the NFC. Furthermore, Kruglanski, Pierro, Higgins, and Capozza (2007) showed in a field study that high-NFC individuals have greater difficulty with organizational change than do low-NFC individuals.

In the same vein, Dechesne, Schultz, Kruglanski, Orehek, and Fishman (2008) found that high-NFC individuals preferred groups with impermeable (vs. permeable) boundaries, but only when the groups in question were perceived as homogeneous in their composition (members being perceived as similar to each other). Thus, if a group represents a foundation for stable social reality, as is the case with a homogeneous group, high-NFC individuals desire the maintenance of that reality, achieved by keeping (potentially dissimilar) others out of the group. In a "real-world" application of this hypothesis, Dechesne et al. (2008) found that high NFC was correlated with endorsement of stricter border policies in the United States.

Preference for sameness and stability is also manifest in the linguistic intergroup bias (LIB). This particular bias reflects the tendency for group members to describe (1) the positive characteristics of the ingroup and the negative characteristics of the outgroup in abstract terms, thereby implying stable traits; (2) the negative characteristics of the ingroup and the positive characteristics of the outgroup in concrete terms, implying the situation-specific nature of such events (Maass & Arcuri, 1992). In this connection, a study by Webster, Kruglanski, and Pattison (1997) found that individuals high (vs. low) in NFC used significantly more abstract (vs. specific) terms when describing positive ingroup and negative outgroup behaviors, thereby exhibiting an enhanced LIB. However, when it comes to negative ingroup characteristics and positive outgroup characteristics, predictions from the NFC and LIB diverge: The NFC drives people toward greater abstraction in this case as well, whereas the LIB implies lesser abstraction. As a consequence, no significant difference in abstraction should distinguish high- versus low-NFC individuals in this case, and none was found.

Taken together, research on group processes and NFC indicates that high-NFC individuals desire consensus and homogeneity among group members. As such, they are willing to engage in processes that achieve and maintain stability, including focusing on the task at hand, pressuring others to change their opinions, rejecting those who hold different opinions, sharing less information with others, and supporting an autocratic leadership style. Moreover, high-NFC individuals are biased toward their own ingroup. They exhibit greater liking for ingroup members and greater LIB. Moreover, high-NFC individuals prefer ingroups that are homogeneous and similar to the self, and once those groups are established, they are supportive of any attempts to maintain the group as is and exclude others (e.g., potential immigrants) from the group.

Conclusion and Implications

Contemporary society is characterized by greater diversity and complexity than ever before. The flow of information conveyed through an ever-increasing number of communication channels, in addition to the increasing pressure to interact with people who are profoundly different from oneself in social, cultural, and religious background, makes it of considerable interest to examine the interplay of cognitive, motivational, and social factors in the regulation of interpersonal information. Uncertainty, and (in)tolerance toward it, can be assumed to play a critical role in this context. It determines whether one is inspired by complexity or turned off, whether one seeks out contact with different-minded others or turns away, and whether one is willing to share and reach out to dissimilar others or deprive them.

Research on the NFC has generated numerous insights that are of considerable pertinence to these issues. The NFC refers to the extent to which one desires quick, simple answers, as opposed to remaining in a state of uncertainty and ambiguity. Greater NFC implies greater stress in dealing with complexity and diversity. Hence, those high in NFC should exhibit strong longing for simpler and more unequivocal times. Indeed, previous research has alluded to a relation between NFC and conservative and traditionalist ideology (Jost, Glaser, Kruglanski, & Sulloway, 2003). However, the conclusions and implications stemming from the research program just reviewed suggest an even richer and more dynamic relationship between uncertainty, information regulation, and social interaction.

We have proposed that knowledge and uncertainty are profoundly relevant for understanding human functioning. Knowledge helps to disambiguate the environment and thereby affords decisions and actions. In this regard, uncertainty hampers progress in action, and the management of uncertainty should, therefore, be given a central place in the analysis of human functioning. Our second proposition holds that the degree to which uncertainty is deemed aversive is assumed to vary across situations and individuals. Urgency to act and limitation in cognitive resources are considered situation-specific initiators of negative attitudes toward uncertainty. Conversely, situations may also promote a need for accuracy or a need to refrain from a definitive opinion, and may thereby make certainty a less desirable state. Moreover, some individuals may simply prefer certainty and base their lives and beliefs on simple structures, whereas others thrive in situations of complexity and ambiguity.

Our third proposition states that the extent to which situations and individuals give rise to enhanced closure seeking is predictive of the extent to which tendencies to quickly seize and rigidly freeze on judgments can be observed. In other words, the NFC accelerates the tendency to accept information as true in the absence of prior beliefs and strengthens the perseverance of beliefs. Fourth, we proposed that such seizing and freezing tendencies can be found in a variety of instances in the context of interpersonal and intergroup interaction. Knowledge formation is to a great extent a social phenomenon. Social communities and interactions constitute the primary contexts in which beliefs about the world are generated and validated. To the extent that social interactions involve the generation and validation of beliefs, NFC is likely to influence seizing and freezing tendencies in the social domain.

In presenting these four propositions, we hope to have provided an evidence-based comprehensive framework for understanding information regulation in social interaction. At its core is the variable of the NFC. It is most appropriately considered a motivational-psychological factor that affects communication and interaction. It is the fit between NFC, task demands, and social context that allows for predictions regarding the smoothness of an interaction or effectiveness of a task group. For instance, high-NFC groups may very well be the most effective in dealing with relatively simple tasks that urgently require completion. At the same time, however, dealing with more complex tasks may benefit from a consideration of multiple options and hence may benefit to a greater extent from individuals low in NFC. Also, when in a hurry, a conversation with someone high in NFC may turn out to be considerably more gratifying than someone with less of that need. But, on a long trip, one may find conversation partners high in NFC to be less-than-optimal travel companions. We hope the framework presented in this chapter will inspire further research that helps to advance insight in the conditions under which uncertainty appraisal, and associated information regulation strategies, impede or facilitate interpersonal and intergroup interaction.

References

Boudreau, L. A., Baron, R., & Oliver, P. V. (1992). Effects of expected communication target expertise and timing of set on trait use in person description. *Personality and Social Psychology Bulletin, 18*, 447–452.

Chiu, C., Morris, M. W., Hong, Y., & Menon, T. (2000). Motivated cultural cognition: The impact of implicit cultural theories on dispositional attribution varies as a function of need for closure. *Journal of Personality and Social Psychology, 78*, 247–259.

Dechesne, M., Schultz, J. M., Kruglanski, A. W., Orehek, E., & Fishman, S. (2008). *A psychology of borders: Need for closure and the allure of group impermeability*. Unpublished manuscript, University of Maryland.

De Grada, E., Kruglanski, A. W., Mannetti, L., & Pierro, A. (1999). Motivated cognition and group interaction: Need for closure affects the contents and processes of collective negotiations. *Journal of Experimental Social Psychology, 35*, 346–365.

Dijksterhuis, A. P., Van Knippenberg, A. D., Kruglanski, A. W., & Schaper, C. (1996). Motivated social cognition: Need for closure effects on memory and judgment. *Journal of Experimental Social Psychology, 32*, 254–270.

Festinger, L. (1950). Informal social communication. *Psychological Review, 57,* 271–282.

Ford, T. E., & Kruglanski, A. W. (1995). Effects of epistemic motivations on the use of accessible constructs in social judgment. *Personality and Social Psychology Bulletin, 21,* 950–962.

Gilbert, D. T., Pelham, B. W., & Krull, D. S. (1988). On cognitive busyness: When person perceivers meet persons perceived. *Journal of Personality and Social Psychology, 54,* 733–740.

Jamieson, D. W., & Zanna, M. P. (1989). Need for structure in attitude formation and expression. In A. R. Pratkanis, S. J. Breckler, & A. G. Greenwald (Eds.), *Attitude structure and function* (pp. 383–406). Hillsdale, NJ: Lawrence Erlbaum.

Jones, E. E. (1979). The rocky road from acts to dispositions. *American Psychologist, 34,* 107–117.

Jost, J. T., Glaser, J., Kruglanski, A. W., & Sulloway, F. J. (2003). Political conservatism as motivated social cognition. *Psychological Bulletin, 129,* 339–375.

Kruglanski, A. W. (1989). *Lay epistemics and human knowledge: Cognitive and motivational bases.* New York: Plenum.

Kruglanski, A., & Freund, T. (1983). The freezing and un-freezing of lay-inferences: Effects on impressional primacy, ethnic stereotyping and numerical anchoring. *Journal of Experimental Social Psychology, 19,* 448–468.

Kruglanski, A. W., Pierro, A., Higgins, E. T., & Capozza, D. (2007). "On the move" or "staying put": Locomotion, need for closure and reactions to organizational change. *Journal of Applied Social Psychology, 37,* 1305–1340.

Kruglanski, A. W., Pierro, A., Mannetti, L., & De Grada, E. (2006). Groups as epistemic providers: Need for closure and the unfolding of group-centrism. *Psychological Review, 113,* 84–100.

Kruglanski, A. W., Shah, J. Y., Fishbach, A., Friedman, R., Chun, W.-Y., & Sleeth-Keppler, D. (2002). A theory of goal systems. In M. P. Zanna (Ed.), *Advances in experimental social psychology* (Vol. 34, pp. 331–376). New York: Academic Press.

Kruglanski, A. W., & Webster, D. M. (1991). Group members' reactions to opinion deviates and conformists at varying degrees of proximity to decision deadline and of environmental noise. *Journal of Personality and Social Psychology, 61,* 212–225.

Kruglanski, A. W., & Webster, D. M. (1996). Motivated closing of the mind: "Seizing" and "freezing." *Psychological Review, 103,* 263–283.

Kruglanski, A. W., Webster, D. M., & Klem, A. (1993). Motivated resistance and openness to persuasion in the presence or absence of prior information. *Journal of Personality and Social Psychology, 65,* 861–876.

Livi, S. (2003). *Il bisogno di chiusura cognitiva e la transmissione delle norme nei piccoli gruppi* [The need for cognitive closure and norm transmission in small groups]. Unpublished doctoral dissertation, University of Rome "La Sapienza," Rome, Italy.

Maass, A., & Arcuri, L. (1992). The role of language in the persistence of stereotypes. In G. Semin & K. Fiedler (Eds.), *Language, interaction and social cognition* (pp. 129–143). Thousand Oaks, CA: Sage.

Mayseless, O., & Kruglanski, A. W. (1987). What makes you so sure? Effects of epistemic motivations on judgmental confidence. *Organizational Behavior and Human Decision Processes, 39,* 162–183.

Mikulincer, M., Yinon, A., & Kabili, D. (1991). Epistemic needs and learned help-lessness. *European Journal of Personality, 5*, 249–258.

Pierro, A., Mannetti, L., De Grada, E., Livi, S., & Kruglanski, A. W. (2003). Autocracy bias in groups under need for closure. *Personality and Social Psychology Bulletin, 29*, 405–417.

Richter, L., & Kruglanski, A. W. (1999). Motivated search for common ground: Need for closure effects on audience design in interpersonal communication. *Personality and Social Psychology Bulletin, 25*, 1101–1114.

Ross, L. (1977). The intuitive psychologist and his shortcomings: Distortions in the attribution process. In L. Berkowitz (Ed.), *Advances in experimental social psychology* (Vol. 10, pp. 173–220). New York: Academic Press.

Rubini, M., & Kruglanski, A. W. (1997). Brief encounters ending in estrangement: Motivated language-use and interpersonal rapport. *Journal of Personality and Social Psychology, 12*, 1047–1060.

Shah, J. Y., Kruglanski, A. W., & Thompson, E. P. (1998). Membership has its (epistemic) rewards: Need for closure effects on ingroup bias. *Journal of Personality and Social Psychology, 75*, 383–393.

Webster, D. M. (1993a). Motivated augmentation and reduction of the overattribution bias. *Journal of Personality and Social Psychology, 65*, 261–271.

Webster, D. M. (1993b). *Groups under the influence: Need for closure effects on information sharing in decision making groups.* Unpublished doctoral dissertation, University of Maryland.

Webster, D. M., & Kruglanski, A. W. (1994). Individual differences in need for cognitive closure. *Journal of Personality and Social Psychology, 67*, 1049–1062.

Webster, D. M., Kruglanski, A. W., & Pattison, D. A. (1997). Motivated language use in intergroup contexts: Need for closure effects on the linguistic intergroup bias. *Journal of Personality and Social Psychology, 72*, 1122–1131.

Webster, D. M., Richter, L., & Kruglanski, A. W. (1996). On leaping to conclusions when feeling tired: Mental fatigue effects on impressional primacy. *Journal of Experimental Social Psychology, 32*, 181–195.

Webster-Nelson, D., Klein, C. T., & Irvin, J. E. (2003). Motivational antecedents of empathy: Inhibiting effects of fatigue. *Basic and Applied Social Psychology, 25*, 37–50.

The Nature of Information Seeking
in Specific Contexts

8   Use of the Risk Perception Attitude (RPA) Framework for Understanding Health Information Seeking

The Role of Anxiety, Risk Perception, and Efficacy Beliefs

Rajiv N. Rimal and Monique Mitchell Turner

Information seeking is an important concept in many areas of communication scholarship. In the uncertainty reduction literature, for example, information seeking is conceptualized as a fundamental process that guides the development of interpersonal encounters (Berger, 1987), including close relationships (Afifi, Dillow, & Morse, 2004). In the organizational communication literature, information seeking is seen as one of the primary behaviors in newcomers' socialization processes (Wanberg & Kammeyer-Mueller, 2000) and in employees' motivations for receiving performance feedback (Ashford & Cummings, 1983; Morrison, 1991). Information seeking is also thought to be one of the primary motivations for individuals' use of the Internet (Murero & Rice, 2006).

In the literature, a number of closely related terms are used to capture the underlying idea pertaining to how individuals engage with information in their environment; some of these terms include *information management* (Afifi & Weiner, 2004), *information behavior* (Pálsdóttir, 2008), *information use* (Wilson, 2000), *willingness to communicate* (McCroskey & Richmond, 1998), and *information scanning* (Niederdeppe et al., 2007). There are, no doubt, subtle but important differences across these terms; for the purpose of this chapter, however, we focus instead on their commonality in a health context—the idea that individuals seek information in order to address a health-related need. We will return to the motivations underlying such decisions later in the chapter, but first we briefly discuss information seeking in a health context.

Information Seeking and Health Issues

Information seeking on the part of patients (Street, 1991) and communication skills training on the part of physicians (for a review, see Cegala & Broz, 2003) are the subjects of an extensive body of work, much of it centering around the role of uncertainty (Afifi & Weiner, 2004; Babrow, Kasch, & Ford, 1998; Brashers, 2001) and the desire to reduce anxiety associated with uncertainty (Afifi et al., 2004). Information seeking is also associated with coping styles; it is positively correlated with problem-focused coping

(Folkman & Lazarus, 1980), which in turn is associated with health benefits, especially among people living with chronic conditions (Kalichman et al., 2006).

Cancer communication researchers are also beginning to pay closer attention to information seeking as an important concept (Johnson, 1997). Among the many unmet psychosocial needs of cancer patients, need for information ranks as one of the most important (Jefford et al., 2005), and not having this need met is associated with anxiety and distress (Fallowfield, Ford, & Lewis, 1995). One study showed that, among women treated with early-stage breast cancer, those who sought information about their illness (rather than focus on their symptoms) experienced greater physical quality-of-life improvements (Ransom, Jacobsen, Schmidt, & Andrykowski, 2005). The need for cancer information is also demonstrated by the widespread use of the National Cancer Institute's Cancer Information System (CIS). Established in 1975 to educate people about various issues related to cancer prevention, treatment, and research, the CIS appears to be meeting the cancer information needs of a broad cross-section of the U.S. population. In 2004, the CIS celebrated its 10 millionth call, and over 4 million inquiries were received by the CIS in 2005 (Niederhuber, 2006).

Data from large-scale public health interventions, including the Stanford Five-City Project (Winkleby, Flora, & Kraemer, 1994) and the Minnesota Heart Health Program (Viswanath & Finnegan, 1996), indicate not only that people's information-seeking motivations can be significantly improved, but also that increases in information-seeking behaviors are positively associated with the durability of intervention effects (Rimal, Flora, & Schooler, 1999).

To the extent that information seeking is an adaptive response, its corollary—that avoiding information is maladaptive—is not necessarily true (Brashers, Goldsmith, & Hsieh, 2002; Brashers et al., 2000). The ways of coping (WOC) model (Folkman & Lazarus, 1980) posits, for example, that emotion-focused coping, which includes information avoidance, is an appropriate strategy when the problem is perceived to be stable and uncontrollable (Ben-Zur, 2004). Brashers et al. (2002) use the term *information management* to capture strategies that people adopt to either seek or avoid information through active means.

Positive and Negative Outcomes

Often, information seeking on the part of patients is viewed as a proactive behavior; it signifies, for example, that they are taking responsibility for their own health. If information seekers become more knowledgeable about their risks and use the information to make effective decisions, healthy outcomes can result. Under this model, medical information seeking should lead to better informed decisions by patients, more tailored treatment decisions, strong relationships between the patient and doctor, and increased patient compliance (Cline & Haynes, 2001).

Information seeking can also have negative outcomes. Miller's (1987) research on monitors and blunters makes this point clear. Monitoring and blunting are described as coping dimensions on which people vary when threatened with an aversive event. In this situation, monitors seek information, whereas blunters distract themselves. Researchers have examined the effect of these personality characteristics on outcomes such as anxiety and stress, finding that those who engage in cognitive avoidance or blunting showed less stress, anxiety, and arousal than those who sought information (Holmes & Houston, 1974).

We also have reasons to be concerned that medical outcomes could sometimes be harmed by information seekers' lack of technical knowledge to process the information they encounter (LaPerriere et al., 1998). When an urgent need for information leads to information that is confusing, deceptive, or difficult to process, the outcome can be anxiety provoking (Cline & Haynes, 2001). This can occur, for example, when newly diagnosed patients, seeking information on the Internet, encounter information that is technical, confusing, or one-sided because of the underlying commercial interest. In fact, concerns about the quality of health information on the Internet led to the *Healthy People 2010* focus on the *quality of Internet health information sources*. In addition, information overload can lead to decreased likelihood of effective decision making on the part of patients (LaPerriere et al., 1998). It is thus critical that we understand what the motivators of information seeking are and what outcomes result from people taking the initiative to seek information on their own.

As such, public health and communication scholars have become increasingly interested in understanding the motivations behind information seeking. For example, Cegala et al. (2008) showed that the diagnosis of a disease is a significant predictor of information seeking: After a prostate cancer diagnosis, patients are far more likely to seek information on the Internet than prior to the diagnosis. Cline and Haynes (2001) reported that people who seek medical information online often do so for the purposes of anonymity, diversity of the information, and convenience of the accessibility of the information. It is also understood that the majority (77%) of consumers seeking health information do so to arm themselves with knowledge they can use for consultation with their doctor (Chi-Lum, 1999). Furthermore, more than 90% of health information seekers want information related to physical illness (Wilkins, 1999).

Given the tremendous appetite and need on the part of patients for health information, many scholars have focused on this topic, trying to understand the underlying motivations for information seeking. Indeed, a number of theories specifically address information-seeking behaviors, some of which include the model of goal-directed behavior (Perugini & Bagozzi, 2001), with a recent modification (Taylor, 2007): the theory of motivated information management (Afifi & Weiner, 2004) and the WOC model (Folkman & Lazarus, 1980). In this chapter, we conceptualize information seeking as a health behavior, and we turn to the rich literature on health behavior change to understand what factors affect individuals' propensity to seek information and how information-seeking behaviors can be modified. Toward that end, we focus on two constructs—risk perception and efficacy beliefs—that have emerged from the literature as important predictors of behavior change and have rich potential as predictors of information-seeking decisions.

Risk Perception and Efficacy Beliefs

Risk perception, individuals' beliefs about their vulnerability to various diseases and risk factors, is a concept of great interest to health communication scholars. An extensive body of work (Weinstein, 1982) shows that individuals are optimistically biased in their perceptions of personal vulnerability: People tend to believe that they are at less risk than the "average person." This finding is noteworthy, of course, because, mathematically at least, everyone cannot have risks less than the average person. Nevertheless, this finding has remained robust across cultures and contexts (Weinstein, 1987). Of particular interest to health communication scholars, the discrepancy between objective and subjective measures of risk can be affected by the manner in which risk information is communicated, or framed (Tversky & Kahneman, 1973).

Risk perception is also a central concept in theories of health behavior change, many of which propose that, when people's beliefs about their personal risk are heightened, they will be motivated to take action to mitigate the threat. This idea is at the heart of the health belief model (Janz & Becker, 1984), protection motivation theory (Rogers, 1975), and the extended parallel process model (Witte, 1992). If perceptions of risk are instrumental in promoting behavior change, as suggested by these theories, then findings from the optimistic bias literature would point to the difficulty involved in promoting behavior change by increasing people's risk perceptions: Such efforts would face enormous challenges because of people's proclivities to minimize their own vulnerabilities. Hence, from a health communication perspective, the challenge is to overcome people's optimistically biased barriers in order to convince people to acknowledge risks they face.

Despite the central role ascribed to risk perception in promoting behavior change, researchers who explicitly test for causal relation between perceived risk and behavioral action have found the evidence to be inconsistent. Whereas some studies do find the hypothesized link (Weinstein, 1983, 1983), others do not (Svenson, Fischhoff, & MacGregor, 1985), and still others show a negative correlation (Svenson et al., 1985).

A number of explanations, both methodological and conceptual, have been proposed to explain the lack of consistent findings in the relationship between risk perception and behavioral action. Weinstein and Nicolich (1993) pointed out that the causal link between the two is often reciprocal. Just as heightened risk perceptions (cause) can promote a behavioral response (effect), engagement in the risk-reducing behaviors (cause) can also reduce people's perceptions of risk (effect). It is logical for people who exercise, refrain from smoking, and eat healthy foods to believe that they have lower levels of risk to various diseases. Longitudinal studies are clearly needed to understand this complex relationship. Most of the studies in the literature, however, are cross-sectional in nature, making it difficult to disentangle the cause from the effect.

Conceptually, there are at least two considerations that deserve closer scrutiny. First, researchers very seldom distinguish among the different classes of behaviors that can result from heightened risk perceptions. Whereas the central concern in disease prevention pertains to specific acts that people do to remain healthy (e.g., exercising, eating healthy foods, getting screened for diseases), more and more health communication scholars are focusing on the role that people's use of health information has on their health and well-being. Relatively little is known, however, about how perceptions of risk affect information-seeking behaviors. We present two explanations: One explanation (a mediator account) is based on appraisal processes that invoke particular emotions, and another explanation (a moderator account) focuses on the role of efficacy in determining how risk information is processed.

The mediator account. Among the many underlying dimensions of risk that have been identified in the literature (see Slovic, 1987; Smith & Ellsworth, 1985) two of particular interest to risk communication researchers are the dimensions of certainty (the degree to which future events seem predictable and comprehensible) and control (the degree to which events seem to be brought about by individual agency vs. situational agency). Two commonly experienced emotions in risk-related situations, anger and fear, for example, are differentiated by these two dimensions: Anger arises from appraisals of negative events as (a) predictable (certainty), and (b) under the control of and brought about by others (other-control), whereas fear arises from perceptions of negative events as (a) unpredictable, and (b) under situational control. Lerner and Keltner (2001) found that these two distinct emotions influenced individuals' risk judgments: Fearful people expressed pessimistic risk estimates and risk-averse choices, whereas angry people expressed optimistic risk estimates and risk-seeking choices.

Nabi's (1999) cognitive function model suggests that emotions affect information-seeking processes (what she and others call motivated processing). Accordingly, people seek information that is congruent with the goals of the emotion they are experiencing. Fearful people seek information that tells them how to control a threat, whereas angry people tend to seek information that tells them how to gain retribution. Similarly, Shiloh, Ben-Sinai, and Keinan (1999) argue that there are two main reasons why people seek information about risk: for its pragmatic value and for emotional reasons. The emotional value in information seeking lies in the belief that certainty can provide rewards; thus, people seek information to attain certainty. Furthermore, uncertainty causes conflict and increases arousal; information seeking can lower that arousal.

The above argument suggests that risks lead people to make cognitive appraisals regarding control and certainty. Such appraisals cause distinct emotions, which in turn lead to unique patterns of information seeking. Parts of this argument have also been tested by Afifi et al. (2004), who studied how uncertainty discrepancy (the gap between the level of certainty possessed and desired by individuals) affects information seeking. They found that anxiety and efficacy are important mediators in the process: a large uncertainty discrepancy results in higher anxiety, which suppresses efficacy (and subsequently information seeking).

The moderator account. A second explanation that links risk assessments with information-seeking behaviors is based on the moderating role of efficacy beliefs. When people believe that they are at risk, they are more willing to act to avert the threat if they also believe that they have the ability to affect the outcome. In other words, individuals are likely to translate high-risk perceptions into behavioral actions if they possess strong efficacy beliefs.

Self-efficacy is one of the most consistent predictors of behavior change across numerous health domains, and social cognitive theory (Bandura, 1986) conceptualizes it as the primary motivator of action. Self-efficacy—defined as people's confidence in their ability to exert personal control over specific behaviors—affects behaviors both directly and indirectly through outcome expectations, goal setting, and construal processes (Bandura, 2004). Outcome expectations, which refer to people's beliefs that engaging in specific behaviors will produce desired benefits, tend to be more positive among those with heightened efficacy beliefs than among those with weaker ones (Bandura, 1986). Persons with positive efficacy beliefs also set more challenging goals for themselves and construe impediments to change as barriers to be overcome through effort and perseverance, not impenetrable barricades. Efficacy beliefs also influence meaning that people derive from their behavioral outcomes. Whereas those with strong efficacy perceptions construe failures as consequences of inadequate effort, those with weak efficacy perceptions tend to view failures as further evidence of their own inability. Given its central role in behavior change, self-efficacy is envisioned as a critical construct in a number of theories, including the health belief model (Janz & Becker, 1984), transactional model of stress and coping (Lazarus & Cohen, 1977), protection motivation theory (Rogers, 1975), and the extended parallel process model (Witte, 1992).

The combined role of risk perception and efficacy beliefs in information seeking is addressed by the risk perception attitude (RPA) framework (Rimal & Real, 2003), a topic we turn to next.

The Risk Perception Attitude Framework

The RPA framework is based on the premise that motivations to engage in a health behavior are guided by the joint influence of risk perceptions and efficacy beliefs. People will take action to avert a threat if they believe that

Table 8.1 The Four Groups in the Risk Perception Attitude (RPA) Framework

Risk perceptions	Efficacy beliefs	
	Strong	Weak
High	Responsive	Avoidance
Low	Proactive	Indifference

they are at risk and that there is something they can do to avert the threat. This is also the central idea behind the extended parallel process model (EPPM; Witte, 1992). On the basis of people's risk perceptions and efficacy beliefs, the RPA framework formulates four attitudinal groups, which are then used to predict health information-seeking and other behaviors. The four groups are shown in Table 8.1.

Those with high-risk perceptions and strong efficacy beliefs are classified into the *responsive* group; this group is thought to be both highly motivated (because of high-risk perceptions) and able (because of efficacy beliefs) to translate motivations into action. In the elaboration-likelihood model (Petty & Cacioppo, 1986), individuals who have both the motivation and the ability to process information are thought to process information through the "central route." Members of the responsive group can be conceptualized in this way as well, and the prediction would be that the responsive group engages in high levels of information seeking. Furthermore, if members of the responsive group process information through the central route, they are also expected to retain much of the information they encounter.

In the RPA framework, individuals with high-risk perceptions and weak efficacy beliefs are described as the *avoidance* group. Members of the avoidance group believe that they are vulnerable to a disease or risk factor and simultaneously feel incapable of addressing the threat. This combination of heightened risk perceptions and dampened efficacy beliefs are thought to lead to defensive behaviors, including the active avoidance of information that can make their risk status more salient. In the EPPM, this is characterized as a fear-control response: When people's perceptions of threat outweigh their levels of personal efficacy, they attempt to manage their emotional response to the threat, not the source of the threat itself. Hence, both the RPA framework and the EPPM predict lower levels of information seeking and higher levels of information avoidance among this group.

The *indifference* group comprises individuals with low-risk perceptions and weak efficacy beliefs. Members of this group are thought to be least motivated to act. Because of the low-risk perceptions, their motivations to enact healthy behaviors are thought to be low, and weak efficacy beliefs are thought to further diminish the likelihood of behavior change. According to the EPPM, perceptions of threat are critical in promoting behavior change; hence, individuals who do not perceive they are at risk are likely to be unmotivated to act. Among members of the indifference group, the low motivations are further reinforced by weak efficacy beliefs.

Finally, members of the *proactive* group—those with low-risk perceptions and strong efficacy beliefs—are able to take action because of their strong efficacy beliefs. Because they perceive that they are able to take the requisite action to protect themselves against diseases, they are likely to experience little, if any, anxiety about their health status; after all, believing in one's ability to bring about change is highly comforting. From a health behavior-change perspective, the proactive group's lack of personal vulnerability (especially if actual levels of risk to a disease are high) presents challenges in motivating this group to act. Because of low levels of perceived risk, this group is not motivated to take action. This feeling of invulnerability, combined with high perceptions of efficacy, can lull individuals to inaction.

Correspondence with the Extended Parallel Process Model

Although the formulation of the four RPA framework groups is derived from the EPPM, there are two noteworthy differences between the two. First, the primary motivation of change in the EPPM is *perceived threat*, whereas the corresponding factor in the RPA framework is *perceived risk*. Perceived threat is generally conceptualized as a property of the message; it speaks to the level of danger that an action, disease, or risk factor implies. Perceived risk, on the other hand, is generally conceptualized as a property of individuals; it signifies the extent to which people believe that they are likely to acquire a disease or be subjected to an adverse event. The two constructs, perceived threat and perceived risk, are isomorphic to the extent that the threat in a message has a one-to-one correspondence with perceptions of risk that it engenders.

Often, high-threat messages do induce heightened perceptions of risk, but this relationship is considerably diminished if people believe that the threat does not apply to them. As an example, consider the use of a high fear-provoking message—one that shows pictures of dirty lungs—that highlights the effects of smoking. This high-threat message is likely to induce high perceptions of risk to the extent that people believe the message applies to them. If they believe that it does not apply to them (either because they are nonsmokers or because they are optimistically biased), the high-threat message will not translate into high risk.

The second difference between the EPPM and the RPA framework is the distinction between the indifference and the proactive groups. According to the EPPM, when perceptions of threat are low, efficacy beliefs will not exercise a differential impact on individuals' behaviors. The EPPM posits that a certain, "threshold" level of threat is required before individuals take preventive action; it is only after this threshold is reached that efficacy beliefs will determine the nature of the behavioral response. By contrast, the RPA framework predicts that, even when risk perceptions are low, efficacy beliefs have a bearing on individuals' actions. Thus, according to the RPA framework, the proactive group (low-risk perceptions and strong efficacy beliefs) is expected to engage in healthier behaviors than the indifference group (low-risk perceptions and weak efficacy beliefs).

Based on this description of the four RPA framework groups, we can summarize the overall theoretical predictions in this way: The responsive group and the indifference group constitute the ends of the behavior-change continuum, from the highest to the lowest level of change, respectively; the avoidance and the proactive group are hypothesized to occupy intermediate positions in terms of their likelihood of taking self-protective action. Predictions derived from the RPA framework have met with mixed success. We next review some of that literature and suggest future studies that can test specific propositions.

Empirical Evidence from the Literature

Rimal (2001) analyzed the effects of the RPA framework classification in a longitudinal data-set. The classification of individuals into one of the four groups was able to predict their use of health information and their information-seeking behaviors 2 and 6 years later. Furthermore, it was shown that the heightened levels of use of health information were significantly associated with gains in health knowledge. The baseline categorization of people into one of the four RPA framework groups accounted for 12% of the variance in knowledge 2 years later ($p < .001$) and 11% of the variance in knowledge 6 years later ($p < .001$; Rimal, 2001). This led to the conclusion that the RPA framework could be used to classify individuals into meaningful information-seeking groups and the ensuing information-seeking behaviors resulted in corresponding increases in health knowledge.

Subsequently, a number of studies, using both experimental (study 1 in Rimal & Real, 2003; Turner, Rimal, Morrison, & Kim, 2006) and correlational designs (study 2 in Rimal & Real, 2003; Rimal, Böse, Brown, Mkandawire, & Folda, in press; Rimal & Juon, in press), have shown that risk perceptions and efficacy beliefs jointly affect health outcomes. When experiment participants' risk and efficacy perceptions have been manipulated, however, members of the avoidance group typically display greater motivation and information-seeking intentions, in comparison to the control group. Rimal and Real (2003) use the term *affective interference* to explain this finding; it refers to the attenuation in information processing and information retention that typically accompanies anxiety-induced information seeking. In other words, anxiety promotes higher levels of information seeking, but it also reduces the ability to remember the information that one encounters. Based on findings reviewed in this chapter, a number of implications emerge for both health interventions and future studies, two topics we turn to next.

Intervention Implications

Communication scholars are interested not only in understanding information-seeking behaviors, but also in being able to develop messages that motivate such behaviors. Findings from the RPA framework in this effort would lead to recommendations that we develop messages that bolster people's risk perceptions and efficacy to move them toward the responsive group.

Prior studies have shown that the responsive group—with high-risk perceptions and strong efficacy beliefs—consistently displays the most positive levels of self-protective motivations and behaviors. This group's perceptions of personal vulnerability motivate and strong efficacy beliefs facilitate behavioral action. By contrast, the indifference group's low perceptions of risk and weak efficacy beliefs both act to deter self-protective action.

It is standard practice for health campaigns to spend considerable resources conducting formative evaluation before designing and implementing the intervention. Findings summarized in this chapter imply that two variables on which to focus the formative evaluation are *risk perceptions* and *efficacy beliefs*. The extent to which members of the target audience perceive that they are at risk to a disease and the extent to which they feel efficacious in enacting effective behaviors are two variables that need to be measured in order to understand what the focus of the intervention needs to be. If both variables are high, intervention messages may need to focus on means through which these beliefs can be reinforced. If these variables are found to be lacking, then interventions may need to develop strategies for enhancing them.

Earlier, we noted findings from the optimistic bias literature that highlight the challenges inherent in enhancing people's risk perceptions. People have a tendency to minimize threats that they are likely to encounter, and hence messages that highlight potential threats are likely to be dismissed as pertaining only to others. One way around this issue may be to use role models perceived as highly similar by the target audience. There is evidence to indicate, for example, that the more similar the referent, the more we gauge their attitudes and behaviors relative to our own (Menon, Bickart, Sudman, & Blair, 1995), with the result that optimistic bias is almost completely eliminated when we gauge our risks relative to a referent similar to ourselves (Menon, Block, & Ramanathan, 2002; Rimal & Morrison, 2006). This implies that, in order to increase perceptions of risk among the target audience, interventions should consider using role models similar to the target audience.

The RPA framework indicates that efficacy beliefs are key in improving behavioral action. This is also the central proposition of Bandura's (1977, 1986) social cognitive theory (SCT). Given the central role of efficacy beliefs in health behavior change, interventions need to consider ways of enhancing these beliefs among their target audience. According to SCT, efficacy beliefs can be enhanced through four different mechanisms: verbal persuasion (by convincing others that making the requisite behavior change is within their control), affective arousal (focusing on positive feelings that come with mastery experiences), vicarious reinforcement (modeling others who are successful), and performance accomplishment (using prior behaviors to reinforce subsequent efficacy). Depending on the nature of the campaign, some of these four mechanisms may be more suitable than others, but focusing on them to enhance efficacy beliefs is key.

Implications for Research

The RPA framework-based studies reviewed in this chapter reveal that studying the relationship between risk perceptions and efficacy beliefs can greatly enhance our understanding about information seeking. We next outline some avenues for future research that can use this framework to make more precise predictions about individuals' information-seeking behaviors. In particular, we urge future scholars to focus on predicting the types of information people seek, predicting the scope of information sought and understanding the behavioral attributes that underlie the domain of information.

Nature of Information Being Sought

In laboratory settings when risk perceptions and efficacy beliefs are manipulated, Turner et al. (2006) have found that the avoidance group engages in greater information seeking because of the need to reduce anxiety. This implies that, to lessen the anxiety, individuals are likely to be selective in the information they seek—avoiding information that makes their risk status more salient and seeking information that reduces their anxiety. This further implies that, in making predictions about information seeking, we need to make distinctions between the different kinds of information being sought by individuals. Thus, the practice of seeking information about a disease, its risk factors, and symptoms may be rather different than that of seeking information about how to manage one's emotions, where to seek help, and so on. We can characterize the former as an *instrumentally* focused and the latter as an *emotionally* focused form of information seeking. It is likely that the determinants of these two forms of information seeking are somewhat different, and future research could explore how they differ. For example, one could hypothesize that an instrumentally focused motivation is concerned primarily with prevention and hence the perception of risk may be a greater motivation than beliefs about personal efficacy. On the other hand, emotionally focused motivations are likely to be invoked when the risk factor is already present and anxiety levels are high. If so, it is likely that efficacy beliefs (particularly around coping skills) are likely to predominate. Though speculative, this line of reasoning leads to testable hypotheses.

The scope of information. Human beings tend to be cognitive misers; they tend to seek information only to the extent that they believe that their repertoire of information is insufficient for the task at hand. Even if individuals perceive that they are at high risk, their information seeking may still be curtailed if they believe that they already possess the requisite information. In other words, not all high-risk outcomes are governed by information deficiency. For example, for most smokers, their knowledge about the link between smoking and lung cancer is likely to be quite high, and so information seeking would not necessarily be the logical outcome of their high-risk perceptions. We thus need to pursue research questions that seek to understand the conditions under which individuals' high-risk perceptions are likely to result in greater information seeking and those under which high-risk perceptions result in other outcomes. An important moderator in this relationship is likely to be prior knowledge about the topic, or more precisely, individuals' *perceptions* about their knowledge. If people believe that they already possess the requisite knowledge about a disease or risk factor, then there is no reason to seek further information. In that case, actions to avert the threat may result directly from enhanced perceptions of risk. If, however, prior knowledge about the topic is low, then uncertainty about the proper course of action is likely to be high, and hence high-risk perceptions are likely to be strong motivators of action. Under these conditions, risk perception's influence on information-seeking behaviors will likely be moderated by efficacy beliefs, as predicted by the RPA framework.

Understanding behavioral attributes. The precision with which social science theories are able to predict health behavior is likely due not only to the vagaries and complexity of behaviors themselves, but also to the inadequacies of the prevailing theories. Theories of health behavior focus on characteristics of the actors or the contexts in which behaviors are enacted. The theory of reasoned action (Ajzen & Fishbein, 1980), for example, highlights the role of perceptions about norms and attitudinal assessments in predicting behavioral intentions. SCT (Bandura, 1986) proposes that human behavior influences and is influenced by perceptions of efficacy and the social environment in which the behaviors are enacted. Predictions made by other prominent health behavior theories are also limited to characteristics of individuals and the social context in which behaviors are enacted. Neglected in these theories is the role played by behavioral attributes that underlie the behavior that is being studied or targeted for change.

Behavioral attributes refer to the constituent characteristics that define a behavioral domain. Any behavioral domain can be decomposed into theoretically meaningful attributes (Lapinski, Rimal, DeVries, & Lee, 2007). For example, some of the attributes that constitute the behavioral domain of HIV testing may include its confidential nature, stigma associated with the outcome, its capacity to produce anxiety, and so on. A focus on behavioral attributes allows researchers to choose an appropriate theory for modifying the behavior on the premise that some theories are more appropriate for certain behavioral attributes, and less so for others.

In the context of this chapter, one consequence of a focus on behavioral attributes is that we begin to raise questions about characteristics (i.e., attributes) of diseases that make them more (or less) amenable to information seeking. For example, a novel disease, one about which very little information exists or one that is newly emerging (e.g., avian flu), may engender a greater amount of information seeking on the part of individuals who perceive to be at high risk. By contrast, diseases whose preventive methods are perceived to be fairly well understood (e.g., heart disease) may not engender the same level of need for information.

Focus on other emotions. Future RPA framework studies might include emotions other than anxiety that are salient to individuals in a given context. Some of the studies reviewed in this chapter (Turner et al., 2006) found that anxiety was a mediator in the relationship between perceived risk and information seeking: high-risk individuals become anxious and then turned to information seeking for reducing their anxiety. There may, however, be other emotions that might serve as key determinants of information seeking. For example, certain health threats might cause increased feelings of anger, especially if patients perceive a lack of control over getting sick: if they perceive, for example, that large corporations were responsible for environmental contaminants that made them sick. Anger in these conditions might lead to activist-type actions (Turner, 2007), where respondents seek more information (regardless of efficacy levels), process that information carefully, assess the information for blame and revenge goals, and engage in activist behaviors.

Consistency of available information. There may be additional mediators and moderators to be included in deriving predictions from the RPA framework. For example, future models may include consistency of the information being sought. If consumers of health information seek greater knowledge but encounter inconsistent findings, then, regardless of their information-processing depths or styles, their knowledge will likely be compromised. However, the consistency of information available for public consumption is not a topic that has received a great deal of attention in the health communication literature. Vardeman and Aldoory's (2008) research found, for example, that women of childbearing age perceived that information regarding fish consumption was inconsistent. Data from their qualitative interviews suggest that these inconsistencies led to feelings of anger, perceptions that they did not know what behaviors to engage in, and frustration with the medical community. After encountering inconsistent information in this fashion, people may give up seeking information, even though the initial search may have been guided by risk perceptions and efficacy beliefs. In other words, people's engagement with risk information is likely a dynamic and iterative process, one in which they make initial assessments, take appropriate action, evaluate the ensuing (though tentative) outcome, and modify further actions accordingly. If the initial outcomes are favorable, they will likely pursue further; if the initial outcome is unfavorable, unpredictable, or inconsistent, they will likely abandon the effort. The point here is that we need to conceptualize information-seeking behaviors (and their determinants) as iterative processes that individuals modify according to whether they perceive that their particular needs are being met.

Conclusion

Information seeking is a topic that is becoming increasingly important in the health communication literature, not only because of the ever-increasing pool of readily available information obtainable through the Internet (Fox, Anderson, & Rainie, 2005), but also because information consumption, in and of itself, is a worthy outcome of health promotion campaigns (Rimal et al., 1999). Information seeking can serve as a form of adaptation to anxiety-provoking situations (Folkman & Lazarus, 1980), especially if the efficacy surrounding the utility and ease of acquiring information are perceived to be high (Witte, 1992). Information avoidance can also serve as a productive response to a stressful situation, especially if the decision to avoid information is deliberate (Brashers et al., 2000, 2002).

The RPA framework (Rimal & Real, 2003) classifies people into one of four groups (responsive, avoidance, indifference, and proactive) on the basis of their risk perceptions and efficacy beliefs. Individuals with a responsive attitude tend to seek information the most, those with an indifference attitude the least, and the other two seek information at intermediate levels. The RPA framework-based research (Turner et al., 2006) finds that people's anxiety is heightened when they receive high-risk and low-efficacy information (as may be the case, for example, when patients receive a deadly diagnosis). This anxiety can promote information seeking, but information processing and retention are hampered because of the affective interference. Under conditions of high anxiety, people may also seek information without the cognitive capacity to process it. This can have counterproductive effects, particularly if the information is inaccurate, misleading, or biased, as it can further exacerbate anxiety (Cline & Haynes, 2001).

One upshot of this finding, therefore, is that scholars must seek to understand what kinds of messages motivate information seeking without heightening anxiety. Although it is generally accepted that messages must contain efficacy-enhancing information, there is a dearth of studies explaining how to develop health-risk messages that create feelings of efficacy. Health communication scholars might turn their attention to warmth appeals, positively framed messages, positive narrative appeals, and even anger appeals (Turner, 2007) to see if and how they might promote efficacy. Moreover, these studies must pay attention to the cognitive capacities of the receivers after consuming the message.

Finally, we note the need for researchers to begin raising questions about the role that certain behavioral attributes may play in determining information seeking under conditions of heightened risk and enhanced efficacy. For certain behaviors (e.g., those characterized by their habitual nature or lack of uncertainty), there may not be any need for further information seeking;

in this case, health campaigns may simply promote the preferred behavioral change. For other behaviors (those characterized by uncertainty and novelty, for example) the meaningful behavior in question may be to seek further information. Hence, theoretical approaches that make these sorts of distinctions are likely to enhance their precision and predictive ability.

References

Afifi, W. A., Dillow, M. R., & Morse, C. (2004). Examining predictors and consequences of information seeking in close relationships. *Personal Relationships, 11,* 429–449.

Afifi, W. A., & Weiner, J. L. (2004). Toward a theory of motivated information management. *Communication Theory, 14,* 167–190.

Ajzen, I., & Fishbein, M. (1980). *Understanding attitudes and predicting social behavior.* Englewood Cliffs, NJ: Prentice Hall.

Ashford, S. J., & Cummings, L. L. (1983). Feedback as an individual resource: Personal strategies for creating information. *Organizational Behavior and Human Performance, 32,* 370–398.

Babrow, A. S., Kasch, C. R., & Ford, L. A. (1998). The many meanings of uncertainty in illness: Toward a systematic accounting. *Health Communication, 10,* 1–23.

Bandura, A. (1977). *Social learning theory.* Englewood Cliffs, NJ: Prentice-Hall.

Bandura, A. (1986). *Social foundations of thought and action.* Englewood Cliffs, NJ: Prentice-Hall.

Bandura, A. (2004). Health promotion by social cognitive means. *Health Education and Behavior, 31,* 143–164.

Ben-Zur, H. (2004). Monitoring/blunting and social support: Associations with coping and affect. *International Journal of Stress Management, 9,* 357–373.

Berger, C. R. (1987). Communicating under uncertainty. In M. E. Roloff & G. R. Miller (Eds.), *Interpersonal processes: New direction in communication research* (pp. 39–62). Beverly Hills, CA: Sage.

Beisecker, A. E., & Beisecker, T. D. (1990). Patient information-seeking behaviors when communicating with doctors. *Medical Care, 28,* 19–28.

Brashers, D. E. (2001). Communication and uncertainty management. *Journal of Communication, 51,* 477–497.

Brashers, D. E., Goldsmith, D. J., & Hsieh, E. (2002). Information seeking and avoiding in health contexts. *Human Communication Research, 28,* 258–271.

Brashers, D. E., Neidig, J. L., Haas, S. M., Dobbs, L. K., Cardillo, L. W., & Russell, J. A. (2000). Communication in the management of uncertainty: The case of persons living with HIV or AIDS. *Communication Monographs, 67,* 63–84.

Brucks, M. (1985). The effects of product class knowledge on information search behavior. *Journal of Consumer Research, 12,* 1–16.

Cegala, D. J., Bahnson, R. R., Clinton, S. K., David, P., Gong, M. C., Monk, J. P., Nag, S., & Pohar, K. S. (2008). Information seeking and satisfaction with physician–patient communication among prostate cancer survivors. *Health Communication, 23,* 62–69.

Cegala, D. J., & Broz, S. L. (2003). Provider and patient communication skills training. In T. L. Thompson, A. M. Dorsey, K. I. Miller, & R. Parrott (Eds.), *Handbook of health communication* (pp. 95–119). Mahwah, NJ: Erlbaum.

Chaffee, S. H., & McLeod, J. M. (1973). Individual vs. social predictors of information-seeking. *Journalism Quarterly, 50,* 237–245.

Chaffee, S. H., & Roser, C. (1986). Involvement and the consistency of knowledge, attitudes, and behaviors. *Communication Research, 13,* 373–399.

Chi-Lum, B. (1999). Friend or foe? Consumers using the Internet for medical information. *Journal of Medical Practice Management, 14,* 196–198.

Cline, R. J. W., & Haynes, K. M. (2001). Consumer health information seeking on the Internet: The state of the art. *Health Education Research, 16,* 671–692.

Czaja, R., Manfredi, C., & Price, J. (2003). The determinants and consequences of information seeking among cancer patients. *Journal of Health Communication, 8,* 529–562.

Donohew, L., & Tipton, L. (1973). A conceptual model of information seeking, avoiding and processing. In P. Clarke (Ed.), *New Models for Mass Communication Research* (pp. 243–268). Beverly Hills, CA: Sage.

Dutta-Bergman, M. J. (2004). Primary sources of health information: Comparisons in the domain of health attitudes, health cognitions, and health behaviors. *Health Communication, 16,* 273–288.

Eysenbach, G., & Diepgen, T. (1998). Responses to unsolicited patient e-mail requests for medical advice on the World Wide Web. *Journal of the American Medical Association, 280,* 1333–1346.

Fallowfield, L., Ford, S., & Lewis, S. (1995). No news is not good news. *Psychoncology, 4,* 197–202.

Farquhar, J. W., Fortmann, S. P., Flora, J. A., Taylor, B., Haskell, W. L., Williams, P. T., Maccobby, N., & Wood, P. D. (1990). Effects of community-wide education on cardiovascular disease risk factors: The Stanford Five-City Project. *Journal of the American Medical Association, 264,* 359–365.

Folkman, S., & Lazarus, R. S. (1980). An analysis of coping in a middle-aged community sample. *Journal of Health and Social Behavior, 21,* 219–239.

Fox, S., Anderson, J. Q., & Rainie, L. (2005, January 9). The future of the Internet. Retrieved July 1, 2008, from http://www.pewinternet.org/pdfs/PIP_Future_of_Internet.pdf

Holmes, D. S., & Houston, B. K. (1974). Effectiveness of situation redefinition and affective isolation in coping with stress. *Journal of Personality and Social Psychology, 1,* 290–302.

Jadad, A. R., & Gagliari, A. (1998). Rating health information on the Internet: Navigating to knowledge or to Babel? *Journal of the American Medical Association, 279,* 611–614.

Janz, N. K., & Becker, M. H. (1984). The health belief model: A decade later. *Health Education Quarterly, 11,* 1–47.

Jefford, M., Black, C., Grogan, S., Yeoman, G., White, V., & Akkerman, D. (2005). Information and support needs of callers to the Cancer Helpline. *European Journal of Cancer Care, 14,* 113–123.

Johnson, J. D. (1997). *Cancer-related information seeking.* Cresskill, NJ: Hampton Press.

Johnson, J. D. (2003). On contexts of information seeking. *Information Processing and Management, 39,* 735–760.

Johnson, J. D., Meischke, H., Grau, J., & Johnson, S. H. (1992). Cancer-related channel selection. *Health Communication, 4,* 183–196.

Kalichman, S. C., Cherry, C., Cain, D., Weinhardt, L. S., Benotsch, E., Pope, H., & Kalichman, M. (2006). Health information on the Internet and people living with HIV/AIDS: Information evaluation and coping styles. *Health Psychology, 25,* 205–210.

Knaus, C. S., Pinkelton, B. E., & Austin, E. W. (2000). The ability of the AIDS quilt to motivate information seeking, personal discussion, and preventative behavior as a health communication intervention. *Health Communication, 12*, 301–316.

LaPerriere, B., Edwards, P., Romeder, J. M., & Maxwell-Young, L. (1998). Using the Internet to support self-care. *Canadian Nurse, 94*, 47–48.

Lapinski, M., Rimal, R. N., DeVries, R., & Lee, E. L. (2007). The role of group orientation and descriptive norms on water conservation attitudes and behaviors. *Health Communication, 22*, 133–142.

Lazarus, R. S., & Cohen, J. B. (1977). Environmental stress. In I. Altman and J. F. Wohlwill (Eds.), *Human Behavior and Environment* (Vol. 2, pp. 89–127). New York: Penum.

Lerner, J. S., & Keltner, D. (2000). Beyond valence: Toward a model of emotion-specific influences on judgement and choice. *Cognition and Emotion, 14*, 473–493.

Lerner, J. S., & Keltner, D. (2001). Fear, anger, and risk. *Journal of Personality and Social Psychology, 81*, 146–159.

McCroskey, J. C., & Richmond, V. P. (1998). Willingness to communicate. In J. C. McCroskey, J. A. Daly, M. M. Martin, & M. J. Beatty (Eds.), *Communication and personality: Trait perspectives* (pp. 118–131). Cresskill, NJ: Hampton Press.

Menon, G., Bickart, B., Sudman, S., & Blair, J. (1995). How well do you know your partner? Strategies for formulating proxy-reports and their effects on convergence to self-reports. *Journal of Marketing Research, 32*, 75–84.

Menon, G., Block, L. G., & Ramanathan, S. (2002). We're at as much risk as we are led to believe: Effects of message cues on judgments of health risk. *Journal of Consumer Research, 28*, 533–549.

Miller, S. M. (1987). Monitoring and blunting: Validation of a questionnaire to assess styles of information processing under threat. *Journal of Personality and Social Psychology*, 52, 345–353.

Mills, M., & Sullivan, K. (1999). The importance of information giving for patients newly diagnosed with cancer: A review of the literature. *Journal of Clinical Nursing, 8*, 631–641.

Morrison, E. W. (1991). Impression management in the feedback-seeking process: A literature review and research agenda. *Academy of Management Review, 15*, 522–541.

Morrison, E. W. (1993). Longitudinal study of the effects of information seeking on newcomer socialization. *Journal of Applied Psychology, 78*, 173–183.

Murero, M., & Rice, R. E. (Eds.). (2006). *The Internet and health care: Theory, research and practice*. Mahwah, NJ: Lawrence Erlbaum Associates.

Nabi, R. L. (1999). A cognitive functional model for the effects of discrete negative emotions on information processing, attitude change and recall. *Communication Theory, 9*, 292–320.

Niederdeppe, J., Hornik, R. C., Kelly, B. J., Frosch, D. L., Romantan, A., Stevens, R. S., Barg, F. K., Weiner, J. L., & Schwartz, J. S. (2007). Examining the dimensions of cancer-related information seeking and scanning behavior. *Health Communication, 22*, 153–167.

Niederhuber, J. D. (2006). NCI's CIS celebrates 30 years. *NCI Cancer Bulletin*. Retrieved June 9, 2006, from http://www.cancer.gov/ncicancerbulletin/NCI_Cancer_Bulletin_032806

Pálsdóttir, A. (2008). Information behaviour, health self-efficacy beliefs and health behaviour in Icelanders' everyday life. *Information Research, 13*, 1–23.

Perugini, M., & Bagozzi, R. P. (2001). The role of desires and anticipated emotions in goal-directed behaviours: Broadening and deepening the theory of planned behaviors. *British Journal of Social Psychology, 40*, 79–98.

Petty, R. E., & Cacioppo, J. T. (1986). *Communication and persuasion: Central and peripheral routes to attitude change.* New York: Springer.

Ransom, S., Jacobsen, P. B., Schmidt, J. E., & Andrykowski, M. A. (2005). Relationship of problem-focused coping strategies to changes in quality of life following treatment for early stage breast cancer. *Journal of Pain and Symptom Management, 30*, 243–253.

Rees, C., & Bath, P. (2001). Information-seeking behaviors of women with breast cancer. *Oncology Nursing Forum, 28*, 691–698.

Rimal, R. N. (2001). Perceived risk and self-efficacy as motivators: Understanding individuals' long-term use of health information. *Journal of Communication, 51*, 633–654.

Rimal, R. N., & Morrison, D. (2006). A uniqueness to personal threat (UPT) hypothesis: How similarity affects perceptions of susceptibility and severity in risk assessment. *Health Communication, 20*, 209–219.

Rimal, R. N., Böse, K., Brown, J., Mkandawire, G., & Folda, L. (in press). Extending the purview of the risk perception attitude (RPA) framework: Findings from HIV/AIDS prevention research in Malawi. *Health Communication.*

Rimal, R. N., Flora, J. A., & Schooler, C. (1999). Achieving improvements in overall health orientation: Effects of campaign exposure, information seeking, and health media use. *Communication Research, 26*, 322–348.

Rimal, R. N., & Juon, H. S. (in press). Use of the risk perception attitude (RPA) framework to understand attention paid to breast cancer information and prevention behaviors among immigrant Indian women. *Journal of Applied Social Psychology.*

Rimal, R. N., & Real, K. (2003). Perceived risk and efficacy beliefs as motivators of change: Use of the risk perception attitude (RPA) framework to understand health behaviors. *Human Communication Research, 29*, 370–399.

Rogers, R. W. (1975). A protection motivation theory of fear appeals and attitude change. *Journal of Psychology, 91*, 93–114.

Shiloh, S., Ben-Sinai, R., & Keinan, G. (1999). Effects of controllability, predictability, and information-seeking style on interest in predictive genetic testing. *Personality and Social Psychology Bulletin, 25*, 1187–1195.

Silberg, W. M., Lundberg, G. D., & Musaccio, R. A. (1997). Assessing, controlling, and assuring the quality of medical information on the Internet: Caveat lector et viewor—let the reader and viewer beware. *Journal of the American Medical Association, 277*, 1244–1245.

Slovic, P. (1987). Perception of risk. *Science, 236*, 280–285.

Smith, C. A., & Ellsworth, P. C. (1985). Patterns of cognitive appraisal in emotion. *Journal of Personality and Social Psychology, 48*, 813–838.

Street, R. L., Jr. (1991). Information-giving in medical consultations: The influence of parents' communicative styles and personal characteristics. *Social Science and Medicine, 32*, 541–548.

Svenson, O., Fischhoff, B., & MacGregor, D. (1985). Perceived driving safety and seatbelt usage. *Accident Analysis and Prevention, 17*, 119–133.

Taylor, S. A. (2007). The addition of anticipated regret to attitudinally based, goal-directed models of information search behaviours under conditions of uncertainty. *British Journal of Social Psychology, 46*, 739–768.

Tidwell, M., & Sias, P. (2005). Personality and information seeking: Understanding how traits influence information seeking behaviors. *Journal of Business Communication, 42,* 51–77.

Turner, M. M. (2007). Using emotion to prevent risky behavior: The anger activism model. *Public Relations Review, 33,* 114–119.

Turner, M. M., Rimal, R. N., Morrison, D., & Kim, H. (2006). The role of anxiety in processing risk information: Testing the risk perception attitude framework in two studies. *Human Communication Research, 32,* 130–156.

Tversky, A., & Kahneman, D. (1973). Availability: A heuristic for judging frequency and probability. *Cognitive Psychology, 5,* 207–232.

Vardeman, J. E., & Aldoory, L. (2008). A qualitative study of how women make meaning of contradictory media messages about the risks of eating fish. *Health Communication, 23,* 282–291.

Viswanath, K., & Finnegan, J. R., Jr. (1996). The knowledge gap hypothesis: Twenty-five years later. In B. Burleson (Ed.), *Communication Yearbook* (Vol. 19, pp. 187–227). Thousand Oaks, CA: Sage.

Wanberg, C. R., & Kammeyer-Mueller, J. D. (2000). Predictors and outcomes of proactivity in the socialization process. *Journal of Applied Psychology, 85,* 373–385.

Weinstein, N. D. (1982). Unrealistic optimism about susceptibility to health problems. *Journal of Behavioral Medicine, 5,* 441–460.

Weinstein, N. D. (1983). Reducing unrealistic optimism about illness susceptibility. *Health Psychology, 2,* 11–20.

Weinstein, N. D. (1987). Unrealistic optimism about susceptibility to health problems: Conclusions from a community-wide sample. *Journal of Behavioral Medicine, 10,* 481–500.

Weinstein, N. D., & Nicolich, M. (1993). Correct and incorrect interpretations of correlations between risk perceptions and risk behaviors. *Health Psychology, 12,* 3, 235–245.

Wilkins, A. S. (1999). Expanding Internet access for health care consumers. *Health Care Management Review, 24,* 30–41.

Wilkinson, G. S., & Wilson, J. (1983). An evaluation of demographic differences in the utilization of a cancer information service. *Social Science and Medicine, 17,* 169–175.

Wilson, T. D. (2000). Human information behavior. *Informing Science, 3,* 49–56.

Winkleby, M. A., Flora, J. A., & Kraemer, H. C. (1994). A community-based heart disease intervention: Predictors of change. *American Journal of Public Health, 84,* 767–772.

Witte, K. (1992). Putting the fear back in fear appeals: The extended parallel process model. *Communication Monographs, 59,* 225–249.

9   Managing Uncertainty in Work
       Interactions

Michael W. Kramer

Even though uncertainty reduction theory (URT) originated in interpersonal communication (Berger & Calabrese, 1975), the topic of uncertainty in organizational contexts has been and continues to be a common research area. Some of the research (e.g., organizational leaders' perceptions of environmental uncertainty; Beam, 1996) is beyond the scope of this volume because it does not focus on uncertainty in interactions. However, a significant amount of organizational research has examined uncertainty in interpersonal interactions within organizational contexts. The purpose of this chapter is to review some of that research, especially as it relates to assimilation or socialization processes, and then build upon Kramer's (2004) theory of managing uncertainty (TMU) to develop specific hypotheses and research questions to guide future research on managing uncertainty in workplace interactions.

Socialization Research

Perhaps the most prominent area of research exploring uncertainty in interpersonal interactions in organizational settings examines organizational newcomers' experiences with uncertainty as part of the assimilation or socialization process (for reviews see Jablin, 2001; Waldeck & Myers, 2008). Assimilation research examines the communication experiences of individuals from prior to joining organizations until after they leave. Typically, stage models are used to describe the process. The stages often include the following: *anticipatory socialization*, the time period during which individuals choose careers (anticipatory occupational socialization) and organizations (anticipatory organizational socialization); *encounter,* the first days, weeks, or months as organizational newcomers; *metamorphosis*, the time during which individuals feel they are full organizational members, even though they may experience various transitions such as promotions, transfers, and mergers during this time; and *exit*, the period leading up to and following formal voluntary or involuntary departure from organizational membership (Jablin, 2001).

Much of the research based on this model or similar ones has explicitly or implicitly used URT to explore employees' experiences. Illustrative of this research, scholars have identified different types of uncertainty that newcomers experience (e.g., such as task, role, culture/norms, and group in Ostroff & Kozlowski, 1992; or referent, relational, and appraisal in Miller & Jablin, 1991). Others have focused on sources of information individuals use to reduce uncertainty (e.g., coworkers, supervisors, subordinates, friends, partners, and family in Teboul, 1994; or peers, supervisors, and secretaries/staff in Nelson & Quick, 1991). Still others have focused on the strategies newcomers use to reduce uncertainty (e.g., overt questions, indirect questions, third party, testing, disguising, observing, and surveillance in Miller & Jablin, 1991; or inquiry, observation, or passive in Morrison, 1995). As a logical extension of this type of research, scholars examined the impact of these variables on uncertainty reduction or assimilation (e.g., job satisfaction, performance, and intention to say in Morrison, 1993; or involvement, commitment, and acceptance in Myers & McPhee, 2006). In general, the results find that, as employees communicate with other organizational members to reduce their uncertainty, they are more satisfied, involved, and committed, perform better, and are less likely to leave. Of course, some strategies and sources are more effective than others. Overall, results from this line of research have generally been consistent with Berger's original conceptualizations of URT that as uncertainty decreases positive attitudes increase.

Beyond attention to newcomers' uncertainty reduction experiences, researchers have also explored organizational members' uncertainty during the metamorphosis phase. For example, URT has been applied to job transitions, such as job transfers (Kramer, 1993, 1994). Other research has examined employee interactions after layoffs (Johnson, Bernhagen, Miller, & Allen, 1996) or after mergers and acquisitions (Kramer, Dougherty, & Pierce, 2004). Thus, URT has been used broadly to examine workplace interactions beyond initial interactions.

As the body of research based on uncertainty during interactions in organizational settings has grown, results have demonstrated that some of the original tenets of URT oversimplified the process of responding to uncertainty, partly because uncertainty occurs in settings other than initial interactions. For example, though URT would predict that individuals with the most communication with their supervisors or peers would experience the lowest levels of uncertainty and highest levels of satisfaction, a number of studies have produced alternative results. For example, although not explicitly testing URT, Vecchio and Gobdel (1984) examined bank tellers in closed, middle, or open relationships with their supervisors. Although bank tellers in open-communication relationships with their supervisors were more satisfied than those in closed-communication relationships, those in the middle-group relationships were actually the most satisfied. Kramer (1995) reports similar results in his longitudinal study of transferees. Those in the most closed-communication relationships with their supervisors reported the most stress, role ambiguity, and least satisfaction, those with open-communication relationships with their supervisors reported less stress, less role ambiguity, and more satisfaction, but those in the middle-group reported the lowest levels of stress, least role ambiguity, and most satisfaction. In another setting, Kramer et al. (2004) found that, as airline pilots received more information about an airline merger, they reduced their uncertainty, but also became less satisfied with the merger. The pilots discovered that the merger was going to have a negative impact on their careers as they lost seniority crucial to gaining preferences on flights and equipment. Counter to URT's original premises, uncertainty reduction resulted in dissatisfaction, not satisfaction.

Results like these complement research findings in health and interpersonal communication that have also questioned some of the original conceptualizations of URT. For example, Brashers, Goldsmith, and Hsieh (2002) and Brashers et al. (2000) found that individuals are not always motivated to reduce uncertainty related to health issues. In order to remain hopeful, some individuals will avoid information that would reduce uncertainty if the diagnosis is likely to be negative, whereas others will seek additional information to increase uncertainty after a negative diagnosis. Planalp and Honeycutt (1985) also found that gaining additional information can often lead to increases in uncertainty instead of decreases, such as when something unexpected is discovered about a partner.

Together the results of organizational, health, and interpersonal research have led to a gradual recognition that the original conceptualization of URT by Berger and Calabrese (1975) failed to capture the complexity of uncertainty human interaction. For example, uncertainty does not always motivate individuals to seek information (Axiom 3); information may increase rather than reduce uncertainty (Axiom 1), and reducing uncertainty sometimes leads to negative evaluations (Axiom 7). As a result, scholars now focus on how individuals are motivated to manage uncertainty, not necessarily reduce it; the shift in terminology recognizes that motivations other than uncertainty reduction can direct action (Afifi & Weiner, 2004; Brashers, 2001; Kramer, 2004).

Kramer (2004) proposed a complex and comprehensive model, TMU, to describe the process of managing uncertainty interactions in organizational settings. The model includes key points that were not in the initial conceptualizations of URT. One such addition is that individuals often manage uncertainty internally through cognitive processes without seeking information. Cognitive processes such as scripts or schemas actually reduce the initial experience of uncertainty by making the experience appear predictable. Other cognitive processes, such as denying the uncertainty, tolerating uncertainty, or imagined conversations without seeking information, manage uncertainty as well. The second key addition of TMU is the awareness that competing motives that interact with uncertainty reduction (e.g., impression management or politeness norms) may cause individuals to not seek information despite experiencing uncertainty or cause them to seek information even when they do not experience uncertainty. Finally, Kramer's model proposes that when using a variety of information-seeking strategies, individuals may experience reductions, no change, or increases in uncertainty regardless of their intentions.

The contingency nature of Kramer's (2004) TMU suggests that additional contextual factors will also affect how individuals manage uncertainty in their workplace interactions. One contextual factor that has received limited attention is the source of uncertainty. Individuals are likely to change the way they manage uncertainty (e.g., avoidance, direct information seeking) based on who created it (e.g., customer, supervisor, or CEO). To address this omission, this chapter explores how different interaction relationships likely influence how individuals experience and manage uncertainty in interpersonal interactions in organizational contexts.

Another limitation to most uncertainty research is that it focuses only on how individuals gain information to respond to their own uncertainty. Even Kramer's (2004) model focuses only on how individuals manage their own uncertainty. Although Afifi and Weiner (2004) recognize the importance of the information management strategies of the information giver in managing the information seeker's uncertainty, scholars have not examined how the parties interact to mutually manage uncertainty. Research has shown that information giving and information receiving are both part of the assimilation process (Kramer, Callister, & Turban, 1995). This suggests that information giving and information receiving may serve to manage the uncertainty of both interaction parties. Through giving information, individuals reduce the uncertainty of their interaction partners, making the situation more predictable for both parties.

The remainder of the chapter examines how individuals manage their own and their interaction partner's uncertainty in a variety of personal interactions in organizational settings. It would be impossible to examine the entire range of interpersonal interactions individuals experience in an organization within a single chapter. As a result, organizational relationships are divided into four primary groups based on frequency of interaction and relationship level (see Table 9.1). In particular, the discussion will distinguish between organizational relationships involving frequent interactions (e.g., work-group peers, supervisors, and staff members) and rather infrequent interactions (e.g., upper management, customers). Then each of these groups is further divided into two levels of relationships. The propositions explore how individuals likely manage their own and the other's uncertainty differently depending on the frequency of interaction and level of relationship.

Managing Uncertainty between High-Frequency Interaction Partners

Initial Interactions

During the encounter phase of the socialization process, organizational newcomers identify three primary sources of information for managing

Table 9.1 Communication Strategies for Managing Uncertainty in Interpersonal Interactions in Organizational Contexts

Target of uncertainty	Frequent interactions		Infrequent interactions	
	Close relationship	Distant relationship	High-consequence interaction	Low-consequence interaction
Initial uncertainty	Direct exchange	Direct exchange	Prior information seeking	Cognitive scripts
Task uncertainty	Direct exchange	Direct exchange	Direct exchange	Direct exchange
Relational uncertainty	Direct exchange	Indirect exchange	Limited exchange	Limited exchange
Change uncertainty	Cognitive processes, indirect exchange	Cognitive processes, indirect exchange	Limited information seeking	No exchange
Exit uncertainty	Direct exchange	Limited exchange	Limited information seeking	No exchange

Note: Example relationships for each cell—close relationship/frequent interaction: close peers, partnership supervisors, close staff; distant relationship/frequent interaction: information peers, overseer supervisors, impersonal staff; high consequence/infrequent interactions: upper management; low consequence/infrequent interactions: routine customer, strangers, distant staff.

uncertainty within their work groups: peers, supervisors, and staff. Each of these frequent interaction targets is both a source of uncertainty and a source of information for managing uncertainty. Of these, peers (or coworkers) are considered the most available and helpful sources of information (Louis, Posner, & Powell, 1983; Nelson & Quick, 1991). Newcomers must determine who the peer is, how their jobs are either related or are not related to each other, as well as more personal matters such as if they share common interests and personality traits in order to reduce both task and relational uncertainty in their peer relationships (e.g., Nelson & Quick, 1991). Peers are also a primary source of information for reducing more global uncertainty issues about the organizational culture, identity, and performance standards.

Supervisors are another primary source of uncertainty and information. Although newcomers prefer peers for some types of information, they prefer supervisors for others (Morrison, 1993). For example, newcomers learn their supervisors' expectations through job performance feedback in order to manage their referent and appraisal uncertainty (Miller & Jablin, 1991). As such, supervisors provide resources and information that enable newcomers to function effectively in their new environment.

Interactions with staff (e.g., secretaries, administrative assistants) are frequent for many employees, although these interactions are generally overlooked as an area of interpersonal interactions in typical hierarchical classifications of employee relationships. As staff members are another important source of uncertainty reduction for newcomers (Nelson & Quick, 1991), it is important to consider how newcomers manage their uncertainty with staff members as well. Employees must be able to identify staff members correctly, understand their work relationships with them, and determine whether they have common interests or background.

During these initial interactions, it is not just newcomers who experience uncertainty. The peers, supervisors, and staff members experience uncertainty as they interact with newcomers. Although veteran members experience less uncertainty about their roles and the organizational culture due to their accumulated organizational knowledge, they still must learn to identify the newcomers, gain an understanding of how the newcomers' work habits will affect them, and develop interpersonal relationships with them. As such, interactions between organizational newcomers and veteran peers, supervisors, and staff members occur in an organizational context, but otherwise largely resemble initial interactions as conceived by Berger and Calabrese (1975) in their initial conceptualizations of URT; the individuals involved are seeking information to reduce uncertainty. As a result the first proposition is this:

> Proposition 1: Organizational newcomers and their high-frequency interaction work-group members (peers, supervisors, and staff) will actively seek and give information in their initial interactions to manage their high levels of uncertainty.

Ongoing Relationships

Initial conceptualizations of URT suggested that in interpersonal interactions there is a gradual progression of reducing uncertainty, increasing liking, additional uncertainty reduction, and increasing depth of relationships. Such a progression is consistent with other interpersonal theories, such as social penetration theory (Altman & Taylor, 1973), and various relationship models (e.g., Knapp, 1984). However, the notion that work-group relationships will all follow the same trajectory in an organizational setting is unrealistic. A variety of task factors, such as level of task interdependence and proximity, and relational factors, such as common interests and affective responses from attraction to repulsion, lead to quite different relational outcomes after the initial interactions between newcomers and organizational veterans.

Organizational members develop at least three distinctly different types of peer relationships based on the depth of communication (Kram & Isabella, 1985). Information peers primarily communicate about task information necessary to complete jobs and polite social topics. Collegial peers provide additional job and career feedback and more personal information about families and personal life. Special peers talk frankly about a range of topics, provide emotional support, and rarely keep secrets. Managing uncertainty in these different types of relationships is likely quite different.

Similarly, although at one time there was a belief that supervisors had an average leadership style (ALS) that described their relationships to all subordinates, a large body of research by Graen and his associates, among others, concludes that supervisors develop different types of leader member exchange (LMX) relationships with subordinates (see Graen, 2003). Although in some cases relationships develop from strangers to acquaintance to mature relationships as suggested by interpersonal relational models, supervisors typically develop three distinct types or levels of relationships with their subordinates (Graen & Uhl-Bien, 1995). Supervisors have close, in-group, or partnership relationships characterized by frequent, open communication, inclusion in decision making, and depth of social conversation with some subordinates. With others they have closed, out-group, or overseer relationships characterized by directive, work-related communication and limited polite social conversation. Still others fall in the middle group between the two extremes.

Because interactions between staff members and other work-group members are so understudied, there is little research on the types of relationships they develop. However, based on the peer and supervisor relationship research just cited, it seems probable that work-group members and staff members also develop three different types of relationships. Some develop close, personal relationships despite status differences due to task interdependence, common interests, or compatible personalities. Others develop task-oriented relationships with limited personal interactions, while others fall somewhere in between.

Managing uncertainty within different levels of relational closeness likely involves significantly different communication patterns. Within ongoing close peer relationships, organizational members should have little difficulty managing uncertainty. The experience of uncertainty should be infrequent for both parties due to the depth of communication that occurs in the relationships. Then due to the openness of the relationships, direct inquiry and information giving are readily available methods for managing uncertainty, thus simplifying the limited uncertainty management that is needed. Similarly, supervisors and subordinates in partnership relationships should experience less uncertainty because the inclusive nature of decision making gives them mutual access to information. When they do experience uncertainty, the open communication should provide them opportunity to give and seek information directly from each other. Managing uncertainty for those in close relationships with staff members should similarly pose few problems because there should be limited uncertainty due to the ongoing relationship. When it does occur, individuals should be willing and able to use direct inquiries. Thus, the second proposition for interactions with work-group members in close relationships is this:

Proposition 2: In close personal work relationships with peers, supervisors, and staff members, organizational members will experience low levels of uncertainty and rely on direct methods of seeking and giving information to manage their uncertainty.

In contrast to close relationships, the experience and management of uncertainty is likely quite different in closed or impersonal relationships. For example, with information (distant) peers, uncertainty may be a common experience. Frequent task-oriented interactions may limit the experience of task uncertainty, but the lack of other shared experiences likely results in high levels of relational uncertainty. Furthermore, in some instances, information from peers may develop into various types of unpleasant or difficult relationships in which maintaining relationships is challenging and uncertainty is high (e.g., Fritz, 1997). Similarly, those in overseer or outgroup supervisor relationships are likely to experience high levels of uncertainty. Research indicates that the insider relationship of others is a source of uncertainty for those who are outsiders; as a result, outsiders spend time discussing these relationships with other peers to reduce their uncertainty about the insider relationships (Sias & Jablin, 1995). Distant relationships with staff members likely cause similar uncertainty management problems due to more limited communication.

In addition to experiencing more uncertainty in more distant relationships, the methods of managing uncertainty are likely to be quite different. For example, because relationships with information peers, overseer supervisor relationships, and distant staff relationships are primarily task oriented, a direct communication strategy may still be used to manage task uncertainty. Such an approach of focusing directly on task-related issues may even be a useful way to manage difficult relationships by maintaining distance (e.g., Hess, 2000). In contrast, relational uncertainty (Miller & Jablin, 1991) is likely to be more challenging to manage in these less open relationships. Due to relational distance, impression management concerns, and other competing motives, individuals will likely be reluctant to address relational uncertainty directly with information peers. Politeness norms, emotion management norms, and a variety of other motives make direct inquiry into these types of more personal topics of uncertainty less desirable. As a result, instead of direct inquiry, individuals in these more distant relationships are more likely to rely on indirect methods such as observation and third-party inquiry to manage relational uncertainty. These strategies avoid potentially unpleasant interactions and involve less risk. This suggests a third proposition:

Proposition 3: In task-oriented, distant relationships with peers, supervisors and subordinates, and staff members, organizational members will use direct requests and information giving to manage task uncertainty, but will rely on more indirect methods (e.g., third party, observation) of information seeking and giving to manage relational uncertainty.

Changing Relationships

Relationships in organizational contexts are no more stable than they are in other contexts. In the same way that information can result in increases in uncertainty in interpersonal contexts (Planalp, Rutherford, & Honeycutt, 1988), uncertainty levels fluctuate in organizational relationships. Individuals are particularly likely to experience uncertainty when individuals behave in an uncharacteristic manner. Violations of expected behavior, whether positive or negative, frequently results in changes in levels of uncertainty (Afifi & Burgoon, 2000). For example, the expression of an inappropriate emotion can become a turning point in a relationship, with varying consequences for relational distance (Kramer & Tan, 2006). A variety of personal, behavioral, organizational, and structural changes influence the direction of relational changes (Hess, Omdahl, & Fritz, 2006). Regardless of whether the behavior change is brought on suddenly or is part of a gradual change in relationship behaviors (e.g., Sias, 2006), an organizational member is likely to experience an increase in uncertainty. Although responses vary according to the size, importance, and valence of the changes (Afifi & Burgoon, 2000), individuals are generally motivated to manage uncertainty once they recognize that a change has occurred. Thus, the next proposition is this:

> Proposition 4: After experiencing change in their work-group relationships (with peers, supervisors/subordinates, or staff), organizational members will be motivated to give and seek information to manage uncertainty.

Although generally motivated to manage their uncertainty, organizational members may often be reluctant to use direct communication strategies to manage uncertainty about changes they observe in their relationships. Due to competing motives such as impression management for self- and face-saving concerns for others, and based on their previous experience with these work-group members, individuals may rely on cognitive processes to manage their uncertainty (Kramer, 2004). For example, they may deny that the change has occurred or tolerate the uncertainty it creates for extended periods of time rather than seeking information (Kramer, 2004). They may rely on imaginary conversations (Honeycutt, 1993) in which they speculate about the explanation the individual would provide if asked, rather than actually asking for information. In addition, power differences will also likely influence uncertainty management, particularly between supervisors and subordinates and between work-group members and staff. For example, it may be more important for employees to maintain a positive image with each other than to reduce their uncertainty and so they may prefer to use indirect and third-party requests for information. Thus, the next proposition is this:

> Proposition 5: After experiencing gradual or marked changes in their work-group relationships (with peers, supervisor–subordinate relationships, and

staff), organizational members will rely on cognitive processes and indirect methods of information giving and seeking to manage their uncertainty.

Ending Work Relationships

One of the inevitable changes in interpersonal relationships in organizational settings involves exit. Exit results in the cessation of work relationships, although sometimes personal or friendship relationships continue. Exit is usually separated into either voluntary exit, which occurs when someone retires or takes a new job, or involuntary exit, such as when an individual is dismissed either for individual behaviors or as part of an organizational downsizing or restructuring (Bluedorn, 1978). Managing uncertainty is likely different for these two processes.

Organizational members voluntarily leave organizations for a variety of reasons, from gradual dissatisfaction with their jobs to unexpected events at work or home that shock or disrupt them (e.g., Lee, Mitchell, Wise, & Fireman, 1996). In cases of voluntary exit, employees are frequently motivated to create smooth transitions by finding and training replacements (Jablin, 2001). However, the nature of the relationship likely influences the uncertainty management process. In their close relationships with peers, supervisors, and staff, individuals develop a pattern of sharing personal information and create deep levels of trust. In those relationships, individuals likely feel a need to mutually manage uncertainty. As a result, they likely communicate as they consider leaving, weigh various options, and gradually make a decision to leave. In this way, their close work-group members become sounding boards as they wrestle with their own uncertainty about whether to leave or stay. At the same time, they help these individuals manage their own uncertainty by giving information about why they are leaving and offer task information to allow for a smooth transition. In contrast, those considering exit may be much more reluctant to share information with work-group members with whom they feel more distant. Because these relationships are more task focused, leavers are likely unmotivated to communicate except to announce their imminent departure and offer elementary job transition information. Consistent with this notion, research suggests that people who are exiting frequently do not provide complete or accurate explanations of their departure to many of their work-group members except for those to whom they feel close (Klatzke, 2008). Based on the differences in relational closeness, the following proposition is suggested:

Proposition 6: Employees will manage uncertainty about voluntary exit from an organization with close work-group relationships (peers, supervisors, and staff) differently than with more distant work-group relationships: The former will be characterized by more information exchange concerning their departure, compared to the latter.

In involuntary exit, the employees' dismissals are typically either due to negative evaluations (Fairhurst, Green, & Snavely, 1984) or corporate downsizing (Johnson et al., 1996). Relationships with supervisors are especially likely to be stressed during involuntary exit because the supervisor likely delivers the termination message. For all work-group members, the uncertainty is not about the departure itself, but rather about the reasons for it and the impact it will have on their jobs. Those left behind are typically concerned about how the departure of others will affect their own jobs, especially during layoffs (Johnson et al., 1996). Those leaving are likely more concerned about impression management than about the impact of their departure on an organization that no longer wants them. As a result, their interactions with distant work-group members are likely to be primarily focused on attempts to present their departure in a positive light. With close work-group members those leaving likely attempt to simultaneously put themselves in a positive light and reduce uncertainty to assist their close work-group members in managing the changes related to the exit. This suggests the following proposition:

> Proposition 7: Organizational members experiencing involuntary exit will be primarily motivated by impression management concerns with their distant work-group members, but will also help close work-group members address uncertainty management concerns.

Managing Uncertainty between Low-Frequency Interaction Partners

Most research on uncertainty in interpersonal relationships in organizational settings has focused on uncertainty in the relationships of those who interact frequently. Such a focus fails to consider that organizational members must also manage uncertainty in their interactions with those with whom they interact infrequently. Unlike the relationship with information peers and overseer supervisors that remains distant despite frequent interactions, these infrequent interaction relationships remain distant largely due to a lack of interaction. To provide a more complete examination of the dynamics involved in these interactions, these infrequent-interaction partners are divided into those involving high-consequence relationships and those more routine relationships.

Infrequent High-Consequence Relationships

Especially in larger organizations, other than with their immediate supervisor, the majority of employees have infrequent interactions with higher-level personnel or executives (defined as those two or more levels higher in the hierarchy). Since research suggests that these second-level higher managers influence lower-level employees' careers in important ways (Lee,

1997), these few interactions can be of high consequence for organizational members. Although a virtually untouched area of research, it is important to consider how individuals manage uncertainty in these interactions. Due to the limited number of interactions, the anticipation of these interactions will likely create high levels of uncertainty (Gudykunst, 1995). Despite mutual organizational membership, the interactants often have different organizational values, perspectives, and ways of doing things. The lower-level members of these interactions probably experience additional uncertainty because they may believe the interactions will influence their career opportunities, while the upper-level manager may tolerate the uncertainty and view the interactions more as impression management opportunities. Both parties are likely to want to manage their uncertainty by seeking information about the other individual prior to their interactions. A variety of indirect information-seeking avenues can accomplish this uncertainty management, from asking other organizational members to consulting written documents and personnel files to searching the organizational Web site. Thus, the following hypothesis is suggested:

> Proposition 8: Organizational members will attempt to manage their uncertainty for interactions between upper- and lower-level personnel prior to their interactions by seeking information through indirect methods such as third parties (e.g., peers and other supervisors), observation of public behavior, and reading published (print and Web-based) media.

The interactions between upper- and lower-level organizational members typically occur either at business meetings or official social events, both of which often lack opportunities for extended informal conversations. In addition, the lower-level members are likely to perceive themselves in decidedly different positions of power. As such, lower-level employees are likely to take a passive or reactive approach to managing uncertainty during these interactions. If the upper-level person asks for information, the employee provides it. If the executive provides information, they listen and receive it, but they are probably reluctant to use direct inquiry to gain information. In addition, the setting suggests that politeness norms and job roles are probably strong behavioral motivators that compete with uncertainty reduction to influence communication behavior. The focus of the exchange will primarily be work related, although polite social information may also be exchanged. This suggests the following proposition about interactions with upper-level personnel:

> Proposition 9: To manage uncertainty during interactions between lower- and upper-level personnel, the upper-level personnel will direct the information giving and seeking with a focus on organizational rather than personal topics, and the lower-level employees will primarily react passively by receiving information and by giving information in response to inquiries.

Due to the infrequent interactions between upper- and lower-level organizational members, changes in their relationships are unlikely to occur and the exit of the lower-level member is likely to go unnoticed. However, upper-level members may publicly announce organizational changes through meetings or media presentations, and when they leave the organization there may be official public explanations for their departure. In either case, the uncertainty such changes create is likely to be managed through indirect methods. This suggests the following proposition:

> Proposition 10: To manage uncertainty created by organizational change or the exit of upper-level personnel, lower-level personnel will use indirect methods to the information seeking such as third-party inquiries and consulting mediated materials.

Infrequent Routine Relationships

In contrast to infrequent high-consequence interactions, organizational members have many one-time or infrequent interactions with other individuals as a common part of the organizational experience. These interactions might include communicating with customers or strangers who enter the work environment or with various more distant organizational staff members, such as maintenance or information technology employees. Although these are typically initial interactions, they differ from other initial work-group interactions because it is likely that there will be limited or no future interactions. As a result, relational development or relational uncertainty is relatively unimportant. Managing uncertainty in these interactions has rarely been studied.

Berger and Bradac (1982) provide a partial explanation for why uncertainty in these interactions is likely to be fairly limited. They delineated three levels or types of uncertainty: (a) descriptive uncertainty, being able to reliably identify an individual; (b) predictive uncertainty, being able to predict the behaviors or actions an individual will likely perform; and (c) explanatory uncertainty, being able to explain the behaviors or actions of an individual. In making these distinctions, Berger and Bradac explain that it is not necessary to reduce all three types of uncertainty to manage interactions. Thus, in these infrequent routine interactions, individuals most likely focus only on managing predictive uncertainty. Therefore, for example, front-line employees and customers need to be able to predict each other's behaviors within a certain range in order to complete their goals or tasks, but do not need to be concerned about descriptive and explanatory uncertainty. Neither party needs to be able to explain much about the other's behavior or be able to identify them for future interactions.

In addition, individuals will likely experience limited uncertainty in these routine situations because they can rely on process scripts or schemas to manage uncertainty (Kramer, 2004). Schemas or scripts provide cognitive shortcuts for understanding situations and allow for almost mindless responses to events (Cantor, Mischel, & Schwartz, 1982). In support of this notion, Kramer (2004) found that car salespersons managed uncertainty in interactions with customers by following process scripts. These scripts provide salespersons with the appropriate behaviors to reduce their own uncertainty by allowing them to quickly access the customers' needs and, at the same time, enable the salespersons to provide information to reduce customers' uncertainty. As long as the activities match the scripts, individuals experience little uncertainty because the script provides sufficient understanding of how to act and make sense of the situations. Similar behavioral scripts exist for interacting with strangers who enter the workplace or for infrequently consulted staff members, such as information technology persons.

The uncertainty that is not reduced by process scripts can often be managed through other cognitive processes. When there is little chance for future interactions, individuals often either deny or tolerate the uncertainty in the situation (Kramer, 2004). It is easy to dismiss the descriptive and explanatory uncertainty in the interaction when there will most likely be little or no future interaction. As a result, while a salesperson might wonder about a customer's unusual behavior, as there is limited likelihood of future interaction, it is simpler to dismiss the uncertainty than to seek information to reduce it. Together, this suggests the following proposition for infrequent routine interactions:

> Proposition 11: Organizational members will rely on behavioral scripts and cognitive processes to manage uncertainty in routine interactions with individuals with whom they infrequently interact.

In addition to using scripts to manage uncertainty in these interactions, the nature of these infrequent, routine interactions suggests that the focus of the communication will be mostly task oriented. For example, the customer wants to purchase a product or service and the organizational member wants to complete the sale, or the office worker and the information technology staff member both want to solve a computer problem. There may be some polite or peripheral sharing of social information, but not with the intent of creating long-term relationships. In addition, there would be little chance of these relationships changing due to their short duration. So in order to accomplish their tasks, individuals will rely on direct inquiry to manage uncertainty in order to accomplish their goals because other approaches are either more time-consuming, unavailable, or more likely to lead to incorrect information. Thus the final proposition is this:

> Proposition 12: Organizational members will focus primarily on direct inquiry to manage task uncertainty in routine interactions with individuals with whom they infrequently interact.

Discussion

The study of uncertainty in interpersonal relationships in organizational settings has primarily focused on how newcomers attempt to reduce their uncertainty as part of the socialization or assimilation process. Such a focus has four noticeable limitations. First, while initial conceptualizations of URT focused on reducing uncertainty, more recent theories focus on managing uncertainty. Second, the exclusive focus on uncertainty reduction failed to consider how competing motives may be more important than uncertainty reduction in determining interaction behaviors. Third, by focusing on how newcomers reduce uncertainty, previous research has failed to examine how individuals manage uncertainty in the breadth of organizational relationships and interactions they experience as part of their organizational roles. Finally, uncertainty research has focused on how individuals manage their own uncertainty without recognizing that managing uncertainty is a mutual or interactive process involving giving and receiving information.

In an effort to broaden the scope of uncertainty research on interpersonal interactions in organizational settings, this chapter examined uncertainty management for a range of interaction partners based on the frequency of interaction and the nature of the relationship. It explored how cognitive process and competing motives influence the uncertainty management, and considered how uncertainty is managed for both parties in the interactions. A summary of the propositions is presented in Table 9.1. The choice of the word "exchange" in Table 9.1 emphasizes that uncertainty management is always a mutually accomplished task. By both seeking and giving information, the individuals involved are managing uncertainty for themselves and for others. In some cases, such as initial interactions with peers, the exchange is essentially equal with both parties managing similar levels of uncertainty and assisting each other in roughly equal amounts. In other instances, there is an imbalance, such that one interaction member experiences significantly greater uncertainty than the other, often as a result of differences in access to scripts.

By no means are the propositions advanced in this chapter comprehensive. It would be next to impossible to consider all the nuances of interactions with all of the interaction partners that make up organizational contexts. For example, some organizational members develop long-term relationships with customers; uncertainty management in those relationships might more closely mirror those of frequent, close relationships than infrequent, routine relationships. In a small organization, relationships with upper management may be more similar to other work-group relationships due to the frequency of interaction. The appearance of a threatening stranger in an organization creates different uncertainties than the appearance of someone who appears lost. Those in close work-group relationships should be able to rely on direct inquiry to seek information, but contextual factors and competing motives may result in reliance on indirect approaches to managing uncertainty. So although the suggested propositions oversimplify the complexity of organizational relationships, hopefully they are representative of some of the possibilities for examining uncertainty management for interpersonal interactions in organizational settings and will spur new research in this domain.

References

Afifi, W. A., & Burgoon, J. K. (2000). The impact of violations on uncertainty and the consequences for attractiveness. *Human Communication Research, 26,* 203–233.

Afifi, W. A., & Weiner, J. L. (2004). Toward a theory of motivated information management. *Communication Theory, 14,* 167–190.

Altman, I., & Taylor, D. (1973). *Social penetration: The development of interpersonal relationships.* New York: Holt.

Beam, R. A. (1996). How perceived environmental uncertainty influences the marketing orientation of U.S. daily newspapers. *Journalism and Mass Communication Quarterly, 73,* 285–303.

Berger, C. R., & Bradac, J. J. (1982). *Language and social knowledge: Uncertainty in interpersonal relations.* London: Edward Arnold.

Berger, C. R., & Calabrese, R. J. (1975). Some explorations in initial interaction and beyond: Toward a developmental theory of interpersonal communication. *Human Communication Research, 1,* 99–112.

Bluedorn, A. C. (1978). A taxonomy of turnover. *Academy of Management Review, 3,* 647–651.

Brashers, D. E. (2001). Communication and uncertainty management. *Journal of Communication, 51,* 477–497.

Brashers, D. E., Goldsmith, D. J., & Hsieh, E. (2002). Information seeking and avoiding in health contexts. *Human Communication Research, 28,* 258–271.

Brashers, D. E., Neidig, J. L., Haas, S. M., Dobbs, L. K., Cardillo, L. W., & Russell, J. A. (2000). Communication in the management of uncertainty: The case of persons living with HIV or AIDS. *Communication Monographs, 67,* 63–84.

Cantor, N., Mischel, W., & Schwartz, J. (1982). Social knowledge: Structure, content, use and abuse. In A. H. Hastrof & A. M. Isen (Eds.), *Cognitive social psychology* (pp. 33–72). New York: Elsevier-North Holland.

Fairhurst, G. T., Green, S. G., & Snavely, B. K. (1984). Managerial control and discipline: Whips and chains. In R. N. Bostrom & B. H. Westley (Eds.), *Communication yearbook 8* (pp. 558–593). Beverly Hills, CA: Sage.

Fritz, J. M. H. (1997). Responses to unpleasant work relationships. *Communication Research Reports, 14,* 302–311.

Graen, G. B. (2003). Interpersonal workplace theory at the crossroads. In G. B. Graen (Ed.), *Dealing with diversity. LMX leadership: The series* (Vol. 1, pp. 145–182). Greenwich, CT: Information Age.

Graen, G. B., & Uhl-Bien, M. (1995). Relationship-based approach to leadership: Development of leader-member exchange (LMX) theory of leadership over 25 years—applying a multilevel multidomain perspective. *Leadership Quarterly, 6,* 219–247.

Gudykunst, W. B. (1995). Anxiety/uncertainty management (AUM) theory. In R. L. Wiseman (Ed.), *Intercultural communication theory* (pp. 8–58). Thousand Oaks, CA: Sage.

Hess, J. A. (2000). Maintaining nonvoluntary relationship with disliked partners: An investigation into the use of distancing behaviors. *Human Communication Research, 26*, 458–488.

Hess, J. A., Omdahl, B. L., & Fritz, J. M. H. (2006). Turning points in relationships with disliked co-workers. In J. M. H. Fritz & B. L. Omdahl (Eds.), *Problematic relationships in the workplace* (pp. 89–106). New York: Peter Lang.

Honeycutt, J. M. (1993). Components and functions of communication during initial interaction, with extrapolations to beyond. In S. A. Deetz (Ed.), *Communication yearbook 16* (pp. 461–490). Newbury Park, CA: Sage.

Jablin, F. M. (2001). Organizational entry, assimilation, and disengagement/exit. In F. M. Jablin & L. L. Putnam (Eds.), *The new handbook of organizational communication: Advances in theory, research, and methods* (pp. 732–818). Thousand Oaks, CA: Sage.

Johnson, J. R., Bernhagen, M. J., Miller, V., & Allen, M. (1996). The role of communication in managing reductions in work force. *Journal of Applied Communication Research, 24*, 139–164.

Klatzke, S. R. (2008). *Communication and sensemaking during the exit phase of socialization*. Unpublished dissertation at the University of Missouri.

Knapp, M. L. (1984). *Interpersonal communication and human relationships*. New York: Allyn & Bacon.

Kram, K. E., & Isabella, L. A. (1985). Mentoring alternatives: The role of peer relationships in career development. *Academy of Management Journal, 28*, 110–132.

Kramer, M. W. (1993). Communication and uncertainty reduction during job transfers: Leaving and joining processes. *Communication Monographs, 60*, 178–198.

Kramer, M. W. (1994). Uncertainty reduction during job transitions: An exploratory study of the communication experiences of newcomers and transferees. *Management Communication Quarterly, 7*, 384–412.

Kramer, M. W. (1995). A longitudinal study of superior–subordinate communication during job transfers. *Human Communication Research, 22*, 39–64.

Kramer, M. W. (2004). *Managing uncertainty in organizational communication*. Mahwah, NJ: Lawrence Erlbaum.

Kramer, M. W., Callister, R. R., & Turban, D. B. (1995). Information-giving and information-receiving during job transitions. *Western Journal of Communication, 59*, 151–170.

Kramer, M. W., Dougherty, D. S., & Pierce, T. A. (2004). Communication during a corporate merger: A case of managing uncertainty during organizational change. *Human Communication Research, 30*, 71–101.

Kramer, M. W., & Tan, C. L. (2006). Emotion management in dealing with difficult people. In J. M. H. Fritz & B. L. Omdahl (Eds.), *Communicating in the workplace with difficult others* (pp. 153–178). New York: Peter Lang.

Lee, J. (1997). Leader–member exchange, the "Pelz Effect," and cooperative communication between group members. *Management Communication Quarterly, 11*, 266–287.

Lee, T. W., Mitchell, T. R., Wise, L., & Fireman, S. (1996). An unfolding model of voluntary employee turnover. *Academy of Management Journal, 39*, 5–36.

Louis, M. R., Posner, B. Z., & Powell, G. N. (1983). The availability and helpfulness of socialization practices. *Personnel Psychology, 36*, 857–866.

Miller, V. D., & Jablin, F. M. (1991). Information seeking during organization entry: Influences, tactics, and a model of the process. *Academy of Management Review, 16,* 92–120.

Morrison, E. W. (1993). Newcomer information seeking: Exploring types, modes, sources, and outcomes. *Academy of Management Journal, 36,* 557–589.

Morrison, E. W. (1995). Information usefulness and acquisition during organizational encounter. *Management Communication Quarterly, 9,* 131–155.

Myers, K. K., & McPhee, R. D. (2006). Influences on member assimilation in workgroups in high-reliability organizations: A multi-level analysis. *Human Communication Research, 32,* 440–468.

Nelson, D. L., & Quick, J. C. (1991). Social support and newcomer adjustment in organizations: Attachment theory at work. *Journal of Organizational Behavior, 12,* 543–554.

Ostroff, C., & Kozlowski, S. W. J. (1992). Organizational socialization as a learning process: The role of information acquisition. *Personnel Psychology, 45,* 849–874.

Planalp, S., & Honeycutt, J. M. (1985). Events that increase uncertainty in personal relationships. *Human Communication Research, 11,* 593–604.

Planalp, S., Rutherford, D. K., & Honeycutt, J. M. (1988). Events that increase uncertainty in personal relationships II: Replication and extension. *Human Communication Research, 14,* 516–547.

Sias, P. M. (2006). Workplace friendship deterioration. In J. M. H. Fritz & B. L. Omdahl (Eds.), *Communicating in the workplace with difficult others* (pp. 69–87). New York: Peter Lang.

Sias, P. M., & Jablin, F. M. (1995). Differential superior–subordinate relations, perceptions of fairness, and coworker communication. *Human Communication Research, 22,* 5–38.

Teboul, J. C. B. (1994). Facing and coping with uncertainty during organizational encounters. *Management Communication Quarterly, 8,* 190–224.

Vecchio, R. P., & Gobdel, B. C. (1984). The vertical dyad linkage model of leaderships: Problems and prospects. *Organizational Behavior and Human Performance, 34,* 5–20.

Waldeck, J., & Myers, K. (2008). Organizational assimilation theory, research, and implications for multiple areas of the discipline: A state of the art review. In C. S. Beck (Ed.), *Communication yearbook 31* (pp. 322–367). New York: Lawrence Erlbaum.

10 Information Regulation in Work–Life

Applying the Comprehensive Model of Information Seeking to Organizational Networks

J. David Johnson

While there has been considerable research focused on work–life (WL) issues, in their exhaustive review Eby, Casper, Lockwood, Bordeaux, and Brinley (2005) noted that it lacked a theoretical base and that very few studies focused on classic communication issues, such as how people went about seeking information or the impact of social networks. This chapter seeks to redress these shortcomings by integrating divergent literatures on WL, information seeking, and network analysis to highlight important issues of information regulation and uncertainty management for members of organizations. First, I will review general problems in WL, with a special focus on employee assistance programs (EAPs) that are designed to ameliorate them. Second, I will extend the framework of the comprehensive model of information seeking (CMIS) to this particular context. Third, I will focus particularly on information-seeking actions that relate to WL in communication networks. Finally, I will discuss the theoretic and pragmatic implications of this work for understanding how people regulate their information seeking related to these issues. Throughout, propositions will be offered that stem from the application of the CMIS framework to the context of EAPs and that are intended to serve as guides for future inquiry into work–life information-seeking decisions.

Work–Life Overview

The issue of work–life balance has received increasing attention across a host of disciplines (Kossek & Lambert, 2005), in part because of the wide range of problems confronting the contemporary workforce. Obviously, work and family are two of the most important realms of an individual's life, but these two realms can be detrimental to each other (Kossek & Ozeki, 1998), with competing time demands and energy requirements leading to a need to mutual adjustments in an individual's multiplexed communication networks.

The depth of an organizational member's struggle with work–life balance is troubling. It is estimated that 10% of employees are impaired sufficiently to need behavioral health intervention (Poverny & Dodd, 2000). Organizations typically use formal EAPs to address these issues, so they will be our pragmatic focus here. Historically, EAP programs primarily focused on substance and alcohol abuse. Recently, though, there has been a move toward more broad-based programs that offer a wide range of benefits and approaches to address these complex problems (Poverny & Dodd, 2000). More comprehensive EAP services for employees might include programs addressing the following: depression, stress, relationships, marital problems, compulsive gambling, career issues, financial and legal concerns, lactation difficulties, child and elder care, health and wellness, violence, and so on. Typically users of these programs are the most vulnerable organizational members (Poverny & Dodd, 2000).

However, the very complexity of these formal programs increases the difficulty of effectively communicating their nature and increasing awareness of them, so that employees can make informed choices (Picherit-Duthler & Freitag, 2004). Partly as a result, people often find employee benefit communication confusing, complicated, and frustrating (Picherit-Duthler & Freitag, 2004). Another challenge to EAPs is employee resistance to help. EAPs are impacted by confidentiality, face, and information regulation issues that hamper individuals in their efforts to seek information to deal with their problems.

As I will detail in the remainder of this chapter, finding help in organizations is a complex phenomenon and there are many barriers that seekers must overcome. Ignorance of employee benefits, which has a direct bearing on the employee's personal life, is widespread (Picherit-Duthler & Freitag, 2004), often in spite of government-mandated procedures for informing employees. Lack of trust and concerns over confidentiality may result in workers seeking informal or external sources of information for dealing with their problems because they want to avoid being labeled or categorized in a way that is hard to remove (Geist-Martin, Horsley, & Farrell, 2003). As a result, some employees may simply withdraw, often perceiving that their organization's culture demands that they suffer in silence (that they should just "buck it up"). Unfortunately, the literature in this area has generally overlooked the motivations that lead employees to seek answers to WL questions they pose for themselves and the factors that lead them to decide on strategies for negotiating them (Johnson, 1996). One approach for examining these issues is found in the CMIS and its application to communication networks in the workplace.

The Comprehensive Model of Information Seeking

Information seeking can be defined simply as the purposive acquisition of information from selected information carriers (Johnson, 1996, 1997). There are many, often contradictory, senses of information. Here we will focus on the classic one of being able to discern patterns of matter and energy in the world around us (Case, 2007; Johnson, 1996). A focus on information seeking develops a true receiver's perspective and forces us to

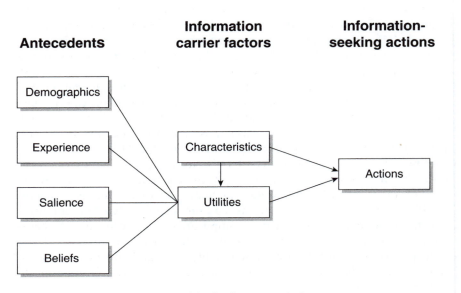

Figure 10.1 Comprehensive Model of Information Seeking

examine how an individual acts within an information field containing multiple information carriers.

I will organize our discussion of the information-seeking strategies of individuals relating to EAPs on the theoretical foundation provided by Johnson's (1997) CMIS. That framework has been empirically tested in a variety of cancer (Johnson, 1993; Johnson & Meischke, 1993) and organizational contexts (Johnson, Donohue, Atkin, & Johnson, 1995). Johnson (2003) has systematically compared these two contexts and their implications for the CMIS. These empirical tests rest on a foundation of rigorous scale development, unique in this area of research, and tests of the entire model. Like other encompassing models, portions of the CMIS have been tested in subsequent empirical research (e.g., Kelly, Andrews, Case, Allard, & Johnson, 2007). The CMIS has also been reviewed and used in the information science, communication, and health literatures (e.g., Babrow, 2001; Case, 2007; Wilson, 1997). The CMIS focuses on the antecedents that explain why people become information seekers, the information carrier characteristics that shape how people go about looking for information, and the information-seeking actions that reflect the nature of the search itself (see Figure 10.1).

Antecedents

There are four classes of CMIS antecedents: demographics, personal experience, salience, and beliefs. These factors determine an individual's natural predisposition to search for information from particular information carriers.

Demographics

Organizational demography refers to the composition of the human membership of the organization in terms of such basic attributes as sex and age. A common theme related to demographic research, which bears directly on communication networks, is the relative isolation of certain groups (Kanter, 1977). This notion of isolation could be extended to the stigma associated with substance abuse, a key component of most EAPs (Dietz, Cook, & Hersch, 2005).

Indeed, one way in which demographic characteristics serve as antecedents to information-seeking decisions is that individuals look to others of similar status to share information when facing uncertainty. Thus, as uncertainty about one's job increases, organizational members will have a tendency to communicate with individuals with whom they share the same status. In turn, cohesive groups may form negative perceptions of outgroup members (e.g., nondrug users), further isolating them (Hansen, Mors, & Lovas, 2005). This sort of isolation is especially likely when social categorization processes impede information use (Dahlin, Weingart, & Hinds, 2005). This, in turn, often means that women and minorities are excluded from informal networks, denying them access to restricted knowledge (Johnson, 1996), which can dissuade even the most active seekers.

> P1: Younger, disadvantaged workers will have a greater need to develop rich social networks and utilize formal EAP systems.

Personal Experience

The CMIS conceptualizes personal experience as individuals' direct, personal exposure to the issue. In the context of EAPs, it suggests that employees' direct or indirect prior involvement with the problem at hand (e.g., coworker's substance abuse) affects the directness of their search for information related to EAPs.

> P2: Those with limited personal experience with EAP problems receive greater benefits from developing rich social networks and the utilization of formal EAP systems.

Salience

Salience refers to the personal significance of information to the individual. An individual might wonder, "Is it important that I do something?" Potential costs of seeking information from others (e.g., interpersonal risk of admitting ignorance) often inhibit the development of wide-ranging ties in networks (Nebus, 2006). Indeed, the face and status costs of seeking information within the organization may be so troublesome that people prefer to seek information outside of the organization itself, rather than to ask overt questions (Johnson, 1996).

There are also a host of motivations for people not to seek information related to EAPs. First, it is not uncommon for managers to avoid information that would force them to make a decision to overcome some problem, especially difficult personal issues (Johnson, 1996). Second, ignorance can be used as a justification for inaction. Third, trust (a major mediator of the open exchange of information) may be lacking in EAP situations. Fourth, seeking information in proscribed; taboo areas could result in sanctions that make ignorance a preferable alternative. Fifth, often ignorance provides a way of avoiding conflict. Sixth, ignorance can often be reassuring of a comfortable inertial state, whereas knowledge might lead to arousal to take action. Finally, the very act of seeking information involves admitting one's ignorance. Admissions of ignorance come at substantial costs to one's own ego. In fact, if it is an area in which an employee is expected to be competent, then ignorance may have untold consequences. As a result, individuals will only admit ignorance in certain limited situations.

Acquiring more information and enhancing awareness can increase a person's uncertainty and, relatedly, their stress levels. More generally, it has been argued that information seeking may not resolve ambiguity, it may create more, as it forces us to confront an often mysterious and unknowable universe (Babrow, 1992). As a result, individuals and organizations often choose to reduce this uncomfortable state through processes associated with denial, inertia, and apathy (Johnson, 1996). Organizations, and the individuals within them, often deny the presence of disturbing information rather than confronting it. They do not want to know certain things or they hope problems will just go away. However, in this context, where life problems can interfere with work, salience may be further enhanced by formal managerial interventions such as referral to drug treatment programs.

In sum, some individuals just do not have the interpersonal skills necessary to develop the informal network relationships necessary to acquire information. Others have such low self-esteem they are afraid that any information they get will confirm their already low self-concept. Any approach to providing personally significant information to employees about EAPs must recognize and deal with these dynamics.

> P3: Workers must appreciate the salience of their problems to receive more positive outcomes from social networks and formal EAP systems.

Beliefs

EAP information seeking is also affected by various cultural factors, such as clusters of attitudes associated with beliefs or expectations about various information carriers, because all cultures develop rules that limit the sharing of information. Natural language is well suited for ambiguity and deception and often concerns for politeness lead us to equivocate, dissemble, and to tell others "white lies" (Smithson, 1989). We may be limited in polite discourse in the extent to which we can self-disclose personal information. Conversely, others may be limited in the questions they feel they can ask us and the strategies they can pursue in seeking information. Fundamentally, individuals' attempts to establish relations with others for the purposes of sharing information must be accepted by the other, and utilitarian concerns for both the value of information and the social standing of individuals determine acceptance (Nebus, 2006). This may be why advice networks are so characterized with sporadic, asymmetric, and/or nonreciprocating relationships (Nebus, 2006), which may be especially true for EAP-driven interactions.

Individuals' perception of the extent to which they can shape or control events also impacts their level of awareness of WL problems. For many individuals it does not make much sense to learn more about things over which they have no control, so the powerless tend not to seek information (Katz, 1968). Case, Andrews, Johnson, and Allard (2005) have articulated systematically why the avoidance of information may be very rational in particular situations where people have low self-efficacy, or where face-threatening information about job performance might result (Ashford, Blatt, & VandeWalle, 2003). It may be perfectly rational then to avoid information when there is nothing one can do with the answers one may obtain. If the threat is extreme, or if any potential responses are not expected to be effective, then an attractive alternative is to ignore the threat entirely, which in turn promotes cognitive consistency (Case et al., 2005). People who are officially referred to programs often have limited abilities to cope with their problems (Poverny & Dodd, 2000). They do not have a sense of self-efficacy that they will be able to correctly interpret and react to new information with which they are presented. Use of the Web and formal on-site and off-site sources often require some sense of self-efficacy. An individual's belief in the efficacy of various programs also plays a role.

> P4: Workers must believe that their actions will make a difference to receive more positive outcomes from rich social networks and formal EAP systems.

Information Carrier Factors

The information carrier factors contained in the CMIS are drawn from a model of media exposure and appraisal (MEA) that has been tested on a variety of information carriers, including both sources and channels, and in a variety of cultural settings (Johnson, 1983, 1984a, 1984b, 1987; Johnson & Oliveira, 1988). Following the MEA, the CMIS (Johnson, 1993; Johnson et al., 1995; Johnson & Meischke, 1993) focuses on editorial tone, communication potential, and utility of the information source. Editorial tone captures an audience member's perception of credibility. In network, organizational terms, the concept translates to perceptions of the source's trust. Communication potential relates to issues of style and comprehensiveness.

Finally, utility involves the degree to which qualities of the medium correspond to the needs of an individual and shares much with uses and gratifications perspectives (Johnson, 1997). In other words, individuals will ask whether the medium is relevant, topical, and important for their purposes, factors that have led to increased use of the Web and off-site counseling for EAPs.

Information carrier factors entail the following specific propositions relating to the actions we will examine in the next section:

P5: Characteristic factors of trust and communication potential determine the activation of network ties and perceptions of their utility.

P6: Workers must perceive high utilities to engage in active searches within their social networks.

Information-Seeking Actions

The area related to individual information-seeking action in organizations that has probably received the most research attention over the past decade or so has been feedback seeking related to individual performance, especially during organizational entry or job changing (Ashford et al., 2003). Of particular interest have been the strategies that individuals use to uncover information about task, cultural, and other expectations an organization might have related to their performance (Miller & Jablin, 1991). The information newcomers acquire is critical for determining their adjustment to the organization and their performance within it; thus, it becomes a significant coping mechanism for individuals, especially those who have WL issues. Active information seeking is often necessary because organizations withhold information inadvertently or purposively (Miller & Jablin, 1991).

The vast array of information to which newcomers are exposed and the gaps in the information they are provided often result in high levels of uncertainty. This uncertainty affects people's perceptions of role ambiguity and can impede an employee's job satisfaction, productivity, and ultimately affect his or her tenure. This, in itself, increases stress and the need for EAPs. With such uncomfortable feelings, employees are driven to seek information to reduce uncertainty they are experiencing (Miller & Jablin, 1991). But here they may be doubly vexed because they may be inexperienced information seekers who don't know what strategies are appropriate or useful in their organization. Hence, naive employees will often think that question asking is the only available tactic they have, little realizing that asking direct/overt questions about sensitive areas may be taboo. Individuals may also feel uncomfortable asking direct questions if they perceive a question reveals more about themselves than they want others to know. Use of questioning also involves a choice for the target of the question, which in itself may be a difficult one. Similarly, there is also the risk that a question (e.g., "How do I handle stress?") will result in a negative answer that both supervisor and employee would like to avoid. Thus, counterbalancing the uncertainty newcomers are experiencing are the social costs of seeking information and a desire to manage the impression they give others, all factors that act to constrain one's social network.

These factors may result in individuals pursuing less direct, overt means of acquiring information (Miller & Jablin, 1991). Indirect questions are often employed in cases where someone is uncomfortable (Miller & Jablin, 1991). They usually take the form of a simple declarative sentence or observation that is meant to solicit information, often disguised within an apparently casual conversation. Another strategy is to use a third party as an intermediary to gather information. Thus, rather than asking your supervisor, who serves as a primary source, you might go to HR as a secondary source of information (Miller & Jablin, 1991). At times the most approachable individuals to a newcomer are those individuals who are most likely to lead them astray, or who have limited information, thus resulting in a pooling of ignorance. Another, more dangerous strategy in which individuals might engage is testing limits (Miller & Jablin, 1991). Thus, if an individual really wants to find out how his or her supervisor will react to drinking, he or she might try sneaking some during the workday. A less direct strategy is that of observing (Miller & Jablin, 1991). Employees can watch the actual behaviors of their supervisors and coworkers and weigh them against their words. There are limits, however, to what a new employee can directly observe, especially concerning issues related to EAPs that others might want to cloak. Beyond the newcomer information-seeking strategies identified traditionally in the literature, there are other actions (e.g., skimming, berry-picking, chaining, monitoring key sources for developments) that have been identified in the information science literature (Case, 2007) that also might pertain to this problem. This work on feedback seeking provides a foundation for understanding the factors that constrain the development of networks of ties related to EAPs.

In turn, the foundational research on the CMIS suggests it provides the "bare bones" of a causal structure, although the nature of the specific relationships contained in the model appears to be context dependent. Tests of the CMIS in health situations suggests the model works best with authoritative channels, such as doctors, which are the object of intense, goal-directed searches (Johnson, 1993; Johnson & Meischke, 1993), and for rational, programmed tasks that are more proximate to the individual (Johnson et al., 1995). These characteristics certainly relate to the formal role of EAPs in organizations. This chapter provides a chance to extend this framework to a situation that is often emotional and irrational, governed by the dark side of informal networks. Here, we will explore actions primarily in terms of an individual's search for information within organizational communication networks; the topic I will turn to in more detail in the next section.

Information-Seeking Actions in Organizational Communication Networks

Network analysis represents a very systematic means of examining the overall configuration of relationships within an organization. The most common form of graphic portrayal of networks contains nodes that represent social units (e.g., people, groups), and relationships of various sorts between them. Because of its generality, network analysis has been used by almost every science to study specific problems (Watts, 2003). It has been the primary means of studying communication structure in organizations for over three decades (Susskind, Schwartz, Richards, & Johnson, 2005). So much attention has been paid to network analysis that a comprehensive review of all material related to it is beyond the scope of this chapter, so I will focus on the fundamental question of how people come to find answers to their EAP concerns. EAPs traditionally have been individually focused, seldom addressing more macro issues of social health, social capital issues surrounding one's social network of relationships including camaraderie with peers, communicating with superiors, and family connections (Farrell & Geist-Martin, 2005).

How Do People Know Where to Go?

How people come to know who has answers to new questions is a relatively understudied problem. One of the things that characterize effective communication networks is knowing what the other knows and when to turn to them (Cross, Rice, & Parker, 2001). Partly growing from the classic debates relating to the validity of self-reports of network linkages, some have suggested that individuals have strong, albeit often crude, categorical intuitions of surrounding social structures and, by implication, they have some awareness of where information resides (Freeman, 1992).

However, I am not exploring how people get routine information from their strong ties. Rather, I am interested in how people actively search for answers to questions that may exceed the capability of their existing network. This question is given some additional impetus by the classic findings that people will seek information from interpersonal sources who are accessible and can summarize information for them in meaningful terms and that people are not terribly persistent nor sophisticated in their search behaviors (Cross et al., 2001; Johnson, 1997).

Addressing the problem of where to go has traditionally been one compelling advantage of a formal organizational chart, which in effect provides a road map for confronting it. Official guidance on sources of information often comes from formal organizational structures (e.g., "I have to respond to certain information requests because of job requirements"). However, there is some preliminary evidence that informal sources of WL support may be more efficacious (Behson, 2005). We turn, then, to how individuals negotiate the more shadowy informal world for answers to their questions.

Specifically, the literatures on opinion leadership, small world dynamics, and transactive memory provide frameworks from which to understand individual behaviors in this context.

Opinion Leaders

Both the traditional opinion leadership (Katz & Lazarsfeld, 1955) and network role literature suggest that people seek out knowledgeable others in their informal networks for answers to their questions (Johnson, 1997). One key advantage to the use of opinion leaders is that they can sometimes serve as mentors of individual skills. Thus, not only do opinion leaders disseminate ideas, but they also, because of the interpersonal nature of their ties, provide additional pressure to conform as well. This sort of influence is a key factor in the success of drug and alcohol rehabilitation programs (Department of Labor, 2006). However, the literature is less clear on the question of how people come to know who these others are.

Opinion leaders not only serve a relay function, but they also provide social support information to individuals. Generally two crucial dimensions of support are isolated, informational and emotional, with informational support associated with a feeling of mastery and control over one's environment (Freimuth, 1987) and emotional support affiliated with feelings of personal coping, enhanced self-esteem, and needs for affiliation (Albrecht & Adelman, 1987). Support has been associated with such critical organizational outcome variables as stress, absenteeism, burnout, turnover, productivity, and morale (Ray, 1987).

Small World Strategies

The classic small world problem of where to go is couched in terms of an individual who needs to contact a distant target "other" (e.g., someone who knows how to cope with substance abuse), previously unknown to them, through intermediaries. Small world issues have received renewed attention with the advent of the Internet (Watts, 2003). The twist is that we are not seeking a particular target other, but rather targeted information that another may possess. In this sort of "expertise" network, knowledge may substitute for formal authority for identification of targets, but similar problems of access, managing attention, overload, and queuing may result (Krackhardt, 1994).

Watts (2003) has recently given more focused attention to how individuals strategically target particular intermediaries. He suggests individuals start with two broad strategies. One is to engage in a broadcast search in which you tell everyone you know, they in turn tell everyone they know until a target is reached, or in our case an answer is found. This approach is crude and has some obvious problems: (1) It reveals your ignorance broadly; (2) It implicates a large number of others, distracting them from their other tasks; (3) It may produce large volumes of information that need to then be filtered by some criteria (e.g., credibility, relevance, and so on); and (4) It makes your problems visible to a wide range of others, something particularly important in EAP situations. The alternative, a directed search, may start by developing some criteria (e.g., "I will only ask people I can trust with sensitive, confidential information") used to guide contact with others who may have answers to my questions. Retrieval criteria are important components of transactive memory approaches.

Transactive Memory

> ... a knowledge community or network would seem to require a human hub or switch, whose function is as much to know who knows what as to know what is known.
>
> (Earl, 2001, p. 225)

Knowing who knows what (i.e., the know-who question) is a fundamental issue in communication networks (Borgatti & Cross, 2003). Using computer search engines and networks as a metaphor can also lead us to interesting insights into this human systems problem. If people can be considered to be computers, then every social group can be viewed as a computer network with analogous problems and solutions (Wegner, 1995), developing means of retrieving and allocating information to collective tasks (Palazzolo, Serb, She, Su, & Contractor, 2006). But we are not focused here on the hardware and software available to search for expertise: classic knowledge management tools used in many organizations (e.g., SPIFI, directories, "yellow pages"). Perhaps the most serious limit on these technologies is the recurring preference of individuals for interpersonal information sources who can digest and summarize vast quantities of information for individual seekers (Johnson, 1996). Some have argued, then, that the fundamental unit of transactive memory is task–expertise–person (TEP) units that answer in fundamental ways the know-who question (Brandon & Hollingshead, 2004).

Transactive memory explains how people develop cognitive knowledge networks that help them identify the skills and expertise of others (Palazzolo et al., 2006), such as knowledge of drug treatment options. Several interrelated processes are involved, including retrieval coordination, directory updating, and information allocation (Palazzolo et al., 2006; Wegner, 1995). Retrieval coordination specifies procedures for finding information. Directory updating involves learning who knows what, while information allocation assigns memory items for group members. Once someone's expertise is known, they are more likely to become the objects of information searches (Borgatti & Cross, 2003) or action in CMIS terms.

In summary, given the forgoing, the CMIS suggests that the antecedent factors shape perceptions of the utilities of various actions in social networks. Characteristics such as editorial tone (trust) and communication potential (being able to couch answers in understandable ways) then shape both utilities and action in social networks.

Implications

In this section I will examine how the literatures on opinion leadership, small world dynamics, and transactive memory provide frameworks for understanding individual behaviors in this context. Examining information-seeking EAP contexts provides an opportunity to point to several implications for future work on the CMIS. One of the least articulated elements of the CMIS has been the nature of actions. A focus on social networks has uncovered a host of interesting manifestations of actions. It also raises issues of how much assistance one is likely to find in social networks in which they are embedded and how to balance differing networks representing separable WL domains. In this section I also examine what management can do to intervene in these networks.

Implications for Theory

People arrange their information environment in a manner that is consonant with their personal predispositions (Johnson, 1997). Increasingly some organizational members *expect* to experience role ambiguity while performing the duties associated with their role and some prefer a large number of stressors. Indeed, managing the process of uncertainty reduction by information regulation, not necessarily reducing it, may be the critical issue for modern organizational members (Babrow, 1992, 2001).

One set of empirical findings that compels us to advance theory relates to the paradoxical decline in the desire for information as one's proximity to a problem increases (Johnson, Case, Andrews, & Allard, 2005). Due to a lack of efficacy or an unwillingness to make the effort to confront problems, people often seem to prefer to avoid information rather than seek it (Brashers, Goldsmith, & Hsieh, 2002; Case et al., 2005). This creates substantial problems for effective EAPs in organizations because supervisors are often unwilling to confront employees who are having difficulties.

Indeed, the human environment within which relationships are embedded may discourage the widespread transfer and sharing of knowledge. One of the features of organizational life is constraint, which results in highly segmented pools of locally dense knowledge. EAP situations are complicated by a concern for stigma and privacy management (Petronio, 2007) that further impedes one's search for answers. These contextual factors (e.g., culture) need to be more explicitly represented in future work on the CMIS to further capture constraints that govern the development of organizational communication networks.

These limitations often represent the darker side of organizational life in what is often seen as a patriarchal workplace. For example, health and wellness programs are widely touted as ways to reduce rising health care costs, improve worker efficiency, reduce absenteeism, and create employee loyalty and are viewed as mutually beneficial to management and workers (Zoeller, 2003). However, there have been concerns that a health emphasis embodies managerial (and middle class, Protestant) values of individual responsibility, self-denial, and self-control with healthy workers providing competitive advantage by working at full capacity (Zoeller, 2003). Some have gone so far as to suggest that an element of the very definition of "professional" assumes a willingness to manage one's health so as to maximize organizational performance (Kelly & Colquhoun, 2005). Some view EAPs as paternalistic with an emphasis on tailoring the individual to the organization's requirements rather than changing work processes to fit employees who might conceivably focus on relaxation and pleasure as alternative values (Zoeller, 2003).

Official EAPs often mediate structured disadvantages (e.g., gender discrimination) in the workplace for those with lower wages, less discretionary time, and differential coverage under health plans (Poverny & Dodd, 2000). However, informal norms among coworkers also influence usage of organizational work–life benefits such as paternity leave where fellow workers might be influenced by absences (Kirby & Krone, 2002). These informal norms result in concertative control suggesting that dedicated, ambitious employees will forgo work–life benefits. These norms are further reinforced by middle managers (Kirby & Krone, 2002). Issues of equity also emerge for individuals without family obligations (Kirby & Krone, 2002). In the shadowy informal world of organization "behavioral contracts" between workers and supervisors may emerge due to the failure of official policies to deal with the manager's concerns for work performance and effectively dealing with problematic employees. This may lead to informal referral to programs like Alcoholics Anonymous or chats with intermediaries in social networks. All of this creates a structuration dynamic in how official policies are actually implemented (Kirby & Krone, 2002).

In many ways, these issues are more contemporary manifestations of a traditional literature that dealt with role sets in focal network terms and role conflict (Katz & Kahn, 1978). There is now increasing concern with the blurring boundaries of work–family life and the commercialization of intimate life (Kirby, 2006). At the heart of the intersection of work–life is balance and people being successful in both. Indeed, the workplace may serve as a refuge for some people from personal, family, and health issues (Geist-Martin et al., 2003).

Pragmatic/Policy Issues

Individuals need to decide their own strategies for negotiating WL dilemmas, but when uncertainty rises to a high level and people's skills are insufficient to address it, they need the pragmatic interventions that an effective EAP can provide. Most of our major life problems are associated with lack of knowledge, skills, or ability to assess risks. Information and the skills to acquire it are critical to surmounting these problems. This implies that one viable strategy might be to conduct intraorganizational information campaigns and training programs that increase an individual's awareness of sources, how to use them, and for what they are appropriate. Such training programs might address optimal search behaviors (e.g., appropriate key word selection) and acquaint individuals with unfamiliar (and more trustworthy and credible) sources of information. The more people in the social network who know what to do, the greater the likelihood that individuals will find the answers they need. This is especially so in the light of Burt's (2007) recent findings that suggest that only direct contacts are likely to be influential, that friend-of-friend types of indirect ties have minimal influence.

Increasing an individual's familiarity with possible authoritative sources of information should be one aspect of any EAP training component. One objective of training in information seeking should be to sensitize individuals to other sources of communication and to increasing their information-seeking capabilities. A cornerstone of any strategy to facilitate information seeking is the removal of various access barriers. Firms have to support the sharing and using of information. Employees should be able to easily access a common pool of available information through modern telecommunication and database systems. Increasingly, when employees use sources like the Internet, which contains many conflicting voices, they need to be trained in how to weigh the credibility of various sources as well (Case, Johnson, Andrews, Allard, & Kelley, 2004). Another possible approach to enhancing information seeking is to increase the richness of an individual's information fields and the larger organizational information infrastructure through such interventions as comprehensive Web sites.

Organizations should nurture prosocial information seeking associated with personal growth, creativity, curiosity, or sharing information with coworkers by providing individuals with the autonomy to pursue their searches and the ready availability of resources that meet their needs by such means as comprehensive Web sites and off-site, formal counseling, telephone EAP services. The basic task of management is to change structures, information infrastructure and technology, and culture to promote information sharing and seeking. In effect, management should serve as a guide to what areas and sources are most likely to have valuable information; this referral function is critical because managers are typically not equipped to be counselors.

Management campaigns often fail because their recommended beneficial effects are not apparent to employees, which may certainly be the case for some EAP issues where employees are in denial. These campaigns do not identify market segments that require different, tailored communication approaches in line with their specific needs, suggesting that a range of strategies be used to reach employees (Picherit-Duthler & Freitag, 2004), especially a greater appreciation of the role of informal networks. This suggests that finer-grain segmentations of the audience may be necessary to ensure effective communication campaigns and the tailoring of messages. Traditionally, in EAP situations, organizations have relied on supervisors to target likely employees.

Summary

Information seeking is often a great challenge to individuals. We must recognize human limits and be aware that stress related to work–life issues further deteriorates them. People have to be willing to believe that their individual actions can make a difference, that by seeking information they gain some control and mastery over their WL. They also have to overcome the limits of their education and knowledge base. They have to possess skills as information seekers, a knowledge of electronic information resources, familiarity with the Internet, an ability to weigh conflicting sources of information and to make judgments about their credibility. They also need a more sophisticated understanding of the surrounding social network and knowledge of who can help them with difficult problems, the specification of which enriches the CMIS. Absence of any one of the factors on this rather long linked chain could severely impede, if not halt, the acquisition of knowledge that allows individuals to act on their WL problems.

Many of the traditional barriers to information seeking can be addressed. Training programs and support structures can be designed to overcome individual lack of skills and awareness of information sources. They also can increase the salience of EAP issues as an important life/career skill. Perhaps most important, new technologies offer the possibility of overcoming and/or substituting for the traditional problems of confidentiality, accessibility, inertia, and the limitations of humans as information processors. However, perhaps the most serious limit on these technologies is the recurring preference of individuals for interpersonal information sources in social networks that can digest and summarize vast quantities of information for individual seekers.

Acknowledgment

I would like to thank Donald Case for reviewing an earlier version of this chapter.

References

Albrecht, T. L., & Adelman, M. B. (1987). Dilemmas of supportive communication. In T. L. Albrecht & M. B. Adelman (Eds.), *Communicating social support* (pp. 240–254). Newbury Park, CA: Sage.
Ashford, S. J., Blatt, R., & VandeWalle, D. (2003). Reflections on the looking glass: A review of research on feedback seeking behavior in organizations. *Journal of Management, 29*, 773–799.

Babrow, A. S. (1992). Communication and problematic integration: Understanding diverging probability and value, ambiguity, ambivalence and impossibility. *Communication Theory, 2*, 95–130.

Babrow, A. S. (2001). Guest editor's introduction to the special issue on uncertainty, evaluation, and communication. *Journal of Communication, 51*, 453–455.

Behson, S. J. (2005). The relative contribution of formal and informal organizational work–family support. *Journal of Vocational Behavior, 66*, 487–500.

Borgatti, S. P., & Cross, S. P. (2003). A relational view of information seeking and learning in social networks. *Management Science, 49*, 432–445.

Brandon, D. P., & Hollingshead, A. B. (2004). Transactive memory systems in organizations: Matching tasks, expertise, and people. *Organization Science, 15*, 633–644.

Brashers, D. E., Goldsmith, D. J., & Hsieh, E. (2002). Information seeking and avoiding in health contexts. *Human Communication Research, 28*, 258–271.

Burt, R. S. (2007). Secondhand brokerage: Evidence on the importance of local structure for managers, bankers, and analysts. *Academy of Management Journal, 50*, 119–148.

Case, D. O. (2007). *Looking for information* (2nd ed.). New York: Academic Press.

Case, D. O., Andrews, J. E., Johnson, J. D., & Allard, S. L. (2005). Avoiding versus seeking: The relationship of information seeking to avoidance, blunting, coping, dissonance and related concepts. *Journal of Medical Libraries Association, 93*, 48–57.

Case, D. O., Johnson, J. D., Andrews, J. E., Allard, S. L., & Kelley, K. M. (2004). From two-step flow to the Internet: The changing array of sources for genetics information seeking. *Journal of the American Society for Information Science and Technology, 55*, 660–669.

Cross, R., Rice, R. E., & Parker, A. (2001). Information seeking in social context: Structural influences and receipt of information benefits. *IEEE Transactions on Systems, Man, and Cybernetics—Part C: Applications and Reviews, 31*, 438–448.

Dahlin, K. B., Weingart, L. R., & Hinds, P. J. (2005). Team diversity and information use. *Academy of Management Journal, 48*, 1107–1123.

Department of Labor. (2006). General workplace impact. Retrieved October 24, 2006, from http://www.dol.gov/asp/programs/drugs/workingpartners/stats/wi.asp

Dietz, D., Cook, R., & Hersch, R. (2005). Workplace health promotion and utilization of health services: Follow-up data findings. *Journal of Behavioral Health Services & Research, 32*, 306–319.

Earl, M. (2001). Knowledge management strategies: Toward a taxonomy. *Journal of Management Information Systems, 18*, 215–233.

Eby, L. T., Casper, W. J., Lockwood, A., Bordeaux, C., & Brinley, A. (2005). Work and family research in IO/OB: Content analysis and review of the literature. *Journal of Vocational Behavior, 66*, 124–197.

Farrell, A., & Geist-Martin, P. (2005). Communicating social health: Perceptions of wellness at work. *Management Communication Quarterly, 18*, 543–592.

Freeman, L. C. (1992). Filling in blanks: A theory of cognitive categories and the structure of social affiliation. *Social Psychology Quarterly, 55*, 118–127.

Freimuth, V. S. (1987). The diffusion of supportive information. In T. L. Albrecht & M. B. Adelman (Eds.), *Communicating social support* (pp. 212–237). Newbury Park, CA: Sage.

Geist-Martin, P., Horsley, K., & Farrell, A. (2003). Working well: Communicating individual and collective wellness initiatives. In T. L. Thompson, A. M. Dorsey, K. I. Miller, & R. Parrott (Eds.), *Handbook of health communication* (pp. 423–443). Mahwah, NJ: Lawrence Erlbaum Associates.

Hansen, M. T., Mors, M. L., & Lovas, B. (2005). Knowledge sharing in organizations: Multiple networks, multiple phases. *Academy of Management Journal, 48,* 776–793.

Johnson, J. D. (1983). A test of a model of magazine exposure and appraisal in India. *Communication Monographs, 50,* 148–157.

Johnson, J. D. (1984a). International communication media appraisal: Tests in Germany. In R. N. Bostrom (Ed.), *Communication yearbook 8* (pp. 645–658). Beverly Hills, CA: Sage.

Johnson, J. D. (1984b). A test of a model of media exposure and appraisal on two magazines in Nigeria. *Journal of Applied Communication Research, 12,* 63–74.

Johnson, J. D. (1987). A model of international communication media appraisal: Phase IV, generalizing the model to film. *International Journal of Intercultural Relations, 11,* 129–142.

Johnson, J. D. (1993). *Tests of a comprehensive model of cancer-related information seeking.* Paper presented at the Annual Convention of the Speech Communication Association, Miami, FL.

Johnson, J. D. (1996). *Information seeking: An organizational dilemma.* Westport, CT: Quorum Books.

Johnson, J. D. (1997). *Cancer-related information seeking.* Cresskill, NJ: Hampton Press.

Johnson, J. D. (2003). On contexts of information seeking. *Information Processing and Management, 39,* 735–760.

Johnson, J. D., Case, D. O., Andrews, J. E., & Allard, S. L. (2005). Genomics—The perfect information seeking research problem. *Journal of Health Communication, 10,* 323–329.

Johnson, J. D., Donohue, W. A., Atkin, C. K., & Johnson, S. H. (1995). A comprehensive model of information seeking: Tests focusing on a technical organization. *Science Communication, 16,* 274–303.

Johnson, J. D., & Meischke, H. (1993). A comprehensive model of cancer-related information seeking applied to magazines. *Human Communication Research, 19,* 343–367.

Johnson, J. D., & Oliveira, O. S. (1988). A model of international communication media appraisal and exposure: A comprehensive test in Belize. *World Communication, 17,* 253–277.

Kanter, R. M. (1977). *Men and women of the corporation.* New York: Basic Books.

Katz, D., & Kahn, R. L. (1978). *The social psychology of organizations* (2nd ed.). New York: Wiley & Sons.

Katz, E. (1968). On reopening the question of selectivity in exposure to mass communications. In R. P. Abelson (Ed.), *Theories of cognitive consistency* (pp. 788–796). New York: Rand McNally.

Katz, E., & Lazarsfeld, P. F. (1955). *Personal influence: The part played by people in the flow of mass communications.* New York: The Free Press.

Kelly, K., Andrews, J. E., Case, D. O., Allard, S. L., & Johnson, J. D. (2007). Information seeking and intentions to have genetic testing for hereditary cancers in rural and Appalachian Kentuckians. *Journal of Rural Health, 23,* 166–172.

Kelly, P., & Colquhoun, D. (2005). The professionalization of stress management: Health and well-being as a professional duty of care? *Critical Public Health, 15,* 135–145.

Kirby, E. L. (2006). "Helping you make room in your life for your needs": When organizations appropriate family roles. *Communication Monographs, 73*, 474–480.

Kirby, E. L., & Krone, K. J. (2002). "The policy exists but you can't really use it": Communication and the structuration of work–family process. *Journal of Applied Communication Research, 30*, 50–77.

Kossek, E. E., & Lambert, S. J. (Eds.). (2005). *Work and life integration: Organizational, cultural, and individual perspectives.* Mahwah, NJ: Lawrence Erlbaum Associates.

Kossek, E. E., & Ozeki, C. (1998). Work–family conflict, policies, and the job–life satisfaction relationships: A review and directions for organizational behavior– human resources research. *Journal of Applied Psychology, 83*, 139–149.

Krackhardt, D. (1994). Constraints on the interactive organization as an ideal type. In C. Heckscher & A. Donnelon (Eds.), *The post-bureaucratic organization: New perspectives on organizational change* (pp. 211–222). Thousand Oaks, CA: Sage.

Miller, V. D., & Jablin, F. M. (1991). Information seeking during organizational entry: Influences, tactics, and a model of the process. *Academy of Management Review, 16*, 92–120.

Nebus, J. (2006). Building collegial information networks: A theory of advice network generation. *Academy of Management Review, 31*, 615–637.

Palazzolo, E. T., Serb, D. A., She, Y., Su, C., & Contractor, N. S. (2006). Coevolution of communication and knowledge networks in transactive memory systems: Using computational models for theoretical development. *Communication Theory, 16*, 223–250.

Petronio, S. (2007). Translational research endeavors and the practice of Communication Privacy Management. *Journal of Applied Communication Research, 35*, 218–222.

Picherit-Duthler, G., & Freitag, A. (2004). Researching employees' perceptions of benefits communication: A communication inquiry on channel preferences, understanding, decision-making, and benefits satisfaction. *Communication Research Reports, 21*, 391–403.

Poverny, L. M., & Dodd, S. J. (2000). Differential patterns of EAP service utilization: A nine year follow-up study of faculty and staff. *Employee Assistance Quarterly, 15*, 29–42.

Ray, E. B. (1987). Supportive relationships and occupational stress in the workplace. In T. L. Albrecht & M. B. Adelman (Eds.), *Communicating social support* (pp. 172–191). Newbury Park, CA: Sage.

Smithson, M. (1989). *Ignorance and uncertainty: Emerging paradigms.* New York: Springer-Verlag.

Susskind, A. M., Schwartz, D. F., Richards, W. D., & Johnson, J. D. (2005). Evolution and diffusion of the Michigan State University tradition of organizational communication network research. *Communication Studies, 56*, 397–418.

Watts, D. J. (2003). *Six degrees: The science of the connected age.* New York: W. W. Norton.

Wegner, D. M. (1995). A computer network of model of human transactive memory. *Social Cognition, 13*, 319–339.

Wilson, T. D. (1997). Information behavior: An interdisciplinary perspective. *Information Processing and Management, 33*, 551–572.

Zoeller, H. M. (2003). Working out: Managerialism in workplace health promotion. *Management Communication Quarterly, 17*, 171–205.

Part II

Disclosure Decisions

The Intersection Between Uncertainty and Disclosure

11 Uncertainty and Communication in Couples Coping with Serious Illness

Daena J. Goldsmith

Paul's heart disease almost went undetected. While seeing his physician for another condition he mentioned an unrelated symptom that led the physician to order a stress test. Within 24 hours, Paul had coronary artery bypass graft surgery. He recalled, "They told me that had I not done anything with this, that I'd have had a 50/50 chance of living a year." Now that he is recovered, however, he feels confident about the future, saying,

> I have so much information from the hospital, visiting nurses and numbers to call if I have any problems. That's why I never really had any concerns that I couldn't get answers. . . . We had one little flare-up the other day, my wife wanted me to call a nurse. I just waited a while and it went away.

In contrast, his wife, Dot, said, "It makes you like a little apprehensive. You know, we had no idea he had heart trouble, he didn't have a heart attack. He was golfing every day and no problems at all." Medical advice and information hasn't completely alleviated her uncertainty: "You read books and everything and you know like the thing he had with his shoulder, I thought, 'Is this a normal thing?' . . . And I said, 'Is it a pain or what is it?' And of course, then that kind of sets me off, I worry about it because I don't know." Paul said his wife asks him about his health more often now but that he didn't mind because these were "just normal wifely concerns."

These accounts illustrate the complexity of uncertainty management for couples coping with serious illness. Even though Paul and Dot were generally satisfied with his treatment, prognosis, and access to information, Paul's illness prompted uncertainty. Paul and Dot agreed that information was readily available from their health care team, yet differed in their access to bodily sensations (Dot must rely on him to tell her how he feels) and in how they applied to daily experience what they had read or been told. Paul's nearly missed diagnosis made him grateful, though not particularly apprehensive, and a vocal advocate of cardiovascular screening. Dot questioned the appearance of wellness and became vigilant about everyday aches and pains. These differences showed up in their interactions with one another, as they discussed when to seek information and when to wait and see if a symptom goes away. Paul chalked up their different orientations to gendered marital roles. This brief glimpse into one couple's story shows how illness uncertainty has implications for identity and relationship, how partners can interpret these issues differently, and that couples may need to coordinate their uncertainties.

This chapter explores how couples coping with serious illness manage uncertainty. I have included the voices of participants in my research to give examples of theoretical issues. The Illinois Heart Care Project involved interviews with 25 patients and 16 partners of patients who had a myocardial infarction (MI; commonly referred to as a "heart attack") and/or coronary artery bypass graft surgery (CABG) in the last year (for study details, see Goldsmith, Bute, & Lindholm, 2007; Goldsmith, Gumminger, & Bute, 2006; Goldsmith, Lindholm, & Bute, 2006). Recently, we completed additional interviews with 19 patients and 16 partners of patients treated for cancer in the last 5 years (see Goldsmith & Moriarty, 2008, for study details).

I begin by discussing how couple interdependence creates distinctive coping demands, a phenomenon variously conceptualized as "relational," "communal," or "dyadic" coping. Then I discuss how these dyadic processes shape interrelated uncertainties about illness, identity, and relationships. Research on uncertainty management and dyadic coping strategies provide a basis for speculating how couples facing illness communicate. Finally, I suggest directions for future research. Throughout, I show how studying uncertainty in the couple-coping-with-illness context extends theory in two ways: (1) We consider not only individual but also dyadic uncertainty management, and (2) We find interrelationships among multiple types of uncertainty.

The Couple Context for Coping with Illness

I didn't tell him [not to mow the lawn] because I knew that would be the wrong thing to do, but I did say to him that I would rather, I would prefer he let someone else do our mowing for quite awhile. And the doctor just gave him the release last week when he asked if he could mow now. Because he dearly loves to mow. . . . So this will be a challenge for me [laughs] probably to just stay and not watch when he goes out to do it. But I feel like he needs to do it. The doctor said he can, he needs to go do it, I need to keep my mouth shut.

(Donna, wife of a man recovering from MI and CABG)

I think I worried more about Joe because me going through this, I was going through it, I knew what I was up against, physically and emotionally what I was up against. He could do nothing and I would go in and have this test that was absolutely the most miserable thing that I could ever imagine and that poor guy would just be sitting out there waiting. I worried about him having to be there with me. He'd, "Oh, you don't have to worry about it," yeah right! And I did, to me that's an inequality, he had to be there and there was nothing that I could do to make it better for him. Everybody was keyed on me that this was my cancer, it was my issue but it was our issue. He didn't have that support system of the doctors and the nurses and everybody saying, "Are you okay? Are you okay? Are you okay?" He'd just sit out there in the waiting room. And I couldn't even be out there saying, "Are you okay? Are you okay?"

(Kathy, a woman treated for lymphoma)

Patients are not the only ones who experience uncertainty related to illness and both patients and partners have concerns not only about the illness but also about its effects on one another and their relationship. The couple context draws attention to dyadic interdependence as a distinctive feature of uncertainty management. When the person experiencing illness is a member of a committed couple (including marriage as well as other committed partners), both partners are affected by demands of treatment, changes to daily life, and concerns for the future. Couple interdependence includes not only intertwined activities and outcomes, but also symbolic interdependence in expectations for self and other (Kelley, Berscheid, Christensen, Harvey, & Huston, 1983). For example, believing partners should stand together "in sickness and in health" means their actions in the face of illness are important not only for illness adaptation but also for how they reflect on the moral standing of each person and the quality of their relationship.

Couples' illness experiences are interdependent. Partners' physical health, mental well-being, and health behaviors are correlated (see Meyler, Stimpson, & Peek, 2007, for a review). Couples experience shared stressors (e.g., financial difficulties) and one partner's stressors affect the other, either directly (e.g., by creating caregiving demands) or indirectly (e.g., through empathic distress for the partner's trouble; Bodenmann, 2005; O'Brien & DeLongis, 1997; Westman & Vinokur, 1998). How well one person copes with illness-related stressors affects the other's adjustment (e.g., Ben-Zur, Gilbar, & Lev, 2001; Manne & Zautra, 1990).

Illness has often been viewed as a stressor, leading researchers to investigate how a patient copes and how social support facilitates coping. Recently, scholars have recognized that coping and social support concepts miss something important about coping in interdependent relationships (e.g., Revenson, Kayser, & Bodenmann, 2005). Coping research typically focuses on the individual perspective, ignoring how stressors simultaneously affect others in one's life. As Afifi, Hutchinson, and Krouse (2006) observe, "Family members respond and adapt to stress based on their interactions with other family members. Their responses to stress are often a function of other family members' stress and their ability (effectively or ineffectively) to adapt to it, as well as their ability to cope by communicating with one another" (p. 383).

Social support research seldom corrects this individualistic bias; instead, it treats others as resources for one person's coping. In interdependent relationships, it may not be clear who is a provider and who is a recipient of support (Goldsmith, 2004). Assuming that one partner's illness is *the* stressor, and the other partner is only a source of coping assistance, ignores the complexity of illness and the interdependence of partners. Illness prompts many interrelated stressors, including changes in household routines, financial burdens, and worries about the future. These stressors affect partners as much or more than they affect the patient (e.g., Moser & Dracup, 2004; Northouse, Laten, & Reddy, 1995). The *patient*'s ability to reciprocally support the partner is important for partner adjustment and relational satisfaction (Wright & Aquilino, 1998).

To further complicate matters, directly seeking and providing support are not the only ways partners assist each other. One may aid the other without that person's knowledge and ordinary routines help partners cope together without explicitly doing social support. For example, when wives of men recovering from a heart attack shielded their husbands from household concerns and the wives' own anxieties, their husbands experienced improved self-efficacy, well-being, and physical health (Coyne & Smith, 1994). Everyday conversations, routines, and shared activities can assist recovery from MI or CABG without the explicit talk about the stresses of heart disease that we would conventionally recognize as social support (Goldsmith, 2004). In close relationships, needing to ask for or offer support may be the exception rather than the rule and could represent a breakdown of mutual responsiveness, shared meaning, and routines through which couples normally cope (Coyne, Ellard, & Smith, 1990).

Theories of relationship-focused coping (e.g., Coyne et al., 1990; O'Brien & DeLongis, 1997), communal coping (e.g., Afifi et al., 2006; Lyons, Mickelson, Sullivan, & Coyne, 1998), and dyadic coping (e.g., Revenson, Kayser, & Bodenmann, 2005) developed out of a recognition that one partner's stress affects the other, that each partner's coping affects the other, and that dyadic interaction patterns affect individual adjustment and relational functioning. During difficult times, one's partner and relationship may be a source of stress as well as support. When one's partner is upset and trying to cope, responding to her or his distress and coordinating responses requires cognitive, emotional, and behavioral energy, or what Coyne and Smith (1991) refer to as "grappling with each other's presence and emotional needs" (p. 405). A review of this growing body of work and distinctions among the related concepts are beyond the scope of this chapter (see Afifi et al., 2006; Berg & Upchurch, 2007; Revenson, Kayser, & Bodenmann, 2005). I refer to "dyadic coping" to capture features common to these various concepts and I identify key contributions of this work to set the stage for discussion of dyadic uncertainty management.

Forms of Dyadic Coping

Couples vary in how they "grapple" with each other's distress and sustain their relationship. No single typology of strategies has emerged but some common dimensions differentiate couples' responses. First, couples vary in how openly they communicate about one another's distress and coping. For example, Coyne and his colleagues (e.g., Coyne et al., 1990; Coyne & Smith, 1991, 1994) differentiate "active engagement" (in which couples discuss feelings and engage in joint problem solving) from "protective buffering" (in which one or both partners hide concerns from the other to avoid upset or conflict).

Second, couples differ in appraising stress and coping as shared rather than individual. For example, Lyons and colleagues (1998) differentiate responses to stressors along two dimensions: responsibility for the problem and responsibility for a solution. "Communal coping" occurs when a problem is appraised as shared (our problem) and requiring joint actions (our solutions) and is characterized by communication about coping and cooperative action (see also Afifi et al., 2006, for an expanded conceptualization). Alternatively, Berg and Upchurch (2007) propose a single continuum of dyadic coping responses, ranging from partners who are uninvolved, to supportive, then collaborative, and, finally, overinvolved.

Third, responses range from positive to negative. For example, Bodenmann (2005) contrasts positive supportive dyadic coping (e.g., helping with tasks, giving advice, expressing empathy, showing solidarity) with negative dyadic coping (e.g., support given in a hostile, ambivalent, or superficial way). Overprotection (doing for the patient tasks that he or she could do alone) is harmful for patients when it arises from a partner's hostility, criticism, and frustration that the patient is not trying; however, overprotection that is caring and supportive has neutral or even positive effects on the patient (Fiske, Coyne, & Smith, 1991; Riegel & Dracup, 1992).

Fourth, couples may differ in awareness of one another's intentions and explicitness of coordination. For example, Afifi and colleagues (2006) found that protective buffering could occur with or without the other's knowledge that he or she was being protected. Awareness is also related to empathic understanding of the other's experience (O'Brien & DeLongis, 1997), and to relational awareness (Acetelli & Badr, 2005).

Effects of Dyadic Coping

The variety of dyadic coping forms has led to research on whether some ways of coping are more satisfying and productive than others. Not surprisingly, positive behaviors fare better than negative ones (Berg & Upchurch, 2007; Bodenmann, 2005) but, with respect to the other dimensions, it is not clear that one pattern is necessarily best. Nonetheless, it is possible to identify factors that shape the course of dyadic coping and outcomes.

The benefits of dyadic coping strategies sometimes vary for each partner and for different outcomes. For example, it was distressing for wives of men recovering from MI to engage in protective buffering but it promoted better self-efficacy and physical recovery for their husbands (Coyne & Smith, 1991,

1994). The intersection of patient and partner roles with gender also affects the efficacy of open discussion versus protective withholding (Revenson, Abraido-Lanza, Majerovitz, & Jordan, 2005). Women (patients and partners) experience more cancer-related distress than men (Hagedoorn, Sanderman, Bolks, Tuinstra, & Coyne, 2008) and the ability to discuss and collaborate may have more impact on women than men (Hagedoorn et al., 2000). Men are more likely to be actively engaged when they are the patient, but they tend to do protective buffering when their wives are ill; wives do active engagement when well and protective buffering when ill (Badr, 2004).

Congruency of coping influences satisfaction and effectiveness. Similar coping strategies can be mutually reinforcing; however, complementary strategies may extend the range of coping actions and enable one partner's strengths to compensate for another's weaknesses (Berghuis & Stanton, 2002; Revenson, 1994). The type of coping matters: It is unlikely to be productive if both partners engage in individual avoidance, denial, and negativity or in mutual negative dyadic coping (Bodenmann, 2005; Pakenham, 1998). When one partner engages in high levels of protective buffering or avoidance, it is better if the other reports low levels of these forms of coping; in contrast, marital adjustment was related to *similarity* in levels of active engagement but not to the *amount* of active engagement (Badr, 2004).

Coping patterns may have different effects depending upon preexisting couple satisfaction (Berg & Upchurch, 2007). For example, Coyne and Smith (1991) found protective buffering was more distressing in unhappy than in happy marriages. They speculated that, in unhappy marriages, protective buffering may be experienced as antagonistic cooperation rather than sincere concern. While it is tempting to presume dyadic coping affects marital satisfaction, we must also consider the possibility that those who are more satisfied and adjusted find it easier to relate to one another in desirable ways. However, there is evidence from Bodenmann's longitudinal studies that shared dyadic coping at earlier time periods does predict marital satisfaction and stability 5 years later (Bodenmann, 2005).

In addition to patient and partner roles, gender roles, congruency of coping, and marital satisfaction, Berg and Upchurch (2007) suggest additional factors to consider. Specifically, they propose that cultural differences, life span differences (e.g., due to age and cohort effects), and illness differences can all impact the types of dyadic coping that occur and their effects.

Relevance to Understanding Uncertainty

Dyadic coping draws attention to the distinctively social components of experiencing a stressful life event in the context of a close, committed, interdependent dyadic bond. Like the research on individual coping and social support to which dyadic coping was a critical response, research related to uncertainty and illness has frequently adopted the individual point of view to the relative neglect of the dyadic. We can usefully insert "uncertainty management" in place of "coping" to focus attention on *dyadic uncertainty management*. This would lead us to ask questions akin to those asked in dyadic coping research, such as: How are partners' uncertainty management efforts intertwined? How does one partner's uncertainty management shape the other's outcomes? What are some of the ways partners attempt to coordinate their uncertainty management efforts? What factors shape the effectiveness of dyadic efforts?

Multilayered Uncertainties in Illness

Illness is the other contextual feature of uncertainty management that is highlighted by studying the couples-coping-with-illness context. Our improving capabilities to diagnose and treat serious illnesses create new uncertainties. For example, heart disease and cancer are leading causes of death in the developed world and yet these conditions are no longer seen as a near-certain death sentence. While this is good news for patients and their loved ones, it sets the stage for numerous sources of uncertainty. Some concerns are about the *illness*: What treatment is best for me? Should I seek additional information? Can I trust the information I have received? What symptoms of illness or side effects can I expect? What is the likelihood of my condition worsening or recurring? Will I survive this illness and for how long? There are often additional uncertainties about whether and how the illness may change one's *identity*: Will I be the same person I once was? Can I still care for my loved ones, make a living, and enjoy activities? Couples who go through illness together also experience *relational* uncertainty. Interdependence can create a need to coordinate sense making, emotional expression, and behavior related to the illness. How each partner is affected, how each partner can care for the other, and how their relationship may change can become additional sources of ambiguity.

Research on illness uncertainty and illness identity does sometimes recognize the partner's significant role in managing uncertainty; however, the patient is usually focal. Relational uncertainty research has frequently been conducted in young, mostly healthy populations whose uncertainty arises from getting acquainted and making a commitment. In what follows, I show how studying illness, identity, and relational uncertainty in couples coping with serious illness can broaden our understanding of uncertainty and how appreciating this context requires considering how multiple sources of uncertainty are interrelated.

Uncertainty about Illness

> Our interview protocol asked partners of heart patients, "Do you ever feel anxious about your husband having another heart attack?" Faith replied: "I was with him when he had the [MI] and even to this day, I wouldn't have perceived him as having a heart attack. I just didn't realize that's what he was having. So, yeah, I am. Sure."
>
> (Faith, wife of a man recovering from MI and CABG)

Well, I'm concerned, he's concerned too. He wants to know when all that strength will come back, you know, or when his chest will quit hurting and that type of thing.

(Lois, wife of man recovering from MI and CABG)

If I can't function, I'll refuse treatment. Cindy, my wife, of course wants to have me around as long as possible. The only potential cure for this thing is a bone marrow transplant . . . she was hoping, I think, that would be the next step for us. . . . [W]e decided against the bone marrow transplant. We did extensive research on just how long can you keep going with transfusions, had conversations with a number of doctors. . . . [When I was first diagnosed], I said, "Worst case, what have I got?" He says, "Four months." Okay, um . . . we dealt [chuckling] with that. I've been going now for a year and a half and if this transfusion thing continues to work, I could be going for a long, long-time, with the hope that they are making so many advances now in MDS treatment that six months down the road from now, they may have a major breakthrough that will enable me to return to a normal life.

(Ryan, treated for a bone marrow disorder)

As Faith's description of her husband's MI shows, illness disrupts the otherwise taken-for-granted state of health (Becker, 1997). Faith, Lois, and Ryan each comment on the range of uncertainties associated with illness. We may be uncertain if we are ill and, even if medical professionals confirm that something is amiss, we may experience uncertainty about the correct diagnosis, prognosis, treatment, and side effects. Even when one has recovered health, uncertainty about recurrence may loom. Partners experience these uncertainties, too, and couples may need to coordinate uncertainty management.

Many factors shape the nature and level of uncertainty a patient experiences, including the familiarity and severity of symptoms, patient familiarity with health care settings, and the availability of personal and social resources for imposing structure on the illness experience (Mast, 1995; Mishel, 1988; Mishel & Braden, 1988). Illnesses may have complex causes, the information we find may be insufficient or unreliable, probabilistic information about illness may be difficult to interpret or apply, or we may doubt whether the future can be predicted (Babrow, Kasch, & Ford, 1998).

Illness uncertainty takes many forms (Brashers et al., 2003). Medical uncertainty occurs when there is insufficient information about diagnosis, ambiguous symptom patterns, complex symptoms of treatment and care, and unpredictable disease progression or prognosis. In addition, personal uncertainty (e.g., "Am I sick or well?" "What are the financial ramifications of my illness?") and social uncertainty (e.g., "Will I be stigmatized?" "Will my relationships be affected?") arise from the consequences of illness and its treatment. Even recovery and successful treatment can create uncertainty about how to live again (Brashers et al., 1999) or about whether a condition will recur (Mast, 1998). Over the course of an illness, uncertainty may shift from one topic or form to another and may be transformed from an individual to a social experience, either by interacting with specific others or through the use of culturally shared forms and meanings (Babrow, 2007).

How patients respond to illness uncertainty depends upon how it is appraised (Brashers et al., 2000; Mishel, 1988). Uncertainty may threaten one's goals and sense of control, creating anxiety and fear, but it can also be an opportunity when ambiguity about the likelihood of death or disability enables a patient to retain hope. Appraisals shape an individual's response: Threat appraisals prompt attempts to seek information to reduce uncertainty, whereas opportunity appraisals lead to avoiding information or seeking information that will enhance hope (Brashers et al., 2000). Some conditions entail living with chronic uncertainty (Mishel, 1990). Accepting uncertainty may be facilitated by information management, reorienting plans and goals, and shifting focus from an uncertain future to daily life (Brashers et al., 2000). Uncertainty is not always associated with negative emotions or outcomes! Managing uncertainty associated with cancer and myocardial infarction can result in "increased tolerance and appreciation for others, greater self-acceptance, and increased optimism and joy in life" (Mast, 1995, p. 19).

Significant others influence how patients appraise and manage illness-related uncertainty. Social support has been conceptualized as assisted uncertainty reduction (Albrecht & Adelman, 1987) or management (Brashers, Neidig, & Goldsmith, 2004; Ford, Babrow, & Stohl, 1996). Just as individuals seek to increase, maintain, or reduce uncertainty, supportive messages to breast cancer patients exhibited parallel forms of uncertainty management (Ford et al., 1996). Brashers and colleagues found social support aided uncertainty management for persons with HIV/AIDS by assisting with information seeking and avoiding, providing instrumental support, facilitating skill development, giving acceptance, allowing ventilation, and encouraging perspective shifts. Significant others were sources of information, collaborators in information gathering, evaluators of information, and buffers against information. However, they could also hinder uncertainty management by giving information a patient wanted to avoid or providing information that disagreed with conclusions the patients had reached. When one's own and others' uncertainty management were uncoordinated, this added relational uncertainty to illness uncertainty and created the burden of managing others' uncertainty in addition to one's own.

A focus on dyadic uncertainty management reminds us that significant others are not only potential collaborators in uncertainty management but also persons with uncertainties of their own. Partners often have comparable or greater levels of uncertainty than patients (Moser, Dracup, & Marsden, 1993; Northouse et al., 1995) and may be concerned about many of the same issues as patients. In addition, partners experience some distinctive uncertainties. Partners lack firsthand access to bodily sensations that could increase or decrease uncertainty. For example, heart patients recovering from MI or CABG must watch for discomfort during activities and cancer patients who have completed treatment may continue to monitor their bodies for signs of recurrence. Partners have to rely on patients to know whether an activity hurts or a lump shows up. Patients can shield partners from such information but, if partners suspect patients are withholding alarming information, they experience uncertainty nonetheless, wondering, "Is he or she experiencing a symptom and just not telling me?"

Partner uncertainty is also shaped by constraints on their information seeking. Partners may be very involved in seeking information relevant to treatment decision making, yet the structure of medical interactions can exclude partners and make it difficult to obtain information from health care providers (for a review, see Goldsmith & Moriarty, 2008). Contact between physicians and care providers of persons with HIV/AIDS enabled partners to help with home care, monitor symptoms, and advocate for the patient, yet the normative model of medical care constrained partner–physician interaction (Miller & Zook, 1997). The quality of interaction between partners of heart patients and health care providers influenced couple interactions at home, with implications for partner distress and patient self-efficacy (Coyne & Smith, 1991).

Partners may also have some information needs that differ from those of patients. In a study of couples 5 months following a cardiac event, Moser and colleagues (1993) found both patients and spouses identified the need for information as most important compared with all other needs; however, they wanted different types of information. Partners most wanted information about the patient's feelings and psychological recovery, whereas emotional concerns were given low rankings by patients, who placed more emphasis on information about their physical condition. Frequently, partners' needs for emotional information went unmet.

Uncertainty about Identity

> I'm uncertain about her work. I think work, for her, is something that's extremely important . . . some mornings she's able to work and others she isn't. And she feels the tug about, "but I should be in the office more," and I honestly don't know what to encourage her to do, you know. So I'm really uncertain as to what's the best thing for her and what my role should be in that.
>
> (Gregory, husband of woman with brain cancer)

> I mean actually I thought about [how to talk about possible impotence after prostate surgery], but you know, a lot of identity is tied up in that self-image, so it's not that it's difficult because it's sex, but it's difficult because of what it could mean, you know, and what one would, you know, need to deal with, and not simply in terms of like, plumbing, you know, but in terms of, you know, self-image and, you know, all that kind of stuff. So that's, that would be the difficult part, I think, of trying to figure out how to, um . . . you know, best talk about that without adding insult to injury.
>
> (Anita, wife of a man treated for prostate cancer)

Will I grow older? Because I want to! And so [my partner and I] did a lot of talking about that, about everything that I still wanted to do and the goals that I wanted to accomplish.

(Carrie, woman treated for breast cancer)

An essential issue in studies of illness identity and illness narratives is how individuals come to grips with uncertainty about who they are in the wake of a serious illness. Gregory recognizes how illness encroaches on his wife's valued work identity and he reports uncertainty about when and whether she should let that identity go. Anita acknowledges how treatment for cancer can threaten sexual identity. Carrie speaks to perhaps the most fundamental identity issue of all: whether she will live out the biography she had envisioned for her and with her partner.

Serious illness calls taken-for-granted identities into question (Becker, 1997). When serious illness is chronic, life may become a series of good days and bad days requiring ongoing attempts to reconcile one's sense of self with the constraints of illness and to impose coherence on an uncertain future (Charmaz, 1991). "People with serious chronic illnesses must repeatedly rethink how they live and who they are becoming. . . . Self and social identities are intertwined in daily actions and endeavors" (Charmaz, 2000, p. 286). It is not only that the activities involved in our various identities are disrupted, but illness also calls into question our ability to take for granted that our body will cooperate as we perform our identities (Kirmayer, 1992). Our sense of self includes the physical (our body) and temporal (past, present, future); illness disrupts the linkages between self, body, and biography (Corbin & Strauss, 1987).

Patients' stories about illness can reveal how they are managing uncertainty about identity. Frank (1995) has identified three recurring genres of illness narratives. Restitution narratives tell of health disrupted by illness and an eventual return to one's previous state. Chaos narratives lack order and express difficulty understanding physical suffering and dismay that one's condition may never improve. Quest narratives portray illness as a challenge that has changed the narrator for the better. One prototype tends to dominate an individual's story but elements of each may be present and patients may have to revise their stories over time (Charmaz, 1987). Narratives help manage uncertainty by giving voice to concerns about who one is, what illness means, and what life will be like.

A considerable literature addresses illness identity, but nearly all of it focuses on patient identity as revealed in narratives told to an interviewer. Observing couples coping with illness reminds us that narratives have multiple characters and multiple audiences, both of which include partners. Although they do not analyze the structure and function of narrative per se, two studies that collected partner narratives show how partners' identities may become uncertain and how they cope. Öhman and Söderberg (2004) found wives of persons with serious chronic illness suffered a shrinking sense of self as their activities and relational roles were constrained and they felt forced to take responsibility. Living in the present, feeling joy in being together, and committing to be together until the end were some of the ways these partners coped. Wives in another study (Eriksson & Svedlund, 2006) reported their husband's chronic illness had limited their social roles and activities and changed their marital roles. Though illness generated change, their lives felt less spontaneous because extensive planning and routine were required to care for their husbands. They reported needing to "permanently adapt," a concept that captures both the certainty of illness demands and their evolving nature. Similarly, "living with incessant harassment" captured their certainty that they would continue to feel uncertain about the adequacy of the patient's care and the coming of his death. Wives coped by normalizing illness, achieving balance, and seeking support and attention for themselves.

For many individuals, the performance of husband, wife, or partner is among their valued identities. It takes two to tango and, if one partner can no longer manage the footwork, the other person's interlocking identity performances will also be affected. Likewise, partners are the recipients of patient narratives, shaping them through their response (Charmaz, 2000). Partners may also become tellers or coperformers of patient stories. The story of illness is their story, too, suggesting we need greater attention to partners' narratives in their own right. Changes in partner identities, coordination of patient and partner identity performances, and partners' narrative collaborations can be powerful influences on patient and partner illness identities.

Uncertainty about the Relationship

> I feel a certain amount of stress or a big responsibility to do it [cooking a heart-healthy diet] right. . . . I think he appreciates very much what I'm doing. He sometimes will act like maybe this isn't what he wants, but I think that in reality he is. You know. In fact, just the other day I said, "You know," jokingly, I said, "Do you feel like I've taken all the control away from you and what you eat?" And he said, "No, never, not at all." So I do think that he is very appreciative of it, even though he probably kind of gives me a little static on it once in a while, I don't think it's sincere.
>
> (Rose, wife of a man recovering from CABG)

> We're just kind of coping with pain and so she got into this mode where it was like I was breakable and so I had to encourage her not to treat me as if I was breakable. And so a lot of that was physical and asking for what I needed and you talk about things that were hard to talk about. That goes right into the sexual relation and the breakable aspect of it because she's not wanting to do something to hurt me but you're as you're going through all these physical changes you're needing to know that you're still attractive.
>
> (Monica, treated for breast cancer)

If you're married a long time, you might as well realize that you'll probably have to take care of him, and she's been very good about that. . . . I think in some ways [our relationship] is better. But I feel sorry for her having to put up with all that. And I appreciate her taking care of me all the time.

(Wendall, who had multiple MIs and was
recovering from a recent CABG)

We don't know how much time we have left together.

(Rhonda, a woman with brain cancer)

Illness affects not only patient and partner individually, but also their relationship. Ken and Rose grapple with ambiguity about whether her actions show desirable concern or undesirable control. Recovery from breast surgery requires ongoing negotiation in Monica's sexual relationship. Wendall's physical decline and his wife's caregiving provoke mixed feelings of closeness, gratitude, regret, and inequality. Rhonda articulates uncertainty about her prognosis ("How long will *I* live?") in relational terms ("How much time do *we* have left *together*?").

Uncertainty reduction theory (Berger & Calabrese, 1975) directed our attention to uncertainty about strangers, their likely behavior, and our own appropriate responses. Subsequent work showed uncertainty does not end once we get to know a person but can recur through uncertainty-prompting events (Planalp, Rutherford, & Honeycutt, 1988). In addition to uncertainty about our own and our partner's attitudes and behaviors, we may also experience *relational uncertainty* about our involvement (Knobloch & Solomon, 1999), including ambiguity in our own commitment to, goals for, and definition of the relationship; inability to predict our partner's involvement; and/or uncertainty about where the relationship is headed. Inequity in relationships can contribute to relational uncertainty (Dainton, 2003). As Berger and Bradac (1982, p. 13) pointed out, ". . . in order for a relationship to continue, it is important that the persons involved in the relationship consistently update their fund of knowledge about themselves, their relational partner, and their relationship."

Both uncertainty and predictability are intrinsic to relationships (Baxter & Montgomery, 1996). Uncertainty about own and partner behavior and cognition may interfere with smooth coordination and evoke negative emotions but it can also be a source of novelty, spontaneity, and desire. Relational uncertainty can produce negative judgments of a partner's behaviors and upsetting events (Knobloch, 2007), but it can also sustain hope about the future of the relationship and partners may not always seek to remove relational ambiguity. The process of reducing uncertainty together may be reaffirming (Knobloch & Solomon, 2002a).

Knobloch and Solomon (2005) differentiate global relational uncertainty (overall doubts about involvement) from episodic relational uncertainty triggered by discrete events. They observe that, in intimate relationships, "[U]ncertainty[-]increasing episodes are important because they influence people's perceptions of closeness, companionship, emotional involvement, fairness, and trust within the relationship" (Knobloch & Solomon, 2002b, p. 460). How individuals respond to episodic relational uncertainty depends upon the intimacy of the relationship, the appraisal of the event, and the emotions experienced (Knobloch, 2005). Intimate partners who experience fear are more likely to respond positively, either by openly discussing their fears or indirectly increasing time spent together or expressing affection. In contrast, when episodic relational uncertainty triggers anger, or when a relationship is not very close, a person may be more likely to express negativity by yelling or quarreling. Sadness tends to provoke neutrally valenced avoidance.

Relational uncertainty makes it more difficult for partners to formulate messages and has been associated with less fluency, affiliativeness, relationship focus, explicitness, and perceived effectiveness (Knobloch, 2006; Knobloch & Solomon, 2005). In one study, married couples who reported even modest uncertainty about commitment reported more negative emotion, more perceived threat to self and relationship, more partner dominance, and less affiliation and involvement (Knobloch, Miller, Bond, & Mannone, 2007). Add to this the physical and emotional vulnerability entailed in coping with illness and we can imagine communication could become especially challenging, even for couples in long-standing satisfying relationships.

Studying couples coping with serious illness extends theorizing about episodic relational uncertainty. Identity-related uncertainties prompted by illness are a poignant reminder that self and other are not static. Even when we know one another quite well, illness can shake up our sense of self and reintroduce uncertainty about how each person thinks and acts in response to a new set of demands. Likewise, this context extends relational uncertainty past premarital relationships, enriching our notion of uncertainty about "involvement" from "Will this relationship continue into the future?" to "Having committed to the future, what will it be like?" Illness can be a significant stressor on a relationship, yet most relationships endure (e.g., Revenson, 1994; Taylor-Brown, Kilpatrick, Maunsell, & Dorval, 2000). Consequently, relational uncertainty in illness surrounds qualitative changes in involvement such as control, affection, dependence, obligation, equity, and intimacy. Paradoxically, the relative certainty of one's commitment heightens concerns about what life together will be like now.

Communication as Source and Resource

> I was pretty set, right from the beginning, on surgery. . . . My wife, being a researcher, she wanted to kind of take time and research things to make sure that was the right choice, and so she took the kind of more analytical and less emotional approach to the decision and I took the kind of immediate emotional approach and said, "Let's cut it out, let's get rid of it," . . . so it was a nice division of labor that way [laughs].
>
> (James, treated for prostate cancer)

I don't know what to say, I don't know what to do. I don't know, I don't have any words to say to make that fear subside. . . . I'm wrestling trying to find a word or something that may be profound enough to make a difference and I can't find it, it's not there. . . . I'm somewhat satisfied with our communication. It could be better.

(Joe, husband of a woman treated for lymphoma)

I've experienced a lot of uncertainty. We occasionally talk about it. . . . I'm uncertain about certain topics like whether to bring them up or not . . . it's not just a matter of treatment decisions, it's the other things. It's talking to the son, talking to her parents, talking to other family members about it. Uncertainty about when and how to enlist the support of others.

(Gregory, husband of a woman with brain cancer)

I think it was usually at night after our daughter goes to bed, that's generally the time. . . . It was just on our minds [laughs], so I think we were both kind of thinking about it and talking about it. None of the conversations were frantic or emotional, to me it all seemed pretty normal course of, you know, conversation. It wasn't quite at the level of, you know, what do we need to buy at the store today but, you know, it was all kind of part of the routine of life, you know, in the decision making.

(James, treated for prostate cancer)

Communication can be a source of uncertainty as well as a resource for managing it. Problem-solving communication between James and his wife helped them manage their individual uncertainties and coordinate preferences about treatment for his prostate cancer. Yet not all couples took this approach and a couple might use a different strategy for other topics. At another point in his interview (not included above), Joe said he and his wife were a "team" in seeking information about treatment; yet when it came to talking about their fears for the future, they felt less sure of whether and how to talk. Gregory mentions that communication with others outside the relationship is not only a source of potential assistance with uncertainty management but also a source of uncertainty for him: "When and how should I enlist support?" "Do I make those decisions on my own or discuss them with my wife?" The final excerpt shows that, in addition to intentional problem-solving discussions, couples also manage uncertainty in ordinary conversations that emerge from everyday routines. Illness uncertainty may prompt a desire to talk with one's partner, yet the changes they are experiencing may make partners unsure about how to communicate. Couples communicate about uncertainty created by illness, identity, or relationship, and may also need to talk about their uncertainty management efforts.

Communication between Partners to Manage Illness, Identity, and Relational Uncertainty

Researchers have identified several ways close relational partners communicate with one another in response to uncertainty. For example, Afifi and colleagues' theory of motivated information management (Afifi, Dillow, & Morse, 2004; Afifi & Weiner, 2004) differentiates direct information seeking (e.g., initiating discussions with the target about the issue in question) from indirect information seeking (e.g., heightened awareness about target-related cues surrounding the issue with a corresponding absence of intentional action intended to gather that information). They also recognize active avoidance strategies, which entail intentional efforts to steer clear of information relevant to the issue at hand. Knobloch and Solomon (2003) suggest that communicative management of relational uncertainty can be conceptualized as varying along an approach–avoid dimension and a valence dimension, yielding five strategies: integrative strategies (positive approach; for example, calm discussion, direct questioning), distributive behaviors (negative approach; for example, yelling, quarreling), closeness (positive avoidance; for example, spending more time together, increasing affection), distance (negative avoidance; for example, ignoring partner, decreasing affection), and avoidance (neutral avoidance; for example, hiding feelings, pretending).

Both direct and indirect strategies can be functional under different circumstances. If directly asking a partner about changes in identity or relationship is expected to reveal hurtful information, there may be wisdom in approaching the issue indirectly or avoiding it altogether (Afifi et al., 2004). Avoiding communication is usually relationally dissatisfying, but avoidance that is motivated by a desire to protect the relationship is an exception (Caughlin & Golish, 2002). In a review of research on open communication and avoidance among couples coping with cancer, Goldsmith, Miller, and Caughlin (2007) found open communication could improve coordination, closeness, and commitment; however, couples gave numerous reasons why they sometimes avoided open discussion, including protecting self or partner from distress, reluctance to express negative feelings, desire for privacy, sustaining hope and normalcy, avoiding the unnecessary, and preserving identities and relational qualities. The utility of direct, indirect, or avoidant strategies depended upon culture, gender, patient/partner role, age, length of relationship, and illness characteristics. Feeling able to talk if needed, perceiving one's partner as responsive, and steering clear of negative strategies (conflict, hostility, criticism) were associated with individual well-being and relational satisfaction.

In addition to intentional strategies, couples can manage uncertainty through daily routines. Among couples coping with MI or CABG (Goldsmith, 2004), ordinary talk surrounding everyday events (e.g., small talk over breakfast; evening talk about their respective days; making plans to shop for groceries, or have lunch following a doctor's appointment) provided a comfortable context in which issues relevant to illness arose spontaneously. These ordinary conversations could also substitute for more explicit talk by providing information and enabling inferences. Partners sometimes raised topics indirectly in the course of a conversation that was ostensibly about something else. Finally, talk about daily activities such as work, meals, or recreation could normalize new illness-related regimens and their corresponding implications for identity and relationship, obviating the need for a more explicit discussion of changes in lifestyle.

Communication between Partners to Coordinate Uncertainty Management

Dyadic uncertainty management draws our attention to the notion that partners may experience uncertainty about their communication and a need to coordinate their uncertainty management. I was unable to locate research that was specific to dyadic uncertainty management in the context of illness, but relevant options and issues may be inferred from related studies.

Brashers and his colleagues (2004) found that well-meaning significant others sometimes interfered with the preferred uncertainty management strategies employed by persons with HIV or AIDS. Patients avoiding information to sustain hope or relieve information overload were frustrated by friends and family who sent them information and patients who felt satisfied with their medical care were distressed when partners created uncertainty by questioning that care. Respondents reported several responses. Some took an active role in managing their own uncertainty independent of what others did or became selective about allowing others to help with uncertainty management. Some found ways to reframe undesired support as relationally meaningful even when it was not useful for managing illness uncertainty. Some accepted a lack of support from others, withdrew from problematic social situations, or asserted relational boundaries to prevent interference. Some of these strategies (e.g., withdrawal) may be less feasible for committed couples and the study focused only on the patient point of view; however, these findings suggest some dyadic uncertainty management strategies.

Dyadic uncertainty management is one domain of dyadic coping so dyadic coping strategies yield clues as to how couples coordinate uncertainty management. As indicated above, couples vary in how openly they discuss relational coping, how involved partners are in the patient's illness, the valence of interactions, and awareness of one another's relational coping. Active engagement is open and positive, with both partners involved and aware. There is evidence that active engagement is beneficial for individual functioning and relational satisfaction (see Berg & Upchurch, 2007, for a review); however, the benefits may be most applicable when distress, patient limitations, and illness are most severe (Hagedoorn et al., 2000; Kuijer et al., 2000). Protective buffering and overprotection may be most common when partners are very distressed, raising the question: Do these patterns produce distress or do they represent couples doing the best they can in a bad situation (Fiske et al., 1991)?

Juxtaposing individual uncertainty management options with dyadic coping strategies makes clear that the active engagement concept conflates dimensions that need to be examined separately. The most often studied dyadic coping options entail dichotomous contrasts between open and closed styles of communicating (i.e., open discussion versus withholding worries) or between collaborative and controlling styles of problem solving (i.e., joint problem solving versus partner overprotection), leaving uninvestigated the potential benefits of indirect communication that have been shown to be useful individual uncertainty management strategies.

Directions for Research

I have synthesized bodies of research that usually are distinct to show how the couples-coping-with-illness context is useful for studying uncertainty and communication. Considering how couples manage multiple layers of uncertainty raises several questions for future research.

Serious illness prompts a need for patients and partners to manage illness uncertainty. While patient uncertainty has been examined, we know little about partners' illness uncertainty. Likewise, we should investigate how patterns of communication (e.g., with health care providers and social network members) affect partners' illness uncertainty and how couples coordinate their meanings of the illness and their efforts to manage both persons' illness uncertainty.

Illness can threaten identity, motivating patient narratives that reconstruct a sense of self and biography. We know little about how partners serve as audiences for and participants in these narratives. In addition, we should study partner narratives in their own right. Coordination of narratives or the development of couple narratives could be examined for contributions to individual distress and relational satisfaction. We should also study what purposes and audiences may be served by distinct patient and partner narratives. Some stories may be too painful to tell one's partner, but could productively be told to a support group or confidant.

Serious illnesses can draw couples together or impose stresses that threaten relational dissolution. Do uncertainty management patterns differ for couples whose commitment is strengthened compared to couples who drift apart? Do intimacy and commitment offset or intensify uncertainty about illness, identity, and relationship? In addition, we should probe what other facets of a relational definition become uncertain in illness (e.g., equity, affection, control), how couples manage relational uncertainty, and what factors shape their responses.

Communication can be both a source of uncertainty and a resource for managing uncertainty. Little research has addressed how couples communicate with one another to reduce uncertainty in the face of illness or how they coordinate their uncertainty management efforts. Consequently, basic descriptive questions need to be addressed: What challenges do couples face in coordinating their uncertainty management efforts? Does uncertainty motivate couple communication and mediate its effects? What strategies do couples have available for uncertainty management and what factors shape their use? In addition to strategic efforts, how can ordinary communication routines manage uncertainty?

The uncertainty that ripples outward from an individual's illness experience is multifaceted and complex. As Babrow (2001) observes,

> [U]ncertainty is multilayered, interconnected, and temporal. . . . The layers of context suggest that people experience multiple sources of uncertainty at once, that manipulation of one type of uncertainty can impact uncertainties of other types, and that experiences of uncertainty are ongoing and changing features of life. (p. 481)

Dyadic uncertainty management adds to this complexity! At the very least, it doubles the possible sources, appraisals, and responses by adding partner to patient uncertainty. Furthermore, patients and partners seldom lead parallel lives; more often, their uncertainties interpenetrate, adding uncertainty that is distinctly dyadic. Communication, a powerful tool for managing uncertainty, may itself become a source of uncertainty. Though challenging to conceptualize and study, dyadic uncertainty management among couples coping with illness captures an experience that has often been overlooked. This chapter has suggested some of the issues at stake as we broaden our focus to encompass these additional uncertainties.

References

Acetelli, L. K., & Badr, H. (2005). My illness or our illness? Attending to the relationship when one partner is ill. In T. A. Revenson, K. Kayser, & G. Bodenmann (Eds.), *Couples coping with stress: Emerging perspectives on dyadic coping* (pp. 121–136). Washington, DC: APA.

Afifi, T. D., Hutchinson, S., & Krouse, S. (2006). Toward a theoretical model of communal coping in postdivorce families and other naturally occurring groups. *Communication Theory, 16*, 378–409.

Afifi, W., Dillow, M., & Morse, C. (2004). Examining predictors and consequences of information seeking in close relationships. *Personal Relationships, 11*, 429–449.

Afifi, W., & Weiner, J. (2004). Toward a theory of motivated information management. *Communication Theory, 14*, 167–190.

Albrecht, T. L., & Adelman, M. B. (1987). *Communicating social support.* Newbury Park, CA: Sage.

Babrow, A. S. (2001). Uncertainty, value, communication, and problematic integration. *Journal of Communication, 51*, 553–573.

Babrow, A. S. (2007). Problematic integration theory. In B. B. Whaley & S. Samter (Eds.), *Explaining communication: Contemporary theories and exemplars* (pp. 181–200). Mahwah, NJ: Erlbaum.

Babrow, A. S., Kasch, C. R., & Ford, L. A. (1998). The many meanings of *uncertainty* in illness: Toward a systematic accounting. *Health Communication, 10*, 1–23.

Badr, H. (2004). Coping in marital dyads: A contextual perspective on the role of gender and health. *Personal Relationships, 11*, 197–211.

Baxter, L. A., & Montgomery, B. M. (1996). *Relating: Dialogues and dialectics.* New York: Guilford.

Becker, G. (1997). *Disrupted lives: How people create meaning in a chaotic world.* Berkeley, CA: University of California Press.

Ben-Zur, H., Gilbar, O., & Lev, S. (2001). Coping with breast cancer: Patient, spouse, and dyad models. *Psychosomatic Medicine, 63,* 32–39.

Berg, C. A., & Upchurch, R. (2007). A developmental-contextual model of couples coping with illness across the adult life span. *Psychological Bulletin, 133,* 920–954.

Berger, C. R., & Bradac, J. J. (1982). *Language and social knowledge: Uncertainty in interpersonal relationships.* London: Edward Arnold.

Berger, C. R., & Calabrese, R. J. (1975). Some explorations in initial interactions and beyond: Toward a developmental theory of interpersonal communication. *Human Communication Research, 1,* 99–112.

Berghuis, J. P., & Stanton, A. L. (2002). Adjustment to a dyadic stressor: A longitudinal study of coping and depressive symptoms in infertile couples over an insemination attempt. *Journal of Consulting & Clinical Psychology, 70,* 433–438.

Bodenmann, G. (2005). Dyadic coping and its significance for marital functioning. In T. A. Revenson, K. Kayser, & G. Bodenmann (Eds.), *Couples coping with stress: Emerging perspectives on dyadic coping* (pp. 33–49). Washington, DC: APA.

Brashers, D. E., Neidig, J. L., Cardillo, L. W., Dobbs, L. K., Russell, J. A., & Haas, S. M. (1999). "In an important way, I did die": Uncertainty and revival in persons living with HIV or AIDS. *AIDS Care, 11,* 201–219.

Brashers, D. E., Neidig, J. L., & Goldsmith, D. J. (2004). Social support and the management of uncertainty for persons living with HIV or AIDS. *Health Communication, 16,* 305–332.

Brashers, D. E., Neidig, J. L., Haas, S. M., Dobbs, L. K., Cardillo, L. W., & Russell, J. A. (2000). Communication in the management of uncertainty: The case of persons living with HIV or AIDS. *Communication Monographs, 67,* 63–84.

Brashers, D. E., Neidig, J. L., Russell, J. A., Cardillo, L. W., Haas, S. M., Dobbs, L. K. et al. (2003). The medical, personal, and social causes of uncertainty in HIV illness. *Issues in Mental Health Nursing, 24,* 497–522.

Caughlin, J. P., & Golish, T. D. (2002). An analysis of the association between topic avoidance and dissatisfaction: Comparing perceptual and interpersonal explanations. *Communication Monographs, 69,* 275–295.

Charmaz, K. (1987). Struggling for a self: Identity levels of the chronically ill. In J. Roth & P. Conrad (Eds.), *Research in the sociology of health care* (Vol. 6, pp. 283–321). Greenwich, CT: JAI Press.

Charmaz, K. (1991). *Good days, bad days: The self in chronic illness and time.* New Brunswick, NJ: Rutgers University Press.

Charmaz, K. (2000). Experiencing chronic illness. In G. L. Albrecht, R. Fitzpatrick, & S. C. Scrimshaw (Eds.), *Handbook of social studies in health and medicine* (pp. 277–292). London: Sage.

Corbin, J., & Strauss, A. L. (1987). Accompaniments of chronic illness: Changes in body, self, biography, and biographical time. *Research in the Sociology of Health Care, 6,* 249–281.

Coyne, J. C., Ellard, J. H., & Smith, D. (1990). Social support, interdependence, and the dilemmas of helping. In B. R. Sarason, I. G. Sarason, & G. R. Pierce (Eds.), *Social support: An interactional view* (pp. 129–149). New York: Wiley.

Coyne, J. C., & Smith, D. A. (1991). Couples coping with a myocardial infarction: A contextual perspective on wives' distress. *Journal of Personality and Social Psychology, 61*, 404–412.

Coyne, J. C., & Smith, D. A. F. (1994). Couples coping with a myocardial infarction: Contextual perspective on patient self-efficacy. *Journal of Family Psychology, 8*, 43–54.

Dainton, M. (2003). Equity and uncertainty in relational maintenance. *Western Journal of Communication, 67*, 164–186.

Eriksson, M., & Svedlund, M. (2006). "The intruder": Spouses' narratives about life with a chronically ill partner. *Journal of Clinical Nursing, 15*, 324–333.

Fiske, V., Coyne, J. C., & Smith, D. A. (1991). Couples coping with myocardial infarction: An empirical investigation of the role of overprotectiveness. *Journal of Family Psychology, 5*, 4–20.

Ford, L. A., Babrow, A. S., & Stohl, C. (1996). Social support messages and the management of uncertainty in the experience of breast cancer: An application of problematic integration theory. *Communication Monographs, 63*, 189–207.

Frank, A. W. (1995). *The wounded storyteller.* Chicago: The University of Chicago Press.

Goldsmith, D. J. (2004). *Communicating social support.* New York: Cambridge University Press.

Goldsmith, D. J., Bute, J. J., & Lindholm, K. A. (2007, November). *Couples' strategies for talking about lifestyle change following a cardiac event.* Paper presented at the meeting of the National Communication Association, Chicago, IL.

Goldsmith, D. J., Gumminger, K. A. L., & Bute, J. J. (2006). Communication about lifestyle change between cardiac patients and their partners. In B. LePoire & R. M. Dailey (Eds.), *Socially meaningful applied research in interpersonal communication* (pp. 95–118). New York: Peter Lang.

Goldsmith, D. J., Lindholm, K. A., & Bute, J. J. (2006). Dilemmas of talking about lifestyle changes among couples coping with a cardiac event. *Social Science & Medicine, 63*, 2079–2090.

Goldsmith, D. J., Miller, L. E., & Caughlin, J. P. (2007). Openness and avoidance in couples communicating about cancer. In C. Beck (Ed.), *Communication yearbook 31* (pp. 62–115). Malden, MA: Blackwell.

Goldsmith, D. J., & Moriarty, C. (2008, May). *Partner involvement in cancer treatment decision-making.* Paper presented at the meeting of the International Communication Association, Montreal, Canada.

Hagedoorn, M., Kuijer, R. G., Buunk, B. P., DeJong, G. M., Wobbes, T., & Sanderman, R. (2000). Marital satisfaction in patients with cancer: Does support from intimate partners particularly affect those who need it most? *Health Psychology, 19*, 274–282.

Hagedoorn, M., Sanderman, R., Bolks, H. N., Tuinstra, J., & Coyne, J. C. (2008). Distress in couples coping with cancer: A meta-analysis and critical review of role and gender effects. *Psychological Bulletin, 134*, 1–30.

Kelley, H. H., Berscheid, E., Christensen, A., Harvey, J. H., & Huston, T. L. (1983). *Close relationships.* New York: W. H. Freeman & Co.

Kirmayer, L. J. (1992). The body's insistence on meaning: Metaphor as presentation and representation in illness experience. *Medical Anthropology Quarterly, 6*, 323–346.

Knobloch, L. K. (2005). Evaluating a contextual model of responses to relational uncertainty increasing events. *Human Communication Research, 31,* 60–101.

Knobloch, L. K. (2006). Relational uncertainty and message production within courtship: Features of date request messages. *Human Communication Research, 32,* 244–273.

Knobloch, L. K. (2007). Uncertainty reduction theory: Communicating under conditions of ambiguity. In L. A. Baxter & D. O. Braithwaite (Eds.), *Engaging theories in interpersonal communication: Multiple perspectives* (pp. 133–144). Los Angeles: Sage.

Knobloch, L. K., Miller, L. E., Bond, B. J., & Mannone, S. E. (2007). Relational uncertainty and message processing in marriage. *Communication Monographs, 74,* 154–180.

Knobloch, L. K., & Solomon, D. H. (1999). Measuring the sources and content of relational uncertainty. *Communication Studies, 50,* 261–278.

Knobloch, L. K., & Solomon, D. H. (2002a). Information seeking beyond initial interaction: Negotiating relational uncertainty within close relationships. *Human Communication Research, 28,* 243–257.

Knobloch, L. K., & Solomon, D. H. (2002b). Intimacy and the magnitude and experience of episodic relational uncertainty within romantic relationships. *Personal Relationships, 9,* 457–478.

Knobloch, L. K., & Solomon, D. H. (2003). Responses to changes in relational uncertainty within dating relationships: Emotions and communication strategies. *Communication Studies, 54,* 282–305.

Knobloch, L. K., & Solomon, D. H. (2005). Relational uncertainty and relational information processing: Questions with answers? *Communication Research, 32,* 349–388.

Kuijer, R. G., Ybema, J. F., Buunk, B. P., DeJong, G. M., Thijs-Boer, F., & Sanderman, R. (2000). Active engagement, protective buffering, and overprotection: Three ways of giving support by intimate partners of patients with cancer. *Journal of Social and Clinical Psychology, 19,* 256–275.

Lyons, R. F., Mickelson, K. D., Sullivan, M. J. L., & Coyne, J. C. (1998). Coping as a communal process. *Journal of Social and Personal Relationships, 15,* 579–605.

Manne, S. L., & Zautra, A. J. (1990). Couples coping with chronic illness: Women with rheumatoid arthritis and their healthy husbands. *Journal of Behavioral Medicine, 13,* 327–342.

Mast, M. E. (1995). Adult uncertainty in illness: A critical review of research. *Scholarly Inquiry for Nursing Practice, 9,* 3–29.

Mast, M. E. (1998). Survivors of breast cancer: Illness uncertainty, positive reappraisal, and emotional distress. *Oncology Nursing Forum, 25,* 555–562.

Meyler, D., Stimpson, J. P., & Peek, M. K. (2007). Health concordance within couples: A systematic review. *Social Science & Medicine, 64,* 2297–2310.

Miller, K., & Zook, E. G. (1997). Care partners for persons with AIDS: Implications for health communication. *Journal of Applied Communication Research, 25,* 57–74.

Mishel, M. H. (1988). Uncertainty in illness. *Image: Journal of Nursing Scholarship, 20,* 225–231.

Mishel, M. H. (1990). Reconceptualization of the uncertainty in illness theory. *Image: Journal of Nursing Scholarship, 22,* 256–262.

Mishel, M. H., & Braden, C. J. (1988). Finding meaning: Antecedents of uncertainty in illness. *Nursing Research, 37,* 98–103.

Moser, D. K., & Dracup, K. (2004). Role of spousal anxiety and depression in patients' psychosocial recovery after a cardiac event. *Psychosomatic Medicine, 66,* 527–532.

Moser, D. K., Dracup, K. A., & Marsden, C. (1993). Needs of recovering cardiac patients and their spouses: Compared views. *International Journal of Nursing Studies, 30,* 105–114.

Northouse, L. L., Laten, D., & Reddy, P. (1995). Adjustment of women and their husbands to recurrent breast cancer. *Research in Nursing & Health, 18,* 515–524.

O'Brien, T. B., & DeLongis, A. (1997). Coping with chronic stress: An interpersonal perspective. In B. H. Gottlieb (Ed.), *Coping with chronic stress* (pp. 161–190). New York: Plenum.

Öhman, M., & Söderberg, S. (2004). The experiences of close relatives living with a person with serious chronic illness. *Qualitative Health Research, 14,* 396–410.

Pakenham, K. F. (1998). Couple coping and adjustment to multiple sclerosis in care receiver–carer dyads. *Family Relations, 47,* 269–277.

Planalp, S., Rutherford, D. K., & Honeycutt, J. M. (1988). Events that increase uncertainty in personal relationships II: Replication and extension. *Human Communication Research, 14,* 516–547.

Revenson, T. A. (1994). Social support and marital coping with chronic illness. *Annals of Behavioral Medicine, 16,* 122–130.

Revenson, T. A., Abraido-Lanza, A. F., Majerovitz, S. D., & Jordan, C. (2005). Couples coping with chronic illness: What's gender got to do with it? In T. A. Revenson, K. Kayser, & G. Bodenmann (Eds.), *Couples coping with stress: Emerging perspectives on dyadic coping* (pp. 137–156). Washington, DC: APA.

Revenson, T. A., Kayser, K., & Bodenmann, G. (2005). *Couples coping with stress: Emerging perspectives on dyadic coping.* Washington, DC: APA.

Riegel, B. J., & Dracup, K. A. (1992). Does overprotection cause cardiac invalidism after acute myocardial infarction? *Heart and Lung, 21,* 529–535.

Taylor-Brown, J., Kilpatrick, M., Maunsell, E., & Dorval, M. (2000). Partner abandonment of women with breast cancer. *Cancer Practice, 8,* 160–164.

Westman, M., & Vinokur, A. D. (1998). Unraveling the relationship of distress levels within couples: Common stressors, empathic reactions, or crossover via social interaction? *Human Relations, 51,* 137–156.

Wright, D. L., & Aquilino, W. S. (1998). Influence of emotional support exchange in marriage on caregiving wives' burden and marital satisfaction. *Family Relations, 47,* 195–204.

12 An Integrated Model of Health Disclosure Decision-Making[1]

Kathryn Greene

People receiving a health diagnosis experience a range of emotions, including uncertainty and fear, and may average 1 hour a day or more dealing with illnesses such as diabetes (Braitman et al., in press) or cancer. Most patients are overwhelmed by the sheer amount of health information they receive (Epstein & Street, 2007). They will face challenges in adhering to regimens, deciding on treatment, and may require social support. Researchers need more sophisticated understandings of how people manage information in these situations, especially how they manage the tension surrounding disclosure or sharing the information with others.

Scholars recently sought reconceptualizations of uncertainty and information management. Brashers (2001) called for scholars to abandon the assumption that uncertainty produces anxiety and focus on *how* people manage uncertainty. Several recent theories, including uncertainty management theory (UMT; Brashers, 2001), problematic integration theory (PI; Babrow, 2001), the revelation risk model (RRM; Afifi & Steuber, in press), and the theory of motivated information management (TMIM; Afifi & Weiner, 2004), advance conceptualizations in the information management arena. Some of these theories focus on information-seeking behaviors, yet people with health diagnoses must also manage sharing the information. Thus, we need to explore how disclosure decision-making unfolds in situations of health uncertainty.

Individuals presume a right to privacy (Petronio, 2002) or believe they have a choice in what information they share, when they share it, and with whom. Initial conceptualizations of the process of disclosing information involve confounding dilemmas about whether to reveal highly intimate personal information to significant others. That is, people balance the risks inherent in disclosure along with the benefits they might gain. A health disclosure decision involves coping with these dialectical dilemmas (Greene, Derlega, & Mathews, 2006) and attempts to reconcile these needs in a comparative weighting process for self, other, and relationships (see Afifi, Olson, & Armstrong, 2005; Derlega, Sherburne, & Lewis, 1998; Derlega, Winstead, & Folk-Barron, 2000). What is less clear are the factors that people weigh in these disclosure decision processes, and the model presented in this chapter addresses this gap.

Information regulation has been explored in literatures such as disclosure, avoidance, privacy, and secrets. Widespread scholarly interest has been devoted to examining these phenomena, but there are relatively few integrating frameworks or overarching theories that guide operationalization of these processes and generate testable hypotheses. Generally rooted in catharsis principles (see Stiles, 1987), much of this research assumes that people will purge troubling information. The crucial question is what underlies the decision processes and creates conditions for likely disclosure that are relatively consistent across situations, goals, and individual differences (Omarzu, 2000).

Much disclosure research has focused on reasons or motivations for disclosure but not always on the decision process. Reasons for disclosure are multifaceted and vary in complexity, and people generally pursue multiple goals simultaneously (Caughlin & Vangelisti, this volume; Dillard, 1990; Goldsmith, 2004; O'Keefe, 1988). Afifi and Caughlin (2006) describe a clash of motivational forces leading to a complex picture of when people are likely to disclose or not. Some reasons spring from common processes, yet others pertain to specific situations and cannot be generalized (Goldsmith, Miller, & Caughlin, 2007). Thus, these relevant decision factors are unclear in form and number, and the solution does not lie in typologies. Instead, researchers need a model to explain steps in the process leading to a decision to disclose. A clearer articulation of the sequence of the decision process will enable a more complex understanding of it, especially what variables interact to produce disclosure decisions (and the outcomes thereof). Consequently, the proposed model advances research by integrating and providing a framework to predict decisions to disclose. At the foundation of this new model are disclosure uncertainty, managing uncertainty regarding the information, the relationship, and efficacy in evaluating whether or not to share.

Model Overview

The first model presented in this chapter is an overview of the global process of a disclosure decision-making episode (see Figure 12.1). According to this model, explicated in greater detail by Greene, Derlega, Yep, and Petronio (2003) and Greene et al. (2006), a number of features are taken into account when a potential discloser assesses information and recipients for possible sharing. If a decision is made to disclose, the discloser carefully considers message features (e.g., setting and timing). Finally, the disclosure episode includes outcomes affecting the self, other, and relationship as well as subsequent disclosures. Portions of the model have been elaborated and tested previously, although there are many available avenues for future research.

The model depicted in Figure 12.2 addresses the call for a better understanding of decisions to manage uncertainty through disclosure (explicating the first component of the model in Figure 12.1) and possible moderators of disclosure decisions. This is conceptualized as a process including both direct and indirect effects (prior to the disclosure enactment). The first part

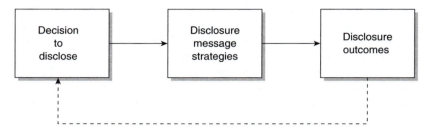

Figure 12.1 Simplified Disclosure Process Model

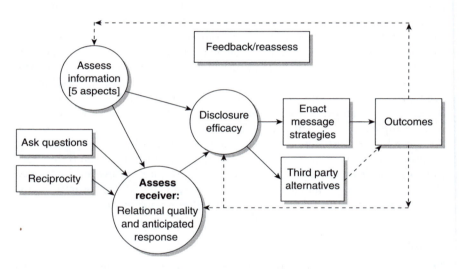

Figure 12.2 Health Disclosure Decision-Making Model

of this process is to assess the diagnosis or information (Propositions 1–5), followed by an evaluation of a potential receiver (Propositions 6–7), and finally exploration of perceived disclosure efficacy (Proposition 8) in predicting willingness to disclose. What is argued is that disclosures are encouraged or discouraged by the relative assessment of these factors. Interruptions to the most predictable decision patterns are also included (Propositions 9–10), along with potential feedback loops. Propositions are included to allow for testable hypotheses and to examine more complex associations accounting for moderation and interruptions in the general decision-making process.

The Proposed Disclosure Decision-Making Model (DD-MM)

The DD-MM separates the disclosure decision-making process into several components perceived by the discloser. Initially, the person assesses the information or diagnosis; this process is repeated for various targets, but it is also cycled through in the disease process when new pieces of information become available. The DD-MM illuminates how people evaluate information as one part of this complex initial process of information management. The assessment of information includes weighing five components that are likely interrelated: stigma, preparation, prognosis, symptoms, and relevance to others. These five aspects are not intended to represent an ordered process; each could occur in a different progression, simultaneously, or not be relevant for a particular piece of information. In an instance such as a sexually transmitted infection (STI), a person might evaluate stigma and relation to others initially, but with another situation a prognosis assessment might come first. Based on the evaluation of information, if the evaluated risk is not too great and the process lends itself to continued consideration of revealing, the discloser will then move to consider the specific potential receiver. A potential discloser can also exit the disclosure process at this point by not disclosing or waiting to potentially disclose in the future when some aspect of the information is reconsidered.

The second component of the DD-MM is consideration of the potential receiver, and this variable includes two factors: relational quality and anticipated response. First, the discloser considers the quality of the relationship (including intimacy or closeness and anticipated contact). Anticipated response is the second factor and includes the discloser's subjective assessment of how the receiver might respond or react to the shared information. If, after consideration of these two receiver factors, this part of the decision process is still favorable for sharing, the discloser will then examine his or her disclosure efficacy. The discloser can also exit the process at this point by not disclosing to this person and potentially reassess the decision at a later point in time.

The last portion of the model, disclosure efficacy, has not received a great deal of attention, although it has been included as a reason for nondisclosure or reported as a disclosure concern. Disclosure efficacy is a person's perception of his or her ability to share the message to produce the desired results (Bandura, 1977), and this is a narrower conceptualization than communication efficacy that spans varied situations and communication behaviors. The initial disclosures of a piece of information may be especially salient in people's assessment of their efficacy. One aspect that has not been fully considered is the use of intentional third party disclosures and alternate message strategies (see Greene et al., 2003, p. 116f). If people do not perceive that they have the ability to disclose, they may enlist another to disclose or choose other options. If disclosers do not perceive efficacy or select another strategy to disclose the information, they may decide not to disclose at the current time (and exit the model).

Finally, in the DD-MM, if disclosers perceive adequate efficacy and all other components of the model lead to a disclosure decision, they will enact the message. This part of the process includes the discloser planning the setting, timing, channel/mode, and the message features, which may also include practice or rehearsal. The aspects of the process that are not explicated in this chapter due to space limitations include disclosure enactment and disclosure outcomes, but some of these components have been articulated elsewhere (e.g., Afifi & Caughlin, 2006; Derlega, Winstead, Greene, Serovich, & Elwood, 2004; Caughlin, Afifi, Carpenter-Theune, & Miller, 2005; Greene et al., 2003, 2006).

Outcome variable. One question to address is the nature of the outcome variable, which is the intention to disclose or likelihood of disclosure in the DD-MM. The most commonly utilized measure, disclose/not disclose, has a number of limitations beyond its dichotomous nature, including the inability to separate goals from behavior. Utilizing intention or willingness to disclose allows for more focus on planning and the process of disclosure, with consideration of interruptions. Similar to behavior change models such as the theory of reasoned action (TRA; Ajzen & Fishbein, 1980), the DD-MM also recognizes that intentions, although highly correlated with behavior in certain circumstances, do not always lead to the planned disclosure behavior.

Scope

The DD-MM focuses on interpersonal contexts, including face-to-face or mediated interaction, but it would not include public disclosure or announcing information to a large group. The DD-MM is best suited for conditions where people have a personal relationship, rather than, for example, considering disclosure to a medical professional who may be visited based on the information in question (e.g., getting a scan to track cancer progression or X-rays to follow arthritis progression). However, there is research available on the disclosure of HIV to medical professionals (e.g., Jeffe et al., 2000) or workplace disclosure (Munir, Leka, & Griffiths, 2005).

Certain communication interactions are more planned or mindful, and this may be the case with health disclosures. The decision to disclose important information is generally preceded by considerable effort in strategically planning the disclosure (Afifi, Dillow, & Morse, 2004). Similar to other information management models, the DD-MM assumes we strategically manage our information, yet it is likely that different parts of this process are more automatic (e.g., oft-repeated disclosures), while others are more cautiously planned (Omarzu, 2000). We must grapple with the reality that the entire disclosure process is rife with unpredictability, and this is revealed in numerous predicted interruptions in the model.

Self-disclosure and private information. Knowing how people define, assess, and manage their private information is crucial in coping with disease. This chapter adopts Derlega, Metts, Petronio, and Margulis's (1993) focus on self-disclosure as an interaction between at least two individuals where one intends to deliberately divulge something personal to another. There is less agreement about "what" people do or do not disclose. Mathews, Derlega, and Morrow (2006) asked people to identify their personal information, and many of their reported personal topics had negative valence (see also Vangelisti's or T. Afifi's research on secrets). When participants are asked to describe secrets, most are negatively valenced. Health "issues" are also often negatively valenced, with positive disclosure moments in the progression such as "The biopsy was negative" or "My PSA is still low." The influence of the level of perceived privacy of a piece of information remains a question for future research (see Venetis, Greene, Banerjee, & Bagdasarov, 2008a), but it is clear that perceptions of the intimacy of secrets vary and affect disclosure decisions. For example, having an eating disorder is secret to some, private to some, and open to others. The assessment of information is present in the DD-MM but not most disclosure models (for exception see valence in RRM; Afifi & Steuber, in press).

The DD-MM is conceptualized to include both disclosure and privacy and can address secrets and avoidance. Nondisclosure is different from avoidance because people fail to introduce topics, such as not discussing new symptoms or treatment options with a person even after sharing the initial diagnosis. We know little about conditions in which avoidance of health information is productive or functional for relationships (see Goldsmith et al., 2007, for review with cancer). There is a growing body of research on secrets that may also illuminate nondisclosure decisions (see Kelly, 2002; Vangelisti, 1994). Keeping secrets is an active process that uses cognitive resources (Kelly & McKillop, 1996; Wegner & Lane, 1995), compared to privacy. This research points to how potential disclosers view the information, as private or secret (see Venetis et al., 2008a), and assessment of information is a crucial first step in the DD-MM.

Definition of health. The DD-MM explains the health information decision-making process; most traditionally this would apply to physical or psychological health topics. Thus, it can be applied to health, yet disclosing divorce (family health) or infidelity (relational health) could be considered using the DD-MM, but a physician sharing a diagnosis with a patient or disclosure to a therapist would not fit the model as well because of the situational demands as well as the nature of the information and relationship. The DD-MM may not have the same applicability for traumas such as a car crash, breaking a bone, or receiving stitches. For example, "I was in the hospital" could in some situations be a health disclosure of an ongoing illness or condition. Recent topics of disclosure studies have ranged widely, from epilepsy (Santosh, Kumar, Sarma, & Radhakrishnan, 2007) to rape (Ahrens, Campbell, Ternier-Thames, Wasco, & Sefl, 2007), from genital herpes (Green et al., 2003) to psychiatric disorders (Corrigan & Matthews, 2003), demonstrating the range of potential applicability of the DD-MM.

One additional question is whether the information is about the self, other, or the relationship. There are genetic diseases where siblings might consider testing (family information), or a parent has Alzheimer's, and this information could be considered relational in nature. The focus of the DD-MM is generally on health information about the self, yet "We are pregnant" can be relational news and fit within the DD-MM. Sharing others' health information is labeled *third party* or *gossip* and is also discussed in the DD-MM, but this is not considered disclosure because it is not personal information revealed by the discloser.

Process. The interactive nature of the disclosure process is not captured well by current disclosure models, although several models, like the DD-MM and RRM, contain variables similar to relational quality. Disclosure is an iterative process where people share and then incorporate perceived responses to disclosure into their future disclosure decisions as feedback mechanisms. The DD-MM is designed to proceed through the decision-making process with exits for nondisclosure. Disclosure itself is cumulative (of a diagnosis) in that, for one piece of information, disclosers increase the number of people who know (or are told), yet nondisclosure decisions may be reassessed (disclosure decisions can only be regretted and perhaps new information not shared). People can and do reevaluate receivers not told and decide whether or not they want to share further. There is little research to date on the order of disclosure or who people tell first (and last) and how initial reactions—positive and negative—affect subsequent sharing (see Afifi & Steuber, 2008). People also do not simply disclose about an illness diagnosis (the initial consideration of the DD-MM). Rather, there is a continual disclosure process regarding treatment options, coping, and disease progression. People are constantly in a process where decisions have to be made about sharing updates, not simply the initial diagnosis. Thus, the process is complex, and people can simultaneously disclose some aspects yet avoid sharing other information.

Assessing Information

The DD-MM proposes that the first stage of disclosure decision-making involves assessing the diagnosed information. How a person appraises the information is crucial, as there are many responses to the same diagnosis (PI theory; Babrow, 2001). Aspects of assessing the diagnosis include stigma, preparation, prognosis, symptoms, and relevance to others, conceptualized globally in other work as valence (e.g., Afifi & Steuber, in press).

Stigma

Disclosure involves vulnerability and potential risk, and this risk is elevated when the information is viewed as stigmatized. Depending on perceptions of the topic and stigma, there may be more pressure to conceal. Goffman's

(1963) initial conceptualizations of stigma and spoiled identity underlie most research in this area, but the most complete treatment of health-related stigma is Leary and Schreindorfer's model (1998; see also Greene et al., 2003). Recent research on stigma has centered on HIV, but there are also many investigations with cancer and sexual orientation. For some people, attribution of responsibility for a disease is a critical facet of both disclosure and response, perhaps related to labeling such as with mental illness. Recent studies of stigma and disclosure have ranged from obesity (Brown, Ueno, Smith, Austin, & Bickman, 2007) to erectile dysfunction (Rowland, Thornton, & Burnett, 2005), among others.

Stigma literature has developed extensively to incorporate health, yet we still know little about the effect on disclosure intentions, particularly how relational quality might moderate this association. If a person has a good relationship with the potential recipient, she or he may be willing to disclose even highly stigmatized information. Research consistently reports negative correlations between perceived stigma and willingness to disclose (and negative outcomes of disclosure). However, despite all these possible draw-backs or risks, people do choose to selectively share stigmatized information. We know little about the conditions under which some variable, such as anticipated response, "overcomes" stigma and leads to a disclosure decision. If a person believes that she or he will receive a positive response to a disclosure (likely correlated with relational quality), she or he may be willing to disclose even highly stigmatized information. With this information in mind, the first propositions are set forth:

Proposition 1A: Perceptions of stigma decrease intentions to disclose.

1B: The effect of stigma on intention to disclose is partly moderated by anticipated response and relational quality.

Preparation

Preparation addresses the discloser's expectations prior to receiving the information. People may anticipate a diagnosis if they are aware of symptoms and this leads to visiting a physician. It is possible, however, that a routine exam (or an unrelated test) uncovers cancer, for example, leaving a person less prepared for a diagnosis. Age may also influence preparation, given that as people age they may become more prepared for certain types of health diagnoses. Another component of preparation is whether the person has any prior knowledge of the disease. A person may have some general awareness of arthritis but not his or her particular type. Family history or group membership may also prepare a person for a diagnosis if the disease is hereditary or genetically linked, such as for diabetes.

The relation of preparation to disclosure decisions is complex. On one hand, if the person was prepared to some degree and expected the diagnosis, she or he may have already considered the disclosure decision process and waited to share the news (or selected one close confidant for initial disclosure). According to Berger (1997), increased time for planning leads to more complex plans (and perhaps greater success). Alternatively, it is possible that, without having preparation or readiness, a person unprepared for the diagnosis might disclose immediately to relieve distress (see Stiles' 1987 fever model). In this case, emotions may overcome a more rational model of disclosure decision-making, and people may vent in search of expressive social support (or instrumental support if they need assistance such as research on the Internet). The association between preparation and disclosure may also be influenced by relational quality and anticipated response, such that we seek out a target with good relationship features accompanied by a positive anticipated response, especially if we are unprepared for the diagnosis. Therefore, the next set of propositions suggests that associations exist among these variables, but their direction remains unclear:

2A: What is the association between preparation and intention to disclose?

2B: Is the association between preparation and intention to disclose partly moderated by the assessment of the receiver (relational quality and anticipated response)?

Prognosis

There is a great deal of variability in prognosis and intrusiveness by disease stage. Goldsmith et al. (2007) argue that we need to theorize about these relations and not simply control for or sample by disease features, as addressed by this portion of the DD-MM. When receiving a diagnosis, a person may subjectively evaluate the disease prognosis. Is the disease chronic, treatable, or terminal? What are the treatment options? This is a classic case where having additional information (the diagnosis) decreases one form of uncertainty yet increases another. Assessing the prognosis may include considering the relative probability of various outcomes (see PI; Babrow, 2001). One of the greatest concerns for breast cancer patients is the uncertainty of progression and recurrence (e.g., Gill & Babrow, 2007). Patients may need to transition to coping with death, which could include disclosure decisions and preparing social networks. The topic of death "inspires some of the greatest variability in communication" (Goldsmith et al., 2007, p. 72), including disclosure decisions. Death may be an especially ominous topic, and people may find it easier to share treatments or facts rather than feelings, especially if they are uncertain of how the other might react. A terminal prognosis may also create greater interaction urgency (see Berger, 1997) where people feel pressure to disclose. In the final weeks, people may openly discuss death (Hinton, 1998) or conversely they may discuss death initially at diagnosis and then drop the topic.

Although clinicians report that they are discussing illness prognoses with patients, patients and caregivers do not generally confirm these reports (Fried, Bradley, & O'Leary, 2003), and patients may not desire prognostic information or probability information in assessing risk (Beresford, Seymour, Vincent, & Moat, 2001). Terminal cancer patients may want to know less information (Jiang et al., 2007). For instance, Fujimori et al. (2007) reported that 30% of Japanese cancer patients did not want life expectancy information. Desire for prognosis information may need to be addressed for a patient before she or he proceeds with disclosure decisions. In addition, receivers may ask about the disease prognosis ("How long do you have?" or "How bad is it?"), thus the discloser must prepare for possible disclosure outcomes such as varied responses.

Differences in the desire for prognosis information are best explained theoretically by Babrow's (2001; Babrow & Matthias, this volume) PI theory that describes uncertainty as a central feature of illness experience. According to PI theory, people form probabilistic and evaluative orientations to the world, and these two features are interdependent and affect how people integrate an illness experience. According to this perspective, more information may not reduce uncertainty (or lead to disclosure): "many uncertainties cannot be resolved by more information" (Babrow, 2001, p. 563). PI explains why some people may avoid not only prognosis information but may more extensively avoid through strategies such as not seeing a doctor or declining offers for testing (e.g., genetic testing; Lerman et al., 1999). Some of these strategies may be more active than others: Avoid seeing a doctor or not returning a phone call are more passive, yet telling a physician that you do not want surgery or information about treatment options are more active. Finally, PI theory proposes that people can "cognitively reappraise" and reassess information, and thus they can potentially abort the disclosure process and decide not to share. For example, people can reframe even definitive diagnostic information as "preliminary," choosing as well to await results of surgery, initial chemo or other therapy, before disclosing their condition. Therefore, the following propositions are proposed:

3A: Is the relation between prognosis and disclosure intention curvilinear?

3B: The effect of prognosis on disclosure intention is moderated by anticipated response.

3C: Prognosis uncertainty will lead to delay in disclosure intentions.

Symptoms

There are risks of complications and visible symptoms associated with the progression of many diseases that vary over the illness trajectory. However, there have not been many studies of the relationship between disclosure and disease progression except in the context of HIV. Most HIV studies report that disclosure is positively associated with physical symptoms, including CD4 count and illness severity (e.g., Greene et al., 2003, pp. 99–100; Vallerand, Hough, Pittiglio, & Marvicsin, 2005; for exception see Klitzman et al., 2007). Some people do refrain from disclosing a disease until they are symptomatic or too ill to care for themselves. For example, Asians disclosed HIV status to relatives only when necessitated by declining health (Yoshioka & Schustack, 2001).

People who are symptomatic may disclose more than those who are in the earlier stages of their illness. We still need a better understanding of the disclosure process with other diseases, such as those progressing rapidly or with few or no external symptoms. With longer-course illnesses, it might be a matter of time before some people share (Emlet, 2006; Zea, Reisen, Poppen, Echeverry, & Bianchi, 2004), or people may feel a sense of inevitability about others' knowing. Some people feel that circumstances will reveal the information anyway and cite this as a reason for disclosure (e.g., Greene et al., 2003; Vangelisti, Caughlin, & Timmerman, 2001).

Noticeable symptoms may affect the timing of disclosure or interrupt plans, perhaps leading receivers to ask questions about an illness (discussed later in the chapter). Some people feel the process of disclosure is forced on them because of declining health status (e.g., Vallerand et al., 2005) and need for social support. Symptoms or disease progression may force changes in routine, which can result in people trying to hide symptoms (see Leary & Schreindorfer, 1998, p. 26). As health begins to decline, others may begin to notice changes in a person's normal activities, such as eating patterns or not going out in public (due to compromised immune system). This leads to the next set of propositions below:

4A: Disease progression and symptom visibility are associated with increased disclosure intentions.

4B: What is the association between progression and disclosure intentions for diseases with few visible symptoms?

Relevance to Others

One last part of assessing the decision to disclose is consideration of the diagnosis in relation to the potential recipient of the information: Are others directly or indirectly affected by the diagnosis? Most research in this area has been conducted with STIs, where people consider the possible risk of transmission to their sexual partners. In this context, a partner may seek an explanation for changes in safer sex practices, such as the introduction of condoms (see Mattson & Roberts, 2001). Public health recommendations include STI disclosure to all sexual partners, yet data indicate that this particular decision is complex with STI information not shared with all or even most sexual partners (e.g., Ciccarone et al., 2003; Simbayi et al., 2007). These decisions are complicated by perceptions of stigma and potential anticipated responses; if people fear loss of the relationship or view the information as stigmatized, they are less likely to disclose, even if the information is relevant to the other or they believe the other "has a right to know."

Several related topics are also worthy of consideration. Noncommunicable diseases that may still affect others are unaddressed in the disclosure literature. First, consider disclosure of illnesses with genetic links such as cystic fibrosis, Huntington's syndrome, or hemophilia. People receiving such diagnoses may want to share the information with siblings, children, or other family members. Second, there may be environmental issues, such as being exposed to lead poisoning, where people would be motivated to tell others at the workplace (yet an employer may or may not share this motivation to reveal the information). In cases such as rape (see Ahrens et al., 2007) or sexual abuse, where the perpetrator might place additional others at risk, a survivor might feel compelled to disclose to protect others and/or prevent future crimes. Finally, even a person losing a job may directly or indirectly affect the family (e.g., their financial health). Thus, it is suggested that:

5A: The perceived relevance of a diagnosis to others' health increases intentions to disclose.

5B: This association is moderated by stigma and anticipated response.

Assessing the Receiver

If, after evaluating the information, people continue to consider disclosing, the next portion of the DD-MM involves assessing the receiver. Two receiver variables, relational quality and anticipated response, are factors people use when they consider whether or not they should disclose. These two variables are likely positively associated (e.g., Afifi & Olson, 2005). That is, the closer people feel toward the respondent, the more likely they will be to expect a positive response (see also Afifi & Steuber, 2008).

Who is told. Much attention has been paid to comparisons of who is told a specific piece of information. This research, however, has confounded relational role or type with relational quality and is thus limited conceptually. People have varying levels of intimacy with a particular "role" such as a sibling. Some researchers sum the number of people told to create a "disclosure measure," and this operationalization confounds family or network size with the proportion of possible persons told, leading to inflated measures for those with large networks.

Disclosure involves a pattern of selective sharing or target selection. Target selection in rare cases is determined by the situation; most often we have a range of options for choosing disclosure targets (Omarzu, 2000). People often begin the disclosure process by assessing their social network, or answering the question, "Who might I tell (or not tell)?" People are relatively selective about who they choose as recipients (Vangelisti et al., 2001), especially with important information, and thus select confidants to minimize risk. An illness takes a tremendous toll on families/partners who are available and willing to provide support. Consequently, we need more information about when and why some disclosers choose not to share their health status, perhaps due to the quality of these relationships or character-istics of the information/diagnosis.

Relational Quality

Disclosure plays a critical role in the kind of relationships people have with each other (Greene et al., 2006; Harvey & Omarzu, 1997; Prager, 1995), and the quality of a relationship with a recipient is associated with the like-lihood of disclosure (e.g., Altman & Taylor, 1973; Chaiken & Derlega, 1974). Some research, however, confounds relational quality or intimacy and disclosure both conceptually and operationally (Altman & Taylor, 1973; Sullivan, 1953). Current views of intimacy are broader, separating the disclosure process from the relationship development process (see Morr & Petronio, 2007), yet even discussing private topics increases intimacy (see Derlega et al., 1993), making it important to consider the reciprocal nature of this relationship.

Generally, better relational quality is related to increased intentions to disclose and may even overcome the suppressive effect of stigma, yet there are situations where people disclose to those with whom they have poor relation-ships. We need to better understand the conditions under which people choose to disclose to recipients where the relationships are poor or conflictual (and the consequences of such disclosures), as these particular disclosure events are likely to have heightened uncertainty. Factors that might predict disclosing based on poor relational quality include telling a former lover that she or he should be tested, feeling a duty to inform, or perhaps to make amends before dying. Caughlin and Afifi (2004) and others reported a lack of closeness as a reason for avoiding.

Despite the centrality of relational quality in research on disclosure over the past 40 years, there are a number of unanswered questions regarding relational quality, including measurement and sampling. Relational quality may also be confounded with variables such as anticipated contact. A dis-closer could easily delay sharing (e.g., disclosure of pregnancy) for months if she or he would not be seeing a potential recipient face-to-face in contrast to a case where a person is surrounded daily by potential disclosure recipients (Afifi & Steuber, 2008). We also need to consider social changes in modes of contact including e-mail, IM, and mobile phones, rather than simply face-to-face contact (see Greene et al., 2003, p. 85f). A lack of contact is also cited as a reason for not sharing (e.g., Golish & Caughlin, 2002).

Research to date has not been well designed to assess the impact of rela-tional quality in disclosure decisions or how relational quality moderates associations. If there is not enough variance in measurement (e.g., why bring a friend with whom you have a poor relationship to a lab study, but also how could a person have a close relationship with a stranger?) this will attenuate associations in model testing, perhaps underestimating the role of relational quality. This leads to the following:

6A: Better relational quality will be associated with increased disclosure intentions.

6B: Relational quality moderates the association between perceived stigma and disclosure.

Anticipated Reactions

People often consider what would happen if they did reveal to a specific person (Greene & Faulkner, 2002; Vangelisti et al., 2001) and make estimates about the likely reaction of a receiver before deciding whether to share the information, including the relative probability of the outcome or reaction from the receiver (see Babrow, 2001). An unresponsive reaction is cited as a reason for topic avoidance (e.g., Caughlin & Afifi, 2004). Kelly and McKillop (1996) proposed that prior to disclosure people should evaluate three qualities of a recipient that could be captured under the umbrella of anticipated response: Is the person discreet, nonjudgmental, and able to help them? Alternately, Reis and Shaver's (1988) interpersonal process model of intimacy (IPMI) emphasizes the role of partner responsiveness, and Manne et al. (2004a) reported a very strong association between perceived responsiveness and intimacy among couples (range .72–.88). This research suggests the need for more tests of the role of response using models like the DD-MM.

Generally, a discloser must anticipate a positive (not negative or neutral) response before being willing to disclose (Altman & Taylor, 1973; Greene & Serovich, 1996), although exceptions have been reported and are not well understood. A rejecting response will decrease the likelihood of additional disclosure and could be viewed as feedback. We know little about situations where a discloser is neutral or uncertain about a receiver's likely response (for exception, see Greene & Faulkner, 2002), and these may be the source of greatest uncertainty. In these ambiguous situations, disclosers may focus additional attention on maximizing either recipient or relational goals (see Sunnafrank, 1986) in deciding whether to disclose. People can also test reactions by observing others (Kelly & McKillop, 1996) or use incremental disclosure to gauge reactions before fully disclosing (e.g., Greene et al., 2003; Petronio, Reeder, Hecht, & Mon't Ros-Mendoza, 1996).

Research to date has failed to consider the discloser's confidence in the potential receiver's reaction. If a partner might leave the relationship, being "nearly certain" that this will not occur may not be sufficient to overcome fear and result in nondisclosure. For example, less than half of women with epilepsy in India disclosed their illness prior to marriage, fearing breakup of marriage negotiations (Santosh et al., 2007). Other specific relational challenges with anticipated response include sharing with elderly people or those who are ill where a discloser may not want to burden someone or increase his or her stress. A potential receiver may also be seen by the discloser as "unsophisticated" or might not know much about the disease, thus limiting disclosure.

Gossip and PRPs. As one possible outcome from disclosure, recipients may repeat information to others, even if specifically asked not to do so. Thus, people consider the discretion of the potential recipient (Kelly & McKillop, 1996) and choose recipients who will respect their privacy requests. According to communication privacy management (CPM; see Petronio, 2002; Petronio & Reierson, this volume), recipients are viewed as shareholders or co-owners of the information, even though the recipient does not always treat the information with the same caution as the discloser. Some people feel a great deal of ownership of their health information (DeMatteo et al., 2002), but there are no quantitative tests of this phenomenon, including whether ownership perceptions are shared by the receiver and how this affects the receiver's subsequent disclosure decisions and perceived responsibility for the other's information. If a receiver does share the information despite a discloser's request to remain private (Greene & Faulkner, 2002, labeled this gossip), this may affect the subsequent disclosure decisions such that a discloser will share with fewer people.

The area of gossip and third party disclosure has received some attention, but only two studies to date have examined prior restraint phrases (PRPs). PRPs mark the disclosed information for others and signal how the discloser wants the information to be managed (e.g., "Please don't tell anyone else, but ..."). According to Petronio and Bantz (1991), people who receive PRPs do not necessarily keep the information secret. Even the discloser recognizes that the information will likely be shared—but hopefully only to select others, such as the receiver's partner. Nevertheless, the discloser intends the PRP to result in the receiver sharing with few others (but not zero others). Venetis, Greene, Banerjee, and Bagdasarov (2008b) described how both implicitly and explicitly stated privacy rules generally serve to safeguard disclosed information from further revealing, but they differ based on the participant's role as recipient or discloser, motivations to not further reveal, and the type of information disclosed. How disclosers' expectations about privacy responses are communicated to—and perceived by—receivers is deserving of future research.

Prior reactions. One component of the DD-MM that forms the basis of anticipated response is prior reactions. People may consider the target's previous responses in deciding whether to reveal (Afifi & Caughlin, 2006). Past histories with potential disclosure recipients form the basis for expectations (positive or negative). If the respondent has responded positively to prior revelations, this may increase the likelihood of sharing again, but if prior responses were negative this may delay disclosure or result in not sharing. In a longitudinal study of family secrets, people were less likely to reveal (and reported decreased closeness) if they expected negative reactions (Afifi & Steuber, 2008). A related phenomenon was labeled the *chilling effect*, where partners withhold relational complaints if they believe a partner will respond negatively such as with anger or aggression (see Afifi & Olson, 2005; Cloven & Roloff, 1993; Roloff & Cloven, 1990). It is also likely that perceived prior response is positively associated with relational quality, or we tend to like those who respond positively (or vice versa).

Biased perceptions? Evaluating anticipated consequences assumes individuals are able to accurately predict outcomes or others' responses, yet people have biased perceptions (Caughlin et al., 2005). People may expect negative reactions to sharing and delay their disclosure as a result; then when they finally do disclose and receive a negative reaction, is the negative reaction atttributable to the delay in sharing or to the information itself (see Afifi et al., 2005)? There are few studies that untangle these questions, especially with regard to health information.

There may also be bias in retrospective reports where the discloser considers that "telling was not as bad as I thought" with the passage of time. Greene and Faulkner (2002), however, reported unexpected gossip and threats of violence (toward the source of HIV infection) as unanticipated reactions from recipients. Measures of targets' responses, however, are based on disclosers' perceptions rather than on the receivers' actual or reported reactions. Kelly (2002) argues that the discloser's perception of a receiver's response is more crucial than actual recipient behaviors or responses. There are few studies measuring both the discloser and the receiver that could help address this gap (see Caughlin et al., 2005). Both perspectives can assess the congruence of views, even if both are biased, despite the fact that it is the discloser's view that is pivotal in information-sharing models.

Actual reactions. We may expect the worst outcomes to disclosure. Actual reactions to disclosure may be far less dramatic than anticipated reactions (Rutledge, 2007), although some extremely negative reactions are reported (e.g., Greene et al., 2003; Greene & Faulkner, 2002). Caughlin et al. (2005) found that people were generally relieved that their partner's reactions were more positive than expected, yet Ahrens et al. (2007) found that only about half of their sample reported receiving positive responses to first disclosures of rape. Greene and Faulkner (2002) reported that five categories captured perceived reactions to HIV disclosure (three that would be labeled *negative*) including treated differently, negative emotional reactions, provided support, told others, and treated no differently. Thus, actual reactions to disclosure may be more positive than expected, with crucial negative instances being evaluated as people assess the relative risk of disclosing.

Even well-intentioned people may respond in unsupportive or distressing ways (see Barbee, Derlega, Sherburne, & Grimshaw, 1998; Ingram, Betz, Mindes, Schmitt, & Smith, 2001; Wortman & Lehman, 1985). People can be surprised by close others' reactions, both positively and negatively. This is best explained by expectancy violation theory (Burgoon, Buller, Dillman, & Walther, 1995), where uncertainty is increased when expectations are not met, such as when a discloser expects a positive response and receives a negative or ambiguous one. A person may overreward a receiver if she or he receives a more positive—or less intensely negative—response than expected, yet negative responses likely decrease future disclosure to others and may have negative effects on relational quality. Thus, the same behavior some-times increases and decreases uncertainty, depending on what the discloser expected prior to sharing (see Afifi & Olson, 2005). Positive violations will likely increase perceived efficacy and future disclosure. Disconfirming responses will lead to tighter boundaries (CPM; see Petronio, 2002; Petronio & Reierson, this volume). Consequently,

> 7A: If the anticipated response is positive, people are likely to disclose to this receiver, even if the information is assessed as stigmatized.

> 7B: There is a positive association between relational quality and anticipated response.

> 7C: If the perceived actual response is more negative (or less positive) than expected, this will result in less future disclosure intentions.

> 7D: If a PRP is perceived to be violated, there will be decreased rela-tional quality and decreased future disclosure intentions.

> 7E: Gossip or unsolicited third party disclosure will decrease future disclosure intentions.

Disclosure Efficacy

If, after evaluations of the information and potential target, people continue to consider disclosing the information, they must evaluate their ability to send this message to this specific person. Both confidence and skills are needed to share a difficult message such as a health diagnosis, although at times disclos-ers *do* share with trepidation, apprehension, and considerable uncertainty. Efficacy is the perception of one's ability to perform an action or produce an outcome (Bandura, 1977; Makoul & Roloff, 1998; see also Afifi & Weiner, 2004). People can design message strategies but know that "in the moment" they would not be able to articulate or enact the message. Thus, people may not act upon a disclosure plan unless they are confident in their ability (see Afifi et al., 2005), and this efficacy is also affected by the information assessed. In fact, the strongest path in the RRM is between risk assessment and efficacy (Afifi & Steuber, in press; see also Afifi et al., 2005).

Does repetition or practice affect disclosure efficacy? Afifi and Steuber (in press) reported that decreased communication efficacy was related to increased rehearsal (and incremental disclosure). For some people, disclosure becomes easier after the first few times, yet others retain their anxiety throughout each disclosure. Miller and Rubin (2007) reported that some people discuss disclosure strategies with a trusted person to facilitate planning, and this could potentially include choosing words ("I'm sick" vs. "I have cancer"; see Greene et al., 2003; Hosek, Harper, & Domanico, 2000) and other message features, akin to creating a script (see Afifi et al., 2005). Many disclosure recommendations encourage practice or preparing details, including choosing time, phrasing, and location for disclosure to maximize confidence in skills.

One framework that is useful for considering the efficacy component is impression management, or people's desire to decrease potential loss of face and protect their identity (Afifi & Caughlin, 2006). People have complex identity needs that affect disclosure decisions, often motivated by the need to avoid negative impressions (Afifi & Guerrero, 2000; Rosenfeld, 1979). Some information is assessed as more face threatening, such as the fear of being seen as weak, thus one would expect that increased relational quality and perceived anticipated response would be required in addition to perceived efficacy to share this type of message. A discloser could also perceive that his or her efficacy might be higher at a later time and wait to disclose, perhaps when there is more pressure due to symptoms or the receiver notices and asks.

If people feel unable to share yet are still motivated to disclose, they may resort to alternate message strategies to accomplish sharing the information. That is, they could ask another person to share the information (see third party disclosure). Options for disclosure enactment also include sending an e-mail or letter if the discloser feels unable to verbalize the message or experience the verbal/nonverbal reactions in person (see Greene et al., 2003; Petronio et al., 1996). Correspondingly, it is argued that:

8A: Increased stigma will lead to decreased disclosure efficacy (and this may be partially moderated by relational quality and anticipated responses).

8B: Decreased relational quality and anticipated negative responses will lead to decreased disclosure efficacy.

8C: Perceived negative outcomes of disclosure will result in decreased efficacy and decreased future intentions to disclose to others.

Third Party

One phenomenon worthy of additional scrutiny is when people share information that is not their "own." Although this is not self-disclosure per se, it captures some information management strategies utilized. This phenomenon has been labeled *third party* (intentional or not) *disclosure*, using intermediaries, and gossip.

Several studies report intentional third party disclosure as a vehicle for HIV disclosure (see Greene et al., 2003). Miller and Rubin (2007) describe intermediation where some people selected a relative with whom they were close (often a cousin or sibling) and "sent this person with explicit instructions to inform those in the family who needed to know the diagnosis" (p. 593). Schrodt and Afifi (2007) also report how disclosure may place a person in the role as messenger of information in divorced families. Although this third party strategy is practical in some cases and may serve to protect the person from the stress and burden of retelling, there may be side effects such as placing the third party in the middle or lack of clarity about who this person can tell. Third party disclosure could also result in the recipient feeling betrayed or not respected by receiving the information indirectly (from another person). However, recipients may appreciate knowing, even if the delivery is not directly from the diagnosed person. Given the lack of research in this area, research questions are presented:

9A: What is the effect of intentional third party disclosure on perceived reactions to disclosure?

9B: Does intentional third party disclosure result in increased sharing by recipients?

9C: Use of intentional third party disclosure will increase relational quality for the intermediary but decreased perceptions of relational quality for the recipient.

Interruptions in the Model

At times the disclosure process is nonlinear and foundationally unpredictable. Despite having a clear disclosure plan, circumstances may alter intentions, or a context may create an unanticipated opening for spontaneous disclosure. This section examines two conversational events that can interrupt an overall disclosure plan: asking questions and reciprocity. The fever model (Stiles, 1987) assumes that disclosure tension is an internal state, yet these are external pressures (Afifi & Steuber, in press) that are brought to the discloser (see also PI; Babrow, 2001). The DD-MM conceptualizes these interruptions as occurring prior to evaluation of the receiver. That is, depending on who asks the question or discloses first, a potential discloser may still lie, avoid, or choose to disclose depending on evaluation of the specific person.

Questions. Asking questions impedes the normal disclosure decision process, and plans (including setting, order, timing, etc.) can be bypassed by both direct and indirect questions. Invitations to disclose are recognized by others (Caughlin & Golish, 2002). Even a general question can be interpreted as an opportunity for disclosure (Petronio et al., 1996), with the inquiry taken as permission to share. For example, a general question such as "How was your break?" could receive the response, "Well, I had surgery to explore a suspicious growth." Petronio et al. described how sexual abuse survivors look for cues that signal tacit permission to disclose, similar to Greene et al.'s (2003) reports for people with HIV. It is unclear whether asking questions is related to relational quality, or whether those closer to us tend to ask more questions or perhaps wait to give the discloser time and space to share on their own terms. In addition, if the question askers are relationally close, are they more likely to receive full disclosures?

Asking questions has been included as a reason for disclosure (e.g., Agne, Thompson, & Cusella, 2000; Vangelisti et al., 2001). Ahrens et al. (2007) reported that, of first disclosures of rape, one third were not initiated by the survivor but rather were "initiated by others" to explain why the survivor was acting strangely or the survivor was asked, "What's wrong?" (see Allagia, 2004). The person asking questions may already have some information: The discloser had a doctor's appointment or she or he may be present when a medical office calls with test results. In these situations, disclosure may be difficult to avoid without directly lying. In situations where someone asks or implies interest, however, the potential discloser has a wider range of options, such as avoiding, lying, or partial disclosure (see Berger & Kellerman, 1989). If people see an opportunity to share, they may choose to disclose, even without a clear anticipated response. With this in mind, the next set of propositions are set forth:

10A: The potential recipient asking questions increases disclosure.

10B: What are the consequences of unplanned disclosure in response to a question?

10C: What is the association between relational quality and question asking?

10D: Does the directness of the question predict the disclosure response?

Reciprocity. Another feature that interrupts the planned disclosure decision process may be reciprocity. People report that they generally share if they receive equivalent disclosure. Many communication behaviors are reciprocated: We respond to disclosure with disclosure, especially if the topic is shared (Dindia, 1982, 2000; Gouldner, 1960; Jourard, 1971).

There is little systematic research on this reciprocity phenomenon in health, yet it is reported as a reason for disclosure in some studies (e.g., Greene et al., 2003; Vangelisti et al., 2001) with low occurrence. Thus, it does not account for a great deal of variance in disclosure, but it is a phenomenon that interrupts the regular/planned process and is recognized by participants as such (e.g., "I hadn't planned to talk about it, but she was talking about her violent boyfriend and it just seemed right to share"). One example of research on health disclosure reciprocity is Manne et al. (2004b) who reported that reciprocal self-disclosure during videotaped discussions between partners (where one had breast cancer) was associated with lower overall levels of distress. Additional dyadic studies such as Manne et al.'s using the IPMI would increase understanding of this phenomenon. This research begs the questions below:

> 11A: What level of initial disclosure must occur before reciprocity is enacted?

> 11B: What are the perceived consequences of unplanned reciprocal disclosure?

Future Research

This chapter presents the DD-MM to integrate existing frameworks and research on disclosure processes. The chapter has noted a number of under-explored areas and unanswered questions, and this section elaborates on areas for future research. There are few studies of dyads interacting in the health disclosure context (for exception, see Manne et al., 2004b). Studies generally rely on individual data to examine dyadic relationship processes and draw relationship conclusions (Caughlin & Golish, 2002). We need studies generalizing across diseases or illness states and replications across samples and topics. Increased longitudinal research would also allow exploration of decision processes, order of disclosure, and consequences, among other factors. Studies including outcomes for the relationship and for the health of the discloser and recipient would be beneficial. Research often purports that disclosure is unilaterally beneficial, but we know much less about situations where sharing is harmful and concealment is healthy.

Self-disclosure is a social action that must be accomplished in interaction, and this emphasizes message enactment and efficacy. Beach and Anderson (2003) suggest that conversational analysis is a tool for studying how families "interactively accomplish" cancer communication. Researchers know little about how disclosure messages are processed, including how receiver reactions are viewed and integrated into future decisions. Why does disclosure fail to produce desired outcomes (Hines, Babrow, Badzek, & Moss, 2001)? Is this related to disclosers' expectations, or are receivers unprepared to support disclosers?

What information is disclosed is also worth exploring. A person may disclose the health diagnosis but not update the receiver on treatments or progression, perhaps based on the receiver's initial response. The DD-MM examines one point in time, yet people constantly reassess disclosure decisions, especially with those receivers who were not told. The order of who was told (and why) is likely linked to relational quality, anticipated response, and confidence in keeping the secret, which could be explored further. In addition, we need to include culture as a factor, as there may be fundamental differences in perceptions of privacy and expectations for relational openness. Privacy could also be a relational choice managed by the couple (Goldsmith et al., 2007).

Different reactions to disclosure and outcomes are difficult to compare across studies because the methodology is difficult to replicate (e.g., focus groups or interviews) or different variables are measured. Operational definitions vary widely, including measuring disclosure as "Did you tell X?" instead of "Does X know?" to assess third party disclosure or other information discovery modes such as guessing or reading a person's e-mail (see Caughlin, Scotts, Miller, & Hefner, 2008, putative secrets). In addition, disclosure is secondary to some investigations, measured by one or two items (exceptions are HIV and recent studies of breast cancer), which poses a significant limitation in understanding disclosure as a process. Other measures are even less nuanced. For example, reaction to disclosure is a complex phenomenon operationalized in some studies (e.g., Jonzon & Lindblad, 2005) as positive or negative, often based on one primary code that obscures multiple goals. The present chapter encourages quantitative measurement of variables that are weighed in each part of the disclosure decision process.

This chapter has presented an integrated model of health information sharing, the DD-MM, focusing on the decision process prior to revealing/ concealing. The DD-MM proposes evaluation of uncertainty related to information, relationship, and efficacy and describes a possible sequence that can cut across contexts. The model was developed to integrate and organize lines of research, as well as lay a foundation for future examinations. The disclosure process outlined by the DD-MM includes a nuanced selection of disclosure recipients based on relative assessments of identified components. The DD-MM emphasizes the process of disclosure decision-making, and a next step will be to test these relations and link these variables to the type of disclosure made (e.g., breadth, depth, and duration, Omarzu, 2000; directness, Afifi & Steuber, 2008). The model has heuristic potential, with a wide range of applicability including health contexts.

Note

1 The author would like to thank Austin Babrow, Val Derlega, Sandra Faulkner, Tammy Afifi, and Walid Afifi for comments on earlier drafts of this chapter.

References

Afifi, T. D., & Olson, L. N. (2005). The chilling effect in families and the pressure to conceal secrets. *Communication Monographs, 72*, 192–216.

Afifi, T. D., Olson, L. N., & Armstrong, C. (2005). The chilling effect and family secrets: Examining the role of self protection, other protection, and communication efficacy. *Human Communication Research, 31*, 564–598.

Afifi, T. D., & Steuber, K. (2008). *The Cycle of Concealment Model: An examination of how secrets, and the strategies used to reveal them, affect family relationships over time.* Manuscript submitted for publication.

Afifi, T. D., & Steuber, K. (in press). The Revelation Risk Model (RRM): Factors that predict the revelation of secrets and the strategies used to reveal them. *Communication Monographs.*

Afifi, W. A., & Caughlin, J. P. (2006). A close look at revealing secrets and some consequences that follow. *Communication Research, 33,* 467–488.

Afifi, W. A., Dillow, M. R., & Morse, C. (2004). Examining predictors and consequences of information seeking in close relationships. *Personal Relationships, 11,* 429–449.

Afifi, W. A., & Guerrero, L. K. (2000). Motivations underlying topic avoidance in close relationships. In S. Petronio (Ed.), *Balancing the secrets of private disclosures* (pp. 165–179). Mahwah, NJ: Erlbaum.

Afifi, W. A., & Weiner, J. L. (2004). Toward a theory of motivated information management. *Communication Theory, 14,* 167–190.

Agne, R. R., Thompson, T. L., & Cusella, L. P. (2000). Stigma in the line of face: Self disclosure of patients' HIV status to health care providers. *Journal of Applied Communication Research, 28,* 235–261.

Ahrens, C. E., Campbell, R., Ternier-Thames, N. K., Wasco, S. M., & Sefl, T. (2007). Deciding whom to tell: Expectations and outcomes of rape survivors' first disclosures. *Psychology of Women Quarterly, 31,* 38–49.

Ajzen, I., & Fishbein, M. (1980). *Understanding attitudes and predicting social behavior.* Englewood Cliffs, NJ: Prentice-Hall.

Allagia, R. (2004). Many ways of telling: Expanding conceptualizations of child sexual abuse disclosure. *Child Abuse & Neglect, 28,* 1213–1227.

Altman, I., & Taylor, D. A. (1973). *Social penetration: The development of interpersonal relationships.* New York: Holt, Rinehart, & Winston.

Babrow, A. S. (2001). Uncertainty, value, communication, and problematic integration. *Journal of Communication, 51,* 553–573.

Bandura, A. (1977). Self-efficacy: Toward a unifying theory of behavior change. *Psychological Review, 84,* 191–215.

Barbee, A. P., Derlega, V. J., Sherburne, S. P., & Grimshaw, A. (1998). Helpful and unhelpful forms of social support for HIV-positive individuals. In V. J. Derlega & A. P. Barbee (Eds.), *HIV and social interaction* (pp. 83–105). Thousand Oaks, CA: Sage.

Beach, W. A., & Anderson, J. K. (2003). Communication and cancer? Part I: The noticeable absence of interactional research. *Journal of Psychosocial Oncology, 21,* 1–23.

Beresford, N., Seymour, L., Vincent, C., & Moat, N. (2001). Risks of elective cardiac surgery: What do patients want to know? *Heart, 86,* 626–631.

Berger, C., & Kellerman, K. (1989). Personal opacity and social information gathering: Explorations in strategic communication. *Communication Research, 16,* 314–351.

Berger, C. R. (1997). Producing messages under uncertainty. In J. Greene (Ed.), *Message production: Advances in communication theory* (pp. 221–244). Mahwah, NJ: Erlbaum.

Braitman, A. L., Derlega, V. J., Henson, J. M., Robinett, I., Saadeh, G. M., Janda, L. J., et al. (in press). Social constraints in talking about diabetes to significant others and diabetes self-care: A social-cognitive processing perspective. *Journal of Social and Clinical Psychology.*

Brashers, D. E. (2001). Communication and uncertainty management. *Journal of Communication, 51*, 477–497.

Brown, T. N., Ueno, K., Smith, C. L., Austin, N. S., & Bickman, L. (2007). Communication patterns in medical encounters for the treatment of child psychological problems: Does pediatrician–parent concordance matter? *Health Communication, 21*, 247–256.

Burgoon, J. K., Buller, D. B., Dillman, L., & Walther, J. (1995). Interpersonal deception: IV. Effects of suspicion on perceived communication and nonverbal behavior dynamics. *Human Communication Research, 22*, 163–196.

Burgoon, J. K., Stern, L. A., & Dillman, L. (1995). *Dyadic adaptation: Dyadic interaction pattern*. Newbury Park, CA: Sage.

Caughlin, J. P., & Afifi, T. D. (2004). When is topic avoidance unsatisfying? Examining moderators of the association between avoidance and dissatisfaction. *Human Communication Research, 30*, 479–513.

Caughlin, J. P., Afifi, W. A., Carpenter-Theune, K. E., & Miller, L. E. (2005). Reasons for, and consequences of, revealing personal secrets in close relationships: A longitudinal study. *Personal Relationships, 12*, 43–59.

Caughlin, J. P., & Golish, T. D. (2002). An analysis of the association between topic avoidance and dissatisfaction: Comparing perceptual and interpersonal explanations. *Communication Monographs, 69*, 275–296.

Caughlin, J. P., Scotts, A. M., Miller, L. E., & Hefner, V. (2008, November). *Putative secrets: When information is supposedly a secret*. Paper presented at the annual convention of the National Communication Association, San Diego, CA.

Chaiken, A. L., & Derlega, V. J. (1974). *Self-disclosure*. Morristown, NJ: General Learning Press.

Ciccarone, D. H., Kanouse, D. E., Collins, R. L., Miu, A., Chen, J. L., Morton, S. C., et al. (2003). Sex without disclosure of positive HIV serostatus in a US probability sample of persons receiving medical care for HIV infection. *American Journal of Public Health, 93*, 949–954.

Cloven, D. H., & Roloff, M. E. (1993). The chilling effect of aggressive potential on the expression of complaints in intimate relationships. *Communication Monographs, 60*, 199–219.

Corrigan, P., & Matthews, A. (2003). Stigma and disclosure: Implications for coming out of the closet. *Journal of Mental Health, 12*, 235–248.

DeMatteo, D., Harrison, C., Arneson, C., Goldie, R. S., Lefebvre, A., Read, S. E., et al. (2002). Disclosing HIV/AIDS to children: The paths families take to truth-telling. *Psychology, Health, & Medicine, 7*, 339–356.

Derlega, V. J., Metts, S., Petronio, S., & Margulis, S. T. (1993). *Self-disclosure*. Newbury Park, CA: Sage.

Derlega, V. J., Sherburne, S. P., & Lewis, R. J. (1998). Reactions to an HIV-positive man: Impact of his sexual orientation, cause of infection, and research participants' gender. *AIDS and Behavior, 2*, 239–248.

Derlega, V. J., Winstead, B. A., & Folk-Barron, L. (2000). Reasons for and against disclosing HIV-seropositive test results to an intimate partner: A functional perspective. In S. Petronio (Ed.), *Balancing the secrets of private disclosures* (pp. 53–69). Mahwah, NJ: Erlbaum.

Derlega, V. J., Winstead, B. A., Greene, K., Serovich, J., & Elwood, W. N. (2004). Reasons for HIV disclosure/nondisclosure in close relationships: Testing a model of HIV-disclosure decision making. *Journal of Social & Clinical Psychology, 23*, 747–767.

Dillard, J. P. (1990). A goal-driven model of interpersonal influence. In J. P. Dillard (Ed.), *Seeking compliance: The production of interpersonal influence messages* (pp. 41–56). Scottsdale, AZ: Gorsuch Scarisbrick.

Dindia, K. (1982). Reciprocity of self-disclosure: A sequential analysis. In M. Burgoon (Ed.), *Communication yearbook 5* (pp. 506–528). New Brunswick, NJ: Transaction Books.

Dindia, K. (2000). Sex differences in self-disclosure, reciprocity of self-disclosure, and self-disclosure and liking: Three meta-analyses reviewed. In S. Petronio (Ed.), *Balancing the secrets of private disclosures* (pp. 21–35). Mahwah, NJ: Erlbaum.

Emlet, C. A. (2006). A comparison of HIV stigma and disclosure patterns between older and younger adults living with HIV/AIDS. *AIDS Patient Care and STDs, 20,* 350–358.

Epstein, R. M., & Street, R. L. (2007). *Patient-centered communication in cancer care: Promoting healing and reducing suffering.* Bethesda, MD: National Cancer Institute (NIH Publication No. 07–6225).

Fried, T. R., Bradley, E. H., & O'Leary, J. (2003). Prognosis communication in serious illness: Perceptions of older patients, caregivers, and clinicians. *Journal of the American Geriatrics Society, 51,* 1398–1403.

Fujimori, M., Akechi, T., Morita, T., Inagaki, M., Akizuki, N., Sakano, Y., et al. (2007). Preferences of cancer patients regarding the disclosure of bad news. *Psycho-Oncology, 16,* 573–581.

Gill, E. A., & Babrow, A. S. (2007). To hope or to know: Coping with uncertainty about ambivalence in women's magazine breast cancer articles. *Journal of Applied Communication Research, 35,* 133–155.

Goffman, E. (1963). *Stigma: Notes on the management of spoiled identity.* Englewood Cliffs, NJ: Prentice-Hall.

Goldsmith, D. J. (2004). *Communicating social support.* New York: Cambridge University Press.

Goldsmith, D. J., Miller, L. E., & Caughlin, J. (2007). Openness and avoidance in couples communicating about cancer. *Communication Yearbook, 31,* 62–117.

Golish, T. D., & Caughlin, J. (2002). "I'd rather not talk about it": Adolescents' and young adults' use of topic avoidance in stepfamilies. *Journal of Applied Communication Research, 30,* 78–106.

Gouldner, A. W. (1960). The norm of reciprocity: A preliminary statement. *American Sociological Review, 25,* 161–178.

Green, J., Ferrier, S., Kocsis, A., Shadrick, J., Ukoumunne, O. C., Murphy, S., et al. (2003). Determinants of disclosure of genital herpes to partners. *Sexually Transmitted Infections, 79,* 42–44.

Greene, K. (2000). Disclosure of chronic illness varies by topic and target: The role of stigma and boundaries in willingness to disclose. In S. Petronio (Ed.), *Balancing the secrets of private disclosures* (pp. 123–135). Mahwah, NJ: Erlbaum.

Greene, K., Derlega, V. J., & Mathews, A. (2006). Self-disclosure in personal relationships. In A. L. Vangelisti & D. Perlman (Eds.), *The Cambridge handbook of personal relationships* (pp. 409–427). Cambridge, UK: Cambridge University Press.

Greene, K., Derlega, V. J., Yep, G. A., & Petronio, S. (2003). *Privacy and disclosure of HIV in interpersonal relationships: A sourcebook for researchers and practitioners.* Mahwah, NJ: Erlbaum.

Greene, K., & Faulkner, S. L. (2002). Self-disclosure in relationships of HIV-positive African-American adolescent females. *Communication Studies, 53,* 297–313.

Greene, K., & Serovich, J. M. (1996). Appropriateness of disclosure of HIV testing information: The perspective of PLWAs. *Journal of Applied Communication Research, 24,* 50–65.

Harvey, J. H., & Omarzu, J. (1997). Minding the close relationship. *Personality and Social Psychology Review, 1,* 224–240.

Hines, S. C., Babrow, A. S., Badzek, L., & Moss, A. (2001). From coping with life to coping with death: Problematic integration for the seriously ill elderly. *Health Communication, 13,* 327–342.

Hinton, J. (1998). An assessment of open communication between people with terminal cancer, caring relatives, and others during home care. *Journal of Palliative Care, 14,* 15–23.

Hosek, S. G., Harper, G. W., & Domanico, R. (2000). Psychological and social difficulties of adolescents living with HIV: A qualitative analysis. *Journal of Sex Education and Therapy, 25,* 269–276.

Ingram, K. M., Bentz, N. E., Mindes, E. J., Schmitt, M. M., & Smith, N. G. (2001). Unsupportive responses from others concerning a stressful life event: Development of the Unsupportive Social Interactions Inventory. *Journal of Social and Clinical Psychology, 20,* 173–207.

Jeffe, D. B., Khan, S. R., Meredith, K. L., Schlesinger, M., Fraser, V. J., & Mundy, L. M. (2000). Disclosure of HIV status to medical providers: Differences by gender, "race," and immune function. *Public Health Reports, 115,* 38–45.

Jiang, Y., Liu, C., Li, J. Y., Huang, M. J., Yao, W. X., Zhang, R., et al. (2007). Different attitudes of Chinese patients and their families toward truth telling of different stages of cancer. *Psycho-Oncology, 16,* 928–936.

Jonzon, E., & Lindblad, F. (2005). Adult female victims of child sexual abuse. *Journal of Interpersonal Violence, 20,* 651–666.

Jourard, S. M. (1971). *Self-disclosure: An experimental analysis of the transparent self.* New York: Wiley-Interscience.

Kelly, A. E. (2002). *The psychology of secrets.* New York: Kluwer Academic/Plenum.

Kelly, A. E., & McKillop, K. J. (1996). Consequences of revealing personal secrets. *Psychological Bulletin, 120,* 450–465.

Klitzman, R., Exner, T., Correale, J., Kirshenbaum, S. B., Remien, R., Ehrhardt, A. A., et al. (2007). It's not just what you say: Relationships of HIV disclosure and risk reduction among MSM in the post-HAART era. *AIDS Care, 19,* 749–756.

Leary, M. R., & Schreindorfer, L. S. (1998). The stigmatization of HIV and AIDS: Rubbing salt in the wound. In V. J. Derlega & A. P. Barbee (Eds.), *HIV and social interaction* (pp. 12–29). Thousand Oaks, CA: Sage.

Lerman, C., Hughes, C., Trock, B. J., Myers, R. E., Main, D., Bonney, A., et al. (1999). Genetic testing in families with hereditary nonpolyposis colon cancer. *JAMA, 281,* 1618–1622.

Makoul, G., & Roloff, M. (1998). The role of efficacy and outcome expectations in the decision to withhold relational complaints. *Communication Research, 25,* 5–29.

Manne, S., Ostroff, J., Rini, C., Fox, K., Goldstein, L., & Grana, G. (2004a). The interpersonal process model of intimacy: The role of self-disclosure, partner disclosure and partner responsiveness in interactions between breast cancer patients and their partners. *Journal of Family Psychology, 18,* 589–599.

Manne, S., Ostroff, J., Sherman, M., Heyman, R., Ross, S., & Fox, K. (2004b). Couples' support-related communication, psychological distress, and relationship satisfaction among women with early stage breast cancer. *Journal of Consulting and Clinical Psychology, 72*, 660–670.

Mathews, A., Derlega, V. J., & Morrow, J. (2006). What is highly personal information and how is it related to self-disclosure decision-making? The perspective of college students. *Communication Research Reports, 23*, 85–92.

Mattson, M., & Roberts, F. (2001). Overcoming truth telling as an obstacle to initiating safer sex: Clients and health practitioners planning deception during HIV test counseling. *Health Communication, 13*, 343–362.

Miller, A. N., & Rubin, D. L. (2007). Factors leading to self-disclosure of a positive HIV diagnosis in Nairobi, Kenya. *Qualitative Health Research, 17*, 586–598.

Morr, M. C., & Petronio, S. (2007). Communication privacy management theory. In B. B. Whaley & W. Samter (Eds.), *Explaining communication: Contemporary theories and exemplars* (pp. 257–274). Mahwah, NJ: Erlbaum.

Munir, F., Leka, S., & Griffiths, A. (2005). Dealing with self-management of chronic illness at work: Predictors for self-disclosure. *Social Science & Medicine, 60*, 1397–1407.

O'Keefe, B. J. (1988). The logic of message design: Individual differences in reasoning about communication. *Communication Monographs, 55*, 80–103.

Omarzu, J. (2000). A disclosure decision model: Determining how and when individuals will self-disclose. *Personality and Social Psychology Review, 4*, 174–185.

Petronio, S. (2002). *Boundaries of privacy: Dialectics of disclosure.* Albany, NY: State University of New York Press.

Petronio, S., & Bantz, C. (1991). Controlling the ramifications of disclosure: "Don't tell anybody but . . ." *Journal of Language & Social Psychology, 10*, 263–269.

Petronio, S., Reeder, H. M., Hecht, M. L., & Mon't Ros-Mendoza, T. (1996). Disclosure of sexual abuse by children and adolescents. *Journal of Applied Communication Research, 24*, 181–199.

Prager, K. J. (1995). *The psychology of intimacy.* New York: Guilford Press.

Reis, H. T., & Shaver, P. (1988). Intimacy as an interpersonal process. In S. W. Duck (Ed.), *Handbook of personal relationships: Theory, research and interventions* (pp. 376–389). Chichester, England: Wiley.

Roloff, M. E., & Cloven, D. H. (1990). The chilling effect in interpersonal relationships: The reluctance to speak one's mind. In D. D. Cahn (Ed.), *Intimates in conflict: A communication perspective* (pp. 49–76). Hillsdale, NJ: Erlbaum.

Rosenfeld, L. B. (1979). Self-disclosure avoidance: Why am I afraid to tell you who I am? *Communication Monographs, 46*, 63–74.

Rowland, D. L., Thornton, J. A., & Burnett, A. L. (2005). Recognizing the risk of erectile dysfunction in a urology clinic practice. *BJU International, 95*, 1034–1038.

Rutledge, S. E. (2007). Enacting personal HIV disclosure policies for sexual situations: HIV-positive gay men's experiences. *Qualitative Health Research, 17*, 1040–1059.

Santosh, D., Kumar, T. S., Sarma, P. S., & Radhakrishnan, K. (2007). Women with onset of epilepsy prior to marriage: Disclose or conceal? *Epilepsia, 48*, 1007–1010.

Schrodt, P., & Afifi, T. (2007). Communication processes that predict young adults' feelings of being caught and their associations with mental health and family satisfaction. *Communication Monographs, 74*, 200–228.

Simbayi, L. C., Kalichman, S. C., Strebel, A., Cloete, A., Henda, N., & Mqeketo, A. (2007). Disclosure of HIV status to sex partners and sexual risk behaviors among

HIV-positive men and women, Cape Town, South Africa. *Sexually Transmitted Infections, 83*, 29–34.

Stiles, W. B. (1987). "I have to talk to somebody." A fever model of disclosure. In V. J. Derlega & J. H. Berg (Eds.), *Self-disclosure: Theory, research, and therapy* (pp. 257–282). New York: Plenum.

Sullivan, H. S. (1953). *The interpersonal theory of psychiatry.* New York: Norton.

Sunnafrank, M. (1986). Predicted outcome value during initial interactions: A reformulation of uncertainty reduction theory. *Human Communication Research, 13*, 3–33.

Vallerand, A. H., Hough, E., Pittiglio, L., & Marvicsin, D. (2005). The process of disclosing HIV serostatus between HIV-positive mothers and their HIV-negative children. *AIDS Patient Care and STDs, 19*, 100–109.

Vangelisti, A. L. (1994). Family secrets: Forms, functions and correlates. *Journal of Social and Personal Relationships, 11*, 113–135.

Vangelisti, A. L., Caughlin, J. P., & Timmerman, L. (2001). Criteria for revealing family secrets. *Communication Monographs, 68*, 1–27.

Venetis, M. K., Greene, K., Banerjee, S. C., & Bagdasarov, Z. (2008a, May). *Labeling private and secret information in disclosure decisions.* Paper presented at the annual meeting of the International Communication Association, Montreal, Canada.

Venetis, M. K., Greene, K., Banerjee, S. C., & Bagdasarov, Z. (2008b, November). *Exploring explicitly and implicitly stated privacy rules used in third party disclosure and gossip.* Paper presented at the annual meeting of the National Communication Association, San Diego, CA.

Wegner, D. M., & Lane, J. D. (1995). From secrecy to psychopathology. In J. W. Pennebaker (Ed.), *Emotion, disclosure, and health* (pp. 25–46). Washington, DC: American Psychological Association.

Wortman, C. B., & Lehman, D. R. (1985). Reactions to victims of life crises: Support attempts that fail. In I. G. Sarason & B. R. Sarason (Eds.), *Social support: Theory, research and applications* (pp. 463–489). Dordrecht, The Netherlands: Martinus Nijhoff.

Yoshioka, M. R., & Schustack, A. (2001). Disclosure of HIV status: Cultural issues of Asian parents. *AIDS Patient Care & STDs, 15*, 77–82.

Zea, M. C., Reisen, C. A., Poppen, P. J., Echeverry, J. J., & Bianchi, F. T. (2004). Disclosure of HIV-positive status to Latino gay men's social networks. *American Journal of Community Psychology, 33*, 107–116.

13 Information, Uncertainty, and Sexual Disclosures in the Era of HIV/AIDS

Serena C. Lo, María Cecilia Zea, and Paul J. Poppen

The continuing high levels of HIV as well as other sexually transmitted infections (STIs) remain a top public health concern in the United States and other countries. The risk posed by HIV in particular has intensified the consequential nature of sexual behavior and the need to manage uncertainties involved in sexual decision making. When engaging in sexual behavior, individuals may bring about potential outcomes ranging from pleasure and intimacy to infection. Some outcomes will be more or less probable depending on the behaviors in which an individual engages, the precautions the individual takes, and the people with whom sexual activities are carried out. With respect to the latter, the uncertainty around the risk of contracting HIV/AIDS and other STIs has made the desire to know the sexual histories of current and prospective sexual partners more salient than ever before.

In this chapter, we will discuss the kinds of sexual history information that people might want to know about their partners in order to reduce uncertainty about the potential risks of having sex. We describe common assumptions and barriers that can interfere with the process of verifying the sexual health status of one's sexual partners. We then shift our focus to the mutually related act of disclosing one's own sexual history and health information to a sexual partner, whether current or prospective, and explore difficulties encountered on the discloser's side of sexual history discussions. We specifically consider the case of HIV status disclosure and the role of stigma and other culturally based factors that can affect people's disclosure decisions. We also highlight our research on Latino men who have sex with men as a way of exploring HIV disclosure in a specific sociocultural context. Finally, we discuss the interrelationships between sexual self-disclosure and sexual behavior, and the practical implications of sexual history disclosures relative to public health efforts to reduce the prevalence of STIs. In general, much of the peer-reviewed literature on the "discovery" side of sexual communication has focused primarily on discussions of sexual history, STIs, and safer sex topics among heterosexual adolescents and young adults. On the disclosure side of sexual communication, the vast majority of recent published literature has focused specifically on the issue of HIV disclosure in populations of men who have sex with men (MSM). As a

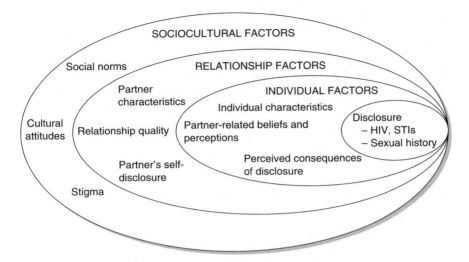

Figure 13.1 Conceptual Model of Sexual Health Disclosure

result, our chapter reflects the asymmetries in the literature on which we have relied.

Drawing from a tradition originated by developmental psychologist Urie Bronfenbrenner (1979), our discussion attempts to bridge seemingly disparate topics by employing an ecological approach to conceptualizing HIV disclosure and disclosure of sexual history. The conceptual model of this ecological approach, illustrated in Figure 13.1, also builds on a social influence perspective proposed by Zea, Reisen, Poppen, Bianchi, and Echeverry (2007). As depicted in Figure 13.1, sexual disclosure behavior is nested within multiple interrelated levels of influences, including individual, interpersonal relationship, and sociocultural factors. At the individual level, individual characteristics and perceptions influence disclosure decisions. However, individuals are situated within a relationship context, and the relationship is, in turn, situated in a sociocultural context. Thus, factors at the relationship and sociocultural levels also determine the dynamics of disclosure at the level of the individual.

Discovery and the Public Health Perspective

From both a public health and individual perspective, it is important for people to know the sexual health status of their sexual partners, especially in the absence of consistent condom use. It is particularly important to know whether a sexual partner has a sexually transmitted infection, including HIV or STDs. In cases where a single sexual encounter occurs between partners, use of a barrier method (e.g., condoms) might appear to make discussions of sexual health status moot. However, many sexual partnerships involve numerous sexual encounters spread over a period of weeks, months, or years. For such ongoing partnerships, an eventual progression from sex with to sex without the use of physical barriers is a normative transition (Conley & Rabinowitz, 2004; Reisen & Poppen, 1995). At the time this transition occurs, the risk of STI exposure may increase. Indeed STIs may continue to pose a risk throughout the course of the relationship, depending on the behaviors in which partners engage both within and outside the context of the current partnership. Moreover, although consistent, correct use of condoms significantly reduces the risk of transmission of HIV and other STIs, condoms do not eliminate risks of these infections in their entirety (National Institutes of Health, 2001).

Biased Reasoning and Faulty Appraisals of Partner Risk

Egon Brunswik was one of the first psychologists to suggest that organisms must learn to operate within a complex environment, which by virtue of its complex nature subjects organisms to uncertainty (Tolman & Brunswik, 1935; Weary & Edwards, 1996). Jerome Kagan (1972) subsequently proposed that a fundamental class of human motives is the resolution of uncertainty. Because there are adaptive advantages to holding correct beliefs about, and making accurate appraisals of, the environment, accumulating uncertainty can induce feelings of anxiety or other psychological distress. Thus, Kagan argued that most people are motivated to reduce or manage uncertainty in order to avoid such negative sequelae.

In interpersonal contexts, people may be similarly motivated to resolve uncertainty about their relationship partners. Because one method of reducing interpersonal uncertainty involves communication with others, a number of communication researchers have formulated and advanced theoretical frameworks to explain processes involved in uncertainty management (e.g., Afifi & Weiner, 2006; Berger & Calabrese, 1975; Brashers et al., 2000). A review of these uncertainty management theories is beyond the scope of the current chapter. However, one theoretical distinction described by Brashers et al. (2000) seems especially useful for the present discussion: that individuals appraise the uncertainty they face in a given situation, and these appraisals influence how a person will react to the uncertainty (see Hogan & Brashers' chapter in this volume for a review). Appraisal is a key consideration in situations in which individuals face uncertainty about a sexual partner. When an individual is uncertain about his or her partner's sexual risk potential, positive and negative appraisals of that uncertainty may result in varying efforts to maintain or reduce the uncertainty, as noted by Brashers and colleagues. However, we believe that, in the case of sexual partner perceptions, people may also engage in spontaneous *reappraisals* of the uncertainties about their partners. These reappraisals involve cognitive processes that often lead people to judge that the uncertainty about their sexual partners is insignificant. Indeed, cognitive biases can prompt individuals to dispel partner-related uncertainty altogether through error-prone reasoning or information that is irrelevant to sexual risk. Ultimately, these cognitive processes essentially bypass the need for subsequent uncertainty management by diminishing levels of perceived uncertainty and reducing individuals' motivation to confirm the status of current and prospective partners' sexual health.

In sexual relationships, a number of assumptions can lead people to perceive low levels of uncertainty concerning their partners. For example, people might assume that spouses and other steady partners pose little to no sexual risk to each other. Mosher, Chandra, and Jones (2005) reflected this widely held assumption in a report on the 2002 National Survey of Family Growth (NSFG) by referring to never married, sexually active men and women as "groups that may be at higher risk of STIs" (p. 16) in comparison with married or cohabiting individuals. Rather than relying on medical test results or explicit discussions with their partner, people often make assumptions about their partners based on error-prone decision-making rules. The characterization of "known" partners as "safe" partners is an example of a heuristic, a mental shortcut or simple rule that people employ relatively automatically when forming impressions and making judgments about other people, the environment, or themselves (Nisbett & Wilson, 1977; Tversky & Kahneman, 1974). Due to such heuristics, partners who are perceived as familiar, attractive, trustworthy, and likeable may automatically be deemed "safe" sexual partners even in the absence of objective knowledge to support that conclusion (Kershaw, Ethier, Niccolai, Lewis, & Ickovics, 2003; Misovich, Fisher, & Fisher, 1997; Noar, Zimmerman, & Atwood, 2004; Swann & Gill, 1997; Williams et al., 1992). Once this conclusion is reached, it is unlikely to change, as new information about the partner will be subject to biased processing (e.g., selective attention to conclusion-consistent information), thereby allowing judgments of the partner to remain unchallenged (Nickerson, 1998; Rusbult, Van Lange, Wildschut, Yovetich, & Verette, 2000).

Another heuristic that can contribute to inaccurate partner risk perceptions is the tendency to rely on feelings of confidence to judge the correctness of one's knowledge (Koriat & Levy-Sadot, 1999). Such confidence does not always correspond with accuracy. In the context of sexually intimate relationships, people may be especially likely to feel confident in their knowledge about their partners. Swann and Gill (1997) observed this overconfidence in a study conducted with individuals involved in heterosexual dating relationships. As relationship length and degree of involvement increased, so did the confidence people had in their impressions of their partner's sexual history. However, length and involvement did not predict greater *accuracy* of those impressions.

Feelings of emotional safety may also be erroneously extended to presumed physical safety (i.e., absence of STIs). An experiment by Comer and Nemeroff (2000) vividly demonstrated such halo effects (i.e., influences of global evaluations on the evaluation of a specific attribute [Nisbett & Wilson, 1977]). In this study, college students were presented with one of three randomly selected scenarios describing a casual partner, a regular "emotionally safe" partner, or a regular objectively safe partner. In the casual partner condition, participants read a scenario in which they imagined meeting a sexual partner for the first time at a bar. The emotionally safe scenario described a situation where the participant was sexually involved with a dating partner with whom the participant had developed a trusting, caring relationship. The objectively safe scenario was identical to the emotionally safe scenario, but explicitly noted that monogamy had been discussed and agreed to and also noted the partner's tested HIV/AIDS status. As predicted, the study results demonstrated that participants rated the physical risk posed by the casual partner as significantly higher than the risk posed by either of the regular partner types. However, participants' ratings of the risk posed by the "emotionally safe" partner did not significantly differ from the ratings for the objectively safe partner. In other words, perceived risk ratings of regular partners were not affected by the presence or absence of explicit monogamy intentions or HIV/AIDS test results. Thus, participants appeared to perceive less uncertainty about sexual partners when provided with emotionally based information (presence of a trusting, caring relationship) versus fact-based information (explicit monogamy and HIV/AIDS test results).

Comer and Nemeroff (2000) also found that 61% of participants assigned to the emotionally safe scenario either mistakenly recalled or assumed monogamy and 32% indicated the hypothetical partner had been tested for HIV, even though this scenario mentioned nothing about monogamy or HIV testing. These findings imply that, in conditions where emotional safety is salient, people often assume monogamy, even if no explicit agreement about monogamy has been expressed, and people may even assume the absence of infection. Assumptions regarding monogamy are problematic because, as some empirical evidence suggests, these assumptions are not always accurate (e.g., Drumright, Gorbach, & Holmes, 2004; Harvey, Bird, Henderson, Beckman, & Huszti, 2004; Riehman, Wechsberg, Francis, Moore, & Morgan-Lopez, 2006). An additional problem with inferring physical safety from emotional safety is that it fails to account for serial monogamy. Current trends indicate that, because many adolescents and young adults practice serial monogamy, there may be short gaps between sexual partners. If these gaps are shorter than the duration of infectivity of any untreated STI, this could result in transmission of infection from the first partner to the second partner (Aral, 2002). STIs are also asymptomatic in many cases; people infected by earlier partners may not be aware of their infection, which could contribute to the possibility of monogamous partners being vectors of infection. Thus, even if monogamy perceptions are accurate, the assumption that monogamy fully protects people from STIs is not entirely valid.

Another major reason that people do not obtain sexual health information about their partners is that competing motivations may reduce a person's willingness to seek such information. For example, people in relationships are commonly motivated to justify their positive beliefs about their partners as well as their desires to engage in potentially unsafe sexual activity. These motivations can lead people to rely on irrelevant information (e.g., the partner was raised in a religious family) in order to rationalize desired conclusions (e.g., the partner is uninfected) and actions (e.g., sex without a condom). Indeed, studies have demonstrated that variables such as partner attractiveness and relationship commitment increase people's reliance on nondiagnostic personality information that is irrelevant to the potential riskiness of the partner, which is in turn related to greater willingness to engage in potentially less safe sexual behavior (Agocha & Cooper, 1999; Blanton & Gerrard, 1997; Knäuper, Kornik, Atkinson, Guberman, & Aydin, 2005).

In sum, people often believe that they already have the information they need in order to assess a partner's risk, due to feelings of emotional safety, trust and familiarity, confidence in one's knowledge, and so on. Moreover, motives stemming from sexual desire or relationship commitment may conflict with motives to protect one's health. These heuristics and biases, therefore, decrease the perceptions of uncertainty about actual and potential sexual partners, as well as the likelihood that individuals will obtain the factual information necessary to judge partner-associated sexual risk. However, as depicted in our conceptual model in Figure 13.1, intrapersonal factors such as partner-related beliefs, feelings, and perceptions, along with motivated and heuristic-driven reasoning processes, constitute only one of multiple levels of influences that can affect individuals' seeking of sexual health information. When individuals enter into the process of discovering and disclosing sexual health information, they engage in actions that are inherently interpersonal and reciprocal. The following section explores some of the interpersonal aspects involved in the exchange (or withholding) of sexual health information.

Disclosure: Interpersonal Influences

Communication between partners is a two-way interaction and typically involves reciprocal self-disclosure as a relationship develops. Rather than being individually driven, relationship partners construct shared rules and restrictions, either explicit or implicit, concerning information seeking and self-disclosure. As a result, certain topics may be openly discussed whereas other topics are mutually avoided (Caughlin & Afifi, 2004; Derlega, Metts, Petronio, & Margulis, 1993; Knobloch & Carpenter-Theune, 2004). Sexual history is one topic that people often prefer to avoid. For example, a survey of college-aged Canadian blood donors revealed that 68% of respondents did not fully disclose their sexual history and, more surprisingly, 69% of respondents actually *preferred* that their partner not fully disclose their sexual history (Mair, Barrett, Campbell, & Ditto, 2003). Hence, if a person goes so far as to venture an inquiry, and it is met with silence, censure, or withholding of information, such responses are likely to discourage a person from probing any further. In addition, by asking a partner about personal topics such as past sexual experiences and HIV status, a person may invite questions about his or her own situation. Thus, people may be less willing to seek information that they themselves would be uncomfortable revealing.

Although discussions of sexual history may include topics ranging from the number of sexual partners a person has had to past or present diagnoses of STIs, the most extensive amount of research in the past decade has focused on disclosure of HIV-positive status. As with general self-disclosure, numerous studies suggest that communication between partners about HIV serostatus occurs in a reciprocal fashion: those most likely to know the HIV status of their partner are also more likely to have disclosed their own serostatus, particularly when both partners are seroconcordant (Wolitski, Parsons, & Gómez, 2004). For example, Zea, Reisen, Poppen, and Díaz (2003) found that asking and telling a sexual partner about HIV status were highly correlated ($r = .59$, $p < .0001$). The correspondence between asking and telling partners about one's sexual health status is a reflection of not only the reciprocal nature of disclosure, but also the fact that many barriers to asking about sexual health information overlap with the barriers to revealing such information. Personal barriers such as embarrassment and lack of self-efficacy, as well as expectations of negative partner reactions and relationship disruption, impede both directions of dialogue in discussions of sexual risk. Given the multiple drawbacks to initiating conversations about safer sex, people may decide that avoiding the topic altogether is the best course of action.

Just as there are important facts that people should ideally know about the sexual health of their partners, people who currently have a sexually transmitted infection often have a corresponding sense of responsibility to tell their sexual partners about the presence of infection. However, as in many behavioral domains, what people believe they should do does not necessarily match what they *actually* do. For example, Ciccarone and colleagues (2003) found that, in a U.S. probability sample of HIV-positive adults ($N = 1,421$), 42% of gay or bisexual men, 19% of heterosexual men, and 17% of women had engaged in oral, anal, or vaginal sex without disclosing their serostatus at least once in the past 6 months. A variety of situational factors, such as the type of infection, the perceived quality of the relationship between partners, and the anticipated consequences of revealing and hiding information, are among the variables that can affect a person's decision to disclose his or her sexual health status and associated sexual history information.

Out of all the possible types of personal information that an individual may choose to disclose to or withhold from a current or prospective sexual partner, sexual health and sexual history information have unique features. For instance, in contrast to other types of background information (e.g., educational background, family history), sexually related disclosures are likely to elicit a more extreme response in the recipient of these disclosures, and depending on the target–discloser relationship, there is perhaps greater self-interest in sexual history information. Echoing the research on people's failures to obtain accurate sexual history information from their partners, people's desire to be honest with their relationship partners must be weighed against competing motivations to avoid a host of potential consequences, such as embarrassment, rejection, loss of privacy, relationship disruption, and lost opportunities for sexual gratification. Because these concerns are perhaps most acute when it comes to disclosure of one's HIV-positive status, the subsequent sections will emphasize this domain of sexual disclosure, drawing parallels with other sexual disclosures where applicable.

Theoretical Perspectives on HIV Disclosure

Although there has been extensive theorizing and research on self-disclosure as a general interpersonal process, empirically validated theories specific to disclosure of HIV status and sexual history are few in number. Proposed HIV disclosure theories have included disease progression theory and consequence theory. Disease progression theory (Kalichman, 1995) asserts that individuals disclose their HIV diagnosis because it becomes more difficult to hide the condition as they become ill. The consequence theory (Serovich, 2001) posits that one's anticipated consequences of disclosure moderate the relationship between disease progression and disclosure. Both of these theories have fallen short in predicting disclosure to sexual partners (Simoni & Pantalone, 2005). Serovich expressed the need for broader measures of HIV disclosure consequences, including variables such as power differentials and the strength of the partnership. An alternative perspective, communication privacy management theory, has been advanced by Petronio (2007; see also Petronio & Reierson's chapter in this book). An applied theory in the communication field, communication privacy management theory extends beyond the realm of HIV-specific disclosures and focuses on the idea that individuals control the flow of private information and use privacy rules to decide whether to disclose or conceal information. In other words, the desire to maintain privacy competes with motivations to disclose personal information. Thus far, the communication privacy management theory has been used as an organizing framework for exploring HIV disclosure on a conceptual and theoretical level (e.g., Greene, Derlega, Yep, & Petronio, 2003). However, the theory has not yet been employed as a model for hypothesis testing in empirical, quantitative research on HIV disclosure.

A common theme among both general and HIV-specific models of disclosure is that disclosure often involves risk, and people who anticipate negative consequences from disclosure are less likely to reveal the information than those who do not envision such negative reactions (Derlega, Winstead, Greene, Serovich, & Elwood, 2004; Omarzu, 2000). This overarching view of HIV disclosure is consistent with reasoned action perspectives (i.e., theory of reasoned action and theory of planned behavior), which behavioral researchers have utilized in a broad range of behavioral domains (e.g., Albarracin, Johnson, Fishbein, & Muellerleile, 2001; Armitage & Conner, 2001; Fishbein & Ajzen, 1975). In addition to perceived consequences, theoretical models such as the theory of reasoned action and the theory of planned behavior incorporate broader social factors, specifically norms and beliefs, which are socioculturally derived. Thus, Zea and colleagues (2007) proposed a social influence theory to describe the antecedents of disclosure. To test a conceptual model based on this social influence theory, Zea et al. conducted a study that combined expected utility (e.g., perceived consequence) approaches, normative components reflected in reasoned action models, and additional cultural factors. Zea and colleagues hypothesized that, consistent with consequence theory, HIV-positive Latino gay men would report greater serostatus disclosure when they perceived greater potential for positive outcomes as a result of disclosure. However, beyond perceived consequences, Zea et al. also predicted that those individuals who saw disclosure as normative among their peers would reveal their HIV status to a greater proportion of their social networks. Zea et al. also examined whether social factors such as U.S. acculturation, gay community involvement, and ethnic and sexual orientation discrimination experiences played a role in levels of HIV disclosure.

In support of the consequence theory of disclosure, Zea et al. (2007) found that individuals who anticipated positive consequences of disclosure revealed their serostatus to a greater proportion of casual sexual partners, close friends, and family members. Moreover, those who perceived greater barriers to disclosure reported less disclosure to friends and family members, although there was no statistically significant association between perceived negative consequences and disclosure to casual sexual partners. Findings from the study also supported the researchers' broader social influence model: individuals who regarded serostatus disclosure as more normative among their peers tended to disclose to a greater extent to their casual sexual partners, close friends, and family members. However, gay community involvement had a more complex relationship with disclosure. Specifically, greater identification and involvement with the gay community were negatively associated with disclosure to casual partners, positively associated with disclosure to close friends, and unrelated to disclosure to family members. Disclosure was also unrelated to U.S. acculturation and experiences of discrimination due to ethnicity or sexual orientation.

The overall results of the study by Zea and colleagues (2007) are consistent with the ecological model of sexual health disclosures depicted in Figure 13.1 of this chapter. In addition to demonstrating the importance of perceived consequences of disclosure (an individual-level factor), the study showed how disclosure varies depending on the nature of the relationship context (e.g., casual sexual partner, close friend, or family). Furthermore, the study showed that social and cultural factors such as norms and gay community involvement may also play a role in disclosure decision making.

Risks of Sexual Disclosure Vary by Cultural and Social Context

Cultural and social contexts shape people's views and attitudes concerning acceptable and appropriate behavior and modes of interaction, including self-disclosure, and socioculturally based differences often correspond to different patterns of behavior. For example, Considine, Sabag-Cohen, and Krivoshekova (2007) measured general self-disclosure for a list of topic categories (e.g., sexual activities, shameful events, personal health, feelings, relationships, beliefs, and traumas) in a sample of U.S.-born African American and European American university students and found interactive effects of ethnicity and target on variation in levels of disclosure. In particular, Considine and colleagues found lower levels of overall disclosure among African Americans to closer-relationship targets (lovers/partners, female friends, male friends, and fathers) in comparison to European Americans. Also notable was the fact that, among seven topic domains, disclosure regarding sexual experiences as a general category was lower than disclosure regarding any other topic, including shaming experiences and traumas. Rates of disclosure about sexual experiences in general were universally low; no significant differences were found between the African Americans and European Americans on this disclosure topic.

Disclosure decisions regarding STIs other than HIV are similarly interrelated with cultural context. For example, U.S. cultural values generally support sexual activity within heterosexual, committed relationships and discourage sexual activity with same-sex or casual, less well-known partners (Misovich et al., 1997). Behavior that is inconsistent with these cultural standards is often negatively evaluated. Thus, expectations of disapproval can motivate individuals to conceal or even lie about their past behaviors. This adds to a sense of secrecy and self-defensiveness around the topic of sexuality, which can impede open, honest, and nonjudgmental discussions of sexual health between partners (Cline, Johnson, & Freeman, 1992; Institute of Medicine, 1997; Lear, 1995; Pliskin, 1997; U.S. Department of Health and Human Services, 2000). In addition, notions about romantic relationships are shaped in part by cultural ideas about the nature of love and its relationship with sex. Idealized images of romance in literature, film, and television shows emphasize spontaneity, rarely portraying condom use in sexual encounters, or discussions between partners about sexual histories or STI testing. Media images of sexual activity unencumbered by health concerns and free of adverse consequences have been shown to affect people's attitudes toward safe sex and relationships (Diekman, McDonald, & Gardner, 2000).

Socioeconomic factors are also relevant to individuals' HIV disclosure decisions (Emlet, 2006; Gielen, McDonnell, Burke, & O'Campo, 2000; World Health Organization, 2004). Individuals of low socioeconomic status (SES) who have limited social networks or social capital, such as women in developing countries and some U.S. immigrant populations, may be especially fearful of abandonment and loss of economic support from a partner. Moreover, many of these same individuals may be vulnerable to violence as well as social isolation and discrimination if they disclose their HIV-positive status. Avoiding such consequences is often a matter of survival, whether for individuals in resource-poor areas such as sub-Saharan Africa or socially isolated, low-SES individuals living in the United States. Thus, benefits of disclosing one's HIV-positive status may not outweigh the potential for severe personal harm in some situations.

Stigma: A Cross-Culturally Relevant Barrier to HIV and STI Disclosure

Although there is cross-cultural variation in stigmatizing attitudes, STIs, HIV, and nonheterosexuality are rarely regarded positively in any sociocultural context. The taboo nature of these topics is implicit in the fact that most theoretical perspectives on HIV and STI disclosure include anticipation of negative consequences as a predictor of disclosure. Cultural stigmatization of those with STIs and HIV, as well as certain behavioral characteristics associated with these conditions (e.g., promiscuity, injection drug use, homosexual behavior), renders communication regarding sexual matters and STIs a virtual minefield of potentially embarrassing, negative, or emotionally intense revelations and discoveries. Sexual health disclosure is, therefore, a uniquely difficult domain of self-disclosure. Furthermore, the possibility of sexual or otherwise personal rejection can heighten the emotional vulnerability and uncertainty experienced when individuals consider disclosing sexual history information. Compounding these interpersonal risks are broader social attitudes and sanctions concerning morality and disease, all of which can reinforce and perpetuate a culture of silence regarding sexuality, homosexuality, and other topics relevant to HIV and other STIs.

HIV Stigma

Although HIV-positive individuals in the United States do not experience the same extent of social isolation and discrimination experienced by those in many other countries, people living with HIV in the United States still face a substantial degree of negative sentiment. Much research suggests that both homophobia and stigmatization of HIV discourage open discussions of topics related to HIV risk and transmission (Herek, 1999; Herek & Capitanio, 1999; Herek, Capitanio, & Widaman, 2002). When HIV was first identified in the United States in the 1980s, many of the earliest victims of HIV and AIDS were gay men and injection drug users. Despite the evolving dynamics of the epidemic, popular conceptions of HIV/AIDS in the United States and other societies continue to associate the condition with behaviors often thought of as aberrant. HIV-positive individuals who live in communities where homophobia is commonplace may incur ridicule, rejection, or even physical violence as a consequence of revealing their HIV-positive diagnosis, regardless of their sexual orientation. Because people may assume that a man with HIV is gay, or that people with HIV have engaged in drug use or other risky behaviors, those who wish to avoid such suspicions may be hesitant to disclose the presence of HIV infection.

Homophobia and negative attitudes toward drug use feed into generalized HIV stigma, which is in turn reinforced by HIV stigmatization at a structural and an institutional level. For example, the U.S. Immigration and Nationality Act (8 U.S.C. 1182) prohibits individuals with HIV from entering the United States as tourists, workers, or immigrants. In addition, a 2006 Kaiser Family Foundation survey showed that 81% of those surveyed said that there was "some" or "a lot" of prejudice and discrimination against people living with HIV and AIDS in the United States. Thus, a majority of the public appears to recognize the generally negative connotations associated with HIV and AIDS, and these negative perceptions are manifested at not only the individual level, but also the national level.

Besides homophobia and negative attitudes about sexual behaviors and drug use, fears of illness and death combined with serious misconceptions about how HIV/AIDS is transmitted also fuel stigmatization of HIV. In the United States, for example, 16% of Americans surveyed in 2006 believed that HIV infection could result from sharing a drinking glass with someone who has HIV (Kaiser Family Foundation, 2006a); inclusion of respondents who said they did not know the correct answer raised this percentage to 22%. In turn, 33% of those who agreed HIV could be transmitted through sharing a drinking glass (or did not know) said that they would be uncomfortable working with someone with HIV versus 17% of those who did not harbor this misunderstanding (Kaiser Family Foundation, 2006b). Thus, the persistence of such misconceptions is likely to contribute to the sense of personal rejection and shame often experienced by persons living with HIV/AIDS.

Stereotypes and Stigmatization of People with STIs in General

The stigma attached to STIs other than HIV may be less complicated by sexual orientation issues or ramifications beyond the immediate interpersonal context, yet negative attitudes and judgments of people with STIs prevail nonetheless. Healthy People 2010 explicitly acknowledged stigma as a fundamental barrier to stemming the spread of STIs in the United States (U.S. Department of Health and Human Services, 2000). STIs have long been regarded as punishment for immoral behavior and promiscuity (Institute of Medicine, 1997; Roberts, 1997). This history feeds into stereotypes about people who contract STIs, stereotypes that are decidedly negative. For example, qualitative research has found that individuals have described and sometimes endorsed the common belief that "nice" people do not get STIs (Barth, Cook, Downs, Switzer, & Fischhoff, 2002; Duncan, Hart, Scoular, & Bigrigg, 2001). These stereotypes, in turn, affect how people perceive themselves, their partners, and the behaviors in which they and their partners engage. Even the act of getting tested for STIs or attending a sexual health clinic can connote shameful conduct because these activities in and of themselves suggest that one has been "loose," "dirty," or "irresponsible" (Barth et al., 2002, p. 155; Mulholland & Van Wersch, 2007). In light of these stereotypical beliefs about people who have STIs, people sometimes believe that they can distinguish an uninfected partner from an infected partner simply on the basis of appearance, and this belief has been associated with decreased condom use in adolescents and college students (Noar et al., 2004).

Because of the negative connotations associated with STIs, the characteristics and behaviors associated with STIs may be viewed negatively as well. For example, having numerous past sexual partners, having a history of risky sexual behavior or injection drug use, and seeking STI testing on a regular basis may be seen as indicative of promiscuity, low moral integrity, or other generally negative personal attributes. In turn, such negative connotations make it difficult for people to discuss their sexual histories, particularly if those histories have involved one or more of these stigmatized elements or experiences. The risk of negative evaluation may convince some individuals that it is better to avoid discussions of sexual history altogether, or at least those aspects relevant to sexual risk (e.g., past unprotected sexual activity, past STI diagnoses, and recency of STI testing). If topic avoidance proves unsuccessful, individuals may lie in order to protect themselves from stigmatizing reactions. Due to social desirability concerns, the prevalence of sexual dishonesty is difficult to assess, but some researchers have found that lying about sexual history information is not uncommon (Cochran & Mays, 1990; Marelich & Clark, 2004). For instance, one online survey by GayHealth (2007) found that nearly 10% of respondents had lied to a sexual partner about their HIV status. Depending on the context, the consequences of these lies may vary in severity (e.g., reporting a lower number of sexual partners than one has actually had vs. concealing the presence of a current STI and engaging in unprotected sex). Nevertheless, such surveys indicate that people do, on occasion, misrepresent important aspects of their sexual histories, including their HIV status, to sexual partners.

Although it is justifiable to hold individuals accountable when deliberate distortion of their sexual histories places a sexual partner at risk, unequivocal condemnation of individual dishonesty glosses over the role that society plays in these deceptions through its stigmatization of people with STIs. By encouraging the devaluation of individuals with HIV or other STIs, stigmatization makes full and honest disclosure difficult not only for infected individuals, but also for almost any sexually experienced individual. In turn, such disincentive to disclose sexual history information is compounded by a virtual absence of established norms for initiating health protective sexual communication prior to the onset of sexual activity in a relationship.

HIV Disclosure and Relationship Factors

Although disclosure of HIV-positive serostatus is somewhat distinct from disclosure concerning the presence of other STIs, in both cases the norms concerning disclosure vary across targets and depend on the nature of the relationship between partners. As previously mentioned, sexual health information is more commonly disclosed to main sexual partners than to nonsexual partners or to casual partners (Duru et al., 2006; O'Brien et al., 2003; Zea, Reisen, Poppen, Echeverry, & Bianchi, 2004). Target-specific differences in disclosure norms are especially evident among some populations of MSM, many of whom may view a general absence of discussion of serostatus between casual sexual partners as normative (Sheon & Crosby, 2004). In the case of MSM, disclosure may be more likely to targets who are already aware of the individual's sexual orientation (Marks, Bundek, Richardson, & Ruiz, 1992; O'Brien et al., 2003; Zea et al., 2004). Cultural values and beliefs also influence target-specific decisions about sexual health disclosure. For example, cultural values that emphasize relational harmony and protecting the family from shame or embarrassment can be factors that make disclosure to particular family members less likely among Latino and Asian immigrants in the United States (Yoshioka & Schustack, 2001; Zea, 2008).

For a given target, decisions about disclosure may be influenced by the nature and quality of the relationship, with higher levels of closeness and trust being associated with greater likelihood of disclosure (Zea et al., 2004). Another factor that may vary by target is motivation. Motivations for disclosure or nondisclosure to sexual partners differ from motivations that are relevant in other types of relationships. Differences in relationship goals, in turn, are likely to give rise to differences in disclosure decisions. Consistent with this idea, Derlega et al. (2004) found that reasons for and against HIV disclosure varied depending on whether the target was a close friend, intimate partner, or parent. For example, men and women were more likely to endorse testing the other's reactions as a reason for HIV disclosure to an intimate partner than to a parent. Thus, protecting the health of oneself or one's partner must be weighed against goals such as maintaining a certain self-image, avoiding rejection and interpersonal conflicts, and protecting one's privacy.

It is important to note that, in addition to relationship characteristics, other situational factors are also important determinants of HIV serostatus disclosure and related disclosures. For example, when individuals are in a state of sexual arousal, the desire to experience physical pleasure or intimacy with a partner may overpower other motivations. Situational factors such as whether a condom is used, the location where a sexual encounter occurs (e.g., at home or in a public place), alcohol or drug use, and the partner's HIV status also show associations with HIV disclosure (Marks & Crepaz, 2001; Serovich & Mosack, 2003; Simoni & Pantalone, 2005). Moreover, with respect to the latter, Poppen, Reisen, Zea, Bianchi, and Echeverry (2005) found that individuals' disclosure of their HIV-positive status is interrelated with individuals' knowledge of their partner's serostatus and the emotional relationship between partners. That is, individuals who disclosed their serostatus to a partner typically knew the serostatus of that partner, knowledge of a partner's serostatus was more likely in more emotionally intimate relationships, and disclosure of serostatus was more common in emotionally intimate relationships.

Thus, the appraisal of uncertainty surrounding a sexual interaction depends on the type of disclosure target (e.g., casual sexual partner vs. steady partner), the status and quality of the relationship between partners, and situational features such as concurrent behaviors (e.g., condom use, alcohol use, or drug use) and the prospective partner's sexual health status. When a sexual interaction involves a casual sex partner and condoms are used, individuals may perceive little need to reduce uncertainty. When a sexual interaction involves a prospective long-term relationship partner or a desire to forgo condom use, individuals may have greater interest in eliminating uncertainties about the prospective partner's sexual health and sexual history.

Disclosure among HIV-Positive Latino Men Who Have Sex with Men (MSM)

HIV serostatus disclosure among HIV-positive Latino MSM is one area of research that illustrates how the complex interplay of individual differences and relationship, social, and cultural factors can influence HIV disclosure. For example, a study of disclosure by HIV-positive Latino MSM to different members of the social network indicated that, when parents, friends, or other family members were unaware of participants' gay or bisexual orientation, participants were less likely to share with these individuals the fact that they were living with HIV (Zea et al., 2004). Greater emotional closeness was associated with greater likelihood of disclosure to mothers and fathers, but emotional closeness was less strongly associated with disclosure than knowledge of sexual orientation and was not related to disclosure to closest friends. The study also found that men who were more acculturated into U.S. culture were more likely to disclose to fathers than those who were less acculturated.

With respect to individual differences, a more recent study by Zea and colleagues (cited in Zea, 2008) provided evidence that failure to disclose one's HIV-positive status to a sexual partner may be linked to depressed mood. In this study, a mixed serostatus sample consisting of Brazilian, Colombian, and Dominican MSM provided information on their most recent sexual encounter.

Participants reported on their mood and whether they felt depressed at the time of the encounter. Participants also reported whether the sexual partner knew their serostatus. The study results revealed that, if the partner knew the participant's serostatus, the participant was less depressed than if the partner did not. Although knowledge of a partner's serostatus does not necessarily mean that the partner has disclosed this information directly, these findings are consistent with the idea that concealing one's HIV status from a sexual partner may play a role in adverse mental health outcomes (Pachankis, 2007).

In sum, individual characteristics as well as relationship, social, and cultural factors can influence HIV disclosure. Interpersonal factors such as emotional closeness and target knowledge of sexual orientation act in conjunction with culturally rooted experience to shape the process of disclosure in terms of timing and selection of disclosure recipients. In turn, HIV disclosure can influence interpersonal relationship dynamics and access to social support as well as individuals' mental health.

Conclusions and Summary

Public health campaigns have generally encouraged three primary strategies for reducing sexual risk: abstinence, monogamy (i.e., "being faithful"), and condom use. This three-pronged public health campaign is popularly referred to as the "ABC" approach. Depending on which route of sexual risk reduction is pursued, there are different requirements for developing and implementing sexual history discovery and disclosure skills. For example, a monogamous person who employs regular, correct, and consistent condom use throughout his or her lifetime may have limited need for health-protective sexual discovery and disclosure skills. On the other hand, those who engage in serial monogamy or at some point transition to sexual activity in the absence of any barrier method would likely benefit from such communication skills.

In addition to multiple sexual-risk reduction strategies, there are varying motivations associated with sexual behavior and, correspondingly, different discovery and disclosure concerns. In casual sex encounters, the primary pursuit may be pleasure as opposed to true intimacy. Casual sex seekers likely differ from "serious" sex seekers in terms of what they desire to know about prospective partners. If one is concerned about his or her own sexual health, the sole interest may be to verify that a partner is disease free; other aspects of sexual history, such as number of previous partners or sexual activity preferences, may not be of interest. In contrast, individuals in ongoing sexual partnerships or steady relationships probably want to know more than the casual sex seeker wants to know. Concerns may range from the prospective partner's sexual skills and habits to his or her number of prior sexual partners, in addition to prior STIs. These features are important because they presumably provide information about the character and personality of the prospective partner; also, these might be features that would enhance the desirability of or disqualify the partner. Whether the

range of information of interest is narrow or broad, discovery and disclosure of sexual health information such as being HIV positive are important
for both casual and more serious sex seekers. However, as a two-person
process, each party risks personal rejection, threat, or disappointment in the
course of exchanging sexual health information. Consequently, sexual history topics are often broached indirectly, disclosures may be less than truth-
ful, and individuals are prone to rely on cues and their own personal
feelings to draw conclusions.

From a public health perspective, there is a logical appeal to assuring that
people know their sexual partners' health status because this allows individuals to make informed choices about the risks to which they may expose
themselves if they engage in unprotected sex. It is important to note, however,
that studies in the domain of HIV disclosure have produced mixed findings
concerning the question of whether disclosure of HIV-positive status promotes safer sexual behavior. Some individuals with HIV may adopt a strategy
of consistently engaging in safer sex practices in the absence of disclosure,
whereas other HIV-positive individuals may use disclosure simply as a way
of verifying that both partners are HIV positive (i.e., seroconcordant;
Gorbach et al., 2004; Parsons et al., 2005; Xia et al., 2006). In the latter case,
if two individuals discover that they are both HIV positive, they may decide
to engage in unprotected sex based on the assumption that sexual risk concerns are not applicable. Selectively engaging in unprotected sex in seroconcordant partnerships has been termed "serosorting" (Truong et al., 2006).
Alternatively, upon establishing serodiscordance, where one partner is HIV
positive and the other negative, male partners may employ strategic positioning by assigning the HIV-positive partner a receptive role in the sexual
encounter or by avoiding ejaculation during anal and oral sex (Parsons et al.,
2005). As confirmed by Poppen et al. (2005), seroconcordance between partners is a significant negative predictor of condom use during anal intercourse.
However, honest disclosure of serostatus is a precondition of establishing
seroconcordance, and disclosure is more likely to occur in the context of a
steady relationship. In addition, relationship characteristics such as emotional
closeness and familiarity affect sexual practices, with steady-relationship
partners showing an increased likelihood of sex without the use of condoms.
Thus, disclosure can have differential associations with unprotected sex
depending on the relationship context, in addition to individual characteristics and motivations.

Although the vast majority of recent published literature concerning sexual
health disclosure has focused specifically on the issue of HIV disclosure,
many of the same motivational conflicts and barriers apply to disclosures of
other STIs and related health information. Ultimately, the failure to disclose
the presence of STIs and past sexual risk behaviors not only poses potential
harm, but also precludes positive and proactive behaviors to curb the spread
of STIs. For example, STI disclosure may motivate sexual partners to seek
testing and take precautions to reduce risk. Nondisclosure also can lead to

greater isolation and psychological distress over time, as well as exacerbate the shame and discomfort surrounding sexuality and the stigmatization of STIs. The burden of concealing one's HIV status can also exact a toll in terms of access and adherence to treatment regimens and reduce opportunities to plan for the future. However, discussing sexual health and sexual risk with a sexual partner is often difficult. The process of disclosing as well as discovering personal sexual history information depends on the content of the information, disclosers' perceptions and expectations of their sexual partners, the quality of the relationship between the discloser and the recipient, and socioeconomic and cultural factors. With respect to the latter, U.S. cultural values that impede open and nonjudgmental discussions of sexual health, whether between sexual partners or in public arenas, appear to have shown little change since the 1997 IOM report that referred to sexually transmitted diseases as "hidden" epidemics. Societal recognition of and counteraction against the insidious effects of stigmatization on the perpetuation of STI epidemics is a necessary complement to efforts aimed at increasing effective sexual health communication on an individual level. Should cultural shifts toward less judgmental perspectives on STIs, HIV, and nonheterosexuality occur, researchers may begin to observe a corresponding shift in the balance of individuals' perceived risks and uncertainties involved in health-protective sexual discovery and disclosure.

References

Afifi, W. A., & Weiner, J. L. (2006). Seeking information about sexual health: Applying the theory of motivated information management. *Human Communication Research, 32*, 35–57.

Agocha, V. B., & Cooper, M. L. (1999). Risk perceptions and safer-sex intentions: Does a partner's physical attractiveness undermine the use of risk relevant information? *Personality and Social Psychology Bulletin, 25*, 746–759.

Albarracin, D., Johnson, B. T., Fishbein, M., & Muellerleile, P. A. (2001). Theories of reasoned action and planned behavior as models of condom use: A meta-analysis. *Psychological Bulletin, 127*, 142–161.

Aral, S. O. (2002). Determinants of STD epidemics: Implications for phase appropriate intervention strategies. *Sexually Transmitted Infections, 78*(Suppl. 1), i3–i13.

Armitage, C. J., & Conner, M. (2001). Efficacy of the theory of planned behavior: A meta-analytic review. *British Journal of Social Psychology, 40*, 471–499.

Barth, K. R., Cook, R. L., Downs, J. S., Switzer, G. E., & Fischhoff, B. (2002). Social stigma and negative consequences: Factors that influence college students' decisions to seek testing for sexually transmitted infections. *Journal of American College Health, 50*, 153–159.

Berger, C. R., & Calabrese, R. J. (1975). Some explorations in initial interaction and beyond: Toward a developmental theory of interpersonal communication. *Human Communication Research, 1*, 99–112.

Blanton, H., & Gerrard, M. (1997). Effect of sexual motivation on men's risk perception for sexually transmitted disease: There must be 50 ways to justify a lover. *Health Psychology, 16*, 374–379.

Brashers, D. E., Neidig, J. L., Haas, S. M., Dobbs, L. K., Cardillo, L. W., & Russell, J. A. (2000). Communication in the management of uncertainty: The case of persons living with HIV or AIDS. *Communication Monographs, 67*, 63–84.

Bronfenbrenner, U. (1979). Toward an experimental ecology of human development. *American Psychologist, 32*, 513–531.

Caughlin, J. P., & Afifi, T. D. (2004). When is topic avoidance unsatisfying? Examining moderators of the association between avoidance and dissatisfaction. *Human Communication Research, 30*, 479–513.

Ciccarone, D. H., Kanouse, D. E., Collins, R. L., Miu, A., Chen, J. L., Morton, S. C., & Stall, R. (2003). Sex without disclosure of positive HIV serostatus in a US probability sample of persons receiving medical care for HIV infection. *American Journal of Public Health, 93*, 949–954.

Cline, R. J. W., Johnson, S. J., & Freeman, K. E. (1992). Talk among sexual partners about AIDS: Interpersonal communication for risk reduction or risk enhancement? *Health Communication, 4*, 39–56.

Cochran, S. D., & Mays, V. M. (1990). Sex, lies, and HIV [Letter to the editor]. *New England Journal of Medicine, 322*, 774–775.

Comer, L. K., & Nemeroff, C. J. (2000). Blurring emotional safety with physical safety in AIDS and STD risk estimations: The casual/regular partner distinction. *Journal of Applied Social Psychology, 30*, 2467–2490.

Conley, T. D., & Rabinowitz, J. L. (2004). Scripts, close relationships, and symbolic meanings of contraceptives. *Personal Relationships, 11*, 539–558.

Consedine, N. S., Sabag-Cohen, S., & Krivoshekova, Y. S. (2007). Ethnic, gender, and socioeconomic differences in young adults' self-disclosure: Who discloses what and to whom? *Cultural Diversity and Ethnic Minority Psychology, 13*, 254–263.

Derlega, V. J., Metts, S., Petronio, S., & Margulis, S. T. (1993). *Self-disclosure.* Newbury Park, CA: Sage.

Derlega, V. J., Winstead, B. A., Greene, K., Serovich, J., & Elwood, W. N. (2004). Reasons for HIV disclosure/nondisclosure in close relationships: Testing a model of HIV-disclosure decision making. *Journal of Social and Clinical Psychology, 23*, 747–767.

Diekman, A. B., McDonald, M., & Gardner, W. L. (2000). Love means never having to be careful. *Psychology of Women Quarterly, 24*, 179–188.

Drumright, L. N., Gorbach, P. M., & Holmes, K. K. (2004). Do people really know their sex partners? Concurrency, knowledge of partner behavior, and sexually transmitted infections within partnerships. *Sexually Transmitted Diseases, 31*, 437–442.

Duncan, B., Hart, G., Scoular, A., & Bigrigg, A. (2001). Qualitative analysis of psychosocial impact of diagnosis of *Chlamydia trachomatis*: Implications for screening. *BMJ, 322*, 195–199.

Duru, O. K., Collins, R. L., Ciccarone, D. H., Morton, S. C., Stall, R., Beckman, R., et al. (2006). Correlates of sex without serostatus disclosure among a national probability sample of HIV patients. *AIDS and Behavior, 10*, 495–507.

Emlet, C. A. (2006). A comparison of HIV stigma and disclosure patterns between older and younger adults living with HIV/AIDS. *AIDS Patient Care and STDs, 20*, 350–358.

Fishbein, M., & Ajzen, I. (1975). *Belief, attitudes, intention, and behavior: An introduction to theory and research.* Reading, MA: Addison-Wesley.

GayHealth. (2007). HIV: Secrets and lies survey. Retrieved December 18, 2007, from http://www.gayhealth.com/templates/sex/aids?record=1197

Gielen, A. C., McDonnell, K. A., Burke, J. G., & O'Campo, P. (2000). Women's lives after an HIV-positive diagnosis: Disclosure and violence. *Maternal and Child Health Journal, 4,* 111–120.

Gorbach, P. M., Galea, J. T., Amani, B., Shin, A., Celum, C., Kerndt, P., & Golden, M. R. (2004). Don't ask, don't tell: Patterns of HIV disclosure among HIV positive men who have sex with men with recent STI practising high risk behaviour in Los Angeles and Seattle. *Sexually Transmitted Infections, 80,* 512–517.

Greene, K., Derlega, V. J., Yep, G. A., & Petronio, S. (2003). *Privacy and disclosure of HIV in interpersonal relationships: A sourcebook for researchers and practitioners.* Mahwah, NJ: LEA Publishers.

Harvey, S. M., Bird, S. T., Henderson, J. T., Beckman, L. J., & Huszti, H. C. (2004). He said, she said: Concordance between sexual partners. *Sexually Transmitted Diseases, 31,* 185–191.

Herek, G. M. (1999). AIDS and stigma. *American Behavioral Scientist, 42,* 1106–1116.

Herek, G. M., & Capitanio, J. P. (1999). AIDS and stigma and sexual prejudice. *American Behavioral Scientist, 42,* 1130–1147.

Herek, G. M., Capitanio, J. P., & Widaman, K. F. (2002). HIV-related stigma and knowledge in the United States: Prevalence and trends, 1991–1999. *American Journal of Public Health, 92,* 371–377.

Immigration and Nationality Act, 8 U.S.C. §1182.

Institute of Medicine. (1997). *The hidden epidemic: Confronting sexually transmitted diseases.* Washington, DC: National Academy Press.

Kagan, J. (1972). Motives and development. *Journal of Personality and Social Psychology, 22,* 51–66.

Kaiser Family Foundation. (2006a). Kaiser public opinion spotlight: The public's knowledge and perceptions about HIV/AIDS. Retrieved November 20, 2007, from http://www.kff.org/spotlight/hiv/upload/Spotlight_Aug06_Knowledge.pdf

Kaiser Family Foundation. (2006b). Kaiser public opinion spotlight: Attitudes about stigma and discrimination related to HIV/AIDS. Retrieved June 17, 2008, from http://www.kff.org/spotlight/hivstigma/upload/Spotlight_Aug06_Stigma-pdf.pdf

Kalichman, S. C. (1995). *Understanding AIDS: A guide for mental health professionals.* Washington, DC: American Psychological Association.

Kershaw, T. S., Ethier, K. A., Niccolai, L. M., Lewis, J. B., & Ickovics, J. R. (2003). Misperceived risk among female adolescents: Social and psychological factors associated with sexual risk accuracy. *Health Psychology, 22,* 523–532.

Knäuper, B., Kornik, R., Atkinson, K., Guberman, C., & Aydin, C. (2005). Motivation influences the underestimation of cumulative risk. *Personality and Social Psychology Bulletin, 31,* 1511–1523.

Knobloch, L. K., & Carpenter-Theune, K. E. (2004). Topic avoidance in developing romantic relationships. Associations with intimacy and relational uncertainty. *Communication Research, 31,* 173–205.

Koriat, A., & Levy-Sadot, R. (1999). Processes underlying metacognitive judgments: Information-based and experience-based monitoring of one's own knowledge. In S. Chaiken & Y. Trope (Eds.), *Dual process theories in social psychology* (pp. 483–502). New York: Guilford.

Lear, D. (1995). Sexual communication in the age of AIDS: The construction of risk and trust among young adults. *Social Science and Medicine, 9,* 1311–1323.

Mair, M., Barrett, S. P., Campbell, T., & Ditto, B. (2003). Prevalence, disclosure and interpretations of sexual activities in a sample of Canadian college-aged blood donors. *International Journal of STD & AIDS, 14,* 399–403.

Marelich, W. D., & Clark, T. (2004). Human immunodeficiency virus (HIV) testing and false disclosures in heterosexual college students. *Journal of American College Health, 53,* 109–115.

Marks, G., Bundek, N. I., Richardson, J. L., & Ruiz, M. S. (1992). Self-disclosure of HIV infection: Preliminary results from a sample of Hispanic men. *Health Psychology, 11,* 300–306.

Marks, G., & Crepaz, N. (2001). HIV-positive men's sexual practices in the context of self-disclosure of HIV status. *Journal of Acquired Immune Deficiency Syndromes, 27,* 79–85.

Misovich, S. J., Fisher, J. D., & Fisher, W. A. (1997). Close relationships and elevated HIV risk behavior: Evidence and possible underlying psychological processes. *Review of General Psychology, 1,* 72–107.

Mosher, W. D., Chandra, A., & Jones, J. (2005). Sexual behavior and selected health measures: Men and women 15–44 years of age, United States, 2002. *Advance data from vital and health statistics, 362.* Hyattsville, MD: National Center for Health Statistics. Retrieved November 6, 2007, from http://www.cdc.gov/nchs/data/ad/ad362.pdf

Mulholland, E., & Van Wersch, A. (2007). Stigma, sexually transmitted infections and attendance at the GUM clinic: An exploratory study with implications for the theory of planned behavior. *Journal of Health Psychology, 12,* 17–31.

National Institutes of Health. (2001). Workshop summary: Scientific evidence on condom effectiveness for sexually transmitted disease infection, July 20, 2001. Retrieved December 11, 2007, from http://www3.niaid.nih.gov/about/organization/dmid/PDF/condomReport.pdf

Nickerson, R. (1998). Confirmation bias: A ubiquitous phenomenon in many guises. *Review of General Psychology, 2,* 175–220.

Nisbett, R. E., & Wilson, T. D. (1977). The halo effect: Evidence for unconscious alteration of judgments. *Journal of Personality and Social Psychology, 35,* 250–256.

Noar, S. M., Zimmerman, R. S., & Atwood, K. A. (2004). Safer sex and sexually transmitted infections from a relationship perspective. In J. H. Harvey, A. Wenzel, & S. Sprecher (Eds.), *The handbook of sexuality in close relationships* (pp. 519–544). Mahwah, NJ: Lawrence Erlbaum.

O'Brien, M. E., Richardson-Alston, G., Ayoub, M., Magnus, M., Peterman, T. A., & Kissinger, P. (2003). Prevalence and correlates of HIV serostatus disclosure. *Sexually Transmitted Diseases, 30,* 731–735.

Omarzu, J. (2000). A disclosure decision model: Determining how and when individuals will self-disclose. *Personality and Social Psychology Review, 4,* 174–185.

Pachankis, J. E. (2007). The psychological implications of concealing a stigma: A cognitive-affective-behavioral model. *Psychological Bulletin, 133,* 328–345.

Parsons, J. T., Schrimshaw, E. W., Wolitski, R. J., Halkitis, P. N., Purcell, D. W., Hoff, C. C., et al. (2005). Sexual harm reduction practices of HIV-seropositive gay and bisexual men: Serosorting, strategic positioning, and withdrawal before ejaculation. *AIDS, 19*(Suppl. 1), S13–S25.

Petronio, S. (2007). Translational research endeavors and the practices of communication privacy management. *Journal of Applied Communication Research, 35,* 218–222.

Pliskin, K. L. (1997). Verbal intercourse and sexual communication: Impediments to STD prevention. *Medical Anthropology Quarterly, 11*, 89–109.

Poppen, P. J., Reisen, C. A., Zea, M. C., Bianchi, F. T., & Echeverry, J. J. (2005). Serostatus disclosure, seroconcordance, partner relationship, and unprotected anal intercourse among HIV-positive Latino MSM. *AIDS Education and Prevention, 17*, 227–237.

Reisen, C. A., & Poppen, P. J. (1995). College women and condom use: Importance of partner relationship. *Journal of Applied Social Psychology, 25*, 1485–1498.

Riehman, K. S., Wechsberg, W. M., Francis, S. A., Moore, M., & Morgan-Lopez, A. (2006). Discordance in monogamy beliefs, sexual concurrency, and condom use among young adult substance-involved couples: Implications for risk of sexually transmitted infections. *Sexually Transmitted Diseases, 33*, 677–682.

Roberts, R. E. L. (1997). Power/knowledge and discredited identities: Media representations of herpes. *Sociological Quarterly, 38*, 265–284.

Rusbult, C. E., Van Lange, P. A. M., Wildschut, T., Yovetich, N., & Verette, J. (2000). Perceived superiority in close relationships: Why it exists and persists. *Journal of Personality and Social Psychology, 79*, 521–545.

Serovich, J. M. (2001). A test of two HIV disclosure theories. *AIDS Education and Prevention, 13*, 355–364.

Serovich, J. M., & Mosack, K. E. (2003). Reasons for HIV disclosure or nondisclosure to casual sexual partners. *AIDS Education and Prevention, 15*, 70–80.

Sheon, N., & Crosby, G. M. (2004). Ambivalent tales of HIV disclosure in San Francisco. *Social Science & Medicine, 58*, 2105–2118.

Simoni, J. M., & Pantalone, D. W. (2005). HIV disclosure and safer sex. In S. C. Kalichman (Ed.), *Positive prevention: Reducing HIV transmission among people living with HIV/AIDS* (pp. 65–98). New York: Springer.

Swann, W. B., Jr., & Gill, M. J. (1997). Confidence and accuracy in person perception: Do we know what we think we know about our relationship partners? *Journal of Personality and Social Psychology, 73*, 747–757.

Tolman, E., & Brunswik, E. (1935). The organism and the causal texture of the environment. *Psychological Review, 42*, 43–77.

Truong, H. H. M., Kellogg, T., Klausner, J. D., Katz, M. H., Dilley, J., Knapper, K., et al. (2006). Increases in sexually transmitted infections and sexual risk behaviour without a concurrent increase in HIV incidence among men who have sex with men in San Francisco: A suggestion of HIV serosorting? *Sexually Transmitted Infections, 82*, 461–466.

Tversky, A., & Kahneman, D. (1974). Judgment under uncertainty: Heuristics and biases. *Science, 185*, 1124–1131.

U.S. Department of Health and Human Services. (2000). *Healthy People 2010: Understanding and improving health*, 2nd ed. Washington, DC: U.S. Government Printing Office, November 2000. Retrieved June 12, 2008, from http://www.healthypeople.gov/Document/tableofcontents.htm#under

Weary, G., & Edwards, J. A. (1996). Causal-uncertainty beliefs and related goal structures. In R. M. Sorrentino & E. T. Higgins (Eds.), *Handbook of motivation and cognition. Volume 3: The interpersonal context*. New York: Guilford.

Williams, S. S., Kimble, D. L., Covell, N. H., Weiss, L. H., Newton, K. J., Fisher, J. D., & Fisher, W. A. (1992). College students use implicit personality theory instead of safer sex. *Journal of Applied Social Psychology, 22*, 921–933.

Wolitski, R. J., Parsons, J. T., & Gómez, C. A., for the SUMS & SUMIT Study Teams. (2004). Prevention with HIV-seropositive men who have sex with men: Lessons from the Seropositive Urban Men's Study (SUMS) and the Seropositive Urban Men's Intervention Trial (SUMIT). *Journal of Acquired Immune Deficiency Syndromes, 37*(Suppl. 2), S101–S109.

World Health Organization. (2004). Gender dimensions of HIV status disclosure to sexual partners: Rates, barriers and outcomes. Retrieved June 12, 2008, from http://www.who.int/gender/documents/en/genderdimensions.pdf

Xia, Q., Osmond, D. H., Tholandi, M., Pollack, L. M., Zhou, W., Ruiz, J. D., & Catania, J. A. (2006). HIV prevalence and sexual risk behaviors among men who have sex with men: Results from a statewide population-based survey in California. *Journal of Acquired Immune Deficiency Syndromes, 41*, 238–245.

Yoshioka, M. R., & Schustack, A. (2001). Disclosure of HIV status: Cultural issues of Asian patients. *AIDS Patient Care and STD's, 15*, 77–82.

Zea, M. C. (2008). Disclosure of HIV status and mental health among Latino men who have sex with men. In S. Loue (Ed.), *Health issues confronting minority men who have sex with men* (pp. 217–228). New York: Springer.

Zea, M. C., Reisen, C. A., Poppen, P. J., Bianchi, F. T., & Echeverry, J. J. (2007). Predictors of disclosure of human immunovirus-positive serostatus among Latino gay men. *Cultural Diversity and Ethnic Minority Psychology, 13*, 304–312.

Zea, M. C., Reisen, C. A., Poppen, P. J., & Díaz, R. M. (2003). Asking and telling: Communication about HIV status among Latino HIV-positive gay men. *AIDS and Behavior, 7*, 143–152.

Zea, M. C., Reisen, C. A., Poppen, P. J., Echeverry, J. J., & Bianchi, F. T. (2004). Disclosure of HIV-positive status to Latino gay men's social networks. *American Journal of Community Psychology, 33*, 107–116.

Predictors and Consequences of Withholding Information

14 Why People Conceal or Reveal Secrets

A Multiple Goals Theory Perspective

John P. Caughlin and Anita L. Vangelisti

The reasons people keep secrets and the criteria they use when deciding to reveal secrets offer insights into the goals people bring to their social interactions. Individuals who keep secrets to avoid being negatively evaluated are using secrecy to achieve different objectives than are those who keep secrets to strengthen their relational ties with others. Similarly, people who decide to reveal secrets because the information happens to fit well in a conversation have different goals than do those who reveal secrets only when someone urgently needs to know the information.

The purpose of the current chapter is to examine the reasons people conceal or reveal secrets from a multiple goals theory perspective. Our main argument is not only that individuals are acting on multiple goals when they decide to conceal or reveal secret information, but also that the goals that people bring to their decisions about keeping or revealing secrets provide important information about individuals, their social interactions, and their relationships. In making this argument, we first critically examine how scholars have conceptualized secrecy. Then, we discuss the implications of viewing secrecy from a multiple goals perspective. Next, we review the literatures on reasons for concealing secrets as well as criteria for revealing secrets. We also consider issues that emerge from examining these two literatures together. Finally, we put forth a number of general propositions that illustrate the heuristic value of studying concealing and revealing secrets from a multiple goals perspective.

Conceptual Issues

Scholars have defined secrets in various ways. One of the most common conceptualizations of secrets involves a distinction between privacy and secrecy (e.g., Bellman, 1981; Kelly, 2002). Bellman (1981) wrote that "the term *private* usually establishes that the other person does not have a right to some knowledge" but that secrets involve "information that the other person may have rights to, but that the possessor chooses, is told to, or is obligated to withhold" (p. 4). Reference to who has rights to information may seem useful when there is widespread consensus about those rights.

After the first reports of his liaisons with prostitutes, for example, former New York State Governor Eliot Spitzer tried to claim that his actions were a "private matter" (Reuters, 2008), but the general consensus was that the public had a right to know this information, and Spitzer was viewed as keeping secrets.

Unfortunately, privacy and secrecy cannot always be so neatly distinguished. First, it is not always clear who has the right to know information; for instance, adolescents and parents often disagree about the children's obligation to reveal information to their parents (Smetana, Metzger, Gettman, & Campione-Barr, 2006). Moreover, lay understandings of privacy and secrecy do not make a definitive distinction. People asked to explain why they keep family secrets, for instance, often report that they do so because the information is private (Vangelisti, 1994). In short, privacy and secrecy appear to be overlapping rather than mutually exclusive.

Another prominent conceptualization of secrecy is based on Petronio's (2002) communication privacy management (CPM) theory. According to CPM, any information that is restricted from others is considered private, and granting access to such private information involves various risks. Based on this perspective, secrets "are a highly restricted set of private information" (Petronio, 2002, p. 31). Because of the particularly rigid restrictions surrounding them, Petronio argues that secrets involve a form of private information that is viewed as particularly risky to reveal.

Although CPM avoids the problems associated with treating privacy and secrecy as mutually exclusive, treating secrets as a subset of private information is problematic because some secrets are not typically considered private information. To be considered private, information usually has to be personal (Bellman, 1981), but many secrets are not about personal issues. For instance, government officials and corporate employees often keep secrets on behalf of their institutions. Moreover, whereas some secrets involve information that is risky, others do not correspond with the usual connotations of risky; for example, people often report keeping secrets about surprise parties or gifts (Caughlin, Afifi, Carpenter-Theune, & Miller, 2005).

A third definition of secrets is Bok's (1983) idea that secrets involve information that individuals purposefully conceal from others. We adopt this definition for several reasons. First, this definition implicitly defers to individuals' judgments about what they consider to be secret; if they act as if information is secret, their concealment constitutes an instance of secret keeping. Second, Bok's definition does not make problematic implications about the association between privacy and secrecy; by this definition information can be both secret and private (e.g., personal information that is intentionally concealed), secret but not private (e.g., a closely guarded state secret), or private but not secret (e.g., intimate information that is not intentionally concealed). Moreover, Bok's definition avoids making negative assumptions about secrecy. Secrets are often discussed as if they are inherently sinister and traumatic (e.g., Bradshaw, 1995; Webster, 1991), which contradicts evidence that practically everyone reports keeping secrets and that some secrets are perceived to be fairly positive (Caughlin et al., 2005; Vangelisti, 1994).

Multiple Goals

Conceptualizing secret keeping as purposeful has important theoretical implications. If keeping secrets is something people do on purpose, it implies that individuals keep secrets to achieve some objective. That is, keeping a secret can be viewed as goal oriented. There is, of course, nothing new about suggesting that communication behaviors are often oriented toward goals. Berger (2005) argued that "it is a truism that individuals generally pursue multiple goals simultaneously during their interactions with others" (p. 422), and numerous scholars (e.g., Clark & Delia, 1979; Goldsmith, 2004; Wilson, 2002) have developed theories assuming that communication serves various purposes (for a review, see Wilson & Feng, 2007).

Although multiple goals perspectives have been used widely for understanding communicative behaviors, such perspectives have not been prominent in the secrets literature (cf. Goldsmith, Miller, & Caughlin, 2008). One possible reason why multiple goals have not been applied to secrecy is that multiple goals perspectives are often associated with message production (Berger, 2005), and secret keeping may be viewed as the absence of message production. The fact that secrets are kept purposefully, however, implies that individuals act, or are at least willing to act, to keep their secrets. Concealing a secret may involve communicative behaviors such as lying, trying to act normally, and changing conversational topics (Caughlin, Scott, Miller, & Hefner, in press-b). Keeping a secret is not merely the absence of a disclosure message; it involves the presence of purposeful concealment (see Finkenauer & Hazam, 2000).

To analyze secret keeping as a goal-oriented activity, it is useful to consider the kinds of objectives that are commonly relevant when people keep secrets. One difficulty with doing so is that individuals are not necessarily aware of their goals, even when their communication demonstrably attends to some purpose (Kellermann, 1992). Nevertheless, people can provide insights into their communicative purposes, and given that secret keeping often leads to reflection and rumination (Afifi & Caughlin, 2006; Wegner, Lane, & Dimitri, 1994), people are probably more conscious of their reasons for keeping secrets than they are of many other communicative goals. Individuals also can articulate the criteria they would use for deciding when to reveal a secret (Vangelisti, Caughlin, & Timmerman, 2001), which may provide insights into the objectives that secret keepers have for keeping and potentially revealing secrets. Thus, examining individuals' reported reasons for keeping secrets, as well as their criteria for revealing secrets, should provide important information about the processes of keeping and revealing secrets and the personal and relational consequences of keeping or revealing those secrets.

Reasons for Concealing Secrets

Individuals' reasons for keeping secrets often are linked to their particular secret and circumstances. Consider, for instance, two different secret keeping scenarios: one in which a person living with HIV keeps the diagnosis a secret and another in which a victim of child abuse keeps the crime a secret. People living with HIV often keep this information secret because they believe others who learn of their diagnosis will be afraid of them (Derlega, Winstead, & Folk-Barron, 2000). Children who are victims of child abuse frequently do not reveal the abuse because they think others will not believe them (Paine & Hansen, 2002). Clearly, such reasons are related to the particular situation. Although concern about being believed is salient for abuse victims, it is unlikely to be a prominent issue for individuals considering whether to disclose an HIV-positive diagnosis. Whereas people living with HIV may keep their status a secret because others may fear becoming ill, children deciding whether to reveal abuse are unlikely to be concerned that potential confidants would fear becoming infected.

Because people's reasons for keeping secrets are tied to their particular secrets and circumstances, there are perhaps as many reasons for secrecy as there are secrets. Given the complexity of the links between secrets and the reasons they are kept, it makes sense that scholars have commonly focused their attention on specific secret topics; for instance, the scholarly literature on abuse is largely separate from that concerning HIV. Because of the unique aspects of certain secrets, understanding individuals' decisions about keeping or revealing secrets requires consideration of the particular secrets and the situations surrounding them.

Despite the variety of specific reasons for keeping secrets, there are also some common themes in people's reported reasons for keeping secrets. One salient theme across many contexts involves trying to keep others from forming *negative evaluations* (Vangelisti, 1994). Concerns about being evaluated negatively are a prominent reason why some people living with HIV keep their status secret (Alonzo & Reynolds, 1995; Herek, Capitanio, & Widaman, 2002), why sexual abuse victims sometimes do not tell others about the abuse (Paine & Hansen, 2002), and why people keep secrets about their sexual history from their romantic partners (Caughlin et al., 2005). The possibility of negative evaluations from outsiders is one reason why small groups, such as university search committees, withhold information about their deliberations (Eisenberg, Murphy, & Andrews, 1998). Obviously, the nature of the negative judgments varies across situations; the identity threat associated with having secrets about one's sexual history, for instance, is not the same as the stigma associated with having HIV. Still, the concern about being evaluated negatively can be thought of as a general reason for keeping secrets that cuts across many specific contexts.

Another general reason for keeping secrets involves *relational maintenance* (Vangelisti, 1994). Individuals sometimes try to protect relational bonds by keeping secrets, or they hope to shield others from stress (Brown-Smith, 1998). Cancer patients, for instance, sometimes withhold information about symptoms or specific prognoses so as not to burden people close to them (Goldsmith et al., 2008). Parents who have HIV often try to shield their children from excessive worrying by concealing aspects of their illness (Schrimshaw & Siegel, 2002).

People also sometimes report keeping secrets because of concerns about *communication competence* (Vangelisti, 1994). Individuals who keep secrets may have concerns about their own or the potential confidant's ability to discuss the issue (Afifi, Caughlin, & Afifi, 2007). They also may believe that discussing a secret would violate a *communicative norm*; some people say their families keep secrets because they simply are not very open (Vangelisti, 1994).

In addition, individuals sometimes keep secrets to *defend themselves* from social threats (Vangelisti, 1994). There are situations when others can take advantage of an individual or a group if they learn a secret. A common way that people can take advantage is by divulging the information to others (Petronio & Bantz, 1991). Concerns about subsequent disclosures to third parties are particularly salient when the secret involves potentially stigmatizing information, such as having HIV (Derlega, Winstead, Greene, Serovich, & Elwood, 2004).

Another commonly reported reason for keeping secrets involves *privacy* (Vangelisti, 1994). That is, people sometimes purposefully conceal information because the information is personal or not relevant to others. Although cases like Eliot Spitzer's suggest that secret keepers can claim privacy even when others would not agree with the legitimacy of the claim, privacy is sometimes recognized as a legitimate reason for keeping secrets. Indeed, one study that examined people's perceptions of why others kept secrets found that privacy was listed as a common reason for keeping secrets and that secrets attributed to privacy were not seen as having particularly harmful relational impacts (Caughlin et al., in press-b).

Finally, people sometimes keep secrets to serve a *relational bonding* function (Vangelisti, 1994). When people collaborate to keep a secret, it can promote identification among those who keep the secret, demonstrating who is an insider and who is an outsider (Goffman, 1959). There is also evidence that keeping a secret with another person—even a secret as trivial as unobserved foot contact—can promote attraction between the individuals sharing the secret (Wegner et al., 1994).

Taken as a whole, the literature on individuals' reasons for keeping secrets suggests tremendous complexity. Even when focusing on major themes, there are a number of distinct reasons for keeping secrets. Given this complexity, researchers may find it useful to occasionally conceptualize the reasons for keeping secrets at an even higher level of abstraction; for instance, Afifi, Olson, and Armstrong (2005) suggested that most of people's reasons for keeping secrets can be thought of as some form of protection. Concerns about negative evaluation and defense might be considered examples of self protection, for example.

Conceptualizing the reasons for secrecy in terms of a single dimension like protection (or a few dimensions like self, other, and relational protection) is probably useful in some circumstances, such as when the secrecy involves a family member who is so aggressive that protection becomes the overriding concern (Afifi et al., 2005). Notwithstanding such potential uses, it is important to be cautious about conceptualizing the reasons for keeping secrets at a level that is too abstract. Trying to summarize the reasons for keeping secrets on a single dimension will inevitably leave out some reasons that are commonly salient; for example, the notion of protection does not capture the idea that people sometimes keep secrets to bond. Moreover, higher-order conceptualizations may ignore differences among constructs that are known to be empirically meaningful. For instance, Vangelisti and Caughlin (1997) found that keeping secrets because of bonding or privacy reasons was positively and significantly associated with family satisfaction, but keeping secrets because of negative evaluation or defense was negatively associated with family satisfaction. That is, the reasons vary significantly in their associations with a third construct (satisfaction), which undermines the idea that they are unidimensional. Moreover, recent research on people's perceptions of why others try to keep secrets indicates a number of interactions among reasons for keeping secrets; for instance, there was generally a positive association between believing the other person kept a secret to avoid negative evaluation and reports of relational distancing and hurt feelings, but these positive associations were mitigated when individuals reported that the other person had dispositional reasons for keeping the secrets (Caughlin et al., in press-b). Obviously, such interactions cannot be examined if the various reasons are lumped into too few dimensions.

Criteria for Revealing Secrets

There is an extensive literature on reasons why individuals self-disclose (for reviews, see Greene, Derlega, & Mathews, 2006; Omarzu, 2000; Petronio, 2002). This research is relevant to understanding why people sometimes reveal secrets, especially when the information is something frequently concealed from others, such as having HIV (Derlega et al., 2000, 2004). Nevertheless, it is important to recognize that the decisions to reveal secrets are different from most other self-disclosures. Because people have been purposefully keeping something secret, deciding to reveal a secret involves more than just evaluating reasons to disclose. One commonly cited reason for self-disclosure, for example, is self-expression (Derlega, Metts, Petronio, & Margulis, 1993; Omarzu, 2000). Even if individuals keeping a secret desire self-expression, the aforementioned reasons for keeping secrets may outweigh their desire to express themselves. Alternatively, individuals may express themselves in a different way, such as cases when people disclose some personal information specifically selected to help conceal a secret (Cooper, 1994; Greene et al., 2006). For instance, a person who is keeping a relationship secret from his or her parents might disclose information about challenges at work to avoid the topic of dating. In short, revealing secrets is distinct from most self-disclosures, and our focus here is on criteria for the former rather than the reasons for the latter.

Vangelisti and her colleagues (2001) conducted a study on the criteria that individuals would use for deciding whether to reveal a secret. In this study, participants were asked to describe a secret that their entire family kept from nonfamily members, and then they were asked what (if anything) would need to happen for them to reveal the secret to a particular person outside the family. Some participants reported that they would never divulge their family secret, but most reported at least one criterion that they would use to decide to reveal the secret.

There were a number of different types of criteria reported (Vangelisti et al., 2001). Some of the criteria corresponded with well-known findings from the self-disclosure literature. One such criterion was *equivalent disclosure*, meaning that individuals would reveal the secret if the other person first divulged similar information. The notion of equivalent disclosure is consistent with the dyadic effect, in which one person's disclosures tend to elicit comparably intimate disclosures from the other (e.g., Greene et al., 2006). Another commonly cited reason for disclosures is catharsis (e.g., Derlega et al., 1993; Omarzu, 2000). Similarly, some individuals reported that they would reveal their family secret if they felt an important *need to talk*. Also, given the general connection between intimacy and self-disclosure (Derlega et al., 1993), it is not surprising that many participants reported a criterion of *relational security*; that is, they stated that they would reveal the secret if they developed a significantly closer or more trusting relationship with the potential confidant. Another criterion was *acceptance*, which referred to having a suitably responsive and supportive confidant. Again, research on disclosure generally is consistent with the idea that a supportive confidant is a reason for disclosure (e.g., Greene et al., 2006; Petronio, 2002). Studies on self-disclosure also point to the importance of the conversational moment or "flow" (Greene et al., 2006, p. 414), and this was echoed in the criterion of *conversational appropriateness* for revealing secrets.

Whereas several of the criteria for revealing secrets fit nicely with the larger literature on self-disclosure, others seem specifically tied to decisions about revealing secrets. Some participants, for instance, reported that they would only divulge the secret if *circumstances would reveal the secret anyway*. Such responses are theoretically interesting because they imply that respondents would not be swayed by any of the usual reasons for disclosing; they did not want the person to find out about the secret. If the person was going to find out anyway, however, participants would reveal the secret. Given that secret keeping itself has negative connotations (Caughlin

& Petronio, 2004; Vangelisti, 1994), perhaps people would rather make a preemptive disclosure than be caught having kept a secret. If individuals reveal a secret before others discover it, they may be able to adopt the pretense of communicating openly about the issue. Disclosing the secret also may provide people with an opportunity to frame the information in a way that mitigates any pertinent risks of revealing, such as being evaluated negatively (Caughlin et al., in press-a).

In the Vangelisti et al. (2001) study, some individuals reported that they would reveal their family secret if the other person *asked directly* about the secret. It is possible that people who are asked directly about a secret assume that the other person probably knows or suspects the secret anyway, which might make them assume that further attempts to conceal the information are futile. Another explanation is that, if someone explicitly asks about the secret, continuing to conceal the secret would necessitate an overt lie. There is evidence that people believe lying to keep secrets is more hurtful and aversive than using other means to keep a secret, such as simply not mentioning the issue (Caughlin et al., in press-b; Engels, Finkenauer, & van Kooten, 2006). Consequently, individuals sometimes may be unwilling to use explicit lies to conceal a secret.

Another common criterion for revealing a secret was to *help the other person*, especially if the other person was in a similar situation and telling might help the other get through it. Some individuals also reported that they would divulge the secret if there were an *escalation or recurrence of a problem* associated with a secret. One participant, for instance, stated that her father's alcoholism would remain a secret unless he began drinking again. Participants also reported that they would reveal their secret if there was an *important reason* to do so (e.g., the other person needed to know the information). Interestingly, having an important reason seemed to supersede the other criteria: People reported that they probably would reveal the secret if there was an important reason, regardless of other factors. Even if they did not have a close and trusting relationship with someone, for example, people typically reported that they would reveal their family secret if there was an important reason.

Not only are some of the criteria for revealing secrets distinct from common reasons for making self-disclosures, but also, as Vangelisti et al. (2001) found, there are two criteria that are specifically pertinent to revelations of family secrets: (a) *family membership*, meaning that the person would be told the secret if he or she became a member of the family (e.g., through marriage); and (b) *permission*, which involved securing permission from other family members before telling anyone outside the family the secret.

Considering the Reasons for Concealing and the Criteria for Revealing Together

In juxtaposing the literatures on reasons for concealing and criteria for revealing secrets one thing becomes apparent: Reasons for concealing secrets and criteria for revealing secrets do not operate in opposition to each other. That is to say, the presence of a criterion for revealing a secret does not necessarily indicate the absence of a reason for keeping the same secret. People who opt to reveal a secret because they believe there is an important reason to do so or because they want to help another person may simultaneously be very concerned that others will take advantage of them once the information is revealed.

Treating reasons and criteria for keeping and revealing secrets, respectively, as separate cognitive processes that can function independently of each other raises several interesting issues for researchers to consider. First, it is likely that the factors that encourage people to conceal secrets differ from those that encourage them to reveal secrets. Keeping secrets can be viewed, in part, as a consequence of an avoidance motivation. When people keep secrets, their effort is to avoid divulging the secret information to others and, perhaps, to avoid discussions concerning the information with particular individuals. By contrast, revealing secrets can be conceived as a result of an approach motivation. When individuals decide to reveal secrets, they opt to approach the information by discussing it with particular others.[1] Although some researchers suggest that classifying individuals' motivations and behaviors in terms of approach and avoidance is too simplistic (e.g., Cappella & Greene, 1982), most agree that many of the feelings, behaviors, and events that encourage people to approach social interaction differ from those that encourage them to avoid it (e.g., Baxter & Montgomery, 1996). Similarly, the factors that push individuals to reveal secrets should differ from those that push them to conceal secrets. Of course, people may experience motivations to approach and avoid information simultaneously. When that occurs, they are likely to evaluate their goals as well as the various factors that are pressing them toward concealing and revealing the information.

A second issue raised by the notion that reasons for keeping and criteria for revealing secrets can operate separately is that they likely are associated with each other in predictable ways. For instance, most people who keep a secret to avoid being negatively evaluated by others probably would not reveal the secret just because it fits nicely into a conversation. At the same time, someone who keeps a secret to avoid negative evaluation may be willing to divulge the information if the situation at hand is urgent. The associations illustrated in examples such as these may be explained by examining reasons for keeping secrets and criteria for revealing secrets in terms of individuals' goals. Although individuals generally pursue multiple goals when interacting with others, they also distinguish some goals as more important than others (Berger, 2005). While there are certainly idiosyncratic variations in the weight people place on various objectives, it is also likely that there are some commonalities in how people rank the importance of various objectives. For example, a common goal hierarchy is implied by Vangelisti et al.'s (2001) finding that—regardless of other factors—people are likely to reveal secrets if there is an urgent need. When the objective of helping another person with an urgent need is relevant, it likely ranks very high in importance.

A third issue raised by the idea that reasons for keeping and criteria for revealing secrets can function separately is that the factors that encourage people to conceal or reveal secrets are embedded in, and influenced by, social relationships. In part as a consequence, it is unlikely that individuals' decisions to conceal or reveal secrets will be fully explained by the reasons they report keeping the secrets or the criteria they say they would use in deciding to reveal them. People who keep a particular secret to protect their family may not feel the need to be so guarded in the context of a close romantic relationship. If, in fact, their main reason for keeping the secret is unimportant in this relationship, they may opt to reveal the information to their romantic partner whenever it fits into the conversation. In a similar vein, those who say they probably would reveal a secret if the person they were talking to made an equivalent disclosure may decide not to do so if their conversational partner is someone they dislike. In short, the reasons people keep secrets and the criteria they use in evaluating whether to reveal them are only two of a number of factors that influence the decisions that people make when they opt to conceal or reveal a secret from others. Because the factors that push people to conceal or reveal secrets are influenced by relationships, the quality of those relationships, the individual differences of relational partners, partners' typical interaction patterns, and even the characteristics of partners' social networks are likely to affect individuals' decisions about concealing and revealing secrets.

Implications

Conceptualizing secret keeping and revealing as purposeful activities implies that principles from multiple goals theories ought to be relevant to understanding secrecy. The discussion below examines this possibility, focusing on seven general propositions.

Predicting Concealing and Revealing

The first general proposition implied by a multiple goals perspective is that *individuals' reasons for keeping secrets and their criteria for revealing them ought to predict whether people reveal secrets.* The proposition is supported by extant scholarship; there is considerable research pertinent to predicting whether individuals will reveal secrets (for a review, see Kelly, 2002).

One limitation of the existing research is that it typically treats concealing or revealing secrets as a dichotomous variable; the main outcome is simply whether or not the information is revealed (Afifi et al., 2007). A multiple goals perspective, however, suggests that it is important to examine not only whether a secret is revealed but also how it is concealed or how it is revealed. A central tenet in a variety of multiple goals theories is that objectives relevant to communication situations shape how people communicate (see Wilson & Feng, 2007, for a review). Brown and Levinson's (1987) influential politeness theory, for instance, posits that certain objectives are reflected in politeness behaviors. For example, the objective of not imposing too much is relevant when people make requests, and the extent to which this objective is salient predicts attempts to mitigate the potential for threatening the other's autonomy (e.g., by adding politeness redress to requests). If the objective of not imposing is particularly prominent, a request might be even made indirectly; for instance, a person can state a desire in a way that allows a compliant other to grant the request but also allows both communicators to act as if there was no request if the indirect request is not granted. An individual wanting to ask someone on a date, for example, could do so indirectly by making a statement like, "I wish I had somebody to see that new movie with me this weekend."

Clearly, the specific goals that are relevant to concealing and revealing secrets are different from those associated with making requests, but the general principle that goals ought to shape communicators' behaviors should still apply. Concerning the issue of how secrets are concealed, a multiple goals perspective implies that individuals' reasons for keeping secrets and their criteria for revealing them ought to predict the means by which they keep secrets. Not much research has focused on various means for concealing secrets, but there is evidence that individuals discern qualitatively distinct ways of keeping secrets (e.g., Finkenauer, Kubacka, Engels, & Kerkhof, this volume). In one study (Caughlin et al., in press-b), participants reported that there are at least four empirically distinguishable means of keeping secrets: *overt deception* (lying or covering up the secret), *topic avoidance* (not introducing the subject or changing topics), *physical avoidance* (trying to avoid seeing the other person), and *acting normal* (pretending that there was nothing unusual going on).

Based on the multiple goals literature, it is possible to make some predictions about how reasons and criteria may be related to the means of keeping secrets. Previous research has demonstrated that the more individuals are concerned about being evaluated negatively, the less likely they are to reveal their secrets (Caughlin et al., 2005). Such findings suggest that people concerned about negative evaluation would be willing to guard their secrets more aggressively than would those who keep their secrets for other reasons. As Finkenauer and her colleagues (this volume) suggest, overt deception is a more active strategy for keeping a secret than simply not raising an issue or trying to act normal. Moreover, using deception involves potential risks to one's identity. Deception is sometimes viewed as particularly hurtful and aversive (Caughlin et al., in press-b; Engels et al., 2006). Because it is an active strategy that involves risks, overt deception is probably more likely in circumstances when secret keepers are willing to guard their secrets aggressively, such as when their concerns about negative evaluation are intense. Obviously, this theoretical connection has not been directly tested, but it illustrates a second general proposition: *People's reasons for keeping secrets and criteria for revealing them ought to predict the means by which they keep their secrets.*

Our third general proposition is similar to the second except that it focuses on cases in which secrets are revealed. A multiple goals perspective implies that *individuals' reasons for keeping secrets and their criteria for revealing them ought to predict the manner in which they reveal their secrets.* The proposition is fundamentally different from most extant scholarship on reasons for keeping secrets. Typically, the literature conceptualizes reasons for keeping secrets as impediments to revealing the information; divulging a secret implicitly involves overcoming the various reasons for keeping the secret. However, as previously noted, just because a person ends up revealing a secret, it does not necessarily follow that the various reasons for keeping the secret dissipate. A person who has kept a secret for many years due to concerns about negative evaluation, for example, may experience those concerns acutely at the moment that secret is revealed. From a multiple goals perspective, such concerns should be reflected in the general goal of maintaining a positive identity, and the salience of that goal ought to shape the way in which the secret is revealed.

Most research on the revelation of secrets does not differentiate various means of revealing; however, the literature on self-disclosure has begun to consider issues like features of disclosure messages (e.g., Greene et al., 2006). With respect to secrets, Afifi and Steuber (in press) examined various strategies for revealing secrets, which they labeled *preparation and rehearsal* (i.e., practicing how the secret would be told); *directness* (i.e., revealing the secret in a face-to-face interaction); *third party revelations* (i.e., asking someone else to reveal the secret); *incremental disclosures* (i.e., revealing in segments and gauging the other person's reaction before continuing); *entrapment* (i.e., arranging to have the person discover the secret); and *indirect mediums* (i.e., using mediated communication, such as a letter, to reveal the secret).[2] Afifi and Steuber's (in press) findings were consistent with our general proposition; they found that people revealing secrets were more likely to use indirect strategies when they were concerned about the other person's reaction. This finding clearly can be understood within a multiple goals framework; being concerned about the other's reaction is a type of identity concern, and the goal of managing that identity concern may lead to more indirect strategies.

Although directness is an important feature of messages, it is certainly not the only important feature. Messages that reveal a secret can also vary in other important ways. Caughlin et al. (in press-a) presented a theoretical scheme of six different types of messages that varied systematically in terms of the goals that were explicitly addressed. All the messages included explicit disclosures of an HIV-positive test result, but the information accompanying the disclosure varied. Some messages addressed instrumental concerns for obtaining support (e.g., by including a phrase like, "I'm going to need your help"), other messages addressed the concern that others might not protect the information (e.g., "I would hope that you will keep this just between us"), and so on. While a full description of the Caughlin et al. (in press-a) study is not possible in the space of the current chapter, even this brief discussion illustrates our point that various goals can shape disclosure message characteristics besides directness.

Predicting the Effectiveness of Concealing and Revealing

Although the primary focus of many multiple goals theorists has been on message production, multiple goals perspectives can also be applied to assessing the relative quality or competence of communicative behaviors (Goldsmith, 2004; O'Keefe, 1988). A key assumption of multiple goals perspectives on message quality is that some ways of enacting communication are more successful than others at accomplishing the various goals that are relevant to certain scenarios. This way of conceptualizing message quality applies to situations that are complex—those situations in which there are multiple relevant and potentially conflicting goals (O'Keefe, 1988). Although there are simple situations in which everyone communicates in virtually the same way, people respond to complex situations in various ways, some more successful than others.

In some situations, certain goals are conventionally understood to be relevant, even if a particular communicator does not recognize or endorse those goals. The goal of not appearing nosey, for instance, is inherently salient whenever one offers advice (Goldsmith & Fitch, 1997; Kunkel, Wilson, Olufowote, & Robson, 2003). Not attending to conventionally relevant goals is part of what makes some communication ineffective; for instance, regardless of whether an advice giver actually attends to the goal of not being nosey, advice that seems overly intrusive is more likely to elicit anger than advice that is viewed as less intrusive.

Concealing and revealing secrets are both potentially complex situations. First consider concealing secrets. As evidenced by the various reasons for keeping secrets, a number of objectives may be served by keeping secrets. However, the criteria for revealing secrets suggest that people also may have countervailing impulses; for instance, even people with good reasons for keeping a secret may wonder whether revealing their secret might help someone else, or they may feel a need to talk about the secret. Such possibilities suggest the potential for competing goals and perhaps even dilemmas; for instance, the person a secret keeper would most like to talk to about the secret could be the same person who is most likely to react negatively.

In addition to such personal dilemmas, secret keeping is conventionally relevant to certain identity and relational goals. Western cultures value openness (Kirkman, Rosenthal, & Feldman, 2005; Parks, 1982). Consequently, secret keeping is necessarily relevant to a conventional identity goal of not appearing to be a secretive person and a conventional relational goal of maintaining the appearance of openness. It is important to recognize that individuals commonly report that their relationships are open, even when they actually avoid topics and keep secrets (Kirkman et al., 2005). That is, the conventionally relevant identity goal concerns foster an impression that one is open rather than actually being open.

Because secret keeping can be a complex situation, a fourth proposition based on a multiple goals framework is *certain ways of keeping secrets ought to be more effective at achieving multiple objectives than are others*. By *effective* here, we do not refer to the relative effectiveness of keeping a secret concealed (although that would be an interesting line of research). Instead, consistent with multiple goals perspectives, some ways of keeping secrets ought to be better than others at simultaneously addressing various relevant goals. It is fairly common, for example, for secret keepers' secrets to be putative ones (i.e., they believe that they have kept the secret from someone, but unbeknownst to them, the other person already knows). Because secrets are sometimes learned by others without the secret keeper knowing, the savviest strategies for keeping secrets may be those that allow for plausible deniability; that is, they may allow secret keepers to maintain the pretext that they were not keeping a secret. Consistent with this possibility, there is evidence that people judge attempts to keep secrets particularly harshly if the attempts to keep the secret involve overt deception (Caughlin et al., in press-b; Engels et al., 2006). In contrast, when people believe a putative secret keeper attempts to keep the secret by acting normally, the attempt at keeping the secret is not viewed as particularly hurtful or distancing (Caughlin et al., in press-b). From a multiple goals perspective, such findings can be understood in terms of identity goals. A person caught engaging in overt deception to conceal a secret cannot deny being secretive, and being known as a liar is an impression that is generally disfavored. In contrast, keeping a secret by acting normally allows for the possibility that an individual can still maintain an identity as an open and honest person (e.g., "I was not keeping it from you; I would have told you had it come up"). Such a possibility is consistent with research showing that being viewed as open and honest does not require actually discussing issues frankly (Kirkman et al., 2005).

Not only can secret keeping be complex, but secret revealing can constitute a complex situation as well. Imagine, for example, a secret that an individual keeps for one main reason: fear of negative evaluation. Suppose various factors overcame that reason for keeping the secret; perhaps the person decided that there was an important reason to tell someone else. Just because the primary reason for concealing the secret was outweighed by other objectives, it does not mean that the reason for concealing would vanish. Unless something else changed (e.g., a potential confidant indicated acceptance), a person concerned about being evaluated negatively before revealing a secret likely would remain concerned as he or she revealed that secret. Such concerns constitute a relevant identity goal. Even this simple example illustrates that multiple competing goals can be relevant when revealing secrets. The person who needs to know the secret might benefit most from a direct and frank discussion of the secret, but telling about the secret directly may be the greatest threat to the secret keeper's positive identity.

The circumstances of actual secret revelations can be even more complex, with numerous relevant goals. Caughlin et al. (2008), for instance, argued that a person who decides to reveal an HIV-positive test result has to manage multiple concerns such as the potential for negative evaluation, the possibility that the information will be passed on to others, and the chance that one's relationship with the target of the revelation will be harmed. If this information had been kept secret for a while, other issues may become relevant. Sometimes confidants are hurt or insulted that they were not told sooner (Caughlin et al., 2005) or at least before other people (Caughlin & Petronio, 2004). Clearly, such factors imply identity threats (e.g., by implying that the other person is not a favored confidant) and relational threats (e.g., because the confidant considers the timing of the disclosure to be indicative of a lack of closeness).

In short, revealing secrets often involves complex situations. Thus, a fifth proposition implied by a multiple goals perspective is *certain ways of revealing secrets ought to be more effective at achieving multiple objectives than are others.* Although there is limited research specifically addressing this proposition, some findings are consistent with it. For instance, Afifi and Steuber (in press) found that certain means of revealing secrets are associated with decreases in perceived closeness of family relationships, and their findings can be interpreted from a multiple goals framework. One of the strategies associated with diminishing closeness, for instance, was using mediated communication (e.g., e-mail, letters) to reveal a secret (Afifi & Steuber, in press). Using mediated communication is undoubtedly effective at achieving the goal of revealing the information, but it may be less effective at managing other interactional goals. Compared to revealing the information in a face-to-face encounter, such mediated revelations could threaten relevant goals in numerous ways: They may threaten revealers' identities by suggesting they are too ashamed to reveal the information in person, may threaten recipients' identities by suggesting that the revealer believes their reaction will be harsh or judgmental, and may threaten relational goals by contradicting the nearly ubiquitous belief that family members should be able to have frank and open discussions with each other (see Caughlin, 2003).

Although Afifi and Steuber's (in press) findings suggest that some ways of revealing secrets are generally less effective than others at attending to multiple objectives, it is important to recognize that a multiple goals perspective on this issue does not imply that it is possible to compile a list of more and less effective strategies. The utility of particular strategies is likely influenced by the goals that are relevant to a specific encounter. Consider, for instance, Ben-Ari's (1995) research on parents' reactions to a child coming out as gay. Mothers tended to react more favorably when told during a one-on-one conversation, whereas fathers responded more favorably when told with the mother present. Such findings may indicate that the different roles and identities of mothers and fathers create different conditions for what constitutes the most effective strategy for revealing a secret.

In addition to research suggesting the importance of broad strategies (e.g., revealing in person vs. disclosing via another medium), there is some evidence that the specific message used to disclose matters is important too. In the aforementioned Caughlin et al. (in press-a) study, participants received one of six different kinds of messages and were asked to imagine that a sibling revealed having HIV with that particular disclosure message. This study did not examine secrets per se, but the results indicated that features of disclosure messages can influence how people react to important revelations. For example, messages that included an element explicitly addressing the goal of guarding against subsequent disclosures (e.g., "I would really appreciate you not telling anybody else") tended to elicit more negative evaluations from participants than most of the other message types. One explanation for this finding is that explicitly asking a sibling not to tell others may not attend to conventionally relevant goals, such as not threatening the sibling's identity by implying that the sibling is indiscreet. Clearly, there is ample space for much more research on how disclosure message features influence recipients' reactions, but there is already sufficient evidence to conclude that the specific content of disclosure messages matters and that a multiple goals perspective provides a rich framework for assessing the quality of various disclosure messages.

Predicting Relational Outcomes of Concealing and Revealing

Most researchers who have studied reasons for concealing and criteria for revealing secrets have done so from the perspective of individuals who are keeping secrets. As a consequence, we know little about how others—including friends, romantic partners, and family members—evaluate the various reasons people conceal and reveal secret information. The few studies that have examined others' perceptions of secret keepers' behavior suggest that the behaviors associated with concealing secrets are evaluated in predictable ways. For instance, as previously noted, when individuals perceive that a putative secret keeper tries to keep a secret by acting normally, they tend not to view the attempt as particularly hurtful or distancing (Caughlin et al., in press-b).

A vast literature on attributions in close relationships indicates that the way people evaluate the behavior of their relational partners is associated with the quality of their relationship. More specifically, individuals who evaluate their partner's behavior in ways that are likely to enhance their relationship tend to be more satisfied than those who assess their partner's behavior in ways that are likely to promote dissatisfaction or distress (Fincham, Beach, & Baucom, 1987; Grigg, Fletcher, & Fitness, 1989; Holtzworth-Munroe & Jacobson, 1985). The consistency of the link between people's evaluations or interpretations of their partner's behavior and their relational satisfaction suggests a sixth proposition, that *the reasons individuals perceive their relational partner is keeping (or has kept) information secret ought to predict the quality of their relationship.* For example, people who perceive their partner kept a secret for selfish reasons probably will be less satisfied than those who believe their partner kept a secret for more innocuous reasons, such as having a sense of privacy. In the former case, individuals are likely to view their partner as pursuing goals that place personal gain ahead of maintaining the relationship, whereas in the latter they are more likely to view the partner's goals as a matter of personal discretion.

In a similar vein, *the criteria individuals perceive their relational partner use (or used) in deciding to reveal secret information ought to predict the quality of their relationship* (Proposition 7). Those who believe their partner opted to reveal secret information because he or she felt a strong sense of security in the relationship probably will be more satisfied than people who perceive their partner divulged the information because the circumstances at hand would reveal it anyway. Individuals may very well perceive that the partner who used relational security as a criterion was acting on goals consistent with increasing relational intimacy, whereas the one who felt that circumstances would reveal it anyway was trying to preclude personal or relational distress.

The case made by the two aforementioned propositions (Propositions 6 and 7) is that individuals' perceptions of their partner's reasons for concealing and criteria for revealing secrets influence relational quality. It is also important to acknowledge that current relational quality probably affects people's perceptions of reasons for concealing and criteria for revealing secrets. Individuals who already are satisfied may interpret their partner's efforts to protect the relationship in relatively benevolent ways ("She cares enough about our relationship to protect it"), while those who are dissatisfied may view the same efforts as a measure of weakness ("She can't handle the effect it would have on our relationship"). Similarly, people who are happy with their relationship may view a decision based on relational security as a positive sign ("He trusts me enough to tell me his secrets"), whereas individuals who are unhappy may perceive the same criterion as a negative indicator ("He should have trusted me enough to tell me this before now").

Although prior research provides fairly strong evidence for the links between relational satisfaction and individuals' evaluations of their partner's reasons for concealing or criteria for revealing secret information, the cognitive processes that drive these associations still are not well defined. Examining people's perceptions of reasons for concealing or criteria for revealing secrets from a multiple goals perspective could provide telling data on the association between those perceptions and individuals' satisfaction. For instance, people who prioritize the goal of maintaining their relationship above other goals may assess their partner's reasons for keeping a secret differently than do individuals who prioritize their identity concerns above other goals. Those who focus on relational maintenance as a primary goal may look kindly on their partner's decision to keep a secret to protect their relationship because it demonstrates concern for the relationship. By contrast, those who emphasize maintaining a positive identity may be insulted by the same reasoning because it raises questions about their ability to cope with the secret information. A similar case can be made for people's evaluations of their partner's criteria for revealing secrets. Individuals whose primary goal is relational maintenance may view a partner's decision to tell them a secret based on relational security as quite positive, whereas those whose primary goal is to maintain a positive identity may view the same decision in a negative light because it raises questions about their identity as a relational partner prior to the time of the disclosure. In all of these examples, people's idiosyncratic ranking of goal importance may moderate the association between their perceptions of their partner's reasons for concealing and criteria for revealing secrets and their relational satisfaction.

Final Thoughts

The research literature on secrecy has been dominated by two overarching issues: How do people decide whether to reveal their secrets and what are the consequences of keeping secrets? To date, these issues mainly have been examined separately. Taking a multiple goals perspective has the potential to provide a coherent means of addressing both issues. With respect to whether one reveals secrets, the existing research on reasons for concealing and criteria for revealing secrets can be conceptualized as multiple goals that individuals weigh when making choices about revealing secrets. Moreover, various combinations of goals ought to influence how a secret is kept and how it is revealed if it is revealed. Finally, various strategies for concealing or revealing are likely to be more or less successful at attending to the relevant goals in a particular social situation; thus, the outcomes of keeping secrets are theoretically linked to the communicative objectives that are pertinent to a given circumstance.

Notes

1 It is important to note that when we use the phrases "approach motivation" and "avoidance motivation" we do not intend to equate these to the biologically based approach and avoidance systems discussed by some social psychologists (e.g., Gable & Reis, 2001). Indeed, because the approach and avoidance systems described by social psychologists focus on people's tendencies to approach positive stimuli and avoid negative ones, they are inconsistent with our discussion. We do not view individuals' tendency to approach secret information as reflecting a desire for positive stimuli or their tendency to avoid secret information as reflecting an aversion to negative stimuli. Rather, we refer to approach and avoidance motivations as relatively abstract constructs that shape the goals individuals may bring to social interaction.

2 Afifi and Steuber's (in press) use of the terms direct and indirect are somewhat different from the way those terms are typically used in the multiple goals literature. As we noted in our discussion of politeness, Brown and Levinson (1987), for instance, call messages indirect if they imply a kind of action but do not do so overtly, whereas direct messages perform the action explicitly or on the record.

References

Afifi, T. D., Caughlin, J. P., & Afifi, W. A. (2007). The dark side (and light side) of avoidance and secrets. In B. H. Spitzberg & W. R. Cupach (Eds.), *The dark side of interpersonal communication* (2nd ed., pp. 61–92). Mahwah, NJ: Erlbaum.

Afifi, T. D., Olson, L., & Armstrong, C. (2005). The chilling effect and family secrets: Examining the role of self protection, other protection, and communication efficacy. *Human Communication Research, 31*, 564–598.

Afifi, T. D., & Steuber, K. (in press). The Revelation Risk Model (RRM) and the strategies used to reveal secrets. *Communication Monographs.*

Afifi, W. A., & Caughlin, J. P. (2006). A close look at revealing secrets and some consequences that follow. *Communication Research, 33*, 467–488.

Alonzo, A. A., & Reynolds, N. R. (1995). Stigma, HIV, and AIDS: An exploration and elaboration of a stigma trajectory model. *Social Science and Medicine, 41*, 303–315.

Baxter, L. A., & Montgomery, B. (1996). *Relating: Dialogues and dialectics.* New York: Guilford Press.

Bellman, B. L. (1981). The paradox of secrecy. *Human Studies, 4*, 1–24.

Ben-Ari, A. (1995). Coming out: A dialectic of intimacy and privacy. *Families in Society, 76*, 306–314.

Berger, C. R. (2005). Interpersonal communication: Theoretical perspectives, future prospects. *Journal of Communication, 55*, 415–447.

Bok, S. (1983). *Secrets: On the ethics of concealment and revelation.* New York: Vintage Books.

Bradshaw, J. (1995). *Family secrets: What you don't know can hurt you.* New York: Bantam Books.

Brown, P., & Levinson, S. (1987). *Politeness: Some universals in language usage.* Cambridge, England: Cambridge University Press.

Brown-Smith, N. (1998). Family secrets. *Journal of Family Issues, 19*, 20–42.

Cappella, J. N., & Greene, J. O. (1982). A discrepancy-arousal explanation of mutual influence in expressive behavior for adult–adult and infant–adult interaction. *Communication Monographs, 49*, 89–114.

Caughlin, J. P. (2003). Family communication standards: What counts as excellent family communication and how are such standards associated with family satisfaction? *Human Communication Research, 29*, 5–40.

Caughlin, J. P., Afifi, W. A., Carpenter-Theune, K. E., & Miller, C. E. (2005). Reasons for, and consequences of, revealing personal secrets in close relationships: A longitudinal study. *Personal Relationships, 12*, 43–59.

Caughlin, J. P., Brashers, D. E., Ramey, M. E., Kosenko, K. A., Donovan-Kicken, E., & Bute, J. J. (2008). The message design logics of responses to HIV disclosures. *Human Communication Research, 34*, 655–685.

Caughlin, J. P., Bute, J. J., Donovan-Kicken, E., Kosenko, K. A., Ramey, M. E., & Brashers, D. E. (in press-a). Do message features influence reactions to HIV disclosures? A multiple goals perspective. *Health Communication.*

Caughlin, J. P., & Petronio, S. (2004). Privacy in families. In A. L. Vangelisti (Ed.), *Handbook of family communication* (pp. 379–412). Mahwah, NJ: Erlbaum.

Caughlin, J. P., Scott, A. M., Miller, L. E., & Hefner, V. (in press-b). Putative secrets: When information is supposedly a secret. *Journal of Social and Personal Relationships.*

Clark, R. A., & Delia, J. G. (1979). *Topoi* and rhetorical competence. *Quarterly Journal of Speech, 65*, 187–206.

Cooper, V. W. (1994). The disguise of self-disclosure: The relationship ruse of a Soviet spy. *Journal of Applied Communication Research, 22*, 338–347.

Derlega, V. J., Metts, S., Petronio, S., & Margulis, S. T. (1993). *Self-disclosure.* Newbury Park, CA: Sage.

Derlega, V. J., Winstead, B. A., & Folk-Barron, L. (2000). Reasons for and against disclosing HIV-seropositive test results to an intimate partner: A functional perspective. In S. Petronio (Ed.), *Balancing the secrets of private disclosures* (pp. 53–69). Mahwah, NJ: Erlbaum.

Derlega, V. J., Winstead, B. A., Greene, K., Serovich, J., & Elwood, W. N. (2004). Reasons for HIV disclosure/nondisclosure in close relationships: Testing a model of HIV-disclosure decision making. *Journal of Social and Clinical Psychology, 23*, 747–767.

Eisenberg, E. M., Murphy, A., & Andrews, L. (1998). Openness and decision making in the search for a university provost. *Communication Monographs, 65*, 1–23.

Engels, R. C. M. E., Finkenauer, C., & van Kooten, D. C. (2006). Lying behavior, family functioning and adjustment in early adolescence. *Journal of Youth and Adolescence, 35*, 949–958.

Fincham, F. D., Beach, S. R., & Baucom, D. H. (1987). Attribution processes in distressed and nondistressed couples: 4. Self–partner attribution differences. *Journal of Personality and Social Psychology, 52*, 739–748.

Finkenauer, C., & Hazam, H. (2000). Disclosure and secrecy in marriage: Do both contribute to marital satisfaction? *Journal of Social and Personal Relationships, 17*, 245–263.

Gable, S. L., & Reis, H. T. (2001). Appetitive and aversive social interaction. In J. H. Harvey & A. E. Wenzel (Eds.), *Close romantic relationship maintenance and enhancement* (pp. 169–194). Mahwah, NJ: Erlbaum.

Goffman, E. (1959). *The presentation of self in everyday life.* Garden City, NY: Doubleday.

Goldsmith, D. J. (2004). *Communicating social support.* New York: Cambridge University Press.

Goldsmith, D. J., & Fitch, K. (1997). The normative context of advice as social support. *Human Communication Research, 23*, 454–476.

Goldsmith, D. J., Miller, L. E., & Caughlin, J. P. (2008). Openness and avoidance in couples communicating about cancer. *Communication Yearbook, 31*, 62–115.

Greene, K., Derlega, V. J., & Mathews, A. (2006). Self-disclosure in personal relationships. In A. L. Vangelisti & D. Perlman (Eds.), *The Cambridge handbook of personal relationships* (pp. 409–427). New York: Cambridge University Press.

Grigg, F., Fletcher, G. J. O., & Fitness, J. (1989). Spontaneous attributions in happy and unhappy dating relationships. *Journal of Social and Personal Relationships, 6*, 61–68.

Herek, G. M., Capitanio, J. P., & Widaman, K. F. (2002). HIV-related stigma and knowledge in the United States: Prevalence and trends, 1991–1999. *American Journal of Public Health, 92*, 371–377.

Holtzworth-Munroe, A., & Jacobson, N. S. (1985). Causal attributions of married couples: When do they search for causes? What do they conclude when they do? *Journal of Personality and Social Psychology, 48*, 1398–1412.

Kellermann, K. (1992). Communication: Inherently strategic and primarily automatic. *Communication Monographs, 59*, 288–300.

Kelly, A. E. (2002). *The psychology of secrets*. New York: Kluwer Academic/Plenum.

Kirkman, M., Rosenthal, D. A., & Feldman, S. S. (2005). Being open with your mouth shut: The meaning of "openness" in family communication about sexuality. *Sex Education, 5*, 49–66.

Kunkel, A. D., Wilson, S. R., Olofowote, J., & Robson, S. (2003). Identity implications of influence goals: Initiating, intensifying, and ending romantic relationships. *Western Journal of Communication, 67*, 382–412.

O'Keefe, B. J. (1988). The logic of message design: Individual differences in reasoning about communication. *Communication Monographs, 55*, 80–103.

Omarzu, J. (2000). A disclosure decision model: Determining how and when individuals will self-disclose. *Personality and Social Psychology Review, 4*, 174–185.

Paine, M. L., & Hansen, D. J. (2002). Factors influencing children to self-disclose sexual abuse. *Clinical Psychology Review, 22*, 271–295.

Parks, M. R. (1982). Ideology in interpersonal communication: Off the couch and into the world. In M. Burgoon (Ed.), *Communication yearbook 6* (pp. 79–107). Beverly Hills, CA: Sage.

Petronio, S. (2002). *Boundaries of privacy: Dialectics of disclosure*. Albany, NY: SUNY Press.

Petronio, S., & Bantz, C. (1991). Controlling the ramifications of disclosure: "Don't tell anybody but …". *Journal of Language and Social Psychology, 10*, 263–269.

Reuters. (2008, March 10). Instant view: Spitzer apologizes for "private matter." Retrieved March 17, 2008, from http://www.reuters.com/article/politicsNews/idUSN1047511820080310

Schrimshaw, E. W., & Siegel, K. (2002). HIV-infected mothers' disclosure to their uninfected children: Rates, reasons, and reactions. *Journal of Social and Personal Relationships, 19*, 19–43.

Smetana, J. G., Metzger, A., Gettman, D. C., & Campione-Barr, N. (2006). Disclosure and secrecy in adolescent–parent relationships. *Child Development, 77*, 201–217.

Vangelisti, A. L. (1994). Family secrets: Forms, functions, and correlates. *Journal of Social and Personal Relationships, 11*, 113–135.

Vangelisti, A. L., & Caughlin, J. P. (1997). Revealing family secrets: The influence of topic, function, and relationships. *Journal of Social and Personal Relationships, 14*, 679–705.

Vangelisti, A. L., Caughlin, J. P., & Timmerman, L. (2001). Criteria for revealing family secrets. *Communication Monographs, 68*, 1–17.

Webster, H. (1991). *Family secrets: How telling and not telling affects our children, our relationships, and our lives*. Reading, MA: Addison-Wesley.

Wegner, D. M., Lane, J. D., & Dimitri, S. (1994). The allure of secret relationships. *Journal of Personality and Social Psychology, 66*, 287–300.

Wilson, S. R. (2002). *Seeking and resisting compliance: Why people say what they do when trying to influence others*. Thousand Oaks, CA: Sage.

Wilson, S. R., & Feng, H. (2007). Interaction goals and message production: Conceptual and methodological developments. In D. R. Roskos-Ewoldsen & J. L. Monahan (Eds.), *Communication and social cognition: Theories and methods* (pp. 71–95). Mahwah, NJ: Erlbaum.

15 Secrecy in Close Relationships

Investigating its Intrapersonal and Interpersonal Effects

Catrin Finkenauer, Kaska E. Kubacka,
Rutger C. M. E. Engels, and Peter Kerkhof

> While all deception requires secrecy, all secrecy is not meant to deceive.
> Sissela Bok (*Secrets*, 1983, p. 7)

Almost everybody has a secret of some kind. A secret kept all to oneself, a secret shared with one's best friend, or a secret shared with a group of people. A secret about important issues such as incest, illnesses, or drugs, or a secret concerning everyday issues such as surprise parties, presents, or wishes and daydreams. Despite their large variety, all secrets are social phenomena. They all happen between people rather than within one person. People keep their secrets from others. They are careful to protect their secrets from being discovered by others and often go to great lengths to ensure their secret's concealment. Not surprisingly, folk wisdom assumes that keeping secrets in relationships is bad. Close relationships are commonly characterized by trust, caring, honesty, friendship, and respect (Fehr, 1993). Secrecy can be assumed to clash with each of these features. But as implied in the epigraph by Sissela Bok (1983), secrecy may not always be bad, and, more important, may often not be intended to be bad. Indeed, recent research suggests that secrecy can also be beneficial for close relationships and that it may help relationship partners establish boundaries and negotiate closeness and autonomy (Finkenauer, Frijns, Engels, & Kerkhof, 2005; Finkenauer & Hazam, 2000).

By taking a social perspective on secrecy and investigating its implications for relationships, this chapter provides a framework that can account for both the benefits and the harm that secrecy can have for our relationships with others. Often, the divergent interests that lie at the heart of secrets give rise to intense reactions, which may, in turn, strongly influence the quality and the development of the relationship between the person who keeps a secret, the *secret keeper*, and the person from whom the secret is kept, the *secret target*. For a thorough understanding of the relational dynamics of secrecy, it is, therefore, crucial to know how people are influenced by their own and others' secrecy. The purpose of this chapter is to review research that speaks to these *intra-* and *inter*-personal implications of secrecy in close relationships.

Relationship partners affect each other's thoughts, behavior, feelings, and well-being over time. Not surprisingly, secrecy is assumed to be particularly important when partners are highly interdependent, such as in close relationships. Secrecy is more important when people interact on a daily and intimate basis than when they interact only sporadically. Sharing a secret is more important when the partner is close and significant. The present chapter aims to illuminate the role of secrecy in close relationships. We will pay special attention to parent–child relationships. When children enter adolescence, parent–adolescent relationships become more conflictive and strained (Arnett, 1999). Disclosure in parent–adolescent relationships has received considerable attention in research (e.g., Finkenauer, Engels, Branje, & Meeus, 2004; Smetana, Metzger, Gettman, & Campione-Barr, 2006), but little is known about the role of secrecy in parent–child relationships. One line of our research aims to fill this gap in the knowledge on secrecy and concealment. In addition, it offers new insights into the intra- and inter-personal consequences of secrecy not only in parent–child relationships but more generally in relationships between close relationship partners. Instead of taking one side of the debate as to whether secrecy is good or bad for relationships, we reconcile seemingly contradictory findings and perspectives on the role of secrecy in close relationships.

Secrecy is a broad term that encompasses different types of secrets, which may have different implications for relationships (e.g., Finkenauer, Engels, & Kubacka, 2008). In general, secrets protect something that a person considers as intimate or private from unwanted access by others (Bok, 1983; Petronio, 2002). Secret keepers sift apart those who are allowed to access what secret keepers consider their intimate possession, their secret, from those who are not allowed access. In this sense, even though secrets may lie "within" the person, they operate between persons and between groups. They draw a line between those who know the information and those who do not know the information (Petronio). Secrets are thus inherently social phenomena, happening between people rather than within them (Bok; Lane & Wegner, 1995). Given the inherently social nature of secrecy, its implications for relationships and relationship partners may vary considerably depending on whether secrets are kept from or shared with another person. To illustrate, sharing a secret with a close partner may create a feeling of relatedness between the secret keeper and the person with whom the secret is shared. Keeping a secret, such as alcoholism, incest, or rape, from a close other, however, may isolate secret keepers and separate them from close others (e.g., Imber-Black, 1993). Thus, to answer the question whether secrecy is harmful or beneficial for close relationships, we propose that one needs to consider whether secrets are kept from others versus shared with others.

Secrecy in Social Relationships

In conceptualizing the role of secrecy in social relationships, it is useful to distinguish between the intra- and inter-personal effects of secrecy.

Intrapersonal effects refer to the influence secrecy has on the secret keeper, on his or her own psychosocial well-being and behavior. *Interpersonal effects*, on the other hand, refer to the influence secrecy has on the secret target. More important, we propose that these effects will vary across the type of secret under consideration. Before addressing the intra- and interpersonal effects of secrecy, it is, therefore, necessary to differentiate between different types of secrets.

Individual versus Shared Secrets

As defined above, all secrets distinguish between those who know about them and those who do not. Yet the number of secret keepers and secret targets is variable. Some secrets are only known to the secret keeper and are kept from everybody else. For example, a woman keeps a date-rape secret because she fears that others would think that she provoked the attack. In this case, the victim keeps what we call an *individual secret*. Other secrets are shared by a particular group of people (e.g., family, colleagues) and kept from all nongroup members (Simmel, 1950). They occur, for example, when families share a specific secret (e.g., an abortion, a suicide, or the physical illness) but withhold it from nonfamily members (Karpel, 1980; Vangelisti, 1994). We call these secrets *shared secrets*.

The literature supports the suggestion that secrets are shared with a varying number of confidants. To illustrate, in Vangelisti's study (1994) 97% of the participants had a secret that was shared by the entire family but kept from others, 99% had secrets that they shared with one other family member but not with others, and 96% kept secrets from their family. Similarly, in an explorative study among adult professionals, Finkenauer and Baumeister (1996) found that only one third of the respondents reported having an individual secret. The majority had shared their secret with a varying number of confidants: About 25% had shared their secret with one person, 18% with two persons, 14% with three persons, and 17% even with four or more persons. Thus, the extent to which secrets are shared with others varies considerably.

We conducted three studies, with more than 1,000 Dutch adolescents ranging in age from 12 to 19 years, to examine this variation across secrets more systematically. Specifically, we asked adolescents whether they had an individual and a shared secret (Frijns & Finkenauer, 2008). Paralleling the results for adults, about one third of the adolescents in these studies reported having *individual secrets*. The large majority of adolescents reported having *shared secrets* (about 70% across the three studies). These findings support our suggestion that one can meaningfully distinguish between individual and shared secrets. Interestingly, our findings suggest that the two types of secrets do not differ with respect to the specific secret content. As we will argue in the following, whether secrets are shared with others determines whether secrets have harmful or beneficial intrapersonal and interpersonal effects.

Intrapersonal Effects of Secrecy

Most research on the intrapersonal effects of secrecy has examined the harmful effect secrecy can have for the secret keeper, such as health problems (Pennebaker & Susman, 1988), obsessive thoughts (Lane & Wegner, 1995), and emotional distress (Finkenauer & Rimé, 1998). In contrast, little attention has been devoted to the beneficial effects of secrecy. Such effects are sometimes implied in theories on children's development as factors contributing to children's feeling of self-determination (Watson & Valtin, 1993) and in theories on adults' coping with trauma as factors protecting adults from harm and humiliation (Kelly & McKillop, 1996). Their role in adolescent development has not been studied. This neglect is unfortunate because secrecy in adolescence, especially if used skillfully, can be hypothesized to facilitate developmental processes and promote well-being (Finkenauer, Engels, & Meeus, 2002).

To reconcile these seemingly contradictory findings on secrecy's effects, we argue that the effect that secrecy has on secret keepers and people surrounding them is moderated by the type of secret. Most central to our view on secrecy is the suggestion that individual secrets should be more harmful than shared secrets. Although individual secrets may provide intrapersonal benefits for secret keepers such as feelings of independence and self-determination, they also cause (1) intrapersonal harm in that they deprive secret keepers of important social and emotional resources, and (2) interpersonal harm in that they signal separateness and exclusion to close others from whom the secret is kept. Shared secrets, on the contrary, provide secret keepers with the benefits of both: the benefits of keeping secrets from (some) others, including autonomy and self-determination, and the benefits of sharing secrets with others, including interpersonal benefits such as increased feelings of closeness and intimacy. In the following, we will describe research investigating these suggestions.

Harmful Intrapersonal Effects of Secrecy

Both laypeople and researchers often associate secrecy with "having something to hide," something shameful, furtive, or bad (Bok, 1983). Secrecy in this perspective is often seen as a cumulative stressor for the body and mind. Inhibition theory proposes that, comparable to a virus, secrecy poisons the mind and body, ultimately making people physically and mentally sick (e.g., Pennebaker, 1989). Research among adults corroborates this assumption (e.g., Finkenauer & Rimé, 1998; Lane & Wegner, 1995; Larson & Chastain, 1990; Pennebaker & Susman, 1988). In their research, for example, Larson and Chastain found that the dispositional tendency to keep secrets, also called self-concealment, contributed to physical complaints and depression, above and beyond other stress factors associated with physical and psychological problems such as traumatic experiences or lack of social support. Furthermore, both emotional inhibition and psychological secrecy (i.e., the inhibition of social and behavioral impulses associated with homosexuality) are associated with higher incidences of physical illness among (HIV-seronegative) gay men (Cole, Kemeny, Taylor, & Visscher, 1996) and a more rapid progression of the HIV infection among seropositive men who concealed their homosexual identity than among those who openly revealed it (Cole, Kemeny, Taylor, Visscher, & Fahey, 1996). Thus, secrecy may take a psychosocial toll and its harmful intrapersonal effects may be considerable. This research has been extensively reviewed elsewhere (e.g., Kelly, 2002). We will, therefore, confine the present discussion to studies that examine the conditions under which secrecy may have beneficial intrapersonal effects.

Beneficial Intrapersonal Effects of Secrecy

To us, the social nature of secrecy indicates that people actively manage and control information about their selves and their lives. This idea is not new. For example, in her communication privacy management theory, Petronio (1991, 2002) argues that people need to balance openness and concealment in their relationships with others to develop and maintain healthy, harmonious, and lasting relationships. Revealing information about the self is risky because one is potentially vulnerable to being hurt, rejected, ridiculed, or humiliated. Equally, receiving information from others is risky and potentially hurtful (e.g., criticism, revelation of negative feeling, or thoughts). To prevent themselves and others from being hurt, people build a metaphoric boundary between themselves and others (Petronio, 2002). They control this boundary through disclosure and secrecy, thereby regulating others' access to the self. More disclosure increases the permeability of boundaries, allowing a relationship to become closer. Conversely, more secrecy decreases the permeability of boundaries, preventing a relationship from developing any further (e.g., Miell & Duck, 1986). In this sense, people may use disclosure and secrecy as strategic devices to regulate their relationships with others.

Relationship regulation through secrecy may be particularly important during adolescence when adolescents have to develop their identity and try to find out who they are and what they want in various social domains (Finkenauer, Engels, Meeus, & Oosterwegel, 2002). They discover what is unique about themselves and strive to be independent from others so as to develop a sense of their personality. At the same time, they desperately try to fit in and avoid being different. They are particularly vulnerable to feelings of social inadequacy and failure (Seiffge-Krenke, 1998). Adolescents strive to become less dependent on their parents (Smetana, Campione-Barr, & Daddis, 2004) and to develop their own social network of friends on which they can rely as providers of essential resources for their socioemotional and cognitive development (Harris, 1995). Underlining the importance of adolescents' own social network is the fact that having a friend to confide in is considered as a social achievement in adolescence and an indicator of social competence (e.g., Hartup, 1996). Although adolescents strive for independence from their parents, they simultaneously have to maintain a good relationship with them because parents remain important and influential throughout their children's lives (e.g., Harris, 1995; Whiston & Keller, 2004). In this sense, adolescence is one big social challenge for adolescents: They have to develop intimate relationships while striving for independence and autonomy; they have to develop a sense of self and identity while avoiding being different and standing out. The question arises how adolescents can balance these seemingly incompatible developmental tasks. In our view, one possible answer is by skillfully using secrecy.

The scarce literature on secrecy among children supports this suggestion. Watson and Valtin (1993) conducted a comparative study on secret keeping among 200 younger (5 and 6 years) and older children (8, 10, and 12 years). They found that virtually all older children would share a secret with a friend but only half of the younger children would do so. Thus, for older children, secrets represent information that is only shared with a friend. For younger children, secrets represent a personal possession that would be lost if told. These findings suggest that younger children lack the understanding of friendship and trust that older children have in their friends. Friendship and trust were indeed the main reasons why older children shared their secrets (Watson & Valtin). Last and Aharoni-Etzioni (1995) asked children in third-, fifth-, and seventh-grade levels to write about a very important secret. They too found that secrets about possessions (e.g., objects, pets, accessibility to secret places) were much more frequent among younger than older children. Conversely, secrets concerning heterosexual involvement and moral transgressions (e.g., verbal or physical violence, lying, or disobeying) were much more frequent among older than younger children.

Thus, there is an obvious developmental shift from secrets about possessions to secrets about interpersonal relationships, which can be considered as a shift in the developmental tasks of the self. Younger children have to develop a sense of the self as being separate and independent from others. Older children have to develop social skills such as able to form stable and mutually satisfying relationships and fulfilling social demands (e.g., Hartup, 1996). In line with our suggestions then, secrecy may help adolescents regulate their relationships with others. Keeping a secret from a relationship partner indicates separation and distance (Simmel, 1950). Sharing a secret with a relationship partner, on the contrary, indicates intimacy and relatedness (Simmel; Karpel, 1980; Vangelisti, 1994). By oscillating between keeping and sharing secrets with others, adolescents may be able to accomplish contradictory developmental tasks that allow them to relinquish the safety of childhood and parental protection and simultaneously develop a firm hold on the responsibilities and demands of adulthood.

How can secrecy facilitate the accomplishment of developmental tasks in adolescence? Keeping a secret requires adolescents to exert self-control (e.g., resisting the temptation to confide) and make decisions about whom to tell (e.g., not telling my mother but my best friend). These decisions involve the assessment of what will be gained or lost by either choice (Petronio, 2002). For example, by revealing that he is absolutely in love with his class-mate, an adolescent boy may gain the girl's love, but he also risks getting rejected or ridiculed. By the same token, by keeping his love secret, he may gain the protection from getting rejected or becoming too dependent on the girl, but he also loses the possibility to check whether his feelings are mutual. Whether a person reveals or conceals information thus depends on how she or he evaluates the gains and losses of each decision. Often, secret keepers need to negotiate rules about how the secret information should be handled with others (Petronio, 2002). To illustrate, secret keepers often ask their con-fidants to keep the revealed information confidential. Similarly, family secrets (e.g., Vangelisti, 1994) and marital secrets require secret keepers and confi-dants to negotiate privacy rules and determine acceptable levels of secrecy and disclosure (Petronio, 2000).

The exertion of self-control (e.g., inhibiting the impulse to confide the secret) and decision making (e.g., whom to tell what and how much) inherent in secrecy may contribute to the development of identity and independence in several ways (Margolis, 1966). By keeping a secret, adolescents create a meta-phorical boundary between themselves and others (cf. Petronio, 2002), which allows them (1) to perceive themselves as being independent, self-determined, and different from others, and (2) to strategically control others' access to the self, thereby enabling them to, at least in part, control how others view the self (Kelly, 1998, 2000). Furthermore, by keeping secrets from some people and sharing secrets with others, adolescents may actively regulate their relation-ships with others. Sharing a secret may serve as a strategic device to intensify a relationship because sharing a secret should induce feelings of closeness with those with whom the secret is shared (e.g., Bellman, 1984). Conversely, keep-ing a secret from others may serve as a strategic device to prevent relationships from developing any further (cf. Miell & Duck, 1986) because it should emphasize feelings of separation from, and social distance to, the secret target (cf. Leary, Rapp, Herbst, Exum, & Feldman, 1998).

These suggestions give rise to the intriguing possibility that secrecy may be beneficial to the accomplishment of developmental tasks in adolescence. Keeping secrets from parents may enable adolescents to establish and increase their independence from their parents. Through secrecy adoles-cents may exercise self-control and practice decision making regarding their selves and their relationships with their parents (e.g., Allen, Hauser, Bell, & O'Connor, 1994; Steinberg & Silverberg, 1986). This should allow adoles-cents to perceive themselves as being emotionally autonomous and, at least in part, independent from their parents.

To examine this potentially beneficial function of secrecy in adolescence, we conducted a correlational study among two groups of adolescents (Finkenauer, Engels, & Meeus , 2002). Our findings confirmed the hypothesized facilitating effect of secrecy on emotional autonomy. Adolescents rated the extent to which they kept secrets from their parents, the lengths they would go to protect their secret, and the apprehension they experienced when thinking about revealing their secrets to their parents. Adolescents also rated the extent to which they felt emotionally independent from their parents and viewed themselves as independent from them. As predicted, adolescent boys and girls who reported greater concealment from their parents also reported greater levels of emotional autonomy. Conversely, adolescents who reported not keeping secrets from their parents also reported feeling more dependent on them. This result was not explained by the confounding influence of disclosure (e.g., the effects of concealment may be a result of a lack of disclosure to parents), frequency of disclosure to and frequency of contact with friends (e.g., the effects of concealment may be due to a lack of alternative confidants), or the quality of the relationship with parents (e.g., adolescents who have a bad relationship with their parents may conceal more information from them). Thus, keeping secrets from parents in adolescence is related to more feelings of emotional autonomy from parents.

The results also showed that this benefit comes at a price. Specifically, adolescents, girls and boys, and younger and older adolescents, who reported concealing more information from their parents, also reported experiencing more psychosocial problems, such as depressive mood and somatic complaints (see also Frijns, Finkenauer, Vermulst, & Engels, 2005). Thus, concealment from parents may be a double-edged sword in that it may allow adolescents to feel more independent and separate from their parents but at the same time may be stressful and predict feelings of loneliness. Furthermore, keeping a secret from a close relationship partner requires conscious efforts of cognitive and behavioral control that may take a physical and mental toll (e.g., Lane & Wegner, 1995; Pennebaker, 1989). In addition, adolescence, more than any other period in the life span, is characterized by increased self-consciousness and heightened self-presentational concerns (e.g., Finkenauer, Engels, Meeus, & Oosterwegel, 2002). Adolescents feel that it is undesirable to admit their shortcomings because they falsely assume that "everybody else" is normal and coping effectively and they alone are failing. By concealing their worries and concerns from their parents, adolescents deprive themselves of an important source of support and validation. This may contribute to physical complaints and depressed mood.

In sum, our findings converge to suggest that, rather than being exclusively bad and harmful, secrecy in adolescence is a mixed blessing. It may facilitate the accomplishment of emotional autonomy and independence from parents, but has considerable costs in the form of physical complaints and depressive mood. A note of caution is warranted. Although we have argued that concealment may facilitate independence and autonomy, it is equally plausible that an increase in adolescent autonomy leads to more concealment from parents. As adolescents become older, they engage in more activities outside the parental home. Often these activities may not be condoned by parents (e.g., smoking, drinking, playing hooky, sex; Smetana et al., 2006) and adolescents may choose secrecy as a means to conceal them from their parents.

Intrapersonal Effects of Individual and Shared Secrets in Adolescence

As we have discussed above, individual secrets may deprive adolescent secret keepers from socioemotional and cognitive resources (e.g., social support) needed to survive the social and emotional rollercoaster of adolescence. Shared secrets do not. They combine the best of both worlds: They allow secret keepers to distance themselves from certain people by keeping secrets from them, and simultaneously allow them to move closer to other people by sharing their secrets with them. As compared to individual secrets, shared secrets in adolescence should produce fewer psychosocial ill-effects. More important, they may even be related to social benefits, such as the development of social skills needed to form and develop close interpersonal relationships (e.g., knowing when to start revealing personal information versus knowing when to conceal personal information from others) because they may provide adolescents with an opportunity to strengthen their communicative competency and allow them to become competent communicators who selectively use secrecy as a strategic device to skillfully regulate their relationships (cf. Petronio, 2002).

A questionnaire study among 790 adolescents (Frijns & Finkenauer, 2008, study 3) provided support for the suggestion that individual and shared secrets differentially affect adolescents' psychosocial well-being. Consistent with our predictions, adolescents who kept individual secrets reported more depressed mood, lower self-esteem, more physical complaints, and greater feelings of loneliness than adolescents who shared their secrets with at least one confidant. More important, adolescents who reported sharing their secrets with others were more competent communicators than adolescents who reported keeping their secrets all to themselves. For example, they knew, better than adolescents with individual secrets, how to move a conversation with a date or acquaintance beyond superficial talk to really getting to know each other.

These findings are consistent with research showing that the disclosure and expression of trauma-related feelings and thoughts leads to improvement on a variety of health indicators (e.g., Pennebaker, Kiecolt-Glaser, & Glaser, 1988). Pennebaker et al. assigned participants to write about either a traumatic experience or a superficial topic for 20 minutes per day for 4 consecutive days. Respondents in the trauma writing condition showed an enhanced immune function immediately after the last session and a drop in health center visits after 6 weeks. Overall, these findings provide support for the hypothesis that disclosing one's secrets to others has beneficial intrapersonal effects and buffers the potential harmful effects of secrecy.

In short, a number of studies on the intrapersonal effects of secrecy reveal that secrets may be both harmful and beneficial. More important, the harmful effects of secrecy appear to be attenuated by sharing secrets. Because social separation is inherent in secrecy, individual secrets may lead to feelings of isolation and loneliness. After all, individual secrets separate the secret keeper from everybody else. Not surprisingly, these types of secrets are linked to psychosocial problems commonly associated with harmful intrapersonal effects such as loneliness, low self-esteem, frequent depressed mood, and physical complaints (Ichiyama et al., 1993) and predict the development of these problems in the long run (Frijns et al., 2005). Although shared secrets, like individual secrets, separate the secret keeper from those from whom they are kept, they may also provide them with a sense of belonging and control because they are likely to be shared with selected, close others. Shared secrets may thereby allow adolescents to balance contradictory developmental tasks in the relationship realm. By sharing their secrets with friends, adolescents may form new, trusting relationships and by keeping these secrets from their parents they may at the same time assert their independence from their parents.

This section has focused on the intrapersonal effects secrecy may have for the secret keeper, yet it has become clear that these effects are inseparable from the relationships secret keepers have with others. Besides advancing our knowledge on the intrapersonal effects, the investigation of secrecy also highlights the role of secret targets, those people with whom secrets are not shared. Emphasis on the effects of secrecy for other people has been sparse in the literature, yet as we will show in the following, the *inter*personal effects of secrecy are complex and impinge heavily on all aspects of the relationships secret keepers have with others surrounding them, especially close others.

Interpersonal Effects of Secrecy

At the beginning of this chapter, we painted a picture of secrets as social rather than individual phenomena. At the interpersonal level, secrets convey information to others about an individual's feelings about the relationship. Bellman (1984) emphasized that it is not the secret content that contributes to feelings of intimacy between two people sharing a secret, rather it is the "doing secrecy" (p. 147) or having the secret together and exchanging the secret information that creates a feeling of relatedness among secret keepers. According to Bellman (1984), feelings of intimacy and relatedness caused by sharing secrets are far more intense than those that are created by any other type of disclosure. Conversely, keeping a secret from another person may increase feelings of separation and isolation, especially among secret targets (Finkenauer, Kerkhof, Righetti, & Branje, 2008). Irrespective of whether secret keepers have prosocial motives for keeping a secret from someone (e.g., protecting the person from harm; Vangelisti, 1994) or egoistic motives (e.g., protecting their power to increase their superiority; Simmel, 1950), ultimately keeping a secret from someone conveys social exclusion.

Extensive research by Williams and his colleagues (for a review, see Williams, 2007) provides support for this suggestion by showing that people are sensitive to any signs that they are being ignored and excluded. When social exclusion is detected, it elicits reactions comparable to physical pain (Eisenberger, Lieberman, & Williams, 2003), sadness, hurt feelings, anger, and distress (Williams, Cheung, & Choi, 2000). The consequences of social exclusion, especially when it concerns multiple episodes or a single episode that is long-lasting, involve feelings of helplessness, alienation, and despair and often lead to antisocial behavior such as direct and indirect aggression toward and derogation of the person doing the exclusion (Twenge, Baumeister, Tice, & Stucke, 2001). According to our definition, secrecy can be considered a form of social exclusion (i.e., the secret keeper excludes the secret target). And feelings of exclusion caused by detecting secrecy from close others should lead to pain and hurt among secret targets.

The idea that the interpersonal effects of secrecy vary as a function of whether secrets are shared or kept from others is of course highly relevant to the study of the effects of secrecy in close relationships. In this section, we review theories and research on the interpersonal effects of secrecy for people surrounding the secret keeper.

Preliminary Evidence on the Interpersonal Effects of Sharing Secrets in Adolescence

Although there is no empirical evidence that investigates the interpersonal effects of sharing secrets, we would argue that it has beneficial effects and the extant literature, especially the literature on self-disclosure (Derlega, Metts, Petronio, & Margulis, 1993), provides indirect support for this prediction. Sharing a secret makes secret keepers vulnerable to a large variety of hurtful social consequences (e.g., ridicule, rejection, humiliation; Petronio 1991, 2002). Indeed, to share a secret, the secret keeper has to rely on the other's integrity, has to trust her or him with its protection, and has to be willing to become dependent on the other. Adolescents seem to intuitively seek out confidants who are least likely to harm or humiliate them. Their most frequently mentioned confidants are best friends and friends, followed by parents and other family members (e.g., siblings, aunts; Frijns & Finkenauer, 2008). Intimate relationship partners, such as family members or friends, can be nonjudgmental, discreet, and helpful confidants whose listening may make the revelation of the secret a profitable experience (Kelly & McKillop, 1996). That adolescents share their secrets more with friends than parents may suggest that they see parents as potentially more judgmental than friends. Because parents worry about their children's safety and health, adolescents may avoid sharing secrets regarding these issues (e.g., drug and alcohol use, sexual behavior) with their parents (Smetana et al., 2006). Sharing secrets with a friend may also enable adolescents to probe what it would be like to reveal the secret to others (e.g., their parents). Friends may provide advice and insight that may help to verify (or falsify) adolescents' expectations regarding the outcome of the revelation of their anxiously guarded secret (cf. Caughlin, Afifi, Carpenter-Theune, & Miller, 2005).

Sharing secrets also may increase intimacy and relatedness among the secret keepers (Bellman, 1984). Again, this suggestion is consistent with research on self-disclosure (i.e., revealing information about the self to others). In their meta-analysis on self-disclosure and liking, Collins and Miller (1994) revealed that (1) people who disclose intimate information are better liked than people who disclose nonintimate information; (2) the more disclosers like their recipient, the more intimate information they disclose to her or him; and (3) the more people disclose to a recipient, the more they subsequently like her or him. Our research shows that these results extend to relationships between parents and children (Finkenauer et al., 2004). Self-disclosure thus helps people create the mutual liking and intimacy necessary to develop close relationships (e.g., Derlega et al., 1993). Liking and intimacy, in turn, are necessary conditions for revealing more intimate personal information in relationships (e.g., Hendrick, 1981). Because secrets mostly concern intimate, personal information, it is likely that shared secrets increase the mutual trust and intimacy among secret keepers even more than does self-disclosure (i.e., disclosure of information that is commonly known). Thus, evidence converges to confirm our suggestion that sharing secrets with others may have beneficial interpersonal effects and research directly testing these suggestions is urgently needed.

Interpersonal Effects of Keeping Secrets from Others

People are ambivalent toward secrets. On one hand, they believe that they have a "right to secrecy" (Bok, 1983). They cherish their secrets, protect them from discovery, and are offended when others fail to respect their secrecy. On the other hand, people feel they have a "right to know" about others' secrets, especially when those others are close and intimate relationship partners, such as friends, romantic partners, or children (e.g., Smetana et al., 2006). They resent it when close others insist on keeping a secret from them; they feel hurt and rejected (cf. Williams, 2007). This ambivalence toward secrecy suggests that whether secrets are perceived in a positive or negative light varies reliably as a function of whether people are secret keepers or secret targets. From the perspective of the secret keeper, secrets represent precious possessions. From the perspective of the secret targets, however, secrets signal exclusion (cf. Williams). Consequently secret keepers should perceive their secrecy as more positive than secret targets.

Consistent with this prediction, marital partners who conceal difficult issues (e.g., talking about sex, criticizing partner, arguing about topics known to be conflictive) from their partner are also more satisfied with their relationship (Finkenauer & Hazam, 2000; see also Baxter & Wilmot, 1985). In contrast, marital partners who suspect that their partner is concealing information from them are considerably less satisfied with their relationship. Perceiving one's partner to keep secrets appears incompatible with having a close, loving, and accepting relationship. It conveys that one is not a desirable, trusted confidant and signals that one is excluded from one's partner's intimate thoughts and feelings. This message should lead to feelings of hurt, exclusion (Williams, 2007), and loneliness in the marital relationship that reduce relational quality (Flora & Segrin, 2000). Thus, secret keepers perceive secrecy as more positive than secret targets. Secret keepers usually (think they) have good reasons, and mostly good intentions, when concealing certain information from others (e.g., Afifi & Guerrero, 2000). In line with Bok's suggestion (1983), their secrecy is not necessarily meant to deceive. Rather they feel that they are entitled to their secrecy and view it as justified and important for the maintenance of the relationship (e.g., Finkenauer & Hazam, 2000; Vangelisti & Caughlin, 1997). Conversely, secret targets perceive the secret as having an important negative impact on the relationship and suspect negative intentions (cf. Baumeister, Stillwell, & Wotman, 1990; Kowalski, Walker, Wilkinson, Queen, & Sharpe, 2003). These wide discrepancies in people's perceptions of secrets can be assumed to have important implications for the relationship between the secret keeper and secret target that go beyond relationship satisfaction.

Interpersonal effects of secrecy in parent–adolescent relationships. To examine the suggestion that secrecy may have adverse interpersonal effects, we conducted two studies among families with adolescent children (Finkenauer et al., 2005). In the first study, 105 families with both parents and one adolescent ranging in the age group of 10 to 18 years participated. In the second study, 427 mother–adolescent pairs and 134 father–adolescent pairs participated; adolescents were in the age group of 10 to 14 years. In both studies, adolescents reported whether they actually concealed information from their parents, and parents reported whether they perceived their child to keep secrets from them. In addition, parents reported on their own parenting behavior, including parental knowledge, responsiveness, and acceptance.

We expected parents' perception of adolescent concealment to have adverse implications for the adolescent–parent relationship. Even the mere perception that the adolescents are withholding information, above and beyond adolescents' actual concealment, may serve as a clue for parents that the relationship with their adolescent child is not intact (Caughlin & Golish, 2002; Finkenauer & Hazam, 2000). Therefore, parents should experience their (perception of) child's secrecy as hurtful and as a sign of distrust and exclusion (cf. Williams, 2007). In line with this reasoning, parents' perception of their child's concealment should be associated with parents' poorer parenting. Specifically, upon perceiving secrecy from their children, parents should feel hurt, helpless, and alienated (Williams). These feelings should cause parents to withdraw from the relationship with their child and show direct and indirect aggression toward them (cf. Twenge et al., 2001).

Both studies provided results that were consistent with these hypotheses. For both mothers and fathers, we found that, when they perceived their adolescent child to conceal information from them, they reported being less knowledgeable about their child's activities and whereabouts, less responsive to their child's needs, and less accepting of their child. Interestingly, whether adolescents actually kept secrets from their parents did not affect these results, except for parental knowledge. Specifically, we found an interaction between parents' perceptions of concealment and adolescents' reported actual concealment. Parents who perceived high concealment had little knowledge of their child, independent of whether their adolescent child reported actually concealing information from them or not. Parents who perceived no concealment, on the contrary, had significantly more knowledge about their child when their child did not conceal information from them than when their child did conceal information from them. Thus, actual adolescent concealment may limit parents' access to their children's lives (Petronio, 2002) and may in turn restrict parents' knowledge about their activities and whereabouts (Kerr & Stattin, 2000).

These results leave little doubt that the perception of concealment from a close relationship partner is harmful in relationships because it has adverse effects on the quality of the relationship between the secret target and secret keeper. Few studies have investigated the deeper mechanisms underlying the observed link between the perception of the partner's (or child's) concealment of secrets and adverse interpersonal effects. We tried to rectify this gap in the literature in this chapter. Nevertheless, the extant literature provides some evidence that helps illuminate these mechanisms: Research suggests that when people are afraid to express negative information toward relationship partners it can decrease partners' feeling of closeness (Afifi & Olson, 2005) and satisfaction with each other (Vangelisti & Caughlin, 1997). Similarly, when parents perceive that their child is keeping secrets from them, they may interpret this concealment as an indication of their child's increased need for privacy (e.g., "That's none of your business"; cf. Allen et al., 1994), reduced trust and relationship quality (e.g., "I don't trust you enough to tell you about this," "Our relationship is not good enough to tell you"; cf. Imber-Black, 1993), or social exclusion ("I don't want you involved"; cf. Williams, 2007). Not surprisingly, many parents react negatively, with pain and hurt, when they perceive that their children are concealing information from them.

Explaining the Harmful Interpersonal Effects of Secrecy: Secrecy as a Signal of Exclusion

Although the suggestion that secrets carry relational messages that question the reliability of close relationships is appealing, it has not yet been substantiated. In a recent study including a large sample of newlywed couples, we tested one possible mechanism underlying the harmful effects of the perception of secrecy for secret keepers (Finkenauer et al., 2008). As suggested above, we hypothesized that perceiving one's partner's concealment signals exclusion and rejection (e.g., Bok, 1983; Finkenauer et al., 2005). This signal is incompatible with a satisfied, harmonious, and trusting relationship and should communicate a deficiency in closeness, belongingness, and companionship in the marital relationship (Sadava & Matejcic, 1987).

Consequently, the perception of concealment should be associated with feelings of relationship-specific loneliness and exclusion among secret targets—or partners who think they are secret targets. They should feel excluded and rejected by the person with whom they spend most of their time and with whom they are supposedly closest. They should feel lonely in their marriage. These feelings of loneliness in the relationship with one's closest partner, in turn, should negatively affect the quality of their relationship with their partner (e.g., Flora & Segrin, 2000).

To test this prediction, we (Finkenauer et al., 2008) conducted a study in which 199 newlywed couples completed questionnaires 2 months after their marriage assessing their own concealment from their partner and their perception of their partner's concealment. Couples had been romantically involved on average for 6 years and had been living together for an average of 4 years. Confirming our hypotheses, both husbands and wives who perceived high concealment from their partner reported poorer relationship satisfaction, more conflict, and less trust than partners who perceived little concealment from their partner. Whether the partner actually concealed information did not influence these results. In fact, the relation between perceived concealment and actual concealment was marginal ($r = .10-.20$), suggesting that partners are mostly inaccurate in their perception of concealment. Furthermore, partners who reported experiencing feelings of loneliness in their marital relationship were less satisfied, had more conflict, and trusted their partner less. More important, the observed link between perceived concealment and relationship satisfaction was, albeit partially, mediated by feeling excluded and lonely in one's relationship. Perceived concealment contributed independently and directly to relational well-being above and beyond this mediation, which is not surprising given that we focused on only one possible relational message and many more are possible (e.g., lack of trust, love, companionship).

These findings from our newlywed sample and our findings on parental perceptions of child concealment are consistent with the literature showing that partners' unique perceptions shape, at least in part, how they see others and the world surrounding them (e.g., Baldwin, 1992; Berscheid, 1994). The fact that perceived concealment explained variance above and beyond actual concealment by the partner underlines the importance of subjective perceptions in interpersonal relationships. Thus, it is not so much the actual concealment in a relationship that matters but rather what partners make of the perception of concealment. Our study is the first to offer an answer as to what it is that partners make of this perception. Furthermore, it is consistent with research on topic avoidance (e.g., Caughlin & Afifi, 2004; Caughlin & Golish, 2002) showing that partners' awareness that the other person avoids talking about certain topics in the relationship is associated with dissatisfaction with the relationship. In line with our findings, this research has also shown that the perception of topic avoidance from a partner is particularly harmful when it is attributed to a lack of closeness between close relationship partners

(Caughlin & Afifi). This evidence thus suggests that secrecy may backfire and have harmful interpersonal effects if it is directed at a close relationship partner who perceives the secrecy as exclusion and lack of closeness or trust.

Concluding Remarks

The present chapter illuminated a few intrapersonal and interpersonal effects of secrecy in social relationships, but many others can be generated. To illustrate, concealment and secrecy intuitively should come into play when people are being polite and attempt to save another person's face (cf. Mills, 2003) and when people want to protect others (e.g., Karpel, 1980; Vangelisti, 1994). Indeed, without secrecy we would be unable to avoid hurting others, inhibit destructive responses toward them, or to protect them from harm, social disapproval, and embarrassment, or avoid hurting ourselves. Thus, it is likely that, without secrecy, our relationships with others might be less harmonious and more conflictive. Indeed, if someone's primary motivation for keeping a secret is to enhance and maintain the relationship, and secret targets detect such a concern in the secret-keeping partner, secrecy can be hypothesized to benefit relationships (Petronio, 2002). Although existing findings provide first evidence for this suggestion (Caughlin & Afifi, 2004; Finkenauer & Hazam, 2000) more research is needed to investigate the generalizability of the suggestion that secrecy may under certain conditions have beneficial intrapersonal and interpersonal effects in social relationships.

We began this chapter by stating that secrecy may not always be bad, and, more important, may often not be intended to be bad. Much of the existing literature focuses on the harmful nature of secrecy, but we hope that this chapter helps to draw a more complete picture of secrecy by shedding some light at both its harmful and beneficial intra- and inter-personal effects and showing that these effects systematically vary as a function of whether the secrets are kept from or shared with close others. Our review of the intra- and inter-personal effects of secrecy in close relationships suggests a straightforward and robust beneficial effect for secrets that are (selectively) shared with others. For adolescents, keeping secrets from parents but sharing them with their friends may be an adaptive way to deal with the social challenges in adolescence. Sharing secrets with friends may increase feelings of closeness and intimacy. On the contrary, our review also suggests that keeping secrets from close others may have harmful intra- and inter-personal effects. Anxiously keeping secrets from everybody else is stressful and deprives secret keepers from important psychological and social resources. Not surprisingly, these individual secrets have detrimental intrapersonal effects. Harmful interpersonal effects emerge when people perceive close others to keep secrets from them, independent of whether the secrecy occurs in parent–child relationships or marital relationships, and independent of secret keepers' best intentions. Without doubt, the systematic investigation of secrecy in social relationships has helped us better appreciate the pervasive influence secrecy has on close relationships. We have illuminated its intra- and inter-personal effects and are beginning to understand some of the mechanisms through which secrecy exerts these effects. Many questions remain, however, and more research is needed to further enhance our understanding of the role of secrecy in social relationships. It is our hope that the present chapter will help to be a source of inspiration for such research.

References

Afifi, T. D., & Olson, L. (2005). The chilling effect and the pressure to conceal secrets in families. *Communication Monographs, 72,* 192–216.

Afifi, W. A., & Guerrero, L. K. (2000). Motivations underlying topic avoidance in close relationships. In S. Petronio (Ed.), *Balancing the secrets of private disclosures* (pp. 165–180). Mahwah, NJ: Lawrence Erlbaum Associates.

Allen, J. P., Hauser, S. T., Bell, K. L., & O'Connor, T. G. (1994). Longitudinal assessment of autonomy and relatedness in adolescent–family interactions as predictors of adolescent ego development and self-esteem. *Child Development, 65,* 179–194.

Arnett, J. J. (1999). Adolescent storm and stress, reconsidered. *American Psychologist, 54,* 317–326.

Baldwin, M. W. (1992). Relational schemas and the processing of social information. *Psychological Bulletin, 112,* 461–484.

Baumeister, R. F., Stillwell, A., & Wotman, S. R. (1990). Victim and perpetrator accounts of interpersonal conflict: Autobiographical narratives about anger. *Journal of Personality and Social Psychology, 59,* 994–1005.

Baxter, L. A., & Wilmot, W. W. (1985). Taboo topics in close relationships. *Journal of Social and Personal Relationships, 2,* 253–269.

Bellman, B. (1984). *The language of secrecy.* New Brunswick, NJ: Rutgers University Press.

Berscheid, E. (1994). Interpersonal relationships. *Annual Review of Psychology, 45,* 79–129.

Bok, S. (1983). *Secrets: On the Ethics of Concealment and Revelation.* New York: Pantheon Books.

Caughlin, J. P., & Afifi, T. D. (2004). When is conflict avoidance unsatisfying? Examining moderators between avoidance and dissatisfaction. *Human Communication Research, 30,* 479–513.

Caughlin, J. P., Afifi, W. A., Carpenter-Theune, K. E., & Miller, C. E. (2005). Reasons for, and consequences of, revealing personal secrets in close relationships: A longitudinal study. *Personal Relationships, 12,* 43–59.

Caughlin, J. P., & Golish, T. D. (2002). An analysis of the association between topic avoidance and dissatisfaction: Comparing perceptual and interpersonal explanations. *Communication Monographs, 69,* 275–295.

Cole, S. W., Kemeny, M. E., Taylor, S. E., & Visscher, B. R. (1996). Elevated physical health risk among gay men who conceal their homosexual identity. *Health Psychology, 15,* 243–251.

Cole, S. W., Kemeny, M. E., Taylor, S. E., Visscher, B. R., & Fahey, J. L. (1996). Accelerated course of human immunodeficiency virus infection in gay men who conceal their homosexual identity. *Psychosomatic Medicine, 58,* 219–231.

Collins, N. L., & Miller, L. C. (1994). Self-disclosure and liking: A meta-analytic review. *Psychological Bulletin, 116*, 457–475.

Derlega, V. J., Metts, S., Petronio, S., & Margulis, S. T. (1993). *Self-disclosure.* London: Sage.

Eisenberger, N. I., Lieberman, M. D., & Williams, K. D. (2003). Does rejection hurt? An fMRI study of social exclusion. *Science, 302*, 290–292.

Fehr, B. (1993). "How do I love thee? Let me consult my prototype." In S. Duck (Ed.), *Individuals in relationships* (pp. 87–120). Newbury Park, CA: Sage.

Finkenauer, C., & Baumeister, R. (1996). *Secrecy and self-esteem.* Unpublished data, University of Louvain, Louvain-la-Neuve, Belgium.

Finkenauer, C., Engels, R. C. M. E., Branje, S., & Meeus, W. (2004). Disclosure and relationship satisfaction in families. *Journal of Marriage and Family, 66*, 195–209.

Finkenauer, C., Engels, R. C. M. E., & Kubacka, K. E. (2008). Relational implications of secrecy and concealment in parent–adolescent relationships. In M. Kerr, H. Stattin, and R. C. M. E. Engels (Eds.), *New perspectives on parenting* (pp. 42–64). New York: John Wiley.

Finkenauer, C., Engels, R. C. M. E., & Meeus, W. (2002). Keeping secrets from parents: Advantages and disadvantages of secrecy in adolescence. *Journal of Youth and Adolescence, 31*, 123–136.

Finkenauer, C., Engels, R. C. M. E., Meeus, W., & Oosterwegel, A. (2002). Self and identity in early adolescence: The pains and gains of growing up. In T. M. Brinthaupt & R. P. Lipka (Eds.), *Understanding early adolescent self and identity: Applications and interventions* (pp. 25–56). Albany, NY: State University of New York Press.

Finkenauer, C., Frijns, T., Engels, R. C. M. E., & Kerkhof, P. (2005). Perceiving concealment in relationships between parents and adolescents: Links with parental behavior. *Personal Relationships, 12*, 387–406.

Finkenauer, C., & Hazam, H. (2000). Disclosure and secrecy in marriage: Do both contribute to marital satisfaction? *Journal of Social and Personal Relationships, 17*, 245–263.

Finkenauer, C., Kerkhof, P., Righetti, F., & Branje, S. (2008). *Living together apart: Perceived concealment as signal of exclusion in marital relationships.* Manuscript submitted for publication.

Finkenauer, C. & Rimé, B. (1998). Keeping emotional memories secret: Health and subjective well-being when emotions are not shared. *Journal of Health Psychology, 3*, 47–58.

Flora, J., & Segrin, C. (2000). Relationship development in dating couples: Implications for relational and personal well-being. *Journal of Social and Personal Relationships, 17*, 811–825.

Frijns, T., & Finkenauer, C. (2008). *When secrets are shared: Individual versus shared secrets and their links with well-being.* Paper submitted for publication.

Frijns, T., Finkenauer, C., Vermulst, A., & Engels, R. C. M. E. (2005). Keeping secrets from parents: Longitudinal associations of secrecy in adolescence. *Journal of Youth and Adolescence, 34*, 137–148.

Harris, J. R. (1995). Where is the child's environment? A group socialization theory of development. *Psychological Review, 102*, 458–489.

Hartup, W. W. (1996). The company they keep: Friendships and their developmental significance. *Child Development, 67*, 1–13.

Hendrick, S. S. (1981). Self-disclosure and marital satisfaction. *Journal of Personality and Social Psychology, 40,* 980–988.

Ichiyama, M. A., Colbert, D., Laramore, H., Heim, M., Carone, K., & Schmidt, J. (1993). Self-concealment and correlates of adjustment in college students. *Journal of College Student Psychotherapy, 7,* 55–68.

Imber-Black, E. (1993). *Secrets in families and family therapy.* New York: W. W. Norton & Company.

Karpel, M. A. (1980). Family secrets. *Family Process, 19,* 295–306.

Kelly, A. E. (1998). Clients' secret keeping in outpatient therapy. *Journal of Counseling Psychology, 45,* 50–57.

Kelly, A. E. (2000). Helping construct desirable identities: A self-presentational view of psychotherapy. *Psychological Bulletin, 126,* 475–494.

Kelly, A. E. (2002). *The psychology of secrets.* New York: Plenum.

Kelly, A. E., & McKillop, K. J. (1996). Consequences of revealing personal secrets. *Psychological Bulletin, 120,* 450–465.

Kerr, M., & Stattin, H. (2000). What parents know, how they know it, and several forms of adolescent adjustment: Further support for a reinterpretation of Monitoring. *Developmental Psychology, 36,* 366–380.

Kowalski, R. M., Walker, S., Wilkinson, R., Queen, A., & Sharpe, B. (2003). Lying, cheating, complaining, and other aversive interpersonal behaviors: A narrative examination of the darker side of relationships. *Journal of Social and Personal Relationships, 20,* 471–490.

Lane, D. J., & Wegner, D. M. (1995). The cognitive consequences of secrecy. *Journal of Personality and Social Psychology, 69,* 237–253.

Larson, D. G., & Chastain, R. L. (1990). Self-concealment: Conceptualization, measurement, and health implications. *Journal of Social and Clinical Psychology, 9,* 439–455.

Last, U., & Aharoni-Etzioni, A. (1995). Secrets and reasons for secrecy among school-aged children: Developmental trends and gender differences. *Journal of Genetic Psychology, 156,* 191–203.

Leary, M. R., Rapp, S. R., Herbst, K., Exum, L., & Feldman, S. R. (1998). Interpersonal concerns and psychological difficulties of psoriasis patients: Effects of disease severity and fear of negative evaluation. *Health Psychology, 17,* 530–536.

Margolis, G. J. (1966). Secrecy and identity. *International Journal of Psycho-Analysis, 47,* 517–522.

Miell, D. E., & Duck, S. (1986). Strategies in developing friendships. In V. J. Derlega & B. A. Winstead (Eds.), *Friends and social interaction* (pp. 129–143). New York: Springer Verlag.

Mills, S. (2003). *Gender and politeness.* Cambridge: Cambridge University Press.

Pennebaker, J. W. (1989). Confession, inhibition, and disease. In L. Berkowitz (Ed.), *Advances in experimental social psychology* (Vol. 22, pp. 211–244). New York: Academic Press.

Pennebaker, J. W., Kiecolt-Glaser, J. K., & Glaser, R. (1988). Disclosure of traumas and immune function: Health implications for psychotherapy. *Journal of Consulting and Clinical Psychology, 58,* 239–245.

Pennebaker, J. W., & Susman, J. R. (1988). Disclosure of traumas and psychosomatic processes. *Social Science and Medicine, 26,* 327–332.

Petronio, S. (1991). Communication boundary management: A theoretical model of managing disclosure of private information between marital couples. *Communication Theory, 1*, 311–335.

Petronio, S. (2000). The boundaries of privacy: Praxis of everyday life. In S. Petronio (Ed.), *Balancing the secrets of private disclosures* (pp. 37–49). Mahwah, NJ: Lawrence Erlbaum.

Petronio, S. (2002). *Boundaries of privacy: Dialectics of disclosure.* Albany, NY: State University of New York Press.

Sadava, S. W., & Matejcic, C. (1987). Generalized and specific loneliness in early marriage. *Canadian Journal of Behavioral Science, 19*, 56–66.

Seiffge-Krenke, I. (1998). *Adolescents' health: A developmental perspective.* Mahwah, NJ: Lawrence Erlbaum.

Simmel, G. (1950). *The secret and the secret society.* In K. W. Wolff (Ed. and Trans.), *The sociology of Georg Simmel.* New York: Free Press.

Smetana, J. G., Campione-Barr, N., & Daddis, C. (2004). Developmental and longitudinal antecedents of family decision-making: Defining health behavioral autonomy for African American adolescents. *Child Development, 75*, 1–17.

Smetana, J. G., Metzger, A., Gettman, D. C., & Campione-Barr, N. (2006). Disclosure and secrecy in adolescent–parent relationships. *Child Development, 77*, 201–217.

Steinberg, L., & Silverberg, S. B. (1986). The vicissitudes of autonomy in early adolescence. *Child Development, 57*, 841–851.

Twenge, J. M., Baumeister, R. F., Tice, D. M., & Stucke, T. S. (2001). If you can't join them, beat them: Effects of social exclusion on aggressive behavior. *Journal of Personality and Social Psychology, 81*, 1058–1069.

Vangelisti, A. L. (1994). Family secrets: Forms, functions, and correlates. *Journal of Social and Personal Relationships, 11*, 113–135.

Vangelisti, A. L., & Caughlin, J. P. (1997). Revealing family secrets: The influence of topic, function, and relationships. *Journal of Social and Personal Relationships, 14*, 679–705.

Watson, A. J., & Valtin, R. (1993). "It's not telling your mum, only your friend": Children's understanding of secrets. In M. J. Dunkin (Ed.), *St. George papers in education* (Vol. 2, pp. 1–53). Oatley, NSW, Australia: The School of Teacher Education.

Whiston, S. C., & Keller, B. K. (2004). The influences of the family of origin on career development: A review and analysis. *The Counseling Psychologist, 32*, 493–568.

Williams, K. D. (2007). Ostracism. *Annual Review of Psychology, 58*, 425–452.

Williams, K. D., Cheung, C. K. T., & Choi, W. (2000). CyberOstracism: Effects of being ignored over the Internet. *Journal of Personality and Social Psychology, 79*, 748–762.

16 Conflict Avoidance

A Functional Analysis

Michael E. Roloff and Courtney N. Wright

Scholars have long held that conflict is a ubiquitous feature of social interaction (e.g., Dahrendorf, 1958), yet individuals report that verbal conflict or arguing is relatively rare. College student diaries indicate that they average about seven arguments per week, typically with peers, that on average only last 3 minutes (Benoit & Benoit, 1987). Generally, spouses report having one argument per month (Bolger, DeLongis, Kessler, & Wethington, 1989) and about half of spouses report having less than one argument per month (McGonagle, Kessler, & Schilling, 1992). Finally, transcripts of the daily conversations of romantic partners indicate that less than 1% of interactions involve conflict, whereas 75% are focused on descriptions of daily activities, random observations about the current environment, the activities of other people, and television programs (Alberts, Yoshimura, Rabby, & Loschiavo, 2005).

The relative paucity of arguing should not be viewed as a sign of relational harmony. Indeed, relational partners often irritate each other on a daily basis. Studies have shown that 44% of people are irritated by a relational partner each day and that young adults report irritations in their romantic relationships an average of 8.7 times per week (Miller, 1997). Moreover, Kirchler (1988) studied diaries of daily events occurring over a 4-week span and found that happily married individuals reported feeling bad 24% of the time because of something their spouse did, while unhappily married individuals reported experiencing the same negativity 43% of the time. Although arguing is infrequent, the emotional reactions, such as anger, annoyance, and displeasure, which can underlie conflict situations, are not. Hence, there is ample evidence of discord in close relationships other than that of arguing.

Instead of harmony, the absence of arguing may reflect an attempt to avoid disagreement. Using a diary method, Birchler, Weiss, and Vincent (1975) discovered that individuals in nondistressed marriages reported that their spouses engaged in an average of 14 displeasing behaviors over a 5-day span, whereas arguments only occurred once. Similarly, individuals in distressed marriages reported an average of 42 displeasing behaviors, but only three arguments.

Conflict avoidance is used as a management strategy in a variety of relationships and may be the predominant style employed by some individuals in some relationships (Roloff & Ifert, 2000). Although conflict avoidance is recognized as common and is, in some cases, considered a functional form of conflict management, its research is very diverse. Indeed, there are a variety of topics under study and many different theories used to guide conflict avoidance research. Although this diversity can be useful and demonstrates the complexity of conflict avoidance, the absence of a larger theoretical framework to explain it renders this research area somewhat incoherent. The purpose of this chapter is to propose an approach to conflict avoidance that employs a larger framework. Using a functional framework to cast conflict avoidance, we will explicate the construct of conflict avoidance, frame it within a functional approach, and highlight the implications of our analysis.

Conflict Avoidance

Deutsch (1973) posits that conflict exists whenever there are incompatible activities. In his view, incompatibility occurs when a behavior contradicts, prevents, obstructs, interferes with, or makes another action less likely or effective. Although an argument involves expressed disagreement and hence is a common form of conflict, Deutsch's conceptualization allows for the possibility that conflict can occur without an argument. For example, an individual may engage in an action that interferes with our own, but we may choose to remain silent rather than to confront him or her.

Conflict avoidance constitutes attempts to avoid incompatible activities. When avoiding conflict, individuals are trying to avoid stimulating an argument in which they and their partners might express incompatible interpretations of the event and that might expand into other conflict areas. By withholding, they may experience intrapersonal conflict arising from not being able to express themselves about their partner's negative behavior, but they avoid open disagreement. This definition also assumes that avoidant behavior is enacted intentionally. In effect, individuals forecast that certain behaviors may conflict with those of another and purposefully avoid enacting them. For example, individuals often report that they avoid discussing certain topics because they may induce conflict (e.g., Afifi & Guerrero, 2000), withhold complaining about their partner's behavior that conflicts with their own (Roloff & Cloven, 1990), and declare conflict-inducing topics taboo for discussion (Baxter & Wilmot, 1985). In some cases, this forecast is based on personal experiences associated with talking about a problem and in others it may be an inference.

Our definition of *avoidance* is agnostic with regard to several features often attributed to conflict avoidance. First, we do not assume that avoidance is necessarily a passive response to conflict. In some cases, avoidance may indeed appear to others to reflect passivity (e.g., Sillars, Coletti, Parry, & Rogers, 1982), but underlying its use there is often a great deal of cognitive activity as individuals take the perspective of others so as to determine the impact of their behavior and then monitor and modify their own behavior to make it compatible. Indeed, some researchers have observed that individuals who frequently enact conflict avoidance seem exhausted (e.g., Gelles & Straus, 1988). Second, we do not assume that avoidance always reflects a skill deficit. In some cases, conflict avoidance may result from feelings of diminished self or outcome efficacy (e.g., Makoul & Roloff, 1988), but in other cases avoidance may reflect uncertainty about how to respond and is a temporary attempt to buy time in order to form a more cogent response (e.g., Witteman, 1988). Third, we do not assume that conflict avoidance always reflects powerlessness. In some cases, avoidance may result from relational dependency (e.g., Roloff & Cloven, 1990) or fear of a partner's coercive response (e.g., Cloven & Roloff, 1993), but in others it may arise from the perception that the relationship is not sufficiently intimate to confront the problem (Cloven & Roloff, 1994a). We believe that conflict avoidance is enacted primarily because individuals believe it to be functional for them psychologically and/or socially. In the next section, we will cast avoidance in a functional perspective.

A Functional Approach to Conflict Avoidance

Snyder (1993) notes that "a functional analysis is concerned with the reasons and purposes, the needs and goals, the plans and motives that underlie a general psychological phenomena: that is, such an analysis is concerned with the psychological functions served by people's beliefs and their actions . . ." (p. 253). Functional approaches have provided useful insight into a variety of social processes such as persuasion (e.g., Katz, 1960), behavioral confirmation (Snyder, 1992), volunteerism (Snyder, 1993), and organizational citizenship behavior (Rioux & Penner, 2001). At its core, a functional approach assumes that the reasons that people give for their actions provide insights into psychological and social processes that lead to enactment and that people vary with regard to the reasons they give for enacting a given behavior. Hence, two people may engage in the same action but for different reasons. Although understanding the functions of a behavior provides insights into why individuals perform them, it is also important to discover whether research indicates that such actions are actually functional. Hence, beyond merely elucidating the functions served by an action, a functional framework can specify the psychological and social factors that lead to a behavior being associated with a given function, the conditions under which the behavior might actually produce the function, and the conditions that might cause the behavior to become dysfunctional.

Although we are unaware of any studies on conflict avoidance that have adopted a functional approach, research in the area has been conducted in a manner that is consistent with its assumptions. For example, in the area of relational complaints, the typical research method asks individuals to list the reasons why they have not confronted their relational partner about his or her irritating behavior and individuals who provide a given reason are compared with those who have not (Cloven & Roloff, 1993, 1994a; Makoul & Roloff, 1998; Roloff & Cloven, 1990; Roloff & Solomon, 2002). This area of research examines why individuals choose to avoid discussing a conflict that has already occurred and the reasons for it. To illustrate the utility of a functional approach, we will focus on research concerning the withholding of relational complaints.

Cloven and Roloff (1994b) asked undergraduate daters to list things they found irritating about their partners and then to identify how many of their complaints they communicated to the partners. For those complaints that had been withheld, individuals reported why they had not been expressed. These reasons were then content analyzed and subjected to a cluster analysis. The following eight reasons for withholding complaints emerged: the problem is unimportant, negative consequences are feared, self-image would be damaged, communication is futile, the relationship is noninti-mate, complaining is illegitimate, indirect communication is preferred, and the situation inhibits communication. Table 16.1 contains these reasons and sample statements. We will now examine each in greater detail.

Problem Is Unimportant

Some individuals do not find a partner's irritating action to be sufficiently important so as to instigate a confrontation. Statements reflecting this reason included "The problem doesn't bother me that much" and "It's not a big problem." This reason for avoidance implies that some threshold must be passed before individuals are willing to confront another person. Conflict requires the expenditure of valuable resources and prolonged conflict can deplete the supply (Vuchinich & Teachman, 1993). For example, research on serial arguments (arguments that extend over several episodes) indicates that a single hostile encounter can be quite stressful and that afterwards individuals report that they suffer from sleep problems, hyperarousal, and emotional problems that interfere with other activities in their lives (Roloff & Reznik, 2008). To avoid this outcome, individuals may only confront others over important issues; in effect, they learn to pick their battles. For example, Roloff and Solomon (2002) found among daters that relational commitment was positively related to the willingness to confront partners about negative behavior but also was positively related to withholding complaints about minor irritants.

The decision that a problem is insufficiently important to confront could stem from a number of sources. First, viewing a negative behavior as unimportant could result from the relative proportion of positive to negative behaviors enacted by the partner. For example, Gottman (1994) argues that marital satisfaction stems from maintaining a ratio of five positive actions for every negative one. If so, then a partner whose behavior is mostly positive may be forgiven for a particular negative action and it becomes inconsequential.

Table 16.1 Reasons for Withholding Complaints and Exemplars

Reasons	Sample statements
The problem is unimportant	The issue is not that important to me. The situation doesn't bother me that much. It's not a very big problem.
Relationship consequences are negative	My partner would get angry if I brought this up. I want to avoid conflict. I don't want my partner to end our relationship.
Self-image would be damaged	I don't want to sound selfish or appear overbearing. It seems petty and immature, like I'm the jealous type. I would look like I'm cheap or materialistic.
Communication is futile	My partner wouldn't change anyway, so why bother? When I have approached the topic, my partner has ignored it completely. It's just my partner's nature; I can't expect him/her to change.
The relationship is nonintimate	We haven't been dating long enough. The relationship is extremely casual. I'd be asking too much from the relationship.
Complaining is illegitimate	I have no right to tell my partner what to do. It's not really my partner's fault. I feel like it's none of my business.
Indirect communication is preferred	My partner can see that I get frustrated when this happens.
Situation inhibits communication	I haven't found the right time to say something about this. An opportunity hasn't presented itself yet. I think I'll tell my partner about this in a couple of weeks when we aren't so busy. I haven't found the words to articulate the problem. It's hard to tell someone something like this.

Second, reducing the importance of an irritation could also reflect an individual's personal tolerance for frustrating or stressful behavior. Individuals vary with regard to the degree to which they can tolerate stressful situations (Simons & Gaher, 2005) and those with a high tolerance may not be especially bothered by their partner's irritating behavior and, consequently, they see no reason to confront him or her.

It is possible that withholding because a problem is not important may be functional for a relationship. Research suggests that arguing over minor issues is negatively correlated with relational satisfaction (e.g., Cramer,

2002) and, as a result, individuals who withhold minor complaints may be better able to maintain satisfaction than can those who confront them. Indeed, there is some evidence that individuals in long-term marriages tend to avoid conflicts unless the issue is important (Zietlow & Sillars, 1988). Furthermore, individuals who have a more traditional view of marriage often engage in a mixture of avoidance and confrontation that are used selectively depending on the importance of the issue (Fitzpatrick, 1988).

Although not confronting minor problems could be functional in the short term, it may prove to be maladaptive in the long term. If not confronted, minor irritations may continue or possibly increase in frequency. If so, they may eventually overwhelm a person's ability to reduce their importance. With increasing frustration, an angry confrontation may occur, which the partner views as an overreaction to a trivial issue (Baumeister, Stillwell, & Wotman, 1990).

Negative Consequences Are Feared

Not all individuals react positively when confronted about their behavior. Upon being confronted with a personal complaint, individuals may respond aggressively (Stamp, Vangelisti, & Daly, 1992). Therefore, some individuals withhold complaints so as to avoid those negative consequences. Cloven and Roloff (1994b) found some people reported that they feared that a confrontation would make their partners angry, create a conflict, and harm the relationship. Hence, withholding complaints is functional because it allows the withholder to avoid negative personal and relational outcomes. This function is similar to the instrumental function underlying some attitudes (Katz, 1960). Individuals like things that allow them to gain rewards and avoid punishments.

Fear of consequences could result from at least two sources. First, individuals may believe that a complaint is a "hot-button" topic for the partner and angry reactions could occur. For example, Cloven and Roloff (1993) found that individuals anticipated that their partners might react with symbolic or physical aggression to a complaint about the partner's controlling behavior, but not to other types of complaints (e.g., lack of affection or respect). Second, when a partner is perceived to have excellent relational alternatives, an individual may fear that as a result of the confrontation the partner might leave the relationship for a better one (e.g., Roloff & Cloven, 1990).

In some cases, withholding complaints because of anticipated negative reactions may be well founded. Individuals who are fearful of a partner's negative verbal and physical reactions often have experienced similar reactions from him or her in the past (Cloven & Roloff, 1993). Gelles and Straus (1988) found that abused wives tried to avoid discussing topics with their husbands that had previously prompted physical attacks. Moreover, partners with excellent relational alternatives sometimes are not strongly committed to the relationship and prone to exit when dissatisfied (Rusbult,

Johnson, & Morrow, 1986). Indeed, when spouses have good alternatives, they are more likely to divorce (South & Lloyd, 1995).

Although fear of consequences may be a veridical assessment, it is possible that this motive could become dysfunctional in the long term. For example, Roloff, Soule, and Carey (2001) found among individuals who discovered their romantic partner had committed a relational transgression that there exists a positive relationship between choosing to remain in the relationship because of a fear of losing him or her and not confronting the partner about the transgression. Apparently, avoidance proved to be ineffective. Staying because of fear was negatively related to reports that the partner's behavior improved and positively related to reporting that the relationship eventually ended because of the transgression.

Self-Image Would Be Damaged

Some individuals avoid confronting their partners because they perceive that the confrontation would reflect poorly on their image, often noting that they do not want to be perceived as immature, selfish, overbearing, jealous, cheap, or materialistic (Cloven & Roloff, 1994b). Individuals are aware of the potential impressions they create through their communication, and conflict avoidance allows them to avoid creating undesirable images. Katz (1960) noted that some attitudes serve an ego-defensive function such that an attitude allows an individual to mask or avoid acknowledging something negative about oneself. In some cases, this could involve withholding information. For example, some individuals report that they withhold information from their relational partners so that they can maintain their partner's positive impression of them (Metts, 1989).

There is evidence that confronting someone can project a negative image. Confrontation is a form of assertiveness in which a person defends or exerts his or her rights or interests (Lorr & More, 1980). Sometimes assertive behavior, especially behavior that involves expressing negative statements like a disagreement, is seen as socially inappropriate (Wilson & Gallois, 1985). Consequently, individuals who are assertive are sometimes perceived to be more unlikable and inconsiderate than are those who are unassertive (Lowe & Storm, 1986). Furthermore, sometimes individuals delay confronting another until they are very angry, which causes the target of their anger to perceive them as being out of control and overreacting (Baumeister et al., 1990).

When acting in an avoidant fashion, however, individuals may sacrifice the positive impressions arising from acting assertively, which could lead to long-term problems. Assertive individuals often are perceived by others to be competent (Delamater & McNamara, 1986). They express their viewpoints and are willing to stand up for their rights. In contrast, an avoider could appear to be passive, indifferent, or incompetent to his or her partner. If so, the partner of a conflict-avoidant person may acquire greater relational power and may treat the avoidant person in a relatively disparaging manner that eventually becomes humiliating. To restore his or her image, an avoidant person may eventually react aggressively to a partner's behavior (e.g., Bentley, Galliher, & Ferguson, 2007).

Communication Is Futile

Some individuals engage in conflict avoidance because they believe that confrontation will not be effective. Cloven and Roloff (1994b) found that some withholders reported that their partners would not change, could not change, and stonewalled their complaints in the past. Indeed, some spouses report that their partners simply will not change (Eidelson & Epstein, 1982) and some individuals resist influence attempts by others to change their behaviors (e.g., Tucker & Mueller, 2000; Tucker, Orlando, Elliott, & Klein, 2006). Hence, conflict avoidance is an adaptive response to failure. Unlike withholding because of fear of negative consequences, this reason suggests that individuals withhold because confrontation would simply not work and, hence, would be a waste of time.

Withholding because communication is futile may reflect both outcome expectations and self-efficacy. Makoul and Roloff (1993) found that withholding relational complaints was positively related to believing that a confrontation would not successfully change the partner's behavior and feelings that one could not effectively enact a confrontation. These patterns could lead to a self-fulfilling prophecy. The withholder feels that he or she cannot be confrontational and, hence, avoids it. In turn, his or her partner may feel empowered by the lack of resistance, acts independently of the withholder, and further reinforces the withholder's self-view that he or she cannot successfully confront. Hence, the responsibility for failure may reside in both the partner and one's own self-confidence about being confrontational.

Believing that confronting the partner will be ineffective may be accurate. Indeed, some individuals try to avoid being influenced by their partners (Belk & Snell, 1988) and some interpersonal disagreements appear to be intractable (see Miller, Roloff, & Malis, 2007). To reduce the occurrence and negative effects of arguing, some individuals find it useful to declare problematic issues off the table for discussion (Baxter & Wilmot, 1985; Roloff & Ifert, 1998), at least until they can be safely reintroduced (Roloff & Johnson, 2001).

As with many other reasons for avoidance, it is possible that withholding because of the futility of communication may be dysfunctional in the long term. It is possible that circumstances change and communicating about the problem becomes effective (Roloff & Johnson, 2001). Hence, avoidant individuals miss the opportunity to resolve the issue. Moreover, a partner's unwillingness to change may signal a lack of regard for an individual's opinions, and this disrespect may reduce relational satisfaction. Although research does not identify the underlying cause, reporting a partner will not change is negatively related to relational satisfaction (Eidelson & Epstein, 1982).

Relationship Is Nonintimate

Cloven and Roloff (1994b) discovered that some individuals withheld complaints because they had only been involved in their relationship for a short time; they were not really close with their partner and/or felt that to ask the partner to change would be asking too much from the relationship. This reason implies that a certain level of intimacy must be reached before one can confront another. The notion that open communication increases with relational intimacy is not new. Altman and Taylor (1973) characterized the development of relational intimacy as a process by which individuals gradually disclose personal information to each other. Relatively superficial information is disclosed early in the relationship with more individualized information expressed later. The willingness to disclose complaints seems to follow a similar process. Cloven and Roloff (1994a) found that the proportion of withheld relational complaints was most common in newly formed relationships and in relationships at low and moderate levels of intimacy. Moreover, this pattern of withholding was positively related to reporting that the relationship was insufficiently intimate. Although the length of a relationship should make it less likely that withholding results from the nonintimate nature of the relationship, this may not always be true. If one views intimacy as a relational quality reflecting feelings of closeness, it is possible that an established couple could fall out of love, quit sharing information, and essentially become less intimate than they initially were. In such cases, they may start anew withholding complaints because the relationship is not sufficiently intimate.

The notion that disclosure is tied to relational intimacy may result from several sources. First, relational rules and expectations may play a role. Research indicates that people expect communication to be more open in intimate than nonintimate relationships (Knapp, Ellis, & Williams, 1980). The ability to express complaints may be more expected and appropriate in intimate than nonintimate relationships. Hence, conflict avoidance may serve a social adjustment function (Katz, 1960) as individuals conform to social norms. Second, this pattern may reflect relational uncertainty. Some individuals report that they and their partners are uncertain about the relationship and this assessment mediates the relationship between intimacy and the number of topics that daters avoided discussing (Knobloch & Carpenter-Theune, 2004).

Expressing criticism early in a relationship may indeed be harmful. Research indicates that even on the first date individuals expect that they will get to know and evaluate each other (Rose & Frieze, 1993) and will engage in behavior designed to impress one another (Rose & Frieze, 1989). Furthermore, individuals expect that good dates more so than bad ones involve positive experiences, such as being with someone who has similar interests and who compliments them, smiles a great deal, and listens to them (Alksnis, Desmaris, & Wood, 1996). Hence, to complain about another's action in initial stages of dating could be a violation of expectations and bring the relationship to a quick close.

However, the long-term impact of waiting to confront problems may be negative. Avoidance may create an illusion of harmony that may be doomed to fail. Once the relationship becomes sufficiently intimate, a confrontation will occur and a couple may have their first big fight (Siegert & Stamp, 1994). That argument may violate expectations. After all, there was little fighting in the early stages of the relationship and the aggravated partner never complained about the behavior before. This could lead to feelings that the partner changed and the relationship is no longer satisfying (Lloyd & Cate, 1985).

Complaining Is Illegitimate

Individuals have a desire to maintain their decision freedom and often resist when their decision freedom is threatened (Brehm, 1966). Consequently, communicators often adjust their behavior so as to avoid direct challenges to another's autonomy (Brown & Levinson, 1987). Confrontations are especially problematic because they implicitly or explicitly demand a partner do something about his or her unacceptable behavior. Some individuals report that they avoid confronting their relational partners because they do not believe that complaining is legitimate. They make statements such as "I have no right to tell my partner what do to" and "I feel like it's none of my business" (Cloven & Roloff, 1993). These statements imply a value-expressive function (Katz, 1960) in that individuals seem to hold a belief about the appropriateness of confronting others.

Feeling that complaining is legitimate could reflect personal beliefs about an issue. Malis and Roloff (2007) found that believing that personal health lifestyle is a matter of personal choice is negatively related to the legitimacy of confronting another about his or her alcohol problems. In addition, legitimacy could stem from a person's relational orientation. Some individuals approach relationships with a communal orientation in which they believe that they should take care of another who will do the same for them. Individuals who have such an orientation believe that they have a legitimate right to confront another about his or her unhealthy behavior, which of course implies that those who do not share this outlook tend to feel that confrontations are illegitimate (Reznik & Roloff, 2007).

Establishing legitimacy is vital to successfully influencing others. Klein and Lamm (1996) found that, when feeling legitimate, individuals are more willing to express their complaints to partners and their partners are more willing to listen to their complaints when they judge them to be legitimate. Both self-expression and listening facilitate resolving relational problems.

Withholding due to lack of legitimacy implies that a level of tolerance must exist. One must accept another's problematic behavior simply because of a lack of right to confront it. Indeed, Gottman (1994) observed that avoidant couples seem to be very tolerant of their differences and are willing to let each person behave in his or her own way. It is possible that, over time, such tolerance may wane, with growing frustration and irritation overwhelming restraint. There is some evidence that tolerance of one's spouse declines over the course of marriage (Swensen, Eskew, & Kohlhepp, 1981) and, although spouses in mature marriages have few conflicts, those conflicts that are unresolved prompt reciprocal patterns of confrontation (Zietlow & Sillars, 1988).

Indirect Communication Is Preferred

Directly confronting a partner is not the only way to express one's discontent and some individuals report that their withholding reflects a desire to be indirect. Cloven and Roloff (1994b) found that some individuals reported that they withheld complaints because the problem should be obvious to the partner, the partner can see how frustrated they are about the problem, and they have joked and teased the partner about the problem. Relative to the reasons discussed so far, this one indicates that individuals who are withholding are actually engaging the partner, albeit in an indirect way.

Indirect grievance relay could stem from several sources. First, some individuals believe in mindreading in that they think their partners should understand their needs and concerns without having to tell them (Eidelson & Epstein, 1982). Such individuals often communicate their dissatisfaction via the silent treatment. The silent treatment involves the enactment of behaviors that intentionally signal disapproval of another by acting aloof in his or her presence (Williams, 2001). Although it can take a wide variety of forms, the silent treatment most often involves reduced eye contact and being nonresponsive to another's comments or actions (Williams, 2001). Furthermore, when asked by their partner whether they are upset, they respond by stonewalling or admonishing the partner for asking (Wright & Roloff, 2007).

Second, preference for indirectness could reflect a desire to find a "softer" and more playful way to confront the partner by using humor and teasing. Kowalski, Howerton, and McKenzie (2001) conceptualize teasing as "identity confrontation couched in humor" (p. 178). In effect, teasing highlights something about another that is deviant, but does so in a way that is not overtly offensive. Although teasing can be motivated by antisocial motivations (e.g., wanting to hurt another), prosocial (or positive) teasing can afford individuals the ability to confront another with potentially face-threatening information in a manner that is playful and affectionate rather than malicious. Prosocial teasing is high in humor, low in ambiguity, and medium in identity confrontation (Kowalski et al., 2001; cf. Shapiro, Baumeister, & Kessler, 1991). The humor and reduced uncertainty in the meaning of good-natured provocations highlight the playful and friendly elements in prosocial teasing. Although there is identity confrontation, as there is in all teasing (Alberts, Kellar-Guenther, & Corman, 1996; Keltner, Capps, Kring, Yang, & Heerey, 2001), the potential face threat within such teasing is attenuated by the humor. Humor could lessen the target's perception that he or she is being insulted and that also makes the teaser appear to be less insensitive and rude.

Such indirect approaches to confrontations can be useful. For example, teasing provides an outlet for individuals to express negative and/or personally sensitive commentary that they would normally steer clear of communicating (Kowalski et al., 2001). In addition, Alberts (1990) found that adjusted married couples often terminate their conflicts through the use of humor, and Driver and Gottman (2004) found a positive relationship between the degree to which a couple enacted humor during a conflict and the wife's subsequent affection for her husband.

Nevertheless, indirect approaches to confrontations can also be dysfunctional. Research on the silent treatment indicates that it is cognitively taxing to the person using it and negatively impacts the target (Williams, 2001). Moreover, the impact of humor depends on the motive the target attributes to the user. When humor is perceived to be internally motivated, its impact on conflict is negative (Bippus, 2003). Moreover, humor may take a variety of forms such as sarcasm (e.g., Beatty & Dobos, 1993) and ridicule (e.g., Janes & Olson, 2000) that can be hurtful. In addition, although prosocial teasing is positively correlated with relational satisfaction, couples who break up report more prosocial teasing than do those who stay together (Keltner, Young, Heerey, Oemig, & Monarch, 1998). Finally, indirect forms of confrontation may be misperceived. Prosocial teasing is sometimes mistaken for antisocial teasing (e.g., Wright, 2008) and Newell and Stutman (1989/90) found that indirect forms of confrontations are not accurately understood by the target person to be a complaint.

Situation Inhibits Communication

Withholding sometimes stems from not having found an appropriate time to confront the partner. For example, individuals note that withholding complaints results from having busy schedules, an opportunity has not presented itself, and they have not yet figured out what to say (Cloven & Roloff, 1994b). These reasons imply that avoidance is only a temporary response to conflict. Once the appropriate situation presents itself and/or the person formulates a strategy, then confrontation will occur.

Situational inhibition may result from several factors. On one hand, it may stem from a desire to avoid confronting someone until a person has a clear notion of what to do. Witteman (1988) noted that interpersonal problems are often complex and individuals are uncertain about how to resolve them. Consequently, they often try to suspend conflicts by saying they are too tired to discuss the issue, they do not feel like talking about it, or, if they wait, the problem may resolve itself (Witteman, 1988). Alternatively, situational inhibition may result from waiting until the partner is in a better mood. Discussing an issue when an individual is stressed due to other responsibilities could make an effective resolution less likely. Witteman (1988) found that some individuals reported that they avoided confrontation until the partner was in a good mood or that they put them in a good mood before confronting them.

Delaying a confrontation may be useful. Individuals who rehearse prior to a confrontation report greater success in achieving both strategic and performance goals (Stutman & Newell, 1990). Furthermore, waiting for a partner's mood to improve might be useful. Individuals who are in a bad mood relative to those in a good mood respond more negatively to requests and especially to those they consider impolite (Forgas, 1998). Finally, waiting for a less busy time to initiate a confrontation may avoid problems associated with mental fatigue. Individuals who work harried schedules often have difficulty focusing their attention (Akerstedt et al., 2004). This mental fatigue increases irritability and impulsiveness that can stimulate aggression (see Kuo & Sullivan, 2001).

At the same time, delaying a confrontation may be dysfunctional if it prompts intense rumination or mulling about the provocation. Individuals who ruminate about a situation that made them angry are less forgiving and have more thoughts of seeking revenge long after the incident has occurred than are those who avoid thinking about it (Barber, Maltby, & Macaskill, 2005). Hence, for some people, delaying a confrontation may make the situation worse.

Implications

We acknowledge that our exercise in demonstrating the utility of a functional approach is limited by the post hoc nature of our analysis. None of the studies cited in our chapter were designed to test a functional approach and, thus, the methods and results may not fit exactly with the assumptions of functionalism. Furthermore, the Cloven and Roloff (1994b) sample was composed of undergraduate daters who were mostly White and from the United States. As a result, we cannot attest to the generalizability of the reasons that were generated. However, we do believe that several useful insights emerged from our analysis. Specifically, we believe the results link well with other research on topic avoidance and suggest a framework for studying conflict avoidance. We discuss each below.

Links to Topic Avoidance

One primary insight is that some of the reasons for withholding complaints are similar to those found in other research on topic avoidance, among which some were generated from more diverse samples. For example, based upon reasons reported by young adults for avoiding certain topics with their parents (Golish & Caughlin, 2002; Guerrero & Afifi, 1995), Caughlin and Afifi (2004) created a scale focused on six reasons for avoiding topics, four of which are similar to reasons reported by Cloven and Roloff (1994b). The first is self-protection, which combines a portion of the fear of consequences (i.e., fear of partner's negative response) with loss of self-image reasons. The second was relationship protection, which is similar to the portion of the fear of negative consequences reason that is focused on relational harm. The third was partner unresponsiveness that is similar to communication is futile. The fourth was lack of closeness, which seems parallel to withholding because the relationship is nonintimate. Finally, Caughlin and Afifi's notion of conflict avoidance is reflected in the fear of negative consequences arising from the partner's response.

Although observed by Caughlin and Afifi (2004), privacy concerns were not reported by participants in Cloven and Roloff's study as a reason for withholding. It is possible that this stems from Caughlin and Afifi's broader focus on topic avoidance. In their study, some of the topics that were not discussed included the respondent's own behavior (e.g., dating, sex) that would make privacy concerns (e.g., "I want to keep my privacy") critical. However, Cloven and Roloff studied a partner's irritating behavior, which may make an individual less concerned about his or her own privacy.

Cloven and Roloff (1994b) discovered four reasons for withholding irritations that were not part of Caughlin and Afifi's measure: the problem is unimportant, complaining is illegitimate, indirect communication is preferred, and the situation inhibits communication. The first three reasons may also reflect our focus on confrontations. Newell and Stutman (1991) found that individuals often report that they confront another because of urgency (i.e., the problem is important) and because they have a right to confront the other person. They also note that individuals often struggle with decisions about how directly they should confront the person and identifying the appropriate situation in which to do so.

Another significant insight is that the reasons for withholding shed light on the decisions to avoid conflict. Withholding complaints because of fear of negative consequences and the perception that the problem is unimportant implies that decisions to withhold complaints may reflect a trade-off between the negative consequences arising from the partner's irritating behavior and the negative consequences that might occur as a result of confronting the partner about it. In addition, withholding because the relationship is nonintimate and the situation inhibits communication implies that conflict avoidance may be a temporary rather than permanent action. When a relationship becomes more intimate or the situation changes, then presumably a person will confront his or her partner. Finally, withholding because indirect communication is preferred suggests that some people withhold a direct complaint but signal dissatisfaction in a more indirect fashion.

Framework for Understanding Conflict Avoidance

Our functional approach suggests the following set of propositions that provide an explanation why conflict occurs as well as its consequences: First, individuals hold beliefs about the relative efficacy and appropriateness of confronting versus avoiding conflict. Unfortunately, research does not inform us as to the origins of these beliefs. It seems likely that they result from personal experiences with being confrontational/avoidant, observation of others being confrontational/avoidant, and/or advice from others about being confrontational/avoidant. It may also be the case that these beliefs are indirectly influenced by one's genetic background. Some research indicates that temperament (e.g., anger proneness) may be inherited and influences aggressive attitudes and actions (e.g., Cates et al., 1993). If so, individuals who have a passive temperament may be inclined to develop beliefs supporting less overtly aggressive actions like avoidance.

Our second proposition holds that, as long as personal experiences affirm individuals' beliefs that conflict avoidance is more effective and appropriate than confrontation, they use these beliefs to justify their preference for avoidance. Essentially, these reasons allow an individual to maintain a stable pattern of avoidance, which may become a conflict management style. This raises an interesting question for future research concerning the degree to which individuals are willing to express their reasons when confronted about their nonconfrontational style. In other words, do these reasons remain private and if so why? Perhaps providing reasons for conflict-avoidant behavior could indeed lead to conflict if others disagree with them. Hence, individuals may choose not to disclose their reasons when confronted. If the reasons remain private, they also could make it difficult for relational partners or therapists to change a person's avoidant behavior.

The third proposition states that, because reasons for withholding are grounded in individual experiences, conflict avoidance may be perceived as functional by the individual and he or she is motivated to be avoidant rather than confrontational. Functions can serve as the basis for motivations. Motivations energize the individual to take action or, in this case, inaction. In addition, the notion that reasons are grounded in individual experiences leaves open the possibility that two persons may have different experiences and, hence, they may not share the same reasons for withholding and not agree that avoidance is functional. For example, one relational partner may withhold a complaint because it is perceived to be unimportant but the other disagrees and feels that the complaint is of major concern. Two individuals may differ with regard to how intimate their relationship is and, consequently, one may be withholding complaints until the relationship is perceived to be closer, whereas the other is actively disclosing complaints. Moreover, one partner may believe that it is essential to be clear and direct with complaints, whereas the other feels that complaining in an indirect fashion is a better approach.

Finally, when circumstances change, a justification for avoidance may no longer be perceived as valid, and avoidance may be perceived as dysfunctional. In such cases, an individual may choose to confront problems. It is critical that researchers identify the conditions that produce these changes. We suggested some conditions in our earlier analyses. However, we also wonder whether a key factor might be the frequency with which avoidance is used. When avoidance is rarely used, individuals may form a combative union that could become problematic. For example, Gottman (1994) identified some marriages in which both parties are extremely confrontational, but because they perform many positive behaviors, they offset negative byproducts arising from frequent arguing. At the same time, he also notes that such volatile marriages could become hostile and pathological if spouses are unable to control their conflicts or cannot repair it. On the other hand, when avoidance becomes the predominant form of conflict management, relational problems may grow or the relationship will lack emotional vitality. Gottman noted that some avoidant couples seemed to lack conflict management skills and often were emotionally flat (i.e., they rarely became angry or happy). Consistent with the old phrase "moderation in all things," we may find that a moderate and selective use of avoidance may be the best approach.

These propositions provide unique insights into conflict avoidance. Too often, conflict avoidance has been viewed as a passive, powerless response to relationship problems. Although it may be just that for some individuals, a functional approach suggests that conflict avoidance is used to serve a variety of functions. These functions imply that conflict avoidance is often an adaptive response to the negative features of confrontation and conflict, and research suggests that, under some circumstances, conflict avoidance may actually achieve the functions for which it was intended. However, our analysis also indicates that, under some circumstances, conflict avoidance may become dysfunctional and becomes a maladaptive sequence. We intended this chapter to have heuristic value rather than to provide a definitive account of conflict avoidance. Therefore, we believe it is essential that the speculation arising from our functional analysis be directly tested rather than accepted on its face.

References

Afifi, W. A., & Guerrero, L. K. (2000). Motivation underlying topic avoidance in close relationships. In S. Petronio (Ed.), *Balancing the secrets of private disclosures* (pp. 166–179). Mahwah, NJ: Erlbaum.

Akerstedt, T., Knutsson, A., Westerholm, P., Theorell, T., Alfredsson, L., & Kecklund, G. (2004). Mental fatigue, work and sleep: Stress, fibromyalgia and sleep. *Journal of Psychosomatic Research, 57*, 427–433.

Alberts, J. K. (1990). The use of humor in managing couples' conflict interactions. In D. D. Cahn (Ed.), *Intimates in conflict: A communication perspective* (pp. 105–120). Hillsdale, NJ: Erlbaum.

Alberts, J. K., Kellar-Guenther, Y., & Corman, S. R. (1996). That's not funny: Understanding recipients' responses to teasing. *Western Journal of Communication, 60*, 337–357.

Alberts, J. K., Yoshimura, C. G., Rabby, M., & Loschiavo, R. (2005). Mapping the topography of couples' daily conversation. *Journal of Social and Personal Relationships, 22*, 299–322.

Alksnis, C., Desmaris, S., & Wood, E. (1996). Gender differences in scripts for different types of dates. *Sex Roles, 34*, 321–336.

Altman, I., & Taylor, D. A. (1973). *Social penetration: The development of interpersonal relationships.* New York: Holt, Rinehart, & Winston.

Barber, L., Maltby, J., & Macaskill, A. (2005). Angry memories and thoughts of revenge: The relationship between forgiveness and anger rumination. *Personality and Individual Differences, 39*, 253–262.

Baumeister, R. F., Stillwell, A., & Wotman, S. R. (1990). Victim and perpetrator accounts of interpersonal conflict: Autobiographical narratives about anger. *Journal of Personality and Social Psychology, 59*, 994–1005.

Baxter, L. A., & Wilmot, W. W. (1985). Taboo topics in close relationships. *Journal of Social and Personal Relationships, 2*, 253–269.

Beatty, M. J., & Dobos, J. A. (1993). Direct and mediated effects of perceived father criticism and sarcasm on females' perceptions of relational partners' disconfirming behavior. *Communication Quarterly, 41*, 187–197.

Belk, S. S., & Snell, Jr., W. E. (1988). Avoidance strategy use in intimate relationships. *Journal of Social and Clinical Psychology, 7*, 80–96.

Benoit, W. J., & Benoit, P. J. (1987). Everyday argument practices of naive social actors. In J. W. Wentzel (Ed.), *Argument and critical practices* (pp. 465–473). Annandale, VA: Speech Communication Association.

Bentley, C. G., Galliher, R. V., & Ferguson, T. J. (2007). Associations among aspects of interpersonal power and relationship functioning in adolescent romantic couples. *Sex Roles, 57*, 483–495.

Bippus, A. M. (2003). Humor motives, qualities, and reactions in recalled conflict episodes. *Western Journal of Communication, 67*, 413–426.

Birchler, G. R., Weiss, R. L., & Vincent, J. P. (1975). Multimethod analysis of social reinforcement exchange between maritally distress and nondistressed spouse and stranger dyads. *Journal of Personality and Social Psychology, 31*, 349–360.

Bolger, N., DeLongis, A., Kessler, R. C., & Wethington, E. (1989). The contagion of stress across multiple roles. *Journal of Marriage and the Family, 51*, 175–183.

Brehm, J. W. (1966). *A theory of psychological reactance.* New York: Academic Press.

Brown, P., & Levinson, S. C. (1987). *Politeness: Some universals in language usage.* Cambridge: Cambridge University Press.

Cates, D. S., Houston, B. K., Christine, R., Vavak, C. R., Crawford, M. H., & Uttley, M. (1993). Heritability of hostility-related emotions, attitudes, and behaviors. *Journal of Behavioral Medicine, 16*, 237–256.

Caughlin, J. P., & Afifi, T. D. (2004). When is conflict avoidance unsatisfying? Examining moderators between avoidance and dissatisfaction. *Human Communication Research, 30*, 479–513.

Cloven, D. H., & Roloff, M. E. (1993). The chilling effect of aggressive potential on the expression of complaints in intimate relationships. *Communication Monographs, 60*, 199–219.

Cloven, D. H., & Roloff, M. E. (1994a). A developmental model of decisions to withhold relational irritations in romantic relationships. *Personal Relationships, 1*, 143–164.

Cloven, D. H., & Roloff, M. E. (1994b, July). *Conflict avoidance in personal relationships: An examination of motives.* Paper presented at the annual convention of the International Communication Association, Sydney, Australia.

Cramer, D. (2002). Relationship satisfaction and conflict over minor and major issues in romantic relationships. *Journal of Psychology, 136,* 75–81.

Dahrendorf, R. (1958). Out of utopia: Toward a reorientation of sociological analysis. *The American Journal of Sociology, 64,* 115–127.

Delamater, R. J., & McNamara, J. R. (1986). The social impact of assertiveness: Research findings and clinical implications. *Behavior Modification, 10,* 139–158.

Delamater, R. J., & McNamara, J. R. (1991). Perceptions of assertiveness by women involved in a conflict situation. *Behavior Modification, 15,* 173–193.

Deutsch, M. (1973). *The resolution of conflict: Constructive and destructive processes.* New Haven, CT: Yale University Press.

Driver, J. L., & Gottman, J. M. (2004). Daily marital interactions and positive affect during marital conflict among newlywed couples. *Family Process, 43,* 301–314.

Eidelson, R. J., & Epstein, M. (1982). Cognition and relationship maladjustment: Development of a measure of dysfunctional relationship beliefs. *Journal of Consulting and Clinical Psychology, 50,* 715–720.

Fitzpatrick, M. A. (1988). *Between husbands and wives: Communication in marriage.* Thousand Oaks, CA: Sage.

Forgas, J. P. (1998). Asking nicely? The effects of mood on responding to more or less polite requests. *Personality and Social Psychology Bulletin, 24,* 173–185.

Gelles, R. J., & Straus, M. A. (1988). *Intimate violence.* New York: Simon & Schuster.

Golish, T. D., & Caughlin, J. P. (2002). I'd rather not talk about it: Adolescents' and young adults' use of topic avoidance in stepfamilies. *Journal of Applied Communication Research, 30,* 78–106.

Gottman, J. M. (1994). *What predicts divorce: The relationship between marital processes and marital outcomes.* Hillsdale, NJ: LEA.

Guerrero, L. K., & Afifi, W. A. (1995). Some things are better left unsaid: Topic avoidance in family relationships. *Communication Quarterly, 43,* 276–296.

Janes, L. M., & Olson, J. M. (2000). Jeer pressure: The behavioral effects of observing ridicule of others. *Personality and Social Psychology Bulletin, 26,* 474–485.

Katz, D. (1960). The functional approach to the study of attitudes. *Public Opinion Quarterly, 24,* 163–204.

Keltner, D., Capps, L., Kring, A. M., Young, R. C., & Heerey, E. A. (2001). Just teasing: A conceptual analysis and empirical review. *Psychological Bulletin, 127,* 229–248.

Keltner, D., Young, R. C., Heerey, E. A., Oemig, C., & Monarch, N. D. (1998). Teasing in hierarchical and intimate relations. *Journal of Personality and Social Psychology, 75,* 1231–1247.

Kirchler, E. (1988). Marital happiness and interaction in everyday surroundings: A time-sample diary approach for couples. *Journal of Social and Personal Relationships, 5,* 275–382.

Klein, R. C. A., & Lamm, H. (1996). Legitimate interest in couple conflict. *Journal of Social and Personal Relationships, 13,* 619–626.

Knapp, M. L., Ellis, D. G., & Williams, B. A. (1980). Perceptions of communication behavior associated with relationship terms. *Communication Monographs, 47,* 262–278.

Knobloch, L. K., & Carpenter-Theune, K. E. (2004). Topic avoidance in developing romantic relationships: Associations with intimacy and relational uncertainty. *Communication Research, 31,* 173–204.

Kowalski, R. M., Howerton, E., & McKenzie, M. (2001). Permitted disrespect: Teasing in interpersonal interactions. In R. M. Kowalski (Ed.), *Behaving badly: Aversive behaviors in interpersonal relationships* (pp. 177–202). Washington, DC: American Psychological Association.

Kuo, F. E., & Sullivan, W. C. (2001). Aggression and violence in the inner city: Effects of environment via mental fatigue. *Environment and Behavior, 33,* 543–571.

Levin, R. B., & Gross, A. M. (1987). Assertiveness style: Effects on perceptions of assertive behavior. *Behavior Modification, 11,* 229–240.

Lloyd, S. A., & Cate, R. C. (1985). Attributions associated with significant turning points in premarital relationship development and dissolution. *Journal of Social and Personal Relationships, 2,* 419–436.

Lorr, M., & More, W. M. (1980). Four dimensions of assertiveness. *Multivariate Behavioral Research, 2,* 127–138.

Lowe, M. R., & Storm, M. A. (1986). Being assertive or being liked: A genuine dilemma? *Behavior Modification, 10,* 371–390.

Makoul, G., & Roloff, M. E. (1993). The role of efficacy and outcome expectations in the decision to withhold relational complaints. *Communication Research, 25,* 5–29.

Malis, R., & Roloff, M. E. (2007). The effect of legitimacy and intimacy on peer intervention into alcohol abuse. *Western Journal of Communication, 71,* 49–68.

McCorkle, S., & Mills, J. L. (1992). Rowboat in a hurricane: Metaphors of interpersonal conflict management. *Communication Reports, 5,* 57–66.

McGonagle, K. A., Kessler, R. C., & Schilling, E. A. (1992). The frequency and determinants of marital disagreements in a community sample. *Journal of Social and Personal Relationships, 9,* 507–524.

Metts, S. (1989). An exploratory investigation of deception in close relationships. *Journal of Social and Personal Relationships, 6,* 159–179.

Miller, C. W., Roloff, M. E., & Malis, R. S. (2007). Understanding interpersonal conflicts that are difficult to resolve: A review of literature and presentation of an integrated model. In C. S. Beck (Ed.), *Communication yearbook 31* (pp. 118–173). Mahwah, NJ: Erlbaum.

Miller, R. S. (1997). We always hurt the ones we love. In R. M. Kowalski (Ed.), *Aversive interpersonal behaviors* (pp. 11–29). New York: Plenum.

Newell, S. E., & Stutman, R. K. (1989/90). Negotiating confrontation: The problematic nature of initiation and response. *Research on Language and Social Interaction, 23,* 139–162.

Newell, S. E., & Stutman, R. K. (1991). The episodic nature of social confrontation. In J. A. Anderson (Ed.), *Communication yearbook 14* (pp. 359–413). Thousand Oaks, CA: Sage.

Reznik, R. M., & Roloff, M. E. (2007, November). *The role of legitimacy and communal orientation on the use of health influence strategies.* Paper presented at the annual convention of the National Communication Association, Chicago, IL.

Rioux, S. M., & Penner, L. A. (2001). The causes of organizational citizenship behavior: A motivational analysis. *Journal of Applied Psychology, 86,* 1306–1314.

Roloff, M. E., & Cloven, D. H. (1990). The chilling effect in interpersonal relationships: The reluctance to speak one's mind. In D. H. Cahn (Ed.), *Intimates in conflict: A communication perspective* (pp. 49–76). Hillsdale, NJ: LEA.

Roloff, M. E., & Ifert, D. E. (1998). Antecedents and consequences of explicit agreements to declare a topic taboo in dating relationships. *Personal Relationships, 5,* 191–206.

Roloff, M. E., & Ifert, D. E. (2000). Conflict management through avoidance: Withholding complaints, suppressing arguments and declaring topics taboo. In S. Petronio (Ed.), *Balancing the secrets of private disclosures* (pp. 151–164). Mahwah, NJ: Erlbaum.

Roloff, M. E., & Johnson, D. I. (2001). Reintroducing taboo topics: Antecedents and consequences of putting topics back on the table. *Communication Studies, 52,* 37–50.

Roloff, M. E., & Reznik, R. M. (2008). Communication during serial arguments. In M. T. Motely (Ed.), *Studies in applied interpersonal communication* (pp. 97–120). Thousand Oaks, CA: Sage.

Roloff, M. E., & Solomon, D. H. (2002). Conditions under which relational commitment leads to expressing relational complaints. *International Journal for Conflict Management, 13,* 276–291.

Roloff, M. E., Soule, K. P., & Carey, C. M. (2001). Reasons for remaining in a relationship and responses to relational transactions. *Journal of Social and Personal Relationships, 18,* 362–385.

Rose, S., & Frieze, I. H. (1989). Young singles' scripts for a first date. *Gender and Society, 3,* 258–268.

Rose, S., & Frieze, I. H. (1993). Young singles' contemporary dating scripts. *Sex Roles, 28,* 499–509.

Rusbult, C. E., Johnson, D. J., & Morrow, G. D. (1986). Determinants and consequences of exit, voice, loyalty, and neglect: Responses to dissatisfaction in adult romantic involvements. *Human Relations, 39,* 45–63.

Scanzoni, J. (1978). *Sex roles, women's work, and marital conflict.* Lexington, MA: Lexington Books.

Siegert, J. R., & Stamp, G. H. (1994). "Our first big fight" as a milestone in the development of close relationships. *Communication Monographs, 61,* 345–360.

Shapiro, J. P., Baumeister, R. F., & Kessler, J. W. (1991). A three-component model of children's teasing: Aggression, humor, and ambiguity. *Journal of Social and Clinical Psychology, 10,* 459–472.

Sillars, A. L., Coletti, S. F., Parry, D., & Rogers, M. A. (1982). Coding verbal conflict tactics: Nonverbal and perceptual correlates of the "avoidance-distributive-integrative" distinction. *Human Communication Research, 9,* 83–95.

Simons, J. S., & Gaher, R. M. (2005). The distress tolerance scale: Development and validation of a self-report measure. *Motivation and Emotion, 29,* 83–102.

Snyder, M. (1992). Motivational foundations of behavioral confirmation. In M. P. Zanna (Ed.), *Advances in experimental social psychology* (Vol. 25, pp. 67–113). Orlando, FL: Academic Press.

Snyder, M. (1993). Basic research and practical problems: The promise of a "functional" personality and social psychology. *Personality and Social Psychology Bulletin, 19,* 251–264.

South, S. T., & Lloyd, K. M. (1995). Spousal alternatives and marital dissolution. *American Sociological Review, 60,* 21–35.

Stamp, G. H., Vangelisti, A. L., & Daly, J. A. (1992). The creation of defensiveness in social interaction. *Communication Quarterly, 40,* 177–190.

Stutman, R. K., & Newell, S. E. (1990). Rehearsing for confrontation. *Argumentation, 4,* 185–198.

Swensen, C. H., Eskew, R. W., & Kohlhepp, K. A. (1981). Stage of family life cycle, ego development, and the marriage relationship. *Journal of Marriage and the Family, 43,* 841–853.

Tucker, J. S., & Mueller, J. S. (2000). Spouses' social control of health behaviors: Use and effectiveness of specific strategies. *Personality and Social Psychology Bulletin, 26,* 1120–1130.

Tucker, J. S., Orlando, M., Elliott, M. N., & Klein, D. J. (2006). Affective and behavioral responses to health-related social control. *Journal of Personality and Social Psychology, 25,* 715–722.

Vuchinich, S., & Teachman, J. (1993). Influence on the duration of wars, strikes riots, and family arguments. *Journal of Conflict Resolution, 37,* 544–568.

Williams, K. D. (2001). *Ostracism: The power of silence.* New York: Guilford.

Wilson, L. K., & Gallois, C. (1985). Perceptions of assertive behavior: Sex combination, role appropriateness, and message type. *Sex Roles, 12,* 125–141.

Witteman, H. (1988). Interpersonal problem solving: Problem conceptualization and communication use. *Communication Monographs, 55,* 336–359.

Wright, C. N. (2008). *An examination of the relationship of type of teasing and outcome on teasing motivations, construction, and reactions.* Unpublished doctoral dissertation, Northwestern University, Evanston, IL.

Wright, C., & Roloff, M. E. (2007, May). *Why romantic partners won't tell you if they're upset: The relationship between belief in mindreading and type of grievance expression.* Paper presented at the annual convention of the International Communication Association, San Francisco.

Zietlow, P. H., & Sillars, A. L. (1988). Life-stage differences in communication during marital conflicts. *Journal of Social and Personal Relationships, 5,* 223–245.

17 The Standards for Openness Hypothesis

A Gendered Explanation for Why Avoidance is so Dissatisfying

Tamara D. Afifi and Andrea Joseph

The nature of the association between topic avoidance and satisfaction has come under scrutiny in recent years, somewhat in response to its underlying theories. Theories such as dialectical theory (e.g., Baxter, 1990; Baxter & Montgomery, 1996) and communication privacy management (CPM) theory (Petronio, 1991, 2000, 2002) contend that people need a balance of openness and closedness to build and maintain healthy interpersonal relationships. The literature on information regulation (e.g., avoidance, secrets, privacy) also points to the fact that people withhold information from intimate others in an effort to minimize conflict, maintain the current status of their relationships, and protect themselves and others (e.g., Afifi, Olson, & Armstrong, 2005; Greene & Faulkner, 2002; Vangelisti & Caughlin, 1997). Theoretically, most scholars (including the authors) agree that some avoidance is necessary, and even beneficial, in order to maintain satisfying romantic relationships (see Afifi, Caughlin, & Afifi, 2007; Afifi & Guerrero, 2000).

Yet, as Caughlin and Afifi (2004; Caughlin & Golish, 2002) point out, the aforementioned theoretical assumptions often contradict the empirical evidence that has found a linear, positive association between topic avoidance and dissatisfaction. Though theory suggests that avoidance can be beneficial to relationships, the little empirical evidence that is available on this subject suggests that avoidance is dissatisfying (e.g., Afifi & Schrodt, 2003; Caughlin & Golish, 2002; Golish, 2000; Roloff & Ifert, 1998). Even though scholars suggest that avoidance can be beneficial to relationships, more often than not it tends to be associated with dissatisfaction.

In addition, research has assumed that topic avoidance leads to dissatisfaction, but the opposite could also be true with dissatisfaction producing topic avoidance. The research that has suggested that topic avoidance is dissatisfying (e.g., Caughlin & Afifi, 2004; Caughlin & Golish, 2002; Dailey & Palomares, 2004; Golish, 2000) has relied almost exclusively on self-report data collected at one point in time. While it is likely that avoidance produces relational dissatisfaction, it is equally probable that people avoid talking about certain topics with their partners because they are dissatisfied. The relationship may be reciprocal such that avoidance begets dissatisfaction and dissatisfaction begets avoidance. Some research (e.g., Gottman & Krokoff, 1989; Heavey, Layne, & Christensen, 1993) on conflict avoidance suggests that such a nonreciprocal association exists, but little is known about the exact nature of this association and the conditions that prompt it.

We argue in this chapter that the association between topic avoidance and dissatisfaction in romantic relationships is bidirectional, but that this association probably differs for men and women, especially in situations where the topic avoidance turns into conflict avoidance. We contend in our *standards for openness hypothesis* that, when women are avoiding with their partner and/or they think their partner is avoiding with them, it is more likely to make them dissatisfied than it is men because women have been socialized to maintain and identify problems in their relationships. More specifically, the hypothesis states that the discrepancy between how much people think their partner ought to be open with them (standards), and how much they perceive their partner is really open with them, will predict their dissatisfaction. This will be especially the case for women and will be exacerbated in conflict-inducing situations. These standards are grounded in cultural and individual ideals for relationships. Because openness is equated with healthy relationships in the U.S. culture (Bochner, 1982; Parks, 1982), people are likely to equate avoidance with potential trouble areas in their relationships and ruminate about why they (or their partner) are avoiding, which should make them dissatisfied. We also argue that unmet standards for openness should also reduce women's commitment to their relationship, which should result in relational dissatisfaction. This dissatisfaction, in turn, is likely to create an even wider "communication gap" or discrepancy between the standards for openness and reality. The model for this hypothesis is outlined in Figure 17.1. In order to fully explain this hypothesis, we first examine some of the research that links topic avoidance with dissatisfaction, briefly discuss connections to the conflict avoidance literature, and then focus more extensively on the role of gender in relationship standards, commitment, and rumination.

The Link between Topic Avoidance and Dissatisfaction

Two theoretical frameworks that are often used to study information regulation are CPM theory (Petronio, 1991, 2000, 2002) and dialectical theory (e.g., Baxter, 1990; Baxter & Montgomery, 1996). According to dialectical theory, people experience various dialectical tensions that drive change in their relationships (Baxter, 1990; Baxter & Montgomery, 1996). A dialectical tension involves interdependent forces that mutually oppose or negate one another (Baxter & Montgomery, 1996). One of the tensions that is common across relationship types, especially in romantic relationships that are in their initial stages of development (Baxter & Wilmot, 1985), is the tension between wanting to be open about one's thoughts and

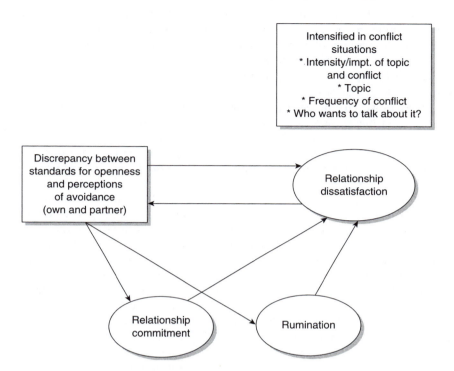

Figure 17.1 Standards for Openness Hypothesis

feelings and the need to be closed or refrain from disclosing certain information. As dialectical theorists argue, people need to be open with their
partners about their backgrounds, feelings, and opinions, to develop and
maintain satisfying relationships (Baxter & Montgomery, 1996). As the
theory also suggests, however, people need to maintain some sense of privacy and too much disclosure can stunt the initial development of a relationship (Baxter, 1990; Baxter & Wilmot, 1985). Individuals need to feel
as if they are able to keep some information private to enhance their
autonomy and sense of self.

Petronio's CPM theory (1991, 2000, 2002) is grounded in the dialectical
tension of openness and closedness. The theory argues that people erect meta-
phorical boundaries around themselves that ebb and flow with the degree of
risk involved with revealing sensitive information. Disclosing sensitive information makes people feel vulnerable, and they often restrict their privacy
boundaries as a result. Topic avoidance is one way in which individuals regulate their privacy boundaries. The more people mistrust their partner's lack
closeness with them, and are afraid of their partner's response to the topic, the
more likely they are to refrain from talking about the topic (Greene &
Faulkner, 2002; Petronio, Reeder, Hecht, & Mon't Ros-Mendoza, 1996;

Vangelisti, 1994). The relative permeability of individuals' boundaries also depends upon motivations for the avoidance, cultural influences, family norms, and other factors such as gender (Petronio, 2002). Part of the underlying premise in both theories, however, is the fact that people are often torn between being open and closed and they need a balance of both in order to sustain healthy relationships.

For the most part, however, the empirical research linking relational satisfaction to topic avoidance (e.g., Afifi & Schrodt, 2003; Caughlin & Afifi, 2004; Golish, 2000; Roloff & Ifert, 1998), and to similar constructs like secret keeping (e.g., Caughlin et al., 2000; Vangelisti, 1994), does not seem to support the theoretical supposition that the association between topic avoidance and satisfaction is curvilinear or that withholding information can be satisfying. For example, Roloff and Ifert (1998) found that the more people reported avoiding topics with their romantic dating partners, the more dissatisfied they were with their relationship. As Caughlin and Golish (2002) also discovered, when dating partners (and parents and children) are avoiding each other, they find their own and their partner's avoidance dissatisfying. In particular, when individuals think their partner is avoiding topics with them, they find it dissatisfying, even if their partners say they are not avoiding topics with them. Individuals' perception of their partner's avoidance was a stronger predictor of their own dissatisfaction than was their perception of their own avoidance. The individual's own topic avoidance, however, was still predictive of their own dissatisfaction.

Caughlin and Golish's (2002) study was an important step in identifying the connection between topic avoidance and satisfaction and how perception influences this association. However, all of the aforementioned studies, including that of Caughlin and Golish, relied on cross-sectional data where dating partners reflected on their overall topic avoidance tendencies in their relationship. An important next step in this line of research would be to analyze the potential bidirectional association between topic avoidance and satisfaction over time in a longitudinal study using a diary method or other means. The potential reciprocal nature of topic avoidance and dissatisfaction is examined next.

The Potential Reciprocal Nature of Topic Avoidance and Dissatisfaction

The research that has examined the connection between topic avoidance and relationship dissatisfaction has relied almost exclusively upon cross-sectional data. For instance, Golish (2000) found that children's topic avoidance with their parents and stepparents was inversely associated with the children's satisfaction with their relationships with them. Likewise, Dailey and Palomares (2004) studied the impact of topic avoidance on relationship dissatisfaction in different relationship types (i.e., significant other relationships, mother–young-adult relationships, and father–young-adult relationships). The authors found that topic avoidance, in general, was inversely associated with relationship satisfaction across relationship types. However, the extent to which the avoidance was dissatisfying and satisfying depended upon the way it was communicated. When the topic avoidance was communicated overtly and sometimes rudely (e.g., becoming defensive, guilt trips, interrupting), it was associated with dissatisfaction. In contrast, when it was communicated more politely (e.g., showing affection, complimenting), it was associated with an increase in *satisfaction*. It may be the case that more overt avoidance attempts where people are probably more cognizant of their avoidance is associated with dissatisfaction but that more covert attempts that "smooth over" the conversation, where people are not as aware of the fact that it is avoidance, may help maintain relationships. Research (e.g., Caughlin & Golish, 2002; Roloff & Ifert, 1998; Sargent, 2002) has also found that the more people avoid talking about certain topics with their romantic partners, the more dissatisfied they are with their relationships. Likewise, research suggests that keeping secrets from one's family members is associated with dissatisfaction in their relationships (Finkenauer & Hazam, 2000; Frijns, 2005; Vangelisti, 1994). In all of these studies, however, the researchers asked their participants to reflect on their topic avoidance and relationship satisfaction at one point in time, prohibiting the ability to determine which variable affected the other.

Yet it is possible that the association between topic avoidance and relationship satisfaction is nonrecursive. The typical argument offered for an inverse association between topic avoidance and satisfaction is that, when people withhold information from their partners, it makes them feel dissatisfied knowing that they cannot be open with their partner (Dailey & Palomares, 2004). Most of the research on disclosure and health (e.g., Pennebaker, Kiecolt-Glaser, & Glaser, 1988; Smyth & Pennebaker, 2001) also supports the contention that disclosure promotes enhanced physical and mental health and relationship well-being. Disclosing information is often accompanied by a cathartic, liberating feeling (Stiles, 1987; Stiles, Shuster, & Harrigan, 1992) and can foster relationship growth (see Afifi et al., 2007). Popular culture also most likely perpetuates these feelings. People are inundated with messages from the media that, in order to have a healthy romantic relationship, they should be completely open with their partner and their partner should be completely open with them (Afifi et al., 2007). Furthermore, the United States is a low-context culture that fosters expectations for openness in relationships (Petronio, 2002). When avoidance is detected and these expectations are unmet, it probably fosters a sense of dissatisfaction. Thus, when dating partners perceive that they, or their partners, are avoiding in their relationship, they may feel as if their relationship is inadequate and, as a result, become dissatisfied.

An alternative explanation, however, is that people refrain from talking about sensitive information with their partners because they are dissatisfied with their relationship. In contrast, when people are in satisfying relationships, they are likely to discuss issues freely and openly with one another. For instance, research on secrets (e.g., Afifi & Steuber, 2009; Vangelisti & Caughlin, 1997) suggests that people are more likely to disclose secrets to others when they have a close relationship with them. Likewise, CPM theory (Petronio, 2002) argues that the more comfortable and trusting people are with their potential respondents, the more likely they are to disclose to them. Given this research, it makes sense that, when people are satisfied with their relationships, they are more likely to open up to their partners about issues that concern them.

In sum, even though scholars have tended to assume that topic avoidance produces dissatisfaction and not vice versa, it seems possible that this association is bidirectional. Individuals could avoid talking about certain topics with their partners because they are dissatisfied and the continued avoidance makes them even further dissatisfied because they feel as if they are not talking about topics that are important to them. Likewise, people could start avoiding topics and become dissatisfied with the fact they are avoiding and this dissatisfaction, in turn, makes them avoid even more information from their partners.

Conflict as a Condition Under Which Topic Avoidance is Especially Likely to be Dissatisfying

While most of the empirical research supports the proposition that topic avoidance is dissatisfying, there may be conditions under which topic avoidance is more or less dissatisfying or even satisfying. One condition in which topic avoidance is probably particularly dissatisfying is when it turns into conflict avoidance. In these situations, avoidance is often indicative of people being reluctant to engage in a potentially conflict-inducing topic. Conflict avoidance may be more likely to ignite feelings of relational dissatisfaction because the topic is important to one or both people. If individuals are unable to voice issues that concern them to their partner or they believe their partner has similar concerns with them, this can be bothersome. Nevertheless, one's dissatisfaction depends upon the importance of the topic, the severity of the conflict that might ensue if it were to be discussed, how often the conflict avoidance occurs, and the extent to which one or both people want to talk about the topic. As Roloff and Ifert (2000) note, conflict avoidance can be beneficial when the topic is trivial. One of the trademarks of strong couples who have been married a long time is the ability to correctly decipher which battles to fight and which ones to let go (e.g., Gottman & Levenson, 2000). They also have the ability to positively reframe their partner's limitations and aversive communication patterns in a way that helps manage conflict and preserve their relationship (Pearson, 1992). In addition, as Caughlin and Afifi (2004) found, people may be more likely to forgive their partner's avoidance if it is for altruistic motives, such as to protect their relationship. Even though Caughlin and Afifi's study was on topic avoidance and not conflict avoidance, these feelings may be exacerbated in conflict situations. That is, people may be less likely to be bothered by their partner's avoidance of potentially conflict-inducing topics if they believe their partner is trying to protect their relationship. However, it should also be noted in the Caughlin and Afifi study that avoidance did not *enhance* relational satisfaction; it merely was not associated with dissatisfaction. Thus, avoidance may be more likely to help maintain dating partners' current level of satisfaction, rather than enhance their satisfaction per se.

A significant amount of information can be gleaned about the association between topic avoidance and dissatisfaction from the research on conflict avoidance. Most notable in this body of literature is the research on demand–withdraw patterns, which have been consistently associated with relationship dissatisfaction and dissolution (Caughlin & Huston, 2002; Weger, 2005). These patterns exist when one person demands to talk about an issue and the other person withdraws or refuses to talk about it (Christensen & Heavey, 1990). Research has overwhelmingly shown women to be more likely to be demanders in heterosexual romantic relationships and men withdrawers (Christensen & Heavey, 1990). Although there are numerous theoretical explanations for this gender difference, two explanations have been given considerable attention: (1) sex role socialization, and (2) the social structural perspective (Christensen & Heavey; Heavey, et al., 1993; Jacobson, 1990). According to the sex role socialization argument, women have been socialized to talk about their problems in relationships from a very early age. They have been taught to more openly diagnose and talk about their problems with others. In contrast, the social structural perspective states that women tend to have less power than men in the U.S. culture. They demand because they desire change in their relationships, whereas men withdraw because they are more satisfied with the status quo (see Caughlin & Vangelisti, 2000, for other explanations).

While much of the research connecting conflict avoidance with dissatisfaction has focused on demand–withdraw patterns, research on conflict avoidance more broadly has also been associated with couples' distress and dissatisfaction (e.g., Bodenmann, Kaiser, Hahlweg, & Fehm-Wolfsdorf, 1998). This pattern has been found regardless of whether avoidance is assessed through observations (e.g., Gottman & Krokoff, 1989; Heavey et al., 1993) or self-reports (e.g., Christensen & Shenk, 1991). In fact, Smith, Heaven, and Ciarrochi (2008) found that avoidance and withdrawing were stronger predictors of relational outcomes like dissatisfaction than constructive conflict management skills and demanding patterns. Similarly, Gottman and Krokoff (1989) discovered that conflict avoidance increased couples' dissatisfaction over time more so than those couples where conflict was pursued. As these authors theorize, couples who avoid conflict over long periods of time may be unable to adequately address their conflict when it happens, creating an increasing emotional barrier between the couple (Gottman & Krokoff, 1989).

While most of the research on conflict avoidance has also been cross-sectional, some research has attempted to understand its causal nature. As we indicate above, when people avoid for extensive periods of time or use that as their predominant conflict style, it may prevent them from openly addressing important issues in their relationship. However, the dissatisfaction that ensues could also create avoidance between the couple (Christensen & Shenk, 1991). Research has found that, when individuals are dissatisfied in their relationship, they are more likely to avoid talking about potentially conflict-inducing topics with their partner (e.g., Noller, Feeney, Bonnell, & Callan, 1994). The emotional distance or "emotional wedge" between the couple reveals itself in avoidance tendencies (Christensen & Shenk, 1991). Conversely, people who are satisfied with their relationship tend to openly address issues with their partner and are more collaborative in nature (Christensen & Shenk, 1991).

In a study examining the reciprocal nature of avoidance and dissatisfaction, Afifi, McManus, Steuber, and Coho (in press) found that, at a basic level, individuals' perception that their dating partner was avoiding them during a potentially conflict-inducing conversation predicted an increase in their dissatisfaction after the conversation was over. They also found that the association between conflict avoidance and dissatisfaction was bidirectional for men, but not for women. The more men were relationally dissatisfied entering the conversation, the more they avoided discussing the topic. Women's satisfaction also seemed to fluctuate more than men's satisfaction.

In short, perceptions of one's own and one's partner's avoidance tend to be dissatisfying. Nevertheless, it is also probably the case that the more people are dissatisfied in their relationship, the more they avoid talking to the person. Consequently, the association between avoidance and dissatisfaction is likely to be bidirectional. The strength of this association is also most likely exacerbated under times of stress or conflict (i.e., conflict avoidance). Given that research (e.g., Lloyd, 1987) tends to suggest that the topic of the conflict, the importance/intensity of it, the frequency of the conflict surrounding the topic and whether one or both people want to talk about the topic influence the nature of the conflict situation and people's avoidance and dissatisfaction tendencies, these types of variables also likely influence the paths in the model. With this information in mind, some initial propositions that provide the foundation for our standards for openness hypothesis (see Figure 17.1) are set forth:

> *Proposition 1*: At a general level, the association between avoidance and dissatisfaction is linear and nonrecursive such that greater perceptions of avoidance (own or partner's avoidance) predicts greater relationship dissatisfaction and greater dissatisfaction predicts greater avoidance.

Proposition 2: The associations in the standards for openness hypothesis should be stronger under times of conflict (i.e., conflict avoidance).

Proposition 3: The associations in the model should also be impacted by the topic of the conflict (or avoidance) and the intensity/importance of the topic and the conflict, whether one or both people want to talk about the topic, and the frequency of the conflict surrounding the topic.

Proposition 4: The avoidance depicted in the model should hold true for people's perceptions of their own avoidance as well as their perceptions of their partner's avoidance.

The association between avoidance and dissatisfaction should also differ for men and women, which, we argue, is largely a function of the discrepancy between standards for openness in relationships and actual avoidance tendencies. These expectations are rooted in cultural and individual ideals for relationships. The implications of gender and relationship standards are discussed next.

Romantic Relationship Standards and Relationship Satisfaction

Relationship Standards

Relationship standards are the beliefs individuals have about what their romantic relationships *should* look like (Baucom, Epstein, Sayers, & Sher, 1989). In other words, relationship standards are concerned with individuals' ideas about the qualities they believe ought to be part of their romantic relationships. Relationship standards are important because they are strongly related to relationship quality: Individuals who report that their partners meet their standards also report a higher-quality relationship (Vangelisti & Daly, 1997).

Before delving into a discussion of relationship standards, it should be noted that, although differences do exist between men and women with regard to their relationship standards, research suggests that these differences are rather minor. For example, in their study on the dimensions of relationship quality, Hasserbrauck and Fehr (2002) found that intimacy, characterized by taking time for each other, talking with each other, and understanding, among other things, was more important to perceptions of relationship quality for women ($r = .80$) than men ($r = .76$). Sexuality, on the other hand, was more important for the relationship satisfaction of men ($r = .58$) than women ($r = .55$). Yet despite these subtle differences between the sexes, overall, intimacy was the most important predictor of relationship quality for both men and women. Sexuality was not nearly as important. In this way, men and women are more similar than different with respect to their relationship standards.

What types of standards do both sexes report are important for healthy romantic relationships? Not surprisingly, given that one component of intimacy is "talking with each other," most individuals claim that open communication is an important standard for their romantic relationships. In their study on gender differences in romantic relationships, Vangelisti and Daly (1997) found that affective accessibility was the best predictor of relationship quality for both sexes. Affective accessibility consists of openness, affection demonstration, and impact. Working on one's relationship by talking out problems and working hard to communicate every day (Weigel, 2008), as well as using affectively oriented communication skills by giving ego support, comfort, and effectively managing conflict with one's partner, are also common relationship standards (Burleson, Kunkel, Samter, & Werking, 1996). Clearly, then, open communication is an important relationship standard that has major implications for the quality of individuals' relationships. Of course, the link between openness and relationship satisfaction should not be surprising given our previous discussion of topic avoidance and romantic relationships.

While there are indeed similarities between women and men's relationship standards, researchers have found a difference in the extent to which men and women feel their standards are met. In particular, women are more likely than men to believe their standards are not being upheld in their current romantic relationships (Vangelisti & Daly, 1997). This is especially true when examining men and women's beliefs about the level of open communication within their relationships. Women, for instance, are more likely than men to desire more openness within their romantic relationships. In fact, although openness is equally important to men and women (Vangelisti & Daly), women are significantly more likely to report using openness within their romantic relationships when compared with men (Aylor & Dainton, 2004). Given this finding, it is not surprising that women are almost 6 times more likely to end their romantic relationships due to a lack of open communication (Baxter, 1986).

The differences in the extent to which relationship standards are fulfilled for men and women also manifest themselves in other ways. Although they are more communal with their same sex friends, women are more quarrelsome and less agreeable with their romantic partners (Suh, Moskowitz, Fournier, & Zuroff, 2004). In fact, in contrast to the stereotype of the quiet, yielding wife or girlfriend, women are more likely than men to quarrel with their romantic partner, while men are more likely than women to be agreeable (Suh et al., 2004). Women are also more likely to see both prototypical relationship violations (e.g., "If I need to talk, my partner will not listen") and nonprototypical relationship violations (e.g., "If I disclose something personal to my partner, my partner will not disclose something important to me in return") as more detrimental to their relationships than men (Hampel & Vangelisti, 2008). In this way, while men and women describe similar relationship standards, their views of their relationship differ in that women are more likely to describe, and be affected by, unmet relationship standards.

Romantic Relationship Standards and Expectations

As we note above, men and women share similar relationship standards, yet men are significantly more likely than women to report that their standards are fulfilled (Vangelisti & Daly, 1997). Given that women's relationship standards are not met as often as men's, women are more likely to act out within their relationships in the form of quarrelsome behavior and decreased agreeableness (Suh et al., 2004). This section will focus on one possible explanation for this discrepancy, namely that relational partners hold different expectations for one another depending on their sex. First, however, the differences between relationship standards and relationship expectations will be explained.

Relationship Expectations

According to Burgoon and Walther (1990), expectations are "cognitions about the anticipated communication behavior of specific others" (p. 236). Within the domain of romantic relationships, expectations can be thought of as the communication processes individuals anticipate their romantic partners will enact. Expectations are conceptually different from standards in that expectations focus on *anticipated* behavior while standards are concerned with how an individual *ought* to act. Certainly there is much overlap between these constructs. For example, individuals' standards may dictate that their partners *ought* to be open with them about a stressful relationship issue. If individuals *anticipate* that their partners will be open with them, then their expectations will probably be fulfilled. On the contrary, some people may believe that romantic relationships should consist of honest, open communication, yet expect their partner to avoid discussing a particularly stressful topic with them.

Relationship Expectations Experienced by Women

Within romantic relationships, women tend to expect—and are expected by others—to fulfill particular roles. Specifically, women are expected to be relationship experts (Fitzpatrick & Sollie, 1999). As such, both men and women anticipate that women will be more aware of the needs of the relationship and have a more developed set of relationship skills to address any problems that may arise. Women are likely to satisfy this role more than men for two main reasons. First, women tend to identify themselves more in terms of their relationships—romantic or otherwise—than men. Second, women have more complex ways of thinking about their relationships.

Research suggests that, across age groups, women tend to be more relationship focused than men. While boys are more likely to spend time engaging in various physical activities with their same sex friends, girls are more likely to talk with, and self-disclose to, their other girl friends (Lever, 1976). In adulthood, women gravitate toward friendships that are emotionally close and communally oriented, while men tend to be more agentic and attempt to assert their dominance over their friends (Suh et al., 2004). In the same vein, women tend to derive a greater sense of self by considering their roles within their relationships (Weigel, 2008), and they report attempting to enhance their relationships in order to increase their self-esteem (Cross & Madson, 1997). Men, on the other hand, prefer to denigrate others, focus on their unique attributes, and overestimate their abilities when they wish to feel better about themselves (Cross & Madson). Given that women place greater importance on their relationships than men, they would be expected to be more knowledgeable in fostering romantic relationships than men.

In addition, it may not be just that women have more experience forming close, intimate friendships. Research also suggests that women have more developed schemas for thinking and talking about their relationships (Martin, 1991). Perhaps as a result of their socialization toward a more relationship-focused orientation, women tend to have much more complex ways of considering their relationships, and their attitudes about their relationships are more accessible to them (Higgins, King, & Mavin, 1982).

As a result of the larger importance women place on relationships, it follows that women are more likely to believe that their relationship standards are not being met. That is, because poor relationships have implications for women's sense of self, and because women are better equipped to discern positive and negative relationship partners, women are more likely to feel that their relationships are not as they ought to be. In the section that follows, we discuss the investment model (Rusbult, 1980, 1983) as one theoretical explanation for the link among relationship standards, avoidance, and relationship satisfaction.

The Investment Model and Relationship Standards and Expectations

Central to the investment model (Rusbult, 1980, 1983) is the notion of commitment, which accounts for partners' willingness to remain in the relationship. According to this model, the greater the relationship quality, the more committed individuals will be to their partnerships. Commitment is based on three main factors. First, drawing from the social exchange theory (Thibaut & Kelley, 1959), individuals want to maximize their rewards and minimize their costs. Relationship costs can consist of any number of things from spending time with one's partner instead of studying to abstaining from romantic partnerships with others. Second, individuals take into account their comparison level of alternatives. The comparison level of alternatives refers to the degree to which individuals believe attractive others are available for them to enter with into a romantic relationship. If individuals believe they have a large comparison level of alternatives, it is likely that their commitment to their current partners will not be as strong. Finally, the investments individuals have already put into the relationship are taken into account. Investments consist of anything that individuals put into the relationship that cannot be gotten back if the relationship were to end. Time and money are two examples of common investments put into romantic relationships.

Given that women tend to be the relationship experts who are primarily responsible for guaranteeing the quality of their partnership, it follows that women should also invest more into their relationships than men. For example, women are likely to devote more cognitive energy to their relationships in the sense that they must continually scan for potential problems. Similarly, because their identities are tied so closely to their relationships, women are likely to invest resources into the partnership to ensure that it is of quality. Expectedly, given their increased investment, women tend to report greater commitment to their relationships, as well as decreased alternatives (Sprecher, 1988). These findings were replicated by Fitzpatrick and Sollie (1999) who contend that women are more invested in their relationships, feel their comparison level is being met to a greater extent than men, and perceive greater rewards and fewer costs of, or alternatives to, their partnership. Moreover, women are more committed to their romantic relationships compared to men.

Ironically, however, given the great investments women put into their relationships, they are also probably more vigilant than men in noting whether their relationship standards are being met; because women put more time into their relationships in terms of costs than men, they are likely to expect more from their partners in terms of rewards. In particular, open communication is one important standard women believe their partners ought to uphold. Open communication is an important part of fostering deep, meaningful relationships. If women sense that their partners are not being open with them, they may feel that their relationships are not developing to the extent that they should be. As such, women are likely to be more dissatisfied with their relationships than men when open communication is not present. In terms of the investment model, women may see a lack of open communication as a large cost, which may lead to decreased commitment. In fact, in their study of social support within marriage, Acitelli and Antonucci (1994) found that wives' marital satisfaction was linked to giving and receiving social support, as well as perceived and actual reciprocity. In other words, open communication about stressful topics predicted positive feelings about the relationship for women. Men were only affected by actual social support reciprocity.

In a related way, women's relationship satisfaction is positively related to the extent to which their husbands talk about their relationship. In her study on gender differences in relationships, Acitelli (1992) looked at relationship awareness, defined as "thinking about interaction patterns, comparisons, or contrasts between himself or herself and the other partner in the relationship. Included are thoughts about the couple or relationship as an entity" (p. 102). In order to measure relationship awareness, couples were interviewed together about their relationship. When men demonstrated more relationship talk, women tended to be more satisfied with their relationships. This was true regardless of the amount of relationship talk the women used. In this way, men who are able to talk easily and freely about their relationships are able to decrease some of the costs usually incurred by women in their relationships; it is fair to conjecture that women whose husbands exhibited a great deal of relationship talk felt that some of the burden of managing the relationship was lifted (Acitelli, 2002).

The investment model provides one explanation for the level of commitment individuals report within their relationships. When people's standards are met, they are likely to stay committed to their relationship and feel satisfied with their relationship as a result; when their standards go unfulfilled, commitment is likely to decrease, which should decrease their satisfaction. Open communication is a particularly important component of relationship satisfaction for women. In fact, husbands who use open communication also have more committed wives. Given the aforementioned research, we set forth the following:

> *Proposition 5*: The discrepancy between the standards (cultural and individual) for openness in relationships and one's perception of the actual avoidance in one's relationship (self and/or partner) should predict relationship dissatisfaction when examined in isolation.

> *Proposition 6*: This discrepancy between standards and reality for openness should be stronger for women than men.

> *Proposition 7*: This discrepancy should predict a decrease in relationship commitment, which should decrease relationship satisfaction.

Rumination and Avoidance

But what happens when wives are not satisfied with the amount of openness in their relationships? What happens, for example, when women believe their partners are avoiding communicating about particular topics? In addition to the decreased feelings of commitment mentioned above, we believe that rumination is likely to occur. When people's standards for openness in relationships go unmet, especially for women, they are likely to ruminate about why these standards are unmet. This rumination, in turn, should predict their relationship dissatisfaction.

According to Martin and Tesser (1996), rumination is defined as a state whereby individuals continually think about topics that revolve around some instrumental theme in the absence of any cues in the direct environment that would require individuals to think about the issue. In other words, rumination is a conscious process that involves repeatedly thinking about or mulling over a topic when the task at hand does not require individuals to consider the topic at all. Rumination occurs when there is a discrepancy between individuals' goals and their ability to meet that goal (Martin & Tesser, 1996). Not surprisingly, individuals do not ruminate about every unattained goal, but rather those goals that are more central to their well-being. Within the context of this current chapter, because women's identities are so closely tied to their romantic relationships, it seems much more likely that a woman would ruminate about the lack of intimacy in their marriage than the fact that her partner does not enjoy watching her favorite movie. Rumination will continue to occur until an individual's goals are reached (e.g., her marriage becomes more intimate) or she decides that the goal is no longer important.

Although not often studied within the context of romantic relationships, rumination is likely to occur as the result of unmet relationship standards. Consider the following: Rumination occurs when individuals are unable to obtain their goals. The more important the goal, the more likely individuals are to ruminate. Because women tend to be the "experts" within their romantic relationships, and their identities are affected by their partnerships with others, it is fair to assume that women desire (or have some sort of innate goal) to form healthy relationships. One important relationship standard for both men and women is open communication. However, women are more likely than men to report that their relationship standards are not being met. In particular, a lack of open communication—in the form of topic avoidance or otherwise—is likely to lead to dissatisfaction. As such, the discrepancies between women's unmet relationship goals for openness within their relationships are likely to produce greater rumination. Because men are not as likely to believe that their relationship standards are unmet and because they are not likely to be dissatisfied with their relationship's level of openness, it follows that women ruminate after topic avoidance more than men. Avoidance is probably really only troubling to the extent that people worry about it or cannot stop thinking about why it exists.

In addition to the fact that women are more likely to feel their relationship goals for openness are unmet, leading to rumination, they are also more likely to ruminate in general (Nolen-Hoeksema & Jackson, 2001). Women are 2 times more likely than men to ruminate, which scholars believe might be related to the fact that women are taught fewer instrumental skills for dealing with their negative emotions (Wupperman, 2003). That is, while men are taught to distract themselves and avoid dwelling on their negative affect, women are likely to believe that they *should* ruminate when they are distressed (Nolen-Hoeksema & Jackson, 2001). In fact, women have significantly higher scores than men on rumination even after taking distress, expressivity, socially desirable responses, and feeling responsible for the emotional tone of the relationship into account (Nolen-Hoeksema & Jackson).

Unfortunately, rumination is responsible for a host of negative outcomes (see Thomsen, 2006, for review). Rumination fosters decreased forgiveness (McCullough, Bono, & Root, 2007), increased aggression toward a transgressor (Bushman, 2002), and decreased problem-solving and decision-making abilities (Ward, Lyubomirsky, Sousa, & Nolen-Hoeksema, 2003). In fact,

Nolen-Hoeksema (1991) contends that ruminative thinking causes individuals to maintain their negative affective state and plays a large role in depression. Given these findings, the implications for women who ruminate due to their own and/or their romantic partner's topic avoidance deserve greater attention.

We argue in our standards for openness hypothesis (see Figure 17.1) that, when the standards for openness in one's relationship go unmet, it decreases people's commitment to their relationship and increases their rumination about why the avoidance exists in their relationship. Rumination and commitment should partially or fully mediate the association between the discrepancy that exists between the standards for openness and perceptions of actual avoidance and relationship satisfaction. Moreover, we contend that the relationship between the discrepancy and dissatisfaction should be nonrecursive in that relationship dissatisfaction should predict not only greater avoidance but a greater "wedge" or discrepancy between what people want from their partner in terms of openness and what they actually receive from their partner. Given the probability that women are more likely to have their standards for openness go unmet, combined with their greater tendency to ruminate, this model should be stronger for women than for men. That is, this model probably holds true for men, but the "fit" of the model and the specific paths in it should be stronger for women. The paths in the model should also be stronger under situations of conflict (i.e., conflict avoidance than topic avoidance per se). Finally, the model should hold true for the perception of one's own avoidance as well as one's perception of one's partner's avoidance. With this information in mind, we propose the remaining propositions:

> *Proposition 8*: The discrepancy between the standards (cultural and individual) for openness in relationships and one's perception of the actual avoidance in one's relationship should predict rumination such that a larger discrepancy should predict greater ruminative tendencies.

> *Proposition 9*: Rumination should partially or fully mediate the association between the discrepancy avoidance score (discrepancy between one's standards for openness in one's relationship and one's perception of the actual avoidance tendencies for self and/or the partner), and relationship dissatisfaction.

> *Proposition 10*: The standards for openness hypothesis should hold true for men and women, but should be significantly stronger for women.

Conclusion

The standards for openness hypothesis provides a new way of thinking about why avoidance might be dissatisfying. As Bochner (1982) and Parks (1982) argued more than two decades ago, there is an ideology of intimacy or openness in the U.S. culture whereby we equate openness with healthy relationships. We argue that, even though times have changed somewhat with the advent of more information regulation literature and theories like dialectical theory (Baxter, 1990; Baxter & Montgomery, 1996) and CPM theory (Petronio, 2002), this bias still exists. However, we go further to contend that this bias is more salient for women because of the way they have been socialized as relationship maintenance experts. While our model should hold true for women and men, the perception of avoidance should evoke stronger feelings of dissatisfaction for women. The hypothesized model we present in this chapter, however, remains to be tested.

Probably one of the strongest heuristic links in the model is the role of rumination. Rumination could offer numerous fruitful avenues of future research for information regulation scholars. For instance, it could be that, when people are dissatisfied with their relationships, it causes them to ruminate, which increases their avoidance. Future research is necessary that can parcel out the various interconnected components of the model more completely. While this chapter offers one explanation for why avoidance tends to be dissatisfying, it is also important to remember that it is only one possible explanation (see Afifi, Caughlin, & Afifi, 2007, for other explanations and benefits of avoidance). Future research should more closely examine the potential bidirectional association between topic avoidance and dissatisfaction using longitudinal research and examine possible gender differences in the process.

References

Acitelli, L. K. (1992). Gender differences in relationship awareness and marital satisfaction among young married couples. *Personality and Social Psychology Bulletin, 18*, 102–110.

Acitelli, L. K., & Antonucci, T. C. (1994). Gender differences in the link between marital support and satisfaction in older couples. *Journal of Personality and Social Psychology, 67*, 688–698.

Afifi, T. D. (2003). "Feeling caught" in stepfamilies: Managing boundary turbulence through appropriate privacy coordination rules. *Journal of Social and Personal Relationships, 20*, 729–756.

Afifi, T. D., Caughlin, J., & Afifi, W. A. (2007). Exploring the dark side (and light side) of avoidance and secrets. In B. Spitzberg and B. Cupach (Eds.), *The dark side of interpersonal relationships* (2nd ed., pp. 61–92). Mahwah, NJ: Lawrence Erlbaum Associates.

Afifi, T. D., McManus, T., Steuber, K., & Coho, A. (in press). Verbal avoidance in intimate conflict situations. *Human Communication Research*.

Afifi, T. D., & Olson, L. (2005). The chilling effect and the pressure to conceal secrets in families. *Communication Monographs, 72*, 192–216.

Afifi, T. D., Olson, L., & Armstrong, C. (2005). The chilling effect and family secrets: Examining the role of self protection, other protection, and communication efficacy. *Human Communication Research, 31*, 564–598.

Afifi, T. D., & Schrodt, P. (2003). "Feeling caught" as a mediator of adolescents' and young adults' avoidance and satisfaction with their parents in divorced and non-divorced households. *Communication Monographs, 70*, 142–173.

Afifi, T. D., & Steuber, K. (2009). *The cycle of concealment and strategies for revealing secrets in families.* Manuscript submitted for publication.

Afifi, W. A., & Guerrero, L. K. (2000). Motivations underlying topic avoidance in close relationships. In S. Petronio (Ed.), *Balancing the secrets of private disclosures* (pp. 165–180). Mahwah, NJ: Lawrence Erlbaum Associates.

Aylor, B., & Dainton, M. (2004). Biological sex and psychological gender as predictors of routine and strategic relationship maintenance. *Sex Roles, 50,* 689–697.

Baucom, D. H., Epstein, N., Sayers, S., & Sher, T. G. (1989). The role of cognitions in marital relationships: Definitional, methodological, and conceptual issues. *Journal of Consulting and Clinical Psychology, 57,* 31–38.

Baxter, L. A. (1986). Gender differences in the heterosexual relationship rules embedded in break-up accounts. *Journal of Social and Personal Relationships, 3,* 289–306.

Baxter, L. A. (1990). Dialectical contradictions in relationship development. *Journal of Social and Personal Relationships, 7,* 69–88.

Baxter, L. A., & Montgomery, B. M. (1996). *Relating: Dialogues & dialectics.* New York: Guilford.

Baxter, L. A., & Wilmot, W. W. (1985). Taboo topics in close relationships. *Journal of Social and Personal Relationships, 2,* 253–269.

Bochner, A. P. (1982). On the efficacy of openness in close relationships. In M. Burgoon (Ed.), *Communication yearbook 6* (pp. 109–123). Beverly Hills, CA: Sage.

Bodenmann, G., Kaiser, A., Hahlweg, K., & Fehm-Wolfsdorf, G. (1998). Communication patterns during marital conflict: A cross-cultural replication. *Personal Relationships, 5,* 343–356.

Burgoon, J. K., & Walther, J. (1990). Nonverbal expectancies and the evaluative consequences of violations. *Human Communication Research, 17,* 232–265.

Burleson, B. R., Kunkel, A., Samter, W., & Werking, K. J. (1996). Men's and women's evaluations of communication skills in personal relationship: When sex differences make a difference—and when they don't. *Journal of Social and Personal Relationships, 13,* 201–224.

Bushman, B. J. (2002). Does venting anger feed or extinguish the flame? Catharsis, rumination, distraction, anger, and aggressive responding. *Personality and Social Psychology Bulletin, 28,* 721–731.

Caughlin, J. (2004). The demand–withdraw pattern of communication as a predictor of marital satisfaction over time: Unresolved issues and future directions. *Human Communication Research, 28,* 49–85.

Caughlin, J., & Afifi, T. D. (2004). When is topic avoidance unsatisfying? A more complete investigation into the underlying links between avoidance and dissatisfaction in parent–child and dating relationships. *Human Communication Research, 30,* 479–513.

Caughlin, J., & Golish, T. (2002). An analysis of the association between topic avoidance and dissatisfaction: Comparing perceptual and interpersonal explanations. *Communication Monographs, 69,* 275–296.

Caughlin, J. P., Golish, T. D., Olson, L. N., Sargent, J. E., Cook, J. S., & Petronio, S. (2000). Intrafamily secrets in various family configurations: A communication boundary management perspective. *Communication Studies, 51,* 116–134.

Caughlin, J. P., & Huston, T. L. (2002). A contextual analysis of the association between demand/withdraw and marital satisfaction. *Personal Relationships, 9,* 95–119.

Caughlin, J. P., & Vangelisti, A. L. (2000). An individual difference explanation of why married couples engage in the demand–withdraw pattern of conflict. *Journal of Social and Personal Relationships, 17*, 523–551.

Christensen, A., & Heavey, C. L. (1990). Gender and social structure in the demand–withdraw pattern of marital conflict. *Journal of Personality and Social Psychology, 59*, 73–81.

Christensen, A., & Shenk, J. L. (1991). Communication, conflict, and psychological distance in nondistressed, clinic, and divorcing couples. *Journal of Counseling and Clinical Psychology, 59*, 458–463.

Cloven, D. H., & Roloff, M. E. (1993). The chilling effect of aggressive potential on the expression of complaints in intimate relationships. *Communication Monographs, 60*, 198–219.

Cross, S. E., & Madson, L. (1997). Models of the self: Self-construals and gender. *Psychological Bulletin, 1*, 5–37.

Cupach, W. R. (2000). Advancing understanding about relational conflict. *Journal of Social and Personal Relationships, 17*, 697–703.

Dailey, R. M., & Palomares, N. A. (2004). Strategic topic avoidance: An investigation of topic avoidance frequency, strategies used, and relational correlates. *Communication Monographs, 71*, 471–496.

Finkenauer, C., & Hazam, H. (2000). Disclosure and secrecy in marriage: Do both contribute to marital satisfaction? *Journal of Social and Personal Relationships, 17*, 245–263.

Fitzpatrick, J., & Sollie, D. L. (1999). Unrealistic gendered and relationship-specific beliefs: Contributions to investments and commitment in dating relationships. *Journal of Social and Personal Relationships, 16*, 852–867.

Frijns, T. (2005). *Keeping secrets: Quantity, quality and consequences.* Amsterdam: De Boelelaan.

Golish, T. D. (2000). Is openness always better? Exploring the role of topic avoidance, satisfaction, and parenting styles of stepparents. *Communication Quarterly, 48*, 137–158.

Gottman, J. M., & Krokoff, L. J. (1989). Marital interaction and satisfaction: A longitudinal view. *Journal of Consulting and Clinical Psychology, 57*, 47–52.

Gottman, J. M., & Levenson, R. W. (2000). The timing of divorce: Predicting when a couple will divorce over a 14-year period. *Journal of Marriage and the Family, 62*, 737–745.

Greene, K., & Faulkner, S. L. (2002). Expected versus actual responses to disclosure in relationships of HIV-positive African American adolescent females. *Communication Studies, 53*, 297–317.

Guerrero, L. K., & Afifi, W. A. (1995). What parents don't know: Topic avoidance in parent–child relationships. In T. Socha & G. Stamp (Eds.), *Parents, children, and communication: Frontiers of theory and research* (pp. 219–247). Mahwah, NJ: Lawrence Erlbaum Associates.

Hampel, A. D., & Vangelisti, A. L. (2008). Commitment expectations in romantic relationships: Application of a prototype interaction-pattern model. *Personal Relationships, 15*, 81–102.

Hasserbrauck, M., & Fehr, B. (2002). Dimensions of relationship quality. *Personal Relationships, 9*, 253–270.

Heavey, C. L., Christensen, A., & Malamuth, N. M. (1995). The longitudinal impact of demand and withdrawal during marital conflict. *Journal of Consulting and Clinical Psychology, 63*, 797–801.

Heavey, C. L., Layne, C., & Christensen, A. (1993). Gender and conflict structure in marital interaction: A replication and extension. *Journal of Consulting and Clinical Psychology, 61*, 16–27.

Higgins, E. T., King, G. A., & Mavin, G. H. (1982). Individual construct accessibility and subjective impressions and recall. *Journal of Personality and Social Psychology, 43*, 35–47.

Huston, T. L., McHale, S. M., & Crouter, A. C. (1986). When the honeymoon's over: Changes in the marriage relationship over the first year. In R. Gilmour & S. Duck (Eds.), *The emerging field of personal relationships* (pp. 109–132). Hillsdale, NJ: Lawrence Erlbaum Associates.

Jacobson, N. S. (1990). Commentary: Contributions from psychology to an understanding of marriage. In F. D. Fincham & T. N. Bradbury (Eds.), *The psychology of marriage* (pp. 258–275). New York: Guilford Press.

Kurdek, L. A. (1995). Predicting change in marital satisfaction from husbands' and wives' conflict resolution styles. *Journal of Marriage and the Family, 57*, 153–164.

Lever, J. (1976). Sex differences in the games children play. *Social Problems, 23*, 478–487.

Lloyd, S. (1987). Conflict in premarital relationships: Differential perceptions of males and females. *Family Relations, 36*, 290–294.

Makoul, G., & Roloff, M. (1998). The role of efficacy and outcome expectations in the decision to withhold relational complaints. *Communication Research, 25*, 5–29.

Malis, R. S., & Roloff, M. E. (2006). Demand–withdraw patterns in serial arguments: Implications for well-being. *Human Communication Research, 32*, 198–216.

Martin, L. L., & Tesser, A. (1996). Some ruminative thoughts. In R. Wyer (Ed.), *Ruminative thought* (pp. 1–48). Mahwah, NJ: Lawrence Erlbaum Associates.

Martin, R. W. (1991). Examining personal relationship thinking: The relational cognition complexity instrument. *Journal of Social and Personal Relationships, 8*, 467–480.

McCullough, M. E., Bono, G., & Root, L. M. (2007). Rumination, emotion, and forgiveness: Three longitudinal studies. *Journal of Personality and Social Psychology, 92*, 490–505.

Nolen-Hoeksema, S. (1991). Responses to depression and their effects on the duration of depressive episodes. *Journal of Abnormal Psychology, 100*, 569–582.

Nolen-Hoeksema, S., & Jackson, B. (2001). Mediators of the gender difference in rumination. *Psychology of Women Quarterly, 25*, 37–47.

Noller, P., Feeney, J. A., Bonnell, D., & Callan, V. J. (1994). A longitudinal study of conflict in early marriage. *Journal of Social and Personal Relationships, 11*, 233–252.

Parks, M. R. (1982). Ideology in interpersonal communication: Off the couch and into the world. In M. Burgoon (Ed.), *Communication yearbook 6* (pp. 79–107). Beverly Hills, CA: Sage.

Pearson, J. C. (1992). *Lasting love: What keeps couples together.* Dubuque, IA: Wm. C. Brown Publishers.

Pennebaker, J. W., Kiecolt-Glaser, J., & Glaser, R. (1988). Disclosure of traumas and immune function: Health implications for psychotherapy. *Journal of Consulting and Clinical Psychology, 56*, 239–245.

Petronio, S. (1991). Communication boundary management: A theoretical model of managing disclosure of private information between marital couples. *Communication Theory, 1,* 311–335.

Petronio, S. (2000). The boundaries of privacy: Praxis of everyday life. In S. Petronio (Ed.), *Balancing the secrets of private disclosures* (pp. 37–49). Mahwah, NJ: Lawrence Erlbaum Associates.

Petronio, S. (2002). *Boundaries of privacy: Dialectics of disclosure.* Albany, NY: SUNY Press.

Petronio, S., Reeder, H. M., Hecht, M. L., & Mon't Ros-Mendoza, T. (1996). Disclosure of sexual abuse by children and adolescents. *Journal of Applied Communication Research, 24,* 181–199.

Roloff, M. E., & Cloven, D. H. (1990). The chilling effect in interpersonal relationships: The reluctance to speak one's mind. In D. D. Cahn (Ed.), *Intimates in conflict: A communication perspective* (pp. 49–76). Hillsdale, NJ: Lawrence Erlbaum Associates.

Roloff, M. E., & Ifert, D. E. (1998). Antecedents and consequences of explicit agreements declaring a taboo topic in dating relationships. *Personal Relationships, 5,* 191–205.

Roloff, M. E., & Ifert, D. E. (2000). Conflict management through avoidance: Withholding complaints, suppressing arguments, and declaring topics taboo. In S. Petronio (Ed.), *Balancing the secrets of private disclosures* (pp. 151–179). Mahwah, NJ: Lawrence Erlbaum Associates.

Rusbult, C. E. (1980). Commitment and satisfaction: A test of the investment model. *Journal of Experimental Social Psychology, 16,* 172–186.

Rusbult, C. E. (1983). A longitudinal test of the investment model. *Journal of Personality and Social Psychology, 45,* 101–117.

Rusbult, C. E., Johnson, D. J., & Morrow, G. D. (1986). Determinants and consequences of exit, voice, loyalty, and neglect: Responses to dissatisfaction in adult romantic involvements. *Human Relations, 39,* 45–63.

Rusbult, C. E., Johnson, D. J., & Morrow, G. D. (1986). Impact of couple patterns of problem solving on distress and nondistress in dating relationships. *Journal of Personality and Social Psychology, 50,* 744–753.

Sabatelli, R. M., & Bartle-Haring, S. (2003). Family-of-origin experiences and adjustment in married couples. *Journal of Marriage and Family, 65,* 159–169.

Sagrestano, L. M., Christensen, A., & Heavey, C. L. (1998). Social influence techniques during marital conflict. *Personal Relationships, 5,* 75–89.

Sargent, J. (2002). Topic avoidance: Is this the way to a more satisfying relationship? *Communication Research Reports, 19,* 175–182.

Sillars, A. L., Roberts, L. J., Leonard, K. E., & Dun, T. (2000). Cognition during marital conflict: The relationship of thought and talk. *Journal of Social and Personal Relationships, 17,* 479–502.

Smith, L., Heaven, P. C. L., & Ciarrochi, J. (2008). Trait emotional intelligence, conflict communication patterns, and relationship satisfaction. *Personality and Individual Differences, 44,* 1314–1325.

Smyth, J. M. (1998). Written emotional expression: Effect sizes, outcome types, and moderating variables. *Journal of Consulting and Clinical Psychology, 66,* 174–184.

Smyth, J. M., & Pennebaker, J. W. (2001). What are the health effects of disclosure? In A. Baum, T. A. Revenson, & J. E. Singer (Eds.), *Handbook of health psychology* (pp. 339–348). Mahwah, NJ: Lawrence Erlbaum Associates.

Solomon, D. H., Knobloch, L. K., & Fitzpatrick, M. A. (2004). Relational power, marital schema, and decisions to withhold complaints: An investigation of the chilling effect on confrontation in marriage. *Communication Studies, 55,* 146–171.

Solomon, D. H., & Samp, J. A. (1998). Power and problem appraisal: Perceptual foundations of the chilling effect in dating relationships. *Journal of Social and Personal Relationships, 15,* 191–209.

Sprecher, S. (1988). Investment model, equity, and social support determinants of relationship commitment. *Social Psychology Quarterly, 51,* 318–328.

Stiles, W. B. (1987). Verbal response modes as intersubjective categories. In R. L. Russell (Ed.), *Language in psychotherapy: Strategies of discovery* (pp. 131–170). New York: Plenum Press.

Stiles, W. B., Shuster, P. L., & Harrigan, J. A. (1992). Disclosure and anxiety: A test of the fever model. *Journal of Personality and Social Psychology, 63,* 980–988.

Suh, E. J., Moskowitz, D. S., Fournier, M. A., & Zuroff, D. C. (2004). Gender and relationship: Influences on agentic and communal behaviors. *Personal Relationships, 1,* 41–49.

Thibaut, J. W., & Kelley, H. H. (1959). *The social psychology of groups.* New York: Wiley.

Thomsen, D. K. (2006). The association between rumination and negative affect: A review. *Cognition and Emotion, 20,* 1216–1235.

Vangelisti, A. L. (1994). Family secrets: Forms, functions and correlates. *Journal of Social and Personal Relationships, 11,* 113–135.

Vangelisti, A. L., & Caughlin, J. P. (1997). Revealing family secrets: The influence of topic, function, and relationships. *Journal of Social and Personal Relationships, 14,* 679–705.

Vangelisti, A. L., Caughlin, J. P., & Timmerman, L. (2001). Criteria for revealing family secrets. *Communication Monographs, 68,* 1–17.

Vangelisti, A. L., & Daly, J. A. (1997). Gender differences in standards for romantic relationships. *Personal Relationships, 4,* 203–219.

Vogel, D. L., Wester, S. R., & Heesacker, M. (1999). Dating relationships and the demand–withdraw pattern of communication. *Sex Roles, 41,* 297–306.

Ward, A., Lyubomirsky, S., Sousa, L., & Nolen-Hoeksema, S. (2003). Can't quite commit: Rumination and uncertainty. *Personality and Social Psychology Bulletin, 29,* 96–107.

Weger, H. (2005). Disconfirming communication and self-verification in marriage: Associations among the demand/withdraw interaction pattern, feeling understood, and marital satisfaction. *Journal of Social and Personal Relationships, 22,* 19–31.

Weigel, D. J. (2008). A dyadic assessment of how couples indicate their commitment to each other. *Personal Relationships, 15,* 17–39.

Wupperman, P. (2003). *Differences in depression as a function of gender.* Unpublished master's thesis, University of North Texas.

Challenges to Disclosure

18 Regulating the Privacy of Confidentiality

Grasping the Complexities through Communication Privacy Management Theory

Sandra Petronio and Jennifer Reierson

In our current world, we often face the concomitant needs of maintaining privacy and revealing to others to attain medical care, establish friendships, sustain family relationships, open bank accounts, get a passport, and talk to our clergy. In all cases, to achieve these goals, we have to tell others our private information. When we make these disclosures, we create a bond with the recipient. There is an implicit or explicit contract that we establish with the "confidant." We think about the targets of our disclosure as people who are likely to keep our information "confidential." Yet, there are many incidents where the contract of confidentiality is breached in ways that violate our trust, undercut our privacy, and compromise our expectations about the nature of confidentiality. While we see these issues in our everyday life, the instability of faith in maintaining privacy has both personal and societal consequences. As Kenneth Prewitt, former director of the U.S. Census Bureau, points out, it is difficult to have the kind of democracy we enjoy in the United States without access to information. He notes that, "if privacy issues [and the belief in confidentiality] begin to erode the information base of our democracy, there is a high price to pay" (Prewitt, 2005, p. 17). This chapter uses communication privacy management theory (Petronio, 2002) to explore the relationship between privacy and confidentiality to better understand the reasons why people are increasingly finding it difficult to have faith in the notion of confidentiality.

Bok (1982) writes that "the principles of confidentiality postulate a duty to protect confidences against third parties under certain circumstances" (p. 119). In assessing the meaning of this well-respected and often desired state of confidentiality, there are several critical components. When we need or wish to confide, we have to give our private information to others, sometimes in response to a request, to achieve a specific goal, or to honor a relationship, thereby telling private information in good faith. There are several circumstances where confidentiality has received considerable attention. One such example is in medical situations. Physician and health care providers have long realized that part of their professional role is to serve the mission of patient confidentiality (Robinson, 1991). However, confidentiality has not been an easy concept to grasp in general or in specific situations such as financial, medical, governmental, social, and relational situations. We find that people are uncertain how to rectify their assumptions about confidentiality and maintaining their privacy with instances where, for example, employers monitor office e-mail (Guernsey, 2000), there is video surveillance of employees (Trevison, 2007), or there is genetic testing that occurs in the workplace (Girion, 2002). As a consequence, the notion of confidentiality has become muddy in our current society. One fundamental concern is the lack of conceptual formulations that give us the apparatus to recognize the underlying paradox of our needs. Given that confidentiality is integral to privacy, one of the more productive ways to grasp the notion of confidentiality regulation is through the lens of communication privacy management (CPM) theory (Petronio, 2002).

Communication Privacy Management

The theory of communication privacy management (Petronio, 2002, 2004, 2007) is a useful framework given understanding the nature of confidentiality requires us to see that (1) privacy and confidentiality work as a tension and (2) the concomitant needs for privacy and granting access function to influence the choices people make to reveal or conceal. Thus, the dialectical push and pull of this tension underpins decision criteria that people use to open up about private issues, thereby establishing a confidant relationship or enabling people to retain their private information. Thus, people often make decisions about revealing based on judging risk-benefits, because of certain motivations to reach a goal, or based on cultural expectations. Further, the decision criteria have the potential to also influence a confidant's judgment about telling or preserving the confidentiality of someone else's information (Petronio, 2000c). Through the use of a boundary metaphor, CPM illustrates the way people manage their privacy both personally and in conjunction with confidants (Petronio, 2000a).

Therefore, this process, where people regulate privacy boundaries as they make choices about the flow of their private information, is guided by six principles: (1) people believe that they own private information, which defines the parameters of what constitutes the meaning of private information; (2) because people believe they own private information, they also believe that they have the right to control that information; (3) to control the flow of their private information, people use privacy rules they develop based on criteria important to them; (4) once they tell others their private information, the nature of that information changes, becoming co-owned by the confidant; (5) once the information is co-owned, ideally the parties negotiate collectively held and agreed-upon privacy rules for third-party dissemination; and (6) because people do not consistently, effectively, or actively negotiate collectively held privacy rules, there is the possibility of "boundary turbulence" which means that there are disruptions in the way that co-owners control and regulate the flow of private information to third parties (Caughlin & Petronio, 2004; Petronio, 2002; Petronio & Durham, 2008; Serewicz & Petronio, 2007).

CPM Parameters of Confidentiality Regulation

CPM helps us recognize the dynamics of confidentiality regulation through the concept of co-ownership (Petronio, 2002). When others choose to tell us their private information, they entrust us with information that they feel belongs to them and should continue to be within their control. Yet, they are willing to reveal the information to us because they judge us to be responsible "confidants." That is, they determined that we could fulfill expectations that are derived from a set of decision criteria used to estimate the target's worthiness of access to their private information (Petronio). CPM argues that people depend on criteria to develop privacy rules. For example, privacy rules are developed based on a person's cultural values, their gender, their motivation to retain something as private or to disclose it, the assessment of risk-benefits, and changes in situational or contextual circumstances that work to modify existing rules, like the changes that occur when individuals divorce. When people divorce, they cannot use the same privacy rules they did with their former spouse. Hence, the situation or context calls for changing the privacy rules that guide choices about managing privacy.

When others meet the needed expectations (according to the privacy rules), they are given access to our private information. However, the act of granting access fundamentally changes the dynamics of how that information is viewed. The information moves from within the domain of the original owner into a shared space or boundary that is controlled, and therefore co-owned, by the original owner and the confidant (Petronio & Durham, 2008). In other words, I disclose to a person I think is my best friend; that act makes my best friend responsible for knowing things about me, a type of co-ownership. My best friend shares in knowing something about me I think is private. This process marks the evolution of private information that transitions from residing solely within a personal privacy boundary to a redefined collective privacy boundary. As such, the information is considered shared property and therefore controlled, not only by the original owner, but also by the confidant who becomes a responsible party. Thus, the privacy boundary advances from a personal to a dyadic or collective organism.

With this metamorphosis, a confidant is created. The original owner gives access to the private information either by disclosing or granting permission to it. However, the original owner does not necessarily perceive that he or she has fully given up control over the private information (Petronio, 2002). Instead, the original owner tends to have expectations for how that entrusted information will be treated after the confidant knows it (Petronio, 2000c). The confidant is seen by the original owner as having fiduciary responsibilities. Original owners often assume that their information will be kept confidential in the way that they themselves would regulate access to third parties. As CPM argues, when these expectations are discussed, the boundary surrounding the private information is managed by mutually negotiated and agreed-upon privacy rules. In CPM terms, this means that the original owner anticipates the privacy rules will be coordinated with the confidant. Coordination reduces the potential for conflict and unwanted breaches of confidentiality as we find in a study by Golish (2003) with step-families. When stepfamilies are able to establish a clear set of privacy rules for how information should flow from custodial to noncustodial family members, they reduce the incidences of conflict and problems among the members (Golish). To accomplish boundary coordination like this, three operations are necessary: negotiating privacy rules for linkages, permeability, and ownership (Petronio, 2002).

Privacy rules for linkages. Linkages refer to the establishment of mutually agreed-upon privacy rules that are used to choose others who might be privy to the collectively held information. A number of parameters are used to make judgments about linkages with others (Petronio, 2002). For example, owners and co-owners may depend on parameters to link others (giving access) such as the status of the potential confidant (e.g., Brooks, 1974); the type of topic discussed (e.g., Aries & Johnson, 1983); the gender of the target confidant (e.g., Cash, 1975); the attractiveness of the target (e.g., Sote & Good, 1974); certain characteristics of the target, including discretion (e.g., Sollie & Fischer, 1985); level of intimacy the owner and confidant perceive they have with the target (e.g., Hill & Stull, 1987); perceived need for control (e.g., Dinger-Duhon & Brown, 1987); and personality traits that might compromise confidentiality (e.g., Brown & Guy, 1983). Because these parameters are "negotiated," the individuals privy to the information determine who may be defined as a coconfidant based on any combination of criteria that meets the needs of controlling or granting access to that information. Of course, the original owner may carry some weight in setting which parameters are more relevant. However, once the information is known, others "in the know" may have their own interpretation of how the information should be managed. Consequently, the act of negotiation is useful to make the desires of the original owner clear and the agreement about a final set of privacy rules for linkages obvious. For every person granted status of "confidant," there are similar negotiations that theoretically take place. In many cases, a finite number of people are given the status of confidant, likely because the spread of information to many others has the potential to compromise the ability to set parameters for information control (Petronio, 2002).

Privacy rules for permeability. Boundary permeability represents rule coordination about the extent to which collectively held privacy boundaries are opened or closed once they are formed. Again, the confidant and the original owner negotiate how much control over the information there should be to restrict or grant access to third parties. These rules regulate the depth, breadth, and amount of private information that is given access.

Depending on the degree of access, the flow of information can be visualized in terms of the thickness or thinness of a boundary wall that allows information to be known. The thicker the boundary, with dense and impenetrable walls, less access is given, and, therefore, less is known about the private information. CPM argues that this condition defines the case where people treat their private information as secrets (Petronio, 2002). However, on the other side of the continuum, the thinner the boundary walls, the more that is known to others. When people define their personal information as less private, the walls are more permeable, making the information easily accessible and open. For the most part, people treat their private information in variable ways, adjusting the level of permeability according to rules that protect and rules that grant access. For example, Greene and Serovich (1996) show that, for people living with HIV/AIDS, their privacy rules for access to testing results reflect a hierarchy of access ranging from who they desire to have the most access to testing information (i.e., their immediate family) to the least desired category of individuals representing nonfamily members (e.g., employers). While this initial set of decisions is predicated on the original owner's protection and access rules, once that information is shared, the original owner expects that confidants understand the fiduciary responsibilities for the information. This translates into the belief that confidants willingly negotiate collectively held privacy rules and abide by the decisions made about third-party disclosures or permission for further access.

Access rules that the confidant and original owner develop to restrict or grant outside others access to the private information function on two levels. On an internal level, when *boundary insiders* are free to discuss the collectively held private information among the coconfidants, it is defined by open access to insiders, all of whom are privileged confidants within a boundary sphere. However, there is also the possibility that, while all confidants within a boundary sphere know certain aspects of the information, they may not be granted the right to openly discuss it with all the members inside the sphere. A curious point about the internal workings of collectively held privacy boundaries is the extent to which confidants linked into a boundary donate their own private information to the existing information.

People who are already privy to someone's private information may, in turn, reveal something equally private about themselves. There are many reasons confidants might contribute their own information to the collective privacy boundary once it has been formed. For example, research has shown that confidants sometimes reveal their own private information as an act of reciprocity. The confidant may reciprocate to put the discloser at ease so he or she tells something about a related experience (Omarzu, 2000). Actions like these may provide social support for the discloser but can also make the confidant feel positive about being called upon to help. Sometimes people decide to reciprocate because they view the act as empathic; they may also gage the likelihood of reciprocation based on perceptions of why they were selected as a confidant (Derlega, Winstead, Wong, & Greenspan, 2004). Perhaps the confidant wants to illustrate competency and, therefore, reveals a way that he or she addressed a similar issue. In addition, a comfort level may be an issue, in that, having the sense of being part of a confidential cocoon, the confidant may feel more at ease talking about a related private matter of his or her own.

For the confidants, contributing their own private information to the collective boundary may differ in depth and breadth (Petronio & Kovach, 1997). That is, the disclosure contributions may not necessarily be of equal weight, intensity, or level of privacy as the original owner's revelation. In particular, the kind of private information the confidant contributes may be disproportionate to the depth and breadth of a disclosure the original owner made to create the privacy boundary. For example, in a nursing home study, research indicated that, while the nursing home residents were expected to give up privacy in many different spheres, the nursing staff did not define their role as necessarily having to contribute to that sphere (Petronio & Kovach). Consequently, little or no contributions were made to the resident's privacy boundary even though the nurses were fully privileged to know all about private matters of the residents. Interestingly, the residents reported feeling disturbed by this disparity and often sought to equalize the incongruity by asking personal, probing questions of the nurses (Petronio & Kovach).

There are a number of dynamics that disproportionate contributions of private information can prompt. Nevertheless, once a contribution is made, the nature of the coordination process shifts to incorporate the expectations of all the co-owners. Each contributor believes that he or she retains ownership rights; however, there is a sense that there may be more trust among the collective because a number of different owners have contributed to the collective whole. However, that level of trust may vary depending on the amount of access the others in the collective find appropriate and whether the trust is breached by either telling insiders forbidden from knowing certain information or by compromising internal information through telling outsiders. For example, in a study on parents' disclosure of medical information about their children, one of the findings indicated that other family members were the most likely to disclose the child's medical condition to other family members not in the know or to individuals outside the family without permission from the parents (Johnson, Kass, & Natowicz, 2005). This is a kind of "unauthorized disclosure," where the rules seemed to be clear about restricted access, yet members of the collective boundary around the medical information determined that they felt it was acceptable for them to disclose but doing so had the potential to compromise the level of trust felt by the parents.

As the aforementioned example suggests, just as there are internal access rules regulating permeability for confidants privy to the information, there are also external privacy rules that control how much *boundary outsiders* can know. For example, in higher education, the Family Educational Rights and Privacy Act (FERPA) regulates the amount and type of information that professors and instructors know about a student's accomplishments and are allowed to share with parents if the child is an emancipated adult (Gilley & Gilley, 2006). Although parents are often invested in their child's performance in classes, the boundary between instructor and student is regulated by privacy rules that evolved into a law (FERPA) governing ways to maintain student privacy (Bernstein, 2007). However, these rules sever parts of an existing boundary in which parents perceive a continuation of control over all matters having to do with their child's welfare. Because they are defined as *boundary outsiders* according to the FERPA regulation, the faculty and university administrators are mandated to deny parental or guardian access to grade or performance information. The conundrum for the parents is that, by the parameters of this legal regulation, other university administrators or personnel may be privy to their child's performance information as grades are entered or financial aid continuance is considered. Although students have the right and may bring their parents into the boundary sphere that is safeguarding performance information, even then the instructor is regulated by external rules of FERPA such that they cannot function by the same privacy rule as the student (Bernstein, 2007).

In addition, the coordination of privacy rules for access often depends on the nature and state of a relationship (e.g., Afifi, 2003). For instance, when relationships are in the process of termination, as decreases in intimacy occur, so too is there a decrease in the breadth of disclosure about private matters (Tolstedt & Stokes, 1984). When the boundaries are more permeable, confidants may know more information, both in depth and breadth, and the permeability may be influenced by the nature and status of the relationship.

On the other hand, protection rules, as opposed to access rules, for collectively held private information reflect many strategies people use to safeguard access to the information. Because there are at least two people represented in collectively held privacy boundaries, the need for negotiation and mutually agreed-upon privacy rules is necessary to achieve a functional level of coordination. While the goal is to limit how much others know, the level of protection achieved often varies with the type of strategy used. CPM argues that there are several different types of protection rules (Petronio & Durham, 2008). For example, topic avoidance tends to be one type of privacy rule that is used to regulate how much information others know (e.g., Afifi & Olson, 2005). There are numerous reasons why people avoid talking about certain topics. Afifi and Guerrero (2000) point out that avoiding revealing information may serve as a safeguard to preserve one's identity. Therefore, telling a confidant information that risks vulnerability is reason enough to assess the likelihood of unresponsiveness or reactions that somehow compromise a sense of self. Consequently, if there is a belief that the confidant might not meet expectations for a particular response, avoiding the disclosure is a viable way to preserve one's identity (Afifi & Guerrero, 1998; Guerrero & Afifi, 1995).

As Afifi and Guerrero (2000) note, topic avoidance also functions both as a means of protecting relationships and as a way to signal the de-escalation of a relationship. In the research on child sexual abuse using CPM, it was clear that topic avoidance was used as a way to shield adults, such as a grandmother, who might have had a relationship with the perpetrator (Petronio, Reeder, Hecht, & Mon't Ros-Mendoza, 1996). However, the children also used incremental disclosure that regulated the information flow to test the confidant's response, measuring whether more information should be told to this person (Petronio et al., 1996). Using topic avoidance with confidants who are relational partners can potentially lead to dissatisfaction with the relationship. However, Caughlin and Afifi (2004) point out that research shows the individual's motivation for avoiding disclosure and the way the partners define the nature of privacy management influences whether a partner might become dissatisfied with a relationship. When people form collective privacy boundaries that include at least one other person, there is a possibility that the type of information being considered is so volatile that the co-owners decide to sustain a thick boundary wall with rigid protection rules by declaring the topic taboo (Petronio, 2002).

Unfortunately, in a number of situations, taboo topic protection rules often are used to shelter harmful information. For example, the perpetrator of incest or sexual abuse typically relies on successfully imposing rules that sustain thick boundaries around the incidents (Ray, 1996; Schultz, 2000). These thick boundaries may be used as protection from social disgrace or legal punishment for the perpetrator, but also function as a means of isolation for the abused. For instance, the proverbial "wall of silence" is successful with sexual abuse of children because the effectiveness of taboo topic protection rules often means that silence lasts for years or even a lifetime. Clearly, many well-kept "family secrets" are such due to pressures imposed by a family member who defines the information to be taboo and off-limits to other members (Afifi & Olson, 2005).

However, for a wall of silence to be effective, those who are members of the boundary must follow the privacy rules that dictate the topic is off-limits for discussion or sharing. While not all privacy boundaries regulated by taboo topic protection rules are as sinister as child sexual abuse, the category of taboo topic protection rules reflects the intensity and volatile nature of information within privacy boundaries. In addition, the motivations for keeping secrets may be to not only protect those in the know within the privacy boundary, but also protect those who do not know (Afifi & Weiner, 2006; Derlega et al., 2004; Greene, Derlega, Yep, & Petronio, 2003).

Thus, these rules can guard such information as diagnosis or prognosis concerning an illness (see Pérez-Cárceles, Pereñiguez, Osuna, & Luna, 2005). To maintain thick boundaries around such information, families, couples, or parents may create a protection rule that excludes the illness as a topic of discussion with targeted others (Duggan & Petronio, in press). Sometimes, these rules are meant to shield children, protect families, or safeguard the employment of the ill person. Although erecting boundary walls and establishing rules to defend the information functions to limit the possibility of others knowing it, sometimes the level of secrecy that prevails also serves to discourage families or those within the privacy boundary from dealing productively with the information. In some situations, avoidance of such topics may be harmful. Infidelity may become taboo between those within the privacy boundary. Individuals that are privy to knowledge of the act may decide not to discuss the topic of infidelity because of the potential for intense repercussions or emotional response. These kinds of issues also have an impact on the privacy rules that are established regarding ownership of the information.

Privacy rules for ownership. The last type of management process that co-owners negotiate is the degree and kind of ownership. Concomitant with ownership is the sense of ownership rights that each of the co-owners assume. People face several issues when it comes to ownership. First, because we live in a world where we manage multiple privacy boundaries, sometimes people find it difficult to know when one boundary ends and another begins (Petronio, 2002). If a brother tells a sister that he was fired from a job, the sister may assume that it is within her purview to have the right to tell their mother. But, it is often difficult to make a decision because there are interconnecting boundary spheres at work given the brother and sister live within a family privacy boundary, each have their own personal privacy boundary, and now they have created a shared sibling privacy boundary around the disclosed information.

The question arises, therefore, about rights of ownership to make dependent decisions concerning who else *can* know the information. The underlying issue is the degree of assumed control over choices about the information. Original owners and confidants (co-owners) ideally negotiate the parameters for rules guiding ownership rights and concurrent obligations. When they do not, potential for conflict arises and this may happen even if a co-owner believes making an independent decision about the collective information is in the best interest of the original owner. For example, if a younger sister tells her older sister that she is pregnant and the older sister feels it is necessary to tell their parents. It is possible that the younger sister would feel betrayed, especially if she explicitly told her older sister not to tell their parents.

Second, ownership may be defined in a number of ways. Confidants are co-owners, yet the level and type of ownership may vary. Confidants may be *shareholders* who have knowledge of private information because they have been given permission to know it. From the perspective of the original owners (the people to whom the information belonged to before being given access), this type of confidant is often viewed as being fully vested in keeping the information according to the original owner's privacy rules. Shareholder confidants are evaluated to be worthy of co-ownership because they are judged to meet the criteria that the original owner used to give access. Besides the benefit of knowing the information, they also share in the cost of knowing through the added responsibility for the information.

Stakeholders are confidants who are perceived as worthy of some level of access because they serve a functional role, providing the original owner a needed outcome. For example, people may be willing to disclose financial information to their banks because they see them as stakeholders. The original owners do not expect their bank to give their "confidential" financial information to uninvited others because doing so compromises the bank's ability to function in a trusted way. Yet the stakes are limited to financial issues and do not extend to other domains. Physicians and health care personnel also represent this category of co-ownership.

For both types, there is a fiduciary responsibility on the part of the co-owner to fulfill the needs of the original owner. However, there may be benefits for the co-owner serving in the role of confidant. For example, the co-owner may become a more trusted friend. There are embedded obligations that theoretically should be negotiated so that a principle of stakeholder fairness is accomplished. In other words, synchronizing the privacy rules for ownership hypothetically allows each party to know the parameters of what is ethically or morally duty bound as a function of serving in a confidant role and they also learn what they must refrain from doing (Phillips, 2003).

Becoming a confidant. There are at least two ways that people become confidants (Petronio, 2002). First, serving as a confidant may result from soliciting private information belonging to someone else. Second, people may find they are recipients of private information, although reluctantly so (Petronio, 2000b, 2000c, 2002; Petronio & Jones, 2006; Petronio, Jones, & Morr, 2003). Deliberate confidants request private information from others either directly, indirectly, or gain permission from them to know the information. The common thread for deliberate confidants is that they purposely seek to know someone else's private information. There are many examples of ways people function as deliberate confidants. For instance, throughout the long history of therapy, the clinician's role is to solicit private thoughts and feelings from clients. Clergy also perform this function. Likewise, physicians depend on learning private medical information either through directly receiving descriptions about the medical symptoms from the patient or through the results of medical tests for which they have been given permission to know. Though the confidant seeks out information, the target does not always willingly give the information (Petronio, 2000c). Instead, there are situations when the discloser tries to thwart the attempts. Nevertheless, confidants pursue the information because they believe they have the right to know.

For reluctant confidants, receiving uninvited private information often is a burden (Petronio et al., 2003). The dilemma is underscored when we remember that reluctant confidants not only may receive information they do not want, but there is also the embedded suggestion of obligation attached to the disclosure (Petronio & Jones, 2007). Learning unwanted private information affects the perceived obligations on the part of the confidant, especially if the messages communicated are directly relevant to the recipient. Petronio and Jones argue that these types of circumstances are often defined as privacy breaches for the reluctant recipient. In studying pregnant couples having their first child, Petronio and Jones learned there were a number of ways these pregnant couples repaired a privacy boundary that was infringed upon when they were told information they did not want but was relevant to their pregnancy. For instance, when pregnant couples defined the unsolicited information as invasive, such as the pregnant woman who was told that she needed to immediately seek medical help because she was carrying the baby low and that meant the baby had the umbilical cord wrapped around its neck, they coped by talking to other people about it, ignoring the uninvited information, and verifying the information with an authority.

Even when the information received by reluctant confidants is not directly pertinent to them, they may still find it necessary to maneuver around expectations that suggest moral obligations to respond in a particular way. For example, bartenders, nursing home care staff, and even airplane passengers can hear confessions, stories, or unwanted information from patrons, residents, or neighboring passengers that they would rather have not heard (Petronio, 2002; Petronio & Kovach, 1997). In many cases, the information leaves the recipient feeling uncertain about privacy obligations or an appropriate response. Confidants may feel pressure to reciprocate the disclosure or help the discloser work through a problem. The recipient may leave the interaction feeling uncomfortably responsible for someone else's private information that he or she did not wish to hear in the first place.

Although the probability is higher that reluctant confidants might be in a position to learn more than they want to know, it is true that there are situations where confidants who solicit may receive private information for which they are not prepared. For example, new partners who solicit information about each other's past relationships might also learn surprising information about multiple partners, STDs, previous abortions, or other promiscuous acts (Afifi & Weiner, 2006). Even physicians' family members soliciting information about their workday may become privy to unexpected medical information about a case (Petronio, 2006). For example, if a physician explains a difficult case to his wife and in the course of the discussion reveals he is worried he made a mistake regarding the course of treatment.

When confidants are able to negotiate the privacy rule parameters with the original owner, reach an agreement about the obligations of knowing, and come to terms with the way they came to be a confidant, it is possible that the nature of the confidant relationship can be productively regulated. However, because negotiations do not consistently or effectively take place, boundary turbulence can occur. As a result, disruptions to the way that confidant and original owner co-create a functional relationship become challenged. Hence, this turbulence may be the product of intentional or unintentional breaches; nevertheless, the nature of the confidant relationship is compromised, requiring repair work to take place (Petronio, 1991, 2002).

Breaches of Confidentiality

Breaching confidentiality is an example of privacy boundary turbulence. The reason this kind of boundary turbulence occurs is because the expectations an original owner had for the way his or her private information would be treated becomes compromised. In these instances, co-owners ignore, disregard, or mistake the kind of responsibility the original owners thought they had toward the security of their information. Violating confidentiality has the potential to disrupt relationships and compromise a sense of trust. In considering the ways that confidentiality is breached or predicted, there appears to be at least three categories that represent these violations; they include *discrepancy breaches of privacy*, *privacy ownership violations*, and times when privacy breaches are predicted or presumed so individuals use *preemptive privacy control* strategies.

Discrepancy breaches of privacy. In general, this breach occurs when anticipated expectations belonging to an original owner about his or her privacy do not match the actual way co-owners regulate third-party access or the way others gain access to become intentional or unintentional co-owners. An example of expectation discrepancies between anticipated and actual privacy regulation is seen in this health care case. Gloria had a biopsy to determine whether she had breast cancer. She was told that she would hear the results from her physician once the tests were completed. She assumed that she would be called at home or called to see the physician in person at his office.

One day, Gloria received a phone call at work. She was a receptionist at a busy organization and this call came during a point when she was registering people for a workshop one of the bosses was conducting. The caller identified herself as a nurse in her physician's office and wanted to let her know that the biopsy tests had just been received. The nurse said, "Gloria, I regret to inform you that the tests were positive, you have stage-four cancer; you need to make arrangements immediately for aggressive treatment. I am very sorry to tell you this. You need to get your affairs in order." She asked if Gloria understood. Gloria said yes. However, Gloria was in shock and could not remember anything the nurse said other than she had to get her affairs in order. She did not expect to receive her confidential medical information in this way.

This example of a discrepancy breach reflects an inconsistency in the expectations that Gloria had for how her private information might be handled by the medical team and the way that it was communicated. She did not expect that the nurse would be the source of the test results. While she understood that the nurse was privy to the information, she did not define the nurse as a primary stakeholder of the information. Instead, she defined the physician playing the primary stakeholder role because, in her estimation, he was managing the case and she put her faith in his hands regarding these tests. The nurse, on the other hand, was considered an auxiliary member of the team and, therefore, the expectation was that she played a supporting role, and not the primary role, when it came to handling the private information.

Privacy ownership violations. In this case, people's ability to exercise ownership and control according to their assumptions about rules for regulating their private information is violated. For example, in this case, a patient explains how she believed her privacy was violated. She states:

> I am a patient in a special unit where the staff has a meeting every week. They discuss the test results and whatever they want to discuss. You sort of find out along the way. They don't tell you what goes on, but you get second-hand information. The nurse will come back and say, "At the meeting the doctor said this . . ." I don't like them discussing me behind my back.
>
> (Braunack-Mayer & Mulligan, 2003, p. 278)

This patient felt violated because she assumed the physician would directly discuss treatment options with her. From her perspective, the integrity of her privacy boundary was compromised because the physician did not negotiate how he should handle talking about private medical information and decision making about her case. The patient defined the lack of direct communication as a breach in confidentiality. This same condition is witnessed in the next example. Another patient from the same study notes:

> I changed to a new GP and he was able to access the results of tests that my previous doctor had done via the computer. I was very surprised that information that one doctor has was available on the computer for another doctor. He did not ask me if that was okay; he did not explain to me; he just said, "I'll check what the tests were . . ." and I was just really surprised and wondered what else was freely available for everyone to read.
>
> (Braunack-Mayer & Mulligan, 2003, p. 278)

As with the first example, the way control over the information is enacted by the physician is contrary to the expectations of the patient. The patient feels violated because she did not have the option of talking about how the medical files and the information would be handled. Her point about not being asked permission illustrates the predicament the patient found herself in regarding the ease of access. Though we do not have information about this, it seems likely that the physician in this case would be perplexed about the patient's statement. Often in these circumstances, the stakeholders are not cognizant of the expectations patients have regarding the care of their private medical information (Rogers, 2006). This example reinforces the usefulness of the original owner and confidant talking about privacy management rules of information.

Preemptive privacy control. We also find cases where individuals have difficulty in confidently predicting the extent to which they will be able to negotiate privacy rules for access and protection to reach the level of confidentiality they desire. This condition may occur because of previous experiences with privacy breaches or a lack of certainty about levels of trust. Consequently, there are instances where people use a strategy of preemptive privacy control to thwart anticipated privacy violations. In this circumstance, people retain control over their information by setting up thick boundary walls preventing disclosure or permission for access. Or else, these individuals develop a test to assess to what degree they might give access. For example, the woman in this case explains why she did not tell a new doctor she previously had gonorrhea that was successfully treated. She stated that "it paints a picture. They don't ask how long ago. They just say, did you have it? It puts something there in their minds that would be negative about you and doesn't necessarily need to be, especially when it's so old" (Jenkins, Merz, & Sankar, 2005, p. 502). Clearly, the patient feels that revealing this medical information from her past directly puts her at risk in terms of the way she predicts her physician will perceive her (Pérez-Cárceles et al., 2005). She determined that given the illness occurred some time ago that it was not directly pertinent to her current case. Thus, in CPM terms, the patient erected thick boundaries around the information and, in a preemptive way, cut off communication about her past medical history.

This type of preemptive control strategy to seek protection from situations that are defined as potentially risking privacy violations also may occur in degrees of control. For instance, in the study on child sexual abuse, we found that children who had been abused tested the potential of harm by incrementally revealing information about the abusive situation to determine the extent of support. In situations where the confidant acted positively to an initial statement, the children were willing to progress to the next stage of revelations (Petronio et al., 1996). In circumstances where the confidant made fun of the child, ignored the child, or ridiculed the child, he or she would regain control over the information and refuse to disclose further. In fact, it is likely that these negative experiences with opening a privacy boundary might reinforce the need to remain silent with others (Petronio, 2002). As such, this type of protection against breaches may be an outgrowth of experiencing negative reactions to disclosures. For example, in a *Los Angeles Times* article, in order to preempt disclosures about their private lives by nannies or other service personnel who would have intimate knowledge of their private lives, celebrities are requiring, as a condition of employment, the signature of a "nondisclosure agreement" to curtail the revelation of potentially private information to unwanted others (Davidow, 2007). In this way, the parameters of confidentiality, or in CPM terms privacy rules, are clearly identified without ambiguity to hinder the possibility of a violation. Of course, actions such as these may not completely hamper the dissemination of private information, yet the fiduciary responsibilities of the co-owners are clearly identified and agreed upon up front. Although there are, no doubt, other types of confidentiality breaches, the three presented serve as the initial step in identifying the way that breaches take place or are thwarted.

Conclusion

Communication Privacy Management theory provides a rich canvas from which to understand the complexities of confidentiality regulation. This chapter illustrates two significant contributions to our understanding of confidentiality. First, unlike other attempts that focus primarily on context, this approach shifts the conceptual landscape to considering confidentiality as a partnership, between original owners and co-owners, where the enterprise of managing private information is built on mutual responsibilities and establishing rules for regulating the flow to others. As a result, it gives a more concrete way to see the *process* of confidentiality. Second, this CPM confidentiality regulation process identifies three kinds of violations individuals encounter, including *discrepancy breaches, privacy ownership violations,* and *preemptive privacy control.* Thus, having a better understanding of the process involved in developing, regulating, and violating confidentiality opens new lines of investigation that help us more clearly comprehend the dynamics of confidentiality regulation.

Future Directions

New directions for research that stem from this discussion include both the expansion of CPM theory and applications that address new research areas within this conceptualization of confidentiality. For instance, within this framework of *confidentiality regulation,* we can better recognize the "dance of establishing confidentiality." Take, for example, patients visiting a doctor for the first time. Undoubtedly, a confidential relationship is necessary, but patients may test the physicians to see whether their reactions to disclosed information yield the kind of response that assures they are being considered credible sources and that they can trust the doctors to protect information. We can also examine the impact of "decision criteria consistency" between the discloser and confidant when regulating confidentiality. For example, there are many situations where disclosers have one set of motivations (decision criteria) for telling or keeping information and confidants have a different set of motivations that influences the rules for third-party disclosure of mutually held information.

We see many examples from genetic counseling that show us the variant motives that have a probability of leading to breaches or conflict. A sister learns that she is a carrier of a disease-causing gene, tells her husband so, but is motivated to keep the information confidential and does not want him to tell her sibling. The husband agrees but has second thoughts because he believes the sister should be tested too. As a result, he violates the confidential agreement by telling her sister. While this husband told the information to protect the sibling, people like the sister withhold because they believe doing so will protect a relationship.

Confidentiality regulation from a CPM perspective can also provide a link to the part social support plays in a confidential relationship. For instance, in order to provide support, a confidant may be more likely to contribute to the mutually owned private information by telling about private experiences as a way to show empathy and understanding. As such, it may be interesting to consider online or community support networks, perhaps those available to new mothers such as La Leche League or those available to cancer patients and their families. These kinds of networks would provide a detailed web of interconnected disclosures with implications for confidentiality and social support. As we increasingly turn to the Internet for relationship building (dating sites, social networking sites, gaming sites), social support, shopping, and services such as banking, bill paying, and medical information, we must consider the implications for the process of confidentiality bound up in such disclosures of our private information. Breaches of confidentiality in these processes could have severe financial and social consequences and could also redefine the systems we currently use and take for granted.

Looking at the regulation system of confidentiality helps us to define the nature of breaches and we are more likely to determine viable repair tools once breaches take place. To better understand breaches and repair tools, researchers might consider the regulation systems for confidentiality between work and life (home). As the boundary between the two spheres becomes increasingly blurred and demands in each more intense, a breach becomes inevitable, constituting a need for viable repair tools that can be determined and explored as they are enacted. We live in a world where, as Bok (1982) suggests, "so much confidential information is now being gathered and recorded and requested by so many about so many that confidentiality, though as strenuously invoked as in the past, is turning out to be a weaker reed than ever" (p. 111). Consequently, we need a better map to discover more viable ways to address the confidentiality needs we face.

References

Afifi, T. D. (2003). "Feeling caught" in stepfamilies: Managing boundary turbulence through appropriate communication privacy rules. *Journal of Social and Personal Relationships, 20,* 729–755.

Afifi, T. D., & Olson, L. N. (2005). The chilling effect in families and the pressure to conceal secrets. *Communication Monographs, 72,* 192–216.

Afifi, W. A., & Guerrero, L. K. (1998). Some things are better left unsaid II: Topic avoidance in friendships. *Communication Quarterly, 36*, 231–249.

Afifi, W. A., & Guerrero, L. K. (2000). Motivations underlying topic avoidance in close relationships. In S. Petronio (Ed.), *Balancing the secrets of private disclosures* (pp. 165–180). Mahwah, NJ: Lawrence Erlbaum.

Afifi, W. A., & Weiner, J. L. (2006). Seeking information about sexual health: Applying the theory of Motivated Information Management. *Human Communication Research, 132*, 35–57.

Aries, E. J., & Johnson, F. L. (1983). Close friendship in adulthood: Conversational content between same-sex friends. *Sex Roles, 9*, 1183–1196.

Bernstein, E. (2007, September 20). Families grapple with student privacy. *Wall Street Journal*, D1–D2.

Bok, S. (1982). *Secrets: On the ethics of concealment and revelation*. New York: Pantheon.

Braunack-Mayer, A. J., & Mulligan, E. C. (2003). Sharing patient information between professionals: Confidentiality and ethics. *Medical Journal of Australia, 178*, 277–279.

Brooks, L. (1974). Interactive effects of sex and status on self-disclosure. *Journal of Counseling Psychology, 21*, 469–474.

Brown, E. C., & Guy, R. F. (1983). The effects of sex and Machiavellianism on self-disclosure patterns. *Social Behavior and Personality, 11*, 93–96.

Cash, T. F. (1975). Self-disclosure in the acquaintance process: Effects of sex, physical attractiveness, and approval motivation. *Dissertation Abstracts International, 35*, 3572B.

Caughlin, J., & Afifi, T. D. (2004). When is topic avoidance unsatisfying? A more complete investigation into the underlying links between avoidance and dissatisfaction in parent–child and dating relationships. *Human Communication Research, 30*, 479–514.

Caughlin, J., & Petronio, S. (2004). Privacy in families. In A. Vangelisti (Ed.), *Handbook of family communication* (pp. 379–412). Mahwah, NJ: Lawrence Erlbaum.

Davidow, A. (2007, July 26). Modern Life; L.A.'s secret service; Confidentiality agreements have become like prenups between Hollywood elite and household help. Those who aren't A-listers are starting to demand them too. *Los Angeles Times*, F-1.

Derlega, V. J., Winstead, B. A., Greene, K., Serovich, J., & Elwood, W. N. (2004). Reasons for HIV disclosure/nondisclosure in close relationships: Testing a model of HIV-disclosure decision making. *Journal of Social and Clinical Psychology, 23*, 747–767.

Dinger-Duhon, M., & Brown, B. B. (1987). Self-disclosure as an influence strategy: Effects of Machiavellianism, androgyny, and sex. *Sex Roles, 16*, 109–123.

Duggan, A., & Petronio, S. (in press). Communication between parents and physicians: A relational approach. In T. Socha & G. Stamp (Eds.), *Parents, children and communication II: Interfacing outside of home*. New York: Routledge.

Gilley, A., & Gilley, J. W. (2006). FERPA: What do faculty know? What can universities do? *College and University, 82*, 17–26.

Girion, L. (2002, May 9). Railroad settles suit over genetic testing workplace: BNSF to pay $2.2 million to 36 workers subjected to secret program. *Los Angeles Times*, p. C3.

Golish, T. D. (2003). Stepfamily communication strengths: Understanding the ties that bind. *Human Communication Research, 29*, 41–80.

Greene, K., Derlega, V., Yep, G., & Petronio, S. (2003). *Privacy and disclosure of HIV/AIDS in interpersonal relationships: A handbook for researchers and practitioners.* Mahwah, NJ: LEA Publishers.

Greene, K. L., & Serovich, J. M. (1996). Appropriateness of disclosure of HIV-testing information: The perspective of PLWAs. *Journal of Applied Communication Research, 24,* 50–65.

Guernsey, L. (2000, April 5). Management: You've got inappropriate mail; Monitoring of office e-mail is increasing. *New York Times,* p. C1.

Guerrero, L. K., & Afifi, W. A. (1995). Some things are better left unsaid: Topic avoidance in family relationships. *Communication Quarterly, 43,* 276–296.

Hill, C. T., & Stull, D. (1987). Gender and self-disclosure: Strategies for exploring the issues. In V. J. Derlega & J. H. Berg (Eds.), *Self-disclosure: Theory, research, and therapy* (pp. 81–96). New York: Plenum Press.

Jenkins, G., Merz, J. F., & Sankar, P. (2005). A qualitative study of women's views on medical confidentiality. *Journal of Medical Ethics, 31,* 499–504.

Johnson, S., Kass, N. E., & Natowicz, M. (2005). Disclosure of personal medical information: Differences among parents and affected adults for genetic and non-genetic conditions. *Genetic Testing, 9,* 269–280.

Omarzu, J. (2000). A disclosure decision model: Determining how and when individuals will self-disclose. *Personality and Social Psychology Review, 4,* 174–185.

Pérez-Cárceles, M. D., Pereñiguez, J. E., Osuna, E., & Luna, A. (2005). Balancing confidentiality and the information provided to families of patients in primary care. *Journal of Medical Ethics, 31,* 531–535.

Petronio, S. (1991). Communication boundary perspective: A model of managing the disclosure of private information between marital couples. *Communication Theory, 4,* 311–332.

Petronio, S. (2000a). The meaning of balance. In S. Petronio (Ed.), *Balancing the secrets of private disclosures* (Preface, pp. xiii–xvi). Mahwah, NJ: LEA Publishers.

Petronio, S. (2000b). The boundaries of privacy: Praxis of everyday life. In S. Petronio (Ed.), *Balancing the secrets of private disclosures* (pp. 37–50). Mahwah, NJ: LEA Publishers.

Petronio, S. (2000c). The ramifications of a reluctant confidant. In A. C. Richards & T. Schumrum (Eds.), *Invitations to dialogue: The legacy of Sidney M. Jourard* (pp. 113–150). Dubuque, IA: Kendall/Hunt Publishers.

Petronio, S. (2002). *Boundaries of privacy: Dialectics of disclosure.* New York: SUNY Press.

Petronio, S. (2004). The road to developing communication privacy management: Narrative in progress, please stand by [Special issue]. *Journal of Family Communication, 4,* 193–208.

Petronio, S. (2006). Impact of medical mistakes: Navigating work–family boundaries for physicians and their families. *Communication Monographs, 73,* 462–467.

Petronio, S. (2007). Translational endeavors and the practices of Communication Privacy Management. *Journal of Applied Communication Research, 35,* 218–222.

Petronio, S., & Durham, W. (2008). Understanding and applying Communication Privacy Management theory. In L. A. Baxter & D. O. Braithwaite (Eds.), *Engaging theories in interpersonal communication.* Thousand Oaks, CA: Sage Publications.

Petronio, S., & Jones, S. M. (2000). Taking stock: Secrets of private disclosures. In S. Petronio (Ed.), *Balancing the secrets of private disclosures* (pp. 301–302). Mahwah, NJ: LEA Publishers.

Petronio, S. & Jones, S. M. (2006). When "friendly advice" becomes a privacy dilemma for pregnant couples: Applying CPM theory. In R. West & L. Turner (Eds.), *Family communication sourcebook* (pp. 201–218). Mahwah, NJ: Lawrence Erlbaum.

Petronio, S., & Jones, S. M. (2007). When "friendly advice" becomes a privacy dilemma for pregnant couples: Applying CPM theory. In R. West & L. Turner (Eds.), *Family communication: A reference of theory and research* (pp. 201–218). Thousand Oaks, CA: Sage Publications.

Petronio, S., & Kovach, S. (1997). Managing privacy boundaries: Health providers' perceptions of resident care in Scottish nursing homes. *Journal of Applied Communication Research, 25*, 115–131.

Petronio, S., Jones, S. M., & Morr, M. C. (2003). Family privacy dilemmas: Managing communication boundaries within family groups. In L. Frey (Ed.), *Group communication in context: Studies of bona fide groups* (pp. 23–56). Mahwah, NJ: LEA Publishers.

Petronio, S., Reeder, H. M., Hecht, M., & Mon't Ros-Mendoza, T. (1996). Disclosure of sexual abuse by children and adolescents. *Journal of Applied Communication Research, 24*, 181–199.

Phillips, R. (2003). *Stakeholder theory and organizational ethics*. San Francisco, CA: Berrett Koehler Publishers.

Prewitt, K. (2005, June 23). Privacy and information collection: Impacts on public policy. Congressional Briefing on privacy to Consortium of Social Science Associations: *Protecting Privacy: "How Much Are We Willing to Give Up?"* Washington, DC.

Ray, E. B. (1996). When the protector is the abuser: Effects of incest on adult survivors. In E. B. Ray (Ed.), *Case studies in communication and disenfranchisement* (pp. 127–140). Mahwah, NJ: LEA Publishers.

Robinson, I. (1991). Confidentiality for whom? *Social Science of Medicine, 32*, 279–286.

Rogers, W. A. (2006). Pressures on confidentiality. *Lancet, 367*, 553–554.

Schultz, P. (2000). Sex offender community notification policies: Balancing privacy and disclosure. In S. Petronio (Ed.), *Balancing the secrets of private disclosures* (pp. 263–274). Mahwah, NJ: Lawrence Erlbaum.

Serewicz, M. C., & Petronio, S. (2007). Communication Privacy Management theory: Ethical considerations. In B. B. Whaley & W. Samter (Eds.), *Explaining communication: Contemporary theories and exemplars*. Mahwah, NJ: Lawrence Erlbaum.

Sollie, D. L., & Fischer, J. L. (1985). Sex-role orientation, intimacy of topic, and target person differences in self-disclosure among women. *Sex Roles, 12*, 917–929.

Sote, G. A., & Good, L. R. (1974). Similarity of self-disclosure and interpersonal attraction. *Psychological Reports, 34*, 491–494.

Tolstedt, B. E., & Stokes, J. P. (1984). Self-disclosure, intimacy, and the depenetration process. *Journal of Personality and Social Psychology, 46*, 84–90.

Trevison, C. (2007, March 29). Secret police cameras catch heat, not crime. *The Oregonian*, p. B1, b5.

19 Why Disclosing to a Confidant Can Be so Good (or Bad) for Us

Anita Kelly and Diane Macready

Imagine that you have finally gotten up the nerve to tell a colleague about something you did wrong at work that has been bothering you for months. You go home and wonder whether you did the right thing. You lie there in bed imagining what your colleague must think of you now and what she might say about you to other colleagues. The next morning, you study her face for signs of judgment and her actions for signs of coolness. There are none. Was your confession good or bad for you from a health standpoint?

The purpose of this chapter is to address this very question and explain the theoretical mechanisms behind the health benefits or detriments of disclosing personal information, especially personal secrets, to others. We begin the chapter by discussing the complexities behind a decision to reveal a personal secret. After that, we highlight studies that have shown that revealing personal information can go well or backfire, depending on the responsiveness of the confidant. We then critically evaluate leading theoretical explanations that have been offered for why personal disclosures can cause health benefits. We also describe as-yet-unpublished data from our own laboratory that require the modification of these existing theories. We conclude by providing an explanation for why disclosing secrets to another person not only can be healthful, as has been emphasized in the literature, but also can be harmful to the revealer. In doing so, we offer a way to predict when the outcomes will be positive or negative. This prediction hinges on whether the disclosure causes one to gain closure on the revealed information.

Defining Terms

Before we unravel the issues to consider in a decision to reveal personal information to another person, we need to define a few key terms. *Self-disclosure* can generally be defined as the information individuals choose to reveal verbally, both orally and in writing, about themselves to others (Derlega, Metts, Petronio, & Margulis, 1993). Typically, disclosures fall in the domain of public behavior (see Rodriguez & Kelly, 2006), which is behavior that is known to others and linked to one's identity (Tice, 1992). *Personal secrets*, in contrast, are defined as hidden information directly involving the secret keeper that he or she deliberately conceals from someone else who expects access to the secret (Kelly, 2002). Secrets always have a relational context and refer to information that is kept from at least one person, but not necessarily from everyone. They are distinct from *private information* in that people do not expect access to private information. For example, if a woman privately colors her graying hair, that is usually nobody's business. But if she is engaged to a man 10 years her junior who assumes that she is around his age, then she is keeping a secret from him because he likely would expect to know that she colors her hair and is older than she appears. In this chapter, we review the relevant research on the disclosure of personal secrets, traumatic experiences, or upsetting events. We start with a closer look at the complexities of a decision to disclose information to others.

Complexities of a Decision to Disclose

Deciding whether and when to reveal personal information to another person is a difficult matter. There are numerous factors to consider when making such a decision, including the characteristics of the discloser, characteristics of the confidant (see Kelly, 2002; Kelly & McKillop, 1996), and relationship between the discloser and confidant (Levesque, Steciuk, & Ledley, 2002). Moreover, there are important consequences of such a decision, given that disclosure serves a key role in the formation and maintenance of relationships (Derlega et al., 1993). Relationships, in turn, play a key role in helping people maintain their physical and psychological well-being (see Uchino, Cacioppo, & Kiecolt-Glaser, 1996, for a review). At the same time, research has demonstrated that relational partners become more judgmental of each other's disclosures as their relationships develop (see Derlega et al., 1993). As such, how much one should disclose to another person puts one in a bit of a dilemma because disclosing too much can lead to negative judgments and social rejection, and disclosing too little can leave one isolated and without the social support necessary to combat many of life's problems. Baxter (1990) has referred to these kinds of dilemmas as dialectical contradictions that occur in interpersonal relationships.

Certainly there is a great deal of evidence that disclosing private traumatic experiences through writing results in health improvements, such as fewer physician visits (e.g., Pennebaker & Beall, 1986; Pennebaker, Colder, & Sharp, 1990; Richards, Beal, Seagal, & Pennebaker, 2000), enhanced immunological functioning (e.g., Booth, Petrie, & Pennebaker, 1997; Petrie, Booth, Pennebaker, Davison, & Thomas, 1995), increased positive affect (e.g., Murray, Lamnin, & Carver, 1989; Smyth, 1998), and reduced stress (e.g., Lepore, Ragan, & Jones, 2000). However, this research on the benefits of writing has focused largely on revealing in confidential, anonymous contexts. Kelly (2002; Kelly & McKillop, 1996) noted that everyday disclosures, including the sharing of personal secrets, usually are not confidential

or anonymous. Kelly (2002) argued that, unlike what happens with anonymous disclosures, when a person reveals a personal secret to someone else
who knows that person, there are implications for the person's identity.
Some of these implications could be negative and harmful to the revealer.

Let's consider an example of the potentially negative implications behind a
decision to reveal distressing information. Imagine that a man comes home
from work distraught because he misplaced $9,000 that was supposed to be
deposited in the company's bank account. He expects to be reprimanded the
next day and feels terrible. He wants to talk to his wife about the incident, so
that he can get her support and thus calm down, and so that he can help her
understand why he is in such a bad mood. But he remembers that his wife had
accused him earlier that week of being irresponsible for forgetting to pay two
overdue bills. What should he do? On the one hand, disclosing to her seems
like an obvious choice—he needs her support and she might learn about the
event anyway. On the other hand, his wife could convey either subtly or overtly
to him that she now sees him as even more financially irresponsible than she
had thought. Such a conclusion is particularly troubling because being depend-
able is ranked as the number one personality trait that both men and women
from various cultures look for in a prospective mate (Shackelford, Schmitt, &
Buss, 2005). If she sees him as undependable, she could become less committed
to the marriage, and he could become angry with her for being so unsupportive. Not only that, as a result of revealing his mistake to her, he could come to
see himself as an undependable person by seeing himself through her eyes.

Support for this last idea comes from a recent experiment in which undergraduates watched an upsetting film clip and then were randomly assigned
either to (a) express their emotions about the clip or (b) describe their previous day to a confederate posing as a counseling psychology graduate student (Yip & Kelly, in press). The confederate then either gave (a) feedback
that the participant was a stable person, (b) feedback that the participant
was a sensitive (i.e., unstable) person, or (c) no feedback. The results
showed that, regardless of the feedback, participants who talked about
their emotions, as compared with those who talked about their previous
day, rated themselves as significantly more neurotic. Yip and Kelly (in
press) suggested that people might see themselves as more neurotic after
sharing negative emotions with others because they imagine that those others see them as less stable and their self-concepts are partly determined by
others' views. These findings are important because they were the first to
provide direct (i.e., experimental) evidence that describing negative emotions to someone else can have negative implications for one's self-concept.
In particular, it can cause people to see themselves as more neurotic, even
though neuroticism is normally construed as a stable personality trait with
a strong hereditary component (e.g., Bouchard & McGue, 1990).

Given such complexity behind a decision to reveal personal information
to others, Kelly (2002) presented a model for whether and when to reveal
a secret within the context of a given relationship that hinges on whether

one's relational partner is an appropriate confidant. An appropriate confidant is defined as someone who (a) can be trusted not to reveal the secret to others, (b) is nonjudgmental, and (c) does not reject the discloser. Having an insightful confidant was mentioned as a bonus. Kelly (2002) argued that if a person has an appropriate confidant, then he or she should reveal it to that confidant, but if the confidant is not appropriate, then the person should consider keeping it to himself or herself.

However, in a recent debate with Kelly on the question of whether revealing secrets is healthful or harmful, Pennebaker (2007) argued that revealing secrets is good and necessary, even in the face of potentially negative reactions from the confidant. Likewise, in his seminal book, *Opening Up: The Healing Power of Confiding in Others*, Pennebaker (1990) approved of a psychiatrist's advice to a traumatized woman to reveal her trauma to everyone she met. In the debate with Kelly, Pennebaker (2007) stated that openness allows the discloser to lead an honest life free of intrusive thoughts about the secret that will interfere with sleep and cause other psychological and physical symptoms. Kelly (2007) responded by noting that there is no evidence that keeping a secret will make a person sick (see also Kelly, 2002). Specifically, no researcher has randomly assigned people to keeping a personal secret or not and then seen if they have become ill.

Panagopoulou and her colleagues (Panagopoulou, Mintziori, Montgomery, Kapoukranidou, & Benos, in press) did, however, conduct an experiment in which they randomly assigned physicians to conditions in which the physicians were either to keep a cancer diagnosis a secret from a dying female patient or to share the diagnosis. The researchers found that the physicians who kept the diagnosis a secret showed physiological signs of reduced stress levels relative to the physicians who revealed the diagnosis. Although that experiment did not involve personal secrets (because the diagnosis was about the patient and not the physician), the results are interesting given the accepted wisdom that keeping a dire secret like a cancer diagnosis would be experienced as burdensome and stressful. Moreover, Kelly and Yip (2006) asked a sample of undergraduates whether they were keeping any major secret at Time 1 and followed up with them 9 weeks later. The researchers found that keeping a major secret did not predict an increase in psychological symptoms.

In a nutshell, it seems that revealing a personal secret or traumatic experience is more complicated than is implied by Pennebaker's (1990) approval of advice to a traumatized woman to reveal her trauma to everyone she met. Revealing to *everyone* might not be as helpful as revealing judiciously to appropriate confidants.

Consequences of Disclosure Can Hinge on the Reaction of the Confidant

What qualities are important in a potential confidant? A sample of undergraduates ranked being nonjudgmental as one of the most essential qualities of a confidant (Kelly, Klusas, von Weiss, & Kenny, 2001, study 1). More specifically, the undergraduates ranked being discreet, understanding, and nonjudgmental as three top qualities in a person with whom they would be most willing to share their personal secrets.

Valuing a discreet confidant makes good sense given the evidence that people often do share the personal information that others disclose to them (Harber & Cohen, 2005; Christophe & Rime, 1997). Christophe and Rime (1997) discovered that people typically share their emotional experiences with others around 96% of the time and that their confidants in turn reveal those experiences about 65% to 78%, telling two people on the average. Harber and Cohen (2005) recently discovered similar rates of social sharing, observing that 97% of a sample of undergraduates shared an emotional event (i.e., a fieldtrip to the morgue) with at least one confidant (note that the confidants were not specifically asked to keep the morgue trip a secret). Those confidants, in turn, shared that event with others, such that just 10 days after the morgue trip by 33 undergraduates, more than 800 other people knew about it. An obvious conclusion from these findings is that personal events can be broadcast widely and rapidly.

Valuing a nonjudgmental confidant also makes good sense given that people often keep secrets to avoid the disapproval or negative reactions from others (Afifi & Olson, 2005; Bok, 1982; Kelly & McKillop, 1996; Larson & Chastain, 1990; Stiles, 1987; Vangelisti, 1994; Wegner & Erber, 1992). This point was demonstrated in a diary study conducted by Macdonald and Morely (2001). The more participants anticipated negative (i.e., labeling or judging) responses to their disclosure of emotional events, the less likely they were to disclose the events (Macdonald & Morely, 2001). Likewise, in families, members keep secrets from particularly aggressive or coercive members to protect themselves and other family members (Afifi, Olson, & Armstrong, 2005). This fear of negative consequences suppresses family members' desire to reveal sensitive information, and this suppression is thought to have a chilling effect on family communication (Afifi & Olson, 2005). Even in psychotherapy, clients often report that they are keeping secrets from their therapists, largely because they feel too ashamed or embarrassed to reveal them (Hill, Thompson, Cogar, & Denman, 1993; Kelly, 1998).

These fears that disclosure will lead to a loss of acceptance may well be justified by research that has shown that, just as supportive social networks have been linked with reduced stress, having unsupportive or critical social networks is associated with increased stress (e.g., Holahan, Moos, Holahan, & Brennan, 1997; Lepore, 1992; Major et al., 1990; Major, Zubek, Cooper, Cozzarelli, & Richards, 1997; Vinokur & Van Ryn, 1993). For instance, Coates, Wortman, and Abbey (1979) found that people who revealed their struggles elicited more rejection from peers than did people who acted as if they were coping well (see also Spiegel, 1992). Moreover, confidants tend to withdraw from those who have revealed secrets to them (Coates et al., 1979; Lazarus, 1985), leaving distressed individuals more socially isolated at a time when they might most benefit from a confidant's support.

Longitudinal evidence of the interaction between self-disclosure and social acceptance was reported by Cole, Kemeny, and Taylor (1997). Specifically, the researchers found that, among a sample of HIV-positive gay men who scored high on rejection sensitivity, those participants who concealed their sexual orientation, as compared with those who disclosed it, experienced a slower progression of AIDS symptoms (Cole et al., 1997). Thus, Cole et al. (1997) were able to show that keeping a secret can serve as a buffer to developing illness when the secret keeper anticipates social rejection as a result of revealing that secret. The findings from this study are especially interesting in light of earlier findings from these same researchers that concealing one's sexual orientation was associated with greater illness rates in samples of gay men who were not necessarily rejection sensitive (Cole, Kemeny, Taylor, & Visscher, 1996; Cole, Kemeny, Taylor, Visscher, & Fahey, 1996).

Research specifically on women, too, has demonstrated that rejecting reactions in a confidant are associated with health detriments for the discloser. Sadly, it is common for women who reveal that they were raped to receive inconsistent support, avoidance, or even hostility from their confidants (Sudderth, 1998). Negative social reactions to rape disclosures have also been shown to significantly predict poor adjustment among adult victims (Ullman, 1996). Major et al. (1990) described similar results among a group of women who told close acquaintances about their abortion. Those women who perceived that their confidants were less than completely supportive experienced poorer psychological adjustment after the abortion than did those women who either shared with a supportive confidant or elected to keep the abortion a secret (Major et al., 1990). However, all of these studies just reviewed have been correlational in nature and thus do not allow us to draw cause-and-effect conclusions about how rejection from a confidant influences health.

In one of the only experiments to examine confidant effects directly, Lepore et al. (2000) investigated cognitive-emotional adjustment to stress as a function of self-disclosure and social support. Participants watched a stress-inducing video and were then assigned to a no-talk control condition or to one of three talk conditions, each of which called on participants to talk about their thoughts and feelings about the film: talk alone, talk to a validating confederate, or talk to an invalidating confederate. Compared to participants in the no-talk condition, participants in the validating and talk-alone conditions reported fewer intrusive thoughts about the film in the 2 days following the initial exposure. In addition, upon being reexposed to the film after the 2-day interim, validating and talk-alone participants reported less stress than did those in the no-talk condition. The authors suggested that talking and validation may have indirectly reduced stress by decreasing the occurrence of intrusive thoughts. However, the invalidating group did not differ from the other three groups on distress and intrusion measures. Lepore et al. (2000) acknowledged that a limitation of their design was that participants might not have perceived the invalidating confederate to be invalidating, thus leaving open the question of how people respond to differentially supportive confidants in an experimental design.

Rodriguez and Kelly (2006) helped fill this gap in the literature by conducting two experiments to determine how disclosing secrets to imagined accepting and nonaccepting confidants might influence health. The first experiment showed that participants who wrote about their secrets with an accepting confidant in mind experienced greater self-reported health benefits 8 weeks later than did those who wrote with a nonaccepting confidant in mind. And the more accepting and discreet those in the accepting group perceived their confidant to be, the fewer illnesses they reported. Moreover, the second experiment showed that, even when participants were not told to imagine their respective confidants until after writing about their secrets, once again those participants in the accepting group reported experiencing significantly fewer illnesses in the 8 weeks following the writing than did the nonaccepting-confidant group. In addition, the more discreet and the less judgmental the accepting and nonaccepting groups found their confidants to be, the fewer symptoms they reported 8 weeks later. Thus, Rodriguez and Kelly demonstrated that the imagined reactions of a confidant can moderate the relation between disclosure and health benefits.

Rodriguez and Kelly (2006) tried to explain their results by suggesting that the imagined acceptance from the confidant allowed participants in the accepting-confidant condition to feel a greater sense of belonging and thus lowered their symptom levels in the period after the writing. These researchers based this idea on the findings reviewed by Baumeister and Leary (1995) that people have a fundamental need to belong and that, when they do not feel they belong, they become distressed and more vulnerable to illnesses. Baumeister and Leary defined the need to belong as the need to have positive relationships with others and regular contact with them. They also suggested that belonging likely served the evolutionarily adaptive function of helping human beings solve problems on the ancestral plain, such as gathering food and fighting predators, which were better addressed by the group as opposed to individuals. However, Rodriguez and Kelly were not able to provide evidence for the idea that a sense of belonging mediates the link between disclosure and health benefits.

Explanations for the Benefits of Written Disclosure

Because the belonging idea seemed so promising, Macready and Kelly (2008) examined whether the health benefits of writing could be explained by the notion that writers feel a greater sense of belonging with the people around them after their disclosure. Thus, we had undergraduate participants write about a personal story—with their names attached—that they believed would be read by their classmates. Upon completion of the writing exercise, however, the participants were randomly assigned to one of two conditions: the essay-read condition or the essay-not-read condition. Those in the essay-read condition were again told that their (nonanonymous) story would be read by their classmates, whereas those in the essay-not-read condition were told that their story would not be read. The dependent variable was the extent to which their self-reported psychological and physical symptoms dropped several weeks after their writing. This methodology was repeated in a second experiment that also measured participants' sense of belonging after 2 weeks and 6 weeks, when the final assessment of symptomatology was made.

The results from both experiments showed that participants in the essay-read condition had greater self-reported health benefits than did participants in the essay-not-read condition (Macready & Kelly, 2008). But when we measured whether feeling a greater sense of belonging mediated the relation between having their stories read and fewer symptoms, we could not find any support for the mediational idea. Still, these findings are important in that they show that having an audience for one's disclosure can be an essential factor in increasing the health benefits derived from writing.

So what *can* be said regarding the question of why written disclosure is healthful? Given the substantial evidence (described earlier) that revealing private traumatic or negative experiences is associated with psychological and physiological benefits, researchers must provide an answer to this question. Pennebaker's (1985) original explanation was based largely on the notion that inhibition is stressful, and thus releasing that inhibition through disclosure allows one to reap health benefits. In this section, we describe how this theory has persisted, even in the face of contradictory data, and describe other mechanisms that have been proposed. We conclude by providing what we consider the most reasonable explanation for the health benefits (or detriments) of disclosure given the available evidence.

Inhibition model. More than two decades ago, Pennebaker and Chew (1985) proposed that the act of inhibiting ongoing behavior requires physiological work. They demonstrated that undergraduates who were induced to inhibit their expression of the truth (i.e., to lie) to experimenters experienced elevated skin-conductance levels relative to their baseline skin-conductance levels. Shortly thereafter, Pennebaker (1985, 1989) proposed a model of the relationship between traumatic experience and psychosomatic disease that included the following three propositions: (a) to inhibit actively one's behavior is stressful and disease related; (b) when individuals do not or cannot express thoughts and feelings concerning a traumatic event (i.e., when they engage in behavioral inhibition), there is an increased probability of having obsessive thoughts about the event and of having illnesses in the long run; and (c) conversely, the act of confiding or otherwise translating the event into language reduces autonomic activity (in the short run) and leads to long-term reductions in disease rates. According to Pennebaker (1997), how the event is discussed, the possibility of ever coming to terms with the event, and the ultimate consequences of discussing the experience are all variables that may influence the outcomes of confiding, inhibition, and, down the road, health. Pennebaker drew his thinking in part from Temoshok's (1983) earlier model of illness, in which Temoshok had depicted a coping style that involves an insufficient expression of thoughts or emotion as a part of the development of psychosomatic disturbances. However, as mentioned earlier, Pennebaker's (e.g., see Pennebaker, 1997) experiments did not demonstrate that keeping secrets causes negative health effects. What his experiments were designed to show, and did show, is that revealing previously undisclosed traumatic experiences in a confidential, anonymous setting leads to health benefits.

Moreover, Greenberg, Wortman, and Stone (1996) were able to challenge directly the notion that the release of inhibition causes the health benefits associated with written disclosure. Specifically, they examined whether disclosing emotions generated by imaginative immersion in a novel traumatic event would enhance health and adjustment in a manner similar to that caused by disclosing real traumatic events. They recruited college women on the basis of their having experienced a traumatic event that was perceived as severe (e.g., rape, violent assault, abandonment by a parent, witnessing a gruesome event). The women then were assigned randomly to write about their own real traumas, imaginary traumas, or trivial events. Those in the imaginary-trauma group were given real traumas to write about, so that the content of their writing would be equivalent to the writing of those in the real-trauma group. The results revealed that, immediately after the experiment, the imaginary-trauma participants were significantly less depressed than real-trauma participants, but they were similarly angry, fearful, and happy. Interestingly enough, at 1-month follow-up, both trauma groups made significantly fewer illness visits than did the control group participants. However, the real-trauma participants reported more fatigue and more avoidance of certain ideas, feelings, or situations than did the other groups. Greenberg et al. (1996) speculated that the health benefits for the participants in the imaginary-trauma group could have resulted from their gaining catharsis (i.e., releasing pent-up emotions), engaging in emotional regulation, or constructing resilient possible selves (i.e., views of self as competent and successful; see Markus & Nurius, 1986). But these researchers provided no mediational evidence to support any one of these explanations. Thus, the key aspect of their findings is that they undermined the notion that the release of previously inhibited material (i.e., from Pennebaker's original inhibition model) is what causes health benefits.

Yet the inhibition model lingers. For example, Niederhoffer and Pennebaker (2002) recently indicated that writing about traumatic events is healthful because the disclosure removes the effort and stress associated with inhibiting the expression of a traumatic event. But until they can provide direct evidence for this explanation, we are left searching for an explanation that better fits the available data.

Meaning making. One such explanation, and one that we support, might be Pennebaker's (2003) second major explanation for the health benefits of writing about traumas. This explanation is that the disclosure allows people to reinterpret and reframe the meaning of the traumatic events and thus experience health benefits. After reviewing the studies on the physical and mental health benefits of revealing private traumatic experience, Pennebaker (1997) concluded that gaining new insights is an important part of recovery from distressing experiences. Pennebaker observed that, although a reduction in inhibition may contribute to the disclosure phenomenon, changes in basic cognitive and linguistic processes during writing predict better health. The key, he noted, was the level of insight people used during their writing. In particular, he found that a high use of positive emotion words and moderate levels of negative emotion words were associated with positive health outcomes.

Suedfeld and Pennebaker (1997) observed this pattern when they explored whether the recall of very unpleasant memories would occur at a different level of complexity in meanings from that of neutral memories and whether differences in such complexity would be related to health outcomes. Two groups of undergraduates wrote an essay each day for four days: One group wrote about a trivial topic, and the other wrote about a negative (traumatic) life event for a previous study. The complexity scores of these two types of essays were compared, and they were correlated with a composite measure of well-being (immunological assays, visits to the Student Health Center, and self-reported distress and substance abuse). As it turned out, the essays about negative experiences were significantly higher in complexity, suggesting that the participants put more mental effort to their writing. Among these essays, there was a significant relationship between the complexity of meanings in the writing and improvement in the participants' health such that moderate levels of complexity (i.e., scores closest to the median for the group) were associated with the most improvement. Apparently, very high levels of complexity represent feeling quite troubled and may be an indication of a continued lack of resolution surrounding the negative event, and low levels of complexity may mean that the person did not put in the mental energy needed to gain closure on the negative event (see Pennebaker, 1997).

This explanation for the health benefits of disclosure is consistent with an extensive literature on the benefits of meaning making. In fact, searching for meaning in life has been described as one of the primary motivations for human beings (see Frankl, 1976/1959), and this search seems particularly acute after a traumatic experience. Making sense of such an experience is considered to be a necessary part of regaining mental and physical health (Antonovsky, 1990; Baumeister, 1991; Lifton, 1986). If people do not talk or write about their traumatic experiences and choose instead to keep them secret, they may miss precious opportunities to get new perspectives on the secrets and develop a sense of closure on the events (Kelly & McKillop, 1996; Pennebaker, 1989, 1997; Pennebaker & Hoover, 1985; Tait & Silver, 1989). People often find meaning in the experiences by getting a new perspective on them and then assimilating them into their worldviews (Horowitz, 1986; Meichenbaum, 1977; Pennebaker, Kiecolt-Glaser, & Glaser, 1988; Silver, Boon, & Stones, 1983).

Pennebaker's (2003) second explanation also is consistent with the fact that many counseling approaches have grown out of the idea that reinterpreting or reframing experiences is critical in helping clients get better (e.g., see Dowd & Milne, 1986; Kelly, 1955). Across many types of brief therapy interventions, interpretations made by the therapist have been found to be associated with client improvement (see Hill, 1992), apparently because the interpretations provide clients with new perspectives on their problems. For example, a therapist might say that her client feeling incompetent at work is a testament to all the valuable time the client devotes to her family's well-being.

One therapy study in particular demonstrated the importance of meaning making by women who had experienced sexual assault (Foa, Molnar, & Cashman, 1995). The women had undergone therapy that involved their repeatedly reliving and recounting their trauma in a treatment referred to as exposure therapy, which is used for treating anxiety disorders such as phobias and posttraumatic stress disorder (PTSD; Foa & Kozak, 1986; Foa & Rothbaum, 1989). Following the treatment, the women had more thoughts in which they attempted to organize the trauma memories, and these organized thoughts were negatively correlated with depression.

Like Foa and her colleagues, Lepore (1997) assessed the mechanism through which making meaning out of distressing experiences can reduce stress surrounding those events. In particular, Lepore explored whether expressive writing improves emotional adaptation to distressing events by reducing event-related intrusive thoughts—unwanted thoughts that pop into people's heads—or by desensitizing people to such thoughts. He asked undergraduates who were preparing for their graduate school entrance exams either to write their deepest thoughts and feelings about the exam (i.e., experimental group) or to write about trivial events (i.e., control group). As it turned out, participants in the experimental group experienced a significant decline in depressive symptoms from 1 month (Time 1) to 3 days (Time 2) before the exam. In contrast, the participants in the control group maintained a relatively high level of depressive symptoms over this same period. Expressive writing did not affect the frequency of intrusive thoughts, but it did seem to affect the impact of intrusive thoughts on depressive symptoms. Specifically, intrusive thoughts at Time 1 were positively related to depressive symptoms at Time 2 in the control group and were unrelated to symptoms in the expressive writing group. Lepore speculated that one possible explanation for this finding was that "people who engage in thinking about and expressing their stress-related thoughts and feelings may gain some insight into the stressor, which in turn renders any reminders or memories of the stressor comprehensible and nonthreatening" (p. 1034). However, he acknowledged that it is not possible to know whether that explanation is better than the notion that the participants habituated to (i.e., got used to) the stressors when they wrote or talked about them (see Bootzin, 1997).

A similar reason why gaining new insights is likely to be curative may be that people are able to find closure on the secrets and avoid what has been termed the Zeigarnik effect (Zeigarnik, 1927)—wherein people actively seek to attain a goal when they have failed to attain the goal or failed to disengage from it (Martin, Tesser, & McIntosh, 1993; see also Pennebaker, 1997). Zeigarnik (1927) showed that people continue to think about and remember interrupted tasks more than finished ones, suggesting that they may have a need for completion or resolution of the events. Thus, revealing a secret and then gaining a new perspective on it may help people feel a sense of resolution about the secret.

Evidence for this idea comes from an experiment in which Kelly et al. (2001, study 2) teased apart the effects of gaining new insights and catharsis to see what makes people feel better about their secrets. Undergraduates were randomly assigned to write about their (a) secrets while trying to gain new insights, (b) secrets while trying to gain catharsis, or (c) previous day. They did this 2 times, 1 week apart. The results revealed that the new insights group felt significantly more positive about their secrets after the second writing than did the other groups. Moreover, they came to terms with their secrets during their second writing to a greater extent than did the catharsis group. In fact, there was a fairly strong correlation ($r = .44$) between participants gaining insights and coming to terms with their secret during their second writing task. Coming to terms with their secrets, in turn, was associated with participants feeling less negative about them. By obtaining these results, Kelly et al. (2001) showed that focusing on getting a new perspective on secrets is a good way to make oneself feel more positive about them. This strategy seems not only to be useful at increasing positive influence, but it also seems to encourage the person to come to terms with the secrets and thus diminish his or her negative emotions surrounding the secrets. Integrating these findings with those of Pennebaker, Mayne, and Francis (1997), and Nolen-Hoeksema, McBride, and Larson (1997), who obtained mixed results regarding the health benefits of high levels of insightful thinking or analysis, Kelly et al. (2001) suggested that attempts at meaning making are valuable to the extent that the person is able to come to terms with their secret or trauma. Continued dwelling on a secret without such closure can backfire, just as venting the negative emotions surrounding a secret without gaining new insights can backfire.

Why Disclosure to a Confidant Can Be so Good (or Bad) for Us

As we have just explained, Pennebaker's (1985) initial notion that the relieving of inhibition would underlie the benefits of disclosure has somehow managed to survive despite its apparent lack of empirical support (e.g., Niederhoffer & Pennebaker, 2002). We argue that any theoretical explanation of why disclosure leads to health benefits must account for the research that has shown that health benefits occurred (a) after writing about imaginary traumas (Greenberg et al., 1996); (b) when writing about a secret to an accepting confidant, but not to a nonaccepting one (Rodriguez & Kelly, 2006); and (c) only when the writers thought someone would read their personal story (Macready & Kelly, 2008). Moreover, we argue that any explanation should be consistent with principles of evolution, because there is cross-cultural evidence that people feel compelled to share their emotional stories with others and do so at an extremely high rate (e.g., Rime, Mesquita, Philippot, & Boca, 1991). A phenomenon that seems so universal points us in the direction of an explanation rooted in our common human ancestry. In particular, we humans may have inherited the disposition to disclose emotional personal events to others because such behavior served an adaptive function for our ancestors, who were able to survive and pass this tendency to us through our genes.

Our explanation or primary propositions in this chapter are as follows: When people disclose a personal story, secret, or trauma to others, this revelation typically allows them to bring closure to the emotions and intrusive thoughts associated with that story. That closure brings a reduction in anxiety and depression and frees mental resources to devote to the tasks of living. Thus, through bringing closure, revelation reduces physical and psychological symptoms. We note that revealing to another person, as opposed to writing it down and having no one read it, puts a spotlight on the implications of that story and prompts the revealer to think it through and bring closure to the story. After all, many studies have shown that public events typically have much greater intrapsychic consequences than do private ones (e.g., Tice, 1992; see Baumeister, 1982, and Leary, 1995, for reviews). We suggest that the process of revealing to another person likely had survival advantages on the human ancestral plain, where dangers often were better addressed by group efforts. We propose that today people continue to reveal their personal stories to others because of a negative reinforcement process: They reveal to others to quell the negative emotions and intrusive thoughts associated with keeping unfinished business to themselves.

But sometimes that primitive reaction to share with others backfires because it makes people ruminate even more about the event they disclosed. For instance, imagine a mother who reveals to a group of close friends that she finally broke down and gave her 3-year-old a painful spanking. She explains that what prompted the spanking was the fact that her toddler had persisted in keeping her locked out of the bathroom with a full tub of water. The mom tells this story looking for validation of her actions. However, her friends respond that they never have resorted to spanking under any circumstances and that perhaps the mom can have the lock removed from the bathroom door. Thus, the mom ends up feeling a bit ostracized from the other women. On the ancestral plain, such ostracism could have translated into the other women cooperating less with this particular mother for fear that she might spank their children; thus, such a disclosure could have been considered maladaptive. At the same time, the mom could have learned something from the other women in terms of protecting her own child's life (i.e., by having the ancestral equivalent of the bathroom lock removed).

The point of this example is that disclosure can be considered an evolved adaptive mechanism even if there are times when disclosure seems to backfire or partially backfire. Cosmides and Tooby (1999) referred to this process in which evolved mechanisms work well on average but necessarily fail in some cases as instance failure. As long as the survival benefits of the mechanism continue to surpass its costs overall, it will continue to be passed to future generations. We are suggesting that the predisposition to disclose emotional events might have been passed down to us from our ancestors who benefited on average from sharing both positive and negative events with others.

Conclusion

In this chapter, we have called attention to the complexities behind disclosure and have offered new data from our laboratory showing that the benefits of written disclosure only occurred when the writer believed that someone would read the disclosure. Moreover, we have elaborated on what we consider to be the best existing explanation for the health benefits of disclosure, and, in doing so, have tried to put to rest the notion that releasing inhibition explains why disclosure can be healthful. We also have offered an explanation for why disclosure can sometimes backfire. In particular, we have argued that disclosure of positive and negative events occurs frequently because it usually serves (and likely did serve on the ancestral plain) an adaptive function to the discloser. Such disclosure puts to rest unfinished business and renders harmless the intrusive thoughts surrounding those events. However, sometimes revealing to another person actually can cause one to ruminate more over the revealed event. We predict if that happens, such as in the case when one reveals to a judgmental or indiscreet confidant, one might experience negative health consequences following disclosure.

An interesting future research direction will be to see how the brain and nervous system respond to disclosures to appropriate versus inappropriate confidants. If what we have argued concerning the evolved adaptive mechanism of disclosing upsetting events to others is valid, we would expect the regions of the brain associated with the experience of fear, especially the amygdala, to show less activity (i.e., in terms of blood flow and secretion of hormones) following disclosure to appropriate confidants.

Finally, we hope that some practical benefits can come from the research and insights we have described in this chapter. In particular, our findings that people benefited even more from writing about personal events that they believed would be read by someone else suggests that people should find appropriate confidants to read their disclosures, such as writing a letter to a confidant instead of writing in a diary. These findings ultimately may have therapeutic implications and could help guide activities used in group or individual therapy. At the same time, we have suggested that our human tendency to share emotional experiences with others might be an adaptive mechanism to which we instinctively turn when we are in trouble. We hope that recognizing this possibility, along with recognizing the possibility that any particular instance of disclosure could backfire, might prompt people to be more judicious in choosing when and with whom to disclose their personal secrets. As scientists' understanding of what makes disclosure helpful or hurtful increases, it will allow people to use disclosure in a way that is beneficial for their health and thus their lives.

References

Afifi, T. D., & Olson, L. (2005). The chilling effect in families and the pressure to conceal secrets. *Communication Monographs, 72*, 192–216.

Afifi, T. D., Olson, L. N., & Armstrong, C. (2005). The chilling effect and family secrets: Examining the role of self protection, other protection, and communication efficacy. *Human Communication Research, 31*, 564–598.

Antonovsky, A. (1990). Pathways leading to successful coping and health. In M. Rosenbaum (Ed.), *Learned resourcefulness: On coping skills, self-control, and adaptive behavior* (Vol. 24, pp. 31–63). New York: Springer.

Baumeister, R. F. (1982). A self-presentational view of social phenomena. *Psychological Bulletin, 91*, 3–26.

Baumeister, R. F. (1991). *Escaping the self*. New York: Basic Books.

Baumeister, R. F., & Leary, M. R. (1995). The need to belong: Desire for interpersonal attachments as a fundamental human motivation. *Psychological Bulletin, 117*, 497–529.

Baxter, L. A. (1990). Dialectical contradictions in relationship development. *Journal of Social and Personal Relationships, 7*, 69–88.

Bok, S. (1982). *Secrets: On the ethics of concealment and revelation*. New York: Pantheon Books.

Booth, R. J., Petrie, K. J., & Pennebaker, J. W. (1997). Changes in circulating lymphocyte numbers following emotional disclosure: Evidence of buffering? *Stress Medicine, 13*, 23–29.

Bootzin, R. R. (1997). Examining the theory and clinical utility of writing about emotional experiences. *Psychological Science, 8*, 167–169.

Bouchard, T. J., & McGue, M. (1990). Genetic and rearing environmental influences on adult personality: An analysis of adopted twins reared apart. *Journal of Personality, 58*, 263–292.

Christophe, V., & Rime, B. (1997). Exposure to the social sharing of emotion: Emotional impact, listener responses and secondary social sharing. *European Journal of Social Psychology, 27*, 37–54.

Coates, D., Wortman, C. B., & Abbey, A. (1979). Reactions to victims. In I. H. Frieze, D. Bar-Tal, & J. S. Carroll (Eds.), *New approaches to social problems* (pp. 21–52). San Francisco: Jossey-Bass.

Cole, S. W., Kemeny, M. E., & Taylor, S. E. (1997). Social identity and physical health: Accelerated HIV progression in rejection-sensitive gay men. *Journal of Personality and Social Psychology, 72,* 320–335.

Cole, S. W., Kemeny, M. E., Taylor, S. E., & Visscher, B. R. (1996). Elevated physical health risk among gay men who conceal their homosexual identity. *Health Psychology, 15,* 243–251.

Cole, S. W., Kemeny, M. E., Taylor, S. E., Visscher, B. R., & Fahey, J. L. (1996). Accelerated course of human immunodeficiency virus infection in gay men who conceal their homosexual identity. *Psychosomatic Medicine, 58,* 219–231.

Cosmides, L., & Tooby, J. (1999). Toward an evolutional taxonomy of treatable conditions. *Journal of Abnormal Psychology, 108,* 453–464.

Derlega, V. J., Metts, S., Petronio, S., & Margulis, S. T. (1993). *Self-disclosure.* Newbury Park, CA: Sage Publications.

Dowd, T. E., & Milne, C. R. (1986). Paradoxical interventions in counseling psychology. *Counseling Psychologist, 14,* 237–282.

Foa, E. B., & Kozak, M. J. (1986). Emotional processing of fear: Exposure to corrective information. *Psychological Bulletin, 99,* 20–35.

Foa, E. B., Molnar, C., & Cashman, L. (1995). Changes in rape narratives during exposure therapy for posttraumatic stress disorder. *Journal of Traumatic Stress, 8,* 675–690.

Foa, E. B., & Rothbaum, B. O. (1989). Behavioural psychotherapy for post-traumatic stress disorder. *International Review of Psychiatry, 1,* 219–226.

Frankl, V. E. (1976/1959). *Man's search for meaning.* New York: Pocket.

Greenberg, M. A., Wortman, C. B., & Stone, A. A. (1996). Emotional expression and physical health: Revising traumatic memories or fostering self-regulation? *Journal of Personality and Social Psychology, 71,* 588–602.

Harber, K. D., & Cohen, D. J. (2005). The Emotional Broadcaster Theory of social sharing. *Journal of Language and Social Psychology, 24,* 382–400.

Hill, C. E. (1992). Research on therapist techniques in brief individual therapy: Implications for practitioners. *Counseling Psychologist, 20,* 689–711.

Hill, C. E., Thompson, B. J., Cogar, M. C., & Denman, D. W. (1993). Beneath the surface of long-term therapy: Therapist and client report of their own and each other's covert processes. *Journal of Counseling Psychology, 40,* 278–287.

Holahan, C. J., Moos, R. H., Holahan, C. K., & Brennan, P. L. (1997). Social context, coping strategies, and depressive symptoms: An expanded model with cardiac patients. *Journal of Personality and Social Psychology, 72,* 918–928.

Horowitz, M. J. (1986). *Stress response syndromes* (2nd ed.). Northvale, NJ: Jason-Aronson.

Kelly, A. E. (1998). Clients' secret keeping in outpatient therapy. *Journal of Counseling Psychology, 45,* 50–57.

Kelly, A. E. (2002). *The psychology of secrets.* New York: Kluwer Academic/Plenum Publishers.

Kelly, A. E. (2007, October). *The good, the bad, the secret keeper, and the liar.* Keynote address offered at the 4th International Emotions Conference, Tilburg University, Netherlands.

Kelly, A. E., Klusas, J. A., von Weiss, R. T., & Kenny, C. (2001). What is it about revealing secrets that is beneficial? *Personality and Social Psychology Bulletin, 27,* 651–665.

Kelly, A. E., & McKillop, K. J. (1996). Consequences of revealing personal secrets. *Psychological Bulletin, 120,* 450–465.

Kelly, A. E., & Yip, J. J. (2006). Is keeping a secret or being a secretive person linked to psychological symptoms? *Journal of Personality, 74,* 1349–1369.

Kelly, G. A. (1955). *The psychology of personal constructs* (Vols. 1 and 2). New York: Norton.

Larson, D. G., & Chastain, R. L. (1990). Self-concealment: Conceptualization, measurement, and health implications. *Journal of Social and Clinical Psychology, 9,* 439–455.

Lazarus, R. S. (1985). The trivialization of distress. In J. C. Rose & L. J. Solomon (Eds.), *Primary prevention of psychopathology: Vol. 8. Prevention in health psychology* (pp. 279–298). Hanover, NH: University Press of New England.

Leary, M. R. (1995). *Self-presentation: Impression management and interpersonal behavior.* Madison, WI: Brown & Benchmark.

Lepore, S. J. (1992). Social conflict, social support, and psychological distress: Evidence of cross-domain buffering effects. *Journal of Personality and Social Psychology, 63,* 857–867.

Lepore, S. J. (1997). Expressive writing moderates the relation between intrusive thoughts and depressive symptoms. *Journal of Personality and Social Psychology, 73,* 1030–1037.

Lepore, S. J., Ragan, J. D., & Jones, S. (2000). Talking facilitates cognitive-emotional processes of adaptation to an acute stressor. *Journal of Personality and Social Psychology, 78,* 499–508.

Levesque, M. J., Steciuk, M., & Ledley, C. (2002). Disclosers, confidants and unique relationships. *Social Behavior and Personality, 30,* 579–592.

Lifton, R. J. (1986). *The Nazi doctors: Medical killing and the psychology of genocide.* New York: Basic Books.

Macdonald, J., & Morely, I. (2001). Shame and non-disclosure: A study of the emotional isolation of people referred for psychotherapy. *British Journal of Medical Psychology, 74,* 1–21.

Macready, D. E., & Kelly, A. E. (2008, August). *Somebody listen to me: Benefits of non-anonymous written disclosure.* Presentation offered at the annual meeting of the American Psychological Association, Boston, MA.

Major, B., Cozzarelli, C., Sciacchittano, A. M., Cooper, M. L., Testa, M., & Mueller, P. M. (1990). Perceived social support, self-efficacy, and adjustment to abortion. *Journal of Personality and Social Psychology, 59,* 452–463.

Major, B., Zubek, J. M., Cooper, M. L., Cozzarelli, C., & Richards, C. (1997). Mixed messages: Implications of social conflict and social support within close relationships for adjustment to a stressful life event. *Journal of Personality and Social Psychology, 72,* 1349–1363.

Markus, H., & Nurius, P. (1986). Possible selves. *American Psychologist, 41,* 954–969.

Martin, L. L., Tesser, A., & McIntosh, W. D. (1993). Wanting but not having: The effects of unattained goals on thoughts and feelings. In D. M. Wegner & J. W. Pennebaker (Eds.), *Handbook of mental control* (pp. 552–572). Englewood Cliffs, NJ: Prentice-Hall.

Meichenbaum, D. (1977). *Cognitive-behavior modification: An integrative approach.* New York: Plenum Press.

Murray, E. J., Lamnin, A. D., & Carver, C. S. (1989). Emotional expression in written essays and psychotherapy. *Journal of Social and Clinical Psychology, 8,* 414–429.

Niederhoffer, K. G., & Pennebaker, J. W. (2002). Sharing one's story: On the benefits of writing or talking about emotional experience. In C. R. Snyder & S. J. Lopez (Eds.), *Handbook of positive psychology* (pp. 573–583). London: Oxford University Press.

Nolen-Hoeksema, S., McBride, A., & Larson, J. (1997). Rumination and psychological distress among bereaved partners. *Journal of Personality and Social Psychology, 72,* 855–862.

Panagopoulou, E., Mintziori, G., Montgomery, A., Kapoukranidou, D., & Benos, A. (in press). Concealment of information in clinical practice: Is lying less stressful than telling the truth? *Journal of Clinical Oncology.*

Pennebaker, J. W. (1985). Traumatic experience and psychosomatic disease: Exploring the roles of behavioural inhibition, obsession, and confiding. *Canadian Psychology, 26,* 82–95.

Pennebaker, J. W. (1989). Confession, inhibition, and disease. *Advances in Experimental Social Psychology, 22,* 211–244.

Pennebaker, J. W. (1990). *Opening up: The healing power of confiding in others.* New York: Morrow.

Pennebaker, J. W. (1997). Writing about emotional experiences as a therapeutic process. *Psychological Science, 8,* 162–166.

Pennebaker, J. W. (2003). The social, linguistic and health consequences of emotional disclosure. In J. Suls and K. A. Wallston (Eds.), *Social psychological foundations of health and illness* (pp. 288–313). Malden, MA: Blackwell Publishers.

Pennebaker, J. W. (2007, October). *The good, the bad, the secret keeper, and the liar.* Keynote address offered at the 4th International Emotions Conference, Tilburg University, Netherlands.

Pennebaker, J. W., & Beall, S. K. (1986). Confronting a traumatic event: Toward an understanding of inhibition and disease. *Journal of Abnormal Psychology, 95,* 274–281.

Pennebaker, J. W., & Chew, C. H. (1985). Behavioral inhibition and electrodermal activity during deception. *Journal of Personality and Social Psychology, 49,* 1427–1433.

Pennebaker, J. W., Colder, M., & Sharp, L. K. (1990). Accelerating the coping process. *Journal of Personality and Social Psychology, 58,* 528–537.

Pennebaker, J. W., & Hoover, C. W. (1985). Inhibition and cognition: Toward an understanding of trauma and disease. In R. J. Davidson, G. E. Schwartz, & D. Shapiro (Eds.), *Consciousness and self-regulation* (Vol. 4, pp. 107–136). New York: Plenum Press.

Pennebaker, J. W., Kiecolt-Glaser, J. K., & Glaser, R. (1988). Disclosure of traumas and immune function: Health implications for psychotherapy. *Journal of Consulting and Clinical Psychology, 56,* 239–245.

Pennebaker, J. W., Mayne, T. J., & Francis, M. E. (1997). Linguistic predictors of adaptive bereavement. *Journal of Personality and Social Psychology, 72,* 863–871.

Petrie, K. J., Booth, R. J., Pennebaker, J. W., Davison, K. P., & Thomas, M. G. (1995). Disclosure of trauma and immune response to a hepatitis B vaccination program. *Journal of Consulting and Clinical Psychology, 63,* 787–792.

Richards, J. M., Beal, W. E., Seagal, J. D., & Pennebaker, J. W. (2000). Effects of disclosure of traumatic events on illness behavior among psychiatric prison inmates. *Journal of Abnormal Psychology, 109*, 156–160.

Rime, B., Mesquita, B., Philippot, P., & Boca, S. (1991). Beyond the emotional event: Six studies on the social sharing of emotion. *Cognition and Emotion, 5*, 435–465.

Rodriguez, R. R., & Kelly, A. E. (2006). Health effects of disclosing personal secrets to imagined accepting versus non-accepting confidants. *Journal of Social and Clinical Psychology, 25*, 1023–1047.

Shackelford, T. K., Schmitt, D. P., & Buss, D. M. (2005). Universal dimensions of human mate preferences. *Personality and Individual Differences, 39*, 447–458.

Silver, R. L., Boon, C., & Stones, M. H. (1983). Searching for meaning in misfortune: Making sense of incest. *Journal of Social Issues, 39*, 81–101.

Smyth, J. M. (1998). Written emotional expression: Effect sizes, outcome types, and moderating variables. *Journal of Consulting and Clinical Psychology, 66*, 174–184.

Spiegel, D. (1992). Effects of psychosocial support on patients with metastatic breast cancer. *Journal of Psychosocial Oncology, 10*, 113–120.

Stiles, W. B. (1987). "I have to talk to somebody." A fever model of disclosure. In V. J. Derlega & J. H. Berg (Eds.), *Self-disclosure: Theory, research, and therapy* (pp. 257–282). New York: Plenum Press.

Sudderth, L. K. (1998). "It'll come right back at me": The interactional context of discussing rape with others. *Violence Against Women, 4*, 572–594.

Suedfeld, P., & Pennebaker, J. W. (1997). Health outcomes and cognitive aspects of recalled negative life events. *Psychosomatic Medicine, 59*, 172–177.

Tait, R., & Silver, R. C. (1989). Coming to terms with major negative life events. In J. A. Bargh & J. S. Uleman (Eds.), *Unintended thought* (pp. 351–382). New York: Guilford Press.

Temoshok, L. (1983). Emotion, adaptation, and disease: A multidimensional theory. In L. Temoshok, C. Van Dyke, & L. S. Zegans (Eds.), *Emotions in health and illness* (pp. 207–233). New York: Grune & Stratton.

Tice, D. M. (1992). Self-concept change and self-presentation: The looking glass self is also a magnifying glass. *Journal of Personality and Social Psychology, 63*, 435–451.

Uchino, B. N., Cacioppo, J. T., & Kiecolt-Glaser, J. K. (1996). The relationship between social support and physiological processes: A review with emphasis on underlying mechanisms and implications for health. *Psychological Bulletin, 119*, 488–531.

Ullman, S. E. (1996). Social reactions, coping strategies, and self-blame attributions in adjustment to sexual assault. *Psychology of Women Quarterly, 20*, 505–526.

Vangelisti, A. L. (1994). Family secrets: Forms, functions and correlates. *Journal of Social and Personal Relationships, 11*, 113–135.

Vinokur, A. D., & Van Ryn, M. (1993). Social support and undermining in close relationships: Their independent effects on the mental health of unemployed persons. *Journal of Personality and Social Psychology, 65*, 350–359.

Wegner, D. M., & Erber, R. (1992). The hyperaccessibility of suppressed thoughts. *Journal of Personality and Social Psychology, 63*, 903–912.

Yip, J. J., & Kelly, A. E. (in press). Can emotional disclosure lead to increased self-reported neuroticism? *Journal of Social and Clinical Psychology*.

Zeigarnik, B. (1927). Uber das behalten von erledigten und unerledigten handlungen. *Psychologische Forschung, 9*, 1–85.

20 The Divorce Disclosure Model (DDM)

Why Parents Disclose Negative Information about the Divorce to their Children and its Effects

Tamara D. Afifi, Paul Schrodt, and Tara McManus

How parents talk about their divorce to their children can have a profound effect on children's well-being and their relationships with their parents. Indeed, children need some information about the divorce to reduce their uncertainty and adapt (Afifi, Coho, & McManus, 2009). Most parents would agree that they need to talk to their children about the divorce. The difficulty rests in knowing what to tell one's children about the divorce, how much to tell them, and how to communicate it. These conversations are complex and often occur throughout the divorce process.

Parents' disclosures about one another, in particular, are essential to determining how well children function after divorce. When parents talk negatively about each other to their children it has an adverse impact on children's physical and mental health (e.g., Koerner, Wallace, Lehman, Lee, & Escalante, 2004; Koerner, Wallace, Lehman, & Raymond, 2002) and can affect the parent–child bond (e.g., Afifi & Schrodt, 2003). Unfortunately, there are no theoretical frameworks that thoroughly explain why parents disclose negative divorce information to their children and the impact of these disclosures. Consequently, the purpose of this chapter is to provide a new theoretical model, the divorce disclosure model (DDM; see Figures 20.1; and 20.2), that explicates the motivations for why parents disclose negative information about the divorce to their adolescent children, the factors that influence these disclosures, and their impact on adolescents' (Figure 20.1) and parents' (Figure 20.2) personal and relational well-being. The aspects of the DDM are discussed in detail in the following sections.

The DDM and the Impact of Parents' Negative Divorce Disclosures on Adolescents

As we note in the DDM for adolescents (see Figure 20.1), parents should have ongoing conversations with their children about the divorce and the changes that are taking place in their family. Children need some information about the divorce, the circumstances of it, how it will affect them and their family relationships, and how they feel about it. These types of conversations should happen over time and are essential to children's ability to cope positively with the divorce. If children are not provided with this information, they may have lingering feelings of uncertainty (e.g., Afifi & Schrodt, 2003), ambiguous loss (Afifi & Keith, 2004), sadness, and resentment (Westberg, Nelson, & Piercy, 2002). From an uncertainty reduction theory (Berger & Calabrese, 1975) standpoint, understanding the divorce can help children manage their uncertainty about the state of their family and provide a sense of closure (Afifi & Schrodt, 2003; Thomas, Booth-Butterfield, & Booth-Butterfield, 1995; Westberg et al., 2002). When children believe they do not have enough information about the divorce, they can feel deceived, which can negatively affect their satisfaction with their communication with their parents (Thomas et al., 1995).

Parents are placed in a difficult position of figuring out what to tell their children about the divorce and how much to tell them. For instance, do parents tell their children about the divorce together or alone? Should they be honest about the reasons for the divorce, even if it involves a serious relational transgression like infidelity? How much should children know about the circumstances of the divorce? As we note in the DDM, one must take into account the age of the child, the context of the divorce, and how long it has been since the divorce, when examining these types of conversations. For instance, communicating about a divorce would be very different with a preschool-age child compared to a teenager. Some researchers (e.g., Buchanan, Maccoby, & Dornbusch, 1991) have argued that adolescents are at most risk for exposure to interparental conflict because they are still living with their parents, are old enough to understand what is going on, and are going through their own identity struggles. While this is true, young adults who have left the home (e.g., college-age children) may actually be more likely to be the recipients of their parents' negative disclosures about the divorce than adolescents because parents are more likely to confide in them as adults (see Afifi & Schrodt, 2003).

Parents disclose about many different divorce-related topics, including financial issues, living arrangements, the reasons for the divorce, personal concerns, and information about the former spouse, to their children (e.g., Afifi, 2003; Dolgin, 1996; Koerner et al., 2004). In fact, Afifi, Afifi, and Coho (in press-a) uncovered 11 different categories of topics that parents talk about with regard to the other parent and marriage/divorce with their adolescents. Our model (Figure 20.1) focuses on the divorce disclosures that are most likely to be problematic for adolescents and young adults. Research suggests that parental divorce disclosures become problematic when they are inappropriate for children to hear. Inappropriate divorce disclosures "constitute private information that a parent reveals to a child about the divorce that is negatively valenced, hurtful toward the other parent, too sensitive for the child's age, or that places the child in an uncomfortable position as a mediator, counselor, or friend" (Afifi, McManus, Hutchinson, & Baker, 2007, p. 79).

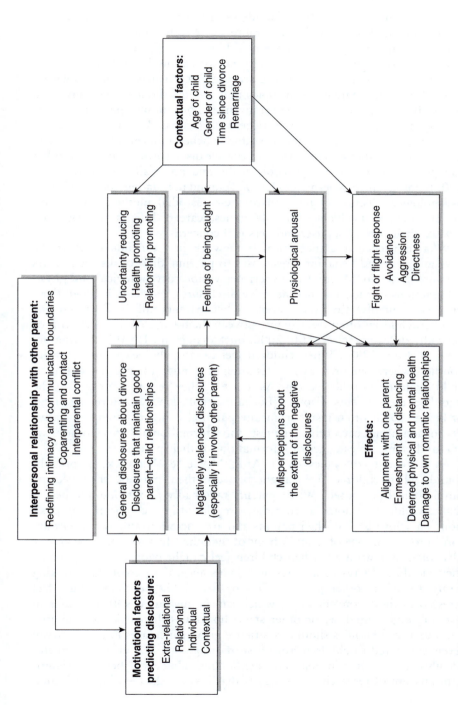

Figure 20.1 Divorce Disclosure Model (DDM)—Adolescents

What we argue in our DDM for adolescents is that it is the intimacy and valence of the divorce disclosures, more so than the amount of disclosure per se, which are of primary concern and interact with the topic of the disclosure. In particular, we contend that the divorce disclosures that are most harmful to children are those that are negatively valenced or derogatory toward the other parent. Even topics that parents disclose that may seem relatively neutral, such as living arrangements or limiting spending, can be anxiety producing for children (Koerner, Jacobs, & Raymond, 2000; Lehman & Koerner, 2002) and are often couched in terms of one's ill feelings about the other parent. Parents' negative disclosures about one another can place children at risk psychologically and physically (Koerner et al., 2002). For instance, Koerner et al. (2002) found that daughters experienced psychological distress in reaction to their custodial mothers' disclosures about financial problems, custody issues, career difficulties, negativity toward their former spouse, and personal concerns.

What is needed is a theoretical framework that can link together the psychological and behavioral responses to parents' divorce disclosures. As we note in the DDM, children experience various psychological and physical reactions to their parents' negative disclosures, particularly when these disclosures involve the other parent. When parents talk badly about one another, children often feel caught between them (e.g., Afifi, 2003; Afifi & Schrodt, 2003; Amato & Afifi, 2006; Buchanan et al., 1991; Hetherington, Cox, & Cox, 1985). When children feel caught, they experience loyalty conflicts where one or both parents attempt to align themselves with their child against the other parent. As a result, they feel torn or put in the middle of their parents' disputes (Buchanan et al., 1991). Children's feelings of being caught often result from interparental conflict, parents' negative disclosures about each other, requests for information about the other parent, and being a messenger of information for their parents.

As Afifi and colleagues (Afifi, Afifi, Morse, & Hamrick, in press-b) found, when children feel caught between their parents, they become physiologically aroused. When parents talk badly about one another, it makes children anxious because they are placed in a compromising position. They love both of their parents and are uncomfortable when they are forced to defend one of them in front of the other. In addition to becoming physiologically aroused, when children feel caught between their parents, they should feel stressed as a result. For instance, if a parent starts talking badly about the other parent to his or her child, the child should feel stressed in these conversations, which can be measured with increases in cortisol, alpha amylase, or other stress hormones. In particular, children from divorced families should experience greater increases in their cortisol levels compared to children from first-marriage families, given the greater likelihood of conflict in first-marriage families. However, there is a significant amount of research that suggests that it is the degree of interparental conflict and not the divorce per se that has the more detrimental effect on children and that children whose parents have a discordant marriage who stay married may actually be the worst off (see Amato & Sobolewski, 2001; Booth & Amato, 2001; Jekielek, 1998). If this is true, then in the aforementioned example, children from first-marriage families whose parents remain in a conflicted relationship may actually experience the greatest rises (both immediate and latent) in cortisol compared to divorced children and children from first-marriage families whose parents get along. Nevertheless, there is also some research (e.g., Granger et al., 1998) that suggests that children who are in highly conflicted or aggressive families may actually have stress levels that are considerably lower than the general population, perhaps because their bodies have gone into a protective mode in order to adapt to the chronic stress. Children who experience chronic interparental conflict may have different latent stress levels than children who experience intermittent or moderate levels of interparental conflict.

As we also argue in the DDM, children's physiological anxiety and stress as a result of their feelings of being caught should give way to various communicative responses. More specifically, adolescents and young adults should respond with a "flight" response by (1) avoiding the topic and/or a "fight" response by (2) directly confronting their parent or (3) responding with aggression. Previous work (e.g., Afifi, 2003; Afifi, Coho, & McManus, 2009; Golish & Caughlin, 2002) suggests that children typically respond to their feelings of being caught between their parents by avoiding talking about their parents' relationship. When they feel caught between their parents, it makes them anxious and their most immediate response is to avoid the discomfort the situation is producing. They often avoid talking about their parents' relationship to prevent conflict, and maintain their relationship with their parents, because they do not know what to say, do not want to make the situation worse, and/or because they want to prevent their parent from getting hurt (Afifi, 2003; Afifi et al., in press-b). Children also avoid in ways that are not topic avoidance. When their parents are fighting, children often use behavioral avoidance, such as exiting the room, listening to music, reading books, playing Nintendo, watching television, or playing with friends, as escape mechanisms (Afifi, 2003). Regardless of the form that adolescents' avoidance assumes, it serves a protective function, shielding them from some of the stress. Unfortunately, parents are often unaware of how much negative information they disclose about the other parent to their children, which is exacerbated by the children's desire to avoid talking about it (Afifi, 2003). This lack of awareness and avoidance can further perpetuate the negative disclosures.

Other children exhibit more of a "fight" response when they feel caught between their parents' conflict. Younger children may not have the cognitive complexity or the communicative competence to tell their parents to stop placing them in the middle of their disputes (Afifi & Schrodt, 2003).

As they age and become more mature, children may be more confident in their communication efficacy or ability to directly confront their parents about the parents' conflict and inappropriate disclosures. They may simply tell their parents to talk to one another about their issues. Still other children may communicate a fight response by becoming aggressive or modeling their parents' conflict behaviors. What is clear from our previous research is that children respond in different ways to their parents' conflict. Future research ought to further delineate how different types of responses influence adolescents' anxiety and stress.

The anxiety, stress, and avoidance that build as a result of children's feelings of being caught can also have a detrimental effect on their relationship with their parents. The research on postdivorce parent–child relationships is somewhat contradictory in that most of it suggests that parent–child relationships weaken after divorce (Afifi & Schrodt, 2003; Booth & Amato, 1994), while some of it indicates that parent–child relationships become closer after divorce (e.g., Arditti, 1999; Orbuch, Thorton, & Cancio, 2000). Both patterns are probably occurring—part of the answer depends upon whether the parent is the custodial or noncustodial parent. Research has consistently shown that children's relationship with their noncustodial fathers diminishes after a divorce, largely due to a decrease in contact with them (see Amato, 2000). Custodial mothers' relationship with their children can also attenuate after a divorce for a variety of reasons, including role burden, financial strain, not having another outlet for their stress, and being absorbed with their own grief (see Tein, Sandler, & Zautra, 2000). Yet there is research that suggests that custodial mothers' relationship with their children, particularly daughters, can become more cohesive throughout the divorce process (e.g., Afifi, Coho, & McManus, 2009; Arditti, 1999). In some instances, parents can become too close to their children because they disclose too much information to them, resulting in emotional parentification whereby the children take on a friendship role (Koerner et al., 2000). Adolescents who act as their divorced parents' confidants tend to worry more about their parents' welfare than adolescents who are not serving in this capacity (Glenwick & Mowrey, 1986; Koerner et al., 2000; Wallerstein, 1985).

What is important to consider is the fact that just because divorce disclosures may enhance closeness between parents and children does not mean they are good for them. As Afifi, Coho, and McManus (2009) found, parents' negative disclosures about the other parent to their children were associated with an increase in closeness between them, but it adversely affected the adolescents' physical and mental health. Therefore, such disclosures may create a cohesive bond between parents and children, but children may become overly anxious and stressed in the process. Research also suggests that, when children feel caught between their parents, they might have a tendency to eventually align themselves with one parent to reduce the cognitive dissonance that such loyalty conflicts produce (see Buchanan

& Waizenhofer, 2001). As a result, their relationship may become more cohesive with one parent and more distant with another.

Motivational Factors for Parents' Divorce Disclosures

As we also depict in the DDM (Figure 20.1), parental divorce disclosures, and the perceived valence of those disclosures, may be shaped by the motives parents ascribe to them. The intended goal for sharing information influences what and how information is revealed (Cody, Canary, & Smith, 1994; McAdams, 1983). While children may perceive or attach certain motives to their parents' disclosures, understanding the parents' intention for disclosing is informative. Parents may be motivated to disclose divorce-related information to their children for a variety of reasons, which are reflected in four factors: extrarelational, relational, individual, and contextual factors.

Extrarelational factors. A parent may be compelled to disclose due to the state of their relationships with others. One of the most consistently influential factors affecting postdivorce adjustment is continued animosity between former spouses (e.g., Jekielek, 1998). Many times parents' negative disclosures are driven by an acrimonious relationship and the perceived inability to control the other person's behaviors. For instance, even if parents agree on privacy rules for how they will talk about one another in front of their children, if one or both parents no longer abide by these rules, it can foster feelings of helplessness. One way to regain a sense of control and restore one's image is to protect it by backing up one's point of view, even if it is at the expense of the other parent. The inability to manage a former spouse's actions may also negatively influence parents' coping efficacy or the belief that they have the ability to cope with the divorce (Holloway & Machida, 1991; Madden-Derich, Leonard, & Christopher, 1999). This could encourage parents to seek out their children for assistance. That is, a lack of control over one's spouse may provoke disclosing this frustration to one's child.

Diminished social support within other relationships may also prompt parents to disclose to offspring. When parents perceive a loss of social support from friends and extended family, they may seek support from their children instead (Koerner et al., 2004; Mayseless, Bartholomew, Henderson, & Trinke, 2004). Depending on the developmental stage of the child, these disclosures may expose children to adult issues or concerns that are beyond their knowledge, skills, and capability to understand (Boszormenyi-Nagy & Spark, 1973; Chase, 1999; Jurkovic, 1997).

Parent–child relational factors. The nature of the parent–child relationship and the roles fulfilled within that relationship may also motivate the parent to disclose. Disclosure might occur in order to build, maintain, or otherwise protect the parent–child relationship (Derlega & Grzelak, 1979; Derlega, Metts, Petronio, & Margulis, 1993; Miller & Stubblefield, 1993; Petronio, 1991, 2002). As with many other relationship types, disclosure can help maintain or alter relational intimacy; thus, parents may choose to reveal information to their children about the divorce to enhance their relationship.

Given the nature of the parent–child relationship, parents may also reveal information to offer guidance or to obtain or provide information. Sharing information about the divorce might allow the parent to teach a child how to manage problems or expose the child to adult issues that the parent believes are important to learn (Koerner et al., 2000). For instance, parents may reveal financial and relational problems to offspring to socialize them about adult concerns and marriage in general (Koerner et al.). In addition, by disclosing, a parent may anticipate gaining information from the child (Derlega, 1984; Derlega et al., 1993). Due to reciprocity expectations, parents may expect their children to disclose in kind if they reveal certain sensitive information (Berger & Kellerman, 1994; Derlega et al.). Alternatively, information, such as good news or alterations in the state of the family, might have inherent importance, and parents may believe that the child ought to know it or is interested in knowing it (Dolgin, 1996), such as good news or alterations in the state of the family. Because the parents' role is to guide, teach, and protect their children, they may disclose to encourage information exchange, which can function to complete these role obligations.

Parents also may disclose to obtain or exchange social support. For instance, if parents feel sad or scared, or need comfort, they might reveal these feelings to their children to obtain support (Dolgin, 1996). Moreover, parents might reveal stressors to receive advice on how they might be resolved or obtain the child's assistance in problem solving (Dolgin). In addition to aiding the parent's individual coping efforts, these disclosures may increase relational closeness because the child appreciates being able to aid the parent (Arditti, 1999). However, adolescents often report greater depressive symptoms when they perceive the need to care for or nurture their divorced parent (Buchanan, Maccoby, & Dornbusch, 1996). While parents may disclose to obtain support and problem-solving assistance, the disclosures made may have both beneficial and detrimental consequences for the child.

Parents may also disclose certain information about the divorce to give their account of it and potentially alter their child's perception of the divorce. By selecting certain information to disclose, parents may be able to control the outcome of the interaction or influence the relationship (Derlega & Grzelak, 1979; Dolgin, 1996). Mothers in Koerner et al.'s (2000) study revealed that one reason they disclosed information regarding their ex-husbands to their child was to alter the child's view about the divorce: Mothers wanted their child to realize that they were not fully to blame for the end of the marriage.

Individual factors. Instead of focusing on relational issues, individual factors motivating parents' negative disclosures refer to the internal characteristics of the parent. Parents' competencies and internal changes, such as their coping abilities, social support skills, emotional intelligence, and grief, may influence how parents disclose and respond to their offspring.

Parents' individual coping abilities may prompt inappropriate disclosures. For example, individuals engage in more problem-focused coping when the stressor is perceived to be changeable; however, when the stressor is not resolvable, more emotion-focused coping tends to be used (Folkman, Lazarus, Dunkel-Schetter, DeLongis, & Gruen, 1986). Divorced parents are probably more likely to discuss stressors with their children when they feel their children will help resolve or alter the stressor (Afifi, McManus et al., 2007). Parents who are less capable of coping with stressors on their own will likely disclose more, and perhaps more inappropriately, to offspring in an attempt to obtain coping assistance.

In addition, parents' negative disclosures may be prompted by a lack of social support skills. Some parents, for instance, may not use very many person-centered supportive messages, which are messages that are developed based on the knowledge of the recipient and needs of that individual (Samter & Burleson, 1984). If the parent is unable to present the disclosed information in an effective, supportive manner, the child may likely be dissatisfied with the information and perceive it as more negative or inappropriate. Parents' inappropriate disclosures may arise due to a lack of skill in creating supportive messages that meet the child's needs.

In some instances, parents may not be socially supportive because they are unable to "read" their child's nonverbal cues of discomfort and distress. The ability to express and understand emotional cues is a critical characteristic of social adjustment and relationship satisfaction, especially in close familial relationships that rely heavily on caregiving and support (Schachner, Shaver, & Mikulincer, 2005). As such, a parent's lack of emotional intelligence may also prompt his or her inappropriate disclosures. Emotional intelligence refers to a set of competencies that (1) provide the ability to perceive and express emotion, (2) facilitate the use of emotions for cognitive processes (e.g., prioritizing thought and information processing, judgment, memory, problem solving), (3) understand and logically reason about emotions, and (4) regulate emotion in one's self and in others without exaggerating or repressing the information emotions convey (Mayer & Salovey, 1997; Mayer, Salovey, & Caruso, 2000). An emotionally intelligent parent would be able to disclose stressful information to the child in a manner that aids in resolving the stressor, demonstrates that she or he understands the emotion and its effects on the child, and do so in a way that regulates the emotion effectively for both individuals. Parents who lack emotional intelligence may continue disclosing inappropriate information because they are unable to perceive their child's nonverbal indicators of discomfort with the information being revealed.

Parents may also sometimes be unable to provide social support to their child and disclose too much information about the divorce because they are consumed with their own grief. Similar to the death of a loved one, divorce involves the loss of a partner, dreams, goals, roles, control, trust, and security (Emery, 1994; Weiss, 1975). However, one difference between the losses associated with divorce and death is that, with divorce, the opportunity for reconciliation exists, making the grieving process unique (Emery, 1994). When experiencing sadness, loneliness and despair are common (Emery, 1994); the parent might be more introspective and less able to attend to the child's needs during this time. During times of sadness, parents may ask about the former spouse or ask the child for reassurance, which may result in inappropriate disclosures (Weiss, 1975).

Parents' divorce disclosures may also be motivated by the parent's need for expression. Revealing personal thoughts, feelings, or emotions to a child can provide catharsis or self-clarification for the parent (Derlega & Grzelak, 1979; Dolgin, 1996; Stiles, 1987). Divorced adults disclose to their offspring often to vent, "let off steam," and to express anger or hurt (Dolgin, 1996). In addition, through voicing the information, the parent may desire to arrive at a better understanding of his or her own position, beliefs, and opinions (Derlega, 1984; Miller & Stubblefield, 1993). Expression may provide a sense of improved well-being for the parent because it permits the parent to examine his or her own thoughts, but it may not be focused on the child's needs. Thus, the parent may express too much detail while attempting to better understand and cope with that information.

Contextual/environmental factors. Parents often experience a cascade of stressors, such as financial stress, role burden, changes in household, and parenting responsibilities, as a result of divorce, which might entice parents to disclose about them to their children. Frequently mothers who struggle to provide financially are experiencing role overload due to their demands outside of the family's home (Jarrett & Burton, 1999; Perry-Jenkins, Seery, & Crouter, 1992). Parents who struggle to fulfill their obligations and are unable to obtain assistance elsewhere might seek help from a child (Jurkovic, 1997). Such requests may place children at an increased risk for emotional and/or instrumental parentification (Carroll & Robinson, 2000; Jurkovic, Thirkield, & Morrell, 2001).

Parents' inappropriate or negative disclosures arise out of a number of factors. The most important factor that likely predicts parents' negative disclosures to their children is the parents' relationship with each other. That one factor alone may override many of the other factors or set them into motion. In addition, although four distinct motivational factors can be identified for parents' disclosures, each disclosure may be motivated by multiple factors that are occurring simultaneously. For instance, conflict and grief may create or exacerbate skill deficits. Because they are distracted and preoccupied by conflict, parents may be emotionally unavailable (Amato & Booth, 1996). This may decrease parents' emotional intelligence, making them unable to monitor their communication and emotions or their child's emotions. In addition, if parents are feeling overwhelmed due to various stressors, they may not have the mental capacity to create a skillful, appropriate message for children. When coupled with a shrinking social network, parents may disclose extensively to their offspring to obtain the assistance and support desired. When working in concert with one another, these factors might magnify, minimize, or otherwise alter the negativity of the disclosure.

The Interpersonal Relationship with the Other (Co)Parent

Of all the factors discussed thus far that could potentially affect how parents and children process divorce disclosures and experience varying levels of well-being as a result, perhaps no factor has a greater influence on every other component in the DDM than the quality of the relationship between former spouses. As some scholars have argued, ex-spouses are often faced with the difficult, and often painful, task of developing a "separate togetherness" while "uncoupling without unfamilying" (Ahrons & Rodgers, 1987; Graham, 1997, 2003; Masheter & Harris, 1986). In what follows, we review two key aspects of the interpersonal relationship between former spouses likely to moderate the frequency, valence, and content of divorce disclosures to children: the (re)negotiation of postdivorce intimacy and boundaries, and the quality of the coparenting relationship.

Postmarital attachment, intimacy, and boundaries. As Masheter (1991, 1994, 1997a, 1997b), Graham (1997, 2003), and others (e.g., Emery, 1994) argue, the previously held belief that the relationship between former spouses ends upon divorce is, in many cases, erroneous. To the contrary, attachment to the ex-spouse is quite common in one form or another when there are children involved; some former spouses become friends (Masheter, 1997b; Masheter & Harris, 1986), advise each other on childrearing, financial, career, and retirement matters (Ahrons, 1994), and serve as confidants for each other regarding new romantic relationships (Ahrons & Rodgers, 1987), whereas others maintain "business-like" partnerships for the purposes of coparenting children in both postdivorce single-parent families and stepfamilies (Braithwaite, McBride, & Schrodt, 2003; Schrodt, Baxter, McBride, Braithwaite, & Fine, 2006). A majority of ex-spouses maintain some form of direct contact well beyond the first year after divorce, although with time the frequency and length of such interactions tend to diminish (Maccoby & Mnookin, 1992). Consequently, at stake in the renegotiation of postmarital relationships is the establishment of healthy and functional boundaries, as interaction patterns relied on in the past no longer suffice in the present relationship (Masheter, 1994).

In her program of research on postdivorce attachment, Masheter (1991, 1997a) identified two key dimensions of postmarital relationships that could potentially influence a parent's decision to disclose information about the divorce and/or the ex-spouse to his or her child: *preoccupation* and *hostility*. First, Masheter (1991, 1997a) has found in two different studies that preoccupation with the ex-spouse is inversely associated with well-being and postdivorce adjustment. Divorced individuals who are highly preoccupied with their former spouses are more likely to exhibit either problematic hostility (e.g., violence or child abduction) or maladaptive affection, including continued love and unrealistic desires for reconciliation (Masheter, 1997a). Thus, it stands to reason that parents who are preoccupied with their former spouses may be more likely to experience thought suppression and rumination over sensitive information concerning their ex-spouses. Thought suppression and rumination over such sensitive information, when coupled with the parents' identity and impression management concerns, may exacerbate the kinds of conditions likely to produce inappropriate and/or negative disclosures to children (see Afifi, Caughlin, & Afifi, 2007).

At the same time, the degree of hostility between former spouses may also prompt parents to disclose inappropriate information to their children. In response to heightened levels of anger and frustration, parents may choose to disclose negative information about each other to (a) re-establish power and control in the family system, (b) renegotiate their parental and post-marital relationships, and/or (c) relieve the stress and tension associated with the "fever" of hostility (among other reasons). As Graham (2003) noted, disclosures are often shared or withheld for the purpose of preventing conflict with former spouses. As such, renegotiating the boundary between disclosing and withholding is particularly critical in postmarital relationships, as too much openness and self-disclosure might signal an unhealthy preoccupation with the former spouse (Graham, 2003).

Intriguingly, Masheter (1997a) examined the combined effects of both preoccupation and hostility on divorced adults' well-being and found that the degree of preoccupation has a stronger association with well-being than the degree of hostility. Specifically, ex-spouses who reported low hostility and low preoccupation had higher well-being than those with low hostility and high preoccupation. As Masheter reasoned, "having a friendly relationship is not enough to ensure high well-being, particularly if the friendly feelings are accompanied by high preoccupation with the ex-spouse" (p. 471). More important, Masheter found that ex-spouses with high hostility and low preoccupation reported *higher* well-being than those who reported either high or low hostility and high preoccupation. Although preoccupation and hostility represent two related yet distinct indicators of postdivorce attachment, Masheter's findings clearly underscore the crucial role that preoccupation plays in distinguishing between healthy and unhealthy friendship, as well as healthy and unhealthy hostility toward ex-spouses. To the extent that ex-spouses can negotiate a postmarital relationship characterized by either high friendship and low preoccupation, or low hostility and low preoccupation (i.e., a complete break), such relationships may be less likely to provoke the kinds of inappropriate disclosures that so often induce feelings of triangulation in children.

The quality of the coparenting relationship. Research on coparenting in general has demonstrated to date that coparenting is more predictive of parenting and child outcomes than is general marital quality (or lack thereof) and that coparenting accounts for variance in parenting and child outcomes after controlling for individual parent characteristics (Feinburg, 2003; Feinburg, Kan, & Hetherington, 2007). According to McHale, Kuersten-Hogan, and Rao (2004), coparental alliances include three core features: (a) the degree of solidarity and support between the coparental partners; (b) the extent to which conflict, strife, and antagonism are present in the adults' coparental communication; and (c) the extent to which both partners participate actively in engaging and directing the children. Not surprisingly, the bulk of postdivorce coparenting research has focused almost exclusively on the nature, frequency, and intensity of conflict and support in coparenting interactions, and with a few notable exceptions (e.g., Braithwaite et al., 2003; Maccoby & Mnookin, 1992; Schrodt et al., 2006), much less is known regarding the role of interpersonal communication and divorce disclosures in creating, sustaining, and altering postmarital coparenting relationships.

To date, the most extensive investigation of communication and coparenting is Maccoby and Mnookin's (1992) longitudinal study of Californian postdivorce families. They identified three basic patterns of coparenting that emerged during the first 3 years following divorce: (1) *disengaged* coparents managed their interpersonal conflict by avoidance and made little to no effort to coordinate their child-rearing activities with each other; (2) *conflicted* coparents maintained regular contact with each other, but were actively involved in conflict that spilled over into the parenting domain; and (3) *cooperative* coparents were able to suppress, mitigate, or insulate their conflicts from their children. More important, Maccoby and Mnookin identified several key factors that undermined cooperative coparenting in postdivorce families, including interparental hostility, legal difficulties over custody and visitation, incompatible values, and a general distrust of a former partner's parenting abilities.

All four of these factors are likely to influence the kinds of disclosures that ex-spouses share with each other and that coparents share with their children, yet the level of *distrust* in the former partner and in his or her parenting abilities is particularly noteworthy when examining inappropriate disclosures in postdivorce relationships. For example, while investigating the role of the divorce decree in coparenting relationships in stepfamilies, Schrodt and his colleagues (2006) found that issues of trust, fairness, and good faith were fundamentally tied to how coparents used the divorce decree to facilitate or hinder the coparenting actions of their former spouses. The most common pattern to emerge involved using the decree as both contract and guide, depending on the coparents' perceptions of whether the other party was coparenting fairly and flexibly.

In general, then, the interpersonal relationship between former spouses is likely to vary as a function of the renegotiation of intimacy and boundaries in postmarital relationships, as well as the quality of the coparenting relationship that emerges in the postdivorce family system. When combined, both dimensions of the ex-spousal relationship are believed to (a) influence the factors that prompt the decision to disclose inappropriate information; (b) provide a relational context within which such disclosures are interpreted and processed; and (c) ultimately impact the psychological, physiological, and relational well-being of both parents and children in postdivorce families.

The DDM and the Impact of Parents' Negative Divorce Disclosures on Parents

In addition to the effects that negative parental disclosures may have on children, such disclosures are also likely to affect the physiological and psychological health and well-being of parents, particularly the well-being of the parent who discloses the information (see Figure 20.2). With one notable exception (i.e., Afifi, McManus et al., 2007), the bulk of extant research on parental disclosures about the divorce process and postdivorce relationships has focused almost exclusively on the attitudinal and health implications for children (e.g., Dennison & Koerner, 2006; Koerner et al., 2004; Westberg et al., 2002). Much less is known about the consequences for parents themselves, yet despite this lacuna, there is indirect evidence to suggest that parents are most likely affected by their own disclosures. In what follows, we proffer a series of direct and indirect effects that could potentially result from disclosing negative information about one's ex-spouse and/or the circumstances surrounding marital dissolution.

Before discussing potential direct and indirect effects of divorce disclosures for parents, however, it is important to note that the effects of such disclosures are likely to depend on (or are moderated by) three key factors: the valence of the disclosure, the quality of the disclosing parent's relationship with the child(ren) acting as the recipient(s), and the quality of the disclosing parent's relationship with his or her ex-spouse. First, the effects of parental disclosures about the divorce process and/or the ex-spouse are likely to vary as a function of the valence of the disclosure. Information that is viewed by both the parent and the child as positive and/or relatively benign (e.g., a parent's hopes and dreams for the future, concerns about being a good parent, or desires for personal change) is much less likely to produce deleterious effects for the parent than information deemed negative or distressing to the parent–child relationship (e.g., complaints about the ex-spouse, feelings about the divorce, or financial concerns; see Dennison & Koerner, 2006; Koerner et al., 2004). Of course, some parents are relatively uninformed and/or inaccurate in assessing the impact of their disclosures concerning the divorce and their former spouses (see Afifi, McManus et al., 2007). Thus, to the extent that parents can accurately discern how the recipient(s) (i.e., their child) will process the valence of their disclosures, such discernment is likely to moderate not only the decision to disclose, but also the intended and unintended consequences of the disclosure. An important key to determining the valence of the disclosure, then, is the parent's *meta-perspective* (Sillars, 1998), which represents his

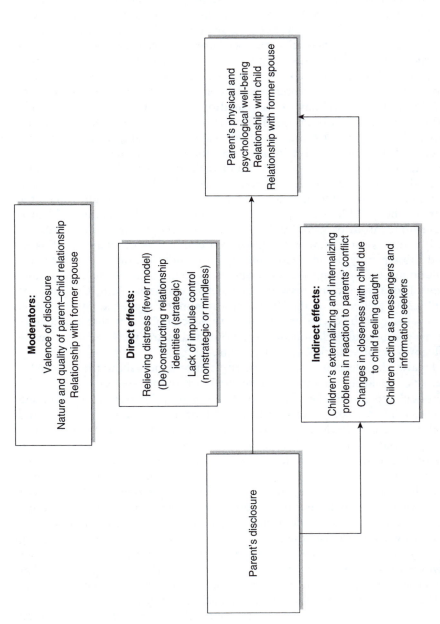

Moderators:

Valence of disclosure
Nature and quality of parent–child relationship
Relationship with former spouse

Direct effects:

Relieving distress (fever model)
(De)constructing relationship identities (strategic)
Lack of impulse control (nonstrategic or mindless)

Indirect effects:

Children's externalizing and internalizing problems in reaction to parents' conflict
Changes in closeness with child due to child feeling caught
Children acting as messengers and information seekers

Parent's physical and psychological well-being
Relationship with child
Relationship with former spouse

Parent's disclosure

Figure 20.2 Divorce Disclosure Model (DDM)—Parents

or her estimate of the child's direct perspective on the valence of the information being disclosed.

The level of congruence, or understanding, between the parent's meta-perspective and the child's direct perspective on the valence of the disclosure is likely to vary as a function of a second moderating factor for determining the effects of divorce disclosures on parents, namely the quality of the parent–child relationship. Some researchers have speculated that relational closeness and concern moderate a number of postdivorce relational processes, such as interparental conflict behaviors (Schrodt & Afifi, 2007), children's feelings of triangulation (Afifi, 2003; Afifi & Schrodt, 2003; Schrodt & Afifi, 2007), and postdivorce adjustment (Koerner et al., 2002). For example, parents who find themselves estranged from their children and disclose negative information about their former spouses in an attempt to "win them over" and bond with them may find that the unintended consequences of their actions produce heightened feelings of triangulation in their children, which in turn produces further withdrawal on the part of their children and greater dissatisfaction in the parent–child relationship (Schrodt & Afifi, 2007). On the other hand, parents (and particularly mothers) may view older adolescent children as peers and confidants and subsequently disclose more information about the divorce and the dissolution of the marriage for the purposes of seeking validation or as a function of identity and impression management concerns (Afifi, Caughlin, & Afifi, 2007; Koerner et al., 2004). At a minimum, then, the interpretation and valence of the disclosure are likely to depend on the nature and quality of the parent–child relationship, and both factors are likely to moderate the effects of divorce disclosures for parents.

Finally, the effects of disclosing negative information about the divorce for parents are likely to vary as a function of the ex-spousal relationship. Although most researchers have found that increased coparental conflict and hostility inhibits successful postdivorce adjustment for both coparents and children alike, Afifi, McManus et al. (2007) recently reported that parents' inappropriate divorce disclosures were inversely associated with their own well-being but only for parents who reported low (not high) levels of conflict with their ex-spouses. Consequently, there is empirical evidence to suggest that the quality of the ex-spousal relationship likely moderates the effects of negative divorce disclosures for the disclosers (or parents) themselves, though the direction and magnitude of this moderation effect remains in question.

Having acknowledged the potential impact that each of these moderating factors may have on the experience of sharing information about one's divorce to one's offspring, the DDM for parents (Figure 20.2) posits that the potential impact of such disclosures on parents themselves can be organized into two broad types: direct and indirect effects.

Direct effects. The direct-effects approach assesses the intrapersonal process and (relatively) the immediate impact of disclosing negative information about the divorce. Here, two competing explanations help provide a foundation for future research examining the direct effects of inappropriate or unwanted disclosures on parents' physiological and psychological well-being. The first explanation stems from a *strategic* approach to disclosing inappropriate information where, in essence, the parent is disclosing to the child for the purposes of either relieving distress or (de)constructing relational identities. For example, the fever model (Stiles, 1987) would predict a direct, positive association between parents' disclosures and their own well-being (Afifi, McManus et al., 2007). According to this model, people who withhold information that is bothering them are likely to become increasingly distressed over time, like a fever that intensifies as the result of a physical infection (Stiles, 1987). Eventually, the fever builds until the person reveals the information in order to relieve the distress. The disclosing of personal information is cathartic in that it allows the body to rid itself of the distress that plagues it and directly or indirectly restore itself to a healthier state (Stiles, Shuster, & Harrigan, 1992). When applied to the context of divorce disclosures, the fever model would suggest that parents who disclose divorce information to their children, regardless of the appropriateness of the disclosure, would experience a cathartic effect that may enhance their psychological and physical well-being (Afifi, McManus et al., 2007). Consequently, the first proposed pathway linking divorce disclosures to parents' well-being involves the parents' attempt to relieve the stress and tension associated with withholding information from the child by disclosing the information and experiencing catharsis.

A second explanation for the direct effects of divorce disclosures on parents' well-being, albeit one that has yet to receive empirical attention, is the strategic disclosure of negative or inappropriate information for the purposes of (de)constructing relational identities and parent–child relationships in the family system. It follows that, if certain coparenting relationships are filled with hostility and animosity, such relationships are likely to foster feelings of distrust and suspicion between former spouses. As the level of distrust grows, parents' abilities to withhold negative disclosures about their ex-partners are likely to diminish, which in turn might lead former spouses to disclose negative information to children for the purposes of impression management, protecting fragile relationships with their children, and/or in an attempt to reestablish parental power and control in the postdivorce family system. Thus, some parents may derive a sense of satisfaction from strategically disclosing negative information about the divorce and their former spouses, if nothing more than out of a desire to enhance their relationships with their children and/or to exact revenge by undermining their children's relationships with their ex-partner.

Of course, what both sets of direct effects (i.e., to relieve stress or to manage relational identities) have in common is that both result from the strategic decision to disclose negative information. Contrary to this goal-directed perspective, some parents may simply disclose negative information to their children as a result of impulsivity or mindlessness. In their research on inappropriate divorce disclosures, Afifi, McManus and colleagues (2007) found that parents' perceived lack of control over divorce-related stressors positively predicted parents' inappropriate disclosures and that this effect was more robust in high- rather than low-conflict families. As Afifi, McManus et al. (2007) reasoned, former spouses who have a conflicted relationship with each other may be less mindful of their disclosures and their appropriateness over time. In effect, such parents may become accustomed to their conflict and be less cognizant and mindful of their inappropriate disclosures to their children.

On the other hand, in low-conflict families, the impulsive disclosure of negative information about the divorce and/or the ex-spouse is likely to engen- der feelings of guilt and anxiety for the parent who discloses such information. For example, Afifi, McManus et al. (2007) discovered that parents' inappro- priate disclosures were inversely associated with parents' well-being, but *only* for parents in low-conflict families. In other words, ex-spouses who have established postdivorce coparenting relationships that are relatively free of conflict and tension are more likely to experience distress and diminished well- being as a function of inappropriately disclosing negative information about the divorce and their former partners to their children. This effect, in turn, lends some initial support to the idea that impulsively disclosing negative information about one's ex-spouse, in the context of a relatively cooperative or harmonious postdivorce relationship, may induce feelings of guilt and anxiety, which in turn undermine parents' mental well-being.

Indirect effects. In contrast to the direct effects that divorce disclosures may have on parents, the indirect-effects approach focuses more so on the inter- personal mechanisms and the relational consequences of disclosing negative information, processes that ultimately affect the disclosers by first affecting other members of the family system (i.e., the unintended consequences of disclosing). Here, we proffer three potential paths that could produce indirect effects on parents' psychological, physiological, and relational well-being. First, as we mentioned earlier in this chapter, researchers have found that interparental hostility, and the heightened feelings of triangulation that often emerge in children as a result, are consistent predictors of externalizing and internalizing behavior problems in children, including heightened levels of disobedience and relational dissatisfaction, reduced self-esteem and subjective well-being, poorer social competence, and increased risk behavior and sub- stance use (Afifi & Schrodt, 2003; Amato, 2000; Amato & Afifi, 2006; Schrodt & Afifi, 2007; Schrodt & Ledbetter, 2007). Thus, one potential indirect effect of parents disclosing negative information to their children may be a heightened sense of parental stress that emerges only after their children react to such disclosures, experience greater distress because of them, and, ultimately, poorer psychological adjustment and well-being.

At the same time, a second indirect effect may emerge as children respond to their feelings of being caught by revealing the inappropriate disclosure to the other parent (i.e., the ex-spouse) to solicit a reaction and/or seek further information about the circumstances and motivations surrounding the disclosure. Here, the strategic disclosure of information for the purposes of managing impressions and constructing identities within the parent–child relationship may only serve to enhance the distrust and interparental hostility between ex-spouses, which again might produce a heightened sense of stress and diminished well-being in the disclosing parent, though such an effect would be, to some extent, "time delayed."

Finally, negative divorce disclosures could potentially produce the unintended, and unwanted, consequence of reduced closeness in the parent–child relationship. Again, negative disclosures are likely to foster feelings of triangulation in adolescent children, which in turn may lead the child to withdraw from one or both parents in an effort to mitigate and/or reduce the stress associated with such loyalty divides. To the extent that children respond adversely to the information being shared by the disclosing parent, then, a final indirect effect of this behavior on the disclosing parent may be reduced closeness in their parent–child relationship.

In sum, disclosing negative information about the divorce process and/ or one's former spouse is likely to have any number of effects on the disclosing parent's psychological, physiological, and relational well-being. Intrapersonally, the parent may experience a release of stress and tension, feelings of guilt and anxiety, and/or a sense of relational satisfaction from disclosing potentially damaging information to the child, whereas interpersonally, the effects that such disclosures may have on the parent–child relationship and the coparenting relationship may ultimately produce undesirable outcomes for the disclosing parent's relationships with both child and ex-spouse. Clearly, continued research is needed to more fully explicate and delineate the potential effects predicted here by the DDM.

References

Afifi, T. D. (2003). "Feeling caught" in stepfamilies: Managing boundary turbulence through appropriate privacy coordination rules. *Journal of Social and Personal Relationships, 20,* 729–756.

Afifi, T. D., Afifi, W. A., Coho, A. (in press-a). Adolescents' physiological reactions to their parents' negative disclosures about the other parent in divorced and non-divorced families. *Journal of Divorce and Remarriage.*

Afifi, T. D., Afifi, W. A., Morse, C., & Hamrick, K. (in press-b). Adolescents' avoidance tendencies and physiological reactions to discussions about their parents' relationship: Implications for post-divorce and non-divorced families. *Communication Monographs.*

Afifi, T. D., Caughlin, J., & Afifi, W. (2007). The dark side (and light side) of avoidance and secrets. In B. H. Spitzberg & W. R. Cupach (Eds.), *The dark side of interpersonal communication* (2nd ed., pp. 61–92). Mahwah, NJ: Lawrence Erlbaum Associates.

Afifi, T. D., Coho, A., & McManus, T. (2009). *Custodial parents' divorce disclosures and their impact on parent–adolescent relational quality and adolescents' physical and mental health.* Manuscript submitted for review.

Afifi, T. D., Hutchinson, S., & Krouse, S. (2006). Toward a theoretical model of communal coping in postdivorce families and other naturally occurring groups. *Communication Theory, 16,* 378–409.

Afifi, T. D., & Keith, S. (2004). A risk and resiliency model of ambiguous loss in post-divorce stepfamilies. *Journal of Family Communication, 4,* 65–98.

Afifi, T. D., McManus, T., Hutchinson, S., & Baker, B. (2007). Inappropriate parental divorce disclosures, the factors that prompt them, and their impact on parents' and adolescents' well-being. *Communication Monographs, 74,* 78–102.

Afifi, T. D., & Schrodt, P. (2003). "Feeling caught" as a mediator of adolescents' and young adults' avoidance and satisfaction with their parents in divorced and non-divorced households. *Communication Monographs, 70,* 142–173.

Ahrons, C. R. (1994). *The good divorce.* New York: HarperCollins.

Ahrons, C. R., & Rodgers, R. H. (1987). *Divorced families: A multidisciplinary developmental view.* New York: Norton.

Amato, P. R. (2000). The consequences of divorce for adults and children. *Journal of Marriage and the Family, 62,* 1269–1287.

Amato, P. R., & Afifi, T. D. (2006). Feeling caught between parents: Adult children's relations with parents and subjective well-being. *Journal of Marriage and Family, 68,* 222–235.

Amato, P. R., & Booth, A. (1996). A prospective study of divorce and parent–child relationships. *Journal of Marriage and the Family, 58,* 356–365.

Amato, P. R., & Sobolewski, J. M. (2001). The effects of divorce and marital discord on adult children's psychological well-being. *American Sociological Review, 66,* 900–921.

Arditti, J. A. (1999). Rethinking relationships between divorced mothers and their children: Capitalizing on family strengths. *Family Relations, 48,* 109–119.

Berger, C. R., & Calabrese, R. J. (1975). Some explorations in initial interactions and beyond: Toward a developmental theory of interpersonal communication. *Human Communication Research, 1,* 99–112.

Berger C. R., & Kellerman, K. (1994). Acquiring social information. In J. A. Daly & J. M. Wiemann (Eds.), *Strategic interpersonal information* (pp. 1–31). Hillsdale, NJ: Lawrence Erlbaum Associates.

Booth, A. & Amato, P. R. (1994). Parental marital quality, parental divorce, and relations with parents. *Journal of Marriage and the Family, 56*(1), 21–34.

Booth, A., & Amato, P. R. (2001). Parental predivorce relations and offspring post-divorce well-being. *Journal of Marriage and the Family, 63,* 197–212.

Boszormenyi-Nagy, I., & Spark, G. M. (1973). *Invisible loyalties: Reciprocity in intergenerational family therapy.* New York: Harper & Row.

Braithwaite, D. O., McBride, M. C., & Schrodt, P. (2003). "Parent teams" and the everyday interactions of co-parenting in stepfamilies. *Communication Reports, 16,* 93–111.

Buchanan, C. M., Maccoby, E. E., & Dornbusch, S. M. (1991). Caught between parents: Adolescents' experience in divorced homes. *Child Development, 62,* 1008–1029.

Buchanan, C. M., Maccoby, E. E., & Dornbusch, S. M. (1996). *Adolescents after divorce.* Cambridge, MA: Harvard University Press.

Buchanan, C. M., & Waizenhofer, R. (2001). The impact of interparental conflict on adolescent children: Considerations of family systems and family structure. In A. Booth, A. C. Crouter, & M. Clements (Eds.), *Couples in conflict* (pp. 149–161). Mahwah, NJ: Lawrence Erlbaum Associates.

Carroll, J. J., & Robinson, B. E. (2000). Depression and parentification among adults as related to parental workaholism and alcoholism. *Family Journal: Counseling and Therapy for Couples and Families, 8,* 360–367.

Chase, N. D. (1999). *Burdened children: Theory, research and treatment of parentification*. Thousand Oaks, CA: Sage.

Cody, M. J., Canary, D. J., & Smith, S. W. (1994). Compliance-gaining goals: An inductive analysis of actor's goal types, strategies, and success. In J. A. Daly & J. M. Wiemann (Eds.), *Strategic interpersonal communication* (pp. 33–90). Hillsdale, NJ: Lawrence Erlbaum Associates.

Dennison, R. P., & Koerner, S. S. (2006). Post-divorce interparental conflict and adolescents' attitudes about marriage: The influence of maternal disclosures and adolescent gender. *Journal of Divorce & Remarriage, 45*, 31–49.

Derlega, V. J. (1984). Self-disclosure and intimate relationships. In V. J. Derlega (Ed.), *Communication, intimacy, and close relationships* (pp. 1–9). Orlando: Academic Press.

Derlega, V. J., & Grzelak, J. (1979). Appropriateness of self-disclosure. In G. J. Chelune (Ed.), *Self-disclosure: Origins, patterns, and implications of openness in interpersonal relationships* (pp. 151–176). San Francisco, CA: Jossey-Bass Publishers.

Derlega, V. J., Metts, S., Petronio, S., & Margulis, S. T. (1993). *Self-disclosure*. Newbury Park, CA: Sage.

Dolgin, K. G. (1996). Parents' disclosure of their own concerns to their adolescent children. *Personal Relationships, 3*, 159–169.

Emery, R. E. (1994). *Renegotiating family relationships: Divorce, child custody, and mediation*. New York: Guilford Press.

Feinburg, M. E. (2003). The internal structure and ecological context of coparenting: A framework for research and intervention. *Parenting: Science and Practice, 3*, 95–131.

Feinburg, M. E., Kan, M. L., & Hetherington, E. M. (2007). The longitudinal influence of coparenting conflict on parental negativity and adolescent maladjustment. *Journal of Marriage and Family, 69*, 687–702.

Folkman, S., Lazarus, R. S., Dunkel-Schetter, C., DeLongis, A., & Gruen, R. J. (1986). Dynamics of a stressful encounter: Cognitive appraisal, coping, and encounter outcomes. *Journal of Personality and Social Psychology, 50*, 992–1003.

Glenwick, D., & Mowrey, J. (1986). When parent becomes peer: Loss of intergenerational boundaries in single parent families. *Family Relations, 35*, 57–62.

Golish, T. D., & Caughlin, J. (2002). "I'd rather not talk about it": Adolescents' and young adults' use of topic avoidance in stepfamilies. *Journal of Applied Communication Research, 30*, 78–106.

Graham, E. E. (1997). Turning points and commitment in post-divorce relationships. *Communication Monographs, 64*, 350–368.

Graham, E. E. (2003). Dialectic contradictions in postmarital relationships. *Journal of Family Communication, 3*, 193–214.

Granger, D., Serbin, L., Schwartzman, A., Lehoux, P., Cooperman, J., & Ikeda, S. (1998). Children's salivary cortisol, internalizing behavior problems, and family environment: Results from the Concordia Longitudinal Risk Project. *International Journal of Behavioral Development, 22*, 707–728.

Hetherington, E. M., Cox, M., & Cox, R. (1985). Long-term effects of divorce and remarriage on the adjustment of children. *Journal of the American Academy of Child Psychiatry, 24*, 518–530.

Holloway, S. D., & Machida, S. (1991). The relationship between divorced mothers' perceived control over child rearing and children's post-divorce development. *Family Relations, 40*, 272–295.

Jarrett, R. J., & Burton, L. M. (1999). Dynamic dimensions of family structure in low-income African American families: Emergent themes in qualitative research. *Journal of Comparative Family Studies, 30*, 177–187.

Jekielek, S. (1998). Parental conflict, marital disruption and children's emotional well-being. *Social Forces, 76*, 905–936.

Jurkovic, G. J. (1997). *Lost childhoods: The plight of the parentified child*. New York: Brunner/Mazel.

Jurkovic, G. J., Thirkield, A., & Morrell, R. (2001). Parentification of adult children of divorce: A multidimensional analysis. *Journal of Youth and Adolescence, 30*, 245–257.

Koerner, S. S., Jacobs, S. L., & Raymond, M. (2000). When mothers turn to their adolescent daughters: Predicting daughters' vulnerability to negative adjustment outcomes. *Family Relations, 49*, 301–309.

Koerner, S. S., Wallace, S., Lehman, S. J., Lee, S., & Escalante, K. A. (2004). Sensitive mother-to-adolescent disclosures after divorce: Is the experience of sons different from that of daughters? *Journal of Family Psychology, 18*, 46–57.

Koerner, S. S., Wallace, S., Lehman, S. J., & Raymond, M. (2002). Mother-to-daughter disclosure after divorce: Are there costs and benefits? *Journal of Child and Family Studies, 11*, 469–483.

Lehman, S. J., & Koerner, S. S. (2002). Family financial hardship and adolescent girls' adjustment: The role of maternal disclosures of financial concerns. *Merill-Palmer Quarterly, 48*, 1–15.

Maccoby, E. E., & Mnookin, R. H. (1992). *Dividing the child: Social and legal dilemmas of custody*. Cambridge, MA: Harvard University Press.

Madden-Derich, D. A., Leonard, S. A., & Christopher, F. S. (1999). Boundary ambiguity and coparental conflict after divorce: An empirical test of a family systems model of the divorce process. *Journal of Marriage and the Family, 61*, 588–598.

Masheter, C. (1991). Postdivorce relationships between exspouses: The roles of attachment and interpersonal conflict. *Journal of Marriage and the Family, 53*, 103–110.

Masheter, C. (1994). Dialogues between ex-spouses: Evidence of dialectic relationship development. In R. Conville (Ed.), *Uses of structure in communication studies* (pp. 83–101). Westport, CT: Praeger.

Masheter, C. (1997a). Healthy and unhealthy friendship and hostility between ex-spouses. *Journal of Marriage and the Family, 59*, 463–475.

Masheter, C. (1997b). Former spouses who are friends: Three case studies. *Journal of Social and Personal Relationships, 14*, 207–222.

Masheter, C., & Harris, L. M. (1986). From divorce to friendship: A study in relationship development. *Journal of Social and Personal Relationships, 3*, 177–189.

Mayer, J. D., & Salovey, P. (1997). What is emotional intelligence? In P. Salovey & D. J. Sluyter (Eds.), *Emotional development and emotional intelligence: Educational implications* (pp. 3–31). New York: Basic Books.

Mayer, J. D., Salovey, P., & Caruso, D. (2000). Models of emotional intelligence. In R. J. Sternberg (Ed.), *Handbook of intelligence* (pp. 396–420). New York: Cambridge University Press.

Mayseless, O., Bartholomew, K., Henderson, A., & Trinke, S. (2004). "I was more her Mom than she was mine": Role reversal in a community sample. *Family Relations, 53*, 78–86.

McAdams, D. P. (1983). Human motives and personal relationships. In V. J. Derlega (Ed.), *Communication, intimacy, and close relationships* (pp. 41–70). Orlando: Academic Press.

McHale, J. P., Kuersten-Hogan, R., & Rao, N. (2004). Growing points for coparenting theory and research. *Journal of Adult Development, 11*, 221–234.

Miller, J. B., & Stubblefield, A. (1993). Parental disclosure from the perspective of late adolescents. *Journal of Adolescents, 16*, 439–455.

Orbuch, T. L., Thorton, A., & Cancio, J. (2000). The impact of marital quality, divorce, and remarriage on the relationships between parents and their children. *Marriage and Family Review, 29*, 221–244.

Perry-Jenkins, M., Seery, B., & Crouter, A. C. (1992). Linkages between provider-role attitudes, psychological well-being, and family relationships. *Psychology of Women, 15*, 311–329.

Petronio, S. (1991). Communication boundary management: A theoretical model of managing disclosure of private information between marital couples. *Communication Theory, 1*, 311–335.

Petronio, S. (2002). *Boundaries of privacy: Dialectics of disclosure.* Albany, NY: SUNY Press.

Samter, W., & Burleson, B. R. (1984). Cognitive and motivational influences on spontaneous comforting behavior. *Human Communication Research, 11*, 231–260.

Schachner, D. A., Shaver, P. R., & Mikulincer, M. (2005). Patterns of nonverbal behavior and sensitivity in the context of attachment relationships. *Journal of Nonverbal Behavior, 29*, 141–169.

Schrodt, P., & Afifi, T. D. (2007). Communication processes that predict young adults' feelings of being caught and their associations with mental health and family satisfaction. *Communication Monographs, 74*, 200–228.

Schrodt, P., Baxter, L. A., McBride, M. C., Braithwaite, D. O., & Fine, M. (2006). The divorce decree, communication, and the structuration of co-parenting relationships in stepfamilies. *Journal of Social and Personal Relationships, 23*, 741–759.

Schrodt, P., & Ledbetter, A. M. (2007). Communication processes that mediate family communication patterns and mental well-being: A mean and covariance structures analysis of young adults from divorced and non-divorced families. *Human Communication Research, 33*, 330–356.

Sillars, A. L. (1998). (Mis)understanding. In B. H. Spitzberg & W. R. Cupach (Eds.), *The dark side of close relationships* (pp. 73–102). Mahwah, NJ: Lawrence Erlbaum Associates.

Stiles, W. B. (1987). Verbal response modes as intersubjective categories. In R. L. Russell (Ed.), *Language in psychotherapy: Strategies of discovery* (pp. 131–170). New York: Plenum Press.

Stiles, W. B., Shuster, P. L., & Harrigan, J. A. (1992). Disclosure and anxiety: A test of the fever model. *Journal of Personality and Social Psychology, 63*, 980–988.

Tein, J., Sandler, I. N., & Zautra, A. J. (2000). Stressful life events, psychological distress, coping, and parenting of divorced mothers: A longitudinal study. *Journal of Family Psychology, 14*, 27–41.

Thomas, C. E., Booth-Butterfield, M., Booth-Butterfield, S. (1995). Perceptions of deception, divorce disclosure, and communication satisfaction with parents. *Western Journal of Communication, 59*, 228–246.

Wallerstein, J. S. (1985). The overburdened child: Some long-term consequences of divorce. *Social Work, 30*, 116–123.

Weiss, R. S. (1975). *Marital separation.* New York: Basic Books.

Westberg, H., Nelson, T. S., & Piercy, K. W. (2002). Disclosure of divorce plans to children: What the children have to say. *Contemporary Family Therapy, 24*, 525–542.

Index